GALLOWAY

GALLOWAY

A LAND APART

Andrew McCulloch

Birlinn

Published in 2000
by Birlinn Limited
8 Canongate Venture
5 New Street
Edinburgh
EH8 8BH
www.birlinn.co.uk

ISBN 1 84158 027 9

British Library Cataloguing-in-Publication Data
A catalogue record for this book is available from the British Library

Typesetting and maps by Edderston Book Design
Printed and bound by Creative Print and Design, Ebbw Vale

CONTENTS

LIST OF ILLUSTRATIONS

1   Ptolemy's map of Scotland.
2   Outline of the Roman camp at Glenlochar.
3   Sweetheart Abbey.
4   The standard layout of a medieval abbey.
5   Whithorn: reconstruction of the Northumbrian minister in about 800.
6   Whithorn: reconstruction of the priory as it would have existed at the time of James IV.
7   Aerial view of the Mote of Urr, near Dalbeattie.
8   Typical layout of a motte-and-bailey castle.
9   Threave Castle on the River Dee.
10 Cardoness Castle, Gatehouse.
11 Kirkdale House, near Carsluith.
12 The former Cardoness House, Gatehouse.
13 The oldest house in Wigtownshire.
14 Barnie McGhie's cottage, Kirkcolm.
15 The cotton mills at Gatehouse in about 1847.
16 The restored bobbin mill at Gatehouse.
17 Transport: brigs at Dub o' Hass in about 1880.
18 Aerial view of Gatehouse.
19 Country life in the early twentieth century: a shooting party at Knockbrex.
20 Life behind the green-baize door: the domestic staff at Terregles House.
21 Steam engine at Kirkcudbright station in 1960.
22 Early twentieth-century agriculture: a steam-driven threshing mill.
23 Early twentieth-century agriculture: a drove of sheep in the main street of Carsphairn.
24 Dry-stone dyking competition on the Cally estate, Gatehouse.
25 James Stewart, earl of Moray.
26 James Douglas, fourth earl of Morton, regent.
27 John Knox.
28 Andrew Melville.
29 James Graham, marquis of Montrose.
30 Samuel Rutherford, one-time minister of Anwoth.
31 James Graham of Claverhouse, later viscount Dundee.
32 Sir James Dalrymple, first viscount Stair.

33   John Dalrymple, second earl of Stair.
34   Admiral the Hon. Keith Stewart of Glasserton.
35   James Murray of Cally.
36   Lady Catherine Stewart, wife of James Murray.
37   Sir William Douglas, bart.
38   The Rev. Professor Alexander Murray.
39   Sir Andrew Agnew of Lochaw, 8th bart.
40   Sir Herbert Maxwell of Monreith, 7th bart. KT, FRS.

GENEALOGICAL TABLES

LIST OF MAPS

ACKNOWLEDGEMENTS

I have been fortunate in reaping the benefit of the comprehensive research which has recently been targeted on Galloway's past, and also in the number of people who have given generously of their time to help me. Particularly, Dr Richard Oram for revising and commenting on the text, offering valuable suggestions for further reading and research, as well as engaging in a number of discussions; and it has been a privilege to have had the advantage of the help, so freely extended, of someone of his academic standing and comprehensive knowledge of medieval Galloway. Also, Mr Peter Hill of the Whithorn Trust who kindly spared the time to give me a résumé of the information which has come to light in the course of the Dig, and to Mr Alastair Penman for his helpful comments on the early chapters, besides bearing patiently with me on my visits to his excavations at Buittle. I am most grateful, too, to Mrs Daphne Brooke for not only reading and commenting on extensive sections of the original draft but for giving me the opportunity of several discussions. And equally so for her generously allowing me to use her published material, particularly her maps indicating the origins of place-names.

Other eminent scholars have also given generously of their time to comment on the chapters relevant to their subjects. They include Dr J.N.G. Ritchie, Head of Archaeology, RCAHMS, Professor Michael Lynch and Dr Pat Denison of Edinburgh University, Professor G.W.S. Barrow, Mr A.E. Truckell, Dr David Breeze of Historic Scotland, Professor Christopher Whately and Dr Derek Craig of Dundee and Durham Universities, and Mr D. Lockwood and Dr David Devereux, curators respectively of the Dumfries and Stewartry museums.

I am grateful, too, to Mr John Davies for his help and support, and also Mr John Jameson, former convenor of Dumfries and Galloway Regional Council, Mr Frank Gourlay, former chairman of the Dumfries and Galloway Tourist Board, for their contributions to the final chapter, my brother Alexander for revising my comments on the current state of farming; and Mr Anthony Wolffe. Also to Mrs Smith for kindly allowing me access to her late husband Dr Ian Smith's thesis, and to Dr John Jones, dean and archivist of Balliol College, Oxford, for permitting me to use Dervorguilla's seal as a motif for the dustjacket. My thanks are due above all, however, to Mrs Diana Phillips for the immense amount of time and effort she spent in scrutinising and amending the text in its previous incarnations to her characteristically high standard. She undertook this challenging task with an enthusiasm matched only by her intellectual rigour, her literary abilities and her wide historical knowledge. Her candid and constructive comments were invariably well-founded, and I am particularly fortunate to have had the benefit of her help.

The illustrations call for a further round of thanks. To Dr Ian Donnachie and Dr Ian Macleod for generously allowing me to reproduce a selection of the illustrations appearing in *Old Galloway* and *The Industrial Archaeology of South-West Scotland.* Mr Charles Balfour-Kinnear and Air Images for their kind permission to use the aerial photographs of Gatehouse, and Cardiness and Threave castles. Mr James Murray Usher and Mrs Jackie Shannon of the Mill on the Fleet for entrusting me with the portrait of James Murray for scanning purposes, and Sir Crispin Agnew Bt for his help and co-operation in reproducing the portrait of his forbear, Sir Andrew Agnew. Also, to Mr Andrew Stewart, Cumloden, and Sir Michael Maxwell Bt, Monreith, for kindly allowing me to use a selection of their ancestral portraits.

I am also indebted to Mr Graham Roberts of the Ewart Library who has cheerfully and helpfully fielded the barrage of queries I invariably confront him with on my visits there. Also for kindly giving me *carte blanche* to use the library's collection of historic photographs: I have taken full advantage of this generous licence. Finally, I must thank Mr Hugh Andrew of Birlinn Ltd for indicating his willingness to publish the book provided it measured up to an acceptable standard; this has given me the encouragement to persevere with what has proved to be a fascinating if time-consuming exercise.

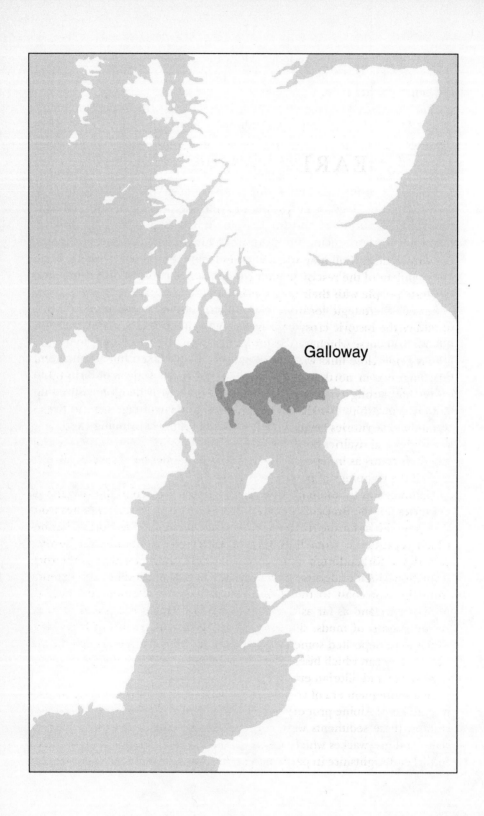

Galloway

1

EARLY MIGRANTS

BACKGROUND

In former times Galloway was an autonomous region which was virtually independent of the rest of Scotland, and its inhabitants were regarded as a separate people with their own special identity. Similarly its history, which reflected its strategic location at the south-west of the country, where it straddles the historic crossroads between England, Scotland and the west, followed a course which was largely exclusive of other parts of the country. The region's close links with Ireland stretch as far back as the arrival of the first migrants in northern Britain, while in medieval times its hereditary rulers had strong connections with the kingdom of Man, as well as the powerful lordships flanking Scotland's western seaboard, and the Norse-dominated territories beyond. These rulers were also intimately involved in the traditional rivalries between the Scots and English kings, and to emphasise their status as independent princes they maintained a semi-regal style and all the trappings of power associated with it.

Galloway was traditionally described as extending from 'the Brigend of Dumfries' to 'the Braes of Glenapp', but more prosaically it stretches from the river Nith as far the fringes of the twenty-one mile wide North Channel which separates it from the coast of Ulster, and embraces the former counties of Kirkcudbright and Wigtown. Geologically, it is part of the rock formation which underlies the Southern Uplands of Scotland and extends from the east coast to the Rhinns of Galloway, and continues through northern Ireland as far as the Atlantic Ocean. This is composed of huge accumulations of muds, silt, sands and pebbles, thousands of feet thick, which were deposited some four to five hundred million years ago on the bed of an ocean which bisected the British Isles in what geologists term the Ordovician and Silurian eras.

In a subsequent era of volcanic activity associated with the emergence of mountains of Alpine proportions, of which the present hills are the eroded stumps, these sediments were compressed and toughened into the hard slates and greywackes which are characteristic of southern Scotland today. In Kirkcudbrightshire in particular, molten lava-like material was forced up into the underlying rock, and its superior resistance to the forces of erosion accounts for the rugged and spectacular scenery of its hinterland today.

During a subsequent epoch of desert conditions, known geologically as the Permian, Galloway lay on the edge of the equator, and wind-blown sand filled the depressions in the land surface to form the sandstone deposits in the region. The most extensive are those in the neighbourhood of Dumfries, where the footprints of a quadruped that roamed the earth millions of years before the age of the dinosaurs have been discovered,[1] and at the opposite end of the region another sandstone formation underlies part of western Wigtownshire.

The present landscape of Galloway began to evolve some fifteen million years ago, when the existing river systems developed and its coastline assumed something approaching its present shape. While the main river valleys run broadly from north to south across the geological grain of the country, the land itself descends in a series of platforms from the high ground in the north to the Solway shore, suggesting that it emerged from the sea at irregular intervals. Consequently, the flat open country to the north of Castle Douglas was formerly an extensive coastal plain that became landlocked as the Solway steadily contracted to become the relatively narrow firth it is today. In stark contrast, the large granite massifs of Criffel, Screel and Cairnsmore of Fleet stand out sentinel-like along the coastline as silent and brooding witnesses to their greater durability.

Wigtownshire is less hilly, having been more heavily ground down by the combined action of water and ice. This has left its northern reaches – aptly termed the Moors – a bare, bleak and windswept country, while the outwash of sand and gravel eroded from the former mountains of Kirkcudbrightshire accounts for the fertility of much of the land to the south. Known as the Machars, this region juts out towards the Isle of Man and separates Wigtown Bay from the shallower waters of Luce Bay to the west. Beyond lies the ridge of low hills known as the Rhinns, and forming the last bastion of mainland Scotland they face Northern Ireland across the marine trench of the North Channel which links the Irish Sea with the Atlantic.

Successive Ice Ages, and the gouging and scouring effects of the glaciers radiating outwards from the ice cap that intermittently covered the Galloway highlands, have been responsible for shaping its hinterland, and particularly those steep declivities that are characteristic of the Merrick and Kells ranges. Besides accounting for the fertility of parts of the Machars, the pulverised débris carried down by the meltwaters draining off the glaciers was also responsible for the formation of the drumlins which are characteristic of much of Wigtownshire, and in the poorer country to the north they constitute islands of fertility in an otherwise bleak and barren landscape. Since this former county was the most accessible part of the region to incoming migrants, most of whom arrived by sea, it is there that evidence of their presence has been mainly found, and the area at the head of Luce Bay in particular has been the most prolific source of archaeological remains in the whole province.

The last Ice Age lasted for roughly a million and a half years, and although it was punctuated by periods of warmer, and even sub-tropical, weather when hippopotami are known to have wallowed in the Thames, Arctic conditions predominated throughout this epoch. Much of Britain lay intermittently under an ice sheet, and while this advanced and receded according to the variations in the climate there were parts of the country where, at its maximum intensity, the accumulation of ice was over a thousand metres thick. This represented a stupendous amount of water, and the consequent fall in the sea level resulted in the emergence of huge tracts of land along the coastline of Britain, including the drying up of much of the North Sea. In the Irish Sea the water receded to the extent that a land bridge connected the Mull of Galloway with the Isle of Man, and between them lay the mouth of an extended River Eden which meandered through the dried-up bed of the Solway Firth and drained the river systems of Galloway.[2]

For much of this time Britain was a frozen waste of sub-Arctic tundra, though temporary relaxations in the icy grip of winter allowed for the establishment of primitive heathland and juniper scrub, and even more advanced types of vegetation. The last break in the ice age occurred around 12,000 BC, and finds of ancient peat interspersed with nettle seeds at sites near Lockerbie and Gretna indicate the existence of cool, steppe-like conditions before colder weather set in again.[3] Known as the Lomond re-advance, this lasted for some three thousand years, and once again an ice cap enshrouded the Scottish mountains, glaciers filled the high valleys in the Galloway hinterland, and permafrost prevailed throughout the land.

The scouring effects of successive ice ages, combined with its diversity of underlying rocks, account for the wide variation of scenery which is such a striking feature of Galloway today. For within this relatively compact area the countryside ranges from the barren, rock-strewn mountain summits to the picturesque orderliness of its rolling farmlands with its neat white farms, and ultimately to the almost sub-tropical, palm-fringed shores of the Irish Sea. Being in the path of the Gulf Stream, the climate is mild if often windy and wet, the rainfall being concentrated in particular in the uplands. From there the water drains into a series of rivers which flow through a number of picturesque lochs and eventually meander through the coastal merselands to reach the Solway Firth. Thus the description of Galloway as 'Scotland in miniature' is amply justified.

EARLY MIGRANTS

Southern England lay beyond the fringes of the ice, and there is evidence
of early man – or his prototype, known as hominids – penetrating there as
far back as 300,000 years ago,[4] but there is considerable uncertainty as to
when he first arrived in Scotland. It is possible that some Stone Age
migrants were lured there during the gaps in the Ice Age,[5] but as all
evidence of their presence was obliterated by the ice as it closed in again[6]
this can only be speculative. It is also possible that some established
settlements on the coastal plains, but here again all traces of their existence
were submerged by the advancing sea. Stone Age implies the use of stone
implements, and pre-historians draw a distinction between the earlier
Palaeolithic (Old Stone Age), Mesolithic (Middle Stone Age) and Neolithic
(New Stone Age), the differences reflecting the advances achieved by the
people in stone-working technology and the development of their social
organisation.

About ten thousand years ago the climate suddenly began to warm – so
rapidly in fact that it is reckoned that within a mere twenty years Arctic
conditions gave way to summer temperatures which were considerably
warmer than today's,[7] and the process continued, albeit at a slower rate, for
the next few millennia until a slight cooling took place.[8] As the ice
retreated, grasslands were established and much of the lower-lying regions
were colonised by trees. At first birch predominated, and later hazel, but
from about 8,000 BC they were superseded by elm, and finally oak.
Meanwhile pine, which had been dominant in the far north-west, gradually
spread over much of the rest of the country to form the Caledonian Forest.[9]

In the wake of this increasingly diverse and luxuriant vegetation came a
variety of wildlife, and bones preserved in peat bogs and caves indicate the
presence of elk, deer and wild boar, horses and ox (or aurochs), as well as
wolves, and that terror of man and beast alike – the brown bear. These in
turn drew early hunter gatherers, known as Mesolithic man, to present-day
Scotland. Stone and flints were the medium from which they fashioned
their weaponry and working utensils, though they also used animal bones
and antlers. Those which have come to light consist mainly of small, barbed
blades or arrowheads, known as microliths, as well as stone axes and
scrapers which were used for scouring away the flesh and fat from animal
skins. Tantalisingly little is known about these people as almost everything
associated with them has long since decayed, and evidence of their
presence is mainly confined to south-west Scotland, though other sites up
the west coast have yielded valuable information.

The earliest known Mesolithic settlement in Scotland is at Kinloch on
the island of Rhum, where a cache of nutshells was found along with traces

of fire and broken hearth stones. As the nutshells have been radio-carbon dated to somewhere between 6800 and 7000 BC,[10] this site is nearly a thousand years older than the earliest Mesolithic settlements which have so far been identified in south-west Scotland. These include sites at Redkirk Point near Gretna, Kirkhill near Lockerbie, and around Loch Doon, all of which have been assigned a date of around 6000 BC.[11] The Mesolithic people themselves were nomads whose wanderings were dictated by the changing seasons, and while most of their camps were temporary ones, others like Kinloch were more permanent.

Where they came from is uncertain, for comparisons between artefacts found on Scottish sites and those in northern England reveal certain cultural differences. Therefore, while some may have penetrated from the south, the fact that Mesolithic people had already settled in Ireland suggests that it was from there that the earliest migrants came to western Scotland and the Hebrides.[12] They are described as hunter gatherers, for while they gathered shellfish, nuts and berries they were primarily hunters of animals, since these were the source of meat, while their skins were used for making clothes (and evidence from European sites shows these could be highly decorative[13]), and their bones and antlers for fashioning implements.

Those who arrived in Galloway would have encountered a coastline which was significantly different from today's, as the meltwaters of the retreating ice had caused a rise in the sea level, and a consequent inundation of much of the low-lying land. Its shape is easily detectable, and it is clear that at that time the region was penetrated by long, tidal inlets, while the lower reaches of the main river valleys, and the merselands along the present coastline, consisted of mudflats which were submerged at high tide. For example, the mouth of the Nith lay to the north of present-day Dumfries, and below it was a large island-studded bay which extended over the whole of the Lochar Moss. Further west, the Cree flowed into the sea at present-day Newton Stewart, while the upper reaches of Wigtown Bay were part of a large tidal basin comprising the entire Moss of Cree, as well as the merselands to the north of Creetown. Beyond Glenluce, the low-lying land between Loch Ryan and Luce Bay consisted of an expanse of sand and mudflats interspersed with channels, and when the sea covered these at high tide the Rhinns were cut off from the mainland to form an island.[14]

During the following millennia, isostatic pressure gradually re-asserted itself as the landmass, freed from the weight of ice, began to rise and the seas receded, leaving behind those raised beaches which are characteristic of the Galloway coastline. The sites of a number of former Mesolithic camps have been found in close proximity to these raised beaches, since fish and shellfish were integral to the diet of these people. Finds of limpet scoops at sites in Argyllshire,[15] together with the remains of harpoon heads and bone hooks, show that they practised line fishing from boats as well.[16]

Evidence from European sites, as well as early rock carvings in Scandinavia, reveal these as being constructed of skins and they were doubtless strengthened with wood or birch bark to render them seaworthy.[17]

The Mesolithic presence in Galloway is particularly apparent in the Luce Sands, an area which consists of some four square miles of sandhills, marsh and moor at the head of Luce Bay. Other sites have been identified along the eastern edge of Luce Bay, notably at Craignarget and on Gillespie Farm near Auchenmalg, while two sites at nearby Barsalloch Point and Low Clone, both of which date from the fifth millennium BC, have yielded a veritable trove of flints. Evidence of a line of stakeholes in the shape of an arc at the former site suggests a rudimentary shelter,[18] while there are signs of fire at Low Clone. This played an important part in the manufacture of flint implements, because heating made it easier to 'knapp' them (i.e. slice them into shape), and a small flint-making industry could well have existed there.[19] There may have been another camp at Cumstoun, near the head of the Dee estuary, since a fish spear fashioned from a red deer's antler was found there.[20] The evidence at Buittle, however, is more conclusive, because the excavations being carried out there have yielded a number of microliths which are believed to have been arrowheads or parts of an implement for slashing grass.[21] Meanwhile, other sites have been identified further up the Solway between Southwick and Carsethorn.[22]

Hitherto it was thought that the Mesolithic people confined themselves to the coastal regions, but artefacts which have come to light as a result of forestry operations, particularly in the Loch Doon/Clatteringshaws area, have shown them to be much more ubiquitous. The location of these finds also throws some light on the routes these people followed between the coast and the upland regions in the course of their seasonal migrations. One of these went up the Dee and Ken valleys and over into the river Doon system in present-day Ayrshire, while another followed a more westerly course up the Fleet valley and past Loch Grannoch and Clatteringshaws, from where it skirted the western flanks of the Rhinns of Kells and ultimately converged in the area round Loch Doon. Artefacts found elsewhere, such as the upper reaches of the Water of Ken, however, are thought to be relics from hunting expeditions rather than being indicative of a migratory route.[23]

Pollen diagrams reveal certain changes in the local vegetation during later Mesolithic times: ivy was spreading into the region, while bracken was becoming more widespread, and trees were colonising much of the uplands.[24] Peat samples found at Brighouse Bay, near Borgue, show alder as invading the coastal fringes from 5500 BC onwards as the brackish lagoons left behind by the retreating seas dried up, though this was later superseded by pine.[25] Other changes were the work of man, and evidence of fire disturbance dating from much the same time in the area of the

Cooran Lane to the north of Loch Dee, combined with a corresponding reduction in birch cover, suggests that these people were also engaged in forest clearance.[26]

Evidence found elsewhere points to an artistic, as well as an arcane, side to Mesolithic life. For the discovery of a contemporary ornamental boat paddle at a site in Denmark suggests an aesthetic dimension,[27] while an analysis of some midden debris found on a site on Oronsay sheds a possible light on their burial practices. It contained traces of human bones, mainly hands and feet, and the remains of some teeth, indicating that these people made a practice of hanging out their dead to allow the flesh to decompose. Smaller bones and teeth would have dropped off, thus accounting for their presence among the refuse, while the remainder of the skeleton was disposed of elsewhere.[28] Evidence from other sites in western Europe indicates that they observed certain well-established funeral rites, involving in some cases the deposition of grave goods – some of them practical, like stone knives, arrowheads and axes, while others were ornamental, and some cemeteries contained the graves of dogs.[29]

EARLY FARMERS

Certain changes become apparent in the excavated material dating from the fourth millenium BC onwards. Shards of pottery appear, and there are signs of new techniques in the fashioning of flint and stone implements. Also, the earliest tombs date from this period and, most important of all, pollen diagrams show evidence of rudimentary farming. This indicates that hunter gathering, which is wholly dependent on nature, was giving place to a partial control over plants and animals. The fact that the crops being grown at this time are not native to Scotland suggests that these changes were associated with the arrival of new groups of people, to whom the term Neolithic has been applied. Meaning literally 'new stone age', this indicates a cultural advance rather than having any ethnic significance, for the evidence points to their infiltrating into Britain from different points of origin. For example, the fact that similar changes were occurring in northern Europe indicates this as being one of them, while certain features in common between the tombs found in western Britain and those in Brittany argue for a northward migration of incomers from that region up the Irish Sea. Some landed on the Galloway coast and settled there, while others penetrated as far as the Hebrides where a number of early sites associated with them have been found.[30]

As the Mesolithic population was comparatively sparse, there was ample land available to be taken up by these incomers, and they carved out settlements by clear-felling tracts of native woodland, using what is known as a 'slash and burn' technique, and ring-barking the larger trees. While much of the cleared land was put down to pasture,[31] the more fertile ground was scratched up with digging sticks to provide a seedbed for their crops of primitive emmer wheat. Yields would have been relatively prolific, thanks in part to the warmer climate, and also to the enrichment of the land from the copious quantities of potash left over from the burnt trees. When yields began to decline through soil exhaustion, the farmers simply carved out further settlements by clear-felling more forest, later returning to the original settlements and removing the secondary growth, which had sprung up in the meantime, in order to bring them back into cultivation.

Axes were needed to cut back the native forest, and in early Neolithic times they were probably fashioned locally from flaked flint, or ground down from hard-grained stone, and mounted in wooden hafts. Later, however, a growing demand for better quality axes led to the emergence of recognised production centres, where the local stone was capable of being knapped more efficiently. Among these were the primitive 'axe factories' at Great Langdale in Cumbria, whose products have been found at a number of sites in Scotland, and also at Tievebulliagh in county Antrim. A third at Creag na Caillich, near Killin in Perthshire, is known to have been in operation around 2000 BC, and the fact that its products have been found on sites as far afield as Lewis and southern England suggests the existence of a well-developed trade network throughout Neolithic Britain.

That trading links between Cumberland and the Machars were part of this nexus is evident from the concentration of axes from the 'factory' at Great Langdale which have come to light in the coastal parishes of Whithorn, Glasserton and Mochrum.[32] Similarly, the resemblance between tools such as flint scrapers, which have come to light on sites in Antrim, and those found at Torrs Warren on the Luce Sands[33] are indicative of trade with Ireland, while the discovery of a microlith fashioned from a Rhum bloodstone at Buittle[34] suggests that these links extended up the west coast as well.

Peat deposits dating from around 3000 BC show a marked fall in tree pollen and a corresponding rise in grass and weed seeds, as well as bracken, and as this becomes increasingly apparent in later peat samples[35] it is clear that the population was expanding, and land was being progressively taken into cultivation. Other factors could have accounted for the decline in tree pollen, because the fact that this was particularly evident in the case of elm[36] suggests that it may have been attributable to the spread of an early form of Dutch elm disease.[37]

Farming activities ranged from pastoral to cultivation depending on local conditions, and while crops were grown on the more fertile land the rest was used for grazing livestock. Some of them were probably indigenous, such as pigs and dogs, though the Neolithic people are thought to have introduced their own sheep, cattle, goats and horses. Their sheep

were small animals with hairy brown fleeces, probably akin to the Soay
sheep of today who could well be their descendants. Two distinct types of
cattle appear to have existed at this time. The indigenous breed, *bos
primogenitus*, was the wild ox or auroch of the native forests,[38] a very large
animal with a wide span of horns which survived in parts of the Continent
until the late Middle Ages. The other breed of cattle, which was almost
certainly imported, was the smaller more easily domesticated *bos longifrons*.
The goats, on the other hand, most likely resembled – and were probably
the ancestors of – their small, grey, modern counterparts which can be seen
roaming the Galloway hills today.

EARLY BURIAL PRACTICES

Much of our knowledge of the Neolithic people is derived from their
tombs, and particularly the grave goods deposited in them. The earlier
ones tended to consist of a burial chamber roofed over with stone slabs,
and these were covered with earth and stones to form elongated mounds,
known appropriately as 'chambered' tombs. An example in Galloway is a
former stone and timber mortuary house at Lochill, near New Abbey,
which dates from about 3700 BC.[39] Through course of time the tombs
became larger and more elaborate, and regional variations developed.
Whereas those found in Orkney and Caithness tend to have a long
entrance passage, the majority of the tombs in the south-west open straight
out of the burial mound, the best examples locally being at Cairnholy, near
Carsluith, and Mid Gleniron in the Luce valley.[40] An alternative type, which
is smaller, circular in shape, and has an entrance passage, is the tomb at
White Cairn of Bargrennan.

Some have the remains of a façade at the entrance, Cairnholy being a
good example. This was part of a forecourt which was used for ritual
activity, while the discovery of scorched pottery shards on similar sites
indicates fire as being integral to these ceremonies. They were probably
elaborate and may have involved an element of mysticism – and a grooved-
ware container found on the site at Balfarg Riding School in Fife suggests
as much, since it was found to have carbonised encrustations containing
henbane. This is a potent narcotic – and poisonous too if taken in large
enough quantities – and the hallucinations it induced may have been an
essential part of these rituals. Similarly, drinking vessels found on the
Neolithic site at Callanish on Lewis show evidence of a potent type of beer
made from heather, and the people are also thought to have distilled a
crude type of whisky which, according to a recent *Times* report,[41] suggests a
'ritualistic and habitual' use of alcohol.

Tomb construction in general, and particularly the later more elaborate
ones which were primarily status symbols, represented a huge investment

of labour which would have lasted for several generations, and the work of
building them must have required considerable organisational skills. This
in turn indicates the emergence of a well-structured, hierarchical society,
which is believed to have consisted of individual priest chieftains and ruling
élites, with an underclass who provided the labour. Although this was
probably less well defined in early Neolithic times, its development was
mainly attributable to the growing population – a fact which is apparent
from the increasing amount of land being taken into cultivation. It is also
evident from the proliferation of cairns which were being built during the
fourth millennium BC, as these are thought to mark the establishment of
new communities which had split off from existing ones, and who erected
them as a symbol of their separate identity.

Burial methods varied. Perhaps in recognition of their status within the
community, some corpses were deposited intact, while shards of pottery
found in the tombs are thought to be the remains of containers for food
and drink to sustain them on their journey to the afterworld.[42] However,
individual burial was the exception, because an alternative practice seems
to have been adopted with lesser mortals. In common with what appears to
have been a Mesolithic practice, their corpses were hung out on 'mortuary
platforms' to allow the flesh to rot away through exposure to the elements,[43]
the process being doubtless assisted by carrion-eating birds, rodents and
stray carnivorous animals. Once the skeletons were picked clean, they were
dismembered and placed in communal tombs according to a well-
established procedure. Skulls were consigned to a specific sector, with
femurs being placed in another, while the remaining bones were dumped
on the communal rubbish heap.

As time went on, the skulls and femurs were removed to make way for
subsequent generations of corpses, and during Bronze Age times many of
the tombs were re-used, when bodies were inserted into the cairn super-
structures, though in most cases the actual burial chambers were left
undisturbed. These practices seem to point to a religion involving an
element of ancestor-worship and a close association with the dead, which is
hardly surprising since the average life expectancy was less than thirty[44] and
the prospect of death was omnipresent.

The groups of standing stones built by the Neolithic people may also
have held a religious significance, perhaps serving as ritualistic focal points
for all the communities in the locality. Alternatively – or perhaps in
complement – it has been suggested that they served as rudimentary
calendars, where the alignment of the sun with certain stones marked the
salient events in the farming year.[45] These groups were evidently fairly
numerous, particularly in Wigtownshire where nineteen possible sites have
been identified.[46] Most have been plundered for building material over the
centuries, but the two best preserved examples are those on Glenquicken

moor, near the old military road from Gatehouse to Creetown, and at Torhouse near Wigtown.

Henges are another type of monument associated with the late Neolithic people. Dating from about 3000 BC onwards, and reflecting an increasingly prosperous society, they consisted of a circle of stones surrounded by a banked or ditched enclosure. Evidence from English sites suggests that they included accommodation for a ruling élite of priest chieftains, and were probably therefore centres of local power. A number of examples exist in Scotland, and the best in Galloway is at Dunragit. Aerial survey shows this as consisting of a triple circle of pits with an overall diameter of three hundred metres, and an avenue of pits leading up to the main entrance – clearly a most impressive ceremonial or funerary complex.[47] Another example can be seen at Pict's Knowe, near Troqueer, where the earliest known ard-type plough was retrieved from the surrounding ditch, along with other articles which were probably ritualistic offerings.[48]

Other finds dating from the Neolithic help to shed some light on the everyday life of the people. Flint scrapers, fixed into handles with birch bark glue, were used to scour the flesh and fat from animal skins, suggesting that these were their main source of clothing. Textiles were used as well, as a piece of Neolithic pottery was found to bear the clear imprint of woollen cloth. Although pottery was mainly used for storage, the appearance of finer, decorated vessels points to it being turned to ornamental purposes as well.

While there are no known examples of Neolithic dwellings in Galloway, those at the Skara Brae complex on Orkney (which dates from between 3000 and 2600 BC) indicate a remarkable degree of sophistication and comfort, as they contain evidence of stone furnishings, free-standing or recessed box beds, the remains of a clay oven, and even signs of water-flushed sanitation. Admittedly this was the centre of an extremely prosperous Neolithic society, but it is not impossible that similar standards of cleanliness and sanitation prevailed among the Neolithic élite in Galloway.

THE 'BEAKER' PEOPLE

From about 2500 BC onwards, certain changes become evident among the skeletons deposited in the tombs, in that they indicate the existence of a taller, more robust people with rounder skulls who were clearly new immigrants. At the same time, there is evidence of a different style of pottery, smaller and more highly decorated than the earlier types, which gave its name to the people associated with it. The previous style grows progressively rarer among contemporary archaeological remains, while the abundance of pottery associated with these new beaker people suggests that they established a cultural – and hence a political – dominance over the native inhabitants. Similarities between their types of pottery and those found in western Europe, including Spain, indicates the Iberian peninsula as their point of origin, and that from there they migrated up through western France and England, probably reaching Galloway by sea, while others continued as far as the Western Isles.[49]

Judging from the location of their earlier burial sites, the beaker people began by colonising virgin land on the peripheries of the more densely populated parts of the country. Through course of time they would have encroached on the more populous regions, perhaps driving out – or simply exterminating – the local ruling élites and establishing a dominance over the existing underclass. Although this is speculative, there is some evidence to support the theory that a degree of physical violence was involved, because at two sites near Stonehaven the skeletons of otherwise apparently healthy Neolithic men in the prime of life were discovered with fractured skulls, from which they had obviously died. Alteratively, beaker dominance could have been achieved in the wake of a collapse of Neolithic society – perhaps as a result of a disease epidemic, or maybe it simply broke down of its own accord as other societies have done in the past.[50] Speculation is endless, but the fact remains that there is little evidence of Neolithic culture among archaeological material dating from the end of the third millenium BC onwards,[51] while the people associated with it would simply have been absorbed by their beaker-making supplanters.

Meanwhile, contemporary pollen diagrams show the native forest being cut back at an accelerating rate, indicating an expansion in farming, and hence a growing population. Although the beaker people were primarily flint-users, the discovery at a site in Argyllshire of an ox-yoke capable of harnessing two animals reveals a more advanced technique. Assuming this was used to draw a conventional ard-type plough, it would have been possible for these people to rip up new pasture to bring it into cultivation, and there are signs, too, that parts of the merselands which had emerged from the retreating seas were being reclaimed.

The beaker people were responsible for erecting groups of stones standing in alignment with one another, the best examples in Galloway being those at Drumtroddan near Port William. Their precise function remains a mystery although they may have marked sanctified spots[52] or territorial areas.[53] Some are decorated with 'cup and ring' markings, spirals or other designs, which were carved with the aid of a driven punch, and there are also examples of outcrops of rock being similarly inscribed.[54]

A radical change took place in contemporary burial practices. Instead of depositing disarticulated remains in communal tombs, corpses were crammed into individual stone 'coffins', sunk into the ground, in a semi-foetal position with the knees drawn up to the chin. The graves were then earthed over, and the site was marked with a cairn of stones. This, however, was by no means the rule, because other corpses were simply inserted into the superstructure of existing Neolithic tombs. Later, cremation became more widely practised, and the ashes were deposited in cinerary urns which were placed in communal graves, this type of burial being particularly evident in south-west Scotland.

Their pottery is extremely distinctive, and from examples found in the Luce Sands and elsewhere two types can be identified, known respectively as 'All-over-cord' and 'European Bell'. Both are characterised as 'low, broad, bell-shaped beakers with narrow mouths and cordoned or collared rims', but whereas the former had a two-stranded cord wound round them before firing, others were decorated by pricking them with short-toothed combs.[55] The small 'pygmy' cups or incense cups, which have been found on a number of sites, were a later refinement. One particular beaker, which was excavated at a site in Fife, was found to contain traces of mead, suggesting that the people not only practised beekeeping but probably fermented other alcoholic drinks as well.

Compared with earlier stone-using societies, the beaker people achieved considerable technological progress. However, the scope for making further advances was limited by the narrow range of raw materials available, as these were confined to stone, flints, and the horns and bones of animals, and therefore if further progress was to be made a more sophisticated medium was needed. Fortunately this was slowly becoming available, because the science of metal-working had already spread from Europe to Britain, and the earliest signs of its presence in Scotland date from around 2000 BC.

NOTES

1. Jardine, 'Holocene raised coastal settlements'. The footprints are identified as those of a primitive four-legged, digital-footed reptile.
2. Spikins, 'Rivers, boundaries and change'.
3. A.E. Truckell, correspondence.
4. Oram, *Scottish Prehistory*, 1: Wickham-Jones, *Scotland's First Settlers*, 32.
5. Theory has it that these variations in the climate related to changes in the direction of the Gulf Stream.
6. Finds of two isolated hand axes, one on Islay and the other at Hillhead in Glasgow, are thought to point to the presence of palaeolithic man during the gap which occurred in the Ice Age some 15,000 years ago, but the evidence is not convincing (Oram, *Scottish Prehistory*, 4).
7. This is based on an analysis of ice core samples taken from Greenland (Mayewski, Climate change events as seen in the Greenland ice core').
8. Bishop and Coope, 'Stratigraphical and faunal evidence in south-west Scotland', 61–88.
9. Oram, *Scottish Prehistory*, 7.

10. *Ibid.*, 1.
11. Wickham-Jones 'Rhum, mesolithic and later sites at Kinloch'.
12. The oldest known Mesolithic site there – at Mount Sandel on the River Bann in northern Ulster – has been radio-carbon dated to some 500 years before the settlement at Kinloch (Wickham-Jones, *Scotland's First Settlers*, 52); and it is also significant that artefacts recovered from Hebridean sites and others in south-west Scotland are comparable with those found on Irish sites. Equally so, that most of the earlier sites associated with the Mesolithic are located in those parts of the country which are immediately accessible to Ireland.
13. Wickham-Jones, *Scotland's First Settlers*, 111–2.
14. Although this subject has been discussed by Morrison in 'Galloway: locality and landscape evolution', these assertions reflect my own findings gleaned from a tour of the coastline armed with the relevant 1:50,000 O.S. maps. An interesting point that emerges from this is that, whereas the former coastline around Dumfries follows broadly the 18m. contour line, in other parts it is rather higher, which confirms the gradual tilting of the land towards the east/south-east.
15. Wickham-Jones, *Scotland's First Settlers*, 93.
16. *Ibid.*, 19 & 93.
17. *Ibid.*, 116–7.
18. Cormack, 'A mesolithic site at Barsalloch', 65.
19. Cormack and Coles 'A mesolithic site at Low Clone, Wigtownshire', 50–3.
20. This is on view in the Stewartry Museum at Kirkcudbright.
21. Miller, 'Interim Report on lithic assemblies from Botel bailey 1992–4'. Also, conversation with A.I.N. Penman, Director of excavations there.
22. Notably at Gillfoot, Maxwellfield, Powilliemount and Tallowquhairn (Cormack, 'A mesolithic site at Barsalloch', 78).
23. Discussed by Edwards and others in, 'New mesolithic sites in south-west Scotland'.
24. *Ibid.*
25. Maynard and others: 'The dune system at Brighouse Bay'.
26. Edwards, 'Meso-neolithic vegetational impacts in Scotland', 143–55.
27. Wickham-Jones, *Scotland's First Settlers*, 117.
28. *Ibid.*, 80.
29. *Ibid.*, 118.
30. Oram, *Scottish Prehistory*, pp 20, 22.
31. Birks, 'Studies in the vegetational history of Scotland', 209–10.
32. Williams, 'Neolithic axes in Dumfries and Galloway', 112.
33. Cowie and others, 'Torrs Warren, Luce Sands, Galloway', 11.
34. Botel bailey excavations: Interim Report 1999.
35. Cowie and others, 'Torrs Warren'.
36. Birks, 'Studies in vegetational history', 208.
37. Wickham-Jones, *Scotland's First Settlers*, 104.
38. The head of one of these animals was found in a marl pit near Whithorn early in the nineteenth century (McKerlie ii, 433).
39. Oram, *Scottish Prehistory*, 23.
40. See Corcoran, 'First Interim Report', 99–110, and 'Second Interim Report', 73–9.
41. February 1996.
42. This is evident from discoveries in some individual tombs of traces of sheep and cattle bones – obviously the remains of cuts of meat which were deposited

for this purpose.

43. Oram, *Scottish Prehistory*, 33.
44. This is evident from bone remains found in a chambered cairn at Isbister on South Ronaldsay on Orkney. (*Ibid*, 34).
45. Ashmore, *Neolithic and Bronze Age Scotland*, 87, 89.
46. Murray, 'The stone circles of Wigtownshire'.
47. Cowie, 'Torrs Warren', 95.
48. Oram, *Scottish Prehistory*, 37.
49. *Ibid.*, 47.
50. Ashmore, *Neolithic and Bronze Age Scotland*, 84–5.
51. *Ibid.*, 85–6.
52. *Ibid.*
53. *Ibid.*, 59.
54. Van Hoek, 'Prehistoric rock art of Galloway', 20–40.
55. Ritchie, 'Beaker pottery in south-west Scotland', 124–135.

2

A DEVELOPING SOCIETY

THE BRONZE AGE

The art of metal-working, in gold, copper and bronze, spread to Europe through the medium of trading links with the ancient civilisations of the Middle East. That it was being practised in Italy by 3300 BC is evident from the recent discovery of a perfectly preserved man, equipped with a copper-bladed axe, in a glacier in the high Alps. It first becomes evident in England by about 2700 BC,[1] but it was not until some seven hundred years later that the earliest signs of it appear in Scotland, when there are indications of the existence of metal-workers in the Moray Firth area.[2]

This represented so huge a technological advance that, to a people accustomed to working with stone and flint, it must have smacked of sorcery, and was doubtless regarded with widespread suspicion. This, combined with the wide range of skills involved in metal-working, could account for the length of time it seems to have taken for it to become accepted. For not only did it involve the technical ability to identify ore-bearing rocks, but considerable expertise was needed to smelt and alloy the metals, as well as to manufacture the casting moulds. However, those chieftains who perceived its advantages, or were perhaps dazzled by the personal adornments associated with it, and who took metal smiths under their patronage, derived immediate benefit. For the superior weaponry which could be manufactured from it gave them an advantage over their stone- and flint-using rivals, and this had predictably far-reaching effects on contemporary society.

It was also a source of wealth for those who controlled the regions where ore-bearing rocks were found. Galloway could have been a case in point, as there are copper deposits around the fringes of the Cairnsmore of Fleet range, and also near Balcary Bay,[3] and although there is no evidence of it these could have been worked during Bronze Age times. By contrast, those parts of the country which lacked minerals, or the means to barter for them, became impoverished and depopulated. A particular example was Orkney whose once prosperous Neolithic society sank into oblivion.

The spread of metal-working resulted in a rapid intensification of

16

trade – both within the British Isles and with the Continent. Bronze, which
was the most widely used of all metals, is a good illustration. This is an alloy
of tin and copper, and while there are a number of copper deposits
throughout the country, tin had a scarcity value since it is found only in
Cornwall and Ireland. This led to a flourishing barter trade within Britain
and across the Irish Sea – both in the base metal itself and in its finished
products. Western Scotland clearly came within this nexus, as carvings of
flat axes of an Irish design have been found incised on burial cists at
Kilmartin in Argyllshire,[4] while a contemporary axe retrieved from the
Luce Sands is thought to have been manufactured in Ireland.[5] Further
confirmation of these links is evident from the presence of shards of
cinerary urns at other coastal sites in Galloway, as these are thought to
suggest 'contact with, if not movement from, Ireland'.[6] Therefore, it seems
likely that Irish smiths would have followed in the wake of these contacts,
and as some may have settled in Galloway it is not impossible that their
expertise enabled them to identify and develop the copper deposits there.

Whether or not this was the case, there is evidence of some affluence in
parts of Galloway. This is apparent from the discovery at Mid Torrs, on the
Luce Sands, of a selection of faience beads dating from about 1600 BC
which originated from the Near East. In fact, the whole area has yielded an
abundance of contemporary artefacts; excavations at Low Torrs have produced a range of buttons, mostly small and conical in shape, while the
articles of personal adornment found at Mid Torrs included a bun-shaped
jet button.[7] This site also yielded up a dagger dating from the sixteenth or
seventeenth century BC, while others were found at nearby Carlochan Cairn
and Dunragit.[8] Buttons were not the only articles associated with clothing,
because a number of jet rings which have come to light are thought to have
been belt fasteners[9]; while dress pins and jewellery have been recovered
from burial cists, and a cache of toggles and jet disc beads was found at a
site near Stoneykirk in the Rhinns.

DISINTEGRATION

The first half of the second millennium BC appears to have been a time of
relative prosperity, with a consequent expansion of the population. This is
apparent from the growing concentration of small villages or communities
in the lower-lying regions, where more land was being taken into cultivation, while the uplands were being reclaimed as pasture. However, the
prosperity was precarious, because it was becoming increasingly dependent
on a continuation of the favourable climate; but in fact this had already
begun to deteriorate, as it was in the process of changing from the relatively
stable Continental pattern to the more variable Atlantic. This was becoming steadily more apparent from about 1500 BC onwards, when hurricane

force winds began to sweep the country and are believed to have been responsible for much of the sand dune formation which exists today along the Galloway coast.

With the onset of cooler weather the growing season shortened, and cereal cultivation gave way to stock-rearing. Higher rainfall is evident from the acceleration of peat formation in the upland regions, and as this intruded into the pasture lands it led to the abandonment of settlements there. Symptomatic of the reduced level of cultivation was the marked decline in hand axes dating from about 1200 BC onwards,[10] which suggests that native forest was no longer being cut back to provide additional grazing land. Therefore, it seems likely that, towards the end of the second millenium BC, the situation had reached a point where middle Bronze Age society was poised on a knife-edge, and it only needed a few seasons of consistently bad weather to tip it over into catastrophe.[11]

This occurred when Mount Hekla in Iceland erupted cataclysmically in 1159 BC. Judging from the fact that nothing remained of it until the emergence of the present one in the fourteenth century AD,[12] the force of the explosion must have blown the whole mountain apart. Volcanic dust, or tephra, was spewed into the atmosphere and blown by winds across northern and western Scotland, where the scale of the disaster is evident from tree pollens preserved in peat and lake sediments, and in the tree rings of timbers found in bogs.[13] Further signs of a deteriorating climate come from a core of peat taken from a site at Torrs Warren in the Luce Sands. This shows certain vegetational changes occurring from about 1100–700 BC, and because these are associated with a rising water table,[14] it is clear that the weather had become much wetter. Land went out of cultivation, while the consequent outbreaks of famine are reckoned to have killed off almost half the population of Britain, and some seven centuries were to elapse before numbers recovered to their former level.[15]

Competition for dwindling resources must have led to increasing violence, and it is significant that a more sophisticated range of weaponry, such as spearheads, rapiers and dirks, date from this time,[16] and there is also growing evidence of settlements being protected by defensive structures. While the short-term results are readily detectable, the longer-term effects are harder to assess, though the presence of such weaponry suggests the emergence of a warrior caste, and hence of warlords, to whom local communities would make voluntary submission and pay tribute in return for their protection. This in turn indicates the development of a better organised, more structured, and increasingly tribalised society.

The existence of an élite group is also reflected in the substantial houses which were being built for local chiefs and community leaders during later Bronze Age times, as well as the earlier hillforts which date from approximately 1000 BC onwards.[17] Most of the contemporary weaponry has been found on sites in the main river valleys of eastern Scotland, though discoveries of a disparate group of long-bladed swords at Drumcoltran near Kirkgunzeon, as well as other weapons in a hoard of bronzeware in Glentrool, could point to a local warrior class in Galloway. However, traces of permanently occupied field systems in southern Scotland, which date from later Bronze Age times,[18] suggest a return to a semblance of prosperity, while fragments of cloth associated with a contemporary axe found in the Luce Sands are indicative of flax being grown in Galloway.[19]

A NEW CULTURE

Meanwhile, trade continued between Britain and the Continent, and these contacts led to a steady flow of people in both directions, with a consequent interchange of cultures and ideas. It was through this medium that the more advanced technology of iron-working was introduced into Britain – a skill which is generally associated with the Celts. A good deal of myth attaches to these people, particularly to 'Celticism' which was mainly concocted by eighteenth- and nineteenth-century romanticists who claimed to have 're-discovered' (but largely invented) a 'Celtic' culture which was perceived to have existed in the Highlands until forcibly suppressed in the aftermath of the 1745 rebellion. The name itself is derived from the word *Keltoi* which was applied by the Greeks to invaders from the north. But, far from having any ethnic significance, the term was simply used to describe a people consisting mainly of Bronze Age farmers, who inhabited part of central Europe extending from Austria across to the lower Rhône.

Early in the first millennium BC these people acquired the technology of iron-working, and while this metal was mainly used in the manufacture of tools, utensils and weaponry, it inspired the development of a bronze-working culture which reflected their latent artistic genius, and in time became highly sophisticated. An early stage in its development was given the name Hallstatt after an ancient cemetery in Austria where a large amount of ornamental weaponry was found. The more advanced level was known as La Tène from a site near Neufchâtel, in Switzerland, where a number of examples were found. More importantly, the weaponry forged from iron had a greater durability, thus giving these people an advantage over their bronze-using neighbours, and this accounted for their success in warfare. They also controlled the large salt deposits in the Salzkammergut region of Austria, and as this commodity was in keen demand it led to an expansion of their trading links with other parts of Europe, including Britain. The earliest evidence of these contacts in Scotland consists of some pieces of bronze metalwork, dating from about 600 BC, which were found on a number of sites in Aberdeenshire, and it is their association with the use of horses which suggests a Celtic influence.

Population pressure was primarily responsible for forcing successive migrations of Celtic people from their homelands into other parts of Europe. This continued at an accelerating rate, and in the course of these they penetrated into the Balkans, posing a formidable threat to the Greeks; they also invaded Italy, sacking Rome in about 390 BC. Classical writers have much to say about these 'barbarians', as they called them. For example, the Greek historian and geographer Strabo describes the terror they inspired in their opponents by their practice of stiffening their hair into lime-coated spikes, allegedly hard enough to impale an apple,[20] claiming that 'the whole race is war-mad and both high spirited and quick for battle'.

Others penetrated northwards, eventually establishing a dominance over the inhabitants of much of Gaul and the Low Countries. Here the prowess of their warriors in battle is well recorded, their women being as doughty fighters as the men. The Roman historian Ammianus Marcellus paints a daunting picture of these amazons, describing how 'no foreigner could cope with them, least of all when she swells her neck and gnashes her teeth and, poising her huge white arms, begins to rain blows mingled with kicks like shots discharged by the twisted cords of a catapult'.[21]

Celtic domination of Gaul and the Low Countries resulted in a growing infiltration of these people into Britain, which eventually swelled to a mass influx of complete tribal entities. An early example were the *Parisii* from the region of the Marne who established themselves in eastern Yorkshire during the fourth century BC, and later the *Belgae* who colonised much of south-eastern England. These bases were the nuclei for the diffusion of Iron Age culture through existing trade routes into other parts of Britain, and this was the prelude to the establishment of a Celtic dominance over these regions, probably involving the overthrow of local ruling élites and a takeover of an existing underclass.

While this was probably the case in much of northern Britain, where the number of Celtic incomers is likely to have been relatively small, the situation was different in the south, where colonisation was more extensive and local populations were massacred, enslaved or driven out of their homelands. Similarities between pieces of contemporary pottery and other artefacts found as far afield as south-west England and the Hebrides suggest that a number of these refugees escaped northwards by sea. Some may have landed in Galloway, and this could account for the existence of a number of coastal settlements, such as McCulloch's castle near Kirkbean, while there is also evidence of their presence in caves near the Dee estuary.[22]

It has been suggested that a flourishing and vibrant Celtic community existed in the district of the lower Nith, though if true this is more likely to have consisted of an iron-using, mainly native, population. In fact, the chances are that only a comparatively small number of incomers settled in south-west Scotland, but it was because of the superiority of their weaponry that they were able to achieve a dominance over the local population and establish themselves as a ruling class. This would have resulted in a diffusion of their Iron Age culture among the native inhabitants, while their Brittonic variant of the Celtic languages became the prevailing speech.[23] Therefore it seems certain that the British population of medieval Galloway, far from being Celtic, were primarily descendants of the Bronze Age inhabitants of the region.

THE IRON AGE

Historians draw a convenient, if somewhat artificial, distinction between the Bronze and Iron Ages, though in fact there was no clear division, and the one simply merged into the other, the only difference being that iron came to be used in addition to bronze. For Iron Age people continued to recycle old bronze, and a thriving trade continued in tin and copper ores to make new metal, and this was the medium for some of their finest craftsmanship. Therefore, it is difficult to say when the Iron Age began, though it is generally regarded as lasting for roughly a thousand years from 500 BC to AD 500, and consequently it continued throughout the whole period of the Roman presence in Britain.

The Iron Age was primarily an extension of the Bronze Age, and this was particularly apparent in the development of a tribally-based society whose origins were almost certainly rooted in Neolithic times. The process was uneven, and much depended on local conditions, though all sources indicate that it had become universal in Britain by the end of the first millennium BC.[24] Our knowledge of the identity of these tribes is mainly derived from the map drawn up by the Alexandrian geographer Ptolemy in the second century AD. It purports to show each individual tribe in Britain with a rough indication of where they were located, though it conceals the fact that these tribes varied in size and cohesiveness according to the local terrain. For example, it has been asserted that 'it is likely from the available evidence that significant centralised social and political groups may have occurred at a local scale in areas like East Lothian, but that over much of Scotland regional groupings were more loosely organised'.[25] On the same theme, another source contends that 'in the north and west . . . it is possible the tribe represented nothing more than a loose alliance of individual petty chieftains and communities'.[26]

The inhabitants of Galloway were a case in point, because its topography clearly dictated a fragmented society consisting of small groups or communities, each having a local chief or 'headman' who would normally occupy a high status dwelling. This could account for the large number of hillforts and local power centres there compared with other parts of the country. While many hillforts can be readily identified, other centres of

local power are less obvious, although one is known to have existed around
Threave, and another at Lochrutton where the remains of a large crannog
have been discovered. Also in Wigtownshire, where the area around
Whithorn was the principal power centre in the Machars, while another
smaller one existed at nearby Rispain, but it is impossible to say whether
this dates from early or later Iron Age times.

Ptolemy's map shows the particular tribe inhabiting south-west Scotland
as having the Romanised name of *Novantae*, but this was no more than a
federation of loosely-knit communities, perhaps under the overall control
of a chieftain whose ruling centre was based at the Moyle. This is a nine-acre
site occupying a commanding position on the crest of a hill overlooking the
Urr estuary, and it is the only earthwork in Galloway that approaches the
larger type of hillforts, known as *oppida*, which were the traditional tribal
ruling centres. The best examples are the forts on the Eildon Hills and on
Traprain Law in East Lothian, which were the respective ruling centres of
the *Selgovae* and the *Votadini* tribes, and it is on sites such as these that
evidence appears of a small-scale domestic industry producing the limited
range of bronze and iron objects which were required to meet local
demand. However, this was not exclusive to the larger forts, because there
are signs of a contemporary metal-working industry at the Mote of Mark,
which is situated immediately below the Moyle on the Urr estuary.

Reflecting their function as refuges in time of danger, most hillforts were
surrounded by a rampart; and while the earlier ones were timber-built it
eventually became the practice to face them with stone, infill them with
turf and rubble, and to insert wooden beams to give them stability. In some
cases they were fired, and the heat caused sections of the stonework to fuse
together into a slaggy mass, thus becoming what are known as 'vitrified'
forts. Traditionally, this was attributed to enemy action, when attackers are
presumed to have set the ramparts on fire in order to destroy them and
smoke out the defenders. However, it has been shown that it would have
taken more than this to achieve vitrification, because it could only be done
by keeping the fire going for a long time and using huge quantities of fuel,
and therefore it was more likely to have been a symbolic demonstration of
the chief's power.[27] There are very few examples in Galloway, though there
is evidence of one at Trusty's Hill, near Gatehouse, which could conceivably
date from this time.

Crannogs were another form of defensive structure, although evidence
from Ireland shows that they also served as high-status settlements. Sited on
lochs, they were built on a foundation of tree trunks with an infill of peat
and stones and weighed down with boulders to form an artificial island,
and in many cases they were connected with the shore by a removable
causeway. While most of them are associated with the Iron Age, some go
back to Bronze Age times, and a crannog at Loch Olavat on Benbecula

dates from the Neolithic. There are believed to have been a large number in Galloway, but only comparatively few are identifiable today. An analysis of the remains of one crannog, which was excavated in Milton Loch during a spell of dry weather in 1953 when the water level was unusually low, shows it to have been built during the fourth century BC and that it continued to be occupied until the second century AD.[28]

Isolated crannogs were probably the exception, since most of them seem to have been built in clusters. For example, when Dowalton Loch in the Machars was drained in 1863 it was found to contain five crannogs, while six smaller stone heaps surrounded by piles are thought to have been the remains of other dwellings. The indications are that the settlement was started in the Bronze Age and added to throughout the Iron Age, and even in medieval times.[29] The quantity of material used for the foundations of these crannogs was prodigious, and it is believed that some three thousand large trees were used in the construction of a small crannog at Barhapple Loch, near Glenluce. They continued to be used as places of refuge throughout the Middle Ages, and it was not until the seventeenth century that an Act of Parliament was passed making it illegal to build them.

Other types of Iron Age fortifications, known as duns and brochs, are mainly confined to northern and western Scotland. Brochs were circular, stone-built towers which tapered towards the top, and if the evidence of one at Mousa on Shetland is anything to go by these could have been upwards of 13m (43 ft) high.[30] Being entirely windowless, and with access given by a single door, protection was bought at the cost of almost total darkness, while even the smallest fire would have rendered it extremely smoky as well. The few that exist in Galloway are confined to the west, where the best example is at Ardwell Point in the Rhinns. A dun, on the other hand, is the name applied to a type of circular or oval stone-walled fort which is found mainly in Argyllshire, the only example known in Galloway being at Castlehaven, near Borgue. There are two schools of thought as to the provenance of these structures in Galloway. Earlier archaeologists attributed them to immigrants from northern Scotland, and while they are now believed to have been commissioned by local chieftains they could nevertheless reflect a different type of social organisation which was attributable to outside influences.

RELIGIOUS CUSTOMS

While chieftains and 'headmen' exercised secular power within their tribes and communities, religious matters were the preserve of the priestly class, and although the latter are popularly associated with druidism there is no evidence that this existed north of Wales. But, druids or not, the priests were responsible for all religious matters and for conducting the ritualistic

ceremonies associated with them. Celtic deities were not seen to exist
exclusively in the sky, but also as lurking in pools, lochs, rivers or streams,
for water was regarded as the principal source of life, and therefore
sacrifices were made to the gods by casting weaponry and other artefacts
into them. The evidence of a hoard of bronzework found in a peat bog
near Corrymuckloch in Perthshire suggests that this practice was a survival
from Bronze Age times, because these artefacts were almost certainly a
votive offering, and being dated to around 800 BC[31] they long preceded the
arrival of Celts in Britain.

The encroachment of peat on the lochs and other watery places, where
votive offerings were deposited, has been responsible for their
preservation, and the best-known example in Galloway is a metal head
band for a pony with holes for its ears, known as a 'chamfrein'. Dating from
the second century BC, this was found, along with a pair of drinking cups,
in a bog at Torrs, near Castle Douglas, and as it has been identified as
reflecting the la Tène culture it was probably non-native, and therefore
most likely acquired through trade, or possibly as an heirloom.[32]

Another important local discovery was a large bronze cauldron
containing approximately a hundred separate pieces of metalware dating
from the first or second centuries AD, which was accidentally dredged up
from Carlingwark Loch by two fishermen in 1866. It is conceivable that they
represented the stock-in-trade of a local smith, which was deposited in the
cauldron and dropped into the loch for safety, though they could equally
well have been a votive offering. They are particularly interesting for the
light they shed on contemporary society in Galloway. Many of the
implements are indicative of a primarily agricultural community consisting
of farmers, peasants, shepherds and smiths, while the eight sword-tips and
fragments of chain mail, which are of native origin, are believed to have
been used by auxiliary troops drafted into the Roman army.[33]

A collection of fine bronzework, including a la Tène crescentic plate and
a magnificent polished hand mirror, was found near Balmaclellan in 1861.
These are thought to have belonged to a Brigantian nobleman and his followers who had taken refuge in Galloway following the suppression of the
unsuccessful revolt in their northern England homeland in the early 70s
AD. During Roman times it became the practice to make offerings to the
deities in the form of coins, and a number have come to light in the
remains of a fourth-century roundhouse, possibly a former shrine, recently
excavated at Buittle. Although identified as counterfeit, this was not
intended to short-change the god in question, but rather to discourage a
subsequent worshipper from appropriating the offerings for himself! In
fact, it is thought there was a considerable amount of forged currency in
circulation, mainly because local smiths found that manufacturing it was a
highly profitable business.[34]

Propitiatory offerings were merely one aspect of contemporary religious practices, for other more barbaric ones involved the ritual sacrifice of animals as well as humans and, on the evidence of Irish sources, even cannibalism. Since religion was an integral part of life, sacrifices were important ceremonial occasions which superstitious dread compelled the people to attend, and Julius Caesar noted that to be banned by the tribal elders from doing so was not only a severe punishment but also a token of extreme disgrace.[35] In some cases the prospective victims are believed to have been eviscerated and their entrails used by the priests to foretell the future[36] – a practice which had long been followed by the Romans. Perhaps the most gruesome of all was a form of sacrifice described by Strabo (and confirmed by Caesar) which involved the construction of a huge, wicker effigy of a god, 'the extremities of which they fill with live men'. Once full and the apertures sealed up it was set on fire and the victims were burned alive.[37]

Ritual strangulation was more often the rule, an example being the Iron Age man who was found in a near-perfect condition in Lindow Moss, near Manchester. A reconstruction of the ceremony revealed that a cord had been wound round his neck, and by twisting it with the aid of a stick the executioner had garotted him and then cut his throat. Beheading was also practised, and an example came to light with the discovery in a cave near Covesea, in Moray, of a quantity of human bones, which included the severed crania and cervical vertebrae of a number of children. Investigation showed that they were first decapitated with a sharp blade, in what was clearly a ritual sacrifice, and their severed heads were impaled on stakes. After the flesh had rotted away and the jaws had fallen off, the skulls were placed on racks for public display.[38]

This rite was symptomatic of the Celts' reverence for the human head, in which the soul was believed to lurk after death, and this accounted for their well-documented practice of hacking off the heads of their enemies slain in battle as trophies. Diodorus Siculus tells us how the Celts 'fasten them about the necks of their horses [and] carry them off as booty . . . and these first-fruits of battle they fasten by nails upon their houses, just as men do in certain kinds of hunting with the heads of wild beasts they have mastered'. They believed, too, that by sucking out the brains of a dead warrior or a tribal elder they could absorb for ever the meritorious qualities for which he had been renowned during his lifetime, while brotherhood with the dead was cemented by drinking, while still warm, the blood of a companion-in-arms slain in battle.

IRON AGE FARMERS

The Iron Age people depended above all on agriculture for their livelihood, and farming settlements were dispersed throughout the countryside. Their size was dictated by the quality of the land and could vary from a group of houses, accommodating an extended family and its dependants, to a single farmstead. In common with those dating from later Bronze Age times, the houses were usually circular with thatched roofs and walls constructed of wood, though later on a growing shortage of native timber led to stone being used instead. In most cases the farmstead was protected by a surrounding bank or ditch to prevent intrusion by livestock, and one example dating from the later Iron Age has been excavated at Rispain camp near Whithorn. Here, a ring of postholes indicates the existence of a former roundhouse which had a diameter of some forty-five metres and is thought to have been one of eight similar structures. Some cattle, sheep and pig bones retrieved from a section of the surrounding ditch are clearly representative of the livestock maintained by the community, while the presence of carbonised seeds of wheat and hulled barley are indicative of the crops which were grown at the time.[39]

These communities were centres of small, localised 'cottage' industries, such as spinning and weaving, as well as curing animal hides for clothing, and fashioning buttons and other artefacts from horn. The existence of a cloth-making industry is apparent from the discovery in a cave at Borness, near Borgue, of stones pierced with holes which have been identified as weights for a handloom, and there is similar evidence at other sites, including Buittle and Whithorn. Also found in the cave at Borness was a comb fashioned from a piece of bone, which is early evidence of an industry that would survive for a long time in Galloway, notably at Whithorn.

Although farming was carried out more extensively during Iron Age times compared with the past, the techniques would have changed little, except that the introduction of iron enabled more durable implements to be manufactured, including an ard-type plough which was capable of scratching the soil more effectively. An example was found in Milton Loch near Crocketford in 1953, while another artefact, tentatively identified as a plough, was retrieved from the site at Pict's Knowe in the 1990s. Other farm implements included wheeled carts with a shaft protruding at the front, to which the oxen were yoked, though the discovery at Blair Drummond in Perthshire of a cart with solid wooden wheels dating from the ninth century BC[40] shows these were already being used by Bronze Age people. The only difference, however, was that the wheels were now equipped with iron rims.

Iron Age farming in Galloway was primarily pastoral, perhaps reflecting Professor Piggott's portrayal of a society of 'Celtic cowboys and shepherds footloose and unpredictable, moving with their animals over rough pasture and moorland'. It appears that their livestock consisted mainly of sheep, cattle and pigs, the last being akin to the wild species, and perhaps even selected from the indigenous stock. The sheep are thought to have resembled the Soay sheep of today[41] and were perhaps descended from those imported by the Neolithic people, though they appear to have been used more for their milk and wool rather than for meat. The wool was dyed with berries and lichens to produce the bright-coloured clothing which is traditionally associated with the Celtic people.

Their cattle included a now-extinct breed known as the Celtic Shorthorn,[42] which is believed to have been akin to the modern-day Highland cattle,[43] and these were bred selectively to produce the compact and powerful oxen which were needed for ploughing and drawing heavy wagons. On the other hand, their horses, which were mostly lightweight ponies resembling the Exmoor of today, were used for warfare rather than farmwork, and judging by Caesar's allusions to the Gauls' partiality for horse dealing, and the high prices paid for good quality animals, there seems to have been a lively trade in them. On the evidence of bone remains and their effigies on pottery, it seems that the type of dogs they kept ranged from small animals, probably domestic pets, to the large hunting dogs mentioned by Strabo.[44] The latter, possibly akin to the Irish wolfhound, was one of Galloway's principal exports during the later Iron Age, as well as in medieval times.

The Celts attached great importance to their domestic animals, for in their society wealth was measured in terms of livestock, and this would remain a feature of native British societies throughout medieval times. Therefore, it was a reflection of their value that the penalties imposed on malefactors frequently involved the forfeiture of cattle. Whereas the ownership of cattle represented wealth, real power depended on the right to control the produce from the land, and therefore this was the preserve of the aristocracy. Any question of landownership became irrelevant, since it was regarded as belonging in common to the occupying kindred, clan or community, and this concept of communal land tenure survived in the British multiple estates in Galloway until well into medieval times.

Modern research has shown that Iron Age farming was highly skilled,[45] though there was only a limited amount of crop growing in Galloway. This was because much of the land consisted of lochs, boggy flows and mosses; and, whereas the uplands were dedicated to livestock rearing, the lower reaches of the main river valleys and the coastal merselands were generally too waterlogged to be worked properly, so they were abandoned as woodland. Therefore, crop growing was limited to those relatively few districts where the land was capable of being cultivated. The partial excavation of two small middens at Brighouse Bay, near Borgue, shows evidence of arable farming in the neighbourhood, as these were found to contain fragments of charcoal and other evidence of fire, which are thought to be the remains of primitive kilns used for rendering sea-shells into lime.[46] The cereal crops consisted mainly of emmer wheat, though the fact that other varieties were found in the gut of the Lindow victim suggests that this was not grown exclusively, while recent research has shown yields to be more prolific than previously thought.[47] Such then were the conditions that prevailed during the time of the Roman presence in Galloway, which began at the end of the first century AD and would continue intermittently for some three centuries.

NOTES

1. Oram, *Scottish Prehistory*, 50.
2. *Ibid.*, 54.
3. Conversation with A.I.N. Penman, the Director of excavations at Buittle.
4. Oram, *Scottish Prehistory*, 54–5.
5. Henshall, 'Report on cloth associated with a socketed axe from Luce Sands', 17.
6. Morrison, 'Cinerary urns and pygmy vessels in south-west Scotland', 95.
7. Ritchie and Shepherd, 'Beaker pottery and associated artefacts in south-west Scotland', 30.
8. *Ibid.*
9. *Ibid.*
10. Oram, *Scottish Prehistory*, 63–4.
11. *Ibid.*, 62.
12. I was told this by a local vulcanologist during a visit to Iceland in 1979. Apparently local farmers found their sheep were dying in inexplicably large numbers, and only later was the cause attributed to lethal gases issuing from the ground before the eruption occurred.
13. There is similar evidence in the narrow growth rings in the remains of oak trees in Ireland dating from this time. (Oram, *Scottish Prehistory*, 62).
14. Cowie and others, 'Torrs Warren, Luce Sands', 86.
15. Oram, *Scottish Prehistory*, 63.
16. *Ibid.*, 63–4.
17. Armit, *Celtic Scotland*, 46.
18. Feacham, 'Ancient agriculture in the high land of Britain', 339–47.
19. Henshall, 'Report on cloth', 17.
20. Ross, *Pagan Celts*, 33.
21. *Ibid*, 34: Loeb, 195: M.A., xv.12.1.
22. Scott-Elliot gives a comprehensive description of this feature in his paper 'McCulloch's castle, Arbigland', 118–124, but he offers no speculation as to its provenance.
23. With possible over-simplification, linguists have identified two principal variants of the tongues spoken by the Celtic people. The older one, known as Goidelic (or Q-Celtic), was the forerunner of Irish Gaelic (or Erse) which

spread to Galloway and Argyllshire, and was the language spoken throughout most of Scotland during medieval times The other, which linguists call P-Celtic, was imported by immigrants from Gaul into Britain, where a variant known as Brittonic (or Brythonic) developed. This was the *lingua franca* of pre-Roman Britain, being the forerunner of Cumbric, which was the speech of the Galloway Britons, modern-day Welsh, Breton, and the now-extinct Cornish.

24. Oram, *Scottish Prehistory*, 73.
25. Hingley, 'Society in Scotland', 34.
26. Oram, *Scottish Prehistory*, 73.
27. Armit, *Celtic Scotland*, 59.
28. Oram, *Scottish Prehistory*, 89.
29. Hunter, 'Dowalton loch re-considered', 53–71. The only visisble sign of a former crannog there is a large clump of rhododendrons standing out incongruously in a reed-infested swamp.
30. Breeze, *Roman Scotland*, 99.
31. Armit, *Celtic Scotland*, pp 22–4.
32. Oram, *Scottish Prehistory*, 92.
33. Piggott, 'Three metal-work hoards': Botel bailey excavations: Interim Report:
34. Hawkins, 'Numismatic Report'. 22–3: Botel bailey excavations: Interim Report 1999.
35. Ross, *Pagan Celts*, 102.
36. Armit, *Celtic Scotland*, 93.
37. Delaney, *The Celts*, 89.
38. Oram, *Scottish Prehistory*, pp 89–90.
39. Haggarty, 'Excavations at Rispain camp, Whithorn', 30–42.
40. Ashmore, *Neolithic and Bronze Age Scotland*, 113.
41. Ross, *Pagan Celts*, 69.
42. Breeze, *Roman Britain*, 84.
43. Ross, *Pagan Celts*, 69.
44. *Ibid.*, 70.
45. Dodghson, *Land and Society*, 24.
46. Maynard and others, 'The dune system at Brighouse Bay'.
47. This was the result of an experimental project carried out at Butser Ancient Farm, near Petersfield in Hampshire, during the 1970s.

3

ROMAN INTERLUDE

EARLY PRESENCE

The Romans are renowned as a militant, methodical and ruthlessly practical people who created the most effective military machine the world had ever known. Through this instrument of aggression, whose commanders included some of the most illustrious generals in the history of warfare, they built up an empire which lasted for half a millennium, and which at its maximum extent covered much of the known world. They first arrived in Britain in 55 BC, when Julius Caesar launched a punitive expedition across the Channel in retaliation for the help given by local mercenaries in opposing his conquest of Gaul. As this was only partially successful, he returned with a larger force the following year, when he succeeded in subduing the whole of the south-east. However, he was forced to break off his campaign and return to Gaul in order to suppress a rebellion which had broken out there, so he was denied the chance to consolidate his gains.

Thereafter, the Romans left the native British to pursue the inter-tribal rivalries which were a feature of their Iron Age society, and it was not until AD 43 that the Emperor Claudius launched a second invasion of the island. He had recently succeeded his nephew, the infamous Caligula, and needed a military success to shore up his political position at home. This coincided with a renewal of the civil war between the native British princes, and it was the appeal for help from the pro-Roman leader Verica that gave him the necessary pretext[1] (the Romans invariably sought to justify their acts of aggression). Therefore, he dispatched an army there under Aulus Plautius, but because resistance proved unexpectedly strong he was eventually compelled to come to Britain and take command in person. According to the Roman commentators, he scored a number of victories, and after subduing the south-east he returned to Rome leaving Aulus Plautius with the somewhat vague instruction 'to conquer the rest'.

During the next fifteen years Plautius and his successors brought much of present-day England under control. However, in 58, while the governor Suetonius Paulinus was engaged in attacking the main centre of British resistance in North Wales, a rebellion broke out in East Anglia under

Boudica (Boadicea), queen of the Iceni, who proceeded to sack the Roman capital of Colchester. This developed into a major crisis, and as it threatened the entire Roman occupation of Britain Paulinus was forced to abandon his campaign and come to the rescue. Although order was restored, it delayed the conquest of the province for some years, so it was not until 78 that this was finally achieved by the new governor, Agricola, who had formerly been one of Paulinus' staff officers.

The conquest of Galloway

The initial period of Roman occupation of southern Scotland is known as the Flavian, after the ruling dynasty of Roman emperors, in order to distinguish it from the subsequent occupations. The first of these emperors was Vespasian, a former legionary commander under Aulus Plautius, who usurped the throne in 79. As he was determined to impose his authority beyond the frontier of Roman Britain, he ordered Agricola to conquer the region to the north, and consequently most of his governorship was spent campaigning there. As a result of a number of successful operations he managed to bring much of southern and central Scotland under Roman rule, and in order to consolidate his gains he built a chain of forts across the Forth-Clyde isthmus and up the Tay.

According to Agricola's son-in-law and biographer Tacitus, it was 'in the fifth season' of his governorship, probably in 81, that he turned his attention to the territories to the west. Tacitus' account states baldly that 'Agricola crossed over in the first ship (*nave prima transgressus*) and, in a string of successful battles, he subdued tribes who had never been heard of till now; and he stationed troops in that part of Britain which faces Ireland'.[2] This poses a number of questions. Which stretch of sea did Agricola cross, even if he did so at all; where were his troops lined up when they faced Ireland; and did his string of successful battles take place in Galloway? Although there are no certain answers, the evidence seems pretty conclusive. For if Agricola had already conquered much of southern Scotland and established a northern frontier along the Forth/Clyde line, it stands to reason that he should have wanted to subjugate the south-west, and since military installations were established in the region shortly afterwards this would seem to clinch the argument. Therefore, it follows that his troops must have been lined up on the Rhinns when they faced Ireland.

Again, it is not known where the campaign was launched from, and the alternative theories depend on the differing interpretations placed on Tacitus' account. Taken at their face value, the words *nave prima* (in the first ship) suggests it was preceded by a sea crossing. But from where? Could it have been across the Solway from present-day Cumbria, or was it from the legionary headquarters at Chester where Agricola's troops would have spent the preceding winter? Even assuming it was a naval operation, which is by no means certain, it begs the question of where the troops would have disembarked. The discovery of a contemporary fort near Annan[3] suggests this as a possibility, though it seems more likely that the fleet was anchored further along the coast at the more accessible Urr estuary, with the soldiery and their equipment being transferred to flat-bottomed barges which served as landing craft. If so, they were probably transported upstream and disembarked at Buittle, which would have been a perfectly feasible operation since the sea level was some 8m higher than it is today.[4]

In conformity with standard Roman practice, Agricola and his sub-ordinate commanders would have gathered as much information as possible about the region and its inhabitants from merchants, travellers and refugees, and perhaps also from spies. Once the campaign was under way, up-to-date news would be obtained from prisoners, deserters, and friendly tribesmen. The number of troops involved can only be surmised, though it was probably substantially less than the 20,000 or so who are thought to have taken part in the following year's advance beyond the Tay, which culminated in Agricola's victory at Mons Graupius.[5]

Judging from Tacitus' reference to 'a string of successful battles', it would seem that the invasion encountered strenuous resistance. On the other hand, the fact of their being 'a string of battles' implies that the local inhabitants were dispersed throughout the region in small, isolated communities and therefore unable to co-ordinate a proper defence. In fact, it has been suggested that these 'so-called tribal groupings had very little potential for corporate action during the whole of the Scottish Iron Age'.[6] Therefore, resistance must have been piecemeal, and Agricola would have been able to pick off local sub-tribes or communities one by one, with others perhaps surrendering voluntarily, and no doubt he took hostages from the families of local chiefs as an earnest of their good behaviour.

Having subdued Galloway, Agricola may have contemplated an invasion of Ireland – in fact this could have been his ultimate objective, and it is thought that a refugee Irish princeling in his retinue was designed to serve as the pretext.[7] Certainly, a conquest of Ireland is believed to have featured in the Romans' plans for the subjugation of the British Isles, but unrest on the northern frontier may have forced Agricola to shelve it, or he may have been instructed to do so by the new Emperor Domitian. As the commentators are silent on this point it has to be a matter for conjecture, and all that is known is that in the following year Agricola was campaigning beyond the Tay.

THE FLAVIAN OCCUPATION

Having conquered Galloway, the Romans established an occupying force in the region, and in conformity with their usual practice they built a number of semi-permanent forts and fortlets to accommodate it. While the fortlets were generally garrisoned by a unit of up to eighty strong, the larger forts provided quartering for a single regiment of between five hundred and a thousand men. These forts were so sited that they controlled the main river valleys, and their grid-like layout included barrack blocks which were occupied by individual units, and these were separated from one another by a series of intersecting thoroughfares. At the centre was the adminis-trative block, the commandant's quarters, and other offices such as the quartermaster's stores. A clear perimeter surrounded the whole complex to allow unimpeded access to the defensive rampart in an emergency, such as a surprise attack. In earlier Roman times forts were built of wood with an infill of earth, but a growing shortage of native timber resulted in the later ones being constructed of stone.

The camp at Dalswinton held the key to the south-west, as this controlled the lower Nith valley. Further upstream, a fortlet was built at Drumlanrig, while another at Ward Law near the Nith estuary was the main access point to the region. A fort was also established on the river Dee at Glenlochar, close to the native power-centre of Threave,[8] this being the first of the three which are known to have been built there.[9] Further west, a fortlet was established on the river Fleet, which was sited some two miles upstream from present-day Gatehouse.[10] As natural erosion combined with subsequent cultivation has removed all visible traces of these structures at ground level they are detectable by crop discolourations which can only be seen from the air. Those at Dalswinton, Glenlochar and Gatehouse are cases in point, as they were all discovered in the course of a series of reconnaissance flights which were carried out during a period of severe drought in the summer of 1949.[11]

A communications network was also established, which included surveil-lance, signalling posts, regular patrols and, most important of all, a road system. During the Flavian period a single spur road was built to connect Dalswinton with the main road through Annandale, which was the western of the two approach routes into Scotland. From Dalswinton, this spur continued up the Nith and Carron valleys, past the camp at Durisdeer, to rejoin the main approach road at the fort near Crawford, on the upper Clyde. It was probably at this time that the road system was extended into Galloway to link Dalswinton with Glenlochar, and perhaps also the fortlet at Gatehouse. As this is considered too small to have been a terminus, theory has it that the road was eventually continued across the hills to the Cree, and perhaps as far as the old native centre of Rerigonium near Loch Ryan.[12]

Much of this is speculative, and because of the dearth of hard evidence relating to this period of the Roman occupation very little is known about it. All the more so since it lasted for such a short time, for the following decade witnessed a series of military reverses on the lower Danube, which compelled the Romans to withdraw one of the four legions that comprised their occupying force in Britain. Consequently, most of their territorial gains in Scotland were abandoned, and the only forts remaining in commission were those which controlled the principal river systems in the south, such as Newstead in Tweeddale, Milton in Annandale, Dalswinton and Glenlochar. These, too, were evacuated sometime between 103 and 105, when they were systematically demolished and burnt by the Romans in the course of their planned withdrawal to a line between the Solway and the Tyne. This, therefore, marked the end of the Flavian occupation of southern Scotland.

For the next fourteen years they maintained a watching presence from their bases along the Tyne/Solway line, but when the northern Britons rebelled in 117[13] the Emperor Hadrian came to Britain in order 'to put things right', to quote his biographer. A brief appraisal of the situation convinced him that it was no longer profitable to maintain a presence beyond Tyne/Solway line, so it was decided to build a wall from Bowness on the Solway as far as the mouth of the Tyne. Named after him, this was mainly designed to control the movements of the local population and, as is evident from the remains which can be seen today, it was such a massive structure that it took most of the remaining sixteen years of his reign to build, and consequently it was not completed until shortly before his death in 138.

THE ANTONINE AND SEVERAN PERIODS

The accession of Hadrian's adopted son Antoninus Pius coincided with outbreaks of unrest in the territories beyond the Wall, and so in the following year the new emperor ordered his legate, Lollius Urbicus, to re-conquer southern Scotland. Urbicus opened his campaign with an advance up Nithsdale and Annandale in order to drive a wedge between the *Selgovae* and the *Novantae* tribesmen.[14] On reaching the line of the Forth and Clyde, he followed Agricola's example by constructing a line of defensive forts, which were reinforced by a stone and turf rampart combined with a large artificial ditch. Known as the Antonine Wall, this was a less elaborate structure than its counterpart further south, though it too was mainly designed to police the movements of the local people.

Reflecting a change of policy, which involved replacing the larger forts with fortlets approximately a day's march apart from each other,[15] the Romans strengthened the defensive line of the Nith by establishing three fortlets at Sanquhar, Barburgh Mill near Auldgirth, and at Lantonside adjacent to the former installation at Ward Law. A fort was established at Carzield, near Kirkton, to replace the abandoned one at Dalswinton, while another was built at Glenlochar. The latter fort was subsequently enlarged to provide accommodation for a *cohors miliaria equitata*,[16] which was a partly mounted unit of about a thousand strong, and was therefore comparable with the fort at Birrens in Dumfriesshire.[17] Since this was at odds with the contemporary practice of building smaller fortlets, it has been suggested that the new fort was intended as a base from which to launch an invasion into southern Ayrshire, though as events turned out this never took place.

During this time the road system in Galloway was extended, but the scarcity of surviving evidence makes it virtually impossible to determine what this involved. All that can be said is that the local topography seems to have dictated an irregular grid with one, or possibly two, lateral roads intersected by roads or tracks penetrating up the main river valleys. Glenlochar seems to have been the focal point, and from there a patrol road is believed to have followed an old-established track up the Dee and Ken valleys and over into Ayrshire to link with the seaport at Girvan.[18] Another one probably followed the Dee southwards to Kirkcudbright, which may have been a seaport in Roman times,[19] while there was most likely a connecting road between Glenlochar and a port on Orchardton Bay.[20] It stands to reason there would have been a road link with Buittle, as this continued to be a disembarking point for supplies and reinforcements destined for Glenlochar. Therefore, an improved Iron Age track is believed to have connected it with the road leading from Glenlochar to Orchardton Bay somewhere near present-day Castle Douglas.[21]

A fresh outbreak of trouble during the 150s resulted in the re-commissioning of the Antonine Wall, but it was abandoned again in about 163 when Hadrian's Wall was re-established as the northern frontier. Notwithstanding this, Cassius Dio tells us that, some twenty years later, in about 180, 'the British tribes crossed the wall [presumably Hadrian's Wall] and slew a general at the head of his army'.[22] The reigning emperor at the time was Commodus, an illegitimate son of the Emperor Marcus Aurelius, who was renowned as much for his brutality as his mental instability (he convinced himself he was the god Hercules). Nevertheless, appreciating the seriousness of the situation, he ordered his governor, Ulpius Marcellus, to counter attack. Initially he was unsuccessful, and it was only after he was sacked and replaced by a new governor that order was eventually restored, on the strength of which the emperor arrogated the title 'Britannicus'.

Thereafter an uneasy peace was maintained, but only at the expense of buying off, 'for a considerable sum of money', the *Caledonii* and *Maeatae* tribes, who inhabited the regions beyond the Forth.[23] By 208 the situation was getting out of hand again; so, in response to an appeal from the governor, the Emperor Septimius Severus came to Britain along with his two sons to restore order, and this resulted in the re-occupation of southern Scotland. Although the Antonine Wall was not put back into commission, forts were established at Cramond on the Forth, and at Carpow near Abernethy on the Tay. Three years later, Severus died at Eboracum (present-day York), whereupon his sons, the new Emperor Caracalla and Geta, 'returned to the fleshpots of Rome', having 'made treaties with the enemy, evacuated their territory and abandoned the forts'.[24]

ROMAN RULE

Relatively few Romans are likely to have set foot in Galloway, or even Scotland for that matter. Those who did would have been administrators and civil servants, since the soldiers were mainly conscripts drawn from other parts of the empire. Supported by the military, these administrators systematically 'romanised' the native populations, and Tacitus gives examples of the methods they used. Apart from levying taxes and requisitioning land, they extended to education, language, religion and dress[25] – all of which is understandable and logical. Education – of the native aristocracy – would have involved a comprehensive indoctrination, while a change to romanised speech and dress was designed to encourage them to assimilate more readily with the new régime. Similarly, it has almost invariably been the practice for conquerors to impose their religion on a defeated people. The Romans would undoubtedly have ordered the dismantling of the remaining hillforts, since they would have regarded them as possible centres of local resistance, and hence a potential threat to their rule, though it appears that most of them had already been abandoned.

How far the native people tolerated Roman rule can only be conjectured, though it would be fair to assume that, while some collaborated and the more courageous were actively resistant, the great majority probably accepted it with sullen acquiescence in the interests of a quiet life. Much would have depended on the local commander, and it is believed that particularly brutal ones were responsible for sporadic outbreaks of rebellion, as happened in southern Britain and Gaul. Their main grudge, however, was the heavy taxation imposed on them, because the Romans invariably tried to render their conquests self-financing operations.[26] In poorer regions, taxes were generally assessed in terms of food render, and the comparatively small amount of coinage found in Galloway suggests that this was standard practice there. It often happened that the commutation prices for food supplies were set at artificially low levels,[27] which rendered the taxes additionally punitive, while the Romans frequently resorted to extortion to obtain their victualling requirements.[28] This was an additional source of grievance, and is believed to have been responsible for the revolt which broke out on the northern frontier at the end of the second century.[29]

The Roman presence was probably more apparent at the higher levels of society, because it was normally their practice to rule conquered territories through existing organs of government, which in Britain were based on tribal groupings.[30] Therefore, only those leaders who were prepared to collaborate would be allowed to act as tribal chiefs, or 'headmen' of local communities, while hostages were taken from their families to ensure their co-operation, and a Roman presence was invariably maintained at tribal meetings. There were a number of recognised assembly points in Galloway – Rerigonium being one, while the standing stone near Kelton Hill marks another.[31] A third may have existed at Lucopibia, which was either at or near Whithorn,[32] and current excavations suggest that this was the site of a military installation during later Roman times.[33]

Roman troops, and their attendant civilians, constituted a valuable market for locally-produced goods – hides for the manufacture of leather being a particular example. This stimulated farmers to expand their cattle-rearing activities, while the demand for wool gave a corresponding fillip to sheep farming. The Romans encouraged this by introducing larger, long-woolled sheep into Britain in an attempt to improve the native stock, and as they are known to have done this in England it is quite possible they did so in southern Scotland as well. They also imported horses, but as the collar which allowed heavy loads to be pulled from the shoulder had not been invented the ox continued to be the main beast of burden, as it would be for centuries to come. Galloway in particular was renowned during Roman times as a source of domestic animals, particularly hunting dogs,[34] and it was also a major exporter of furs. Timber was exported too, and so was charcoal, but this was at the expense of making further inroads into the native forest, much of which had already been cut back to provide additional farmland.

There was also a heavy demand for cereals, and it has been calculated that it took some five hundred hectares to grow enough wheat to feed a single cohort of a thousand men.[35] As this was far in excess of what could be grown locally most of it had to be imported, though the Romans attempted to stimulate local production by introducing the practice of growing oats and rye in areas inimical to wheat. Their diet was primarily vegetarian, and an analysis of the remains of a latrine in the former fort at Bearsden on the Antonine Wall confirms this.[36] These contain traces of the herbs they used, such as coriander, dill and linseed, as well as the opium poppy, which was probably used for medicinal purposes, since the Roman soldiers are known to have suffered from intestinal parasitical worms. They also recognised the medicinal properties of mineral springs, and are believed to have made use of the chalybeate springs in Galloway.

Contact between Roman occupiers and native Britons became progressively closer as time went on. During the Flavian period this was virtually non-existent, and judging from the fact that first-century artefacts are found only on high status sites any such contacts were limited to the upper echelons of local society. Roman artefacts dating from the second century, on the other hand, are found on a wider range of settlements, which suggests that these contacts now extended further down the social scale and were becoming more widespread.[37] A particular example is the statuette of the god Mercury, which came to light in the course of ploughing on Stelloch Farm, near Monreith in Wigtownshire, in 1871.[38] Later, the arrival of an increasing number of civilians fuelled the demand for locally-produced goods, and this encouraged native merchants and traders to establish markets near their settlements, and at other strategic locations in the region.

Discoveries of contemporary coins in Galloway can also be interpreted as evidence of these contacts, although for the reasons stated relatively few have been found there compared with other parts of the country. Nevertheless, coins minted in different parts of the empire, which have come to light at Twynholm, Urr, and Balgreggan in Wigtownshire, could point to a trade between Roman occupiers and the local population. On the other hand, it is equally possible that those at Urr and Balgreggan were buried for safety during a period of unrest,[39] the owners being subsequently killed or otherwise prevented from retrieving them. Another trove of 125 coins was found inside a pottery vessel at Corsock. As these coins had already gone out of circulation, and were therefore valueless, they must have been used for ornamental purposes,[40] and the indications are that they too were buried on purpose.

There is other evidence of a thriving commerce in Galloway. Small industrial enterprises were emerging, and recent excavations reveal more pottery being made in Scotland than previously thought.[41] At the same time, speculators are believed to have been buying up neglected land in the river valleys beyond the militarised zone in order to reclaim it and sell it on at a profit. Meanwhile, the trade in grain, hides and wool gave other entrepreneurs the opportunity to act as middlemen by purchasing these commodities from farmers and other producers at wholesale prices, and retailing them to their customers. Through course of time, their dealings extended to the marketing of locally-produced artefacts as well.

The Roman conquest of western Europe brought a number of advantages to the local populations, because the imposition of their *pax romana* meant that trade could flourish unhindered by war or piracy. Consequently, existing trading links between Whithorn and the Continent expanded, and this is evident from the finds of contemporary imported artefacts. These include shards of Samian pottery manufactured in Gaul,[42] and as this was mainly exported to Britain during the reigns of the emperors Hadrian and Antoninus Pius the indications are that a romanised, or sub-romanised, settlement existed there, or at least in the vicinity, since as early as the second century.[43] Pieces of glass discovered there confirm this, as they have been identified as fragments of a type of imported vessel which is known to have been used at much the same time.[44]

ROMAN DECLINE

The third century was a time of growing pressure on the northern frontier. After the death of the Emperor Severus in 211, and the abandonment of southern Scotland by his sons, a measure of stability was maintained by a combination of alliances with the more powerful tribes of southern Scotland, and a judicious application of bribes and subsidies. However, as these tribesmen were themselves the victims of periodic attacks by others living beyond the Tay, later known as the Picts,[45] the situation remained unstable. Throughout the fourth century the Picts were to prove a constant source of trouble, and the Romans responded by adopting a carrot-and-stick approach. Attempts to buy them off with diplomacy, lubricated with bribes and subsidies, alternated with military action. The first was Constantius Chlorus' invasion of 305/6, and this was followed by another launched by his son, the Emperor Constantine, in 312, while *his* son Constans engaged in a similar campaign in 343. Some years later, in 360, the Picts counter attacked in alliance with the *Scotti*[46] from Antrim, though this was successfully repelled.

Shortly afterwards, there occurred the 'barbarian conspiracy' of 367, when the Romans in Britain were attacked on a number of different fronts by the Picts and *Scotti*, as well as the Saxons and the *Attecotti* (an unknown tribe from Ireland or the Western Isles), all probably acting in concert. Although the Roman general Theodosius managed to beat them off, the Picts and the *Scotti* launched another invasion in 382. Again they were repelled, this time by Magnus Maximus, and they were defeated once again, towards the end of the 390s, by the Roman general Stilicho.

By this time the empire in the west was coming under repeated and increasingly successful attacks from the tribes inhabiting the regions beyond its eastern frontier. Consequently, the Romans were compelled to start withdrawing their troops from Britain, eventually abandoning it altogether in 409/410. Although their presence in England lasted for upwards of three and a half centuries, their intermittent occupation of southern Scotland amounted to a mere fraction of that time. Yet, in spite of this, they had an important influence on the region – so much so, that their *romanitas* would survive for the next two centuries until it was finally extinguished under the impact of the expansion of the kingdom of Northumbria in the seventh century.

NOTES

1. Breeze, *Roman Scotland*, 31.
2. *Agricola* XXIV.
3. Saltway, *Roman Britain*, 145.
4. Maxwell, *A Battle Lost?*, 13–14.
5. Botel bailey excavation: Interim Report 1999. The discovery of ten coins there, dating from 32–31 BC, suggests that trading links between that port and Roman Britain, and perhaps even a Roman presence there, existed before the time of Agricola's invasion.
6. Hingley: 'Society in Scotland', 34.
7. Breeze, *Roman Scotland*, 39.
8. Brooke, *Wild Men*, 303–4.
9. Richmond and St Joseph: 'The Roman fort at Glenlochar', 11–12.
10. St. Joseph, 'The Roman fortlet at Gatehouse of Fleet', 222.
11. *Ibid*, 232.
12. A postulated road system in Galloway during Roman times is discussed in Wilson, 'Roman penetration in west Dumfries and Galloway: a field survey', 7–20.
13. Tradition has it that, in the course of the rebellion, an entire legion – the IX *Hispana* – disappeared. This goes on to assert that it went to ground in the fastnesses of southern Ayrshire, where it integrated with the local population and was allegedly responsible for the recurrence of certain supposedly Roman characteristics among the local population. In fact, it was withdrawn from Britain, first to Gallia-Belgica, then to Syria or Judaea, and finally to the Middle East, where it was either annihilated or cashiered following a major defeat.
14. Williams, 'The frontier policies of Antoninus Pius'.
15. Breeze, *Roman Scotland*, 53–54.
16. Richmond and St Joseph, 'The Roman fort at Glenlochar', 13.
17. *Ibid.*, 12–13.
18. Wilson, 'Roman penetration in west Dumfries and Galloway'.
19. It would have made sense for the Romans to develop a port at Kirkcudbright, given that supplies for their troops in Galloway invariably arrived by sea, and the Dee estuary was deeper than it is now. While not conclusive, the recent discovery (in 1998) of a Roman coin in Kirkcudbright harbour supports the theory.
20. The very obvious straightness of the Ayr/Castle Douglas road A713, and of its continuation along the minor road leading from Carlingwark loch past Gelston suggests they could have been built on the foundations of an old Roman road.
21. Conversation with A.I.N. Penman.
22. *Dio*, LXIII, viii.
23. Breeze, *Roman Scotland*, 104.
24. *Dio*, LXVII, i.

25. Breeze, *Roman Scotland*, pp 89–90.
26. Oram, *Scottish Prehistory*, 99.
27. Breeze, *Roman Scotland*, 84.
28. *Ibid.*, 84–6.
29. Oram, *Scottish Prehistory*, 99.
30. Breeze, *Roman Scotland*, 83.
31. Brooke, *Wild Men*, 52.
32. Rivet and Smith, *The Place-names of Roman Britain*, 389–90. This mentions a document known as the Ravenna Cosmography, which contains a list of place-names referred to as *diversi loci* and believed to have been recognised tribal assembly points (Breeze, *Roman Scotland*, 107). One of these, Lucocion or Lucotion, has been tentatively identified with the settlement of Lucopibia appearing on Ptolemy's map.
33. This seems evident from pieces of glass found at Whithorn, some of which have been identified as fragments of blown window panes similar to those used in army barracks, while others come from a type of bottle which was associated with military installations elsewhere in southern Scotland. The discovery of two early millstones, which are thought to be of Roman origin, are also suggestive, since they are described as being 'appropriate to the mill of a small town or large military establishment' (Hill, *Whithorn*, 293–7).
34. L Keppie, *Brittania* in (ed) S Frere (London, 1986).
35. Smith, *The Archaeological Background to the Emergent Kingdoms of the Tweed Basin in the Early Historic Period* (doctoral thesis).
36. Breeze, *Roman Scotland*, 78.
37. *Ibid.*, 88.
38. Hunter, 'Dowalton loch re-considered', 55.
39. *Ancient Rome, Galloway and Ayrshire*, 29–30.
40. Casey, *Roman Coinage of the Fourth Century in Scotland (Between and Beyond the Walls)* 1984, 302.
41. Breeze, *Roman Scotland*, 87.
42. Hill, *Whithorn*, 293.
43. *Ibid.*
44. *Ibid.*, 294.
45. The term *Picti* was first used by a Roman writer in 297.
46. The name *Scotti* is believed to be derived from an old Irish word meaning 'bandit'.

4

POST-ROMAN TIMES

A SUB-ROMAN SOCIETY

The collapse of the Roman empire in the west marked the onset of what was traditionally known as the Dark Age. This term merely reflects the absence of recorded history during that period, and is essentially a misnomer because enough alternative evidence has since come to light to give a reasonably comprehensive picture of contemporary events. The overthrow of the centralised authority of Rome did not necessarily imply a breakdown of the existing organs of government at local level, or of society generally, nor did it mark the end of Roman influence, culture and civilisation. True, the Germanic tribesmen from the coastal regions of northern Europe were steadily infiltrating into southern and eastern England, where they would eventually establish a ruling class, but for the people living in other parts of the country, life during the immediate post-Roman period would have continued much as before.

This must undoubtedly have been the case with those inhabiting present-day Galloway, while it is evident from discoveries of contemporary artefacts at Whithorn that the settlement there continued to be part of the west European and Mediterranean trading nexus. These include shards of amphorae of western Turkish and north African origin, which are thought to have been used for transporting olive and sesame oil, as well as other more costly oils and unguents.[1] Evidence of links with that part of the world is also confirmed by the contents of a former latrine at Whithorn which included the remains of culinary herbs of Mediterranean origin,[2] while shards of imported wheelmade pottery and glass vessels manufactured in Gaul[3] are indicative of contacts with that region as well.

More importantly, trade routes continued to serve as conduits for the spread of Roman culture, influence and ideas (or *romanitas*), so that sub-Roman trading posts like Whithorn were centres for their diffusion throughout the surrounding district. So, too, were certain larger towns, such as the former *civitas* of Carlisle which continued to be a centre of sub-Roman influence, besides being a source of *romanitas* which could well have extended beyond the Nith. Doubtless other small, semi-Romanised settlements existed along the Galloway coast at places like Kirkcudbright and Buittle, where traders engaged in commerce with their opposite numbers across the Solway and further afield.[4] Therefore, it is possible to visualise the inhabitants of the region comprising present-day Galloway as consisting mainly of rough peasant farmers living in small, clustered communities which were scattered throughout the region, with a ruling élite to whom they paid tribute, and a number of semi-Romanised – and hence more civilised – dwellers in the coastal settlements.

Meanwhile, a combination of factors – Roman influence, raids by Picts from the north, and the *Scotti* from Ireland, and most of all the natural evolution of an increasingly sophisticated society – accounted for the emergence, during the early centuries AD, of a number of small kingdoms ruled by independent princes with the support of a warrior aristocracy. One was Manau Gododdin, which embraced part of the region formerly occupied by the *Votadini* tribe. While Manau extended from the Carse of Forth across to Fife, Gododdin (or Guotodin, identifiable with the name *Votadini*) included the fertile territories of the Lothians as far as the Lammermuirs. To the south lay the kingdom of Bryniach which subsequently gave its name to the Northumbrian province of Bernicia. Another kingdom, centred on Dumbarton Rock, and straddling the lower Clyde basin, was known to the Britons as Cumbria and later as Strathclyde to the Scots. It has been asserted that 'a successful British dynasty with an active warband' was established there by the mid- to late-fifth century,[5] and in the following centuries its influence extended into much of present-day Ayrshire and Lanarkshire.

The Romans' departure from Britain encouraged the Picts and the *Scotti* to intensify their raids on mainland Britain, and the sixth-century British writer, Gildas, draws a lurid picture of them. 'From curroughs in which they had been carried across the valley of the sea', he wrote, 'there emerged foul crowds of *Scotti* and Picts, like dark hordes of maggots from the narrowest cracks and recesses when the sun is overhead and its rays grow warm'.[6] The Picts launched a series of raids down the coast of mainland Britain, though there is no evidence that these extended as far as Galloway. True, a potentially Pictish carving on a rock at Trusty's Hill near Gatehouse has prompted speculation that it marked the grave of a Pictish chief killed during a raid,[7] though this is now thought unlikely. If Galloway had been the victim of Pictish raids more signs would have appeared, so the concept of the Galloway Picts may be relegated to a twelfth-century invention, where it belongs.[8]

On the other hand, Galloway, in common with other parts of western Britain, was the target of repeated raids by the *Scotti*, which are recorded as occurring from the third century onwards.[9] Clearly they must have intensified, because the Roman historian Claudian, writing at the turn of the fifth century, likened these incursions to 'raising all Ireland against me (Britannia)', adding with a flight of fancy that 'the sea foamed under (their) hostile oars'.[10] These raids were the prelude to Irish settlement, and in fact it is suggested that this had been happening since as early as the last two centuries BC.[11] While this is perfectly possible, given the close links that existed between Galloway and Ireland since prehistoric times, the case for Irish settlement there during the fourth and fifth centuries becomes more convincing.

For example, it has been asserted that, because of its proximity to Ireland, the invaders, who were attacking North Wales in the fourth century, and settled in Scottish Dalriada in western Argyllshire in the fifth, are likely to have settled in Galloway as well.[12] In fact, it looks as though they were already founding settlements in south-west Scotland by mid-fourth century, since these bases are believed to have served as the springboards for their raids on the northern reaches of Roman Britain in 360.[13] Certainly, they seem to have been establishing enclaves in western Britain from an early date – or perhaps these expanded very rapidly, because Professor Thomas asserts that by the fifth and sixth centuries the Irish were as numerous there as the Germanic settlers in the south and east.[14] Place-name evidence in south-west Scotland confirms this, because an analysis of those in Galloway and Carrick suggests 'a full-scale and long-lasting settlement of Gaelic speakers there going back to the later fifth or early sixth centuries'.[15]

Irish settlement in Galloway continued throughout the following centuries, and it was a reflection of their numbers, and the influence they came to wield, that their Gaelic speech eventually superseded the Cumbric language of the native British population. More important still, as far as Scotland is concerned, was the colony established by the Scottic kingdom of Dalriada in Argyllshire, because within three hundred years it had expanded to become a major political force in the north, and by the eleventh century its influence was paramount, its ruling dynasty having become kings of much of modern Scotland.

CHRISTIANITY IN GALLOWAY

Christianity may have been introduced into Galloway during Roman times, though firm evidence is lacking. Its spread in Britain was encouraged by the Emperor Constantine's edict proclaiming it as the official religion of the Roman empire, as this led to the establishment of centres of Christianity throughout the province. For, in the course of that century, churches were founded at all the principal towns in Roman Britain, while trading links were responsible for the spread of Christianity into southern Scotland. Since a church was founded at Carlisle, complete with its own bishop, it must almost certainly have penetrated as far as the trading posts along the Solway, including Whithorn.[16]

However, three memorial stones dating from the fifth century onwards,[17] which were discovered in the Rhinns – two at Kirkmadrine and the other at nearby Curghie – provide conclusive evidence of the existence of Christianity in the region by that time. Of the stones at Kirkmadrine, one bears the names VIVENTIUS and MAVORIUS who are described as *sacerdotes*, meaning roughly priests or bishops. The other is incised with FLORENTIUS, clearly visible, and what appears to be TITUS of IUSTUS, though the letters are so badly worn as to be virtually indecipherable.[18] The Curghie stone was lost during the nineteenth century, but fortunately its inscription has been preserved, and this states it to be a memorial to VENTIDIUS who is described as *subdiaconus*,[19] which is a lower rank in clerical orders. As the style of the inscriptions is not native to Galloway but resembles instead that of others found on the Continent, including western Gaul,[20] the indications are that these churchmen were immigrants, while their dates can be established from the style of the *chi-rho* crosses on the stones.

The descriptions given to these churchmen are significant, because the fact that Viventius and Mavorius were priests or bishops, whereas Ventidius was a lower *subdiaconus*, infers an ecclesiastical hierarchy, and hence the possible existence of a diocese in the Rhinns, of which Viventius and Mavorius were successively the bishops. They, or their predecessors, may have been missionaries from the religious communities founded by St Martin of Tours at nearby Ligugé and Marmoutier. A former officer in the Roman army, and subsequently bishop of Tours, Martin was an ascetic who emphasised the austere aspect of the Christian life in contrast to what he saw as the Church's over-identification with the wealthier laity of the cities. He was also responsible for introducing monasticism into Gaul and, reflecting his own preferences, the communities he founded were sited in the less populous and remoter regions.

It is likely that through the medium of trading links missionaries were sent from these communities to evangelise in settlements in Wigtownshire. No doubt they found this relatively empty part of the world conformed with their ideals and were encouraged to found religious communities there, most notably at Whithorn and Kirkmadrine[21] – and excavation of the latter would almost certainly yield fascinating results. The layout of the *monasterium* at Whithorn is recognisably similar to Martin's foundations, and it is possible that the external appearance of the buildings there resembled those at Ligugé and Marmoutier, which would have been built of native Touraine limestone.[22]

This is conjectural, but it is significant that lumps of carbonised grey lime have been found in a rubble bank at Whithorn[23] because this material is not available locally, and therefore it must have been transported there for a specific purpose. Conceivably, it was intended for the construction of the buildings comprising the religious community there in order to give them a superficial resemblance to those in Touraine, and their white appearance is evident from the descriptive name Candida Casa, the 'white' or 'shining' place, given to the settlement. Further evidence of the links between Whithorn and the houses associated with Martin comes from Bede's assertion that the church there was dedicated to that saint.[24]

NINIAN

Once a Christian settlement was established at Whithorn it is reasonable to suppose that churchmen set out to proselytise among the local pagan population, perhaps focusing their efforts on converting the community leaders on the assumption that their dependants would follow suit.[25] Presumably they were successful, and the community's influence expanded to a point where it warranted its own bishop, and it is possible that Ninian was sent from the religious centre at Carlisle for that purpose.[26] An alternative theory holds that the community had become infected by the prevailing heresy of Pelagianism, which was spreading throughout England and Ireland. As this had been anathematised by the pope, the proponents of this theory assert that Ninian was sent there by the orthodox authorities at Carlisle for the purpose of eradicating it.[27]

Supposedly the son of a Romano-British chieftain, and therefore an aristocrat, Ninian's real name is thought to have been Niniau or Nyniau. This was Latinised to Ninauus by Bede, subsequently mis-transcribed as Ninianus and therefore rendered as Ninian.[28] Since there is no primary evidence available, in the form of incised stones or other archaeological data, which can point conclusively to his existence, Ninian remains an essentially shadowy figure, whose cult is based on the testimony of three literary sources, two of them larded with myth, and all to some extent unreliable. The most authoritative is Bede's *Historia Ecclesiastica*, although it was written nearly three centuries later and contains only a passing reference to Ninian, while the later *Miracula Nynie Episcopi*, composed by an Anglian monk sometime between 731 and 804, is more informative about Whithorn in Northumbrian times than about Ninian himself. The third, a twelfth-century hagiography entitled *Vita Niniani*, which is attributed to Ailred, abbot of Rievaulx, claims to be a translation and improvement of a lost *Vita* 'written in a barbarous tongue'.

Uncritical acceptance of these sources has resulted in the traditional view of Ninian as a Briton who was born in the second half of the fourth century, and travelled to Rome, where he received religious instruction and was eventually consecrated a bishop. During his return journey he is supposed to have visited St Martin at Tours, and finally reaching Whithorn he and his followers are credited with building a chapel there, which was known as Candida Casa and dedicated to that saint. Subsequently, he proselytised among the southern Picts and converted them before returning to Whithorn. Numerous miracles attributed to him are responsible for his canonisation, though they can be discounted as politically-slanted inventions of a later date, which were explicitly designed to establish him as a cult figure in order to establish Whithorn's importance as a religious centre.

Bede's reference to him was essentially a footnote to his description of Columba's mission to the northern Picts in 563. In this he mentions the southern Picts as having 'long before, as the story goes, forsaken the error of idolatry and received the faith of truth when the word was preached to them by Nynia, a most reverend bishop and holy man of the nation of Britons, who had been regularly instructed at Rome in the faith and mystery of the truth'. He goes on to say that Ninian's 'episcopal see, distinguished by the name and by the church of St Martin the bishop, where he himself, together with many other saints, rests in the body, the English nation [the Angles] has just now begun to govern'.[29]

Finally, he observes that 'the place, which belongs to the province of the Bernicians, is called in the vernacular *ad candidam casam* because he there built a church of stone in a manner to which the Britons were not accustomed'.[30] This could imply a white appearance, though it has been argued that the name Candida Casa was a literal translation of Lucopibia,[31] a sub-Roman settlement appearing on Ptolemy's map, thus implying that it was the forerunner of Whithorn. The Northumbrians later rendered the settlement which grew up around it into the more prosaic *hwit-aerne*, the white place, from which the name Whithorn is derived.

It must be remembered that Bede was writing some three centuries after Ninian's time when Galloway was under Northumbrian rule, or as he accurately puts it 'a province of the Bernicians'. Moreover, he was a monk living at Jarrow who had never been there himself, and therefore he was forced to rely on hearsay evidence. Quite possibly his friend and fellow cleric, Bishop Pecthelm, was the main source of his information, though he may have drawn on other sources as well. But, because of the passage of time, his informants, whoever they were, are bound to have gleaned at best only a distorted account of the real Ninian. One also has to bear in mind that the Northumbrians were in the business of promoting Ninian as a cult-figure to enhance the reputation of Whithorn, so it is not impossible that Bede tailored his account to reflect this.

There is much speculation as to the date of Ninian's mission. The *Vita* asserts that he actually met Martin on his return journey from Rome, and as the saint died in 397 traditionalists concluded that Ninian must have arrived at Whithorn before that date. Although this cannot be disproved, modern opinion considers he was active around the mid-fifth century or later.[32] The 'Latinus' stone, so-called after its erector, could have a bearing on this. A native stone dating from about that time and found at Whithorn, its inscription has been tentatively interpreted to commemorate the founding of a church there,[33] but as this was not necessarily the first one its connection with Ninian is inconclusive.

While Ninian can be accepted as an early – and perhaps the first – bishop at Whithorn, his mission to the southern Picts is more problematical for, as Macquarrie observes, 'geographically, Whithorn does not look like a base for missionary activity among the Picts'.[34] Referring to Columba's preaching to the northern Picts, who were 'separated from the southern regions by steep and rugged mountain ridges' (the Mounth), Bede asserts that it was these southern Picts who 'long before' had forsaken their idolatry and received the word of faith and truth from Nynia.[35] This could have occurred after the Picts' defeat by the Strathclyde Britons in the mid-fifth century, and a resulting loss of confidence in their own gods may have left them amenable to conversion to a new religion. Yet, in spite of the efforts of scholars to draw on extraneous evidence to substantiate Ninian's alleged missionary activities to the southern Picts, there is considerable doubt as to where they took place,[36] if indeed they did so at all.

Saints are invariably associated with miracles, and both the *Miracula*, as its name implies, and the *Vita* credit Ninian with a number of them. One involved a priest who was accused of fathering a child, but within hours of its birth Ninian caused the infant to speak and identify its true father. On another occasion there was a shortage of vegetables in the *monasterium*, and the brother in charge admitted he had only planted the seeds that day, but when Ninian sent him outside he found 'all kinds of plants sprouting from the seed in the ground'. Other miracles were concerned with moral principles. Once, while Ninian was staying with a farmer in an outlying district to bless the livestock, a band of cattle thieves broke into the compound during the night. They were instantly struck down with paralysis, while a bull gored their leader to death, but Ninian cured them and restored the leader to life, demonstrating both the sin and its merciful forgiveness. In general, however, the span of miracles encompassed physical cures, because they were the most effective form of propaganda for promoting Whithorn as a healing centre.

Early sources indicate the existence of contacts between Whithorn and the Irish church, and it is significant that an early saint, Finnian, whose connection with Galloway is evident in the name Chapel Finnian, near Port William, and possibly also Kirkgunzeon, was trained in Ireland. Therefore, it was logical for Irish clerics to take advantage of the establishment of Christianity in Galloway to found small, isolated communities along its coastline, particularly as their fellow churchman, Columba, was already proselytising among the people of Scottish Dalriada. One example was discovered on Ardwall Island at the entrance to Fleet Bay. When this was excavated in the early 1960s, it was found to consist of an original burial ground, possibly dating from the sixth century, and later expanded into a communal hermitage, comprising a wooden chapel and small stone-built cells similar to other known Irish sites along the western seaboard.[37]

CONTEMPORARY SOCIETY

Excavations at Whithorn suggest the existence of a hierarchical society. This seems evident from the presence of a number of contemporary skeletons in more substantial coffins[38] and buried in consecrated ground,[39] which is indicative of privilege. The skeletons themselves are of more robust people, and the fact that they were obviously better nourished implies that they were members of a local élite.[40] Although Whithorn, being a sub-romanised settlement, was atypical of the region as a whole, one can reasonably assume that contemporary farming methods there, as revealed by the Whithorn Dig, were practised elsewhere, and particularly in the more fertile areas. All the more so since this seems to have been a time of relative peace and prosperity.

These excavations also reveal the existence of a mixed farming enterprise, consisting mainly of cattle-rearing and extensive cropping, particularly of barley. Although oat seeds have been found, it is thought that, rather than being grown as a separate crop, they are more likely to have been weeds growing among the barley.[41] The discovery of plough pebbles there is significant, because these were used to reinforce ploughs in order to give them the durability necessary to break in and cultivate new ground.[42] There are also signs of pig-keeping, but at the same time there is very little evidence of sheep – a fact which is equally apparent at other excavated sites in southern Scotland.[43] Obviously some would have been kept to provide wool for domestic purposes, but the high quality of the land meant it could be put to better use than simply running sheep on it.

Most contemporary cattle bones are those of mature animals, and as they were past the normal age of slaughter for beef they are more likely to have been kept for their milk.[44] Similarly, horse and ox bones show that they were generally used as draft animals and killed at the end of their working life, when they were eaten.[45] Probably only the peasants did so, because Adomnán's *Life of Columba* slates the practice as 'fitting only for thieves',[46] while Pope Gregory II denounced it in a letter to St Boniface as 'a filthy and abominable practice'.[47] These strictures might have reflected a Church proscription, or mere ecclesiastical snobbery, though they could equally easily have referred to a practice among unscrupulous merchants of palming off horse meat as beef or venison.[48]

A further indicator of the prevailing prosperity is the evidence of local markets, and since a number of them are believed to have been sited at former hillforts, the chances are they had a long history, some of them perhaps extending as far back as Bronze Age times. One example is the flat-topped feature near Mochrum, known as the Clays of Airyolland, which was reputed to have been the venue of an important horse-fair associated with the centre at Barhobble.[49] Whithorn had a large market on the crown of the hill there, complete with craftsmens' booths and livestock pens,[50] and until comparatively recent times another existed at Kelton Hill near Castle Douglas where, as we have seen, a standing stone indicates it as being a former tribal assembly point.[51]

During the second half of the fifth century, land beyond the perimeter of the *monasterium* at Whithorn was brought into cultivation. Shortly afterwards, an outer enclosure was built to provide more space for houses, flimsy structures made of wicker[52] or wattle,[53] though by the end of the century they were being replaced by more substantial buildings. The community continued to expand at an accelerating rate, and in the following century the population may have risen to about two hundred,[54] with occasional setbacks caused by harvest failures.

A succession of particularly disastrous years which occurred between 536 and 545 are now attributed to a catastrophic eruption of Mount Krakatoa in Indonesia, when the vast quantity of volcanic ash which was spewed up into the stratosphere resulted in a prolonged dimming of the sun, with a consequent drop in temperature and drought conditions. Moreover, there is strong circumstantial evidence to suggest that this was followed by an outbreak of bubonic plague, which spread to the British population in the west through trading links with the Near East. If so, Whithorn could have been exposed to this, and from there it would inevitably have spread throughout the local population with a potentially calamitous loss of life.[55]

Nevertheless, Whithorn must have recovered something of its former prosperity, because it became an important institution during the sixth century, perhaps identifiable with the *Magnum Monasterium* referred to in Irish sources.[56] Similarly, the surrounding settlement continued to expand, and it now consisted of a clearly identifiable inner and outer precinct. Whereas the former was the religious focus of the community, comprising the church, shrines and a graveyard, the outer zone included separate accommodation for different categories of people – monks, nuns, penitents, schoolboys and others – who comprised the religious element within the community, while a separate area was allocated to craftsmen.[57] Herbs and vegetables were cultivated in the gardens surrounding the complex,[58] while further afield a cluster of small buildings was used as industrial workshops, and beyond that lay the farmland. This was marked off from the outer precinct by a thorn or wattle fence and contained cattle pens, a mill, a corn-

drying kiln, and a smokehouse for curing meat and fish.[59] The discovery of
fish hooks, and what seem to be line weights, indicates that deep-sea fishing
was a source of food, despite the fact that only relatively few fish bones have
been found there.[60]

Domestic industry at Whithorn was also on the increase. Glass manufacture became more sophisticated, probably through the influence of glass-
workers brought in from the Continent to provide the necessary skills, and
this could explain why the site has yielded up the largest assemblage of
imported glass yet identified in the Celtic west.[61] Scraps of crucibles, stone
ingot moulds, and copper alloy[62] indicate the existence of a sixth-century
workshop producing articles such as buckles[63] and nail-headed pins.[64] An
analysis of workshop debris dating from the early sixth century shows evidence of metal-casting being practised at this time,[65] though it was not until
later that signs of sheet-metal working first appear. The local economy of
the Machars must have benefited considerably from this prosperity, and
other communities with access to the sea are bound to have flourished as
well. The Mote of Mark was a notable example,[66] and it is likely that
another existed at Kirkmadrine.

INVADERS FROM RHEGED

While a number of different kingdoms were developing in southern
Scotland during later Iron Age times, another one, which was emerging in
north-west England at much the same time, was Rheged. Theory has it that
its Cumbric name was Yrechwydd, though Welsh sources refer to it as *y
Gogledd*, 'the north'[67] – a tribute to the expansion of the kingdom which
occurred during the sixth century. Initially, it comprised the former tribal
lands of the *Carvetii* and was based on the Eden valley, its original ruling
centre being thought to be located at Brougham, though it seems that by
the mid-sixth century it was established at Carlisle. This coincided with an
apparently mushroom-like expansion of the kingdom, when it came to
embrace modern Cumbria on the west and much of Yorkshire on the east,
while it may have penetrated as far south as Rochdale, since its former
name Recedham is thought to be derived from the name Rheged.

The king who was primarily associated with this expansion was Urien
(otherwise Urbgen, meaning 'city-born'), and our knowledge of him is
mainly derived from the epic poetry of his bard, Taliesin, who hailed him
as lord of Catraeth (Catterick in Yorkshire). According to the Harleian
pedigrees, he was a member of the royal house of Gododdin, so he could
have acquired Rheged by conquest, and if his reputed title of 'true leader
of christendom'[68] is accepted he was also a Christian. A prominent warlord
of his time, he is believed to be one of the composite group of British kings
on whom Nennius' legend of King Arthur is based, but more mundanely

he was described as 'a raider of cattle and a leader who burnt the homes of the English [Angles]'. Under his leadership, the Britons of Rheged invaded the lands beyond the Eden and defeated a coalition of their northern counterparts at the battle of Arderydd in about 573. This is probably identifiable with Arthuret on the Esk some miles north of Carlisle, and his victory there appears to have given Urien control of the lands beyond the Solway.

There is no certainty that his rule extended beyond Annandale and Nithsdale, though it may have reached as far west as the Fleet.[69] Yet, if the theory that the name Dunragit is derived from Dun Rheged, meaning 'fort of Rheged',[70] is true it could have expanded to include much of present-day Wigtownshire, and perhaps southern Ayrshire as well. Urien was murdered in about 585, allegedly by a rival king, and this appears to have resulted in a struggle for the succession between his sons, with a consequent weakening of the kingdom. One of these sons, Ywain, was reputedly the father of Kentigern (or Mungo), who ultimately became the patron saint of the Strathclyde Britons, and hence associated with the diocese of Glasgow, which embraced part of modern Galloway. By the following century Rheged was beginning to crumble in the face of the westward expansion of the Anglian kingdom of Northumbria, and through course of time this would absorb the whole of northern England and virtually all southern Scotland, including Galloway.

NOTES

1. Hill, *Whithorn*, 300, 315, 318–9.
2. *Ibid.*, 124.
3. Ibid., 28. Remains of wheelmade pottery have also been found at Mote of Mark (Thomas, *Celtic Britain*, 94).
4. This seems evident from the discovery at Brighouse of a mould for a false *denarius* of the third century which, it has been asserted, 'should most probably be understood in relation to affairs on the south side of the Solway than [Galloway's] own hinterland' (Maynard, 'The dune system at Brighouse Bay').
5. Macquarrie, 'The Kings of Strathclyde', 17.
6. *Gildas: New Approaches*, (eds) D Dumville and M Lapidge, (Cambridge, 1984).
7. Excavated in 1960 by Thomas, whose findings are reported in 'Excavations at Trusty's hill, Anwoth', 58 et seq.: also, C Cessford, 'Pictish raiders at Trusty's Hill'.
8. Oram, 'The mythical Picts and the monastic pedant', 14 et seq.
9. Saltway, *Roman Britain*, 241.
10. *Claudian* (ed.) Koch. Teubner (1893) xxii. 247.
11. Foster, *Picts Gaels and Scots*, 29.
12. Duncan, *Scotland*, 65.
13. Saltway, *Roman Britain*, 369.
14. Thomas, *Britain and Ireland*, 66.

15. Fellows-Jensen, 'Scandinavians in Dumfriesshire and Galloway – the place-name evidence', 78.
16. Hill, *Whithorn*, 26.
17. Their implications are discussed by Thomas in 'Whithorn's Christian beginnings'.
18. *Ibid.*
19. Reid, 'The Ventidius stone, Kirkmaiden', 184–5.
20. Thomas, 'Whithorn's Christian beginnings'.
21. This was probably the more important of the two centres, since it may have been a pre-Christian holy place – *madrine* being identifiable with the Celtic goddess Madrun – and was within striking distance of the British ruling centre of Rerigonium (Brooke, 'Saints and Goddesses').
22. Hill, *Whithorn*, 15.
23. *Ibid.*, 81: Brooke, *Wild Men*, 16–7.
24. *Bede, HE,* i, 34.
25. The local population must have been converted by the time Ninian arrived at Whithorn – or perhaps he completed the task – otherwise his alleged mission to the southern Picts would make no sense.
26. Thomas, *The Early Christian Archaeology of Northern Britain*, 11–14.
27. Brooke, *Wild Men*, 20–2: Discussion with P. Hill.
28. Gough Cooper, 'Some notes on the name Ninian'.
29. This was a reference to the Northumbrian (or more accurately the Bernician) takeover of Galloway, bearing in mind that Bede was writing in about 731.
30. *Bede: HE* iii.
31. Thomas suggests this in 'Whithorn's Christian beginnings', arguing that the name Lucopibia was derived from the British *leuc-os* meaning 'pure, shining, white' and rendered into Latin as *candidus.*
32. Macquarrie, *The Saints of Scotland,* 55–67.
33. Thomas presented a detailed analysis of its inscription in 'Whithorn's Christian beginnings', 3–7.
34. MacQuarrie, *The Saints of Scotland,* 26.
35. *Bede, HE,* iii, iv.
36. Drawing on a number of ancient legends and church dedications, Daphne Brooke concludes that his mission was concentrated in the region to the south of the Forth-Clyde line (*Wild Men*, 23–6). A.A.M. Duncan suggests it could have been round Peebles and that his converts were Britons not Picts (*Bede, Iona and the Picts*, 23–4), while Thomas concludes that his activities were confined to the regions south of the Forth, where a number of stones suggest the existence of Pictish enclaves (*Christianity in Roman Britain*, 285 et seq.).
37. Thomas, 'Ardwall isle: the excavation of an early Christian site of Irish type', 114 et seq.
38. Hill, *Whithorn*, 70–4.
39. *Ibid.* 74, 112, assuming the skeletons date from this period rather than Northumbrian times.
40. *Ibid.* 169, 557.
41. *Ibid.* 592.
42. Hill and Kucharski, 'Early medieval ploughing at Whithorn': Hill, *Whithorn*, 464–6.
43. Hill, *Whithorn*, 605. This may have been because commercial sheep farming did not develop until the early seventh century in response to the demands of the expanding north European wool markets. (*Ibid.* 607).

44. *Ibid.* 608.
45. *Ibid.* 611.
46. *Ibid.*
47. *Ibid.*
48. *Ibid.*
49. Cormack and others, 'Barhobble, Mochrum', 6.
50. Hill, *Whithorn*, 35.
51. Brooke, *Wild Men*, 52.
52. Hill, *Whithorn*, 70.
53. *Ibid.* 82.
54. *Ibid.* 34.
55. Foster asserts in *Picts, Gaels and Scots* (p 27) that the prolonged cold snap is evident from an analysis of contemporary tree rings, but its attribution to a volcanic explosion was the subject of two TV documentaries (Jul/Aug 1999, and repeated in May 2000).
56. Hill, *Whithorn*, 3–4.
57. *Ibid.* 35.
58. *Ibid.*
59. *Ibid.*
60. *Ibid.* 37.
61. *Ibid.* 299.
62. *Ibid.* 117.
63. *Ibid.* 371.
64. *Ibid.* 363.
65. *Ibid.* 360.
66. Laing, 'The Angles in Scotland and the Mote of Mark'.
67. MacQueen, 'Yvain, Ewen and Owein ap Urien', 110.
68. Clancy, 'Taliesin, The Battle of Gwen Ystrad', 79.
69. Cramp, 'Whithorn and the Northumbrian expansion westwards'.
70. Watson, *History of the Celtic Place-names of Scotland*.
71. MacQuarrie, *The Saints of Scotland*, 120

5

A NORTHUMBRIAN
PROVINCE

Early Anglian expansion

The Angles were a warlike and bloodthirsty people. The epic poetry of the bards describes how their feats of heroism, chanted as they feasted in the halls of their chieftains, were full of the clash of 'hammered blades' and of 'arrows sleeting like hail'. They loved the symbols of death and carnage; the raven who followed the host, his beak dripping with blood, the hungry hawks hovering over the battlefield, the funeral pyre hung with shields and helmets as the companions of the fallen gathered round to sing of the joys of war, and the warrior deeds of the dead.

They are first mentioned by Tacitus who refers to the *Angli* as a maritime people and suggests they came from northern Germany – a fact impliedly confirmed by the passing references of later writers.[1] There is archaeological evidence of Anglian settlement around York during late Roman times,[2] and by the sixth century they established the kingdom of Deira, which comprised central and eastern Yorkshire. From there they expanded northwards as far as the Tweed, and these territories comprised the later kingdom of Bernicia, whose ruling centre was established at Bamburgh.

Its king Aethelfrith, who reigned from about 592 to 627, was responsible for extending the northern frontier beyond the Tweed into present-day Berwickshire and the Lothians. This ruthless warlord was described by Bede as 'a ruler who ravaged the Britons more cruelly and who overran more of their territory than any other English leader, exterminating or enslaving the people, extorting tribute and annexing their land for the English'.[3] At the turn of the century, he defeated a British force at the battle of Catraeth (Catterick Bridge), and in 603 he followed it up with a victory over an alliance between the Scots of Dalriada and the Britons of Strathclyde and Goddodin at the battle of Degsastan (possibly Dawston in Liddesdale, or Addinston in Berwickshire[4]).

Ten years later, in about 613, he defeated a British/Welsh force at Chester and won through to the Irish Sea. Two British kings are reputed to have been killed in the battle, while tradition holds Aethelfrith responsible for the massacre of twelve hundred British monks, who had come in vain to offer up prayers for a victorious outcome. He is believed to have subdued all the territories to the north as far as Dumfriesshire,[6] while his successful conquest of the British kingdoms in the west has been symbolised in Welsh poetry by the image of a dark and roofless hall, stark and deserted after the slaughter of its lord and his warriors, with the songs of his bards silenced forever.[7]

Edwin, a prince of the rival house of Deira, usurped the throne in 627 and ruled both kingdoms until 642. Having first overrun Gododdin and established his rule over all the territory as far as the Firth of Forth, he turned his attention to consolidating his predecessor's gains in the west. Here, his first objective was to subjugate the neighbouring British kingdom of Elmet, as this gave him possession of the southern route into Cumbria. Bede also credits him with bringing the Mevanian islands,[8] thought to be Anglesey and the Isle of Man, under Anglian rule, and if this is correct it would have cut off the Galloway Britons from their counterparts in North Wales, with whom they had a long-standing and close affinity. Thereafter, the two peoples developed a separate identity and their common language diverged, and whereas the northern Britons retained the old Cumbric tongue, those to the south developed the Welsh language of today.

THE TAKEOVER OF GALLOWAY

The conquest of modern Cumbria brought the Northumbrian Angles within sight of south-west Scotland, and this would have impelled them to drive home their attacks on this part of the British kingdom of Rheged. Consequently, they are thought to have re-commissioned the old Roman fort of Bowness as a base for their advance across the Solway fords into Dumfriesshire. This seems to have occurred at a relatively early date, as there is evidence of an Anglian presence at Hoddom in the mid-600s and, if Jocelyn's twelfth-century life of St Kentigern can be believed, they arrived there during the early decades of the century.[9] So it was probably not long after this that they penetrated across the Nith into eastern Galloway. As the lower reaches of the river are unfordable, they are more likely to have crossed it further upstream near the former camp at Dalswinton, and advanced from there along the line of the old Roman road into Galloway. This is conjectural, but as they are known to have used former Roman roads in the course of their advance northwards it would have been logical for them to do so in Galloway.

Place-name evidence throughout the former Northumbrian-controlled territories suggests that they settled in the better quality land, having either slaughtered or enslaved the native inhabitants, or simply evicted them, forcing them to re-settle in the less fertile regions. That wholesale extermination of local populations was carried out in some cases is evident from the life of Wilfred, bishop of Ripon, which describes his diocese as including 'consecrated places . . . which the British clergy had deserted when fleeing the hostile swords of the Northumbrians'.[10] Enslavement of the population was a slightly less drastic alternative, while the third is described by Bede as 'making their lands tributary to the English or ready for English settlement',[11] and it seems that this was the policy they adopted in the case of Galloway. Therefore, it can be presumed that the subjugation of the region to make it 'ready for English settlement' was preceded by a combination of raids, terrorisation of the local population, and the capture of key centres of local power.[12]

Nevertheless, it looks as though it must have taken the Angles far longer to achieve mastery over Galloway than the other regions which they overran. For, if they reached Hoddom by the early decades of the century and the first indications of their presence at Whithorn occurred in the 680s,[13] it seems that the process must have taken up to half a century. Different conclusions can be drawn from this. It is possible that the Angles encountered a determined resistance by the local Britons which it took them a long time to overcome, though there is little archaeological evidence to support this. Alternatively – and perhaps more likely – the conquest of eastern Galloway was achieved relatively quickly, and the Angles paused to consolidate their gains before penetrating further west.

Hill suggests that the takeover of Galloway was achieved relatively peaceably, asserting that 'military conquest and subsequent colonisation would, perhaps, have produced a less sharply-focused distribution of place-names'. He goes on to claim that 'the distribution of Northumbrian settlements is reminiscent of the dispersed territories of the great landed families of the Middle Ages won by dynastic marriages, political intrigue, and the vicious exploitation of mortgage agreements'.[14] However, it is difficult to equate this with the less palatable fact that the Angles were not known for their peaceful colonisation of other conquered Britons, and therefore they are unlikely to have made an exception in the case of Galloway.

More realistically, it was achieved by taking over existing British sub-tribes and communities, probably slaughtering the ruling élites, and forcibly evicting or enslaving local populations to make way for Anglian settlement. No doubt this involved a good deal of intermittent skirmishing, and an example was the storming of the British stronghold of the Mote of Mark, where the ramparts were fired and the fortress was systematically demolished,[15] while the vitrification of the fort at Trusty's Hill, near Gatehouse, might also be a legacy from the Northumbrian takeover.[16]

ANGLIAN SETTLEMENT IN GALLOWAY

The Angles seem to have acquired a tighter control over eastern Galloway than the west, because surviving evidence of an Anglian type of social structure there suggests that they settled more extensively in that region, and this is particularly apparent in the main river valleys and coastal regions. Their settlements tended to consist of small, nucleate communities geared to a fairly intense arable farming, being typical of those in other fertile regions which came under Northumbrian rule. Estates and parishes subsequently developed from these settlements, and examples can be found in the former parishes of Galtway and Dunrod near Kirkcudbright, and also along the Colvend coast and up the Nith estuary.[17] In contrast, the Britons farmed more extensively, being mainly pastoralists, and their type of husbandry was reflected in the larger, more dispersed estates which are associated with the less fertile regions where their traditional form of society survived.[18]

An analysis of place-name associations, church dedications and supporting historical and archaeological material suggests that by the eighth century the Angles had established themselves in certain clearly defined areas in Galloway. Earlier historians contended that their colonisation was 'more in the nature of a scattered upper-crust of landlords than a really thick settlement of peasants',[19] but recent research has shown it to have been more extensive than previously supposed, and that the settlers were mainly small-time farmers.

Place-name evidence indicates the existence of a number of *foci* of local power, the most important being the old-established ruling centre of Kelton.[20] While this served as the nucleus for a group of settlements in central Kirkcudbrightshire, another group, which was based on Buittle, extended as far east as Preston, near Kirkbean, to include Edingham and Richorn on the lower Urr.[21] The seaport of Kirkcudbright, named after the Northumbrian patron saint Cuthbert, controlled a further group, and the discovery of part of an eighth-century stone cross indicates the existence of an early church there, while a similar find at nearby Auchencairn points to an Anglian presence there as well.[22]

Coastal settlements also existed at Senwick and Kirkandrews, and there is evidence of a small contemporary religious community on Ardwall Island,[23] where the existing Irish cell was taken over and redeveloped in the Northumbrian style. Other settlements may have existed at nearby Plunton and at Girthon, and more certainly at Twynholm and Miefield, both of which lie further inland.[24] Anwoth[25] was probably the westernmost of these settlements, for beyond it is the Skyreburn, and the fact that its name is thought to be derived from the Old English *scir-burne*, meaning 'shire stream', suggests it marked a boundary. In fact, it could well have been the western edge of an administrative division known as a 'shire', which comprised most, if not all, the settlements in present-day Kirkcudbrightshire, and the indications are that these were established at an earlier date than those beyond the Cree.

To the west of the Skyreburn lies the hilly region which separates it from the valley of the Cree, and this would have formed a natural barrier between the settlements in eastern Galloway and those in the west. Judging from the preponderance of Cumbric-derived names there – Carsluith, Kirroughtree and Minnigaff – it seems that this district continued to be occupied by Britons throughout the period of Anglian rule.

An analysis of place-names in Wigtownshire suggests that, once they achieved control of that region, the Angles established clusters of settlements there, and these could have comprised a separate shire. One group, which included Penninghame and Merton,[26] appears to have extended as far as the Bladnoch, for beyond it lay the important British estates of Mindork and Manhincon (now Craichlaw). Other settlements based on Wigtown embraced the fertile lands sandwiched between the British estates of Lengest (Longcastle) and Carnmoel (now Kirkinner), and the coast. Place-names in the southern Machars argue for a comparatively dense Anglian settlement there, and a local power centre was established at the former British stronghold of Cruggleton.[27] By contrast, the dearth of place-names derived from Old English in the Rhinns suggests a comparatively limited Anglian settlement there.[28]

Clearly, therefore, the Angles appropriated the best agricultural land, while they also controlled the major ports, river crossings and the navigable stretches of the principal rivers. Being mainly pastoralists, the native British may have grudgingly acquiesced in an arrangement whereby they were allowed to occupy the poorer grazing land, and it is in these regions that their old-established multiple estates survived intact. There appears to have been little contact between the two communities at this stage, but so long as the Britons remained passive and continued to pay tribute to their Anglian masters they probably settled down to a quiescent coexistence. Nevertheless, Anglian colonisation must have involved a large-scale displacement of native Britons, and those who were unable to resettle were faced with the choice of a life of predation, or emigration to Ireland where some are known to have served as mercenaries in the Irish wars between 682 and 709.[29]

Having established control of the south-west, the Angles seem to have gone to considerable lengths in their efforts to persuade the local Britons to acquiesce in their rule, and to steer them away from a potentially threatening affiliation with the Strathclyde Britons to the north.[30] Therefore, in a move that was clearly intended to identify his own dynasty with the former rulers of Rheged, the Northumbrian king Oswiu took as his second wife Urien's great-granddaughter, Rhiemmelth,[31] though perhaps more importantly the Angles deliberately identified themselves with local British traditions. Therefore, when they took over Whithorn they retained its existing name of Candida Casa and systematically promoted the cult of Ninian,[32] building him up into one of the leading figures of medieval times and coining the miracles associated with him. Moreover, they restored that dilapidated centre to a level far above its former eminence, and later on they revived its episcopate.[33]

THE BISHOPRIC RESTORED

The original episcopate, of which Ninian was an early incumbent, survived until the seventh century, but owing to the apparent laxity of the later bishops the church had been allowed to fall into decay, while the settlement had disintegrated. Therefore, when the Northumbrians took it over they set about refurbishing the church with considerable lavishness. Skilled workmen were brought in, building material was imported, while surviving fragments of stained glass give an idea of the scale of the embellishment. For the colours were remarkably diverse, ranging from the characteristic Anglo-Saxon shades of blue, turquoise and green to the more unusual brownish amber, pale olive and purple.[34]

The revival of the episcopate at Whithorn was politically inspired. For, apart from being a sop to the local Britons, it was primarily designed to serve as a bastion against the influence of the Irish Church, with whom the Northumbrian Roman Church was in competition for control of the west. The differences between them were rooted in events which had occurred only comparatively recently. For Christianity – and with it the Roman Church – was originally introduced into Northumbria at the beginning of the seventh century, when St Augustine's emissary Paulinus accompanied a Jutish princess from Kent on her journey north to marry the Northumbrian king, Edwin. Initially his mission was successful, but in the aftermath of Edwin's death in battle against a British coalition under Cadwallon of Powys, parts of the Northumbrian kingdom reverted to paganism. When Cadwallon died in 633 the former dynasty was restored under King Oswald, an erstwhile exile at the court of the king of Dalriada, where he had been converted to the Irish variant of the Roman Church.

Once Oswald had established himself as ruler, he naturally turned to that Church for help in restoring Christianity to Northumbria. It responded by dispatching a small mission under Aidan, who established a centre on the island of Lindisfarne. From there he disseminated the Christian message, although according to Bede this was 'not fully according to knowledge', meaning it did not fully conform with the liturgical and disciplinary customs of the Roman Church. Consequently, Aidan's mission highlighted these differences, and while Bernicia supported his Irish-Scottic Church, Deira adhered to the Roman.

They were partially resolved at the Synod of Whitby in 664, when the Roman doctrine was accepted by the Northumbrian Church, and consequently the Irish-Scottic Church within the Northumbrian-dominated territories in southern Scotland followed suit. Iona also fell into line in 719, but the Church in northern Ireland remained defiant, and it was because Galloway's proximity left it dangerously exposed to its contumacious influence that the ecclesiastical authorities at York decided to create a new diocese based at Whithorn. However, the choice of bishop was important, since a high-ranking and influential churchman was needed who could command the authority necessary to resist any attempt by the Irish Church to gain a foothold in Galloway.

The choice fell on Pecthelm, a former monk and deacon of Malmesbury abbey. He was probably now in his fifties,[35] an elderly man by the standards of the time, though well qualified for the post by his long and distinguished career as a scholar and an authority on ecclesiastical law. During his time at St Malmesbury the abbot was the well-known churchman, Aldhelm, who subsequently became bishop of the West Saxons at Sherborne. Therefore, Pecthelm had assisted him in establishing the Roman Church among the local British population, before undertaking a mission to the pagan Frisians in northern Europe. Consequently his experience and cosmopolitan background rendered him admirably suited to the new and challenging assignment as bishop of Whithorn.[36] He seems to have assumed office sometime before 731, as Bede refers to him in his résumé of the English church, which was written in that year, as bishop of 'Candida Casa, where recently the number of the faithful has increased'.[37] His episcopate lasted for only a short time, as he died in 737, but it was during his reign that an archbishopric was founded at York, when Whithorn became one of its suffragan sees.

WHITHORN'S HEYDAY

The Northumbrian episcopate witnessed a dramatic revival in the fortunes of Whithorn, and during this time it established a commanding reputation as a centre of learning. According to later Irish writers, it was also a prestigious seminary which catered for local ordinands from Galloway, as well as others from further afield, while a number of Irish saints are reputed to have been trained there. The best known of Pecthelm's four immediate successors was Aethelbert, whose episcopate lasted from 777 until his translation to Hexham in 789. He was a close friend of the eminent churchman and scholar, Alcuin of York, who founded and directed an educational establishment at the Emperor Charlemagne's court, besides having extensive contacts on the Continent. Therefore, it was through him that Aethelbert – and hence Whithorn – established wide international links throughout Christendom.

This period saw the Northumbrian kingdom attain a level of civilisation which was unprecedented in Britain. Scholars were attracted to its capital at York, while contacts between the royal court and its counterparts else-where encouraged gifted craftsmen to settle there as well. Their skills inspired a latent native genius among the Northumbrians to blossom into a level of artistic enlightenment which was unrivalled in Anglo-Saxon England, and to some extent this was reflected in the western regions of Northumbria. An outstanding example is the Ruthwell cross in Dumfries-shire. This shows vine stems and tendrils curling about the shapes of animals and birds carved on it, and the quality of the workmanship is a remarkable tribute to the aesthetic sensitivity and artistic technique which were characteristic of the time.

Whithorn was famed above all as a healing centre, focused on Ninian's shrine, where miraculous cures were reportedly achieved, the examples cited in the *Miracula* and *Vita* being concerned with infantile paralysis, blindness, arthritis, and possibly leprosy. While the cures undoubtedly involved an element of faith healing, excavation has revealed evidence of more mundane treatments. For example, an early latrine contained traces of elder, which was used as a remedy for colds, influenza and rheumatism. In addition, there is evidence of woundwort, used for salving wounds, as well as hemlock, which was a strong sedative. Also nettles,[38] for not only were they an antidote to gout and rheumatism, but their stems were used for weaving into a strong, coarse cloth.

In addition, there are traces of climbing corydalis which has narcotic properties, and the fact that this has also been found growing in an atypical environment at Barhobble[39] suggests the existence of a healing centre there as well. This is hardly surprising, since most ecclesiastical centres put a high priority on healing by faith and prayer, combined with herbal remedies, exercise and a dietary regimen, as part of their Christian witness. Whithorn's fame was now widespread, and pilgrims to St Ninian's shrine had become so numerous that it is thought that the 'Petrus' stone (so-called from its inscription LOCI PETRI APOSTVLI – 'of the place of Peter the Apostle'[40]) was erected as a signpost to guide those coming by sea and landing at the Isle of Whithorn.[41]

An analysis of the contents of a contemporary midden shows the senior clergy as living in some luxury. For example, cattle bones are predominantly those from which the better cuts of meat were taken,[42] and, judging from their age of slaughter, both sheep and cattle were kept mainly for this purpose, the cattle being small animals with an average withers height of a mere 107.3 cm (3ft 6ins).[43] Similarly, the remains of roedeer appear to the exclusion of the less gastronomically acceptable red or fallow deer.[44] The abundant evidence of livestock suggests that the community ran an extensive farming enterprise, and that rents, tribute and tithes, exacted from the occupiers of land within its *parochia,* were paid in the form of food. Consisting mainly of bread, honey, fowls and livestock, it also included mead and ale,[45] and probably also cheeses since these were a traditional food render in Galloway during the Middle Ages.

The higher proportion of sheep bones, compared with those of cattle, points to an expansion in sheep farming, and a corresponding increase in wool production. This is apparent from the discovery of contemporary articles associated with wool processing, such as spindle whorls and wool combs,[46] and the growing emphasis on this was undoubtedly attributable to the expansion of the north European woolmarkets which was occurring at this time.

Burials at Whithorn, dating from the mid-sixth to the early eighth centuries, throw some light on the general state of health. Of the 118 graves excavated, 59 produced skeletons, of which about three-quarters were adult. Bone measurements indicate an average height of 176 cm. (5ft 9ins) for men, while the women were on average 8 cm.(3ins) shorter. They also show abundant evidence of trauma and disease, particularly tuberculosis.[47] An analysis of bone material retrieved from a contemporary children's grave reveals a high incidence of *cribra orbitalia.*[48] This is a pitting round the eye sockets, which was probably due to anaemia caused by iron deficiency, or blood loss resulting from hookworm infestation of the intestines – a condition that was probably endemic among the population.

THE LATER EPISCOPATE

In Ninian's time the diocese of Whithorn seems to have been confined to the Machars, because the memorials to the early bishops suggest that a separate one existed in the Rhinns which eventually withered away. In contrast, the diocese to which Pecthelm was appointed could have included the whole of modern Galloway, with the territories to the east coming under the control of Hexham, or possibly Hoddom. The bishop was assisted in his pastoral duties by a number of lay canons or priests, mostly accommodated at Whithorn, who were responsible for undertaking itinerant preaching missions throughout the diocese, including the conducting of baptisms and burials.

Initially, preaching was conducted in the open air, and later these assembly points were marked by stone crosses,[49] which were tangible evidence of the issue of burial licences. Therefore, it was at these sites that the bishop or his lay clergy preached the Word and officiated at baptisms and burials. They were generally surrounded by a wattle fence, and later on rudimentary oratories were erected there, while those that survived as religious *foci* were eventually replaced by stone churches. As these preaching sites were generally located close to the ruling centres of secular estates, it followed that the *parochia*, or area of responsibility, of these field churches was co-terminous with these estates, and in a number of instances this remained the case after the formalisation of a parish system in the twelfth century.[50] In most cases, the crosses, and the churches which were subsequently built on these sites, were commissioned by local secular or ecclesiastical landowners, and in consequence they were known as 'proprietary chapels'. Accordingly, the founding landowners became the patrons of these churches, with an attaching right to appoint its incumbent; and in this lay the roots of patronage which would become an important – and latterly controversial – feature of the Church.

A later development was the emergence of 'mother' churches, or minsters, and their dependent field churches, or 'daughter' churches, as they were called. These minsters accommodated the resident canons or priests who were responsible for the spiritual and pastoral care of their daughter churches, which were collectively known as their *plebiana*. The church at Whithorn functioned as a minster; so too did those at Edingham and Kirkcudbright, and there were doubtless others whose identity has been lost. The minster at Edingham became moribund during the eleventh century, but the one at Kirkcudbright survived into the following century, as 'a little ancient church of rock and stone' is recorded as existing there as late as 1164.[51]

There is evidence of a crisis at Whithorn in about 840. The church was stripped of its liturgical fittings, deconsecrated, and apparently used as a barn for storing grain. Parts of the outer precinct were turned over to cultivation, while the drainage system collapsed, and a section of the site was flooded.[52] The surrounding buildings were either dismantled or left to decay, and a burned gaming counter which was recovered, along with some coinage, from the inner precinct suggests that the chapel had degenerated into a gambling den. Clearly it was a dramatic event, and while the cause remains obscure there is a possible clue. A late and unreliable source[53] records that Alpin, a freebooting Scots warlord, died in Galloway in 841 having 'entirely destroyed and devastated' the area.[54] The place-name Little Laight, in southern Ayrshire, might confirm this, since its former name *Lacht-Alpin*, meaning 'Alpin's gravestone', has been taken to indicate a chieftain of that name being killed in a battle there. With a leap of faith, this somewhat flimsy evidence has been founded on to suggest that it was he who was responsible for attacking and destroying Whithorn.

Shortly afterwards, in 845, a fire broke out in the church, which partially destroyed it. Its cause is uncertain, and while it may have resulted from an accident, it could equally well have occurred in the course of an attack on the centre. For it was a time of political upheaval in Northumbria. Civil war had broken out; King Aethelred was deposed (though he was subsequently restored), and the resulting turmoil could have extended to Whithorn. Alternatively, it may have been burnt in the course of an invasion of Galloway by Alpin's son, the Scots king Kenneth, in revenge for help allegedly given by the Northumbrians to his Pictish enemies. Nor can the possibility of a Viking attack be ruled out, particularly as they were already penetrating the Irish Sea regions and conducting an aggressive campaign in Ireland. If so, it was a foretaste of what was to come, for the ninth century would witness an expansion of these Viking raids which ultimately extended to Galloway.

NOTES

1. Stenton, *Anglo-Saxon England*, 12–13.
2. Correspondence with Dr Oram.
3. *Bede, HE* i, 34.
4. Cramp, 'Whithorn and the Northumbrian expansion westwards'.
5. *Ibid.*
6. Higham, *Northumbria*, 110.
7. Brooke, *Wild Men*, 35.
8. *Bede, H.E* ii, 5–9.
9. *Vita Kentigerni* cap xxxii.
10. Hill, *Whithorn*, 37 (quoting Eddius Stephanus, *Life of Wilfred* XVII, Webb and Farmer 1983, pp 123–4).
11. *Bede, H.E* i, 34.
12. Postulated by Cramp in the case of Anglian settlement on the Cumbrian coastal plain in 'Whithorn and the Northumbrian expansion westwards'.
13. Hill, *Whithorn*, 37, citing as evidence the contemporary introduction of Anglian-style buildings with opposed timber-framed doorways, and the remains of domestic livestock and fowls, which 'can be equated tentatively with new settlements' (p. 18).
14. *Ibid.*,17.
15. Laing, 'The Angles and the Mote of Mark', 39–40.
16. Conversation with Dr Oram.
17. Correspondence with do.
18. Examples include Monreith, Mindork and Manhincon (all in Wigtownshire) which, like Menybrig in the Rhinns, incorporate the Cumbric word *maen*, a 'stone', usually a standing stone. Nearby Leswalt incorporates the word *llys*, a 'court', and Longcastle (Lengest) derives from *lann*, a 'church'. In Kirkcudbrightshire the estate of Minnigaff stems from the Cumbric *mynydd*, a 'mountain'. Kirroughtree and Carsluith both incorporate the word *caer*, a 'stronghold' suggesting that they were former British settlements. So too were Trevercarcou (Balmaclellan), Troquhain and Threave as they all include the word *tref*, a 'homestead' (see Brooke, *Wild Men*, 52, 71: also *Northumbrian*

Settlements in Galloway and Carrick, 295–327).

19. For example, the name Carleton, which occurs near Borgue, and also near Glasserton, is derived from the Old English *ceorla-tun*, 'the settlement of the free peasants' (Fellows-Jensen, 'Scandinavians in Dumfriesshire and Galloway' 86). Hill suggests that the latter Carleton, like the nearby estate of Kidsdale, was held directly from the bishop of Whithorn in return for food render (*Whithorn*, 17–18).

20. This was the focus of a group of settlements which extended as far north as Shirmers (OE *scir-(ge)maere*, 'shire boundary') at the upper end of Loch Ken. Beyond this were the British estates of Trevercarcou and Troquhain. A local ruling centre was established at Arsbotel, now Burned Island on Loch Ken. Probably stretching as far south as Kirkcarswell, this group included parts of the modern parishes of Parton, Balmaghie, Crossmichael and Kelton itself. The church at Kelton was dedicated to the Anglian king, Oswald the martyr, whose name is reflected in Kirkcarswell, while the churches at Balmaghie and Porton (Kirkandrews, near Borgue) were dedicated to the Northumbrian saint, Andrew.

21. Buittle and Edingham are both OE derivatives, and so too is Richorn, which takes its name from *raecc-aern* meaning 'the place (or steading) of the hunting dogs', implying that they were still being exported from Galloway.

22. Brooke, *Wild Men*, 52.

23. Thomas, 'Ardwall Isle: excavation of an early Christian site of Irish type', 93, 102–3. A contemporary memorial stone, which came to light in the course of these excavations, was inscribed with the name 'Cuthgar', presumably a cleric. This is now in the Dumfries museum.

24. Whereas Twynholm and Miefield are obvious OE derivatives, Plunton and Girthon are less so.

25. Although this is a Norse name, it is likely to have been an Anglian settlement at this time.

26. Both these names are positively identified as OE derivatives.

27. This appears to have had a long history as a focus of secular power, and it remained a high status estate until the Middle Ages.

28. The foregoing has been taken virtually in its entirety from Daphne Brooke's comprehensive study of local Anglian-derived place-names in 'The Northumbrian settlements in Galloway and Carrick', and in *Wild Men*, 51–4.

29. Cramp, 'Whithorn and the Northumbrian advance westwards'.

30. *Ibid.*

31. Her name meant literally 'princess of darkness'.

32. Brooke, 'Saints and goddesses'.

33. Hill, *Whithorn*, 18.

34. *Ibid.*, 327.

35. Cramp, 'Whithorn and the Northumbrian advance westwards'.

36. Hill, *Whithorn*, 18–19.

37. *Bede, HE*, V, xxiii.

38. Hill, *Whithorn*, 124.

39. Stewart and Cormack, 'The present botany of a former medieval site: a checklist of plants at Barhobble, Mochrum', 3.

40. Hill, *Whithorn*, 37–8. Its dedication to St Peter reflected the popularity of his cult following the triumph of the Roman party at the Synod of Whitby.

41. It was discovered by the roadside half a mile south of Whithorn, having served as a fence- or gate-post (Thomas, 'Whithorn's Christian beginnings'), and this

could have been close to its original site.

42. Hill, *Whithorn*, 161.
43. *Ibid.* 609, but only a very limited sample was capable of being measured.
44. *Ibid.* 607.
45. *Ibid.* 608.
46. *Ibid.* 607.
47. *Ibid.* 558–9.
48. *Ibid.* 558–9.
49. Craig, 'Pre-Norman sculpture in Galloway'.
50. Examples include the former parishes of Carnmoel (later Kirkinner), Longcastle and Kirkmaiden, the latter probably being identifiable with the British estate of Monreith (Brooke: Saints and goddesses).
51. Reginald of Durham.
52. Hill, *Whithorn*, 162.
53. Anderson, *Kings and Kingship in early Ireland*.
54. Anderson, *Annals*, 270n.

6

SCANDINAVIAN SETTLEMENT

The Vikings

The Vikings have traditionally been a byword for rape, pillage and slaughter, and the epithets given to their leaders – Erik 'bloodaxe', a ninth-century king of Norway, and Thorfinn 'the skullsplitter', a contemporary jarl of Orkney – are evocative of the barbarities which are traditionally associated with them. From their homelands in Norway and Denmark, these seafarers descended in their longships on the coasts of Britain and northern Europe,[1] first as hit-and-run raiders and looters, and later as settlers. Their name means literally 'creek-men', so called because the exceptionally shallow draft of these longships enabled them to sail far up tidal estuaries to launch surprise attacks on unsuspecting and terrified local populations. The reasons for the onset of Viking raids remain obscure, though they may have been driven by a combination of political upheavals at home, land hunger, and the prospect of booty. Beginning in the late 700s, they continued throughout the following century with growing intensity; by the 900s the Vikings controlled substantial tracts of mainland Britain, and in the early eleventh century a Danish dynasty ruled in England.

The northern Vikings, who came from the fjord district of south-western Norway, concentrated their attacks initially on Orkney and Shetland, while the Danish Vikings tended to follow a more southerly route, raiding settlements on the east coast of Britain and the adjacent shores of northern Europe. Others penetrated down the Channel to Ireland, where they launched a series of attacks on the coastal regions around Dublin, and as the native Irish, weakened by internal feuding, offered little resistance, these Danes rapidly established a settlement there. In 850, a band of Norse Vikings attempted to drive them out, and although they were beaten off they returned three years later with a larger force. This time they were successful, and their leader, Olaf, founded a kingdom based on Dublin which expanded so rapidly that within seventy years its authority extended as far afield as York.

Meanwhile, other Danish Vikings were raiding the Northumbrian coast, and in the course of one of these attacks their leader, Ragnar Loðbrok, was taken prisoner and put to death on the orders of King Aelle. Legend has it that an unusual fate was reserved for this chieftain, because he was cast into a snake-pit, and as he lay writhing in the toils of these venomous reptiles he is alleged to have gasped out with his dying breath that 'the little pigs [his sons] will grunt when they hear how it fares with the old boar'.[2] And grunt they did. Landing with a large force in East Anglia, his sons Halfdan and Ivar *Beinlaus* invaded Deira, and by the autumn of 866 they were poised to attack York. The Northumbrians were weakened by a divided kingship, and in spite of maintaining a stout defence the deaths of both kings in battle left them at the mercy of the invaders, and consequently a Danish kingdom was established at York in 875/6.[3] However, some forty years later, in 919, the régime was overthrown by Rognvald, a member of the Norse dynasty at Dublin, who drove out the Danes and usurped the kingship.

During this time, the Norsemen were colonising much of northern and western Scotland. To begin with, their activities were confined to a series of plundering raids, and from their bases in Orkney and Shetland some of these Vikings penetrated far down the east coast. In 793, Lindisfarne was sacked when, according to Alcuin, it was 'spattered with the blood of priests [and] despoiled of all its ornaments', while Bede's monastery of Jarrow was raided the following year. Others concentrated their attacks on the Scottish mainland and the Hebrides, and it was they who were responsible for sacking the monastery on Iona in 794, and burning it again in 802.

Modern opinion inclines to the view that, because the Viking attacks were targeted on religious houses in particular, the monkish chroniclers, who are the main source of information about them, presented an unduly biassed picture, and that in reality the Vikings were primarily farmers who assimilated peacefully with local populations. True, the wealth of the monasteries and their potential for booty was an attraction to them, so it is understandable that these accounts should reflect the chroniclers' horror at the atrocities perpetrated on their fellow monks, as well as their appalled disbelief that anyone should dare attack institutions which represented God's witness on earth.

Nevertheless, this is carrying the current reluctance to accept the violence associated with our forbears too far.[4] For the fact is that Viking attacks did extend to local populations, since it was only by the customary process of slaughter, eviction and enslavement that they succeeded in carving out territories for the colonists, who followed in their wake, to settle as farmers and traders. Although the latter arrived as hostile incomers, and were no doubt feared and resented by the native population, they demonstrated an almost chameleon-like capacity for assimilating with local communities, to the extent that in the regions to the west they, or at least their immediate descendants, adopted Gaelic as their native tongue.

At first, Norse settlement was confined to the Northern Isles, northern Scotland and the Hebrides, and its extent is evident from the density of Scandinavian place-names in those regions. Orkney, in particular, became the centre of a powerful Norse earldom whose authority would extend throughout the north and down the west coast,[5] while other settlements were established in western Argyllshire and Kintyre. From there, the Vikings launched attacks on the regions fringing the Irish Sea, including the Isle of Man, where they founded a kingdom which lasted for some four centuries and became a dominant power in the west. The displacement of native inhabitants to make way for Viking settlement led to a major social upheaval, as large numbers of refugees fled in search of a safe haven, some perhaps seeking refuge in Galloway.

Meanwhile the Danish attacks on Northumbria forced many local Angles to decamp westwards, among them being a band of monks who managed to escape from Lindisfarne when it was sacked in 875. The *Historia Dunelmensis Ecclesiae*, admittedly an unreliable account which was attributed to the eleventh-century chronicler, Symeon of Durham, describes the vicissitudes they encountered in the course of their wanderings. Thanks to the resourcefulness of Bishop Eardulf and their abbot Aenred, they made for the boats in time to save St Cuthbert's coffin and the Lindisfarne Gospels from the raiders. Landing safely further down the coast, they spent the next seven years 'passing through deserted lands ravaged by the Viking invaders', being reduced at one point to subsisting on a cheese and a salted horse's head. Reaching the Cumbrian coast, they attempted to set sail for Ireland but were beaten back by a storm, when the precious Gospels were washed overboard, though they were miraculously recovered intact and still in their jewelled case. Finally, the monks found sanctuary at Whithorn – an outcome which, naturally, was attributed to the divine intervention of St Cuthbert.[6]

Unfortunately, their arrival there coincided with an intensification of Viking raids on the regions fringing the Irish Sea. Although Ireland and the Isle of Man were the principal targets, their attacks extended to modern Cumbria, and evidence of this lies in the recorded flight of Anglian aristocrats from the region in the early tenth century. A case in point was Tilred, abbot of Heversham in southern Westmorland, who decamped to Norham, and later on Aelfred, son of Birhtulf, clearly a man of importance, is reported as fleeing across the Pennines from 'the pirates'.[7] Yet there is no firm evidence of Galloway coming under attack, which seems strange considering its strategic position astride the Irish Sea, while its fertile coastal regions and lush river valleys must positively have invited settlement. Perhaps this was why the refugee monks from Lindisfarne saw it as a safe haven. On the other hand, the destruction of Whithorn in 843 could have been the result of a Viking raid, though perhaps more convincing evidence of upheavals in Galloway could lie in a contemporary hoard of loot found near Talnotrie on the Newton Stewart/New Galloway road, as this may have been buried for safety.[8]

NORSE SETTLEMENT

Surviving evidence points to Norse settlement in Galloway occurring during the 900s. As this was more than a century after the onset of Viking raids on the Scottish coast, these colonists would not have come direct from Norway but are more likely to have been second or third generation settlers from the Isle of Man, or possibly modern Cumbria. Opinion as to the extent of their settlement in Galloway has fluctuated wildly, earlier historians arguing that, because of its proximity to other Scandinavian colonies in the west, it must have been an important centre of Norse power. Founding on their interpretation of unreliable chronicles and sagas, they concluded that the region was at one time part of the earldom of Orkney, and by inference the eleventh-century lords of Galloway were of Norse extraction.

By the 1980s opinion had swung to the opposite extreme, and this was most forcibly expressed by Professor Cowan's dismissive assertion that the Norse presence in Galloway was not significant and 'at most there may have been a few pockets of Scandinavian settlement along the coast'.[9] However, an analysis of local place-names, and the archaeological evidence from Whithorn and Barhobble, while not necessarily conclusive, suggests this was carrying revisionism too far. Norse-derived place-names are strung along the coastline from the Rhinns as far as the Nith estuary, but because many of these stem from coastal navigational features it is only in certain areas, such as the Machars, the district round Borgue and Kirkcudbright, the lower Fleet valley and the merse of Cree, that they can be taken to indicate Norse settlement. The relative scarcity of such names, and the fact that they are confined to certain localities, has prompted the theory that the incomers were invited into the region by the local Angles as part of a deal rather than arriving as raiders, and later settlers.[10]

This speculation is inspired by the rapid expansion of the British kingdom of Strathclyde, possibly as far south as Stainmore Common on the Yorkshire/Lancashire border, and beyond the Nith, perhaps even as far as the Urr, which occurred at about the turn of the tenth century. Therefore, it is conjectured that this encouraged a resurgence by the native Galloway Britons, and, faced with this threat, the local Angles enlisted Viking support in return for surrendering them land. While it is hard to imagine this applying in the case of all the Norse settlement areas in Galloway, it may have been true of the southern Machars. For it is significant that Norse-derived place-names there occur on the peripheries of local ecclesiastical estates,[11] and therefore it is possible that the bishops encircled these with Norse settlers in return for their protection in a potentially hostile and lawless environment. Alternatively, this may have been the price of buying off a threatened attack.

However, Norse-derived place-names are no sure guide to the extent of their settlement since the Norsemen frequently retained the existing names of the estates and habitations they took over. This is known to have applied in the case of Buittle, where there is evidence of a Viking presence,[12] and would doubtless have done so elsewhere in Galloway. In fact, Dr Oram surmises that Norse settlement could have been still more comprehensive, because many former Norse names could have been lost through changes in nomenclature.[13] Yet, the dearth of incised stones reflecting a Norse influence could argue against this, because the only extant example is the slab at Kilmorie on the western shore of Loch Ryan.[14] So the matter will continue to be the subject of debate unless more compelling evidence comes to light.

The presumption must be that Norse settlement in Galloway was achieved by a variety of methods. In some cases, existing estates were appropriated – no doubt by force, and one example was Sorbie which was already a high status estate, and the fact that it must have been seized is evident from the Old Norse origin of its name, which means literally 'swamp farm'.[15] Other settlers may simply have taken over pockets of untilled land and become part of the existing settlement pattern. Less productive land was requisitioned for purposes of summering livestock, and a case in point was the estate of Gaitgil, which straddles the high ground between the Tarff and the Fleet valleys. However, it is unlikely that places like these were extensively colonised, and the native inhabitants were probably allowed to remain there provided they paid tribute to their Norse masters. Therefore, it seems that, while Norse settlement in Galloway may not have been particularly dense, they could nevertheless have controlled substantial areas within the province.

Potentially confirmatory evidence of Norse settlement comes from the observations of two commentators writing nearly a thousand years later. Heron, who travelled through Galloway in 1792, observed that:

> it is worthy of notice that the inhabitants of the district of Borgue . . . were long regarded by other people in the district as a sort of peculiar, insulated tribe. The families of the farmers had been settled there for many generations . . . were all mutually related by intermarriage [and] a person of singular appearance or manners was commonly said by the people of the adjacent country to be a Borgue body . . . I take them to have been a more unmixed race either of Danes or Anglo-Saxons than remained in any other part of this country.[16]

Trotter echoes this in his *Galloway Gossip,* which was written a century later, where he refers to a type he called Fingaels:

> . . . clever-lookin' fellas – maistly lang an' weel-made, wi' lang faces, strecht noses an' blue een [eyes] an' wunnerfu' feet for size. They'r maistly fair-hair't, or licht-broon, an' the lasses is verra bonnie when they'r young, but efter they'r twunty they get verra coorse-lookin'. They'r commonest in Saterness [Southerness], Co'en [Colvend], Borgue, Whithorn an' Kirkmaiden, an' there's odd yins o' them a' ower, but they'r getting' geyly mix't up noo. They'r the descendants o' the Norsemen . . .[17]

Although not conclusive, these accounts could point to the presence of an alien population which appears to have retained its individual identity for an astonishingly long time afterwards.

A CHANGING SOCIETY

While most of the colonists were originally of Norse stock, it seems that parts of eastern Galloway were colonised by Danes – as is evident from the Danish-derived place-name of Mabie in the parish of Troqueer, which was clearly one of a number of settlements they established in the vicinity. This stemmed from Halfdan's capture of York in 875/6, which was the prelude to the conquest of Deira, and its division between the principal Viking leaders. They expanded their territories by filling the vacuum left by the contracting kingdom of Strathclyde, and by early the following century there was extensive Danish settlement in modern Cumbria and Dumfries-shire as far as the Nith valley.

The Scandinavian settlers, however, merely added a further ingredient to the disparate mix of people who already inhabited the region comprising modern Galloway. Apparently the distinction between Angle and Britain was still evident,[18] while there must have been a large Irish population, particularly in the west, and their Gaelic speech was probably already diffusing among the peasantry. The population must therefore have been extremely heterogenous, and clear distinctions would have existed between the inhabitants of different parts of the region, for it was not until later that the Gallovidians came to be regarded as a composite people.

Although the region was still nominally an Anglian province, the authority of the Northumbrian rulers was nugatory, as the kingdom was in the process of disintegrating. While the sons of Ragnar Loðbrok took over Deira, the northern province of Bernicia, which extended as far as the Firth of Forth, continued to be an Anglian stronghold, though it too was about to be dismembered. The expansion of Strathclyde in about 900 cut it off from Galloway, and early in the eleventh century it ceded all the territory north of the Tweed to the Scots king Malcolm II, who was already in the throes of annexing the rump of Strathclyde. The dismemberment of

Northumbria resulted in a resurgence of the native Britons, and a
consequent abandonment by the Anglian population of their Northumbrian names for British ones. This would explain why the principal
landowners in the former Northumbrian-controlled territories had British
names, and it would also account for the dearth of Anglian ones among the
witnesses to early charters relating to Galloway, as well as the disappearance
of the Old English speech there.

From about the tenth century onwards, yet another ingredient was
added to the mix of people inhabiting Galloway with the arrival of Gaelic-
speaking immigrants who were collectively known as the Gall-gaidhil.
Meaning 'stranger Gaels', the term was first used by an Irish annalist in the
seventh century to describe an alien people or those of mixed race. The
mid-ninth century *Annals of Ulster* applied it to warbands, or perhaps
mercenaries, who came from Galloway to take part in the feuding which
was endemic in contemporary Ireland.

In the tenth century it referred to Gaelic-speaking immigrants to
Galloway of mixed ancestry, being first or second generation descendants
of Norse settlers in western Scotland and Ireland who had interbred with
the native population. The fact that the name Galloway is almost certainly
derived from these people[19] inspired the traditional view that they settled
there to the exclusion of anywhere else. This in turn led earlier historians
to assume the reference in the *Annals of Ulster* for 1034 to the death of
Suibhne mac Cinead king of the Gallgaidhil[20] to mean that he was a Viking
ruler of Galloway, and by inference the province was part of the Norse
earldom of Orkney. In fact, the Gall-gaidhil settled throughout the west of
Scotland, and consequently those who owed allegiance to this 'king' would
not necessarily have included people living in Galloway, and almost
certainly did not.

Traditionally they were regarded as pagan freebooters of unbridled
ferocity and violently anti-Christian, but excavations at Whithorn show that
they included influential people, such as churchmen, as well as skilled
craftsmen, among their number. Artefacts of Irish or Norse-Irish design,
dating from the later tenth century,[21] suggest that they were already making
their mark on the community by that stage. But their influence becames
still more pronounced in the following century, when contemporary
buildings there show a marked resemblance to those at Dublin and other
Norse-Irish towns, such as Waterford,[22] while other artefacts replicate those
appearing on Irish sites.

Therefore, the evidence points to the Gall-gaidhil taking over Whithorn
as a trading station and expelling, or possibly massacring, its civic leaders
so that it became a 'potentially Irish-Norse or Irish community'.[23] Other
developments which were occurring in Galloway at this time are also
indicative of their influence. For example, the Chronicle of Man asserts

that the Norwegian king, Magnus Olafsson (1093–1103), claimed overlordship of parts of Galloway and exacted a tribute of timber from the local ecclesiastical and secular landowners,[24] and this could be taken to indicate the existence of a substantial and influential Norse or Gall-gaidhil population in the region.

THE CHURCH

The scarcity of evidence relating to the period from the mid-800s to the 1120s makes it difficult to determine what was happening in Galloway during this time, and therefore historians are left to draw such conclusions as they can from the limited amount available. Nevertheless, it seems likely that Whithorn continued to be a centre of ecclesiastical authority, and that it retained its ties with York,[25] though there is tenuous evidence to suggest that it may at some stage have come under the control of the ecclesiastical authorities on the Isle of Man.[26] If this was the case, it could point to an extensive Norse influence in the province. Galloway east of the Urr, on the other hand, came under the jurisdiction of Glasgow, and this has prompted speculation that its authority extended into western Galloway,[27] though this is now thought unlikely.[28] That there was still a bishop at Whithorn seems evident from the local place-name Bysbie at the Isle of Whithorn, as its former name Biscoby, which dates from the later ninth or early tenth century, is derived from the Old Norse *biscop-byr*, meaning 'bishop's farm'.[29]

The argument in favour of Whithorn continuing to be an ecclesiastical centre throughout this period is supported by the interpretation placed on local sculptured stones, which date from the ninth century onwards. These mark focal points of religious authority, and it is because they are mainly concentrated in the Machars, and nearly all of them post-date the Northumbrian period, that it has been concluded that this region remained under the control of Whithorn. The detailed investigation, which has been carried out on these stones by Dr Craig,[30] shows that those located in the Machars share a basic similarity of design, most notably the inclusion of a disc-headed cross. Since they are thought to have been carved at Whithorn, with a possible subsidiary workshop at Barhobble,[31] they are categorised as belonging to the 'Whithorn school'.

Another group of stones, which have been identified at various locations along the coast from Ardwall Island as far as the Cree, also share certain similarities. For the cross which marked the religious settlement on Ardwall Island has characteristics in common with the one found at Anwoth, while this can be linked with other stones at nearby Kirkclaugh and also at Minnigaff. A third group has been identified in the district between the Dee and the Urr estuaries. As two of these stones are associated with the Northumbrian style of carving, they may pre-date those of the Whithorn school. Moreover, their location to the east of the Dee could be significant, because in Anglian times that river is thought to have marked the boundary between the Northumbrian heartland and the west.[32] If these stones did mark preaching sites, as thought likely, they can be taken to indicate an area of ecclesiastical authority which was probably centred on the local minster at Kirkcudbright.

Another group, which has been identified in the region of Carsphairn, indicate the *parochia* of another ecclesiastical institution, though its precise location, or even if it existed in the vicinity of Carsphairn at all, remains unclear. Superficially, it would seem somewhat incongruous that stones like these, which are primarily an indication of wealth, should exist in such an apparently impoverished region,[33] but in medieval times the grazing land there was in keen demand by pastoralist farmers, and it would have been more densely populated than it is today. Also, because it commanded the main route from Galloway through to Kyle, it was an area of high strategic importance, and probably comprised a group of estates which eventually crystallised into the powerful lordship of Dalmellington.

THE GAELICISATION OF GALLOWAY

By the twelfth century Gaelic had become the speech and culture of the upper classes in Galloway[34] – a fact which is evident from the preponderance of Gaelic names among the witnesses to early charters, and the earliest recorded landowners in the region. This appears to have marked the culmination of a trend whose origins are discernible in the existence of long-established, Gaelic-derived place-names in Galloway. Their connection with natural features, such as a hill or loch, suggests that they were attributable to a Gaelic-speaking peasantry,[35] and this in turn could infer that the Gaelic speech of the Irish settlers in Galloway had been spreading throughout the region over a long period.

However, its percolation up the social scale to the aristocracy ran counter to the usual trend of language changes, which generally diffuse from the upper classes downwards. This might be explained by two interrelated facts. Firstly, the Gaelic-speaking Norse-Irish settlers, who arrived in Galloway from the tenth century onwards, included churchmen and church patrons who appear to have acquired considerable political influence.[36] Secondly, through this influence the Irish Church gained a strong foothold in Galloway – a fact which is evident from the number of eleventh-century and later church dedications to Irish saints identifiable in Kirkcudbrightshire, the Rhinns and southern Carrick.[37] Taken together, therefore, these factors could account for the progressive Gaelicisation of the upper classes, and its supersession of their former British culture.[38]

That no dedications to Irish saints appear in the Machars is further evidence that this region was controlled by Whithorn, though one can only speculate as to how it contrived to remain independent of the Irish Church. Perhaps the link with York was responsible, but more likely the protection of local secular landowners provides an answer, and in particular the early lords of Galloway. One of their principal power centres was at nearby Cruggleton, so they would have been well placed to extend their protection to Whithorn. It is logical to assume that a price was demanded in return, perhaps involving the transfer of ecclesiastical estates, as this could explain why a large part of the demesne lands of the lords of Galloway was concentrated in the Machars. While there are possible arguments for an eleventh-century lordship of Galloway, these early lords remain tantalisingly shadowy, and it is not until the 1100s that they emerge from their obscurity.

NOTES

1. One band of adventurers under Rolf (or Rollo), a Norse princeling, established an enclave in northern France which his descendants eventually enlarged into the dukedom of Normandy. Among them was William 'the bastard', otherwise known as 'the conqueror', who usurped the English throne nearly three centuries later in 1066.
2. Montgomery, *Origin and History of the Montgomerys*, 25. This cites the Anglo-Saxon chronicle as asserting that the event occurred in 865.
3. Dumville, 'The churches of north Britain in the first Viking age', 29.
4. Dumville was particularly scathing about this school of thought. 'I venture to suggest', he said, 'that if Vikings arrived at the door of this church tonight few of us would leave with our lives and those who did might wish they had not' (*ibid.*, 8).
5. Caithness and the Western Isles remained under Norwegian rule until 1266, while Orkney and Shetland continued to do so until 1469, when they were pledged to the Scottish crown and later annexed to it by an act of parliament of 1471.
6. *Historia Dunelmensis ecclesia*, ii, pp 6–13.
7. Symeon of Durham, i, 208–9.
8. Truckell, 'A photo-history of Galloway'.
9. Cowan, 'The Vikings in Galloway', 71.
10. Mooted by Hill and Brooke who discusses it in *Wild Men*, 65–7, and also in 'The Northumbrian settlements in Galloway and Carrick', 299, 321–2.
11. These include Physgill, Appleby, Bysbie and Ardbrack (formerly Arborg), and doubtless there were others as well.
12. A tenth-century Viking bleaching and tanworks have come to light in the course of the excavations there, and similarly furnaces which were used for producing wrought-iron, perhaps for sword-making (*Botel bailey: Interim Report 1999*).
13. Oram, 'Scandinavian settlement in south-west Scotland', 127 et seq.
14. Craig, 'Pre-Norman sculpture in Galloway'.

15. Conversation with Dr Oram.
16. Heron, *Observations* ii, 204.
17. Trotter, *Galloway Gossip*, 181.
18. This seems apparent from the survival of certain cultural distinctions which are evident from the finds at Whithorn and Barhobble, and from certain features among the ninth-century stone crosses.
19. Brooke postulates that it was derived from *coed celidon*, 'the wood of the Caledonians', but the linguistic soundness of this theory has been questioned.
20. *The Annals of Ulster* (eds) Mac Airt and Mac Niocaill, 322–3, but its authority is dubious.
21. Hill, *Whithorn*, 52.
22. *Ibid.*, 56. This was particularly evident in the similarity between the combs manufactured at these centres.
23. *Ibid.*, 59.
24. *Chron. Man*, (Anderson, *Early Sources*), ii, 103. Recently, this assertion has been treated with some reserve, but Dr Oram is beginning to attach greater weight to it.
25. Oram, 'In obedience and reverence', 83 et seq.
26. This could be inferred from a list of Manx bishops and a garbled metrical chronicle of York, which suggests that a Bishop Gamaliel or Gamellinus held the sees of Whithorn and Man in the late eleventh century, though these sources are not wholly reliable (Brooke, *Wild Men*, 78, quoting Anderson, *Early Sources*, 96–228).
27. Skene, *Celtic Scotland* ii, 375.
28. Oram, 'In obedience and reverence', 84–5.
29. Hill, *Whithorn*, 53: Brooke, *Wild Men*, 69.
30. Craig, 'Pre-Norman sculpture in Galloway'.
31. Cormack and others, 'Barhobble, Mochrum', 50.
32. Conversation with Dr Oram.
33. *Ibid.*: Craig, 'Pre-Norman sculpture', 45.
34. Brooke, *Wild Men*, 74.
35. *Ibid.*
36. *Ibid.*
37. For example, the new churches at Urr and Buittle – the one replacing the former minster at Edingham, and the other a field church at Kirkennan, were dedicated to the Irish saint, Colman of Elo. Also, four important parish churches in the heartland of Kirkcudbrightshire, namely St Oswald the Martyr at Kelton and its daughter church of St Michael of Balnacross (now Barncrosh), St Andrew at Balmaghie, and Kirkcormack near Gelston, all came under the control of the Irish church (*ibid.*, 75).
38. Dr Oram has postulated this in course of conversation.

7

FERGUS 'REX GALWITENSIUM'

AN INDEPENDENT PRINCEDOM

Fergus is the earliest known lord of Galloway, and although he first appears as a witness to a royal charter in 1136,[1] the indications are that he had been ruling the territory to the west of the Urr[2] since the 1120s. That his son Uhtred (or Uchtred as he is generally known[3]) was a witness to the same charter suggests that Fergus was by then a middle-aged man. Otherwise, nothing definite is known about his background. He may have been born around 1090,[4] or perhaps earlier, and while he seems more likely to have inherited the lordship than usurping it, the possibility of his being a *parvenu* cannot be ruled out. Judging from the fact that the lordship lands at Kirkcudbright passed to the senior descendants of his great-grandson, Alan, the last of the medieval lords of Galloway, it seems certain that his principal ruling centre was at nearby Lochfergus.[5] He also had a subsidiary power-base at Cruggleton, in the Machars, where he owned extensive lands, as well as a third at Arsbotel, on Loch Ken.

His origins have been the subject of much scholarly debate, the mystery being compounded by his lack of a known patronymic. Founding on the now exploded theory that Galloway was part of the earldom of Orkney, earlier historians suggested a Norse background, though slightly more convincing evidence of this lies in the thirteenth-century romantic poem, the *Roman de Fergus*. Its hero, tentatively equated with Fergus, is portrayed as the youngest son of Somerled, and while this was quite a common Norse name there is no-one on record who can be positively identified with him. Nevertheless, the poem does contain material which could accord with historical fact, and the link it suggests between the dynasties of Galloway and Argyll is arguably supported by the involvement of Fergus and his successors in the politics of the west coast and the Irish Sea. Somerled is portrayed as a boorish peasant, elevated by marriage to a position of wealth and high social status, which might point to a union between one of Fergus's immediate forbears and a native heiress. However, this is mere speculation, and unless more concrete evidence comes to light his origins will remain a matter for conjecture.

Fergus's assertion of his independence of the royal authority was the keynote of his policy throughout his lordship, and this is evident from the contrast in titles accorded him in surviving documents. Whereas English and Scottish charters describe him as Fergus de Galweia or *princeps*, he styled himself 'rex Galwitensium',[6] thus effectively declaring that his authority was derived from the nobility and people he ruled over, and not from the king. At the same time, he was careful to avoid pressing his independence to the point of open rebellion against King David, and it seems that a guarded neutrality was maintained between them throughout the latter's reign.

Fergus's status was greatly enhanced by his marriage to an illegitimate daughter of the English king Henry I.[7] Direct evidence of this is lacking, though it can be inferred from surviving references to a cousinhood between Henry I's successors and Fergus's immediate descendants.[8] The match was essentially political, for Henry made a practice of marrying off his numerous illegitimate daughters to lesser princelings on the peripheries of his realms, and the fact that another daughter was married to the Scots king Alexander I suggests that Henry regarded the rulers of Scotland and Galloway as men of broadly equal status, though inferior to him.[9] This policy was designed to create a bulwark of political alliances for the purpose of protecting Henry's territories, and the fact that Galloway was included in this nexus was a reflection of its strategic importance. Later, Fergus adopted much the same policy by marrying off his own daughter, Affreca, to Olaf Godredsson, king of Man,[10] in order to reinforce his position in the west, and to establish a dynastic link with a powerful lordship which lay outwith the orbit of the Scottish crown.

An early assertion of Fergus's independence is evident from two documents concerning the appointment of the Gallovidian churchman, Gilla-Aldan, to the see of Whithorn – the first recorded bishop since the Northumbrian Hathured in 833/6. The first is a mandate issued by Pope Honorius II in December 1128 ordering an un-named bishop-elect of Whithorn to present himself to the 'appropriate metropolitan' (Archbishop Thurstan of York) for consecration. The other is the oath of obedience sworn by Gilla-Aldan to Thurstan sometime between 1128 and 1140, presumably on the occasion of his consecration. This states that 'from ancient times the Bishop of Candida Casa has owed respect – and in those things that are God's obedience – to his mother the archiepiscopal church of York'.[11] This was a clear affirmation of Whithorn's adherence to that centre,[12] and by implication a firm rebuttal of any attempt by the Scottish Church, particularly the diocese of Glasgow, to establish ecclesiastical authority over Whithorn.

This was essentially a political statement, and doubtless Fergus had a hand in drafting it. The reason was that King David, having seen how successfully the Norman kings used the Church in England as an instrument for consolidating their authority, was determined to apply the same strategy in his own realm. This involved reorganising the diocesan and parochial structure of the Church and securing the appointment of bishops who were prepared to co-operate in reinforcing his authority throughout their dioceses.[13] Therefore, Fergus saw a re-forging of Whithorn's historic ties with York as his best protection against David's ambitions, while its continuing independence of the Scottish Church would give added weight to his own self-professed royal status.

THE ANGLO-NORMANS

Another arm of David's strategy for extending his royal powers was to encourage prominent Anglo-Normans and their dependants to settle in Scotland by granting them substantial fiefs and appointing them to the principal offices in the royal household. This was designed to establish a powerful body of supporters of unquestioned loyalty, whom he could rely upon to strengthen his authority in his newly-acquired kingdom. Fergus, on the other hand, saw the Anglo-Normans as a potential threat to his independence, so he consistently refused to allow them to settle in his domains. Hitherto, the gift of the lands of Borgue to the Anglo-Norman Hugh de Morville was seen as belying this, because it was traditionally thought to have been made sometime before 1150, in which case Fergus would have been the granter. This notion was based on the assertion by an early editor of the *Registrum de Dryburgh* that de Morville endowed his creation of Dryburgh abbey with the church of 'Worgis' in that year,[14] and the consequent inference that he must already have possessed these lands. However, it has now been established that the editor misinterpreted the record and the gift was in fact made in the 1160s by Hugh de Morville's son, another Hugh, suggesting that it was Fergus's son Uchtred, and not himself, who granted the lands.[15]

Most of the foreign settlers whom King David lured to Scotland were first, or at least second, generation Normans, because little more than half a century had elapsed since Duke William of Normandy's conquest of England. This was the prelude to the establishment of a Frankish ruling class there, as increasing numbers of Norman, Breton and Flemish knights were lured across the Channel to this land of opportunity. By Henry I's accession in 1100 they had colonised much of northern England, and ten years later the process was complete. Therefore, by the time David I succeeded to the Scottish throne in 1124 there was pressure to extend their colonising activities to Scotland. He was well placed to take advantage of this, because he himself had become a leading member of the Norman establishment in England.

Although a Scot by birth, David's background was wholly Norman. This was because, as a youth, he had been sent to England for safety during the political upheavals which followed the death of his father, Malcolm III, in 1093. Although a semblance of peace was restored with the accession of his eldest full-brother, Edgar, in 1097, David remained there becoming a protégé of Henry I. Shortly after his accession, Henry married David's sister, Edith, and in consequence David acquired high status at the English court where, according to William of Malmesbury, he had 'the rust of Scottish barbarousness rubbed off him'. In 1113, his power was greatly increased when Henry gave him Maude de Senlis, reputedly the wealthiest widow in England,[16] in marriage. Through her he acquired extensive estates in the Midlands, including the Honour of Huntingdon, as well as an ancestral claim to the earldom of Northumberland. Later still, Henry granted him a large landholding in modern Cumbria and Westmorland, thus establishing him as a prominent marcher lord in the region, and consequently he became one of the most powerful English magnates.

That he was in a position to endow these Anglo-Norman incomers with substantial grants of land stemmed from the fact that he had inherited, along with the Scottish crown, a huge royal patrimony. This consisted of all the lands comprising the former kingdom of Strathclyde, lying to the north of the Solway, as well as much of Lothian and present-day Berwickshire, which had been ceded to the Scottish crown by Northumbria. In addition, his predecessors had annexed the Gaelicised district of northern Ayrshire and Renfrewshire, and it was in these regions that the earliest Anglo-Norman settlers were established. Prominent among them was Robert de Brus, a native of Brix in Normandy. Henry I had already given him extensive lands in Yorkshire for the purpose of maintaining control over that politically unreliable region,[17] and David followed suit by granting him a large tract of land in Annandale in Dumfriesshire. This was a strategically-important lordship, as it controlled the western approach route into Scotland.

Another was Hugh de Morville, a native of Valognes, in the Cotentin peninsula, in northern France, who was already one of David's tenants in his Honour of Huntingdon. He was given substantial lands in Lauderdale, as well as the lordship of Cunninghame in northern Ayrshire, and he was also appointed Constable. This office later became hereditary, and it would eventually pass to the lords of Galloway along with the de Morville lands in Scotland. Other incomers who were given important political office included William Cumin, a clerk in the service of Henry I, whom David appointed his Chancellor, subsequently engineering his preferment to the bishopric of Durham. His collateral descendants, the Comyns, came to dominate the Scottish political scene for upwards of a century, until they fell from power following King Robert Bruce's victory at Bannockburn in 1314.

The lands in modern Cumbria and Westmorland, which David had been granted by Henry I, were also a focus of settlement. Henry himself had already established tenants there, and during the early years of his reign David added to their number. Hugh de Morville was granted territory in Westmorland, while Ranulph de Soulis was given the extensive fief of Liddesdale at the head of the Solway. His family eventually became one of the foremost among the Anglo-Norman establishment in Scotland, while their possessions came to include land in Galloway.[18] Other tenants, however, were natives of modern Cumbria, most of them probably of Anglian origin, and they would become a principal source of incomers to Galloway.

The Anglo-Norman settlers, along with their tenants and dependants, constituted a large alien population in Scotland, and their numbers continued to increase during the reigns of David's grandsons, Malcolm IV and William I. Yet there were clear gradations within their society which were linked to the quality of the land they were given. Aristocrats like Hugh de Morville, who came from the wheat-producing lands of Normandy and were used to eating fine wheaten bread, insisted on being given lands, such as those in Lauderdale, where wheat could be grown. The next category consisted mainly of west Normans, like Robert de Brus, and Bretons such as Walter fitzAlan, the ancestor of the Stewarts. They were prepared to settle in lands which were capable of growing oats and barley, and tending to eat more meat than their social superiors they would also accept pasture land. The Flemings represented the lower end of the social scale, and being essentially pioneers who were willing to make do with black bread made from rye, they settled in poorer regions where this was the only crop that could be cultivated.[19]

The grants made to the Anglo-Normans were founded on the feudal system of land tenure, which up to now was unknown in Scotland. However, the king needed a title to the lands before he could feu them off, so once David had granted away his original patrimony, the process of establishing new tenants-in-chief inevitably slowed down. For it was only through a process of legal forfeitures, or the reversion of lands to the crown for other reasons, that they could be re-granted feudally. In return, his tenants-in-chief undertook various obligations, chiefly of a military character, and most important of all they were obliged to do homage to him, acknowledging him as their feudal superior. As they in turn granted land to their own feudal tenants on a similar basis, a system was created whereby power, patronage and property centred on the king, while at the same time providing him with the means of enforcing his authority and calling out an army when necessary.

THE CAMPAIGN IN NORTHERN ENGLAND

Henry I's death in 1135 resulted in a disputed succession between his daughter, Matilda, and his nephew, Stephen of Blois. Although Matilda had the better claim she was highly unpopular, and besides there was a widespread aversion to the principle of a female ruler. Therefore, seizing the opportunity, Stephen usurped the throne, and civil war broke out in England. King David was poised to intervene in support of Matilda, who was his niece,[20] using this as a pretext for reclaiming the earldom of Northumberland for his son, Henry. Anticipating this, Stephen attempted to buy him off by ceding him the overlordship of his lands in modern Cumbria and Westmorland. David, however, reneged on the agreement by invading northern England, and Fergus dispatched levies from Galloway to serve in his army, as they had done when Malcolm III carried out a similar incursion in 1070. Although their participation might seem at odds with Fergus's assertion of independence, they probably acted as mercenaries since this was a lucrative source of revenue to a ruler. Family ties might have been a consideration as well, as Matilda was a half-sister of Fergus's wife, and this could have encouraged him to support her.

Initially, the campaign was limited to a war of attrition. However, finding themselves unable to make any impression on the Northumbrian strongholds, David's troops turned in rage and frustration on the civilian population, on whom they are alleged to have perpetrated appalling atrocities. According to Richard of Hexham, 'that execrable army . . . harried the whole province and slaughtered everywhere folk of either sex, of every age and condition, destroying, pillaging and burning the villages, churches and houses'. Giving full rein to an obviously fertile imagination, he paints a truly diabolical picture of these men 'slaughtering by the edge of the sword and transfixing with their spears the sick on their pallets, women pregnant and in labour, the babes in the cradles, and other innocents at the breast'.[21]

While Richard of Hexham was referring to the Scots army in general, Abbot Ailred of Rievaulx's highly partial *De Standardo,* written some twenty years later, pinned the blame for the alleged atrocities specifically on the Gallovidians. According to his account, 'these brute beasts devoid of humanity and piety' spared 'neither rank nor age, nor sex or condition and carried off as well the noble widowed matrons and chaste maidens'. He goes on to describe how the Gallovidians stripped them and bound them together 'in troops by cords and thongs' and 'drove them away before them, goading them with their spears and arrows'. Lashing himself into hyperbole, he continues: 'these bestial men who regard as nothing adultery and incest, after they were weary of abusing these hapless creatures after the manner of brute beasts, made them their slaves, or sold them to other barbarians in exchange for cows'. Finally, throwing impartiality to the winds, he asserted that their savagery even extended to small children, describing in gruesome detail how 'a Gallovidian stood, and seizing one after the other by both feet struck their heads against the doorpost, and when he had piled them in a heap, he laughed!'[22]

The army's savagery also turned on religious houses and churches, where the soldiers are alleged to have decapitated the officiating priests and impaled their heads on altar crosses or, as Richard of Hexham put it, they 'irreverently committed acts violent, lewd and execrable'. When news of this reached David, superstitious dread compelled him to issue formal instruments of protection granting his peace to the houses of Hexham and Tynemouth,[23] and orders were issued to his soldiery to respect these on pain of death. However, it seems his protection came at a price, as Richard of Hexham goes on to assert that Tynemouth 'paid the King of Scots and his followers 27 merks of silver to buy for itself, and for those that resided there, peace in the present need'.[24] Despite these measures, the atrocities reached such a pitch that King Stephen ordered Archbishop Thurstan, as his tenant-in-chief, to raise an army to drive out the invading Scots.

Battle was eventually joined on Cowton Moor near Northallerton where, at what became known as the Battle of the Standard, the Scots were routed, and King David fled from the corpse-strewn battlefield with the shattered remnants of his army. Traditionally, the defeat has been attributed to the impetuosity of the Gallovidians who charged into battle in the van of the Scots army and lost contact with them in the melée, adding to the general confusion. True or not, their courage was never questioned. Fighting without the protection of armour, and exposed to the deadly accuracy of the English archers, they are described as wreaking havoc among their enemies with the aid of spears, axes, and long knives. 'Like a hedgehog with its quills', wrote Roger de Howden, 'so you would see a Galwegian bristled all round with arrows and nonetheless brandishing his sword and in blind madness rushing forward now smiting a foe, now lashing the air with useless strokes'.[25] Or, as William of Malmesbury loftily observed, 'who would not laugh rather than fear when to fight against such men [the Normans] runs the worthless Scot [Gallovidian] who with half-bare buttocks exposes his naked hide to our lances, our swords and our arrows, using a mere calf-skin for a shield [and being] inspired by irrational contempt of death rather than by strength'.

MONKISH CASTIGATION

Medieval chroniclers were so successful in blackening the name of the Gallovidians that the image of them as a wild and savage people has never yet been eradicated. One recent aspiring historian, who appears to have accepted this propaganda without equivocation, has obligingly attributed their alleged excesses to a hybrid vigour resulting from their racially mixed ancestry. While the allegations levelled against them by these chroniclers may contain an element of truth, they have to be looked at in perspective. It was an age which set little store on human life and warfare invariably involved atrocities, as it still does, but there is no reason to suppose the Gallovidians were any more guilty of these than their fellow Scots.

More to the point, though, the image they portray of the Scots army in general, and the Gallovidians in particular, is primarily a reflection of the prejudices of the chroniclers themselves. Besides reflecting a Norman, and essentially Frankish, disdain towards the Celts, whom they regarded as an inferior race,[26] they were inspired by deeply-held religious principles. Ailred and his associates were Cistercian monks, and as strict adherents of Pope Gregory's emphasis on clerical celibacy (for which they were known as the 'puritans of Catholicism'), they took exception to the traditionally lax 'Celtic' marriage laws which tolerated informal relationships and allowed for easy 'divorces'.[27] It was these in particular that prompted Walter Daniel's diatribe: '[their] chastity founders as often as lust wills, and the pure is only so far removed from the harlot that the more chaste will change their husbands every month, and a man will sell his wife for a heifer'.[28]

The Cistercians were intent on reforming the Church, and it was the fact that they perceived Whithorn as a bastion of the old ecclesiastical order which accounted for their particular animus against the Gallovidians. Above all, they were highly critical of a system which allowed lay canons to minister to the spiritual needs of the people, and at the same time to marry and own property, because this offended all their moral precepts. This was the subject of another of Walter Daniel's diatribes. While admitting that, 'certain men of that land [Galloway], if regularly established in a religious house, have veritably been transformed into monks', he claimed it was only achieved 'under the counsel and leadership of others, for scarcely have they the perseverence otherwise to reach out for perfection by their own efforts'. Driving the point home, he went on to describe them as 'by nature dull and brutish, having animal appetites which always incline them to the pleasures of the flesh'.[29]

Kirkcudbright, too, was under the charge of secular canons, as is evident from Reginald of Durham's account of an incident which occurred during Ailred's visit there in 1162. Some high-spirited youths were baiting a bull which had been given to the church in alms. When rebuked by their elders one of them sniggered, and challenging the authority of St Cuthbert he released the bull, whereupon at the saint's apparently miraculous intervention it promptly turned round and gored him in the shins.[30] While no doubt a salutary lesson to the offender in question, the point was that these youths are described as *scolocs*, which was a junior order in the pre-reformed Scottish Church.[31] Consequently, this centre must have been under the control of secular canons, while the tale was designed to justify their eviction from it.

Ailred had his own personal reasons for assigning responsibility for the outrages committed during the Northumbrian campaign specifically to the Gallovidians. He was a fervent admirer of King David, having been raised at his court, and was a close friend and contemporary of his son, Henry, earl of Huntingdon. Understandably, therefore, he was concerned to absolve the Scots from blame, but at the same time he was motivated by a personal grudge against Fergus. This arose in consequence of a dispute over the succession to the see of York following Archbishop Thurstan's death in 1140. The two contenders were William fitzHerbert, a relative and nominee of King Stephen, and Henry Murdac, abbot of Fountains, whose candidature was endorsed by King David. As Murdac was a Cistercian, he was naturally supported by Ailred and his fellow members of the order, and they proceeded to issue a stream of invective against fitzHerbert's supporters. These included Fergus, because he feared that if the archbishopric were held by a protégé of the Scottish crown it could risk a repetition of the situation he had managed to avoid in the 1120s.[32]

Although fitzHerbert was successful his tenure was short-lived, for in 1167 Bernard of Clairvaux, a leading protagonist of the Cistercian order, persuaded the pope to depose him in favour of Murdac. However, it was a Pyrrhic victory because Murdac was too terrified of the local citizenry to stay at York, so he abandoned the see and took refuge at his abbey of Fountains. FitzHerbert and his men proceeded to revenge themselves by carrying out a raid on the abbey, castrating an elderly archdeacon as a warning of what lay in store for Murdac.[33] When Murdac died – of natural causes – in 1153, fitzHerbert was reinstated, but again his reign was short as he died the following year. Altogether a sordid tale, though in keeping with the times, but it goes far to explain the Cistercian chroniclers' systematic vilification of Fergus.

Fergus's benefactions

In view of the abuse they heaped on him, Fergus's generosity to the Cistercians seems almost quixotic. For not only did he allow them to found a daughter house of Rievaulx[34] at Dundrennan in 1142,[35] but he also endowed it with a generous grant of land. Moreover, to allow them to establish a citadel of reformism in the heart of his lordship represented a major concession on his part because, conservative by nature and deeply committed to the old order in the Church, he was opposed to all they stood for. The extent of his indulgence is apparent from Walter Daniel's assertion that 'Rievaulx made a plantation in that savage environment [Galloway], which with the help of God who gives increase to a new planting, is now yielding plentiful fruit'.[36]

Clearly Fergus must have been under extreme pressure to consent to this. It may have been designed to placate King David and the Cistercians, but there must have been more compelling reasons. Perhaps he was under threat of ecclesiastical censure for taking up arms against his spiritual overlord, Archbishop Thurstan, and for the reported atrocities of his levies in northern England. In this context, acceptance of a Cistercian presence in Galloway might be seen as an act of atonement which was designed to ward off possible excommunication.[37] This could also explain the munificence of his endowment of Dundrennan, which seems to have consisted of much of the southern and western portions of the modern parish of Rerrick. While Fergus granted the land, the Cistercians were responsible for building the abbey, and the construction costs would most likely have been financed out of loans advanced by the Jewish community at York, since this was generally their practice in the case of the other houses which they founded.

Fergus may also have allowed them to establish an abbey at Soulseat to replace an apparently moribund church, which is thought to have dated from Northumbrian times. For, according to tradition, it was founded as a Cistercian house in 1148 at the behest of the papal legate, Archbishop Malachy (Maelmaedoic) O'Moore of Armagh. However, this is based on an uncertain interpretation of a passage in Bernard of Clairvaux's *Vita Sancti Malachiae* which describes how 'on the third day [after leaving Ireland] he [Malachy] reached a place called *viride stagnum* which he caused to be prepared that he might establish an abbey there'. Having made the necessary arrangements, Malachy left there 'some of his sons, our brothers, as a convent of monks and an abbot'.[38] Meaning 'the green pool', *viride stagnum* has been associated with the loch at Soulseat which is covered by a green algal scum in summertime, and there is also a reference to Viridi Stagni in a charter granted by Soulseat's commendator in 1539. However, there are stronger grounds for believing that the abbey was established after 1148 for the Premonstratensian order, since the Obituary of Prémontré (from which the order took its name) refers to Fergus as its founder.[39] A smaller house than Dundrennan, its endowment was correspondingly modest, as it appears to have consisted of the surrounding lands in the parish of Inch, with outliers in the Machars and the Rhinns.

Fergus had already been instrumental in building a new cathedral at Whithorn,[40] doubtless at the instigation of its bishop Gilla-Aldan. As it was extensively remodelled during the following century, little of the original survives, though the indications are that it conformed to a simple cruciform plan with a short nave,[41] a layout which was designed to meet the requirements of the existing monastic community rather than those of the reformers. Church-building was a recognised act of piety, but Fergus probably had other motives, in that by establishing a cathedral there he was emulating the current fashion among royal patrons for commissioning such institutions, and thus advancing his own regal aspirations.

Changes become apparent at Whithorn with the appointment of Bishop Christian in succession to Gilla-Aldan, who died sometime before 1153. His preferment was probably dictated by the English king, Henry II, and was a reflection of the close ties that had existed between Galloway and England since the time of Fergus's marriage to Henry I's daughter.[42] Although not a Cistercian himself, Christian was a great admirer of the order and clearly an innovative bishop in contrast to his more conservative predecessor. He was responsible for modernising the administrative structure of the diocese, and this involved appointing first an archdeacon and later a dean of Christianity as his assistant. He also replaced the community of secular priests at Whithorn with a priory of canons regular in order to remedy a situation which had become unacceptable to York.[43] For, like Gilla-Aldan, Bishop Christian was a staunch adherent of that centre, as well as being a loyal suffragan of its archbishop, Roger de Pont l'Evêque.

In conformity with the changes which were being introduced by David I, Bishop Christian established a fully-integrated parish system within his diocese, while introducing the compulsory exaction of tithes, or teinds. This was an obligation on farmers and landholders to contribute a tenth share of the produce from their land towards the maintenance of the incumbent of their parish church. Most of these were proprietary churches, where the patronage belonged to secular landowners, and in the course of the following centuries the great majority of these patrons assigned their rights in them to religious houses. These houses would then appoint one of their monks as the parish vicar, while using the teind income to maintain their establishments. However, it soon became the practice to pay the vicar a salary out of the teinds and appropriate the balance. Although this required the consent of the diocesan bishop it was generally granted on the nod, and this laid the foundations of the enormous wealth which the Church eventually accumulated.

WHITHORN

The community at Whithorn continued to prosper, and there is evidence of a thriving trade and considerable industrial activity.[44] Rudimentary planning with signs of a well-defined street system exist,[45] and the pattern of waste debris points to the confining of certain crafts to specific areas within the town. Heavier industries, such as smithying and metal-working, were confined to the outer zone, while the more specialised crafts were practised within the inner precinct.[46] These seem to have ranged from spinning and weaving to needlework, embroidery, leather-working and shoemaking, as well as enamelling[47] and fine metal-working in gold and silver. Combs were made from deer antlers, and the abundance of remains dating from this period shows the extent of this activity, as it was plainly a valuable source of revenue to the community.[48]

The curing and production of cat pelts for the linings of coats was another lucrative business. This was carried on at various sites within the town, and it is known to have been practised at other urban settlements as well.[49] Skeletal remains suggest that the animals were specifically bred for the purpose,[50] while two surviving sheet lead vessels could have been containers for a solution of alum and salt, in which the skins were steeped as part of the curing process.[51] Judging from the fact that the remains of birds of prey have been identified at one of the production sites,[52] it seems that, after skinning them, the cats' carcases were thrown away as offal for scavengers.

There seems to have been a considerable demand for local products, and it is apparent from discoveries of contemporary debris that there was a street market where these could be bought and sold, while there are clear signs of workshops being established along its perimeter. The waste consists predominantly of haberdashery, so tailors' and embroiderers' booths must have formed part of the complex, together with stalls for such items as dress pins.[53] The existence of a wealthy élite can be deduced from finds of the bones of pigs which were slaughtered between the ages of eighteen months and two years, because their meat, though particularly palatable, was expensive to produce, and therefore clearly a luxury.[54] Altogether, the evidence points to a thriving, prosperous, and well-organised community of relatively sophisticated people.

MANX IMBROGLIO

David I died in 1153, and, as his son Earl Henry had recently predeceased him, he was succeeded by his grandson Malcolm IV. Inevitably, the removal of that venerable monarch's firm hand from the helm, and the accession of this young and inexperienced king, resulted in a weakening of the royal authority, and this encouraged Donald MacHeth, a descendant of Donald III, to raise a rebellion in Moray in a bid to overthrow Malcolm and usurp the kingship. His father, Malcolm MacHeth, had made a similar attempt some twenty years before, but his rebellion had proved a fiasco and he was still languishing a prisoner in Roxburgh castle. This time the prospects augured better, and all the more so since Donald had the support of his powerful uncle, Somerled, Lord of the Isles, who controlled Argyll and Kintyre.

The rebellion clearly posed a serious threat, because it was not until 1156 that the situation was finally brought under control, while the fact that MacHeth was eventually captured near Whithorn[55] suggests that he was attempting to enlist local Gallovidian support for his campaign. It must have been a vain hope, since Fergus had his own reasons for opposing MacHeth and his allies, and may even have helped suppress the rebellion and been responsible for MacHeth's capture. This was because MacHeth's uncle, Somerled, was at war with the youthful Godred Olafsson, king of Man, and as Fergus was Godred's grandfather he would naturally have been hostile to the rebels.

Judging from the *Chronicle of Man*, the political situation there seems to have been somewhat chaotic, and it is clear that, because of his kinship with its ruling dynasty, Fergus was closely involved in it. Until recently, the reigning king was his son-in-law, Olaf Godredsson,[56] but he was opposed by his nephews, the sons of his brother Harald. Finally, in 1153, they agreed to a parley, but when the king met his nephews the eldest, Ragnvald, raised his axe in a pretended salute to him and proceeded to 'smite off his head with one blow'. Having thus disposed of their uncle the king, Ragnvald and his brothers carved up the island between them, and thereafter they mustered a fleet and descended on the Galloway coast in what must have been a pre-emptive strike, since Fergus was no doubt preparing to launch an attack on the island in support of Olaf's son, Godred.

However, the invasion was beaten off, Fergus no doubt being instrumental in this, so the brothers withdrew to the Isle of Man, where in retaliation they 'murdered and expelled from the island . . . all the men of Galloway who were resident there'.[57] Meantime, Godred had fled to Norway, where the king, Magnus Erlendsson, supplied him with troops and a fleet of ships. So, when he returned to the Isle of Man shortly afterwards, he succeeded in defeating and capturing the three brothers, blinding two of them and killing the third,[58] only to be driven out in his turn by Somerled, who was another claimant to the kingship. Therefore, it was not until after the latter's death in 1164 that Godred managed to regain the throne.

GALLOVIDIAN REVOLT

Meanwhile, King Stephen had died in 1154, when he was succeeded by the able and vigorous Henry II, the son of his former adversary Matilda. As the MacHeth rebellion had already broken out, Henry was quick to take advantage of Malcolm's predicament by forcing him to return southern Cumbria to the English crown, while his brother William was compelled to give up the earldom of Northumberland.[59] Notwithstanding this, the two kings seem to have remained on friendly terms for, when the rebellion was finally suppressed two years later, Henry successfully played on Malcolm's romantic notions by luring him off with the promise of a knighthood to take part in his war in southern France.

When Malcolm returned in 1159, he found himself confronted by another rebellion, and this time it seems the ringleader – or at least the figurehead – was Fergus. One can only surmise what was happening in Galloway, but it looks as though his sons, Uchtred and Gilbert, probably now in their forties, were impatient to wrest control of the province from their ageing father. In fact, it seems that they were already campaigning against him, because Walter Daniel refers to Galloway as bearing 'the strain of much bloodshed as sons rose against their father, the father against his sons, and brother against brother'.[60] So it is clear that, not only was power slipping from Fergus's grasp, but Uchtred and Gilbert themselves were at odds with each other. Nevertheless, they may have seen Malcolm's absence in France as a golden opportunity to come out in open rebellion, and must have prevailed on their father to abandon his neutrality and join them. That there was a rebellion, and that Fergus was implicated in it, is evident from subsequent events, but what form it took can only be conjectured: suffice it to say that it seems to have been serious.

In fact, so serious was it that when Malcolm returned from France a group of native earls proceeded to carpet him for his ill-timed absence abroad, and may even have threatened to deprive him of his ruling powers and bring him under their tutelage. For the Melrose chronicler tells us that when Malcolm came 'to the city that is called Perth, Earl Fereteth and five other earls [being enraged against the king for going to Toulouse] besieged the city and wished to take the king prisoner; but their presumption did not at all prevail'.[61] Although later historians have called this 'the revolt of the earls', it was no more than an orchestrated protest on their part, and the fact that 'their presumption did not at all prevail' suggests that Malcolm had matured by now and was not prepared to tolerate this sort of conduct from his subjects, however exalted.

Nevertheless, an accommodation seems to have been reached between them, because it was apparently with their support that, according to the

Melrose chronicler, 'King Malcolm went three times with a great army into Galloway and at last subdued them'.[62] Bower confirms this by saying that 'Malcolm got together an army on three occasions in that same year and marched into Galloway against the rebel forces', adding that 'when they [the Gallovidians] had finally been vanquished, brought into alliance and made subject to him, he returned in peace without any loss to his own forces'.[63] Clearly, Malcolm's victory over the Gallovidians was decisive, because Uchtred was delivered up to him as a hostage,[64] while Fergus's subsequent fate shows him as paying the price of failure.

His fortunes were now at their nadir. Galloway was ravaged and defeated, and death – the automatic fate of rebels – looked a certainty. However, this was averted, perhaps on account of his connections with the English royal house, though he was forced to abdicate. At his own request, he retired to become an Augustinian canon regular at Holyrood, which he had already endowed with the patronage of the church of Dunrod, near Kirkcudbright, the adjacent lands of Galtway, as well as the island of Trail, now St Mary's Isle, in Kirkcudbright Bay.[65] Walter Daniel gives the ubiquitous Ailred credit for persuading Fergus to this course, saying that 'he [Ailred] eagerly exhorted Fergus to take up the habit of religion: and by a miracle of persuasion he influenced him towards what he suggested', adding with a sting in the tail that this taught 'a man who had taken the lives of many thousands of men to partake of eternal life'.[66] Nevertheless, the ageing Fergus presents a tragic figure. The prestigious ruler of a semi-independent and politically-important province, and married into the Norman royal house, he was unceremoniously deposed and banished from his lordship to eke out the last year of his life as a humble monk.

NOTES

1. Lawrie, *Charters*.
2. Galloway at this time was an indeterminate region, and generally regarded as comprising much of south-west Scotland extending from Teviotdale to northern Ayrshire, though Fergus's authority was limited to the region to the west of the Urr.
3. He is so described in a royal charter (*RRS* ii, no 443).
4. This is speculative, and is based purely on the fact that Uchtred must have been born in about 1120, if not before.
5. Oram, 'Fergus, Galloway and the Scots', 125.
6. A case in point was the charter which he granted to the Knights of St John of Jerusalem (W Dugdale, *Monasticon Anglicanum*, 1846 (new) vi, i, 267).
7. Brooke, 'Fergus of Galloway'.
8. *Feodora* i, 107–8.
9. Notwithstanding this, Henry himself was married to Alexander's sister, Edith.

10. *Chron. Man,* i, 61 (Anderson: *Early Sources* II, 464: Brown, 'Argyll and the Isles in the Middle Ages', 196.
11. Lawrie, *Charters.*
12. Whithorn's status as a suffragan of York was uncertain at the time, but papal bulls issued in 1176 and 1189 (or 1192) put the matter beyond doubt, as these formally recognised all Scottish sees, collectively known as *ecclesia Scoticana,* as a 'special daughter' of Rome, while expressly omitting Whithorn.
13. David was to achieve this with the sees of Moray, Ross and Caithness. He also aspired to do the same with the archbishopric of York as a means of extending his power into northern England, and although his attempt was unsuccessful he did manage to secure the election of William Cumin to Durham.
14. *Wig Charters,* xvi–xvii.
15. Oram, 'A family business?', 119–20.
16. Maude de Senlis already had sons by her previous marriage who had a prior claim to her lands, and it was at Henry's dictation that they passed to her, and hence to David. This gave Henry a hold over David, in that as feudal superior he could direct them back to Maude's eldest son if he so wished (Scott, 'The partition of Strathclyde').
17. Barrow, *Anglo-Norman Era,* 12.
18. McMichael, 'The feudal family of de Soulis'.
19. Kapelle, *The Norman Conquest of the North,* 169.
20. Her mother was David's sister, Edith, though Stephen's wife was the daughter of another sister.
21. *Richard of Hexham.*
22. *Ailred, de Standardo.*
23. Barrow, *Kingship and Unity,* 38.
24. Anderson, *Annals.*
25. *Roger de Howden.*
26. Bartlett, *The Making of Europe,*101–5.
27. They were somewhat ahead of their time, as the methods of contracting marriage were still in the process of being regularised, and illegitimacy as a consequence of uncanonical marriage did not become a major stigma until the thirteenth century.
28. Daniel, *Ailred.*
29. *Ibid.*
30. *Reginald of Durham.*
31. Though by this time the term *scoloc* was coming to mean a class of peasant bondsman.
32. The episode is discussed by Oram in 'Heirs to Ninian', 55–6.
33. Brooke, *Wild Men,* 90–1.
34. Scott, 'The origins of Dundrennan and Soulseat abbeys', 35.
35. *Chron. Melrose.*
36. Daniel, *Ailred,* 45.
37. Brooke, *Wild Men,* 89.
38. *St Bernard de Clairvaux: Life of St Malachy.*
39. Backmund, 'The Premonstratensian order in Scotland'; Scott, 'The origins of Dundrennan and Soulseat', 35 et seq.
40. Hill, *Whithorn,* 56. Brooke suggests that it was founded between 1125 and 1135 (*Wild Men,* 88).
41. Radford, 'Excavations at Whithorn', 146–50.
42. Oram, 'A family business?', 113.

43. Oram, 'Heirs to Ninian', 57.
44. Hill; *Whithorn*, 56.
45. *Ibid.*, 25.
46. *Ibid.*, 247.
47. *Ibid.*, 244.
48. *Ibid.*, 495.
49. *Ibid.*, 607.
50. *Ibid.*, 612.
51. *Ibid.*, 223.
52. *Ibid.*, 223.
53. *Ibid.*, 232.
54. *Ibid.*, 611.
55. Scott, 'The Partition of a kingdom'.
56. Anderson, *Early Sources* II, 464–8.
57. Stevenson (ed), *Chronicle of Man* v, pt. I, 390 et seq.
58. *Ibid.*
59. William inherited Northumberland from his father, Earl Henry, but as he had been compelled to surrender it under duress he consistently refused to recognise its validity, and his determination to recover it would colour his English policy throughout his reign.
60. Daniel, *Ailred.*
61. *Chron Melrose.*
62. *Ibid.*
63. *Bower* 4, p 259.
64. *Ibid.*
65. A subsequent confirmation of the privileges and possessions of Holyrood abbey, issued by William I in c.1165/6, contains a specific reference to 'the gift of Fergus lord of Galloway of Dunrod with its church, and the Isle of Trail with the land of Galweied' (*RRS* ii, no 147).
66. Daniel, *Ailred*, 45.

8

A HOUSE DIVIDED

The lordship partitioned

The settlement which Malcolm IV imposed on Galloway was stringent, for, besides forcing Fergus to abdicate, he dictated a division of the province between his sons Uchtred and Gilbert, and one can reasonably assume that they were also obliged to acknowledge him as overlord, and possibly their feudal superior.[1] The eastern half of the province was allocated to Uchtred, who continued to use his father's ruling centre at Lochfergus, while the region beyond the Cree went to Gilbert who established his at Cruggleton. While this was primarily a policy of divide and rule, it could nevertheless have reflected a genuine effort on Malcolm's part to conciliate the brothers, and he may have hoped that this arrangement would keep the peace between them. If so, it was in vain, because Walter Daniel tells us that 'the princes of the province were quarrelling with each other [and] the king of Scotland could not repress nor the bishop soften the hatreds and rancours in their minds and their despotic acts towards one another'. Although, obsequious as ever, he goes on to say that Ailred, 'with words of peace and goodness bound the furious brothers together in the firmest of pacts and a single bond of affection',[2] this proved manifestly skin-deep as their mutual antagonism continued to fester.

Traditionally, this is supposed to have sprung from their contrasting attitudes towards foreign settlement in Galloway; that while Uchtred encouraged it, Gilbert was violently opposed to these incomers, and indeed to the whole principle of introducing feudalism into the province. However, the facts belie this because, quite apart from the possibility that Malcolm compelled the two brothers to acknowledge his superiority over their Galloway lands, Gilbert would almost certainly have taken those he subsequently acquired in Carrick[3] under a feudal title. Nor did he have any hesitation in offering to enter into a feudal relationship with Henry II when it suited him. Moreover, he is known to have given a feudal grant to at least one Anglo-Norman, Roger de Skelbrooke, who was established in lands in the Doon valley in modern Ayrshire,[4] and there may well have been other instances where the charters have been lost.

More likely, the brothers' mutual hostility stemmed from Gilbert's obsession with securing the whole of Galloway for himself. Given the traditional view that Uchtred was the elder brother, and that the lordship was his by right of primogeniture, Gilbert's claim would seem entirely unjustified. However, current thinking has it that Uchtred was not the elder son, and that Gilbert was the product of an earlier uncanonical marriage contracted by Fergus – possibly with a west Galloway heiress, before his regular marriage to Henry I's daughter.[5] William of Newburgh was quite specific on this point, as he tells us that 'Gilbert hated his *younger* brother because he had not been allowed to succeed to the whole of his father's right'.[6] As there were no hard-and-fast laws relating to succession rights in a Celtic society, and defect of birth was not regarded as an impediment, this would go far to explain the lengths that Gilbert went to in his efforts to secure the whole lordship. But, elder or not, he seems to have been much the abler of the two, so he may have felt that this alone entitled him to exclusive possession. Although their hostility eventually led to civil war, this did not occur until after Malcolm's death.

Meantime, Malcolm's conquest of Galloway, and the resulting settlement, enabled him to intrude his authority there to a far greater extent than his grandfather had done. One example was his issuing a precept addressed to 'Uchtred son of Fergus and his brother Gilbert, and Ralph the son of Dunegal [lord of Strathnith] and his brother Donald, and all their good men of Galloway and Clydesdale'. This stated that 'he [the king] has given his firm peace to the men going to Galloway to lodge or dwell in the land of Dunrod', while stipulating that 'no-one is to disturb any travelling towards or staying in this land for the purposes mentioned'.[7] This was obviously designed to ensure the personal safety of lay servants travelling between Holyrood and its recently-acquired possessions at Kirkcudbright.

He also seems to have pointedly downgraded the political importance of the province by ceasing to recognise the Gallovidians as a separate people in royal charters. Until as late as 1158[8] these had been variously addressed to 'all my good people, French, English, Scots, Galwegians and Welsh (Britons)' depending on who were affected by them. Similarly, Uchtred and Gilbert were consistently referred to as *domini* (lords), which although an important title, in that it put them on a par with the northern earls, was not the same as the style of *princeps* (literally 'leader', but in this context 'prince') which had been accorded to their father.

Malcolm also extended his grandfather's policy of encircling the province with a shield of loyal supporters. Therefore Flemings, who were renowned as the finest fighting soldiers of the time, were established in the territories extending from Lothian to the upper Clyde. This was designed to plug the gap between the lordships of Annandale and Strathnith on the one side, and King's Kyle in modern Ayrshire on the other, and the names of these settlers are preserved in a number of townships in the region. Their leader, Baldwin,[9] received lands in the neighbourhood of Biggar, which controlled the strategically important route from the Tweed through to the upper Clyde, and to give him added status he was appointed sheriff of Lanark. Another Fleming was established in lands in south Lanarkshire, and his descendants, who adopted the local place-name Douglas as their surname, would become the most powerful members of the Scottish nobility from the fourteenth century onwards.

Malcolm IV died prematurely in 1165, when he was succeeded by his brother William I, whom later historians dubbed 'the Lion'. A forceful and energetic ruler, he greatly extended his royal authority throughout the realm during his long and frequently tempestuous reign of almost fifty years. This is apparent from the number of sheriffdoms he established, for, whereas at his accession there were about twelve in existence, by the time of his death in 1214 the number had risen to some twenty-three.[10] His creations included those of Dumfries and Ayr on the borders of Galloway, and the royal castles he built at these centres to serve as the sheriffs' *capita* were highly visible symbols of the encroachment of his royal authority on the province's traditional independence.

Since they acted as the king's representatives, sheriffs were important functionaries, being almost invariably drawn from the nobility, and their administration of local government entailed a wide range of duties. These included the management of the royal lands in their sheriffdoms, the collection of revenues, and the enforcement of the king's peace, as well as officiating at the elaborate ceremonies connected with the granting of lands. They were also responsible for holding inquests into land ownership – a demanding task, since it involved a formal perambulation of the marches, as well as taking sworn testimony from older people with the longest memories. Initially, their judicial functions were limited to a supervisory presence at the barons' courts to ensure that juries were not unduly influenced by these magnates. Later, however, they acquired their own jurisdictional powers, including the right to try civil and criminal cases, though this excluded the four pleas of the crown, namely, murder, rape, plunder and arson, which continued to be heard by the king's justiciar.

FOREIGN SETTLEMENT

King William's accession coincided with the death of Ralph (or Radulph), lord of Strathnith, when that fief, which included Nithsdale and the territories to the west as far as the Urr, reverted to the crown. Therefore, it was in order to consolidate his authority over these lands that William established a sheriffdom based on the former lordship *caput*, or ruling centre, at Dumfries. He also distributed these lands to a number of tenants-in-chief, and, for reasons which can only be conjectured, they included Uchtred, who was given a feudal grant of the lands to the west of the Nith, which comprised the ecclesiastical deanery of Desnes Ioan. In return, Uchtred was bound in a number of feudal obligations, including the duty to provide a specified number of armed knights in time of war, and to render *cain*.[11] This was a tribute exacted from local landowners towards the maintenance of the king or his representatives while travelling on official duties, and in Galloway it was assessed at a tenth of the locally-produced cheeses.

Since Uchtred was unable to provide the set number of knights on his own, he had to sub-feu the lands. His principal tenant was the king's Chamberlain, Walter de Berkeley, who is believed to have been his son-in-law.[12] De Berkeley's grant was substantial, as it consisted of the entire modern parish of Urr, part of Kirkgunzeon, and possibly a portion of Lochrutton parish as well, because sometime between 1189 and 1193 he granted William fitzRichard the lands of 'Crosswaldef', which is thought to be identifiable with Carswadda in that parish.[13] He established his *caput* on the Urr some two miles upstream from Dalbeattie, where he built the largest motte in Scotland, and the Mote of Urr, as it is known, stands like a huge inverted sugar bowl some 24 m (80 ft) high and occupies an area of nearly a hectare (2 acres). When de Berkeley died in 1193, the Mote of Urr itself, along with half the income from the barony, passed to his younger daughter[14] and her husband Sir Ingelram de Balliol,[15] and ultimately their descendants who died out in the male line at the end of the following century.

Other tenants of the Desnes Ioan lands were drawn from the Normanised establishment in Cumbria, with whom Uchtred was linked by his marriage to Gunnild, the daughter of Waltheof lord of Allerdale, a prominent magnate there.[16] One of the earliest settlers was Richard fitzTroite, a younger brother of the sheriff of Carlisle, who was given the lands of Lochkindeloch[17] (or Lochenelo) in return for the services of one knight.[18] The name is associated with Loch Kindar near New Abbey, and his feu comprised much if not all of that parish, his *caput* being the motte at Ingleston, which overlooks the lower reaches of the New Abbey pow. A number of privileges attached to grant, for besides the possible inclusion of a mill, they extended to the right to hunt deer, keep hawks, take raptors' eggs, as well as a right of pannage, which was a licence to graze pigs in the woods belonging to the lordship demesne during the acorn crop in the autumn.[19] Another incomer was the elderly Gospatrick fitzOrm,[20] who was a cousin of Uchtred's wife. He was given the neighbouring lands of Colvend, a poorer fief, since much of it overlies a bedrock of granite, and his descendants remained there until the fourteenth century.

Uchtred also feued off parts of his hereditary lands, and among the earliest tenants established there was Hugh de Morville the younger[21] who

– probably at King Malcolm's insistence – was given the lands of Borgue, his *caput* being the prominent hilltop feature above present-day Boreland of Borgue. This consisted of a motte with an attaching bailey for the accommodation of soldiery, while the site itself occupies a commanding position overlooking the lower reaches of the Dee. De Morville continued to hold these lands until his death, sometime after 1180, and during this time he gave the patronage of the local church to Dryburgh Abbey, which had been founded by his father, the elder Hugh. The barony subsequently reverted to the lords of Galloway in consequence of Uchtred's son, Roland's, marriage to de Morville's niece, Elena.

Some time later – probably in the early 1170s[22] – David fitzTerrus, a son of the lord of Over Denton, near Gilsland in eastern Cumbria, was granted the lands of Cardiness,[23] to the west of the river Fleet.[24] His *caput* was the large motte-and-bailey feature, known as the Green Tower Mote, which lies immediately behind the farm of Boreland of Anwoth at the head of Fleet Bay. Although the sea has since receded, it would at that time have surrounded the motte on two sides, and part of a third, so that it became a promontory at high tide, thus providing a convenient escape route, because fitzTerrus and his retainers were deep inside potentially hostile territory. The lordship passed to his descendants, who adopted the name de Kerdenesse after their lands, and they remained there until the 1340s. There are grounds for thinking that Uchtred was responsible for establishing another Cumbrian, Gamel de Twynam, in the nearby lands of Twynholm,[25] which were adjacent to those of Borgue, and these too remained in the hands of his family for a similar period.

UCHTRED'S ECCLESIASTICAL POLICY

Uchtred's policy towards the Church seems to have been influenced by two mutually opposed factors. On the one hand, he was concerned to maintain Galloway's independence, while on the other he was bound by a number of ties, including his feudal relationship, with King William. This could account for his support for the king in resisting the threat of encroachment on Galloway by the O'Connor high kings of Ireland. They dominated the Irish Church which had expanded to embrace Iona, and as that community already controlled a number of churches in Galloway it was feared that this could open the way for these kings to establish a power-base there. William countered this by transferring those churches most exposed to Irish influence to Holyrood, which was under his authority, and Uchtred followed suit by granting it the churches which lay within his own domains.

He appears to have been supported by his feudal tenants, as David fitzTerrus donated his church of Anwoth and chapel of 'Culenes' to Holyrood, and similarly Gamel de Twynham gave it his church at Twynholm.[27]

Therefore, taking into account the church of Dunrod which Fergus had given them, the canons of Holyrood now owned the patronage of ten churches and two chapels in Galloway.[28]

While Uchtred was prepared to co-operate with the king in resisting the encroachment of Iona, and hence the political ambitions of the high kings of Ireland, he was nevertheless concerned to preserve a measure of independence of him. Since this depended on maintaining close links with York, he willingly co-operated with Bishop Christian in his efforts to reform the Whithorn diocese,[28] though there was a limit to how far he could go, since much of the diocese was controlled by his brother, Gilbert. Still, the endowments he made for the benefit of the Church, such as his grant of a ploughgate of land and a toft in the parish of Troqueer to the hospital of St Peter at York,[29] were probably instigated by the bishop. So, too, was the founding of a Benedictine nunnery at Lincluden,[30] for which Uchtred is thought to have been responsible.

It was doubtless at the bishop's behest that Uchtred granted the lands of Kirkgunzeon to the Cistercian abbey of Holm Cultram[31] in Cumbria. Since these lay within the diocese of Glasgow, the focal point of the Church in Scotland, this grant may have represented an attempt on Bishop Christian's part to intrude the influence of York there. Moreover, he had a strong personal attachment to Holm Cultram, so much so that, at his own request, he was buried within its precincts. The endowment was substantial, as it included all the land between Walter de Berkeley's barony of Urr on the west, and those of Colvend and Lochkindeloch on the south and east.[32] The confirmatory charter issued by the king mentions a saltpan at Colvend as being included in the grant, which was a valuable perquisite as salt was indispensable for preserving meat. Also, 'all easements of wood and in the port of Urr as far as "Polstursheuid"',[33] which was a necessary concession since the monks needed timber to build steadings and stock pens for purposes of running the lands as a self-contained farming unit, or grange.

The higher ground consisted almost entirely of moorland scrub, well suited to sheep farming, in which the Cistercians specialised, while there was ample scope for reclaiming land from the native forest, as well as for draining and improving the low-lying land between Dalbeattie and Kirkgunzeon itself. Judging from the terms of another royal charter to the abbey, the community's activities may have included cattle-rearing, for in this the king granted 'his firm peace to the monks and lay brothers of Holm Cultram Abbey, and their cattle',[34] as well as permission 'to carry their wool and merchandise for sale in burghs in the kingdom of Scotland wherever they wish'. It also contained the warning that 'no-one is to disturb them on the pain of the King's forfeiture'.[35]

It seems that the lay brothers responsible for farming these lands became involved in a dispute with their opposite numbers at Dundrennan, to whom Uchtred had given the nearby lands of Barncailizie, Crofts and Marwhirn in the parish of Kirkpatrick Durham. This was almost inevitable, since they too farmed these lands as a grange,[36] but it came to a head when the monks of Dundrennan formally complained that sheep belonging to Holm Cultram were straying on to their land. The dispute was finally resolved in Dundrennan's favour when Holm Cultram was obliged to give an undertaking that its flocks would not 'go in the adjacent pastures so far as they cannot return at night to their own grange'. It also promised not to 'acquire more land or build more houses or sheepcotes on the western side of the river Nith', which suggests that Dundrennan may have owned land there as well.[37]

Uchtred himself became embroiled in a dispute with Holm Cultram when he tried to claw back part of his original grant. Evidently, his original charter stipulated that if the monks found it impossible to farm the lands properly they were to return them to him. However, Uchtred took the initiative by appropriating a portion of their lands in order to give it to Walter de Berkeley. The abbot promptly appealed for restitution, so the king ordered an inquest, appointing Roger de Minto as the presiding judge, which suggests that he was the sheriff of Dumfries.[38] He was instructed 'to convene the older men of the district to make a sworn perambulation of the marches of Kirkgunzeon on behalf of Holm Cultram and Christian, Bishop of Galloway'.[39] The upshot was that the decision went against Uchtred, so he was forced to return the disputed land to Holm Cultram.[40]

CIVIL WAR

Meanwhile, Gilbert remained in possession of the region beyond the Cree, nursing his ambition to secure the whole lordship for himself, but unable to realise it. However, his opportunity came in 1174. Henry II's sons had rebelled, and as they were supported by the French king, Philip II, this led to war between England and France. Taking advantage of this, King William proceeded to launch a raid across the Border in an attempt to recover the earldom of Northumberland, so a feudal summons was issued, and Uchtred and Gilbert duly responded to the call. After an inconclusive campaign, disaster struck when William and a party of knights were surprised by a contingent of English cavalry. In the ensuing skirmish, William's horse fell, pinning him to the ground, and he was taken prisoner. A number of his vassals surrendered to the English, 'thinking it honourable to share the peril of their lord',[41] but not so Uchtred and Gilbert who promptly galloped off home. In a rare display of solidarity, they seized the opportunity to send a petition to Henry II offering to become his feudal vassals[42] which, as they saw it, would secure Galloway's independence from the Scottish crown once and for all.

The brothers' brief co-operation broke down almost at once and, while the immediate cause is obscure, William of Newburgh offers a plausible explanation. 'Gilbert', he wrote, 'ever hated his brother in his heart, although fear of the King restrained an outburst of the wrath he had conceived. But when the King was taken he was freed from this fear'.[43] Meanwhile, the king's removal from the scene encouraged the disaffected Gallovidians to launch a series of attacks on the principal castles in the region, which they regarded as symbols of his authority, as well as upon his 'bailiffs and wardens'.[44] Walter de Berkeley's *caput* at the Mote of Urr was singled out in particular,[45] though he was a hostage in England at the time, while the royal castle of Dumfries was burned,[46] and it seems almost certain that these attacks were instigated by Gilbert. According to Bower, the foreign settlers were assaulted too, for he asserts that their persecution 'was so intense [that] no consideration was shown to the sex of any, but all were cruelly killed without thought of ransom, wherever they could be found'.[47] The remainder fled, depriving Uchtred of his natural allies, while those natives who rallied to him were outnumbered by Gilbert's supporters. As he dared not abandon his lands to his opponents, he dispatched his wife and family to safety and sought refuge, possibly on the island of Trail.[48]

Meanwhile, Henry II dispatched envoys to Galloway with his terms for accepting the brothers as vassals. But they arrived too late, for Gilbert's son Malcolm had already brutally disposed of Uchtred. Drawing on the evidence of Roger de Howden, who was one of the envoys, the chronicler records that Malcolm 'sent in his butchers, commanding them to put out his [Uchtred's] eyes, and to emasculate him and cut out his tongue: and so it was done. And they went away leaving him half-dead: and shortly after he ended his life'.[49] The brutalities followed the ritual method of dealing with fallen rulers; blinding removed their capacity for leadership in battle, castration lost them both respect and the ability to sire heirs, while the lack of a tongue prevented them from dispensing justice.[50]

Killing a ruler was a cardinal sin in the eyes of the Church, but if the perpetrators simply maimed him and he elected to take his own life they were absolved from blame. So, although it was given out that Uchtred had strangled himself, this was merely a disclaimer by Gilbert, as he is much more likely to have died from shock and loss of blood. When they heard of the details surrounding Uchtred's death, the envoys were so appalled that they refused to treat with Gilbert and returned to England to report the atrocity to Henry.

GILBERT'S LORDSHIP

In the following year King William was allowed to return to Scotland. The extortionate terms of his release were embodied in the treaty of Falaise,

under which he was compelled to swear fealty to Henry, becoming his
vassal, and to acknowledge his overlordship of Scotland. Secular barons
were required to do homage to him for their lands, as were Scottish bishops
and abbots, while a number of castles in southern Scotland were delivered
up to him, and hostages were handed over. However, the fact that William
was now Henry's vassal meant that Gilbert was prevented from exploiting
the differences between them to his advantage. So, instead he tried to buy
Henry's goodwill by offering him an annual payment of two thousand
merks of silver, along with five hundred cows and a like number of swine.
This was angrily rejected, and Gilbert was summoned to appear before
Henry to answer for the crime of killing his near relative.[51]

Gilbert ignored the summons – there was little else he could do, so
Henry ordered William, as his vassal, to send an army into Galloway to
capture him.[52] There is no record of a battle, though the expedition must
have been successful, because William brought Gilbert to Henry at
Feckenham the following year. There, he was compelled to swear fealty to
Henry, guarantee Uchtred's son, Roland,[53] in the peaceable possession of
his inherited lands, and to undertake to pay a thousand silver merks in
restitution for Uchtred's death.[54] However, very little of this sum ever
reached the English treasury despite Gilbert's son, Duncan, being given up
as a hostage in security. Also, it must have been some consolation to Gilbert
that this arrangement specifically excluded King William from any
authority over Galloway, because it meant that to that extent the object of
his rebellion was achieved.

Thereafter, he concentrated on what was referred to as 'maritime
adventure', in other words piracy, on the strength of which he became
notoriously rich. He also launched a series of plundering raids on neighbouring territories, including the royal lands of King's Kyle. These
continued intermittently throughout the rest of his life, and a particularly
violent sortie into eastern Galloway in 1182 may have been a deliberate
attempt to seize Roland's lands by force.

While material demands and guarantees could be evaded, spiritual pressure on Gilbert for penance and restitution was harder to resist. The papal
envoy, Cardinal Vivian, is known to have visited Galloway in 1176, and
presumably it was he who spelt out the terms on which Gilbert could
obtain absolution. These were primarily concerned with Whithorn. Bishop
Christian's efforts to reform that centre had hitherto been frustrated by
Gilbert who, conservative as ever, was determined that the old order
should prevail there. Consequently, it was still under the control of secular
canons, but they had become lax and had allowed the buildings to deteriorate alarmingly.[55]

Then suddenly everything changed, for the annals of Maurice of Prato
for 1177 tell us that 'about this time Christian, Bishop of Candida Casa in

Galloway, a province of Scotland, changed the canons regular of his cathedral church into Premonstratensians. For which reason he is named in the Obituary of Prémontré as founder of that church'. At the same time, a prior was appointed to rule the canons in place of Bishop Christian, who regarded the practice of combining the functions of bishop and abbot, which he had inherited from Gilla-Aldan, as canonically unacceptable. Although in theory these changes could have been carried through without Gilbert's approval, this was not the case in practice, so one can only conclude that his consent to these was the price of absolution.

Moreover, it seems to have been extracted from him under extreme pressure, because he proceeded to revenge himself on the bishop by hounding him remorselessly.[56] This is apparent from a reference in Reginald of Durham's *Life of St Godric* to 'a certain man [Gilbert] in that land [Galloway] who was very wealthy, but the bishop's unrelenting persecutor, a dissipator of the Church's goods [and] most hostile to the bishop'.[57] Eventually, Bishop Christian found his position untenable, as he abandoned Whithorn and established himself at York, where he remained, probably continuing to exercise spiritual jurisdiction over Roland's domains, until his death in 1186.

As an accessory to Uchtred's murder, a pirate, and a persecutor of the bishop, Gilbert appears a distinctly unappealing character, but history is apt to judge losers harshly. For there is no doubt that he and his family commanded a strong popular following in Galloway, while there was equally strong support for his relentless determination to preserve its independence. In pursuing this he displayed a combination of ruthless opportunism, as well as considerable astuteness, in playing off the two kings, Henry and William, against each other. A final instance occurred in 1184, when William took advantage of Henry's absence in France to invade Galloway with the intention of bringing Gilbert to book. However, before he could do so, Henry returned from France and promptly ordered William to withdraw his army, summoning him to appear before him to explain his actions.[58] It was a victory of a sort for Gilbert, though in real terms meaningless, because Galloway remained divided until his death on New Year's day 1185.

Roland triumphant

Meantime, Roland had been ruling in eastern Galloway since about 1176, and was a regular attender at King William's court. Now approaching forty, he had ample time to prepare for Gilbert's death, so he took prompt and decisive action. As Gilbert's son, Duncan, was still a hostage in England, there was nothing to prevent Roland from launching an attack on western Galloway, and in the course of this we are told that he 'slew all that opposed him [and] reduced that land to himself. Moreover he slew all the most powerful and the richest men in Galloway and occupied their lands'.[59] Judging from the large quantity of contemporary ash found at Whithorn, his depredations seem to have included burning that centre as well.[60]

Nevertheless, it seems that Roland encountered a determined resistance under the leadership of a local chieftain, Gillepatrick, who was killed in the course of the campaign,[61] and similarly in Carrick, where his principal adversary was Henry MacKenedi,[62] a leading magnate there. However, Roland finally triumphed and proceeded to occupy the lands of his defeated opponents. Initially, King William seems to have turned a blind eye to this,[63] perhaps out of gratitude to Roland for helping him to hunt down and capture Gillecom, a noted guerilla leader who had been terrorising Lothian.[64] Not so Henry, however, because as custodian of Gilbert's son Duncan he was duty bound to protect his lands, and therefore he ordered William to invade Galloway to put a stop to Roland's attacks, but Roland defied both kings by having trees felled to block the access routes.

Henry now took personal charge, and raising an army of Welsh levies he marched north to Carlisle, where he summoned Roland to appear before him to explain his actions. Roland refused, and it took a deputation led by the bishop of Glasgow, and promises of a safe conduct, to persuade him to change his mind. Henry now took oaths of fealty and homage from him similar to those sworn by Gilbert,[65] while Duncan's claim to his father's lands was upheld pending adjudication. In the following year, William visited Dumfries, and in an attempt to re-assert his authority in Galloway he issued an assize against Gilbert's supporters declaring that 'if anyone is convicted in Galloway, either by combat or in any other way, of breaking the King's peace, he shall give [be fined] twelve score cows and three geldings'.

Henry II died three years later, in 1189, when the overlordship of Scotland became vested in his son, Richard I. As the new king needed to raise money to finance a crusade, he agreed to renounce it for the sum of ten thousand marks, and this was formalised by the Quitclaim of Canterbury in December of that year.[66] As the overlordship of Galloway now reverted to William, he arbitrated a settlement between Roland and Duncan and, reflecting his partiality towards him, he allowed Roland to keep his conquered lands in Wigtownshire. Consequently, he became the first lord of Galloway to rule the whole province from the Nith as far as the western seaboard. Duncan was given his father's lands in Carrick, which was later created an earldom,[67] and he continued to be a powerful political force in the west until his death at an advanced age in 1250.[68] Whithorn, however, still remained under the authority of York, Richard having ratified Henry II's nomination of Bishop John as Christian's successor, and the situation was regularised by the papal bull *cum universi* of 1192, when that see was specifically omitted from the list of dioceses comprising the Scottish Church.

Roland remained a staunch supporter of King William, and in 1187 he played a leading part in the final defeat of Donald MacWilliam (a grandson of Duncan II) whose rebellion had lasted for six years. For the chronicler tells us that the Gallovidians 'slew MacWilliam and carried his head away with them and presented it to the King of Scotland'[69] so that this gory relic could be displayed to the whole army.[70] As a mark of his favour, the king appointed Roland his justiciar for Galloway with a jurisdiction which appears to have included Dumfries, Ayr and Lanark. He was so styled in a writ issued by William commanding 'his responsible men of Galloway' to assist 'the monks of Melrose dwelling in Galloway' in their efforts to track down thieves,[71] and also in two other instances,[72] while there is a record of his presiding as justiciar at Lanark, when it was decided that William was entitled to levy *cain* in eastern Galloway.[73]

Land redistribution

Roland now had a very substantial landholding in Galloway. For, besides those he inherited from his father Uchtred in the eastern half of the province, he also acquired Gilbert's former possessions, as well as those of his leading supporters. Therefore, he was well placed to reward his adherents with grants of land. Although Reid asserts that 'there is little doubt that he must have introduced many Anglo-Normans into Galloway',[74] the resurgence of native landowners which becomes evident towards the end of the thirteenth century[75] belies this, for in fact it was they who were the principal beneficiaries of Roland's land distribution.

This was particularly true in the case of Wigtownshire, probably because Roland found it difficult to attract colonists to the less fertile lands which comprised the principal forfeitures there. In fact, the only recorded Anglo-Norman settler to be established in western Galloway at this time was Sir Ivo de Veteriponte (Vieuxpont), who was a first cousin of Roland's wife, Elena de Morville.[76] He was given the prestigious barony of Sorbie, which consisted of the parishes of St Fillans and St Michael (later called Sorbie Major and Sorbie Minor), near Cruggleton.[77] Other foreign settlers may have included the de Mareschal (Marshall) family, who were established in the fertile lands of Toskerton (Kirkmadrine) in the Rhinns. They are certainly known to have settled there by Roland's son Alan's time, and they subsequently became the principal agents of Dervorguilla's authority in the region.

Judging from the fact that, from this time onwards, native families like the McCullochs rose to prominence in Wigtownshire, it seems that they too were rewarded with lands, perhaps because they had been opponents of Gilbert, or more likely they transferred their allegiance to Roland after his death. Pre-eminent among the native families, however, were the

McDowells. Traditionally, they claimed a vague but unfounded kinship with the medieval lords of Galloway, and it is thought they could be descended from Fergus, a younger son of Uchtred.[78] If true, it would have been logical for Roland to establish his brother as a power in the west, and perhaps it was because they were the nearest male representatives of the lords of Galloway that the McDowells subsequently became the leaders of native society in Galloway.[79]

The most prominent native family in eastern Galloway were the McLellans. Their lands seem to have been concentrated in the Glenkens,[80] and it is thought that one of their number was William de Gevylston,[81] who acquired the lands of Gelston,[82] near modern Castle Douglas, and established his *caput* at the nearby Ingliston motte. The district beyond the Glenkens formed part of the lordship of Dalmellington, and this was granted to Sir Thomas Colville.[83] He in turn gave land in the vicinity of Carsphairn to the monks of Vaudey, a Cistercian house in his native Lincolnshire, for purposes of working the iron and lead deposits there. However, they subsequently resigned these lands to the monks of Melrose, claiming it was 'useless and dangerous' on account of 'the insidious attacks of a barbarous people'.[84] Sir Thomas was appointed constable of Dumfries castle in 1190, but later – for reasons unknown – he was charged with high treason and imprisoned in Edinburgh castle and only released on the payment of a large ransom.

The foreign settlers introduced by Uchtred, and whom Gilbert had driven out, were restored to their lands. As Gospatrick fitzOrm, the former owner of Colvend, had died by this time his barony was divided between his sons, the elder, Thomas lord of Workington, styling himself 'de Culwen', while his brother Gilbert took the lands of Southwick,[85] and both became close associates of Roland and his son Alan. Thomas later feued off part of his lands to Roger de Masculus (Maule), a member of a prominent family in Lauderdale,[86] who is thought to have come to Galloway in the train of Elena de Morville on her marriage to Roland. Certainly, he was established there before 1196, when there is a record of his granting a salt-pan at Colvend to the abbey of St Bees.[87]

Richard fitzTroite, who had been given the barony of Lochkindeloch, was also dead, and as he left no heirs this reverted to Roland and was retained by him as part of his demesne lands.[88] To the south lay the lands of Airdrie, near Kirkbean, which were granted to Gilbert the Despencer in return for the services of one-tenth of a knight,[89] meaning he had to contribute that share of the cost of a fully-armed knight when required by the lord of Galloway as his feudal superior. A possible co-obligant was the owner of neighbouring Arbigland, which was a granted to a family who adopted it as their surname, as Thomas de Erbigland appears as a witness to a charter in 1285,[90] besides featuring in the Ragman Roll.

The twelfth-century landowners were responsible for building the mottes, which are still a feature of the region. These consist of large earthen mounds topped with a timber donjon, some of them being several storeys high. Similar structures went up in other parts of Scotland, though more of them were built in Galloway than anywhere else, with at least twelve in Wigtownshire and thirty-three in Kirkcudbrightshire.[91] Although the practice was introduced by English settlers, native landowners followed their example, and as it continued until the late fourteenth century this probably accounted for the large number which have been identified in the region. Primarily designed for defence, they also served as local administrative centres and seats of baronial justice, while they became the *foci* of the settlements which grew up round them. The English connection is evident from names like Ingliston ('English settlement') and Boreland that generally occur in the vicinity of mottes, the latter being applied to the land which supported these communities.

ROLAND'S BENEFACTIONS

Roland's submission to Henry II included a threat of excommunication if the terms were broken, and it is possible that his acquisition of Gilbert's Wigtownshire lands – though perfectly legal – may have constituted a breach of them in the eyes of the Church. If true, his consent to the establishment of a daughter abbey of Dundrennan at Glenluce in 1192, and the handsome endowment he gave it, can be seen as an act of atonement. For this consisted of a large swathe of territory in western Wigtownshire, which comprised virtually the whole of the modern parishes of Old and New Luce.[92] Alternatively, its foundation could be seen as providing ecclesiastical support for Roland in a politically unreliable region, though these theories are entirely conjectural.

Roland is also credited with founding the Augustinian priory, which was dedicated to St Mary, on the island of Traill in Kirkcudbright Bay, its purpose being to offer up masses for the souls of Fergus and Uchtred. This was constituted a daughter house of Holyrood, and the monks there endowed it with the 'vills', or estates, of Galtway and Dunrod, together with the patronage of the church there which had been given to them by Fergus. For his part, Roland contributed the lands of Pankill (Penkiln), near Garlieston, with the adjacent church of Eggerness, and 'the teind [tenth] of the consumption of food, drink, wax and tallow in his household at Kirkcudbright'.[93]

During his later years, Roland must have lived in hopes of inheriting the extensive de Morville estates, which belonged to his wife's cousin, the childless William de Morville. If so, they were only partially realised, because when William died in 1196 his lands in Westmorland passed to his de Vieuxpont relatives. Nevertheless, Roland acquired all his lands in Cunninghame and Lauderdale, and, perhaps most important of all, the prestigious office of hereditary Contable of the realm. However, there was an attaching liability, because he was required to pay the large sum of seven hundred marks in feudal casualties.[94]

Roland died in 1200.[95] He had been undisputed lord of Galloway for fifteen years, and his success in welding it into a unified, semi-independent province in the face of opposition from Gilbert's supporters, the demands of the Church, and his feudal obligations, was a tribute alike to his ability and ruthlessness – qualities perhaps inherited from his Norman forbears. The least known of all the medieval lords of Galloway, this was an achievement for which he has never been given proper credit.

NOTES

1. This is conjectural, but it is hard to imagine Malcolm failing to insist on it, and it would account for Gilbert's participation in King William's invasion of England in 1174.
2. Daniel, *Ailred*, 45.
3. This can be inferred from the fact that Carrick had hitherto been part of the royal domain and became the portion of Gilbert's son, Duncan.
4. Brooke, *Wild Men*, 109.
5. Conversation with Dr Oram, who is coming to this conclusion.
6. *RRS* i, 13.
7. *Ibid.*, 230. *RRS* i, no 230.
8. Crawford, *Archaeological and Historical Collections of the County of Renfrew* (1883), 26.
9. He was almost certainly the ancestor of Sir Malcolm Fleming, who became David II's tenant-in-chief and principal law enforcer in Wigtownshire during the fourteenth century.
10. *RRS* i, p 39.
11. *Wig Charters*, xix–xx.
12. Conversation with Dr Oram.
13. *Wig Charters*, xxiv (quoting G W S Barrow). The *reddendo* was the services of half a knight (Anderson, *Diplomata Scotiae*, no. 77).
14. Conversation with Dr Oram. His elder daughter inherited his lands at Inverkeilor in Angus, and her descendants took the name Barclay.
15. Reid, 'The Mote of Urr', 19. Sir Ingelram was a great-uncle of the future king, John Balliol.
16. Oram, 'A family business?', 117–8. He suggests that the marriage was arranged by David I, who was probably uneasy at the close family ties that existed between the lords of Galloway and the ruling dynasty in England, and may have hoped that by drawing Uchtred into this milieu these would be loosened. Gunnild's family were members of the Northumbrian aristocracy who had married into the Scottish royal house.
17. *Reg Holm Cultram* no.120a. Kindeloch is thought to be associated with the Welsh saint Cynddelw, to whom the church on an island in the nearby Loch Kindar is

believed to have been dedicated.

18. *Wig Charters*, xx.

19. Oram, 'A family business?', 125.

20. He was Henry II's constable of Appleby when it surrendered to William I in the course of his English invasion in 1174, and was then described as 'a white-haired old man'. (*Jordan Fantosme*, 151).

21. He was a member of Henry II's household and was one of the four knights who murdered Thomas Becket in his cathedral at Canterbury in 1172.

22. This is conjectural and based on the fact that David fitzTerrus gave the church at Over Denton to Lanercost priory on or after its foundation by the de Vaux family in 1160.

23. To avoid confusion, it should be explained that *Cardiness* was the name of the lordship granted to David fitzTerrus, whereas *Cardoness* was that subsequently given to the estate there.

24. Reid opined that the grant comprised the modern parishes of Anwoth and Kirkmabreck, in which case the lands would have extended as far as the Cree (*Wig Charters*, xxxiii). Oram, on the other hand, takes the view that it was confined to Anwoth, though I would submit there are grounds for believing that it included the former parish of Kirkdale as well.

25. This follows from McKerlie's reference (v, 261) to Gamel de Twynam's son, William, granting the church there to the monks of Holyrood, which he asserts was approved by Bishop Christian. As the latter abandoned Whithorn in about 1177, his consent must have been given before then, which implies that the barony would have been granted to de Twynam by Uchtred.

26. *Holyrood Charters* 39: *Wig Charters*, xxxiii: *RRS* ii, 485.

27. See note 24 above.

28. As a first step, the churches of Tongland and St. Cuthbert at Kirkcudbright were transferred to Holyrood (*RRS*, i no. 39). This was followed by the group of churches round Kelton, which included Kelton itself, Kirkcormack (Gelston), Balincros (now Barncrosh), and St Andrew (Balmaghie) (*RRS*, i, no. 141), and likewise the former daughter churches of Edingham, namely, St Calmonel of Urr, St Brigid of Blaiket and St Constantine of Edingham (Brooke, *Wild* Men, 106).

29. *RRS* ii, no. 103,

30. This was suppressed by Archibald the Grim, earl of Douglas, in 1389.

31. *Reg. Holm Cultram*, nos 120, 120a. This abbey was founded by King William's father, Earl Henry, in 1150.

32. The grant was in feu ferme and not in free alms, since Uchtred would have needed the *reddendo* to service his obligations to the king for the Desnes Ioan. This meant the monks were obliged to make a substantial annual cash payment to Uchtred and his successors as lords of Galloway, and this continued to be the case until Edward Bruce quitclaimed the right sometime before 1318.

33. *RRS* ii, no 88 (a literal translation of the Latin). Brooke attempts to identify the place-names referred to in the deed in 'The deanery of the Desnes Cro and the church of Edingham', 54.

34. This did not necessarily infer that the monks actually reared cattle, but the clause followed a set style and would have been inserted to give them an appropriate wayleave right should they do so.

35. *RRS* ii, no 87.

36. The fact that the lands belonging to Dundrennan in the parish of Kirkpatrick Durham were farmed by the monks as a grange is apparent from an Inquest of

1360.
37. *Reg. Holm Cultram.*
38. Scott, 'An early sheriff of Dumfries?', 90.
39. *RRS* ii, no 256.
40. *Ibid.*
41. Anderson: *Annals.*
42. *Roger de Howden*: Anderson, *Annals.*
43. *Benedict of Peterborough*: Anderson, *Annals.*
44. *Ibid.*
45. *Ibid.*, i, 67–8.
46. Hope-Taylor, 'Excavations at Mote of Urr', 167–72.
47. *Bower* 4, p 315.
48. Suggested by J G Scott, though Daphne Brooke prefers Arsbotel (*Wild Men*, 111), but it could equally easily have been Threave island on the river Dee.
49. *Benedict of Peterborough*: Anderson, *Annals.*
50. Disc. Brook, *Wild Men*, 112.
51. Henry II and Uchtred were both grandsons of Henry I.
52. Lawrie, *Charters.*
53. His baptismal name was the Gaelic Lachlan, but he is better known as Roland. Similarly, Gilbert's original name would have been Gaelic. Uchtred (or Uhtred), on the other hand, was a Northumbrian name, and it would be intriguing to know what this implied.
54. *Benedict of Peterborough:* Anderson: *Annals*, i, 126.
55. Hill, *Whithorn*, 57.
56. Diplomatic relations may have existed between the two at this stage, but certainly not later. For, when the cardinal summoned a general council of the Scottish Church at Edinburgh, Bishop Christian refused to attend, claiming (quite correctly) that his obedience lay with York. Notwithstanding this, Cardinal Vivian responded by excommunicating him and suspended him from episcopal office; but, supported by Archbishop Roger, Bishop Christian ignored this and continued in office.
57. *Vita Godrici Eremitae* (Surtees Society, 1848).
58. *Benedict of Peterborough*. Anderson: *annals.*
59. *Ibid.*, 288.
60. Hill, *Whithorn*, 224.
61. *Chron Melrose*: Anderson, *Early Sources*, 310.
62. He is thought to have been the ancestor of the Kennedys, and the traditional loyalty to Gilbert's family was maintained by his descendants, who remained staunch supporters of the earls of Carrick.
63. Duncan, *Scotland*, 183.
64. *Bower* 4, p 367.
65. *Benedict of Peterborough*: Anderson, *Annals* i, 348–9.
66. *Ibid.*, ii, 102–3.
67. *RRS* iii, no 340: Chalmers. *Caledonia*, iii, 530.
68. Although Duncan appears to have got the worst of the deal, his inheritance was to survive the longest for, whereas Roland's possessions were either forfeited or given away by his descendants, the Carrick earldom eventually descended to King Robert Bruce. Thereafter it was merged with the crown, when the title and the attaching comital lands were customarily granted to the heir to the throne, and the earldom still remains a subsidiary title of the princes of Wales.
69. Anderson: *Annals*, 290.
70. *Bower* 4, 337.

71. *RRS* ii, no 406.
72. *Ibid.*, nos 309, 400.
73. *APS* i, 378.
74. *Wig Charters*, xxvii.
75. Disc. Oram 'A family business?', 134–5.
76. De Vieuxpont's mother, Matilda, was a daughter of Hugh de Morville the elder, who was the grandfather of Roland's wife.
77. Sir Ivo gave the churches of St Michael and St Fillans to Dryburgh abbey, thus emphasising their connection with that house through the de Morvilles. Though the lands themselves passed to his sons, their descendants subsequently disappear from the records of Galloway.
78. Oram, 'A family business?', 139.
79. *Ibid.*, 140. It is perhaps significant that from an early date the McDowell family coat of arms incorporated the lion rampant which was used by the lords of Galloway as their heraldic symbol.
80. So it would seem, judging from the fact they are known to have been established there during the late thirteenth century, when they became protégés of Dervorguilla.
81. Conversation with Dr Oram who relayed this theory from W. D. H. Sellar.
82. He first appears on record as a witness to a charter granted by Roland's son, Alan, in 1217 (*Wig Charters*, xxvii), so he could have received his lands from either of them.
83. He was the ancestor of the Colvilles of Ochiltree, who remained prominent landowners in Ayrshire for many centuries, ultimately becoming lords Colville of Culross.
84. *Chron Melrose*: Anderson, *Early Sources*.
85. *Wig Charters*, xxv. Both brothers became closely associated with Roland's son, Alan, and their respective descendants remained there until the fourteenth century.
86. The Maules subsequently became earls of Panmure and are now represented by the earls of Dalhousie.
87. *Register of St Bees*, 91 and 93.
88. And would remain so until Dervorguilla gave them as an endowment to Sweetheart abbey.
89. *Wig Charters*, xxviii.
90. McKerlie iv, 152.
91. Tabraham, 'Norman settlement in Galloway', 87–123.
92. This is evident from the charter conveying the abbey lands to the fourth earl of Cassilis in 1572.
93. *RRS* ii, no 293.
94. Lawrie, *Charters*, 303.
95. *Ibid.*

9

ANNEXATION

A 'MAGNIFICENT PRINCE'

Alan, Lord of Galloway and Constable of Scotland,[1] was one of the most powerful magnates in the realm. Besides falling heir to the former de Morville lands in Cunninghame and Lauderdale, he was the hereditary ruler of a semi-independent province which was pre-eminent in the Celtic west.[2] Later, he became a prominent member of the English baronage, besides acquiring a title to vast territories in northern Ireland. These contrasting roles were reflected in his three marriages; the first to a member of the de Lacy family from Pontefract in Yorkshire, the second to King William's niece, and the third to an Anglo-Irish kinswoman of his first wife. However, it was primarily his position as a Celtic chieftain which accounted for his overriding ambition to dominate the political arena of the west coast and the Irish Sea.

The political scene, within which Alan's loyalties would fluctuate between King William and his rival, the English king John, had already been set when he inherited the Galloway lordship. The mutual animosity between the two kings stemmed from William's attempt, some years previously, to exclude John from the succession by conniving with Richard I's chancellor, William Beauchamp, to promote the rival claims of John's nephew, Arthur of Brittany.[3] Dynastic loyalties drew William to Arthur, since this youth was his great-nephew, but more to the point he calculated that if Arthur were to gain the throne with his support he could reasonably expect to recover the earldom of Northumberland as a reward.

When John took the throne – in the face of widespread opposition[4] – on Richard's death in France in 1199, William, aggrieved that his plans had come to nothing, became belligerent and demanded the cession of Northumberland and Cumberland, threatening to take them by force if necessary. When John summoned him to York to do homage for his lands in Tynedale he refused; though subsequently relenting, he did so at Lincoln in March 1200. But as John declined to entertain William's claim to the northern counties this did nothing to ease the strained relations between them.

Meanwhile, divisions arose within the Angevin possession in France. Whereas Normandy accepted John as Richard's designated heir, some supported Arthur's claim, while others declared for the queen mother, Eleanor of Aquitaine. The French king, Philip II, played a waiting game, and in return for certain territorial concessions he accepted John's homage for the remaining lands, while Arthur was declared John's vassal for Brittany. Matters came to a head in the autumn of 1201, when John seized the lands belonging to the barons of Poitou. They appealed to Philip as feudal overlord for redress, and when judgement was given in their favour John refused to restore them to their lands. In early 1202, Philip decided to enforce his decision by invading Normandy, and having overrun it he evicted John from that fiefdom and declared Arthur as vassal in his place. John retaliated by declaring war on Philip, and during the ensuing campaign he captured Arthur and took him to Rouen, where he is alleged to have murdered him with his bare hands and flung his body into the Seine.[5] Alan of Galloway, in a demonstration of independence of King William, pledged John a fleet of a hundred ships and a large number of foot soldiers as a contribution to his war effort, though the offer was never taken up. Ultimately, the war proved a disaster for John, because it culminated in the loss of Normandy in 1204.

In 1209, relations between the two kings – John and William – reached breaking point, and John mustered a large army to invade Scotland. By the time it reached Norham William, realising that resistance was futile, sued for peace. The terms were humiliating; William was forced to hand over his two daughters, along with his rights in their marriage, to John, and to pay him the gigantic sum of 15,000 marks in return for his 'goodwill'. This left him politically devastated, and his need to secure powerful allies was acute. Therefore, in order to ensure the loyalty of Alan, who was now a widower, he gave him his niece, Margaret of Huntingdon, the daughter of his powerful brother, Earl David, in marriage. It was an extremely prestigious match, since it elevated Alan to the front rank of the Scottish nobility, besides bringing him the lands with which Margaret had been endowed in the Honour of Huntingdon. As he was already a substantial magnate in Westmorland, having inherited his grandmother's estates at Torpenhow, this accretion of lands made him one of the leading members of the English baronage.

FOREIGN ADVENTURES

Alan held these lands as John's tenant-in-chief, and his attaching obligation for military service accounted for Alan's participation in John's Irish campaign in 1210. Ireland had been a constant source of trouble to the Plantagenet kings, and at the beginning of his reign John had sent William de Braose there, along with Hugh de Lacy and others, to bring the region under control.[6] They achieved this, but for various reasons they turned against him and made common cause with a number of native princes. John retaliated by launching a full-scale expedition against them. It was a triumphant success, and with the help of some loyal princes he besieged the rebel leaders in the fortress of Carrickfergus, though Hugh de Lacy and de Braose managed to escape to Scotland.[7] After their flight the garrison surrendered, when severe reprisals were taken and the rebel barons forfeited their lands.[8] Unfortunately, de Braose's wife, Matilda, and their eldest son, fell into the hands of Duncan of Carrick, and he duly handed them over to King John who imprisoned them in Windsor castle where, according to the chroniclers, they were starved to death.[9]

Alan's pay-off was handsome, as he was given a fief in northern Ireland equivalent to a hundred and sixty knights' service.[10] This comprised a large share of the forfeited lands, and included the whole of north Antrim, extending from Larne as far as Coleraine, as well as Hugh de Lacy's former lands in county Derry. Clearly King William was compelled to acquiesce in this, because we are told that 'Alan the Great, lord of Galloway . . . with the consent and permission of his lord the King did homage at Norham to John King of England for the extensive lands in Ireland which he had granted to Alan'.[11] However, the reward proved hollow, because although Alan was given a legal title to these lands he still had to establish his authority over them, and although with the assistance of his brother, Thomas, earl of Atholl, he managed to capture the main seaports on the north-east coast, he found it impossible to gain physical possession of them.

In the following year, John enlisted Alan's help in his Welsh campaign against Llewelyn ap Iorwerth, prince of Gwynedd, who was pre-eminent in north Wales and Anglesey. A former ally of John, he had done homage to him, and in 1204 he was given John's illegitimate daughter in marriage. In 1209, Llewelyn assisted John in his campaign against King William which culminated in the débâcle at Norham, but they fell out shortly afterwards when Llewelyn helped William de Braose to recover some of his Welsh lands. Eventually, he came out in open rebellion, and John assembled an army, which included 1,000 armed men contributed by Alan, at Chester in readiness to march on Llewelyn. Initially, the campaign went badly for John, because Llewelyn's forces harassed his army by using guerilla tactics, but when he eventually captured Bangor, Llewelyn surrendered, though his life was spared at his wife's intercession.

It is impossible to gauge the effectiveness of these Gallovidian levies in the campaign, but it seems that Alan's support for King John led to something approaching friendship between them, cemented perhaps by their kinship (both were descended from Henry I), and the fact that they were much the same age. They are on record as exchanging gifts, John presenting Alan with 'a good hound' and receiving a pair of breeding geese in return.[12] However, this ended with Alan's attendance as one of the rebel barons at the signing of the Magna Carta in June 1215, although when civil war broke out again shortly afterwards John attempted to regain his support with a bribe of '"prests" to the tune of five hundred marks'.[13]

However, Alan was now firmly in the camp of Alexander II who had succeeded King William in 1214. Like his father, the new king was ill disposed to John, all the more so since the latter had made an abortive attempt to kidnap him in the course of a meeting with him when he was deputising for the ageing William.[14] Therefore, in late 1215, Alexander invaded England in support of Robert de Ros[15] who had instigated a rebellion in the north – a venture in which he was joined by Alan, but although they made common cause their objectives were different. Whereas Alexander's aim was to recover Northumberland, Alan was solely concerned with appropriating the former de Morville lands in Westmorland.

Meanwhile, John was already marching northwards to subdue the rebels, and vowing to 'run the fox cub to earth' – a reference to Alexander's red-headedness – he drove him back across the Border, capturing and burning Berwick. However, he was denied the chance to exploit his success, because in May 1216 he had to hurry south to deal with a French invasion under King Philip's son, Louis, in support of the rebel barons. Five months later, John died, still at bay, with Alexander remaining in control of much of the north, and Alan in possession of the de Morville lands in Westmorland.

THE MANX WAR

In 1220, Alan's close family ties with its ruling dynasty drew him into an involvement in a civil war which had broken out in the Isle of Man, and this would occupy him on and off for the next twelve years. Having recovered the throne in 1164, Fergus's grandson, Godred, continued to rule the island (beating off a challenge by his brother Ragnvald whom he castrated and blinded) until his death in 1187, when he was succeeded by his elder son, another Ragnvald.[16]

In what seems to have been virtually a hallowed tradition there, this Ragnvald was under challenge from his half-brother, Olaf 'the black', and in an attempt to buy him off Ragnvald gave Olaf the Isle of Lewis. Apparently this was not enough to satisfy him, and he continued to agitate for more, until Ragnvald eventually contrived to have him captured and handed over to King William. Later, Olaf was freed under a general amnesty, when Ragnvald restored him to Lewis. Nevertheless, this failed to patch up the differences between the brothers, and when Ragnvald's son, Godred, attempted to capture Olaf, he himself was taken prisoner, and in an almost time-honoured ritual he was emasculated and had his eyes gouged out.[17]

Olaf now followed up his success by launching a series of attacks on the Isle of Man, and in desperation Ragnvald appealed to Alan for help. Therefore, with the support of King Alexander, who was deeply suspicious of Olaf's links with the rebellious lord of the Isles, Alan dispatched a fleet of war galleys to Ragnvald's assistance. Initially he was successful; Olaf was driven off, and Alan and Ragnvald pressed home their advantage by attacking Olaf's possessions on Skye and Lewis, or as the Norse chronicler put it 'he [Alan] plundered about the Hebrides [and] made great warfare through the western lands'.[18] Confident that they had crushed Olaf, Alan withdrew, and Ragnvald returned to Man. However, the latter was clearly taking no chances, and in 1225, in order to cement his alliance with Alan against a possible further attack by Olaf, he gave his daughter in marriage to Alan's illegitimate son, Thomas.

Evidently Ragnvald's close identification with Alan was highly unpopular with the Manxmen who had not been consulted about the marriage and felt their views had been overridden, so they deposed Ragnvald, driving him out of the kingdom, and summoned Olaf to the throne in his place. Once again, Ragnvald was compelled to seek help from Alan, and he duly responded by mounting another expedition against the island. This too was successful for, as the Manx chronicler put it, 'Alan, lord of Galloway, Thomas, earl of Atholl and King Reginald [Ragnvald] came to Man with a great army; and devastated the whole southern part of Man and despoiled the Churches, and slew all the men whom they could take; and the southern part of Man was almost reduced to a desert'.[19] Ragnvald was reinstated, and we are told that 'after this Alan returned with his army to his own land; and left his bailiffs in Man to render to him the taxes of the land'[20] – this presumably being the price of his assistance.

Olaf now sought help from his overlord, King Haakon IV of Norway, to whom he owed a tenuous allegiance, and this marked a turning point. The Norwegian king responded by threatening to attack Alan with his fleet, but the latter is alleged to have defiantly retorted that the sea was 'not more difficult to cross to Norway than from Norway to Scotland', meaning that he was equally capable of launching an attack against King Haakon himself. As such blatant challenge to his authority could not be ignored, the king responded by sending a large war fleet under the joint command of Olaf and the lord of the Isles' grandson to invade Scotland. They laid siege to the Steward's castle of Rothesay, on the Isle of Bute, but when news came of the approach of Alan's fleet of a hundred and fifty war-galleys they abandoned it. However, this was merely a feint as Olaf sailed on southwards to the Isle of Man. Landing there, he drove out Alan's bailiffs and reclaimed the kingship, Ragnvald having been killed in a sea engagement in the North Channel.

The failure of the Manx campaign was both a personal and a political blow for Alan. Personal, because Ragnvald's restoration was part of his strategy for securing the kingdom for his illegitimate son Thomas – and it was doubtless with this in mind that he had agreed to the marriage between Thomas and Ragnvald's daughter,[21] and this was now in ruins. Politically, the episode led to a souring of relations with the king, because it showed beyond any doubt that when it came to a pinch Alan was prepared to jeopardise the safety of the realm in the pursuit of his private ambitions. Therefore, Alexander never fully trusted him again.

Alan was now approaching sixty, a widower for the second time, and still without a legitimate male heir. In about 1229 he married for the third time, his bride being Rohesia, the daughter of Hugh de Lacy, now earl of Ulster.[22] This was primarily a political match which was designed to set the seal on an accommodation which Alan had reached with de Lacy. For, when the latter finally made his peace with Henry III in 1224, he was restored to those of his lands in Ulster which had not been signed away by King John to Alan and his brother Earl Thomas. Inevitably, de Lacy set his sights on re-acquiring the remainder, and this led to a state of undeclared war between him and Alan, which the latter looked like losing. Therefore, the marriage may have been arranged as a compromise which allowed him to withdraw without loss of face. It was also intended to produce the longed-for male heir, but tragically for Galloway it failed to do so, as the marriage proved childless.

ALAN'S BENEFACTIONS

Like his predecessors, Alan was a benefactor of the Church, and he is credited with being the founder of Tongland abbey in 1219. Insalubriously situated at the foot of a gorge at the mouth of the Dee, this was a smaller institution than most of its sister houses, and its endowment was correspondingly modest, being limited to the lands in its immediate vicinity, while Holyrood contributed the patronage of the local church.[23] As the Cistercians were currently under excommunication, this was founded for their sister order, the Premonstratensians, and constituted a daughter house of their abbey at Cockersand, in Cumbria. It was to receive some notoriety in the reign of James IV on account of its abbot John Damian the 'fenzeit [feigned] friar'. An eccentric character, and a noted alchemist, he constructed a pair of wings out of hens' feathers in an attempt to fly from the battlements of Stirling castle. This ended ingloriously when he came to earth in a dunghill, attributing his failure to the feathers' 'yearning for the midden and not the skies'!

Alan is also on record as making sundry grants to other religious institutions. For example, he gave some land at Sypland to the nearby church of St Cuthbert at Kirkcudbright, while another holding, amounting

to thirty-two acres of land at Kelton, was granted to the local church of St
Oswald the martyr.[24] In addition, he is thought to have been responsible for
the extensive re-modelling of the cathedral church at Whithorn, which was
carried out during the thirteenth century.[25]

Alan followed his father's example by making grants out of the lordship
patrimony, but the dearth of contemporary charters and other relevant
material makes it difficult to be specific. Nor is it possible to determine
whether those receiving land were natives or incomers (the prefix 'de' to
their names being no sure guide since it was used by both), but as Alan's
lordship depended on the support of the native community[26] it was natural
that they should benefit. A possible example were the de Kyrkonnels,[27] who
first appear in the early thirteenth century as owners of the Kirkconnel
estate, adjacent to the Nith estuary.[28] They are unique, for among all the
landowners in Galloway at this time they alone continue to be represented
there, and their direct descendants, the Maxwells (formerly Maxwell-
Withams), still own part of the lands which were granted to their remote
forbear some eight hundred years ago.[29]

A prominent incomer to Galloway at this time was Ralph de Champaign
(or de Campania), who is thought to have arrived there in the train of
Margaret of Huntingdon on her marriage to Alan. He was given part of the
lands of Borgue, and while he would have used the de Morville's motte-and-
bailey castle at Boreland of Borgue as his *caput*, he was responsible for
building the small subsidiary motte at Barmagachan, near Borgue itself.
These lands ultimately passed to his grandson, who resigned them to
Dervorguilla in 1282.[30] Alan also appointed de Champaign his butler, and
thereafter he was knighted and subsequently became constable of
Roxburgh castle. Meantime, his brother, Robert, was granted Kirkandrews,
his ruling centre being established at 'Castleton of Borgue', which is a
substantial motte near Roberton.[31] This passed to his son, Robert, and
ultimately to the latter's daughter, Margaret, and her husband, Bernard de
Rippelay, the scion of a family of Northumbrian aristocrats who had been
established in Yorkshire since before the Conquest.[32] Another branch of
the de Champaign family was established in unidentified lands in
Wigtownshire, and these passed to their descendants, the McDowells.[33]

REBELLION AND THE AFTERMATH

Alan died in 1234 and was buried in Dundrennan abbey. His failure to
produce a legitimate male heir must have cast a shadow over his later years,
since it meant that the succession would pass to his three daughters, and he
was well aware that Alexander was poised to use the opportunity to
dismantle the lordship. His fears proved abundantly justified, because
Alexander promptly, albeit with questionable legality, ruled that it should

be divided between the three daughters. The eldest Elena, the daughter of Alan's first wife, was married to Roger de Quenci, earl of Winchester, while Christina and Dervorguilla were the offspring of his second marriage. Like her elder sister, Christina married into the Norman aristocracy, her husband being William de Fortez, earl of Aumale, whereas Dervorguilla's husband, John Balliol, was a man of lesser rank who owned estates in county Durham and his native Picardy.

The prospect of losing their independence so alarmed the Gallovidians that it led to the emergence of a body, calling itself the Community of Galloway, who begged Alexander to preserve the integrity of the lordship by taking it under his direct rule. However, he was determined to dismantle it in order to destroy for ever its potential as a hostile power-base, so he threatened to impose his decision by force. The Gallovidians responded defiantly, and power passed to a militant group of magnates, including Alan's father-in-law, Hugh de Lacy, who were prepared to meet force with force. However, there was disagreement over the choice of leader, for although Alan's son, Thomas, was the obvious candidate some saw his illegitimacy as a drawback. These doubters inclined towards Alan's nephew, Patrick, the son of his brother Earl Thomas who had been killed in 1231. But Patrick was still a boy, whereas Thomas was a man of considerable experience, and still more to the point he had the support of Hugh de Lacy and his Irish levies, and possibly also his kinsman, Duncan, earl of Carrick.[34]

Therefore Thomas was declared leader of the resistance movement, and he proceeded to style himself 'Thomas of Galloway'. Then, according to the politically-slanted account of the chronicler, Matthew Paris, he and his leading supporters entered into a blood bond 'which harked back to pagan times' and entailed 'an unheard of covenant, involving a kind of sorcery, in accord nevertheless with a certain abominable custom of their ancient forefathers'. In the course of the ritual 'these barbarians, and their leaders and magistrates shed blood from the precordial vein into a large vessel by bloodletting' and 'after it was drawn they stirred and mixed it [and] drank it as a sign [of their] indissoluble and as it were consanguineal covenant'.[35]

Alexander's threat now became a reality, and he proceeded to invade Galloway, but his campaign nearly ended in disaster when his troops found themselves engulfed in the marshy flows. According to Fordun, 'the natives', taking advantage of their predicament, 'started out of the hills and woods [and] assailed the King and his army who were resting in their tents'.[36] However, he was rescued by the timely arrival of his trusted lieutenant, Farquhar MacTaggart (subsequently earl of Ross), and his Highland levies who turned the course of the battle and enabled Alexander to continue with his conquest of Galloway. Once this was achieved, he was prepared to be magnanimous and, according to the Melrose chronicler, he offered his 'peace to all who came to him'. Many Gallovidian leaders did so, as they reportedly came to him 'with ropes round their necks and begged for peace and the king's favour'.[37] This was granted, but Thomas, who was beyond the pale of forgiveness, fled to Ireland along with others who refused the king's pardon.

Alexander's hold over Galloway was strengthened still further by the outcome of a dispute over the right to elect a successor to Bishop Walter of Whithorn who had died in 1235. The contest was between the 'clergy and people of the diocese', on the one hand, and the cathedral chapter at Whithorn on the other, but in the present unstable situation there were far-reaching political issues at stake. From Alexander's point of view a trustworthy incumbent was vital, for if the cathedral chapter prevailed there was every chance of Whithorn becoming a focus of native opposition. Therefore, putting his weight behind the clergy and people, he engineered the election of Gilbert, a monk of Melrose – a house with which he was closely associated. Also, as a former abbot of Glenluce, Gilbert had sufficient local connections to make him acceptable to the people. However, in order to emphasise that this was the choice of the clergy and people of Galloway, Alexander issued an open letter, giving his formal consent to 'the election of brother Gilbert of Melrose whom you have unanimously chosen as your pastor'. At the same time, he sent another letter to the archbishop of York urging Gilbert's consecration.

Three weeks later, the prior and chapter responded by electing their colleague, Odo Ydonc, former abbot of Dercungal (Holywood). They recommended him to the authorities at York as 'a man literate, honest, modest and religious', while insisting that his election accorded with current papal policy. This was strictly correct, as the pope had recently vested the right of appointing bishops in cathedral chapters, but the prior and chapter at Whithorn wanted formal and unambiguous recognition of their unchallengeable right to appoint bishops both now and in the future. If they achieved this, it would deprive Alexander and his successors of all further right to interfere in Gallovidian ecclesiastical affairs, and therefore this avenue for extending their political influence in the province would be closed to them. The dispute was referred to the archbishop's court at York, where claim and counterclaim were put forward in a lengthy hearing. But while the prior and chapter had a strong canonical case, Alexander was in control of Galloway, so the court, bowing to reality, decided in favour of his nominee Gilbert.[38] This was an important decision, since it established that henceforth the crown had the right to nominate bishops subject to papal approval.[39]

Alexander proceeded to consolidate his authority in Galloway by imposing a reign of terror which was designed to stamp out all opposition, a policy which was euphemistically referred to as the 'pacification of Galloway'. Responsibility for implementing it was assigned to Walter

Comyn, earl of Menteith, the main agent of his authority and his principal trouble-shooter. Therefore, establishing his headquarters at Cruggleton,[40] he set about his task with a vengeance, giving his soldiery full licence to act with the utmost brutality. As the Church had supported Thomas, the religious houses were a prime target. At Tongland the prior and sacristan were murdered in their own church, while a dying monk at Glenluce was stripped of the only sheet covering him as he lay stretched out on the traditional deathbed of straw and ashes.[41] At the same time, Alexander suppressed ecclesiastical opposition by deposing abbots Jordan of Dundrennan and Robert of Glenluce, and replacing them with monks from Melrose.[42]

The 'pacification' was interrupted the following year when Thomas returned from Ireland with a force of Irish 'galloglasses', or mercenaries, and drove out Menteith's forces in disarray. King Alexander immediately sent another army to Galloway under Patrick, earl of Dunbar, and although successful, it seems he achieved this by guile rather than force of arms. For Dunbar persuaded Thomas's principal supporter Gilleruth to defect, thus isolating Thomas, who was left with no alternative but to surrender, and thereafter he disappeared. His Irish gallowglasses were left stranded, as Thomas had taken the precaution of burning their ships to prevent them from deserting back to Ireland,[43] and so this motley rabble drifted northwards, eventually reaching Glasgow, where they were set upon by the mob. Most of them were summarily beheaded, but two of their leaders, who were singled out by the king for special treatment, were sent to Edinburgh, where they were tied to horses and torn limb from limb,[44] presumably for the diversion of the populace.

With the rebellion crushed Galloway was finally subjugated. For the first and only time in its history conquest was not accompanied by land re-distribution, simply because there was no need to, as the daughters' husbands already controlled the patrimonial lands, while Roger de Quenci was a principal agent of Alexander's authority in the region. Therefore, Alexander's primary concern was to divide these lands equitably between the daughters. The traditional view presumed a straightforward division, with Elena de Quenci receiving the lands in the west, Dervorguilla Balliol those in the east, while Christina de Fortez' portion consisted of an indeterminate holding in the middle.[45] While this is broadly true, recent research has shown it to have been more complex.[46] And in addition it seems that Thomas had been given lands there[47] which fell to be divided between his half-sisters.

Reflecting her status as the eldest daughter, Elena was given property at Kirkcudbright, the traditional power-centre of the lordship, and this subsequently passed to her eldest daughter, Margaret de Ferrars.[48] She also received the nearby lands of Senwick, as well as those of Girthon on Fleet,[49] and further east she acquired a half share of the patrimonial lands in the parish of Troqueer.[50] Besides these, she was given most of the lordship lands in Wigtownshire. However, some of these estates came to her through her sister Christina, for when she died without issue in 1245 her Galloway possessions were divided between her sisters,[51] although Dervorguilla acquired the lion's share.[52] Additionally, Elena was awarded the superiority of a large tract of hill country in northern Kirkcudbrightshire, and in consequence of its passing to her son-in-law, Alexander Comyn, earl of Buchan, this became known as the forest of Buchan.

Although Dervorguilla's portion was mainly confined to eastern Galloway, she acquired possessions in Wigtownshire as well. Some were situated in the Rhinns, where she owned land in the parishes of Stoneykirk and Kirkcolm, but the remainder was confined to the southern Machars. This included the important estate of Kidsdale, and part of the lands of Outon which lie to the north of Whithorn.[53] Property in the burgh of Wigtown also came to her, together with land in the adjacent parish of Kirkinner, since this was used to endow the friary she subsequently established at Wigtown. Significantly, the lands she inherited from her sister Christina included Buittle, and it is a measure of its relative unimportance at the time that it should have been given to Christina as the second daughter, whereas Kirkcudbright and Cruggleton were awarded to the eldest daughter, Elena, Dervorguilla meantime being palmed off with the inferior ruling centre of Arsbotel.

THE LAWS OF GALLOWAY

The law which was exercised by the sheriffs and local barons was primarily feudal, although some traditional laws, such as those of *cain* and *conveth*, remained in force. These had a long history in Celtic Scotland, and because they benefited the king and his representatives their validity was formally recognised by Alexander in an assize of 1244. As we have seen, *cain* was a right of food render which was leviable by the king or his representatives during their travels on official business, whereas *conveth* gave them the more comprehensive right to demand hospitality, and any landholder from a tenant-in-chief downwards was liable. The Church seems to have borne the main brunt, probably because its institutions were able to offer better accommodation than the wooden donjons of the feudal magnates and the dwellings of the smaller landholders, though it was also better equipped to articulate a complaint and register the result. For example, a letter addressed by the bishop of Moray to Pope Clement VI referred to 'the evil custom, or rather tyranny and corruption, by which the nobles and powerful men of those parts in their journeys occupy the canons' houses and, driving out their households, therein eat and sleep'.[54]

An important feature of the traditional laws was the concept of *kenkynnol*, derived from the Gaelic for 'head of the kindred'. References to it appear in a number of charters issued during the reign of David II, where Donald Edgar is described as the captain (or chief) of the clan McGowin,[55] similarly Gilbert McGillolane (McLellan) as chief of the clan Connan,[56] and Michael MacGorth the Kenclanan.[57] Its existence was particularly evident in Carrick, where the title of *kenkynnol* was given to successive descendants of Earl Duncan, and latterly to the heads of the Kennedys which, it has been suggested, points to their being his descendants.[58] The kindred chieftainship of the Kennedys was specifically recognised in a charter by David II, which described John Kennedy of Dunure as 'capitain of the Mintirscasduf'.[59]

These chieftains were entitled to rights of food render (*calps*) and hospitality (*frithalos*), analagous to those of *cain* and *conveth*, which were leviable on members of their kindred. At the same time, they had a duty to protect them by enforcing compensation for homicide or injuries inflicted on them by a member of another kindred. The amount was judged according to the victim's *cro*, or status, and was generally assessed in terms of head of cattle or ounces of gold. Edward I is thought to have abolished this particular form of wergild when he took over the government of Scotland in 1304,[60] though other 'special laws' survived until finally suppressed by James I in 1426.

Since the traditional laws were unwritten, they were expounded by *judices*, men regarded as the repositaries of tradition and custom. Justice was frequently conducted in an open-air 'court' and presided over by a judge known as a 'doomsman' or 'dempster'. As his qualifications probably depended on inherited right rather than a knowledge of the laws, he would have relied on advice from 'experts'. Since the verdicts were often arbitrary, aggrieved parties now gained the right to 'fals the doom', meaning they could appeal against the decision to the local sheriff. The application followed a standard form, and in the colourful language of the time the appellant branded the decision of the lower court as 'fals, stynkand and rottin', though he had to show sufficient grounds to warrant an appeal before it could be heard.

Hitherto, most civil disputes beyond the competence of barons' courts were decided by ecclesiastical tribunals rather than secular courts, because it was thought that churchmen with their superior learning were better qualified to deal with more complex issues. This was now becoming less frequent, and in 1270 jurisdiction in such matters was removed from these tribunals altogether. Nevertheless, care was taken to appoint properly qualified men to hear these cases, and a treatise drawn up in John Balliol's reign placed an obligation on magnates to nominate those who had 'the skill and ability to administer law and justice to both poor and rich, and to uphold and supervise the King's rights in all points pertaining to the Crown'.

Jurisdiction in criminal cases depended on the gravity of the offence. Minor matters were disposed of in the baronial courts, with the lord's retainers being responsible for executing sentence. More serious cases, apart from the four pleas of the crown which were the preserve of the king's justiciar, were tried by local sheriffs, and it seems the agents responsible for enforcing their decisions were known as 'sergeants'. The precise definition of the law known as *surdit de sergeant* is unclear, though their duties could have extended to policing the countryside, with powers to arrest suspects. This was certainly the case in England, where sergeants were empowered to execute summary justice, and even to behead robbers caught red-handed. That they had some powers to administer arbitrary justice, or at least to secure convictions on their uncorroborated testimony, seems evident from a charter granted by Robert Bruce, earl of Carrick, in 1285, when he exempted the Carrick tenants of Melrose abbey from the *supradictus* or accusation of 'our sergeants'.

Because their duties extended to tax collection for secular as well as ecclesiastical landowners,[61] these sergeants were understandably highly unpopular, and all the more so since they consistently abused their powers. This is evident from the terms of a petition presented by the Community of Galloway to Edward I in 1304, which complained that the barons and great lords were using the 'strange and ycortenuse [tortious or wrongful] custom called surdit de sergeant to the grievance of the land'.[62] However, judging from the terms of two charters granted by King Robert Bruce in 1324 and 1325 respectively, it seems that the petition must have fallen on deaf ears. The first of these stipulated that 'in any action by the king's sergeant in Galloway' the accused 'shall have a good and faithful assize of his country', and that he should not be tried 'by compurgation according to the ancient laws of Galloway'.[63] In other words, the accused was entitled to be tried by his peers and could not be convicted merely on the strength of unfounded allegations by sergeants. The other charter was more specific, in that it exempted the canons of Whithorn and the tenants of their Glenswinton estate, near Parton, from the sergeants' jurisdiction.[64]

THE COMYNS AND THE BALLIOLS

Alan's hereditary title of Constable passed to his son-in-law, Roger de Quenci, the husband of his eldest daughter Elena,[65] and in spite of the dismantling of the lordship this couple were the recognised leaders of the Gallovidian community. Yet it seems they were not popular – perhaps because de Quenci had been too high-handed towards the local people and had ridden roughshod over their native customs and traditions. The general dissatisfaction came to a head in 1246, when he was 'attacked in his castle by his rebellious subjects' and forced to seek help from King Alexander. While the latter was ready enough to come to the assistance of such an important royal servant as de Quenci, he seems to have exacted a price. For the fact that de Quenci's death in 1264 coincided with the appointment of his son-in-law, Alexander Comyn, earl of Buchan, as sheriff of Wigtown suggests that he may have been required to give a deferred surrender of certain of his judicial powers which would become operative on his death. Following his restoration by Alexander, de Quenci continued to play an important political role, being the principal agent of Henry III's authority in Scotland during Alexander III's minority, while he was also responsible for acting as mediator between the rival Comyn and Durward factions in 1257.[66]

The Comyns prevailed, and as part of their strategy for consolidating their authority they secured the appointment of one of their leaders, John Comyn, lord of Badenoch, as justiciar of Galloway on the death of his uncle, Walter Comyn, earl of Menteith, in 1258.[67] It seems that in addition to being justiciar, the latter had continued to exercise a supervisory role over Galloway following his pacification of the province,[68] because he was accused by the English of giving sanctuary there to the de Marisco (Marsh) brothers[69] who had been outlawed by Henry III and had taken to a life of piracy in the Irish Sea.[70] Earl Walter would almost certainly have been instrumental in arranging the marriage of his half-brother, Alexander Comyn, earl of Buchan, to Elizabeth, the second daughter of Roger and Elena de Quenci, while it is equally likely that Henry III had a hand in the marriages of the other two de Quenci daughters to prominent members of the English baronage,[71] which took place in 1238 and 1242.

Following Roger de Quenci's death, his substantial possessions in England, as well as those in Galloway, were divided between his three daughters, the second one, Elizabeth, being allotted the lands of Cruggleton. This was significant because, being the most prestigious of all the de Quenci possessions in Galloway, they should rightfully have gone to the eldest daughter, Margaret de Ferrars, but the fact that they bypassed her and went to the Comyns instead was doubtless a reflection of their power and influence. It was there that Elizabeth and her husband, Earl Alexander, established their ruling centre[72] and built a new castle, an undertaking which archaeological evidence shows to have been carried out in two stages in the 1260s and 1280s.[73] There was also a practical reason for this, because an attack was imminently expected from the Isle of Man, where Olaf the black's son, Magnus, was king.

This stemmed primarily from the defeat of the Norwegians under their veteran king Haakon IV at Largs in 1263, although the underlying reasons were rooted in the perennially confused political situation on Man. When Olaf the black died in 1237, he was succeeded by his eldest son, Harald, who attempted to consolidate his position by marrying King Haakon's daughter, Cecilia, though without apparent success because they were both beheaded in 1248. Inevitably, this resulted in a disputed succession, and it was only by enlisting Haakon's support and murdering his brother Ragnvald, a rival claimant, that Magnus succeeded in securing the throne. Nevertheless, Haakon's assistance seems to have been conditional on Magnus ackowledging him as overlord of the island, and in that capacity Haakon, following his defeat at Largs, undertook that it would revert to the Scottish crown on Magnus's death. Predictably, Magnus objected – he had not been a party to the agreement, and the undertaking had been given without his consent, and it was for this reason that he was threatening a retaliatory invasion of Scotland.

As this was expected to be launched on the coast of Galloway, Earl Alexander was given responsibility for defending it, and besides building the castle at Cruggleton he also took the precaution of strengthening the defences of Wigtown castle. This seems evident from a record of 1265, which shows forty marks being paid to 'master Peter the mason' for repairing the houses there.[74] Nevertheless, it appears that attempts were made to buy Magnus off by diplomatic means, because the accounts rendered by Earl Alexander as sheriff show a disbursement of money to envoys passing between the kings of Scotland and Man.[75] Although the island was formally annexed to the Scottish crown in 1266, the Scots had still to take physical possession of it, because in 1275 a royal expedition was dispatched there under the justiciar, John Comyn, lord of Badenoch.[76]

While the Comyns were establishing themselves as the *de facto* rulers of Wigtownshire, Dervorguilla was emerging as the supreme power in eastern Galloway, and following the deaths of Elena and Roger de Quenci she was regarded as the principal representative of Alan and his predecessors. Her real name Derbhforgoil was Irish, meaning 'of very high lineage', but it is by her anglicised name that she remains one of the best-known personalities in the history of Galloway. Hitherto, she was of comparatively minor importance there, because being the youngest daughter she ranked behind her sisters, having on that account being given the poorest lands, while she was also downgraded on account of her husband's inferior rank compared with her sisters' husbands.

Initially, she established her *caput* at Arsbotel on Loch Ken, and it was not until the 1250s that she moved it to Buittle. By this time she had fallen heir to a huge access of lands in England as well as in Scotland,[77] and reflecting her growing power and prestige she developed the structure built there by Roland or Alan between 1190 and 1210 into a symbol of her enhanced status in Galloway.[78] Excavations now in progress show that she enlarged it on an extravagant scale, adding a large bailey which was connected to the castle by a drawbridge.[79] Because Buittle was approachable by sea, the settlement which grew up round it developed into a flourishing community, and was eventually constituted a burgh.

Dervorguilla appears to have been regarded as a paragon by her contemporaries, and writing more than a century later, Wyntoun pronounced that 'a bettyr lady than scho [she] was ther nane in al the ile of Mare Bretagne'.[80] This was perhaps a tribute above all to her generosity to the Church. For, along with her husband, she founded a Franciscan friary at Oxford, as well as a Dominican house at Wigtown in the 1260s, to which Alexander III contributed a portion of the burgh's customs.[81] It was on her initiative, too, that at much the same time a Franciscan house was established at Dumfries, which would be the scene of her grandson John Comyn's murder some forty years later.

The most famous of Dervorguilla's foundations in Galloway is the abbey of St Mary of the Sweet Heart, and it was here that her husband John Balliol's embalmed heart is traditionally supposed to be buried. Situated at present-day New Abbey, and now known as Sweetheart Abbey, this was a Cistercian house which was endowed primarily for the souls of Dervorguilla herself and her husband, though her children, her ancestors and all the kings of Scotland were included in its foundation charter.[82] The abbey was completed, or at least habitable, by 1273, and its initial endowment included much of the parish of Lochkindeloch (now New Abbey), some lands in the parish of Kirkpatrick Durham, and the patronage of the churches of Crossmichael, Buittle and Kirkcolm in the Rhinns.[83] Although not recorded, it would also have included access to materials for repair and maintenance purposes, and in particular the right to quarry building stone on the opposite side of the Nith estuary.

Outside Galloway, the most enduring, and certainly the most creative, monument to Dervorguilla's charity is Balliol College, Oxford. According to legend, it originated from a penance imposed on John Balliol to provide lodgings and a weekly stipend for poor students in satisfaction for an assault perpetrated by his retainers on the bishop of Durham. The college itself is thought to have been founded sometime between 1263 and John's death in 1269, and thereafter Dervorguilla assumed the role of patroness, giving it financial support and endowing it with extensive lands in Northumberland, as well as property in Oxford itself. One of the oldest and most prestigious colleges there, its obligation to pray for the souls of Dervorguilla and her husband was observed until the Reformation, and even today a special Bidding Prayer is regularly offered, containing a grateful recognition of 'the liberality of John Balliol and Dervorguilla his wife our pious benefactors'.[84]

Closer to home, Dervorguilla is thought to have been responsible for the erection of a wooden bridge over the Nith at Dumfries. Mundane in comparison with the glories of Balliol College or Sweetheart, its practical value was inestimable. At that time the sea penetrated further inland, with correspondingly higher tides which frequently rendered the Nith unfordable, so the bridge provided a vital link between Galloway and the outside world. Although Margaret, duchess of Touraine, the widow of the fourth earl of Douglas, replaced it with a stone bridge in the 1430s, it is still known by its original name of Dervorguilla's bridge. She survived her husband for many years and died in January 1290 at the age of about seventy six,[85] having lived long enough to see her youngest and only surviving son, John, become the principal claimant to the Scottish throne, though fortunately she was spared witnessing his downfall and the ultimate forfeiture of all her ancestral estates in Scotland to the crown.

NOTES

1. He always gave this title precedence over that of lord of Galloway in his charters (Stringer, 'Periphery and core', 101).
2. *Ibid.*, 82.
3. *Roger de Howden: William of Newburgh*, lib. iv, c. 14. Arthur was the son of John's elder brother, the now-deceased Geoffrey Plantagenet.
4. Poole, *Doomsday Book to Magna Carta*, 429–30.
5. *Ibid.*, 382.
6. Hugh de Lacy was given the lordship of Ulster, while the other trouble-shooters included his brother, Walter, lord of Meath, and William Marshal, earl of Pembroke.
7. Ashley, *King John*, 111.
8. Poole, *Doomsday Book to Magna Carta*, 315.
9. Ashley, *King John*, 111.
10. *Bower* 4, p 463.
11. *Ibid.*
12. Brooke, *Wild Men*, 131.
13. Stringer, 'Periphery and Core', 89.
14. *Bower* 4, 471.
15. He was Alexander's brother-in-law, as his wife was an illegitimate daughter of King William.
16. *Chron. Man*, Stevenson, v, pt. I, 390 et seq.
17. *Ibid.*
18. Saga of Hacon.
19. *Chron Man*: Anderson, *Early Sources*, 465–6.
20. *Ibid.*
21. Stringer, 'Periphery and core'.
22. Stringer, 'A new wife for Alan of Galloway'.
23. Cowan and Easson, *Medieval Religious Houses*, 103. This was one of the churches whose patronage was given by Uchtred to Holyrood.
24. *RRS* ii, no 489.
25. Hill, *Whithorn*, 56.
26. Stringer, 'Periphery and core', 83–4: Oram, 'A family business?', 134–5.

27. Dr Oram has tentatively expressed this view in course of conversation.
28. Dr Oram concludes that there were two separate families of de Kyrkonnel, and that whereas one possessed Kirkconnel, the other owned nearby Mabie. The latter subsequently disappear from the records, and Mabie passed to the Durand family – hence, possibly, the name Kirkpatrick Durham.
29. This estate has recently been put up for sale.
30. *CDS* ii, 212–4.
31. Hence, probably, the name Roberton.
32. Barrow, *The Anglo-Norman Era*, 113.
33. The information concerning the de Champaign family is based on Reid, *Wig Charters*, xvii, conversation with Dr Oram, and Oram, *Lordship of Galloway*.
34. Disc. Brooke, *Wild Men*,134.
35. *Matthew Paris*: Anderson, *Early Sources* 500–1.
36. *Fordun* ii, 286.
37. *Ibid.*: *Bower* 5, p 151.
38. The saga is described in Ashley, 'Odo, elect of Whithorn 1235', and Oram, 'In Obedience and Reverence', 96–8, and 'Heirs to Ninian', 61–3.
39. This was demonstrated following Gilbert's death in 1253, when the regency council, acting for Alexander III then a minor, appointed Henry of Holyrood as his successor. His election was challenged by Dervorguilla's husband, John Balliol, who claimed to be defending the rights of the people of Galloway, but he was overruled (Ash, 'The Church in the reign of Alexander III', 41).
40. Barrow, *Kingship and Unity*, 115.
41. This story is told by Bower (5, p 151). But on his testimony (5, p 85) the same incident occurred in the course of a raid on Holm Cultram during Alexander's invasion of England in 1215, when a dying monk was also stripped of his clothing. On that occasion he and his captors were accidentally drowned in the river Eden. So, either this was standard practice or Bower was simply repeating the story in another context.
42. Oram, 'Heirs to Ninian', 63.
43. *Bower* 5, p 151.
44. *Ibid.*
45. *Wig Charters*, xxxix.
46. The division of the lordship between Alan's daughters is discussed in Oram, 'Dervorgilla, the Balliols and Buittle' 167–171, and *Lordship of Galloway*.
47. *CDS* ii, no. 1541.
48. 'Brevis Descriptio Regni Scotie'. This describes Kirkcudbright as the property of Margaret de Ferrars' son, William (Oram, *Lordship of Galloway*).
49. This is evident from the fact that in an inquest of 1296 her daughter Elena la Zouche is recorded as owning a third part of the 'vill of Girtun', and also land at Senwick (*CDS* 1884. 216. no 824).
50. *CDS* ii, no 824 pt 4.
51. So was her portion of the former de Morville lands, but those she inherited from her mother's family went wholly to Dervorguilla.
52. *CDS* ii, no. 1541.
53. Oram, *Lordship of Galloway*.
54. *CSSR*, i, 200.
55. *RMS* i, app I, 912.
56. *Ibid.*, no 913.
57. *Ibid.*, no 914.
58. MacQueen, 'The Kin of Kennedy', 285.

59. *RMS* i, app 1, no 982.

60. MacQueen, 'The Kin of Kennedy', 285.

61. *RRS* ii, no 374.

62. *Wig Charters*, xxxv.

63. *RMS* i, app 1 no 59.

64. *Ibid.*, no 20.

65. *RRS* iii, no 274. On Roger de Quenci's death, the office passed to his eldest daughter, Margaret de Ferrars. In about 1275, she resigned it to her brother-in-law, Alexander Comyn, earl of Buchan, whose family retained it until forfeited by King Robert I (see Oram, 'Dervorgilla, the Balliols and Buittle', 171).

66. Young, *Comyns*, 57.

67. *RRS* ii, p 45.

68. Barrow, *Kingdom of the Scots*, 107.

69. They may have been given lands in Galloway, but as their name does not feature in any charters there is no certainty about this.

70. Powicke, *Henry III*, 744.

71. The elder, Margaret, was married to William de Ferrars, earl of Derby, while the youngest, Elena, was the wife of Sir Alan la Zouche. All three daughters left a number of descendants, which would complicate the title to the former de Quenci lands in Galloway during the fourteenth century.

72. Oram, *Lordship of Galloway* (quoting *CDS*, ii, no. 616 for its possession in 1292 by his son Earl John).

73. Truckell and Williams, 'Medieval pottery', 133.

74. *ER* i, 31.

75. *Ibid.*, 22.

76. Young, *Comyns*, 79, 149.

77. Following Christina's death, she acquired much of her lands in Galloway and elsewhere, while she became entitled to all the lands which Christina had inherited from their mother. In addition, she inherited a portion of those belonging to her childless uncle, John earl of Huntingdon, (which included those of his father Earl David and his mother, the heiress of the earls of Chester), while Christina's share also fell to her.

78. Oram, 'Dervorgilla, the Balliols and Buittle', 174–6.

79. Discussion with A.I.N. Penman, Director of excavations at Buittle.

80. *Wyntoun* v, 262.

81. McKerlie, i, 331.

82. Laing, *Charters*, 46.

83. McKerrow, 'Sweetheart Abbey'.

84. I am grateful to Dr. John Jones, Dean and Archivist of Balliol College, for this information.

85. So says McKerlie (iii, 236), which could be about right considering she was the second or third child of her parents who were married in 1209.

10

FRAGILE PROSPERITY

AN ERA OF PEACE

Galloway's incorporation into the Scottish realm heralded an era of peace
and relative prosperity which would last for upwards of than half a century.
This was mainly due to the firm rule of Alexander II and his son Alexander
III, though an Act of Parliament passed during the latter's minority ordering people not to 'truble othir mennis lands'[1] suggests some sporadic
outbreaks of unrest. Both kings maintained friendly relations with their
English counterparts, Henry III and Edward I, cemented by the marriages
of Alexander II to Henry's sister, and Alexander III to his daughter. Thus,
the prevailing peace between the two countries meant that merchants
could expand their trading contacts with the Continent without fear of
attack, while farmers could sow their crops in the confidence of being able
to harvest them without the threat of human interference.

The generally favourable climate which prevailed at that time[2] allowed
for increasing productivity, and with the consequent expansion of the
population an increasing amount of land was taken into cultivation. A
growing population had been a feature of north-west Europe generally
since the beginning of the second millennium, and by 1300 that of both
England and France was higher than it had ever been before,[3] and this
would doubtless have applied in the case of the more fertile parts of
Galloway. Nevertheless, recurrent spells of bad weather caused periodic
setbacks. For the chroniclers speak of 'great, dreadful and long' frosts, high
rainfall, severe gales, and 'a great corruption of the air', while Bower tells
us with perhaps a touch of hyperbole that in 1260 'dreadful claps of
thunder were heard' and 'terrifying flashes of lightning burned up men in
the fields and animals far and wide'.[4]

There is also possible evidence of recurrent grain shortages, because
Henry III was periodically obliged to authorise his justiciar in Ireland to sell
'corn, meal, and other necessary victuals' to the abbot and monks of
Glenluce,[5] though this could have been a reflection of Glenluce's under-
endowment with arable land and an over-dependence on sheep. Similarly,
the fact that Dundrennan was issued with permits to buy grain from

England and Ireland during the 1260s could have resulted from an over-emphasis on sheep at the expense of bringing land into cultivation.

Bad years, such as those described by the chroniclers, would have had a calamitous effect on a people living close to subsistence level. But, judging from the contemporary statutes which were designed to increase production in order to feed a growing population, their effects can only have been transitory since numbers continued to grow. For example, an Act of 1209 encouraged farmers to switch from pastoral to arable farming, and took them to task for 'wasting their lands and the country with a multitude of sheep and beasts, thereby troubling God's people with scarcity, poverty and utter hardship'.[6] Another Act of 1214 was more specific. This compelled the owners of livestock to cultivate more land, while stipulating that ploughing was to begin not later than fifteen days before the feast of the Purification[7] (18 January). However, the dearth of similar statutes during the 1300s reflects the population decline resulting from the wars of that time, and it was not until later, when numbers had recovered, that there is evidence of further legislation on the subject.

LAND IMPROVEMENT

Demand for increased production provided a stimulus for land improvement, and there is ample evidence of this on ecclesiastical estates – and doubtless secular ones as well – during the twelfth and thirteenth centuries. This has been attributed above all to the Cistercian monks, since their houses were sited in the remoter regions where there was more scope for it. Their rule forced it on them as well, because it denied them access to other sources of income, such as rents and revenues from appropriated churches, which were available to their sister orders; so they were compelled to rely on farming to maintain their establishments. As they were forbidden to employ outside labour, the monks had to work the land themselves – a task for which their aristocratic background rendered them ill-fitted.

The unrealism of this precept soon became apparent, and even as early as the twelfth century the order was recruiting lay brothers to undertake the farm work. Although these lesser monks were obliged to conform to the monastic rule, they lived apart from the regular brethren, and their sole *raison d'être* was to allow the latter to devote more time to prayer and religious observance. That at least was the theory, but in reality it gave the more enterprising monks the opportunity to engage in commercial activities, while others simply lapsed into indolence. Shortage of accommodation limited the number of lay brothers who could be admitted and, as the scope of their farming operations expanded, the regular monks increasingly employed peasant labour to do the farm work and carry out improvement schemes.

Outlying lands, on the other hand, were either leased to peasant tenants – as Melrose had been doing ever since its foundation in 1136[8] – or they were run as granges and, as we have seen, this was how Holm Cultram managed its lands at Kirkgunzeon, and Dundrennan theirs at Kirkpatrick Durham. The land improvements carried out by the Cistercian houses in Galloway are particularly evident at Kirkgunzeon, where the monks of Holm Cultram were responsible for draining and bringing into cultivation much of the low-lying land there, while a core sample taken from Torrs Warren on the Luce Sands[9] suggests that those at Glenluce were engaged in much the same activity. This shows the dune lands there being under grass during the middle years of the thirteenth century, so the monks were obviously reclaiming this barren stretch of land to bring it into permanent pasture. Also, the remains of wooden stakes preserved in the mud adjacent to nearby Stairhaven indicate mussel culture as another of their enterprises.

The Cistercians were renowned above all for their expertise in sheep farming, and the lay brother responsible for them was known as the 'storemaster'. It was a demanding task, since careful management was essential to prevent stock losses, as well as to ensure a good lamb crop and to guard against disease. Traditionally, the sheep were summered on the upland pastures while the arable ground was under crop, and the shepherds lived in primitive bothies which served as sheilings. For example, Dundrennan had exclusive rights to summer their sheep on part of the hill ground of Screel and Bengairn, the remainder being shared between the tenants of the neighbouring estates of Kelton, Gelston and Buittle.[10] In the autumn, the sheep were brought down to the arable ground to be folded on to the stubble, where they broke up the mat of weed undergrowth, while their dung provided fertility for the following year's cereal crop.

The need to guard against disease was overwhelming because it was rampant, one of the most virulent being 'pilsought' or 'pluk' (probably sheep scab) which is thought to have resulted from overstocking.[11] A particularly serious outbreak during the late thirteenth century is believed to have resulted from the import of an infected batch of Spanish sheep into England in 1274. Its rapid spread was attributed to hoar frost, and as a precaution the sheep were penned up in their enclosures during the winter and only allowed out after the sun had melted the ground. Nevertheless, the disease continued to spread – to the extent that by the 1290s the export of wool and skins from the Border abbeys had dropped to a sixth of its former total. Drastic measures were needed to contain the situation, so King John Balliol ordered his sheriffs to place an embargo on the movement of all stock, to hold an inquest into each reported outbreak, and to slaughter all infected stock.[12] Predation was another problem, and a number of abbey charters imposed an obligation on their moorland tenants to keep 'a couple of good sleuth hounds for fox and wolf, and to be ready at all times when we charge them to hunt with us'.[13]

Most monasteries engaged in cattle rearing as well, and this was particularly evident in Galloway. Melrose is known to have run them on their lands at Dunscore, because the records speak of their acquiring stopover grazing rights in Nithsdale.[14] The local climate and the consequent abundance of grass was the incentive, and so too was its accessibility to the traditional cattle markets in England. The trade with these centres is evident from the name Galgate near Lancaster, which was named from a twelfth-century road running past Kendal called Galwaithgate, meaning 'Galway road'[15] and is believed to refer to its use by cattle drovers from Galloway.[16]

Responsibility for superintending the cattle was delegated to another lay brother, the *studarius*, and he too had to contend with regular outbreaks of disease. A particularly serious one, which was rampant in Scotland in about 1270, was 'lungessouth',[17] being, as its name implies, a form of lung disease.[18] That cattle stealing was rife is evident from an Act of 1175 which stipulated that all animals exposed for sale had to be accompanied by a 'lauchful borch of hamehald',[19] a form of certificate confirming that they were the lawful property of the seller. Regrettably, ill-treatment of stock seems to have been common practice, as an Act of Parliament refers to the 'spoliation of certane oxin and putting furth their ene' (gouging out their eyes),[20] so it is hardly surprising that a contemporary chronicler described how 'they flie the cumpanie or syght of men'.[21]

The demands of the north European cloth manufacturers accounted in particular for the Cistercians' preoccupation with sheep farming. This long-established market had greatly expanded over the last two centuries, and by the late 1100s the religious houses in Scotland were sending regular shipments of wool to the Continent.[22] However, as Scottish wool was coarser, and therefore regarded as inferior to English wool, the dealers lowered their prices accordingly. This encouraged Scottish sheep farmers, particularly the Cistercians, to breed an animal with a better fleece quality, and their success is evident from the lucrative trade that developed with the merchants of Florence and Venice.

One of them, Francisco Pegolotti, kept a record of his wool purchases from the principal Scottish abbeys at the end of the thirteenth century which still survives. His suppliers included Dundrennan and Glenluce,[23] and judging from his purchases it appears that they both maintained a flock of some 3,750 sheep,[24] though the true figure would have been substantially higher, since part of the woolcrop would have been retained for domestic purposes. Although Sweetheart does not feature in this merchant's records, the *quantum* of its claim against the English crown in the early fourteenth century for wool seized suggests that it ran a flock of some 2,000 sheep.[25]

Initially, the monastic houses were limited to selling their wool to itinerant merchants like Pegolotti, but the drawback was that they invariably discounted the price to allow themselves a commercial profit on its resale to the manufacturers. Also, the Cistercians were under the additional disadvantage of being forbidden by their rule from forward-selling their woolcrop to protect themselves against fluctuations in the market. However, this was relaxed – or simply flouted – as the monks began to sell a specified quantity of wool on a three-, five-, or even ten-year contract.[26] This assumed they could meet their commitment, but if not they had to make up the shortfall by purchasing wool, known as the 'collect', from local farmers and landowners.[27] This eventually became the rule, and the monks regularly contracted with these suppliers to buy their annual woolclip, generally at bargain prices, and resold it to the merchants for a substantial profit. Thus they became primarily dealers in wool, and in the heady days of the booming wool market this was a highly lucrative business.

This encouraged the more enterprising houses to go a stage further by acquiring their own ships to take their wool direct to the markets, thus cutting out the merchants. Dundrennan was a case in point, as there is record of its trading with both England and Ireland during the late 1200s. For example, letters of safe conduct were granted to its representatives in 1266 permitting them to sell wool and other goods in England and to buy grain in return.[28] Similarly, in the following year a further permit was issued allowing the monks to purchase up to 240 'crannocks' of wheat, and as much oats, meal and wine as were required, from Dublin and Drogheda, this being reconfirmed in 1280.[29]

ECCLESIASTICAL WEALTH

The growing wealth of the Church was mainly derived from the revenues of appropriated churches, but because the Cistercians were initially forbidden by their rule from accepting such gifts, they were denied this source of income. However, judging from the fact that two churches were included in Sweetheart's endowment, and that in 1307/8 it petitioned Edward II for the gift of the church at Wigtown in compensation for war damage,[30] it seems that the prohibition was waived. These appropriations required the consent of the diocesan bishop, and while most were prepared to sanction them without demur, the more responsible would only do so on condition that an adequate provision was made for the vicar. For example, when Bishop Gilbert, Alexander II's nominee at Whithorn, confirmed the appropriation of the revenues of Borgue church to Dryburgh abbey he insisted that the vicar be paid a stipend of ten marks of silver and given a glebe of six acres of arable and one of meadowland.[31]

As the majority of bishops were less assiduous, it frequently resulted in vicars being under-remunerated, and that this was already becoming a scandal by the beginning of the thirteenth century is evident from a decree issued during the reign of King William. This ordained that the teind income of the religious institutions was to be used 'for the proper remuneration of the parish incumbents and the payment of the dues levied by diocesan bishops'. Similarly, a decree of the fourth Lateran Council of 1215 stated that 'a vicious custom that must be extirpated has grown up in certain parts where the patrons of parish churches, and certain other persons, claiming the profits for themselves leave to the priests deputed to the service of them such a scanty portion that from it they cannot suitably be sustained'. This went on to stipulate that vicars should 'have a fit portion of the profits of the church'.[32]

The obligation to pay teind was a heavy burden on farmers and landholders, as it represented a significant portion of their produce. While the principle behind it – sedulously promoted by churchmen – that as God was responsible for the annual increase in stock and crops, it was fitting to render a portion to the Church as his earthly representative, may have been accepted, the method of collection was widely resented. This could involve considerable inconvenience and frustration, and nowhere was it more apparent than in the case of harvested crops, where the teindholder had physically to remove his one-tenth share before the remainder could be gathered. Consequently, precious opportunities to take advantage of a spell of fine weather to snatch a crop could be lost through failure of the teindholder or his representative to attend when required.

Another imposition on farmers was the landowners' right of thirlage and the obligation to pay multures, and the method of levying these, not to mention the sharp practices involved, was the source of widespread resentment. Thirlage was the right of landowners, ecclesiastical as well as secular, to compel their tenants to have their grain ground at their own mill. It originated from a well-intentioned desire on the part of landowners to spare their tenants the laborious task of grinding their grain with hand querns by constructing water-powered mills to mechanise the process. In order to recoup the cost, they 'thirled' their tenants to the mill, meaning they monopolised the right to grind their grain, and the charge imposed for this was known as the 'multure'. Landowners soon made a practice of contracting out these mills, and their attaching thirlage rights, to millers in return for an annual rent, and an example in Galloway was the lease of the mill at Buittle to Gilbert Gilbertson, a prominent local husbandman.[33]

The millers, being naturally concerned to maximise the return on their investment, invariably raised the multures to extortionate levels. Worse still, if the mill lade was frozen, or if there was insufficient water to drive it, or it was out of action for any other reason, the tenants were still liable to render the miller his multures, despite having to pay for their corn to be ground elsewhere. Understandably, millers were habitually unpopular members of their community, being consistently vilified by the 'suckeners' (tenants thirled to a mill) who regarded them as cheats and parasites.[34]

By the end of the thirteenth century the larger abbeys had become extremely wealthy insitutions. They were profiting enormously from the booming wool trade, while their appropriated churches represented a growing source of income, and this was supplemented by the revenues derived from contracting out their thirlage rights, and other incidentals, such as charges for using their bakehouses and brewhouses. Consequently, there was a growing tendency for monks to relax their efforts, and because farming was both time-consuming and labour-demanding they began progressively to scale down their enterprises and lease out the land instead. Although perhaps less profitable, it at least assured them a steady, trouble-free rental income,[35] and moreover they were insulated from the effects of bad weather, disease, and all the other hazards which farmers have to contend with. The result was that, while prayer and religious observance continued to be integral to thirteenth-century monasticism, the regular monks were unquestionably becoming 'well-fed, comfortable, and in many ways complacent'.[36]

The Church's increasing secularism and lack of responsiveness to the spiritual needs of the people was primarily accountable for the emergence of the friars. Their object was to bring the Christian message to the common people by living among them and – initially at any rate – subsisting on their charity. Thus, they fulfilled a need that was becoming steadily more apparent as the religious houses were progressively abdicating their spiritual responsibilities. The friars originated in Italy during the early thirteenth century, where a number of different orders were founded, and they first arrived in Scotland during the reign of Alexander II. He founded a number of institutions for the Dominicans and Franciscans, but it was not until later that friaries were established in Galloway. The main benefactor there was Dervorguilla, who founded a convent for the Dominican friars at Wigtown, and another for the Franciscans or Grey Friars in Dumfries. Later, the Grey Friars acquired an establishment at Kirkcudbright,[37] and their presence there survives in the name of its episcopal church.

A CHANGING SOCIAL STRUCTURE

Contemporary evidence from elsewhere in lowland Scotland helps to shed some light on the prevailing social structure in Galloway. This consisted of clearly-defined grades, ranging from the nobility down to small-time landholders, on the one hand, and the vastly more numerous peasantry on the other. As most records deal with land transactions, much more is

known about the upper ranks of society, whereas information about the rest
is mainly derived from incidental references in charters, Acts of Parliament,
and other surviving documents. Nevertheless, it appears that, broadly
speaking, the free peasantry consisted of husbandmen (so-called because
they dwelt in a house) and cottars who inhabited a meaner type of dwelling
known as a 'cot',[38] which was basically a stone and turf hut.[39] Both were
small-time farmers who occupied their holdings in return for providing
their landlord with a specified amount of labour service and – when
occasion demanded – military service.[40] The main difference was that,
whereas the cottar performed labour service himself, the husbandman,
who tended to farm on a larger scale and was frequently an employer of
labour, would delegate it to his men. Labour service was almost universal
during the thirteenth century, though it seems that the practice of
commuting it – or at least part of it – into a monetary payment was
becoming increasingly evident.

The unfree-men included bondmen,[41] who were 'astricted' to the land
where they lived and worked – or *ascripti glebae* as it was officially termed,
meaning they were forbidden to leave it without their lord's consent.
Anyone who did so was liable to be seized and forcibly returned to the land
where he belonged, unless he managed to remain at large for more than a
year and a day, in which case he automatically obtained his freedom.
Furthermore, these people were transmissible with the land as an attaching
pertinent in the event of a change of ownership. However, they were not
slaves in the accepted sense of the term, as some possessed means of their
own,[42] while it was also open to them to improve their lot by acquiring the
lease of a small portion of ground, and thus join the ranks of the cottars. In
fact, this was probably becoming the rule, as the evidence points to a gradual
decline in the number of bondmen during the later thirteenth century.[43]

At the lowest end of the social scale were the serfs. They had no rights
in law, and hence no property rights, and they and their families belonged
to their master who could sell or transfer them to another owner at will.
Nevertheless, in certain circumstances they could become free labourers,
and for the ambitious the most common means of self-advancement was to
acquire the lease of a small portion of ground under a 'steelbow' arrangement.[44] In such cases the landlord would provide them with the necessary
equipment in the form of stock, seed and implements to give them a start.
However, in common with bondmen, their numbers declined during the
1200s, and because of the shortage of manpower resulting from the wars of
the following century this continued at an accelerating rate, to the extent
that by the mid-1300s serfdom had disappeared altogether in Scotland.

The husbandmen mainly owed their existence to the changes taking
place in the landowners' approach to their estates. Traditionally, land was
held in common by families or kindreds, but during the twelfth and

thirteenth centuries this form of tenure was giving place to the Norman-ised, land-based feudalism. As theirs was primarily a militaristic society, the new landowners tended to farm out the management of their estates to agents in return for a render in kind,[45] and from this there developed the system of leasehold tenure, the agents being the forerunners of the husbandmen.[46] Yet, there are many instances of landowners, both secular as well as ecclesiastical, acquiring leases of additional lands, and a statute passed in Alexander II's reign makes a clear distinction between knightly tenants, on the one hand, and 'malaris of carls born and thai that ar of foul kyn' (tenants of low birth) on the other.[47]

Occupiers held their lands at the will of the landowner; they had no security of tenure and were liable to summary eviction without notice, or on a change in the ownership of the land. Judging from the terms of a petition presented to Edward I in 1304, the occupiers' lack of security was a source of widespread discontent. This was submitted on behalf of the 'poor husbandmen of the King in Scotland' and craved him to allow them greater security of tenure 'so that they shall no longer hold their land, as hitherto, from one year to the next'. However, it seems to have been ignored and the situation remained unaltered until later in the century, when a dearth of prospective tenants forced landowners to become more accommodating.

CONTEMPORARY FARMING PRACTICES

Available evidence suggests that the concept of the 'ferme-touns', i.e. small communities of peasant farmers holding their lands under multiple tenancies, which would be a feature of the Middle Ages, was not yet fully developed.[48] Nor was the 'infield' and 'outfield' system, which was to become the conventional method of farming, though it was customary for landowners to allow farmers a licence to graze their stock on the less fertile common land. Many enjoyed other easements, such as a right to cut peats on the hill ground where they summered their livestock, as well as permission to gather firewood from neighbouring forests.

Unlike English forests, many of the Scottish ones comprised tracts of barren and rugged country, and those in Galloway were a mix of both, the forest of Buchan for example, which stretched from the Cree towards the upper Glenkens, consisting of some of the wildest country in the south-west. On the other hand, the forest extending from Dalbeattie towards Kirkbean consisted exclusively of woodland, and so too did that of Dalquhairn. This covered much of the lower Cluden valley in the parish of Irongray, and as it became the preserve of the incumbents of Glasgow it was later known as the bishops' forest. Hunting rights were jealously guarded, and those contravening them were liable to severe penalties.

The forests also carried lesser rights, such as pannage, and also warren rights which included a licence to pursue and control lesser game like rabbits, and these were generally leased to neighbouring farmers. The right of pannage – the grazing of pigs in the woods during the acorn crop in the autumn – was much sought after, as pig-keeping was traditionally an important form of husbandry in Galloway until they were displaced by sheep. Evidence of this is apparent from a record in the 1180s of pig herds of up to five hundred head being allowed to graze in the demesne woods of the lords of Galloway, which were adjacent to the lands belonging to Holm Cultram at Kirkgunzeon.[49]

Farming was a demanding occupation, since it involved heavy and unremitting physical labour. Although multiple tenancies were still a rarity, neighbourly co-operation was necessary, particularly at the busiest times of the year. Ploughing, for example, required teamwork, as it was generally beyond the capacity of a small tenant to do this effectively on his own. The conventional plough was a single-share implement drawn by oxen, though a larger type was being used in the Lothians and the Merse of Tweed. The seed was broadcast by hand before being harrowed into the ground with a whin or piece of thorn tied to an ox's tail, and once the corn began to grow a constant watch had to be maintained in order to frighten off birds and rodents. When ripe it was cut with a sickle or scythe, bound into sheaves, and propped up in stooks to allow it to dry out, though sometimes this never happened and the corn simply sprouted in the stooks. Once dry the grain was separated from the stalks by thrashing it with flails, and thereafter it was ground at the landlord's mill.

While yields were primarily weather-dependant, they were frequently reduced by weed infestation. A particularly obnoxious one was corn marigold, or 'gool', whose ubiquity was due to its tolerance of acid soil, which was a feature of much of contemporary Scotland. Although colour-ful when in full flower, it choked the crops, while its succulent stem prevented the grain from drying out properly, and at its most destructive it is believed to have reduced output to as little as a tenth of the normal yield.[50] Therefore, many landowners frequently employed 'gool riders' to check their tenants' crops for the presence of the weed, those failing to eradicate it being punished,[51] and in addition they were liable to a statutory fine of one sheep.[52]

Notwithstanding the unsophisticated farming techniques, the ravages of weeds and pests, and the uncertain weather, the indications are that by the end of the thirteenth century most estates in Galloway – and elsewhere in Scotland – were yielding an abundant surplus. This is apparent from the wardrobe accounts of Edward I, which show the corn grown in Galloway as being sufficient to feed his occupying troops there, as well as the local population. In fact its abundance was such that it swamped local milling capacity, and shipments of grain were regularly sent to Skinburness in Cumberland, and even as far afield as Dublin, to be ground and re-exported to Galloway as meal.

THE BURGHS

Towns have existed in Scotland since time immemorial, but they were essentially settlements which developed in the immediate vicinity of the traditional markets, and were mainly confined to the east coast. The burghs represented a further stage in their development, in that they were clearly defined entities with statutory rights, privileges and obligations, as well as having their own laws. Having seen the contribution they made to the development of trade and commerce in England, and the revenues in terms of rents, tolls and taxes which they yielded to the crown, David I introduced the concept to Scotland by officially designating certain existing towns as royal burghs. William I and Alexander II followed suit by similarly designating most of the major seaports and market towns, as well as the ruling centres of sheriffdoms, including Dumfries which is tradi-tionally thought to have been constituted a royal burgh in 1186.

Also, some ecclesiastical and secular landowners designated the settlements that grew up round their castles as burghs of barony. The object was to monopolise local trade and to levy dues on it as a source of income, in much the same way as the royal burghs provided revenues for the crown. An example in Galloway was the settlement round Walter de Berkeley's *caput* at the Mote of Urr which was formally constituted a burgh of barony, and so too at a later date was Buittle, while another was established at Innermessan, near Stranraer, though none of them survived beyond the fourteenth century.

The most prosperous medieval burghs in Galloway grew up around its major seaports, Kirkcudbright being the principal example in eastern Galloway, while Wigtown and Whithorn vied for supremacy in the west. The indications are that Kirkcudbright owed its burghal status to the lords of Galloway – possibly Alan, as the earliest record of this is in 1237 when one Erkin, a merchant burgess, was licensed to go to Dublin, where he also held burgess status, in order to buy goods for Roger de Quenci.[53] Wigtown's origins, on the other hand, are wrapped in uncertainty, because although it was granted a crown charter in 1457 it is more likely to have been founded in the reign of Alexander III, when a sheriffdom was first established there; but, because there is no proof of this, Whithorn has invariably claimed to be the older. Current excavations there show it as continuing to be a thriving industrial centre,[54] though comb production, which had been a major source of revenue to the community in the past, ceased when the forest laws introduced during William I's reign imposed severe restrictions on deer-hunting, thus cutting off the supply of antlers which served as the raw material.[55]

Locally-produced wool, hides and skins were exported through these seaports in exchange for imported luxuries, such as wine, spices, salt and fine cloth from Flanders and Italy, though these were the perquisite of the baronage. Galloway was renowned in particular for its native horses, which took their name from the region and were widely prized for their sure-footedness, their reputation being such that Shakespeare used them as an analogy for hardiness.[56] The international dimension of Galloway's trade is evident from the early fourteenth-century hoard of coins discovered at Kirkcudbright. This consisted of eighty-four pieces – one Scottish and seven English, while the remainder came from the Low Countries,[57] and is a clear indication of the trading links that existed between Galloway and that part of the world.

During the thirteenth century the burghs developed an elaborate structure of civic administration,[58] where the 'better, more discreet, and more trustworthy'[59] of the indwellers were elected to form a ruling council, and they in turn appointed the provost and baillies. Similarly, the social hierarchy within the burghs, and the rights and duties of the officials responsible for their administration, became more clearly defined and were given statutory force. Burghs were also granted important privileges, such as the monopoly of local trade and a right to hold regular fairs, an example being Edward Bruce's grant to Whithorn of the right to hold a market there on certain stated occasions.[60] Their trading monopoly was a valuable concession, since it frequently embraced the surrounding district, as well as including a long stretch of coastline – Kirkcudbright, for example, controlling the section from the Nith to the Cree, and Wigtown from there to the Ayrshire border.

The council's judicial resposibilities were exercised by the burgh court, which dealt with all civil and criminal cases falling within its jurisdiction and while the latter excluded the four pleas of the crown, the court still had power to impose the death penalty. Trial was normally by compurgation, where the accused had to establish his innocence by persuading men of standing within the community to testify to his character.[61] The court's civil powers were comprehensive, since they included the regulation of commerce and arbitrating in contractual disputes, as well as supervising trading standards. As these were beyond the scope of feudal law, the burghs developed their own law code which was the forerunner of the mercantile law of today.

Reflecting their superior status, the merchants habitually dominated the burgh's ruling council and as they also controlled its trade, many became extremely wealthy. Their privileged status was inevitably a source of resentment, and some considered it fair game to infringe their monopoly illegally – notably the 'chapmen' who conducted an export trade outside the burghs with such success that they became the target of discriminatory legislation. Similarly 'hucksters' who would waylay country suppliers bringing their produce to the burghs and buy it from them at wholesale prices – or simply appropriate it – in order to retail it themselves.[62] Yet, despite these attempts to interfere with their trade the burghs became so wealthy, and their potential for taxation was such that the burgesses eventually comprised one of the three main constituents (the 'thrie estaitis') of the Scottish Parliament.

Contemporary life

Since bere (or barley) and oats were the crops mainly grown in Galloway, oatmeal in the form of oatcakes, porridge, gruel or brose was the staple diet of the people.[63] Bread was a luxury since it could not be baked properly on the turf or wood fires of the peasantry, while the cost of hiring the landlords' bakehouses was beyond the means of most people, so it was generally confined to the upper classes. The bere crop was used mainly for brewing, and as beer was habitually drunk by all classes[64] it is estimated that as much as a third of the annual production in Scotland was used for this purpose.[65] This monotonous fare was leavened by milk and cheese, since most people kept a cow, and also eggs and poultry. Meat was a rarity, and generally only available in the autumn when the surplus stock was slaughtered; otherwise the only source was the carcases of animals which had died from other causes. Fish was available for those living near a river or the sea, but imported goods were beyond the reach of the peasantry.

The diet of the upper classes was more varied, since they had access to wild game killed or trapped on their estates. They could also afford to garnish their food with spices imported from the Levant, and in springtime these would have been essential for rendering the rotting remains of the salted beef more palatable. Wine was also widely drunk, most of it being imported from Gascony through the principal trading entrepôt of Bordeaux.[66] Yet, all classes were victims of the principal killers of the time – cholera, typhus, plague and influenza, and of those who survived childhood few would live beyond middle age.

Although it became fashionable for the chroniclers who lived through the upheavals of the fourteenth century to portray the reigns of Alexander II and Alexander III as something of a golden age, this was far from the case. True, the upper classes appear to have fared reasonably well, but for the common people life was a constant struggle against nature, and while in good years their diet was probably adequate, and they may even have lived quite well, the spectre of famine was omnipresent. For bad years there were, and if the harvest failed famine almost invariably followed and, as

Bower put it, 'the poor died of their poverty'.[67]

NOTES

1. *APS* i, 60.
2. Lamb, *Climate*, chaps 6 and 7.
3. Duncan, *Scotland*, 309.
4. *Bower* 5, p 325.
5. Morton, 'Glenluce Abbey', 228. The licence was renewed in 1226, 1227 and 1252 (*CDS* i, nos 765, 933, 974, 982, 1889).
6. Grant, *Social and Economic Development*, 98.
7. *APS* i, 67.
8. Correspondence with Dr Oram.
9. Cowie, 'Torrs Warren, Luce Sands'.
10. Conversation with Dr Oram.
11. Duncan, *Scotland*, 421.
12. *Iibid.*
13. Agnew i, 247.
14. *Melrose liber* no. 319.
15. Ekwall, *Dictionary*.
16. Brooke, 'Gall-gaidhil and Galloway', 102.
16. Brooke, *Wild Men*.
17. *Chron. Lanercost*, 85.
18. Duncan, *Scotland*, 421.
19. *APS* i, 373.
20. Haldane, *Drove Roads of Scotland*, 8.
21. *Ibid.*, 7.
22. Duncan, *Scotland*, 428.
23. *Ibid.*, 429, 431.
24. Dodghson *Land and Society*, 127.
25. Correspondence with Dr Oram – the claim itself is recorded in the *CDS*.
26. Duncan, *Scotland*, 428–9.
27. *Ibid.*, 428.
28. *CDS* i, no. 2414.
29. *Ibid.* ii, no. 182.
30. *Wig Charters*, 117: *CSSR* i, 221.
31. Oram, 'Heirs to Ninian', 63–4 (quoting *Dryburgh Liber* no. 66).
32. Duncan, *Scotland*, 301.
33. *Reg Morton.*
34. Symon, *Scottish Farming*, 44–6.
35. Duncan, *Scotland*, 425–6.
36. Croft Dickinson, *Scotland to 1603*, 123.
37. The subject of the friars generally is discussed *ibid*, 123–4.
38. *Ibid*, 89–90: Symon, *Scottish Farming*, 26–8. Their comments relate to Scotland generally and are not specific to Galloway.
39. Duncan refers (*Scotland*, 255) to turf huts dating from this period which have been identified on the Isle of Man.
40. *Ibid.*, 378 et seq.

41. That they existed in Galloway is evident from the reference to *bondi* in a charter confirming Sir Andrew Agnew's appointment as hereditary sheriff of Wigtown (*RMS* ii no. 447).
42. Croft Dickinson, *Scotland*, 89–90.
43. Grant, *Social Development*, 92.
44. Serfdom is discussed in Symon, *Scottish Farming*, 37–40.
45. Duncan, *Scotland*, 392.
46. Grant, *Social Development*, 83.
47. *Ibid.*, 82. The word 'malaris' is derived from 'mails' meaning rents, and therefore they were occupiers of land.
48. Grant implies as much (*Social Development*, 100 et seq), citing a number of examples of the different types of tenure which existed in the remoter parts of the country in later times.
49. *Holm Cultram Reg*, no. 121.
50. Symon, *Scottish Farming*, 23–4.
51. Even as late as the eighteenth century, Grierson of Lag, an estate in the Cairn valley in Dumfriesshire, held special gool courts to punish those of his tenants who allowed it to grow unchecked on the lands.
52. Grant, *Social Development*, 83.
53. *CDS* i, no. 1372.
54. Hill, *Whithorn*, 240 et seq.
55. Grant, *Social Development*, 76.
56. This occurs in Henry IV Part 2, Act II, scene iv where Doll Tearsheet tells Falstaff to thrust the drunken Pistol downstairs, and Pistol retorts angrily, 'Thrust him downstairs! Know we not Galloway nags?'.
57. Duncan, *Scotland*, 519.
58. *Ibid.*, 502.
59. 'Statutes of the merchant guild of Berwick', trans. C Innes in *Ancient Laws: the Scottish Burghs*, vol i, 80–1.
60. *RMS* i, app i, no 20.
61. Grant, *Social Development*, 138.
62. Duncan, *Scotland*, 499.
63. *Ibid.*, 354.
64. *Ibid.*, 351.
65. *Ibid.*, 350.
66. *Ibid.*, 508.
67. *Bower* 5, p 387. This referred in particular to the year 1272, when he tells us that 'a great famine hit France, England and Scotland'.

11

THE DISPUTED
SUCCESSION

THE END OF A DYNASTY

Prophets of doom had foretold that the eighteenth of March 1286 would be the Day of Judgement. Although not quite as predicted, the tragedy that occurred that night had such calamitous results for Scotland that their predictions were widely regarded as justified.

An equinoctial gale was raging throughout the country that day, but this failed to deter the king, Alexander III, from setting out from his royal manor at Kinghorn in Fife to attend a meeting of his council at Edinburgh castle. After its conclusion he stayed on to dinner, and with no sign of the storm abating he was pressed to stay the night; but, scorning the advice of courtiers and soothsayers alike, he insisted on travelling back to Kinghorn where his young French bride of barely six months was waiting for him. The ferryman at Dalmeny begged the king not to cross the Forth, but ignoring him Alexander and his retinue continued on their way. Landing safely on the far side, they followed the track along the coast towards Kinghorn, but buffeted by wind and rain Alexander and his companions became separated. In the darkness his horse stumbled and threw the forty-four-year-old king against a rock, where his body was found the next day.

His formally recognised successor was his granddaughter Margaret, the only child of his now-dead daughter and her husband, the king of Norway, but, as she was only three years old, six guardians were appointed to govern the realm in her name. Therefore, not only was the country faced with a long royal minority but, as the young queen was a sickly child and unlikely to survive to adulthood, there was also every prospect of a long and damaging dispute over the succession. While most of the potential claimants were descended from the bastard offspring of William I and Alexander II, the few who could claim a legitimate descent from the royal house included Dervorguilla's son, John Balliol, and the elderly Robert Bruce, known as the Competitor, the grandfather of the celebrated Robert Bruce. They were both descended from David, earl of Huntingdon, the younger brother of

Malcolm IV and William I; but whereas Balliol was the grandson of Earl David's eldest daughter, Margaret, the wife of Alan, lord of Galloway, Bruce was the son of his second daughter, Isabel.

It was Galloway's misfortune that both claimants had a power-base in the south-west, as this accounted for the region becoming one of the principal battlegrounds in the ensuing war. For, whereas Galloway was under the control of Balliol and his Comyn relatives, the Bruces owned the lordship of Annandale, as well as the earldom of Carrick. This belonged to Robert Bruce the Competitor's son, also Robert Bruce, who acquired it through his marriage to Marjorie, the granddaughter of Earl Duncan. Within Galloway itself, the east was dominated by Balliol's mother, Dervorguilla, and the west by the heirs of Elena de Quenci, notably Alexander Comyn, earl of Buchan and sheriff of Wigtown. Their support for Balliol was endorsed by the powerful McDowells and most of the native aristocracy. Separating Galloway from Annandale was Nithsdale, where the dominant power was John Balliol's brother-in-law, John Comyn of Badenoch, who owned the barony of Dalswinton, while another prominent supporter was Sir Thomas Randolph,[2] the lord of Morton. Also sheriff of Dumfries, he was the father of Thomas Randolph, the future earl of Moray, who would become one of King Robert's principal lieutenants.

However, the balance of power was tilted firmly against the Bruce faction, for their territories of Annandale and Carrick counted for little against the combination of Dervorguilla's territories and the vast landholdings of Earl Alexander and his great-nephew, the lord of Badenoch. Similarly, the influence of these two magnates over their fellow guardians far outweighed that of the Bruces' adherent, James the Steward. Therefore, in an attempt to reduce the Balliol/Comyn power in Galloway, Robert Bruce the Competitor, and his son, the earl of Carrick, launched a punitive raid on their lands and fortresses in the region.

Having captured the royal castle of Dumfries, they proceeded to ravage the Balliol lands beyond the Nith, taking Buittle in Dervorguilla's absence, while a successful assault gained them the royal castle at Kirkcudbright. Then, advancing across the Cree, they took possession of the royal castle at Wigtown,[3] and probably also the Comyns' stronghold of Cruggleton, before burning the cathedral church at Whithorn,[4] and leaving the bishop in a state of near-starvation.[5]

The extent of the devastation resulting from the invasion is evident from the Exchequer accounts. For these contain references to remissions granted to tenants 'lest they leave the land uncultivated on account of the war waged after the king's death by the earl of Carrick',[6] while citing instances of lands remaining uncultivated as late as 1290. However, it proved a self-defeating exercise, because all it achieved was to leave a legacy of resentment against the Bruces, and bind the Gallovidians more firmly to the Balliols and the Comyns. At the same time, it prompted the latter to consolidate their hold over the province, and consequently Earl Alexander secured the appointment of his son and heir, John (who would succeed him the following year), as keeper of the royal castle and lands of Sypland at Kirkcudbright, while delegating to him his responsibilities as sheriff of Wigtown.[7]

A KINGDOM WITHOUT A KING

In September 1290, the seven-year-old queen Margaret – known as the Maid of Norway – set sail for her foreign realm of Scotland, and the magnates assembled at Perth in readiness for her inauguration. But they waited in vain, as she died at Orkney during the voyage. Now their worst fears were realised, and when no less than thirteen relatives of the royal house put forward competing claims to the throne a disputed succession looked a virtual certainty. The main contenders were John Balliol, already styling himself 'heir of Scotland', and the seventy-nine-year-old Robert Bruce. He had a long and distinguished career as a prominent member of Alexander II's court, a veteran of the crusades, former companion-in-arms of the English king, Edward I, and despite his age he was still a man of undiminished vigour. Since neither of them were prepared to concede the other's claim, there was every prospect of an outbreak of civil war. This so alarmed the guardians that they instructed Bishop Fraser of St Andrews to write to Edward I imploring him to adjudicate on the succession.[8]

The invitation was accepted, and this opened the way for that ambitious and power-hungry monarch to make a further attempt to establish his authority over Scotland. A man of commanding physical presence (he was well over six foot tall[9]) and immense personal authority, he was one of the ablest of the Plantagenet kings, while his reputation as lawgiver was renowned throughout Europe. He had already tried to gain control of the country by engineering a match between his son, Edward, and the Maid of Norway on terms which had recently agreed at the treaty of Birgham, but as her death had thwarted his plans he was quick to take advantage of this second opportunity. Many Scots were uncomfortably aware of his ambitions, and his recent seizure of the Isle of Man, which had been in Scottish hands since 1266, added to their fears. Even more sinister was the fact that his appointment of the bellicose bishop, Antony Bek of Durham, as lieutenant of the realm, allegedly made on behalf of Prince Edward and the Maid of Norway, had never been revoked following her death. Their concerns were to prove abundantly justified.

As a preliminary, Edward summoned the claimants and all the Scottish leaders to meet him at Norham. To reassure them of his pacific intentions, he issued letters patent specifically renouncing any claim to the overlordship of Scotland, while emphasising his role as that of 'a friendly arbiter and respected neighbour' who was there 'to settle a disagreement by his wisdom [as] a friendly conciliator'.[10] However, when Edward met the representatives he attempted to browbeat them into acknowledging him as feudal overlord, and it was only after they had solemnly undertaken to give his demands urgent consideration that he allowed them a respite to deliberate. Once free from his intimidating presence, they summoned up the courage to give him a courteous but firm refusal, arguing that only a ruling king and his council could validly recognise him as overlord,[11] that they were not entitled to do so, and still less could they bind a future sovereign in such an obligation.

Edward nevertheless persisted, informing the guardians that he would not proceed with the adjudication until his demands were met and the principal Scottish castles handed over to him. The guardians conceded, and among those given up were the royal castles of Dumfries, Kirkcudbright and Wigtown, which were put under the custodianship of Sir William de Boyville.[12] When he died later that year, Sir Walter de Curry was appointed in his place,[13] and was later succeeded by Sir Richard Siward of Tibbers, near Thornhill in Dumfriesshire.[14] Fealty was taken from other noblemen, and the Gallovidian magnates made their submissions to the justiciar, Sir William St Clair, the bishop of Galloway, and Sir William de Boyville,[15] as the king's representatives.

A commission was now appointed to adjudicate on the succession. This consisted of 104 auditors: 40 representing Balliol, another 40 Bruce, and the remaining 24 King Edward as its president. Anxious to preserve his reputation as a scrupulous exponent of the law, he acted meticulously in reaching a decision on all the technical points put forward, even summoning experts from Oxford and Cambridge to provide legal counsel where necessary.[16] Most of the claims were either withdrawn or dismissed, and the issue finally narrowed down to those of Balliol and Bruce. By the laws of primogeniture Balliol seemed to have the better right, but Bruce argued that as a member of the senior generation (he was a first cousin of Dervorguilla) he was more closely related to the royal house. After two years of intermittent deliberations the commission found in favour of Balliol, and accordingly he was crowned at Scone in 1292. Robert Bruce declined to accept the decision, and to prevent his claim from lapsing on his death he assigned it to his son, the earl of Carrick, and both men refused to do homage to the new king, John.

KING JOHN

Pro-Bruce propagandists have portrayed John as a feeble puppet king, but his was an impossible task, as Edward deliberately set out to make life difficult for him. The homage demanded of him was all-embracing and included fealty not only for the kingdom of Scotland but his own lands as well, while Edward proceeded to interfere in Scottish affairs to an extent far beyond anything King John or his advisers had ever anticipated. In spite of this, there were occasions when John tried to assert his authority, and the crisis came in 1293 when he was coerced into obeying a summons to appear before Edward in connection with an unresolved court case. When he attempted to defend himself he was subjected to one of that awe-inspiring monarch's terrifying 'dressing-downs' (a similar tongue-lashing was to cause the dean of St Paul's a heart attack[17]). Having reduced him to speechlessness, Edward formally judged John to be in his mercy for contempt of court, and threatened him with dire penalties should he remain contumacious. The result was inevitable: John was forced to back down and plead for time to consult his advisers, while undertaking to appear before the next English parliament.

The Scots parliament, however, refused to endorse their king's capit-ulation and stripped him of his ruling powers, delegating them to a representative council of twelve. These events were grist to the mill of the Bruces who were doing everything possible to undermine John's author-ity. One example was Robert Bruce the Competitor's success in securing the appointment of his chaplain, Thomas de Dalton, as bishop of Whithorn in the face of the king's formal objections to the archbishop of York,[18] which suggests he may have commanded more influence in Galloway than seems apparent. But that redoubtable old man was denied the opportunity to exploit this, as he died shortly afterwards at the advanced age of eighty-four.[19]

Meanwhile, King Edward issued a summons to King John and other Scottish magnates to perform feudal service for him in his French war. After some deliberation, the council of twelve not only refused but they decided to enter into a hostile alliance with the French king, Philip IV, instead. Edward retaliated by declaring war on Scotland and summoned his army. The council responded by issuing a call to arms, but some of the nobility remained in allegiance to Edward, notably the Competitor's son, Robert Bruce, lord of Annandale. In return for paying homage to Edward earlier that year, he was given the keepership of Carlisle castle and a vague promise of the reversion of the Scottish crown in the event of King John being deposed. Now he was expelled from the kingdom, his lands of Annandale being confiscated and put in the hands of John Comyn, who had succeeded his father as earl of Buchan.[20] Bruce had already handed over the Carrick earldom to his son Robert, the future king,[21] and as the latter had fled to England his comital lands were also forfeited.[22]

Meantime, Edward resorted to an imaginative, if somewhat over-optimistic, scheme to undermine King John's influence in Galloway. This involved resurrecting, like a ghost from the past, a man who had been a prominent figure there more than sixty years before, but who had long since disappeared into oblivion. Still alive at the extreme age of almost ninety, Thomas, the bastard son of Alan, the last lord of Galloway, was released from the Balliol stronghold of Barnard castle, where he had been languishing a prisoner for almost all that time,[23] and taken to Carlisle. The object of the exercise was to use Thomas as a focus for Gallovidian loyalties in place of his nephew, King John. Therefore, at Thomas's alleged request, Edward proceeded to issue letters patent to 'the goodmen and whole community of Galloway' granting them 'all their liberties and customs as they and their ancestors held these in the time of King David and of Alan, the said Thomas's father'. Thereafter, Thomas was returned to prison and was heard of no more,[24] and this somewhat bizarre episode achieved nothing.

Edward now embarked on an invasion of Scotland and laid siege to Berwick, that great emporium of northern trade, whose keeper was Sir William Douglas. The walls were quickly breached, and the English soldiers poured into the town, sacking it and massacring the inhabitants, to the extent that 'for two days blood flowed from the bodies of the slain'.[25] It reached such appalling proportions that corpses lay heaped in the streets, and only the desperate pleas of the clergy finally persuaded Edward to call a halt to the killings. A witness described how the stench from the carcases was so overpowering that huge pits had to be dug to bury them, though stories of Edward helping to cart them away in a wheelbarrow are probably apocryphal.[26] So, too, was the tradition that it was the sight of a woman being slaughtered while in the act of giving birth that prompted his change of heart.

Leaving the smoking ruins of Berwick behind them, Edward's troops advanced northwards, and routing the Scots at Dunbar they pursued them across the Forth. When the army reached Perth, King John was compelled to surrender unconditionally, and his captors brought him to Edward's court at Brechin, where in the course of an extraordinarily degrading ceremony he was forced to abdicate. The royal arms were wrenched off his tunic, his hood and knightly girdle torn away from him, and in the words of a contemporary chronicler he was reduced to a 'toom tabard', meaning an 'empty surcoat'. Stretching even his ability to interpret the law to his advantage, Edward claimed that John's abdication entailed a resignation to him of all his own lands, including his estates and jurisdictional powers in Galloway.[27] Thereafter, the deposed king was dispatched to the Tower, along with the leaders of the Comyn faction, including Sir Richard Siward who subsequently entered King Edward's service.[28]

A FOREIGN DICTATORSHIP

Edward now took the country under his direct rule, appointing his own
servants as the principal administrators. All the symbols of Scotland's
independence were removed to England – the national records, the
regalia, and worst of all for Scottish pride the Stone of Destiny was taken
from Scone and placed in Westminster abbey. It was at this point that the
elder Robert Bruce is supposed to have reminded him of his promise of the
reversion of the throne in the event of Balliol's deposition. But Edward,
who had no intention of replacing a failed Balliol kingship with a Bruce
dynasty, dismissed his plea with the withering retort, 'Ne avonis ren autre
chosis a fer que a vous reaymys ganere [have we nothing else to do than win
kingdoms for you]?'[29]

Four months later, Edward held a court at Berwick, where he issued an
ordinance for the government of Scotland. All secular and ecclesiastical
landholders in Scotland, including Englishmen owning land north of the
Border, were required to do homage to him in person, or to their local
sheriff as his representative, acknowledging him as feudal overlord. Some
two thousand landowners did so, and their names were recorded in
documents drawn up for each sheriffdom. As many attached their seals as
well, the completed instruments resembled a stage prop used in a popular
game in contemporary court circles, and was therefore sarcastically dubbed
the Ragman Roll.[30]

All the principal castles were garrisoned with English troops, and Henry
de Percy, who had recently been appointed governor of Ayrshire and
Galloway, took over the Comyn- and Balliol-owned castles of Cruggleton
and Buittle.[31] He was also given the custodianship of the royal castles of Ayr
and Wigtown in place of Sir Richard Siward, while Sir John de Hodleston
was appointed their keeper.[32] Englishmen were installed in almost all the
sheriffships, though an exception was made in the case of Wigtown, where
the Kirkcudbrightshire landowner, Sir Walter de Twynam, temporarily held
office. Edward also established clerks of his household in positions of
influence in Galloway, and to give them additional powers he presented
them to the churches of Buittle, Wigtown and Kirkinner,[33] while Henry de
Percy was confirmed in the ownership of the barony of Urr,[34] to the
exclusion of the competing claims of his relatives.[35] The lieutenancy of
Scotland was vested in the veteran John de Warenne, earl of Surrey,[36] who
coincidentally was Henry de Percy's maternal grandfather. As an old
comrade-in-arms, Edward is alleged to have remarked to him, as he
departed south, that 'it was a good business to rid oneself of shit [merde]'[37]
– an earthy reflection of his contempt for the Scots.

Percy's governorship was harsh, and in order to stamp out local opposition he dispatched his deputy, Sir Robert Clifford, to scour the south-west with mounted contingents of armed men to round up potential rebels. All trade with the Continent was cut off to prevent petitions for help from reaching the French king, and only a few selected ports, such as Kirkcudbright, were allowed to remain open. Although Edward had extended his personal protection to all ecclesiastical institutions, he issued a highly unpopular edict stipulating that, because Whithorn was subject to York, only Englishmen could be presented to vacant benefices within that diocese, later extending this to the Scottish Church as well. So long as John Balliol was king, Bishop Thomas was torn by conflicting loyalties between him and the archbishop of York, to whom he was bound by his oath of obedience. Now there was no longer a king he could give his wholehearted allegiance to the archbishop, and consequently he became a leading sup- porter of the unpopular English cause in Galloway.

REBELLION

The English regime was so harsh and oppressive that it was bound sooner or later to trigger off a rebellion. This eventually broke out in the north in 1297. Although attributable to a number of causes, it was mainly provoked by the demands made on the people to provide for the English occupying troops, and Edward's calls on them for money and men to prop up his campaigns in France and Flanders. He was already in desperate financial straits, and there are many instances of officers having to petition for arrears of pay; so to make ends meet he confiscated much of the Scottish woolcrop and sold it abroad, reducing many sheep farmers to beggary. Above all, his attempts to raise troops were deeply resented, because it was claimed that 'the king would have seized all the middle people [i.e the gentry and tenant farmers] of Scotland to send them overseas in his war, to their great damage and destruction'.[38] Therefore, it was these 'middling folk' who were the mainspring of the rebellion, although it subsequently gained wide popular support.

Sporadic outbreaks of unrest had already occurred in the Highlands and Aberdeenshire, and these were co-ordinated into a full-scale rebellion by the Comyn relatives, Andrew Moray, who had recently escaped from imprisonment in England, and Alexander Macdougall of Argyll. Shortly afterwards, another rebellion broke out in the south, which was a combination of an aristocratic revolt and a popular uprising. The former was led by James the Steward and Bishop Robert Wishart of Glasgow, and later joined by Robert Bruce, the future king, who, having concluded there was nothing to be gained from continuing his allegiance to King Edward, threw in his lot with the resistance movement. The popular uprising, on the other hand, consisted mainly of minor landowners and husbandmen, and this was sparked off in May 1297 when William Wallace, the younger son of a crown tenant in Ayrshire, murdered William Hazelrig, the notoriously cruel sheriff of Lanark, in the course of a private vendetta.

The revolt of the nobles proved a muted affair, and when in July 1297 they encountered a superior English force at Irvine under Henry de Percy and Sir Robert Clifford and were offered terms, they surrendered. A number of hostages were taken, including men from Galloway and Niths-dale, many of whom were starved to death in captivity.[39] Wallace's revolt, on the other hand, was much more successful, and when he and Moray joined forces at Stirling they inflicted a decisive defeat on the English troops while they were in the act of crossing the bridge over the river Forth. Afterwards, the bloated corpse of the loathed Hugh de Cressingham, the English treasurer of Scotland, was flayed and pieces of his skin displayed as symbols of liberty from English oppression, Wallace being reputed to have used one to make a sword belt for himself.[40]

Moray and Wallace's overwhelming victory at Stirling bridge gave them the leadership of the resistance movement, and together they set up a government in opposition,[41] so when later that year Moray died of the wounds he received in the battle, Wallace appointed himself sole guardian 'in the name of the famous Prince, Lord John, by God's grace illustrious King of Scotland'. This designation proved controversial because, by so styling himself, Wallace alienated the Bruces and their supporters, while the Comyns and their associates resented being outshone by him.[42] However, this was inevitable, because their leaders were prisoners in England at the time, and although they were released later that year most of them were pledged to serve in King Edward's campaign in Flanders. The earl of Buchan and John Comyn, lord of Badenoch, on the other hand, were allowed to return to Scotland on condition that they undertook to promote Edward's interests in Scotland, which meant that they could not be seen to be taking part in the rebellion – at least not for the time being.

Meanwhile, the younger Robert Bruce, having returned to his allegiance to King Edward, was ordered to raise levies from Kyle, Cunninghame, and his native Carrick. Two leading Galloway magnates, Gibon fitzCan and Duncan McDowell, who had also submitted to him, were directed to do the same in Galloway, and similarly Sir Richard Siward (who had now entered King Edward's service) in Nithsdale. This triggered off a rebellion in the south-west under the earl of Buchan who, in breach of his undertaking to King Edward, had now reverted to his traditional role of leader of the Scottish political community, and was aspiring to take over control of the resistance movement. Wallace was quick to exploit the situation by descending with a small force on Dumfriesshire, where he captured the stronghold of Sanquhar before advancing on Dumfries.[43]

Henry de Percy moved quickly, and summonses were issued to the magnates who had recently submitted to Edward to join in suppressing the rebellion. Among them were Robert Bruce himself, Sir William Douglas the former keeper of Berwick castle, Sir Alexander Lindsay, and Sir Herbert Maxwell of Caerlaverock. They were successful, and the fact that those who were formally thanked for 'putting down the evil-doers and re-taking castles in their country' included the Gallovidian magnates Donald McCan and Gillemichael suggests that support for the Balliol/Comyn faction there was less than universal.

Percy now demanded, in King Edward's name, the formal submission of all those who were involved in the rebellion, and an extant document gives the names of the kindred of Afren (the McGhies) who were concentrated in the Glenkens.[44] Admitting their support for John Balliol in his 'fole emprise' – misguided undertaking – the document narrates that they had been informed of Edward's intention to lead an army into Galloway to punish them, that they had therefore confessed their fault on behalf of the whole kindred and swore on the saints to support him in his campaign against the recalcitrant Scots.[45]

Edward, meanwhile, was preoccupied with his war in Flanders, but notwithstanding the suppression of the revolt in Galloway, the situation in Scotland had become so serious that he was forced to take command in person. Therefore, arriving at York in April 1298, he summoned an army of some 28,000 men to assemble at Roxburgh; but campaigning proved diffi-cult, because much of the country had been ravaged by the Scots, and as Edward's victualling arrangements proved inadequate, supplies ran short. A few shipments did succeed in reaching his army through the east coast ports, including a consignment of 200 tuns of wine, but when this was distributed to the troops the unreliable Welsh levies got so drunk that they rioted and had to be quelled by the English cavalry at the cost of a number of lives.[46]

A pitched battle took place at Falkirk, and after a particularly hard-fought and sanguinary encounter Edward's superior generalship won the day. However, he was helped by the early demise of the Scottish cavalry who broke and fled. According to the suspect evidence of Fordun, this was attributable to 'the ill-will, begotten of the spring of envy, which the Comyns had conceived towards Wallace', as a result of which 'they, with their accomplices, forsook the field and escaped unhurt'.[47] Nevertheless, casualties were high on both sides, and a terrible toll was inflicted on the Scottish foot soldiers, who gallantly stood their ground in the face of a continual hail of English arrows. The main casualty, however, was Wallace's reputation. As his political power depended on military success he was now of no further account, so he resigned the guardianship and left for the Continent, where he spent the next few years trying to enlist French support for the resistance movement.

Although Robert Bruce's father had fought on the English side, he himself was not present at the battle, having taken refuge in Carrick. Later that year, he was appointed a joint guardian along with John Comyn, the heir of Badenoch, who was John Balliol's nephew. Although the partnership was designed to unite these two rival families, it was doomed from the start. According to a report by a spy in the pay of the English constable of Roxburgh castle, an example of their mutual hostility occurred at a meeting of the council at Peebles when 'John Comyn leapt at the earl of Carrick and seized him by the throat'.[48] Clearly relations must have deteriorated still further, because in early 1300 Bruce was forced out of the guardianship and once again threw in his lot with the resistance movement. This left the government in the hands of Comyn, Bishop Lamberton and Sir Ingram de Umfraville, though the latter two were later replaced by Sir John de Soulis, and when he left for France in 1302 John Comyn, now lord of Badenoch, became the sole guardian.

THE CAMPAIGN IN GALLOWAY.

In the summer of 1300, Edward decided to make a show of strength in Galloway, for in spite of all Henry de Percy's efforts the English position in the region was crumbling and needed shoring up, while Edward was determined to deny it as a regional power-base to the Comyns. The campaign opened at Carlisle with the muster of an army of 9,000 men, while a fleet of fifty-seven ships was dispatched to the Solway for the ferrying of supplies from the Cumbrian port of Skinburness. Crossing into Dumfriesshire by the Solway fords, the army advanced in a splendour vividly described in the 'Song of Caerlaverock'.[49] Composed by a herald serving in the king's army, this gives the names of all the knights and nobles on 'powerful and costly chargers' caparisoned with rich trappings, their bright banners fluttering from their lances, 'filling the sun-lit countryside'.

In front of them the massive Criffel range loomed over the lower reaches of the Nith, guarding what the troops must have perceived as the mysterious hinterland of Galloway beyond. In their path lay Sir Herbert Maxwell's recently-built fortress stronghold of Caerlaverock, and as he and his family were long-standing supporters of the Comyns, Edward was determined to take it. According to one account the garrison offered to surrender, but Edward, 'furious like a lioness whose cubs are taken from her', promptly rejected it and ordered a full-scale attack on the castle. Eventually, his siege-breaking equipment succeeded in breaching the walls, and his soldiery poured into the fortress and captured it.[50] Many of the garrison were hanged, including its constable Robert Cunningham, a nephew of the Steward, whose severed head was impaled on a pike and displayed on the battlements.

Fording the Nith, Edward's army advanced into Galloway, his route taking him past Lochrutton, where he stayed the night and is recorded as making an oblation.[51] It appears to have been a relatively peaceful progress, since Edward was anxious to win the support of the Gallovidians, and therefore his troops were under strict orders to refrain from looting and pillaging so as to avoid needlessly antagonising them. When his army reached the Bridge of Dee, he was met by Bishop Thomas de Dalton who had been sent as an emissary by the earl of Buchan with an offer of mediation.[52] Contemptuously rejecting it, Edward continued his advance down river to Kirkcudbright, where he encountered Buchan and his kinsman John Comyn, the younger, who made a further attempt to negotiate peace terms. This time Edward did condescend to parley with them, but they departed empty-handed.

Edward and his court remained there for ten days, during which time he made an oblation at the convent of Greyfriars. Although a present of eighty hogsheads of wine was reportedly shipped to him from the Irish port of Drogheda,[53] supplies were otherwise slow to reach him, and this could account for his prolonged stay at that centre. His next halt was at Twynholm, where he remained for a further six days. Resuming his advance, he set up camp a few miles away on the site of the present-day farm of Enrick, which is situated on the high ground above the river Fleet. There he made a donation of seven shillings to the church of Girthon, and, exercising his self-appropriated jurisdictional powers, he levied fines of forty shillings on the settlement by the Fleet for using defective weights and measures, and 13s 4d on a local miller for indulging in illegal practices.[54]

From there, a foraging party was sent forward with an armed escort, and when they ran into some Scottish troops at the Cree a skirmish ensued, in the course of which the Scottish marshal was captured. The next day Edward ordered his army to advance, but when it reached the Cree it found three Scottish cavalry brigades drawn up on the far side commanded by Buchan, John Comyn, and Sir Ingram de Umfraville. Archers exchanged shots, and when the tide went out the English army advanced across the river and charged the Scots who fled 'like hares before greyhounds', many abandoning their horses in the melée as they took to the hills, leaving their baggage and equipment behind them.

However, it was a token victory, because desertions became so rife that Edward was forced to abandon what was beginning to look like a futile campaign and return to England. This time he followed the coastal route to Dumfries, passing by way of Southwick, where he is recorded as making an oblation, eventually reaching Sweetheart abbey. There he was met by Archbishop Winchelsey of Canterbury, who in some fear and trepidation (he had been threatened with suspension from office if he failed to deliver it) presented him with a disturbing papal bull issued by Boniface VIII.

Reflecting the success of the Scottish party at Rome, this contained a lengthy indictment of Edward's invasions of Scotland and demanded that his feudal claim to the country be adjudicated in the papal curia. This was a serious diplomatic reverse, but Edward played for time by sending a non-committal acknowledgement, because he was already planning another invasion.

Following his abortive campaign in Galloway, Edward dismissed Henry de Percy from the governorship, replacing him with Sir John de St John who had proved a capable administrator during his time as governor of Aquitaine. To consolidate his power in the region, Edward gave him the lands of Kidsdale in the southern Machars, along with the prestigious estates of Buittle, Kenmure and Preston,[55] all of which had been forfeited by Balliol. St John's powers were extensive, as they included the command-ership of the western marches, while he was authorised to raise troops, conduct raids, and admit to the king's peace those Galloway magnates who were prepared to collaborate. Many did, including the heads of the McCan, the McDowell, and the McCulloch kindreds,[56] while the de Quenci heirs, William de Ferrars and Alan la Zouche, being Englishmen and therefore supporters of Edward, were established in the former patrimonial lands in Wigtownshire to buttress his authority there.[57]

THE FINAL COLLAPSE

In June 1301, Edward invaded Scotland for the third time. This was a two-pronged attack which was partly designed to isolate the south-west from the rest of the country. While Edward himself planned to lead the main army from Berwick through Tweeddale into the Lothians, his son Edward, prince of Wales, was given the task of crushing the remaining resistance in the south-west, thus gaining the honour, as his father put it, of 'taming the pride of the Scots'. Once this was accomplished, the prince was to advance up the Ayrshire coast and join his father at the line of the Forth and Clyde. Initially, Prince Edward's campaign was successful, mainly because of the lack of co-ordination among the partisans in eastern Galloway, and as his army advanced they retreated northwards past the Rhinns of Kells and down the Cairn valley into Nithsdale.[58] However, once he crossed the Cree, the prince encountered stiffer resistance under the leadership of the earl of Buchan, and eventually the defenders succeeded in holding up his advance at Loch Ryan. Although his forward detachments managed to take the younger Bruce's stronghold of Turnberry, the main body of the army could get no further and he was compelled to withdraw. Eventually he met up with his father, who had been equally unsuccessful on account of mass desertions, at Linlithgow where they remained for the winter, while a truce was patched up with the Scots.

Scotland's fate was now determined by events in Europe. In 1301, Philip IV of France persuaded the pope, to whom Edward had handed over John Balliol, to deliver him into his custody, and thereafter he was allowed to live on his family estates in Picardy. Nevertheless, rumours began to circulate that he was about to be restored to the Scottish throne with French help, and as this threatened a death-knell to the younger Bruce's hopes of securing the kingship he resumed his allegiance to King Edward. Not surprisingly, Edward was sceptical about his protestations of loyalty, and in order to make doubly sure of this he insisted that Bruce, who was now a widower, should marry Elizabeth de Burgh, a daughter of the earl of Ulster, who was his principal adherent in Ireland.

In July 1302, the French suffered a devastating defeat at the hands of Edward's Flemish allies at Courtrai, and Philip IV was compelled to sue for peace. Negotiations were concluded by the treaty of Paris, which was sealed with the marriage of King Edward, now a widower in his sixties, to King Philip's sister Margaret (by whom he was to have further offspring), while his daughter Isabella (later known as the she-wolf of France) was betrothed to Edward's son, the prince of Wales. The treaty put paid to all hopes of French support for the Scots, and as this had been the mainstay of their resistance it was now in danger of collapsing. King Philip attempted to allay their fears with bland assurances that their interests would be protected by another treaty, and although this never materialised these promises were enough to persuade Wallace to return to Scotland.

The following year, Edward launched another invasion of Scotland. Although lack of money limited the number of troops he could muster, his army of 7,500 men was still a formidable fighting force. So the Scots wisely avoided being drawn into a pitched battle, preferring to concentrate their efforts on conducting a guerilla campaign, and a prominent participant was Wallace, who harried King Edward's army with a series of raids conducted from his base in the forest of Selkirk. Nevertheless, the Scots were disheartened by the withdrawal of French support, and consequently Edward encountered little difficulty in capturing the key power centres in the Comyn heartland of the north-east. As a result, Scottish resistance collapsed, and led by John Comyn, lord of Badenoch, the principal magnates sued for peace. Thus, with the capture of Stirling castle some months later, Edward's conquest of Scotland was complete.

THE DICTATORSHIP RE-ESTABLISHED

In marked contrast to those of 1296, the peace terms which he imposed this time were, generally speaking, conciliatory and statesmanlike. The country was placed under the lieutenancy of his nephew, John of Brittany, and two justiciars – one English and the other Scots – were installed in each of the principal regions. In the south-west, Sir William St Clair was replaced by Sir Roger Kirkpatrick of Closeburn, whose English counterpart, Sir Richard Siward, was re-appointed custodian of the principal castles in Galloway and given the sheriffship of Dumfries. His opposite number at Wigtown was the English loyalist, Sir Thomas McCulloch, who replaced the earl of Buchan, though his appointment can have been no sinecure, since he would have to contend with the plundering raids subsequently perpetrated by Bruce and his partisans on Wigtownshire.

Wallace, however, was still at large, conducting a guerilla campaign at the head of a dwindling band of supporters. Although he had pardoned other rebels, Edward displayed a vindictiveness towards him amounting to an obsession. Wallace is supposed to have offered to surrender to him conditionally, but Edward angrily rejected it, as he regarded him as a traitor and was determined to bring him to justice.[59] So he ordered Comyn and three other confederates to hunt him down, adding a warning that as men who had not come into his peace he would 'watch to see how each of them conducts himself so that he can do most favour to whoever shall capture Wallace, with regard to exile or legal claims or expiation of past misdeeds'.[60]

In fact Wallace was betrayed in 1305 – allegedly by Sir John Stewart of Menteith – and taken to London where he was subjected to a mock trial before undergoing the hideous fate reserved for traitors. Lashed to a hurdle, he was dragged by a horse for four miles through jeering crowds to the public gallows, and there he was hanged, cut down while still alive, castrated and disembowelled, his entrails being burnt in front of him, before he was finally beheaded. The mutilated remains of this physically huge man were then hacked into quarters and his head was nailed above London Bridge. The dismembered portions were dispatched to be displayed as a salutary warning in the key towns of Newcastle, Berwick, Stirling and Perth.

His fame rests on being a main instigator of the Scottish resistance movement, while his shared responsibility for the victory at Stirling Bridge helped keep it alive during its early stages, although he failed to achieve his objective of restoring John Balliol to the kingship. In spite of this, the hagiographical writings of later chroniclers, the nineteenth-century romantic historians, and more recently the promoters of Scottish independence and the myth-makers of Holywood, have built him up into a folk-hero, portraying him as the principal architect of Scottish independence. Although this is a gross exaggeration, it was, ironically, Edward's obsession with hunting him down, and the obloquy heaped on him by contemporary English chroniclers, which is the most genuine tribute to the contribution he made to it.

THE SEEDS OF REVOLUTION

Robert Bruce inherited his family's claim to the kingship on his father's death in 1304, but as there was no chance of his being able to pursue it for the time being, he was prepared to make a show of co-operation with the new régime. Therefore, besides being a party to the preliminary discussions concerning its administrative structure, he was appointed sheriff of Lanark, and in the previous year he and Sir John de Botetourt, King Edward's bastard son and one of his leading commanders, had been ordered to arrange for the installation of the king's officers in southern Scotland. Yet, he never deviated from his ambition to gain the crown, and it was to that end that, in June 1305, he entered into a secret league with Bishop William Lamberton of St Andrews, the supreme Church dignitary and a member of John of Brittany's ruling council, to promote the cause of Scottish independence.

Whereas Bruce saw this as instrumental to the fulfilment of his ambitions, Lamberton and his colleague, Bishop Robert Wishart of Glasgow, regarded it as vital to the survival of the Scottish Church. As independence could only be achieved by a popular revolution, it was agreed that if Bruce were to engineer it by publicly declaring against King Edward, and take over the leadership of the resistance movement, the bishops would use their influence to deliver the Church. It was a huge gamble, but Bruce was the man to take it.

The prospects boded well, as King Edward was now an old man in failing health and not expected to live much longer, while Prince Edward was a man of lesser calibre than his father. However, if the scheme was to stand any chance of success it was vital that Bruce should come to an accommodation with the Comyns; for, besides being the foremost political and military power in the realm, they were still in effective control of the north. Thus, it was essential for him to win over his former adversary, John Comyn; so there could be some truth in the chroniclers' assertions that Bruce was prepared to go to the limit by offering Comyn all his lands in return for his help in securing the kingship.[61]

Fordun claims that no sooner had Bruce made the offer than Comyn blabbed the details to King Edward – a fact which could explain the outcome of the fateful meeting between Bruce and Comyn at the Church of the Grey Friars in Dumfries. Their discussion quickly degenerated into acrimony, and when Comyn charged Bruce with being a traitor the latter, in a fit of temper, drew his dagger and stabbed him. Alerted by the noise and imagining him to be in danger, Bruce's attendants, who had been waiting outside, burst into the church, and when they saw Comyn lying wounded by the altar they slashed him to death with their swords.

His murder was a blunder of the first magnitude. Bruce's whole strategy was blown apart, and he had unwittingly propelled himself into the leadership of a rebellion for which he was completely unprepared. Moreover, he had plunged himself into a blood-feud with the entire Balliol/Comyn kindred and incurred the hostility of all their adherents. Worse still, he had misjudged King Edward whose formidable remaining energies were now concentrated with a single-minded determination on hunting him down and bringing him to justice. The odds against him seemed insuperable, and few would have given a thought for his success.

NOTES

1. She was the widow of Adam de Kilconquhar who had been killed on a crusade. According to Fordun, she first encountered the younger Robert Bruce while out hunting and was so infatuated by him that she had him kidnapped and carried off to her castle at Turnberry, where she seduced him, and later married him. A romantic story; but, more prosaically, the marriage was dictated by strictly political considerations, as the acquisition of the Carrick earldom represented an important accretion to the Bruces' power. Nevertheless, it seems to have been contracted without the consent of Alexander III, who had the gift of Countess Marjorie's marriage, because when he heard about it he was so enraged that he seized her castle and much of her lands, only returning them to her on payment of a substantial fine (Duncan, *Scotland*, 400).
2. His support for Balliol seems somewhat perverse considering he was married to the half-sister of the future king Robert Bruce, she being the daughter of Marjorie of Carrick by her first husband.
3. McKerlie i, 331.
4. Brooke, *Wild Men*, 149: Oram, 'Dervorgilla, the Balliols and Buittle', 176 and 'Bruce, Balliol and the lordship of Galloway', 30.
5. Register of Archbishop John le Romeyn, Surtees Soc 128, vol ii.
6. *ER* i, 35–9.
7. Young, *Comyns*, 101.
8. Barrow, *Robert Bruce*, 30 (quoting *Nat. MSS Scot.* i, no 70).
9. When his coffin was opened in 1774 his corpse, even shrunken by age, was found to measure six feet two inches (1.88 m) which was extremely tall for the time (Prestwich, *Edward I*, 567).
10. *Bower* 6, p 7.
11. Barrow, *Bruce*, 32.
12. *Bain*, ii, 520, 547.
13. *Rot. Scot.* i, 7.
14. *Ibid.* i, 12: *Wig Charters*, xlv. Siward was a brother-in-law of John Comyn, lord of Badenoch, and his appointment was part of King Edward's strategy (which he subsequently abandoned) to rule Scotland through the agency of the Comyn kindred.
15. Barrow, *Bruce*, 38.
16. Prestwich, *Edward I*, 368.
17. Barrow, *Bruce*, 59.

18. *RRS* iv, p 368; *Bain, Northern Regs.* 104-5.
19. Nicholson, *The Later Middle Ages*, 49.
20. Barrow, *Bruce*, 67.
21. The elder Bruce's purpose in doing this was to render himself landless so as to avoid having to pay homage for them to Edward in the event of his succeeding to the kingship.
22. *Chron. Lanercost*, 115-6.
23. Alexander II clearly dared not put Thomas to death for fear of triggering off another rebellion in Galloway, and instead he consigned him to life imprisonment, though one would assume that he was reasonably well treated by his half-sister Dervorguilla. In fact, it was at the instance of John Balliol, and doubtless with her consent, that the question of his release was discussed at the meeting of the council at which Alexander III presided before setting off on his fateful journey back to Kinghorn.
24. *Wig Charters* (p xl) refers to an inventory of missing documents, which includes letters of John Balliol concerning the surrender to the king of Scotland (Alexander III) of 'Thomas of Galloway, his wife and son'. Considering Thomas was married as long ago as 1225 it is not impossible that this son, if alive, could be approaching seventy, and it would be intriguing to know what became of him and whether he left descendants.
25. *Bower* 6, p 59.
26. In fact, it was when a start was made on rebuilding Berwick in the following January that Edward ceremoniously wheeled the first barrowload of soil.
27. Oram, 'Bruce, Balliol', 35.
28. Young, *Comyns*, 162, 186.
29. *Bower* 2, p 166.
30. This is a highly informative document, since it gives a comprehensive picture of landownership throughout Scotland. However, it has its limitations in the case of Galloway, for whereas there is a separate roll for the sheriffdom of Wigtown, the landowners in present-day Kirkcudbrightshire and Dumfriesshire are included in the roll for Dumfries, so it is not always easy to differentiate between them. Nor is it always possible to distinguish between native and incoming landowners.
31. *Rot. Scot.* i, 31: CDS ii, no. 853, pp 224–5: Stevenson, Docs. ii. no. 100.
32. *Ibid.* 46, 47.
33. *Ibid.* 998, 1023: Stevenson, *Docs.* ii, no 423.
34. According to Reid's 'The Mote of Urr', Walter de Berkeley's daughter and her husband Sir Ingelram de Balliol had a son Eustace who inherited his parents' interests in the Urr barony, and a daughter who married William de Percy. When Eustace Balliol's son Ingelram died without issue at the end of the thirteenth century (*CDS* ii, 479, 1060) an inquest was held to determine the succession, and it found in favour of Henry de Percy, as William's grandson and heir of line. So, Edward's grant effectively confirmed him in possession.
35. Conversation with Dr Oram.
36. He is a good example of how closely interrelated the Norman aristocracy in both Scotland and England were. While his wife was a much younger half-sister of Edward's father Henry III (they both had the same mother), one of his daughters was married to John Balliol, while another was the mother of Henry de Percy. His wife was also an aunt of Sir Aymer de Valence, whose sister, Joan, was married to John Balliol's nephew, John Comyn, the guardian (*Europäischen Stammtafeln*, III/4, tab. 816).

37. Barrow, *Bruce*, 193.
38. Prestwich, *Edward I*, 476.
39. Cameron Smith, 'Wallace's capture of Sanquhar and the rising in the south-west', 3.
40. Prestwich, *Edward I*, 479.
41. This is evident from the fact that they set up their own chancery and proceeded to issue acts of parliament in the names of 'Andrew de Moray and William Wallace as leaders of the army of the kingdom of Scotland, and the community of the same, for King John'. (*RRS* iv).
42. The Comyns were descended through the female line from Donald III, who had usurped the kingship following the death of his brother Malcolm III. There were two branches of the family, the senior one being the lords of Badenoch, while the junior one inherited the Buchan earldom through marriage.
43. Cameron Smith, 'Wallace's capture of Sanquhar', 25 et seq.
44. The somewhat uncouth sounding names of these kindred members are recorded as: Gillenef MacGilherf, Neel, Gillcrist, Hoen and Cuthbert McEthe, Duncan MacGilleuras, Adam McGilleconil, Gillespie and Cuthbert McEuri, the two brothers Kalman and Michael McKelli, Auchmacath and Michael McGilmocha, and Duncan McGillauenan. ('Wallace's capture of Sanquhar', 35: *CDS* ii, 990).
45. Brooke, *Wild Men*, 156.
46. Prestwich, *Edward I*, 480.
47. *Fordun* ii, 321–4.
48. Barrow, *Bruce*, 107.
49. *The Siege of Caerlaverock* (ed.) Nicholas (London, 1828).
50. This was the first time trebuchets were used in Scotland, and highly effective they proved to be. Working on the counterweight principle, they were capable of hurling some fifteen kilos of rock for a distance of up to 300 metres, which was enough to breach the stoutest defences. In some cases they were reputed to have been used for lobbing disease-ridden animal carcases or decomposing human corpses into a fortress in order to spread disease among the garrison.
51. McKerlie iv, 337.
52. *Rishanger*, 440.
53. McKerlie iv, 166.
54. *Ibid.* iii, 470.
55. *CDS* ii, no. 1338, 1630. When Sir John de St John died in 1302 these estates, though not his position as warden, passed to his son, John.
56. Oram, 'Bruce, Balliol', 37.
57. Oram, 'Dervorgilla, the Balliols and Buittle', 178.
58. *CDS* ii, no. 1225.
59. Watson refers to this in *Under the Hammer*, citing the English chronicler Pierre Langtoft, ii, 353.
60. *Chron. Lanercost*, 190: *Flores historiarum* (Rolls series) iii, 123, 321: *Rishanger*, 385–6.
61. *Wyntoun*, v, 355: *Fordun*, iv, pp 330–1. They add that, as an alternative, Bruce, in return for Comyn giving him his lands, offered to support him in a bid for the kingship, and being a son of John Balliol's sister he had the better claim to it, a fact which seems to be generally overlooked.

12

THE PATRIOTIC WAR

REVOLUTION

Robert Bruce was in dire straits. Confronted by a formidable array of enemies, the target of King Edward's remorseless vindictiveness, he was also under threat of excommunication for his part in Comyn's sacrilegious murder. His only allies among the nobility were his relatives, the earls of Atholl and Lennox, though the baronage were generally more supportive. Here, his principal adherents were his elderly cousin, James the Steward,[1] John de Soulis, lord of Liddesdale,[2] and the Steward's nephew, James Douglas (son of Sir William, the former keeper of Berwick), who became one of his principal lieutenants. Most of his supporters were drawn from the minor lairds or gentry, such as Robert Boyd of Noddsdale, near Largs, and his fellow Ayrshire laird, Sir Alexander Lindsay,[3] who were subsequently rewarded with grants of land in Galloway.[4] The strongest support of all, however, came from his own family, as three of his brothers, as well as his brother-in-law, Sir Christopher Seton, died in his cause, while his surviving brother, Edward, remained his right-hand man throughout his entire campaign.

Comyn's murder provoked an outbreak of violence in Galloway, where suspected Bruce sympathisers were singled out for attack. The principal victim was Bishop Thomas de Dalton who had compounded the sin of being a Bruce appointee by supporting the English, and threats of physical violence and the systematic plundering of his lands reached such a pitch that he was forced to flee to England, where he remained until his death in about 1320. Bruce's clerical brother, Alexander, to whom their grandfather had given the wealthy living of Kirkinner, was subjected to the same treatment, and he too had to flee the province.

Bruce and his supporters moved quickly to 'take castles, towns and people as fast as he could', in order to establish control over as much territory as possible. His immediate objective was to secure his native Carrick, since this was his principal power-base and would give him a vital lifeline to Ireland for supplies and reinforcements, but as its southern flank was exposed to the hostile Gallovidians that province had to be neutralised.

As the castles at Dumfries, Dalswinton, Tibbers, and Loch Doon guarded the main access routes into Galloway, they were captured as a first priority. Command of the western approaches was also vital, and therefore Robert Boyd captured Rothesay castle on Bute and laid siege to Inverkip, while the key fortress of Dunaverty, at the southern end of Kintyre, was also taken.

Bruce depended heavily on the promised support from the Church – in fact without it his whole campaign would have collapsed. Initially, Comyn's murder and the likelihood of Bruce's excommunication inhibited many clergy from declaring for him. Bishops William Lamberton and Robert Wishart, however, were more stout-hearted, Wishart in particular exhorting his flock to fight for him 'as though it were a crusade',[5] and anticipating Bruce's excommunication he granted him absolution in advance. The support of these bishops was crucial, because it was not until 1309 that the Church finally declared for him,[6] and even that was remarkable considering that Scotland lay under a ban of interdict and Bruce himself was excommunicated.

Nevertheless, members of the clergy were willing to officiate at Bruce's crowning at Scone, on 25 March 1306, in a ceremony which was conducted with as much splendour as circumstances allowed. The choice of Scone echoed the traditional inaugurations of Bruce's predecessors, while the accompanying pageantry was designed to emphasise the restoration of the kingship in him as the legitimate successor of Alexander III. Ironically, since her husband, Earl John, was one of Bruce's leading opponents, Isabel, countess of Buchan, insisted on exercising the traditional right of her family, the earls of Fife, to place the crown on his head.

News of Comyn's murder, Bruce's rebellion, and his subsequent coronation was slow to reach King Edward, but when it did his response was swift and uncompromising. He ordered Sir Aylmer de Valence, who had temporarily replaced John of Brittany as his lieutenant in Scotland, 'to burn and slay and raise dragon'[7] in the east of Scotland, while Henry de Percy was instructed to do the same in the west. This held a particular significance, because 'raising dragon' meant that all conventions of contemporary warfare were to be disregarded and no mercy shown on any account whatever. Spurred into action by this terrible decree, Valence and Percy moved swiftly. The contumacious Bishops Lamberton and Wishart were arrested and dispatched to imprisonment in England, while Valence occupied Perth which was the key to the north. Meantime, Bruce had been steadily gathering recruits, but when he attempted to relieve the city he was defeated so overwhelmingly at nearby Methven that his cause was almost extinguished.

In a desperate attempt to evade capture, his queen, his daughter and their attendants escaped across the mountains to Kildrummy castle in Aberdeenshire, escorted by Bruce's brother Neil, the earl of Atholl, and other prominent supporters. When the castle was besieged they fled, hoping to escape to Norway, where Bruce's sister was the dowager queen. However, they were intercepted at Tain by the earl of Ross, a Comyn ally, who handed them over to the English, and on Edward's specific instructions the men were hanged, drawn and quartered. When the earl of Atholl begged for mercy on the grounds of his kinship with Edward, the latter with grim humour ordered him to be hanged from a higher gallows than the others in recognition of his superior status.[8]

Edward's ferocity was particularly apparent in his treatment of Bruce's sister, Mary, and the countess of Buchan. On his express instructions, they were shut up in iron cages fixed to the towers of Berwick and Roxburgh castles respectively, where the only concession allowed them was a privy.[9] Contact with their fellow Scots was forbidden, and only Englishwomen were allowed to bring them food and water, and in these appalling conditions the wretched victims languished for the next four years until they were removed to more salubrious quarters. As Bruce's daughter, Marjorie, was only twelve, her youth must have persuaded Edward to abandon his original intention of shutting her up in a cage as well, so she was kept in confinement in England, where her stepmother the queen was also a prisoner.

Retribution continued as Bruce's captured adherents were hanged or beheaded, while Edward confiscated their lands on the grounds of treason. Reflecting the lack of support for him in Galloway, there are very few recorded forfeitures there. One was Roland Askeloc (or McGachen), a member of an old native family in Wigtownshire, where he owned estates, as well as others at Borgue.[10] But, because he was a Bruce tenant in Carrick, feudal loyalty demanded that he support him even at the cost of losing these lands. The only other victims were Thomas and Robert de Kyrconnel who had declared for Bruce at the outset.[11]

THE KINGSHIP IN ABEYANCE

After Methven, Bruce's position was so desperate that he was forced to escape from the mainland before his routes to safety were stopped up. So, making his way through difficult and dangerous territory, he reached the fortress of Dunaverty on Kintyre, from where he is thought to have taken ship for Ireland. There is some doubt as to where he spent the winter of 1306–7, but he probably found refuge on the lands there which he acquired with his Carrick earldom.[12]

By the following spring, he had managed to build up sufficient strength to attempt two assaults on the Scottish mainland. One, led by Bruce in person, landed on the coast of Carrick, while the other, which consisted of eighteen ships and a detachment of foot soldiers under the command of his brothers, Thomas and Alexander, landed near Loch Ryan. The latter ended in disaster when it was defeated by a Gallovidian force under Dougal McDowell. Many prisoners were taken, and while most were summarily beheaded the leaders, including Thomas and Alexander, were handed over to the English and taken to Carlisle. Thomas was singled out for special treatment, as he was roped to a horse and dragged through the streets[13] before joining his fellow victims on the scaffold, where they were duly executed and their heads impaled on the city gates.

Bruce's expedition, on the other hand, was more successful, as he managed to secure a bridgehead on the Carrick coast and re-took his castle of Turnberry. Nevertheless, his position was extremely precarious, since lord Percy (as he had now become) was in control of the region, and all the main castles in the south-west were in English hands.[14] Moreover, Edward's most experienced generals, Sir John de Botetourt and Sir John de Mowbray, were in command of the English troops in Carrick, while Sir Aymer de Valence was waiting for him at Ayr. Therefore, all Bruce could do was to conduct a guerilla campaign from the fastnesses of Carrick, making repeated descents on Galloway and ravaging much of the country. This had a devastating effect on the Gallovidians, since not only were their crops being systematically destroyed by Bruce and his men, but the English troops requisitioned such grain as they managed to harvest, while commandeering their wool and livestock.

Their distress is evident from the anguished pleas sent to King Edward. Holm Cultram claimed compensation for 'eight and a half sacks of good, teazed wool taken . . . for the King's use . . . out of [their] grange where it had been stored for fear of the Scots',[15] while Dundrennan made a similar petition for 'the burning of its granges and the destruction of its stores'. The resulting food shortage is evident from the orders issued by Edward to his depots in England and Ireland, directing that supplies be sent to Skinburness and Kirkcudbright 'with utmost haste'.[16] An embargo was also placed on the export of 'corn, beasts or any other victuals' from the southern English ports to the Continent so that they could be diverted to his troops in the north, because 'the land of Scotland [i.e. Galloway and Dumfriesshire]' was being 'wasted, destroyed and denuded'.[17]

Meanwhile, Bruce's plundering raids became so widespread that Edward was compelled to order his local commander, Sir Robert de Clifford (now lord Clifford), to stiffen the English presence in Wigtownshire, while Sir John de Botetourt was instructed to do the same in Nithsdale. This seems to have achieved little, because Sir Dougal MacDowell (knighted for his capture of Thomas and Alexander Bruce), and lord St John (as he had now become) joined the chorus of petitions to Edward, claiming that they were unable to prevent Bruce and his followers from 'burning and plundering and compelling the inhabitants to rebel'.[18] Reflecting the devastation inflicted on the countryside as a result of these raids was Hugh de

Champaign's petition to the king, requesting that the feudal casualties of relief for his lands in Wigtownshire should be calculated 'according to their present value, not the old valuation before the Scottish War as they have been so wasted thereby'.[19]

These appeals became so insistent that Edward ordered John of Brittany, who had resumed the lieutenancy, to lead an army into Galloway in a final effort to hunt down Bruce and his associates. This proved well-nigh impossible, because much of the country straddling the border between Galloway and Carrick was covered by birch and pine forests, which enabled Bruce and his men to hide from their pursuers and continue their attacks. Blackmail seems to have been freely extorted, as the records state that 'he took tribute under the agreement that it [Galloway] should be left in peace'.[20] However, the English troops achieved a modest success when they defeated Bruce in a minor engagement in Glentrool in April 1307. Far from being the victory claimed by the local commemorative stone, his defeat was the result of a botched attempt to ambush and capture the English treasurer, in the course of which Bruce only narrowly escaped capture himself.

The position was reversed the following month when Bruce routed Sir Aymer de Valence's forces at Loudon Hill, in Ayrshire,[21] and followed this up with a victory over another force under the earl of Gloucester. These successes amounted to little, since they were essentially skirmishes rather than pitched battles, but they had a tremendous morale-raising effect on Bruce's supporters, and recruits now flocked to join him from far and wide. For it was believed that, as the English commander at Forfar put it, 'God is openly for him, as he has destroyed all the King's power both among the English and the Scots, and the English force is in retreat'.[22]

So enraged was King Edward at these setbacks that, mortally ill though he was, his indomitable will spurred him into a further effort to capture Bruce. Therefore, he launched another invasion of Scotland, but no longer able to ride a horse he was carried in a litter at the head of his army. However, the effort proved too much, and he died at Burgh-on-Sands a few miles north of Carlisle within sight of the Scottish hills, where Bruce still lurked, unconquered and a free man. As he had already become something of a legend in his own lifetime, it was only natural that his reputation should be further enhanced after his death, and the chronicler, Froissart, gives it colourful embellishment. He tells a gruesome story of how Edward refused even death to deny him victory over the Scots, and how as he was nearing his end he ordered that his corpse should be boiled in a cauldron until the flesh fell from the bones. These were to be carried at the head of his army, and only when the Scots were finally subdued were they to be allowed a ceremonial burial.

THE TIDE TURNS

With the death of this ferocious old monarch and the accession of Edward
II, who lacked his father's remorseless determination, the English will for
campaigning wavered. His army advanced no further than Cumnock, in
southern Ayrshire, before he decided to return to England. Sir Aymer de
Valence and John of Brittany were now left to hold the line of Clydesdale,
in order to contain Bruce in the south-west. This gave him the initiative,
and contemporary records are eloquent of the ferocity of his raids and the
resulting privations suffered by the people, Sweetheart abbey for example
being compelled to petition Edward II for the gift of the church at Wigtown
to compensate it for the losses it sustained. Although this was refused,
Edward was more accommodating to the desperate Gallovidians who were
forced to drive their sheep and cattle across the Solway fords to the safety
of England, for he allowed them to feed their animals in Inglewood forest
in modern Cumbria, 'whither they had come to take refuge from Robert
the Bruce and his accomplices'.[23] Eventually these attacks reached such a
pitch that the Gallovidians were reduced to paying Bruce a substantial
ransom in return for a respite.[24]

The lacklustre English opposition gave him the opportunity to break out
to the north and join forces with his supporters in the Highlands. He
inflicted a crushing defeat on the earl of Buchan at Old Meldrum, and
since Buchan was head of the mighty Comyn faction, as well as being his
principal opponent, Bruce proceeded systematically to destroy his power-
base in the north in order to minimalise his influence there. Therefore, the
resulting devastation of his lands, which was described by the chroniclers as
'the herschip [harrying] of Buchan', was so extensive that it was said to
have taken fifty years for them to recover.[25] Much of northern Scotland, as
well as a large swathe of territory in the Lowlands, stretching from Ayrshire
across to the Borders, was now in Bruce's hands, but as Galloway was still
hostile it needed to be brought under control.

Therefore, when the truce with the Gallovidians expired in 1308, Bruce
dispatched a force to subdue the province and capture the principal castles
there,[26] and since his brother Edward was put in command, and his
lieutenants included James Douglas, Alexander Lindsay and Robert Boyd,[27]
he was clearly leaving nothing to chance. Grasping at this opportunity to
avenge the deaths of his brothers, Edward Bruce embarked on a savage war
of attrition which was tantamount to a reign of terror, and so sudden was
his onslaught that the local inhabitants were caught unawares and unable
to mount a proper defence. Many were killed, while others were driven out
of their homesteads and their lands ravaged and burned.

Eventually Sir Dougal McDowell managed to scrape together a local force, but when it encountered Edward Bruce's army near Kirroughtree, it was put to flight and McDowell himself was killed. This, however, was merely the prelude to a major battle, which took place at the fords of Dee against a combined English and Gallovidian force under the command of lord St John. Edward Bruce scored an overwhelming victory, and in the course of this sanguinary encounter a number of local chiefs were killed, while Sir Donald McCan was taken prisoner.[28] Edward now focused his efforts on the McDowells, since they were the leaders of the native opposition, besides being responsible for putting his brothers to death. Therefore, he launched an attack on their local power centre of Hestan Island and burnt the fortifications there, though Sir Dougal McDowell's son, Duncan, managed to escape to England[29] and lived to play a leading if ignoble part in Galloway's subsequent history.

Although Edward Bruce defeated the Gallovidians in the field, he was unable to recapture the English-held castles in the region, which was the key to achieving complete mastery of the province. Nevertheless, he had effectively broken the local resistance, and as a reward he was given the lordship of Galloway along with the patrimonial lands in 1309,[30] though it was to take him another five years of savage campaigning to establish his authority over the region. He finally achieved this in 1314, but as he was put in charge of his brother's Irish campaign in 1316, and was killed at Faughard near Dundalk in 1318, he was only in a position to exercise his lordship powers for a bare two years.[31]

However, he seems to have made a determined effort to win over the local Church which, being under the control of York, was naturally hostile to the Bruce dynasty. His benefactions included a gift of the lands of Outon in the southern Machars, as well as the revenues from the churches of Kirkinner and Wigtown, to Whithorn priory. In addition he gave it certain more esoteric rights which included fishings on the Cree, 'half a salmon fishing of Dee with a salmon haul in the Dee at Kirkcudbright', and 'six stones of wax for St Ninian's light'.[32] He also relieved the monks of Holm Cultram of all further obligation to pay feuduty to him and his heirs, as lords of Galloway, for their lands at Kirkgunzeon.

By 1313 all the castles in the south-west had been recaptured and their garrisons either expelled or annihilated. The most important one locally was Buittle, since it held the key to eastern Galloway, and as John Balliol still had a contingent right in it there was a danger of the fiction of a government in opposition being maintained there. The siege lasted for several months until the castle finally fell in February 1313, and was thereafter razed to the ground. Dumfries was another important centre, and though this was stubbornly defended by Dougal MacDowell it was eventually starved into surrender in March 1313,[33] when Bruce with a magnanimity verging on imprudence allowed MacDowell to go free. With singular ingratitude he promptly took himself off to the Isle of Man, where he took over responsibility for strengthening its defences against an expected attack by Bruce's forces.

As control of the island was crucial to his strategy for dominating the Irish Sea and disrupting the trade between England and its Irish colony, Bruce placed a high priority on its capture. Therefore, the invasion took place within a bare three months of McDowell's arrival there. Landing at Ramsey with a large fleet, Bruce proceeded to lay siege to the castle of Rushen (now Castletown), and when it fell MacDowell was captured once again. In the light of his previous conduct, the clemency shown him seems almost quixotic, though this time he and his family were exiled to England, where they remained pensioners of the English crown.

By 1314, Stirling was the only important fortress beyond southern Scotland still in English hands. In the previous year, Edward Bruce had entered into an ill-advised pact with its commander, which allowed him a year's respite from attack in return for his undertaking to surrender it if not relieved by then. Although he was later reprimanded for this by his brother, it was too late because the challenge had already been accepted and Edward II was planning a massive invasion to relieve the stronghold, and 'to put down and suppress the wicked rebellion of Robert Bruce and his accomplices in the king's land of Scotland'.[34]

This was the finest army the English could put in the field, being led by Edward in person with the assistance of some of his ablest commanders. Eventually, on 23 June 1314, it encountered Bruce's forces, who had established themselves in prepared positions on the carse of Stirling at Bannockburn. As their army was more than twice the size of the Scots', an English victory looked a foregone conclusion, but Edward failed to give effective leadership, only narrowly escaping capture himself. Therefore, after a two-day battle his army was routed, Stirling castle surrendered and Bruce ordered it to be dismantled. Although the war with England would continue for another fourteen years, Bannockburn marked the turning point, and Bruce's victory gave him undisputed mastery of the realm.

THE FRUITS OF VICTORY

Statesmanlike, King Robert (as he can now justifiably be called) was prepared to be conciliatory towards his opponents, his policy being enshrined in the statute of Cambuskenneth. This gave Scottish landowners who possessed estates in England a choice; if they came into his peace without reservation and renounced their homage to Edward II (with the consequent forfeiture of their English lands), they would be allowed to keep their Scottish estates, but those who failed to do so would stand to forfeit them. This ordinance affected almost the entire nobility, because most of them had, through inheritance or otherwise, acquired lands in England. Some leading magnates refused to come into King Robert's peace and thus automatically forfeited their estates, and these 'disinherited', as they were called, became a powerful political force in England, where they subsequently used their influence to enlist support in an attempt to recover their Scottish lands.

They included a number of Galloway landowners, such as lords St John and Percy[35] whose lands, including Buittle and Urr, were confiscated. Also, a number of the de Quenci heirs forfeited their rights in the former patrimonial lands in Wigtownshire, among them being Alan, lord Zouche,[36] and also Sir Henry de Beaumont[37] who became a leader of the disinherited. Some minor barons, notably Gilbert of Southwick and Gilbert of Colvend,[38] the descendants of Gospatrick fitzOrm, chose to retain their lands in Cumbria in preference to those in Galloway, and they too were dispossessed. The only native Gallovidian landowners who are known to have been penalised were Gylbricht McMalene and Gilruth McMolene (McMillan),[39] who forfeited their lands in the Glenkens. These were given to Sir Robert Boyd,[40] one of King Robert's original supporters, and a principal commander at Bannockburn, though the king subsequently resumed them in order to establish a hunting reserve in the region.[41]

A man who became pre-eminent in Galloway was Thomas Randolph, now earl of Moray. He was already a substantial landowner there, having acquired the barony of Garlies through his wife, who was a descendant of the Stewards.[42] Having already given him much of the forfeited Comyn lands in the north, his uncle the king added to his landholding in Galloway by granting him half the barony of Urr,[43] as well as the lands of Corsock, and those of Glenswinton in the parish of Parton, though Randolph subsequently gave the latter to Whithorn priory.[44] On his death, the remainder of his Galloway estates went to his son, John Randolph, from whom they passed to his maternal uncle, Sir Walter Stewart,[45] and his descendant, the earl of Galloway, continues to own part of the former Garlies barony.

There is no record of the de Kyrkonnels being restored to their lands, though they must have been, since they remained in the possession of their descendants. On the other hand, Roland Asceloc's son, Hector, was not restored to his father's lands at Borgue, nor those in Wigtownshire, because Roland subsequently changed sides and was killed fighting against Edward Bruce during his campaign in Galloway.[46] These lands had already been re-granted elsewhere, and although Borgue was beyond hope of recovery Hector attempted to regain those in Wigtownshire by other means. As Edward I had given them to a Cumbrian landowner, John de Wigton, Hector married de Wigton's sister and then tried to reclaim the lands in her right. This involved him in an expensive lawsuit, in the course of which, as Reid put it, 'the lawyers ate up all the estate'.[47]

King Robert and his brother Edward used the forfeited lands in Galloway to establish a network of loyal supporters in the region. Consequently, Sir Alexander Lindsay was given those of Bombie on the lower Dee,[48] while the former de Quenci lands of Girton on Fleet were given to John de Cragy (or Craigie).[49] Similarly, Thomas Edzear (or Edgar), a native of Nithsdale, was given the lands of Kildonan in the Rhinns,[50] where his alleged descendants, the Adairs, became prominent landowners during the following centuries. In addition, Sir Walter fitzGilbert, who was responsible for handing over Bothwell castle to Edward Bruce, was given the barony of Craichlaw,[51] while Fergus of Ardrossan, a tenant of the Steward and signatory of the Declaration of Arbroath,[52] was given the lands of Sypland,[53] near Kirkcudbright. Significantly, those of Poulton, near Garlieston, were given to King Robert's loyal adherent, Malcolm Fleming,[54] as this was a foretaste of the far more extensive landholding which David II subsequently gave him in order to establish him as overlord of western Galloway.

Edward Bruce had no legitimate issue, so when he was killed in 1318 the Galloway lordship, together with its patrimonial lands, reverted to the king, who later re-granted the lordship, along with part of these lands, to Edward's bastard son, Alexander Bruce. This included estates in the parishes of Senwick, Kelton and Colvend[55] in eastern Galloway, and others in the parishes of Kirkinner[56] and Mochrum[57] in Wigtownshire. At the same time, Robert pensioned off Alexander's mother, Isabel, countess of Atholl, with the lands of Barnhourie near Colvend.[58] Later, Robert gave Alexander the earldom of Carrick, which he had originally bestowed on his father in 1313. However, when Alexander was subsequently killed at Halidon Hill in 1333 without leaving male issue, his possessions, including the Galloway lordship and the earldom of Carrick, reverted once more to the crown.

Some forfeitures resulted from the de Soulis conspiracy of 1320, so-called after its main instigator, Sir William de Soulis. He was a high-ranking nobleman, as well as being hereditary butler to the king, and on the strength of an illegitimate descent from Alexander II his father, Sir Nicholas, had been one of the claimants to the throne in 1290. His mother was a daughter of Alexander, earl of Buchan, and through her he inherited the barony of Cruggleton, though he subsequently gave away half to Whithorn.[59] Although his family were traditionally allies, as well as neighbours, of the Bruces he, unlike his elder brother John who had been one of King Robert's original supporters, had joined his Comyn relatives in opposing him. In fact, he had only recently come into his peace, having been one of the signatories to the Declaration of Arbroath. Notwithstanding this, he seems to have remained covertly hostile to the king, because the plot, which is believed to have had English backing,[60] involved assassinating him and appropriating the crown for himself.

The conspiracy came to light; de Soulis was arrested, and he, along with his accomplices, was charged with treason. They included John de Moubray, a relative of the Badenoch Comyns, but he died a prisoner in the 'stone tower' of Dunbarton before he could be brought to trial. The evidence against him was damning, and his lands stood to be forfeited. However, the law demanded the presence of the accused in court before decree of forfeiture could be pronounced, so in a macabre ritual de Moubray's corpse was brought before parliament. It was duly sentenced to be hanged, beheaded and pulled apart by horses, though the king intervened to prevent this final indignity by ordering the body to be decently buried,[61] though all his lands, including those at Borgue, were forfeited to the crown.[62] The other conspirators were hanged, but at the king's intercession the sentence passed on de Soulis was commuted to life imprisonment, though his lands, including his half share of Cruggleton, were forfeited. Sir Eustace Maxwell of Caerlaverock was more fortunate, as the charges laid against him could not be proved and he was acquitted.

In 1323 Sir James Douglas was given the barony of Buittle. This comprised a substantial landholding which seems to have extended well beyond the confines of the present-day parish, though the charter specifically excepted 'Corbieton and the lands of Patrick McGilbothyn'.[63] The fact that Douglas was given a regality title, which incorporated wider jurisdictional powers than those attaching to a barony title, has prompted speculation about the significance of the grant. Buittle was now the most important barony in Galloway, but its associations with the Balliols, and hence the traditions of the lords of Galloway, rendered it a potential rallying point for local opposition to the Bruce régime. Therefore, it seems that by detaching it from the Galloway lordship King Robert was deliberately downgrading the political importance of both, while his purpose in establishing so powerful an adherent as Sir James Douglas there was to eliminate the risk of a rebellion breaking out in the province.[64]

Robert was instrumental in continuing his brother's policy of winning over the Church in Galloway. It was a difficult task, since it was still fundamentally hostile,[65] so bribery was the only answer. Therefore, in recognition of 'the great harm suffered by Whithorn as a result of the war', Robert gave it the patronage of the church of Kells.[66] In 1322, he granted it the potentially much more lucrative right to a tenth share of the feudal casualties of 'ward, relief and marriage, and all other escheats' arising to the crown from the lordship patrimony in Wigtownshire,[67] and in 1325 he granted it a charter erecting its lands into a free barony.[68] Dundrennan was also a beneficiary, since it received a gift of the lands of Polles.[69] While these grants may have gone some way towards pacifying the local clergy, it was not until King Robert secured the appointment of his loyal supporter, Simon of Wedale, abbot of Holyrood, as bishop in succession to Thomas de Dalton that he finally achieved control over the Church there.

GOOD KING ROBERT

After Bannockburn, Robert's visits to the south-west were infrequent. However, at the end of that year, he travelled to Dumfries to supervise the exchange of a number of high-ranking English prisoners in return for the release of his queen, Elizabeth of Ulster, and Marjorie, the daughter of his first marriage, both of whom had remained in captivity in England since 1306. As Marjorie was now of marriageable age, and her father's only legitimate child, it was important to find a suitable husband for her, so in the following year she was married to Walter the Steward. The union strengthened Robert's already close dynastic links with that powerful family, and in 1316 it produced a son, Robert. As Marjorie died in childbirth, this infant was King Robert's only legitimate descendant, and after Edward Bruce's death in 1318 he became the heir-presumptive to the throne,[70] and remained so until the birth of King Robert's son, David, in 1324.

In January 1327, Edward II's queen, Isabella of France, and her paramour, Roger Mortimer, launched a coup d'état; Edward II was deposed, and later hideously murdered,[71] and they proceeded to exercise power in name of the fourteen-year-old Edward III. Accordingly, they entered into negotiations for an end to the war with the Scots, and these were concluded by the treaty of Northampton in the following year. In return for a military alliance and the payment of a large monthly subsidy, the English recognised Robert and his descendants as the legitimate kings of an independent Scotland, while formally renouncing Edward I's claims to it. Its terms are thought to have included an undertaking by Robert to restore the disinherited to their former estates, perhaps pressured into it by fears that a refusal might imperil a treaty which was vital to the future security of his dynasty.[72] The complexities resulting from such an undertaking were endless, since it would have involved buying out the existing owners, or compensating them with other lands. Whether such an undertaking was given or not, there is evidence of some of the disinherited being restored to their former lands in Galloway,[73] though it is impossible to tell whether this took place during King Robert's reign or later.

The treaty was sealed by the marriage of King Robert's four-year-old son, David, to Edward III's equally youthful sister, Joan – a wedding which he claimed to be too ill to attend. The prolonged hardships sustained during his years of campaigning had begun to take their toll. Old before his time – he was still only in his early fifties – he was subject to increasing disability, which Barbour attributed to 'a benumbing brought on by his cold lying' in the course of the privations he had endured for so long. Perhaps a partial paralysis, it was exacerbated by a skin disease which the chroniclers claim to have been leprosy, and this was gaining on him. A contemporary observer draws a pathetic picture of the husk of a man to which this once heroic figure had been reduced, describing him as 'so weak and wasted [that] he could scarce move anything save his tongue'.[74]

Evidently in search of a cure, King Robert undertook a long drawn-out, and one would imagine painful, pilgrimage to the shrine of St Ninian at Whithorn. Setting out from his manor house at Cardross on the Clyde in January 1329, he travelled by sea to his castle at Turnberry. During his stay there, he is recorded as granting a charter of the lands of Craigcaffie and Beoch, in northern Wigtownshire, to John, son of Neil, a native of Carrick,[75] who was most likely a relative. No longer able to ride a horse, he was transported in a litter to Girvan, and from there to Innermessan near Loch Ryan, but the strain must have been too much for him, as he was forced to linger at nearby Inchmichael (present-day Lochinch) for over a month. Nevertheless, during his stay there he granted a charter of lands adjacent to the Cree to Martin McGech,[76] possibly an ancestor of the McLurgs, since legend asserts that the family acquired their lands from King Robert. He seems to have made a partial recovery, as he continued his slow and laborious journey by way of Glenluce and Monreith, and finally to Whithorn.

He spent some weeks there, and, incapacitated though he was, he persevered with his strategy of establishing families of proven loyalty in the region. This was designed to consolidate his authority over Galloway for the benefit of his son David who, as he was well aware, would shortly inherit the crown.[77] This was clearly the motive behind the grants of land which he made in the course of his final journey. For example, the powerful McCans had now come into his peace, so Sir Donald's grandson, John, was given the lands of 'Sauchayche' (Southwick).[78] John, son of Gilbert McNeil (possibly a relative of the owner of Craigcaffie), received 'the five penny land of Larglanfeld' in the Rhinns,[79] while Richard McGuffog was given Kilsture, an estate consisting of 'eight bovates [ox-gangs]' of land overlooking the Moss of Cree.[80] Having regained sufficient strength during his stay at Whithorn, the king embarked on the return journey to Cardross, where he arrived towards the end of April. However, the respite proved short-lived, as he died there a few weeks later, on 7 June 1329, at the age of fifty-four.

King Robert's triumph has inevitably inspired a sychophantic press from the chroniclers; yet, notwithstanding this, his achievements are indisputable. Moreover, he was by the standards of the time a humane and merciful man who was ready to be magnanimous to his enemies, even though this was not always reciprocated. Genial and approachable by nature, he inspired the affection and loyalty of his followers who were invariably ready to lay down their lives for him. Despite the unedifying track record of his earlier years, and his usurpation of the throne, he proved to be the man of the hour, as it was he who was primarily responsible for freeing Scotland from the yoke of English domination. Bannockburn was his greatest triumph, and here his leadership and gift for strategy won an outstanding victory for his country, which finally secured its independence. Even more importantly, he forged a nation, while giving his people a self-confidence which would never desert them throughout their subsequent turbulent history.

NOTES

1. He was a first cousin of Bruce's mother, Marjorie, countess of Carrick, since her father, Earl Neil, had married a daughter of the third Steward. Therefore, Bruce was a second cousin of both Sir James Douglas and his future son-in-law, Walter, the sixth Steward.
2. John de Soulis was a great-nephew of Sir John de Soulis, the former guardian.
3. A brother-in-law of the Steward, having married his sister, Lindsay had formerly been in King Edward's service but subsequently defected to the Scottish resistance, for which he paid a heavy forfeit following its collapse in 1304. His collateral descendants included the earls of Crawford, Sir James Lindsay, who was later established as a landowner in the Glenkens, and the Lindsays of Fairgirth.
4. Oram, 'Heirs to Ninian', 67.
5. Palgrave, 348.
6. *Scot. Hist. Docs.*, 48–50.
7. *Barbour, The Bruce* i, 35.
8. *Scalachronica*, 131.
9. Palgrave, 358.
10. These formerly belonged to Sir Robert de Champaign, and when he resigned them to Dervorguilla in 1282 she re-granted them to Roland Askeloc.
11. In the appendix to *Bruce,* Professor Barrow indicates their lands as being in Dumfriesshire. Although in the sheriffdom of Dumfries, they were almost certainly identifiable with those of that name in present-day Kirkcudbrightshire.
12. Barrow, *Bruce,* 26.
13. McNamee, *The Wars of the Bruces,* 44.
14. The last to fall was the island fortress on Loch Doon. This was a particularly serious blow for Bruce, as it resulted in the capture and death of his brother-in-law, Sir Christopher Seton, who was one of his closest friends. Later, Letters of Rancour were formally issued against Bruce's cousin, Gilbert of Carrick, who was its constable and therefore held responsible for its fall, though these were subsequently withdrawn (*RRS* v, no. 384).
15. Palgrave iii, no 69.
16. Brooke, *Wild Men,* 153.
17. *Close Rolls,* 522.
18. Palgrave iii, no 15.
19. *Ibid.,* ii, no 1984.
20. *Chron. Lanercost,* 210.
21. *Barbour, The Bruce* viii, 192–200.
22. Prestwich, *Edward I,* 510–1: Barrow, *Bruce,* 172–3.

23. Palgrave ii, no 14.
24. *Ibid.*, nos 14–15.
25. *Barbour, The Bruce,* i, 219.
26. *Bower* 6, pp 343–5.
27. *Chron. Lanercost,* 188.
28. *Ibid.* 6, 343. He is thought to have been a son of Cane McGillolane, the probable head of the McLellan kindred, who had been one of the witnesses to Dervorguilla's foundation charter of Sweetheart. He had been given lands in Kirkcudbrightshire by John Balliol and consequently appears as 'Dovenald fiz Can' in the Ragman Roll (Oram, 'A Family Business?', 137–8).
29. *Chron. Lanercost,* 212.
30. *APS* i, 459.
31. Oram, 'Bruce Balliol', 40.
32. *RRS* v no 275.
33. *CDS* iii, no 304.
34. *Rot. Scot.* i, 118, 119b, etc.
35. It is conceivable that they were restored to some of their lands at the end of King Robert's reign, but this seems unlikely (see Maxwell-Irving, 'Kenmure Castle').
36. He was the grandson and namesake of Sir Alan la Zouche and his wife, Elena, who was a daughter of Elena de Quenci.
37. A former governor of the Isle of Man, who had commanded an English cavalry division at Bannockburn, Beaumont lost out most of all. He was married to Alicia, one of the two daughters of Sir Alexander Comyn. As the latter predeceased his elder brother, the childless earl of Buchan, Alicia and her sister were the joint inheritors of the vast Buchan estates on their uncle, Earl John's death in 1308. Although Beaumont subsequently regained some of the Buchan lands, those in Galloway remained beyond his reach.
38. This is evident from the rubric of the charter granting the lands of Barnhourie to Edward Bruce's abandoned mistress, Isabel of Atholl, as this adds the rider, 'whilk Gilbert Culquen forisfecit [which Gilbert of Colvend forfeited]' (*RMS* i, app.2, no 1113).
39. The McMillans may have regained their lands. For McKerlie asserts (iii, 301) that there were McMillan landowners in the present parish of Carsphairn in the sixteenth century, and two branches of the family continue to be landowners in northern Kirkcudbrightshire.
40. *RRS* v, no 67.
41. There were several changes of ownership before King Robert resumed the lands. When Sir Robert Boyd resigned them shortly afterwards, in exchange for the barony of Kilmarnock, they reverted to Edward Bruce, as lord of Galloway. He granted them to Sir Walter Ross, who then transferred them to his brother, Hugh, earl of Ross (husband of Bruce's sister Maude). Earl Hugh then resigned them to King Robert in return for a grant of the fertile lands of Kinfauns, on the Carse of Gowrie in Perthshire (*RMS* ii, app 1, no. 108).
42. She inherited them from her father, Sir John Stewart of Bonkyl, he having acquired them as a portion from his father, Alexander, the fourth Steward, who was given them as a reward for his share in defeating the Norwegian invasion at Largs in 1263.
43. *RMS* i app.2, no 211, which adds the rider 'quilke Henry Percy forisfecit'. The award of half the barony probably implied an entitlement to a half share of its revenues rather than an actual territorial division.

44. *RRS* v, no 275.
45. *RMS* i app. 2 no 1260.
46. McNamee, *The Wars of the Bruces*, 44.
47. *Wig Charters*, xxxi–xxxii.
48. This is evident from a charter of these lands which was subsequently granted by David II, and which describes them laconically as 'whilk [which] were Lindsays' (*RMS* i, app 2 no 834), they having reverted to the crown on Sir Alexander Lindsay's death without issue.
49. *RMS* i app.2 no 625, the lands being referred to as 'Gortoun de Larganefeild'.
50. *Ibid.* no 681.
51. Morton, 'Craichlaw'. The progenitor of the Hamiltons, he was also given the forfeited Comyn lands in Clydesdale, while his descendants continued to own Craichlaw until the sixteenth century. When they died out in the male line, it passed to an heiress who married into the Keith family (subsequently the earls Marischal). Later, it passed to two co-heiresses, one of whom married a McKie and the other a Mure (*Wig Charters*, 171–2), and this explains why Torhouse, which was formerly part of Craichlaw, was divided into Torhousemuir and Torhousekie.
52. This was a letter addressed to Pope John XXII by the Scottish baronage appealing to him to lift the ban of interdict which had been re-imposed on Scotland in 1318. Although the pope rejected the plea, it is nevertheless an important historical document, as it sets out to justify Scotland's nationhood based on its own mythological past and Robert Bruce's right to the kingship.
53. *RMS* i app 2 no 326.
54. *Ibid.* no. 325.
55. *RMS* i app.2 no 319.
56. *Ibid.* no 320.
57. *Ibid.* no 623.
58. Her ownership of these was subsequently confirmed by David II (*RMS* i, app 2, no 1113).
59. *RRS* v, 275. Again, this implied a half share of the revenues rather than a physical division of the lands.
60. Reid, 'Crown and Community under Robert I', 215.
61. *Bower* 7, p.3.
62. *RMS* i app 2 no 839.
63. The deed itself is narrated at length (in Latin) in *RRS* v, no 267. As some of the place-names mentioned in it have been lost, it is difficult to identify the lands precisely, though they seem to have extended as far as 'the land of Crossmichael' on the north, and those of Kelton and Gelston on the west. In return, Douglas and his successors in title were obliged to render the king a pair of gilt spurs annually.
64. Conversation with Dr Oram.
65. Oram, 'Bruce Balliol', 56.
66. *RRS* v, no 10.
67. *Ibid.*, no 212.
68. *RRS* v, no 275.
69. *RMS* i app 2, no 86. The terms of the rubric suggest that these were part of the lands forfeited by John Balliol. Although it is impossible to identify them, the name suggests low-lying coastal lands, probably somewhere in the neighbourhood of Auchencairn or Orchardton Bay.
70. The possibility of the crown passing to Marjorie was clearly a source of concern

to Robert, as a female ruler was considered unfit to cope with the prevailing situation. Therefore, with her consent, he entailed the succession on his brother Edward (*APS* i, 464–5).

71. Red-hot irons rammed up his fundament burnt his bowels out.
72. Cameron and Ross 'The Treaty of Edinburgh and the Disinherited', 237–56: *RRS* v, nos 353, 457.
73. Maxwell-Irving, 'Kenmure Castle'.
74. Nicholson, 'A sequel to Edward Bruce's invasion of Ireland', 34.
75. *RRS* v no 362. *RMS* i app 2 no 616. He may have been an ancestor of the Neilsons of Craigcaffie.
76. *RRS* v, no 367. During the fifteenth century these passed through an heiress into the Heron family, and their descendants remained at Kirroughtree until the 1930s.
77. Oram, 'Bruce, Balliol', 409.
78. *Ibid.* no 614.
79. *Ibid.* no 626.
80. *Ibid.* no 615. Richard McGuffog was probably the son of Patrick McGuffog, who had been a supporter of the Competitor's raid into Galloway over forty years before. He could also have been an ancestor of the McGuffogs of Rusco, who rose to prominence at the end of the seventeenth century.

13

A BALLIOL RESURGENCE

RIVAL KINGS

King Robert had consolidated his position by a combination of military success, establishing loyal adherents in strategically important regions, conciliating his former enemies, and above all through his ability and force of character. But, because it was a highly personal authority, there was no certainty of it being maintained with a five-year-old boy on the throne. All the more so, since in the eyes of many Robert's was an illegal régime, founded on a successful usurpation rather than an inherited right. He had long been aware that its questionable legitimacy, and the lack of a suitably qualified heir, were fundamental weaknesses, and it was because a strong man was needed at the helm that he had by-passed his daughter and designated his brother, Edward, as his heir.[1] However, when Edward was killed in 1318, Robert's two-year-old grandson, the future Robert II, became his heir until he was edged aside by the birth of his own son, David.

Therefore, anticipating the likelihood of David being a minor at his accession, Robert had executed an entail committing 'the custody, charge and guardianship of the whole kingdom and people' to Thomas Randolph, earl of Moray, and failing him to Sir James Douglas, 'until such time as his heir was of an age to rule'.[2] Consequently, power passed automatically on his death to the earl of Moray, and as he proved a strong and capable guardian there was every prospect of King David's authority being maintained until he was of an age to assume full ruling powers. Moreover, it excluded the possibility of John Balliol's son, Edward, making a successful attempt to claim the throne.

Edward Balliol had inherited his father's right to it on his death in 1313, but as he was well aware that there was no chance of pursuing it during King Robert's lifetime, he was forced to play a waiting game. However, once the king was dead, he conspired with the leaders of the disinherited to launch an invasion of Scotland in order to wrest the kingship. This had the tacit support of Edward III, who had ousted his mother and Mortimer and was now determined to abrogate the treaty of Northampton as soon as his subsidy payments under it had ceased. Therefore, he accepted Balliol's homage for his prospective kingdom in return for the promise of military assistance, but there was little chance of an invasion being successful so long as Moray held the guardianship. However, Balliol was now approaching the age of fifty and growing impatient.

In 1132, the situation suddenly changed because Moray died unexpectedly, having allegedly been poisoned by his personal chaplain with Balliol's connivance.[3] Although Balliol is unlikely to have been a party to this, his opportunity had come at last, and he was determined to seize it. Meanwhile, the council, being well aware of his intentions, embarked on a frantic search for a new guardian, but as there was no obvious candidate they were forced into a 'gret and lang dyssentyown'.[4] Eventually, the choice fell on King Robert's nephew, Donald earl of Mar, but as his was a compromise choice it was inevitable that he was ill-qualified for the task, particularly as he was tainted with too close an association with the English. He had been a lifelong friend of Edward II, and it was only after the latter had been deposed that he returned to Scotland, when his uncle the king had restored him to his earldom. However, as events turned out, he had little chance to prove himself.

Four days after Mar's appointment, Edward Balliol and his younger brother Henry, accompanied by the leaders of the disinherited and a force of some six hundred men, landed at Kinghorn on the coast of Fife. Within a week they had advanced as far as the river Earn, where they encountered a hastily-summoned Scots army encamped on the far side, near Dupplin. As the river was unfordable at this point, the Scots were over-confident of their position and kept only a token watch. However, Balliol's men managed to ford the river further upstream, and launching a flanking attack on the unsuspecting Scots, they slaughtered them 'like cattle in the meat-markets'.[5] Once the survivors managed to extricate themselves and battle was joined, they were routed, Mar himself being among the slain, having held the guardianship for just over a week. Balliol went on to take Perth, and in the following month he had himself crowned at Scone.

This meant there were now two kings in Scotland,[6] and it resulted in a civil war which would last for nearly a quarter of a century. Both sides had to build up their strength, and therefore as soon as Balliol had been crowned he set out for the north to rally support among the leading magnates there. During his absence the Bruce loyalists re-grouped, being joined by the earl of March, who had failed to reach Dupplin in time to take part in the battle. Therefore, when Balliol returned from the north, he found himself confronted by a far stronger force than he had anticipated, and these Bruce adherents besieged him in Perth. However, he was rescued from his predicament by the timely arrival of a detachment of supporters under Sir Eustace Maxwell of Caerlaverock[7] and, successfully eluding the besiegers, he escaped to the safety of the south-west, where he proceeded to establish himself in the new earl of Moray's territories of Annandale and Nithsdale.

His authority was already well entrenched in neighbouring Galloway, where the eastern half of the province was under the control of Sir Eustace Maxwell, while Duncan McDowell was his principal supporter in the west. He was the son of Sir Dougal, who had betrayed King Robert's brothers to the English, and as his family had been consistently hostile to the Bruces it seemed only natural that he should align himself with the Balliol cause. But his support was less than wholehearted, for Duncan was a natural opportunist who was primarily motivated by self-interest. Although he had made his submission to Moray,[8] he defected to Balliol following his success at Dupplin, and his subsequent kaleidoscopic changes of allegiance were such as to give new meaning to the word 'turncoat'. Other Wigtownshire landowners came out in support of Balliol, notably Sir Patrick McCulloch and Sir John le Mareschal, and – surprisingly – Edward Bruce's son, Alexander, lord of Galloway.[9]

Having established his authority in the south-west, Balliol based himself at Roxburgh castle, but no sooner had he done so than he was attacked by a force of Bruce loyalists under the new guardian, Sir Andrew Moray,[10] and Sir Archibald Douglas.[11] In the course of this, Moray was taken prisoner, and so the guardianship passed to Douglas. He affected to conclude a truce with the unsuspecting Balliol, but it proved a sham, as he, along with the earl of Moray and Robert the Steward,[12] launched a surprise attack on him at Annan. Balliol's troops were put to flight and his brother was killed, while he himself narrowly avoided capture, escaping 'with one leg in a boot and the other one bare'.[13]

On reaching Carlisle, Balliol sent envoys to Edward III to request the military assistance which he had promised. Although Edward was prepared to honour his commitment, his terms were steep because, in addition to renewing his homage, Balliol was required to give an undertaking to surrender Berwick castle once it had been captured, and to cede Edward lands in southern Scotland which were sufficient to yield £2,000 a year. Therefore, in March 1333, Balliol returned to Scotland at the head of an English army and laid siege to Berwick, where he was later joined by King Edward in person. The Scots sent a relieving force under Sir Archibald Douglas, but when it encountered the English at Halidon Hill it was routed, Sir Andrew Moray being taken prisoner, while Douglas was killed along with many of the Scottish nobility. Berwick was now abandoned; its keeper, the earl of March, delivered up the castle, and in terms of his undertaking Balliol handed it over to King Edward.

Balliol supremacy

Exercising his kingly powers, Balliol restored the disinherited to their lands. In Galloway, lord St John was restored to the lands of Kenmure,[14] Gilbert of Colvend was reinstated in his former barony,[15] while Balliol himself repossessed much of the lands which had been confiscated from his father. He also ejected Bruce supporters from the principal offices of state, replacing them with members of the disinherited, de Beaumont's son-in-law, David de Strathbogie (a grandson of the murdered John Comyn), for example, being restored to his family earldom of Atholl and given the stewardship. Meanwhile, the dispossessed Robert escaped across the Firth of Clyde to the sanctuary of Dunbarton castle, where the young king and queen were living under the protection of its keeper, Sir Malcolm Fleming. Shortly afterwards, the royal couple set sail for France, where they would remain for the next seven years.

In February 1334 Balliol summoned a parliament at Holyrood, but in spite of packing it with loyal bishops and the restored disinherited, he had difficulty in persuading it to ratify his undertaking to cede land in southern Scotland to King Edward. Nevertheless approval was given, and accordingly a large tract of territory was given up 'to be annexed to the Crown of England for all time to come'.[16] The principal castles were garrisoned with English troops, and Englishmen were appointed sheriffs of Berwick and Roxburgh, while Sir Eustace Maxwell was installed as sheriff of Dumfries.

By this time the tide was turning in favour of the Bruce faction. The cession of these lands was highly unpopular, costing Balliol much valuable support, and even some of the disinherited began to desert him. More importantly, Sir Andrew Moray was released from captivity, while the earl of March defected from his temporary allegiance to Balliol, and at the same time the earl of Moray obtained promises of French assistance. This encouraged the Bruce loyalists to go on the offensive, and Sir Andrew Moray, Robert the Steward, and Sir William Douglas of Liddesdale launched a savage raid on Sir Eustace Maxwell's territories in the south-west, which extended into Galloway. Although this prompted McDowell to switch the dubious commodity of his allegiance to the Bruce cause, the majority of Kirkcudbrightshire landowners remained loyal to Balliol, and this resulted in a civil war between the rival factions in Galloway where, according to the Lanercost chronicler, 'they mutually destroyed one another'.[17]

Balliol's régime was becoming increasingly precarious, and the English were compelled to launch a series of invasions to shore it up. In 1334, Kirkcudbright was a target of attack,[18] and in July 1335 King Edward III led an army of some 13,000 men across the Border, while another one under Balliol set out from Berwick. After scoring a few minor successes, in the course of which the earl of Moray was taken prisoner, the two armies converged on Perth, where King Edward and Balliol established their headquarters. Confident that their show of strength would convince the Bruce supporters of the futility of further resistance, the two kings offered a general amnesty – known as the Pacification of Perth – to those who were willing to submit. Some did, including Robert the Steward, whose lands in the west were under threat of attack from Ireland. Balliol now appointed the earl of Atholl his lieutenant of the north, and, confident that the other Bruce leaders such as Sir Andrew Moray would submit, he and King Edward disbanded their armies and returned to Berwick.

They miscalculated. Moray had no intention of submitting, and instead he and Douglas of Liddesdale defeated Atholl in the forest of Culblean in Aberdeenshire. This gave the Bruce party new heart, all the more so since those of their leaders, such as the Steward, who had submitted at Perth, soon reneged on their undertakings and joined them. In 1336, Sir Andrew Moray was re-appointed to the guardianship, and almost immediately afterwards he launched an attack on the Balliol heartland of Galloway. A token resistance was offered under the leadership of Sir Eustace Maxwell and Duncan McDowell, who had now returned to the Balliol camp, but it was soon overwhelmed, and this prompted McDowell to change sides once again.

The English were now forced to change their strategy. Repeated invasions were proving too expensive, and besides they were becoming progressively less effective; so, instead, they reinforced the garrisons of the castles which Balliol handed over to them, and Sir Eustace Maxwell was instructed to repair the defences of Caerlaverock. This strategy proved equally unsuccessful as many of them were re-taken, and by 1337 King Edward is reported to have 'lost all the castles and towns that he had caused to be fortified in Scotland'.[19] Among them was Caerlaverock. Moray's successful raid into Galloway had shaken Maxwell's resolve, and he had probably already decided to abandon Balliol, but he prudently waited until King Edward had provided him with money and supplies for reinforcing the defence of Caerlaverock before doing so.[20]

As Maxwell had been Balliol's principal supporter in the south-west, his defection marked a nadir in his fortunes at this time, and all the more so since Edward was threatening to withdraw his support. He was planning an invasion of France in pursuit of his dynastic claims to its throne, but because it was likely to be costly he could not afford to maintain the war against the Bruce loyalists, and was anxious to abandon it. As a temporary measure, he declared a truce which was to last until Michaelmas 1339. However, by the time it expired the pendulum of fortune was swinging back to Balliol again. Sir Andrew Moray had died the previous year, and Robert the Steward was appointed guardian in his place, which meant that instead of having a battle-hardened veteran the Scots now had a youth in his early twenties as their leader. As he lacked his predecessor's authority, the Bruce offensive slackened and Balliol was able to take the initiative. This encouraged McDowell and Maxwell to come over to his side again, along with another local magnate, Michael McGhie, while Sir Patrick McCulloch and Sir John le Mareschal, who had been consistently loyal to him, now formally entered the service of Edward III.[21]

In June 1340 the situation changed once again, for the earl of Moray was released from captivity, where he had remained since 1335, and this encouraged the Bruce supporters to go on the offensive again. Therefore, a two-pronged attack was mounted against the south, and, while Moray drove the English out of his own lands of Annandale, Douglas of Liddesdale captured Edinburgh castle and invaded the Border country. By the following year, much of Scotland, including the Border marches, was back in Bruce hands, while support for Balliol was mainly confined to Galloway. This meant the king could now safely return from France, and when he arrived in Scotland he was 'ressavyd [received] with blythnes' by his people.[22]

BRUCE DYNASTY RE-ESTABLISHED

David was now faced with the daunting task of establishing his authority over a realm which had been riven by nine years of civil war, devastated by repeated English invasions, and where Balliol was still a force to be reckoned with. This would have daunted even the most experienced ruler, let alone a seventeen-year-old youth, and the fact that David ultimately achieved an ascendancy over the realm unparalleled by any of his predecessors is a clear indication that he had inherited all the ability, tough-mindedness and determination of his illustrious father.

Since Balliol's power was concentrated on Galloway, priority had to be given to bringing this region under control, and because it was more deeply entrenched in eastern Galloway David was compelled to focus his initial efforts on Wigtownshire. McDowell held the key to it, but as he was not to be trusted David put his former guardian, Sir Malcolm Fleming, in charge of the region. He was already a powerful magnate, owning extensive lands in Clydesdale, besides being sheriff of Dunbarton and having strong links with the leading families in Carrick.[23] However, in order to give him a power-base in the region, David granted him in 1342 a charter of 'all our lands of Farynes and Rynnes' from the Cree to the 'Molerennysnage', and from there to the borders with Carrick,[24] which broadly comprised all the lands in Wigtownshire which had reverted to the crown on the deaths of Edward Bruce and his son, Alexander.[25] Finally, David created Fleming earl of Wigtown, giving him full jurisdictional powers, including the four pleas of the crown.[26]

At this point a snag arose, because the earl of March challenged the king's right to grant these lands to Fleming on the grounds that he had inherited an interest in them through his mother, Marjorie Comyn.[27] As March was a loyal supporter of David his claim could not be overlooked, so he was bought off with the grant of the barony of Mochrum, as well as land in the Glenkens.[28] This meant that Mochrum had to be recovered from Sir Malcolm Fleming, so in compensation he was given the barony of Cardiness,[29] which had recently been confiscated from its de Kerdenesse owners. Forfeitures were also imposed on Balliol supporters in Wigtownshire, such as Sir John de Mareschal, and although he may have died by then his widow and children were dispossessed, being compensated with a pension from the English crown.[30] So too was Sir Patrick McCulloch, whose lands of Myretoun[31] were given to 'John Carrik in liferent'.[32]

In spite of David's authority being more tenuous in eastern Galloway, he seems to have made some changes among the landowners there as well. Out went the de Kerdennesse family, and likewise John de Gevylstoun, whose barony of Gelston was given to James Boyd,[33] probably a younger son of Sir Robert. The de Twynames were another casualty. Although two members of the family held high office under King Robert,[34] it seems they must have defected to Balliol, since their 'ten merk lands of Twynholm' were given to the Bruce supporter, Thomas Crawford.[35] Another beneficiary was Lachlan Edzear (Edgar) whose family had already been rewarded with lands in the Rhinns, as he was given those of Bombie.[36]

One beneficiary in particular was Andrew Buttergask, sheriff of Perth and clerk of the king's wardrobe, who had already been given lands in his native Perthshire and elsewhere. Now he was granted the remainder of the barony of Urr,[37] as well as lands in the parishes of Colvend, Senwick and Kelton,[38] which had previously belonged to Alexander Bruce. As the latter two were high-status estates, their grant to Buttergask is a clear reflection of his political importance and close attachment to David. In 1342, David granted Sir Archibald Douglas's son, William, the future earl of Douglas, and at that time a minor, the forfeited de Moubray lands at Borgue,[39] which presumably was part of a strategy for building up the Douglas power in the region.

Both kings – Edward Balliol and David Bruce – recognised that the support of the local Church was crucial to securing control of Galloway. However, Balliol was not in a position to give it land, since the validity of his title to his family's former possessions was contingent on his securing exclusive control of the kingship. Nevertheless, styling himself 'Edward King of Scots and Lord of Galloway', he successfully petitioned Edward III to restore to the monks of Dundrennan certain lands and privileges belonging to them in Ireland, which in fact he was duty bound to do under the treaty of Northampton. Nevertheless, it is possible that their gift to him of Hestan Island, which he subsequently used as his base in Galloway, was his reward.[40] Later, in 1347, he assigned to Sweetheart abbey half the income from Buittle church – presumably to compensate it for losses suffered during his campaign.

On the other hand, because David was seen as controlling the legitimate government of Scotland, he was in a position to grant a better title to the lands belonging to the royal patrimony. Dundrennan appears to have been the main object of his charity, as it seems he was responsible for granting it the estates of Biskeby (Bysbie),[41] near the Isle of Whithorn, and Culfadden (Culscadden) in the parish of Sorbie. The indications are that David also gave it a tract of hill ground near Creetown in the parish of Kirkmabreck,[42] while he is known to have given them the lands of Culindach,[43] perhaps identifiable with Cullendoch in the neighbouring parish of Girthon. In addition, he confirmed the monks in their possession of the lands of Collin near Auchencairn,[44] and they also received unidentifiable lands described as 'Dungarnok in the Water of Dee'.[45]

It could have been at David's instigation that Sir Malcolm Fleming gave the monks of Glenluce the estates of Barness and Kirkchrist in the parish of Kirkinner,[46] and possibly the lands adjacent to the Knock of Luce, which he is also known to have given them. Even if David did not initiate these gifts, he certainly endorsed them, because he issued a royal charter shortly afterwards confirming the monks in possession of all their lands, including these additional grants.[47] Tongland and Trail (St Mary's Isle) were also given certain rights and privileges,[48] while the lands of 'Dermore in the rins within the town of Innermessan'[49] were added to the bishop's *mensa*.[50]

BALLIOL REVIVAL

David's return to Scotland had coincided with a renewal of the truce with England, but by 1344 it was threatening to break down. Therefore, King Edward instructed Balliol to put the English-held lands in the Borders in a proper state of defence,[51] and he in turn charged McDowell with responsibility for strengthening the garrison on Hestan Island.[52] The Bruce supporters responded by blockading it, and although an English expeditionary force managed to win through with supplies (including a consignment of ten tuns of wine) McDowell's support for Balliol was becoming increasingly precarious.

Learning of this, David bribed him to defect by offering him lands in eastern Galloway,[53] while threatening to confiscate his Wigtownshire possessions if he refused. The result was predictable: McDowell changed sides once again. The English retaliated by attacking the island by sea, taking McDowell prisoner, along with his sons, his servants and 'thirty squires and sergeands of the country'. Thereafter, he was consigned to the Tower, where conditions were so unpleasant that, after enduring them for two years, he readily accepted an offer of release on condition of returning to the Balliol camp. However, he was forced to leave his wife and family in England as hostages for his future conduct.[54]

In October 1346, David took advantage of Edward III's preoccupation with the siege of Calais by launching an invasion of England, in the course of which he sacked the priories of Hexham and Lanercost. However, when he finally encountered the English at Nevill's Cross, near Durham, he was overwhelmingly defeated. Nevertheless, it was a hard-fought battle, and in spite of being struck by two arrows[55] David fought bravely, apparently knocking two teeth out of his principal assailant, until he was finally over-powered and taken prisoner. His nephew, Robert the Steward, on the other hand, seeing the Scots in danger of defeat, escaped from the field and galloped back to Scotland where, in the king's absence, he was appointed lieutenant of the realm. The casualties were enormous, and while the earl of Moray and the Galloway landowner, Andrew Buttergask,[56] were among the slain, many nobles, including Sir Malcolm Fleming, were taken prisoner.

David's imprisonment gave a substantial fillip to the Balliol cause. Therefore, mustering a force of Gallovidians, he led a plundering raid into southern Scotland and, joining forces with Henry, lord Percy, he invaded the Lothians, 'devastating it with fire and sword', before sweeping through Ayrshire and down into Dumfriesshire.[57] David's absence also encouraged King Edward to renew his support for Balliol, so he established him at Caerlaverock castle, giving him semi-regal powers in order to emphasise his kingly status. However, this was only a temporary respite, because Balliol's dwindling support in Scotland persuaded Edward that he was backing a losing cause, and consequently he had no option but to cut his losses and abandon him to make shift for himself as best he could.

In 1346, Balliol established himself in his grandmother, Dervorguilla's, former stronghold of Arsbotel on Loch Ken, from where he conducted a long rearguard action. In spite of its strategic position, where it command-ed the main access route into Galloway from the north, it was dangerously exposed, and this became uncomfortably apparent when Balliol came within an ace of being captured by John Kennedy and Sir Alan Stewart in the course of a plundering raid from their base in Carrick.[58] So, in 1347, with the help of an English expeditionary force, he transferred his headquar-ters to Hestan Island, where he proceeded to rebuild the manor house, but as this proved an inconvenient location he eventually retired to Buittle. As the castle had been demolished by Edward Bruce in 1313, he built a tim-bered manor house to replace it, but, because this was financed through the improper diversion of loans advanced by Edward III for other purposes, it was a shoddily-built affair which eventually collapsed of its own accord.[59]

Balliol was the last of his dynasty and, judging from the amount of lands he transferred to him, it seems he regarded his *scutifer*, or equerry, Sir

William de Aldeburgh, as a surrogate son. For example, in 1352 he gave him the barony of Kells, as well as Arsbotel itself, and later he gave him lands at Crossmichael, and those of Kidsdale, near Whithorn[60] – not that this amounted to much, since he lacked a valid title to them, while the list of witnesses to these charters reflects the limited amount of support for him in Galloway. For they were confined to the faithful Sir Patrick McCulloch and Matthew McLellan and their sons, as well as Sir Roger de Moubray, John de Rerrick, and Dougal McDowell,[61] probably Duncan's brother.

Thereafter support for the Balliol cause crumbled rapidly. In 1353, Douglas of Liddesdale led another raid into Galloway, and although he was defeated by a local force under McDowell, he left a trail of devastation, inflicting yet more hardships on a population which was already reeling from the effects of a plague epidemic. Two years later, the hostages which McDowell had left behind in England were released, so he was open to being suborned again. This time the bait was David's promise to confirm him in possession of all his lands, including those in eastern Galloway, on condition that he came into his peace. This was more than the acquisitive McDowell could resist, and he duly changed sides once more. Thus, his defection, coupled with the fall of Buittle and the capture and destruction of the English-held castles of Dalswinton and Caerlaverock by the Bruce loyalists,[62] dealt a mortal blow to Balliol's position in Galloway.

His final defeat was sealed in 1355, when the French king, John II, who was still at war with Edward III, confiscated his lands in Picardy on the pretext that as he was Edward's vassal he was automatically an enemy of France. This was the last straw, and Edward had little difficulty in persuading Balliol to assign him his rights in the Scottish crown in return for a handsome pension. The English records attribute this to his 'great age and feebleness and his inability to continue the great labour he had to sustain',[63] which was probably true, since he was now well over seventy.[64] Nevertheless, there was still plenty of fight left in the old man, as he is reported to have appeared at King Edward's court at Roxburgh 'like a roaring lion'.[65] There, in a dramatic gesture he tore the crown from his head, and grasping a handfull of earth and stones he thrust them at the king in a symbolic resignation of the kingdom into his hands.[66]

King David

In 1357 King David was released from captivity, where he had remained since 1346. The ransom was 100,000 marks (equivalent to £63,000) payable over ten years, and he was required to surrender hostages in security for the unpaid instalments. A truce was agreed, and this gave David the opportunity to re-establish his authority uninterrupted by the threat of English invasion. Most of Balliol's supporters had already come into his peace, although a notable exception in Galloway was Sir Patrick McCulloch. He had followed Balliol into exile in England, where he remained until the latter's death in 1364. Thereafter, he sued for pardon and was received into the king's peace,[67] when it seems he was restored to part of his former lands.[68]

Judging from the plethora of charters of lands in eastern Galloway, which were granted to members of the McDowell family at this time, it seems that they too were rehabilitated,[69] though it is difficult to establish precisely what was happening. However, the indications are that Duncan McDowell had died and King David was dividing up the lands which had been given to him in 1355 between members of his family in order to reduce their power.[70] For example, those at Borgue were split between Dougal and Fergus McDowell,[71] obviously his sons, and as Dougal received the lion's share of all Duncan's lands in eastern Galloway it seems that he must have been the eldest, though his younger brother, Fergus, is the better known.

Unlike his father, Fergus seems to have been a consistent supporter of David, had fought for him against the English, and was rewarded with a knighthood and the offices of coroner and constable of Kirkcudbright.[72] The story has it that, at one point, the English planned to kidnap him while he was asleep, but St Ninian appeared to him in a dream, warning him of the plot, and consequently Fergus managed to escape from from his would-be captors. In token of his thanks for the saint's intervention, he is believed to have been responsible for repairing the roof of Whithorn cathedral, part of which had collapsed.[73] His wife was Margaret, the daughter of William Cunningham, who was one of David's principal supporters, but their marriage was invalid because they were related to each other and had omitted to obtain papal dispensation.[74] In 1364, they decided to rectify matters, and with David's support they presented a petition to the pope, pleading that if it was refused it would result in 'loss, scandal and slaughter'.[75] Quite why the withholding of papal sanction should have such dramatic results can only be conjectured, but in the event dispensation was granted, so all was well.

David was now in undisputed possession of all the former Balliol lands in Galloway, and one of his first disposals was the prestigious barony of Kenmure to his cousin, Sir Gilbert of Carrick.[76] However, his attention was primarily focused on the Glenkens. Strategically, it was an important region, since it straddled the main access route from the north, but as a result of the wars it had become depopulated and had reverted to a wilderness. It had already been abandoned as an ecclesiastical deanery by the 1350s, while King Robert's hunting reserve had fallen into disuse. Therefore, it is clear from the changes which he made in the pattern of landownership there that David was attempting to rehabilitate the region. He had ample scope to do so, because much of it had reverted to him, having formerly been part of the Balliol patrimony, while George, earl of March, had resigned to him the lands there which he had inherited from his predecessor, Earl Patrick.[77]

As a first step, he re-constituted the forest, and in 1358 he appointed John Crawford of Cumnock its forester or keeper.[78] In the same year, William de Gordon, who was already a landowner in the region,[79] was given 'the whole lordship, administration and safekeeping of the New Forest of the Glenkenne'.[80] Later, in 1366, David granted the forest itself to his cousin Euphemia, countess of Ross, and her husband, Sir Walter Leslie,[81] who was one of his close circle of intimates in whom he reposed supreme political power. The McLellans were also major landowners in the region, and as they owed their advancement to Dervorguilla they naturally supported the Balliols. However, as they had made their peace with David, Gilbert McGillolane, the head of the family, was confirmed in possession of his lands of Balmaclellan and formally designated captain of the kindred of the clan Connon.[82]

One of David's most trusted adherents was Sir John Herries, whose family were former Bruce tenants in Annandale, while he himself was a fellow captive of David in England and had accompanied him on his return to Scotland. David had obviously marked him out as a principal supporter of his authority in Galloway, so when the earl of Mar resigned the barony of Terregles in 1358 he gave it to Herries.[83] Meanwhile, the monks of Holm Cultram were complaining about the difficulties they were encountering in trying to manage their Galloway lands 'on account of the hostility to the English which had resulted from the recent wars'. This was hardly surprising since they represented an English institution in a land which had suffered so much at the hands of their fellow countrymen. So, when they surrendered these lands to David in 1368, he constituted them a barony and gave it to Herries,[84] and as he was also granted him Andrew Buttergask's portion of the barony of Urr, Herries became a leading magnate in eastern Galloway.

THE EMERGENCE OF THE DOUGLASES

Endowing trusted adherents like Sir John Herries with grants of land in eastern Galloway was part of David's strategy for consolidating his authority there; but, for this to be fully effective he needed to appoint an overlord who commanded sufficient power to enable him to exercise supreme control of the region. While he had been in a position to establish Sir Malcolm Fleming as his viceroy in Wigtownshire in 1342, it was impossible for him to do the same in eastern Galloway so long as Edward Balliol was established there. Yet, it was not until twelve years after Balliol's departure that an overlord was finally appointed, and one can only conclude that this was because David had some difficulty in finding the right man.

His choice eventually fell on Sir James Douglas's illegitimate son, Sir Archibald 'the Grim'. His credentials were impeccable. He and his family had been consistently loyal to David throughout Edward Balliol's campaign, while he himself had a distinguished war record, having made a daring escape from the English after his capture at Poitiers.[85] He was one of David's trusted circle of intimates, to whom he confided supreme political power, and it was a measure of his trust in him that David had appointed Archibald keeper of Edinburgh castle and warden of the west marches. This was a difficult and challenging assignment, and his success in stamping his authority on that troublesome region demonstrated beyond all doubt his ability to achieve the same in Galloway.

However, he needed a power-base there, so David proceeded to endow him with all the lands in eastern Galloway which had reverted to the crown. Therefore, in 1369, he granted him a blanket charter of 'all our existing lands in Galloway between the river Cree and the river Nith . . . as our dearest uncle Edward Bruce of good memory held or possessed the said lands while he lived'.[86] Thus, not only did Archibald become entitled to the rents from these estates, but as his was a regality title he was entitled to retain all fines imposed on malefactors within these domains as well. As he was also given the 'fermes' (rents) of the burghs of Kirkcudbright and Wigtown, and (for a limited time) all the customs received at the former, the sum of these grants represented a huge source of revenue.

Meanwhile, in Wigtownshire the veteran Sir Malcolm Fleming had recently died, having been succeeded by his grandson, Thomas.[87] Unfortunately for him, he had been one of the hostages given up in security of David's ransom, and as this had never been paid in full he was compelled to buy his freedom at the cost of selling off some of his lands and wadsetting others.[88] Among those he disposed of was the Cardiness barony, the purchaser being a member of the McCulloch kindred who had recently made their peace with the king.[89] (Legend has it that the McCullochs inherited the barony from the original de Kerdenesse owners,[90] but this is almost certainly fictitious,[91] while the alternative theory that they acquired it from Margaret, duchess of Touraine, the widow of the fourth earl of Douglas, during the mid-fifteenth century, is also unlikely.[92])

Tradition attributes Thomas's inability to control the Wigtownshire baronage to his youth and lack of his grandfather's authority,[93] but it was more likely to have been due to financial stringency. Although he persevered for some years the situation was clearly beyond him, so in 1372 he sold his earldom, along with his remaining lands in Wigtownshire, to Archibald the Grim. Consequently, Archibald now owned most of the former patrimony of the lords of Galloway, and was appropriately styled as such in all subsequent royal charters.

APPENDIX

Note on the ownership of Buittle

The subsequent destination of Buittle is complex. When Sir James Douglas was killed on a crusade in 1330 all his lands, including Buittle, passed to his legitimate son William Douglas. He was killed three years later at Halidon Hill, and as he had no issue his lands passed to his father's half-brother, Hugh 'the dull'. Being a cleric, Hugh had no issue either, and therefore his lands should in the normal course of events have reverted to the crown on his death.

However, in 1342, in recognition of the support given him by the Douglases during Edward Balliol's campaign, David II granted Hugh a concession whereby, in return for resigning his lands to him, he re-granted them under an entail. This specified a series of heirs, starting with Hugh himself, and after him his nephew, William Douglas (the son of his younger brother, Sir Archibald, who was also killed at Halidon Hill), and his male heirs. Should these fail, there was a destination to his kinsman, Sir William Douglas of Liddesdale and his male issue, failing whom to Sir James Douglas's illegitimate son, Archibald the Grim.

When Hugh died in 1347, the Douglas lands passed under the entail to his nephew William, who subsequently became the first earl of Douglas. As he was a minor, his lands were controlled by his tutor, Douglas of Liddesdale, who was coincidentally the next heir. He proceeded to abuse his office by appropriating the feu rights in certain of the entailed lands, including Buittle, thus leaving William with the bare superiority. When Douglas of Liddesdale was killed by his aggrieved ward, his feu right in Buittle passed to his daughter, and on her death without issue it devolved on her father's nephew, Sir James Douglas of Dalkeith, from whom it passed to his descendants, the earls of Morton. They continued to own Buittle until the sixteenth century, when the third earl forfeited it to James V. In 1535, James re-granted it to the fifth lord Maxwell, whose son, the sixth lord, later married the third earl of Morton's daughter, and their descendants, which included the Maxwells of Munches, continued to own part of the former barony.

William Douglas's superiority right in Buittle, on the other hand, passed to his son, the second earl. When he was killed at Otterburn, this right passed along with the entailed Douglas lands to Archibald the Grim, and thereafter it belonged to his successors as earls of Douglas until it was forfeited to the crown, along with the rest of the entailed lands, by the ninth earl in 1455.

NOTES

1. *APS* i, 464–5.
2. *Ibid*, 464: *Bower* 7, p.41.
3. *Bower* 7, p.43.
4. *Wyntoun* ii, 384.
5. *Bower* 7, p 77.
6. To avoid confusion, I will continue to refer to him as Balliol and his rival as King David, though in the eyes of their contemporaries they were both kings.
7. *Chron. Lanercost*, 269.
8. Oram, 'Bruce, Balliol', 42.
9. *Bower* 7, p 83.
10. He was the son of Wallace's former colleague, and also a brother-in-law of King Robert having married his sister Christian.
11. He was Sir James Douglas's youngest half-brother, and father of the first earl of Douglas.
12. King Robert's grandson, the future Robert II, who had inherited the office of Steward on his father's death in 1326.
13. *Bower* 7, p 77.
14. Maxwell-Irving, 'Kenmure Castle'.
15. Conversation with Dr Oram, though he thinks de Colvend could have been restored at the end of King Robert's reign.
16. *Rot. Scot.* i, 273, 391.
17. *Chron. Lanercost*, 278.
18. *CDS* iii, no 911.
19. *Scalachronica*, 166–7.
20. *Chron. Lanercost*, 290–1.
21. *Rot. Scot.* I, 612 It seems that Edward III rewarded him with a grant of the rents from Kirkcudbright (which in war-torn Galloway would have amounted to little), until such time as he could provide him with a 20-merk land in Scotland (*Wig Charters*, xxx).
22. *Fordun* i, 365.
23. Sir Malcolm was one of King David's trusted circle of intimates, in whom he reposed supreme political power.
24. *RMS* app 1 no 119. Farynes and Rynnes were the two ecclesiastical deaneries in Wigtownshire, while 'Molerennysnage' was the Mull of Galloway.
25. Sometime after 1346 a pretender turned up in Galloway claiming to be Alexander Bruce, that he had survived Halidon Hill, and was entitled to have his lands and honours restored to him. As this posed a serious threat to Sir Malcolm Fleming's position in Wigtownshire, and also the Steward who was concerned for the Carrick earldom, they had him put to death in short order.
26. *RRS* vi no 39.
27. The implications of this are discussed in *Wig Charters*, xlii. Marjorie Comyn was a granddaughter of Elena de Quenci.
28. The charter of 1368 confirming Earl Patrick's successor George earl of March in the possession of these lands (RMS i, no 291) refers to them as having belonged to Patrick earl of Dunbar, which was his other title. Although the lands in the Glenkens were later resigned by his successor Earl George, Mochrum remained in the family until the eighteenth century.

29. *RRS* vi no 52: *RMS* i app 2 no 325.

30. Brooke, *Wild Men*, 155: *Wig Charters*, xxx.

31. McKerlie i, 237.

32. *RMS* i app 2 no 1114. This John Carrik was almost certainly the same as the John Carrick who was King David's secretary and later his Chancellor.

33. *RMS* i app 2 no 751. This entry adds the rider 'quhilk [which] John Gamilstoun forisfecit [forfeited]' on the grounds of being 'inimici nostri et rebellis [our enemy and a rebel]'.

34. John de Twynham was his *provoris* (revenue collector) in 1329, while Walter de Twynam, probably a brother, was his Chancellor during the last two years of his reign.

35. *RMS* i app 2 no 838.

36. *Ibid.* no 834.

37. *Ibid.* no 840.

38. *Ibid.* no 792.

39. *RMS* i app 2 no 839. The rubric of this charter refers to the lands as having belonged to the de Moubrays, who are tersely described as 'slaine traitors'.

40. Brooke asserts in *Wild Men* (p 160) that this belonged to Dundrennan in the fourteenth century.

41. The grant of Biskeby was to lead to a long and acrimonious dispute between Dundrennan and Whithorn in the following century, when its contentious prior, William Douglas, tried to appropriate the teinds from these lands.

42. This can be inferred from the fact that Dundrennan owned these at the time of the Reformation (see McKerlie ii, 215).

43. *RMS* i app 2 no 1153. If this was identifiable with Cullendoch, it would have consisted of a tract of barren moorland which was probably contiguous with Dundrennan's lands at Kirkmabreck.

44. *Ibid.* no 1208.

45. *Ibid.* no 836.

46. *Ibid.* no 1148. That these were the lands granted to Glenluce can be inferred from the fact that, whereas its original endowment was confined to the modern parishes of Old and New Luce, the 1572 charter of the abbey lands to the fourth earl of Cassilis shows these as being the only two properties outwith these parishes.

47. *RMS* i app 2 no 1194.

48. *Ibid.* nos. 1170, 1374.

49. *Ibid.* no 837.

50. Meaning literally 'a table', the *mensa* was the collective description of the lands given to the bishopric at one time or another for maintaining the episcopal establishment.

51. *Rot. Parl* II, 147: Nicholson, *The Later Middle Ages*, 145.

52. Oram, 'Bruce, Balliol', 45.

53. These lands included estates in the parishes of Senwick, Twynholm, Kelton and Borgue, as well as another at Edingham near Dalbeattie, all of which were subsequently divided among his family.

54. *Rot. Scot.* i, 722.

55. One struck him in the face, while the head of the other remained embedded in his skull, causing him recurrent headaches at the time of the new moon until it was removed some years later in the course of a visit to Whithorn.

56. *Bower* 7, p 261. As Buttergask died without male heirs, his lands of Urr reverted to the crown.

57. *Ibid.*
58. *Wyntoun* ii, 477.
59. Conversation with A.I.N. Penman.
60. Brooke, *Wild Men,* 164.
61. *CDS* iii, no 1578.
62. *Wyntoun* ii, 487.
63. *CDS* iii, no 1591: *Rot. Scot.* i, p 800.
64. As Balliol was old enough to be attached to the prince of Wales's household in 1296, he would have been at least twelve, and therefore he must have been born in 1284 at the latest (Brooke, *Wild Men,* chap. 7 note 29).
65. *Wyntoun* ii, 485: *Scalachronica* p 304.
66. *Fordun* i, 373.
67. *CDS* iv, no 92.
68. Reid advances this theory in 'Myreton castle'. While the example he gives is demonstrably wrong, the theory could be right, as Sir Patrick may not have been restored to his lands in the parish of Glasserton (McKerlie i, 508), and this could explain how they came to be granted to Sir William Stewart of Garlies in 1426.
69. *RMS* i, app 2 nos 1006, 1147, 1193, 835, 1221, 1176.
70. This theory has been advanced by Oram in 'Bruce, Balliol', 45.
71. *RMS* i, app 2 no 1147.
72. *RMS* i, app 2 no 1007.
73. *The Legends of SS Ninian and Machor,* 74: *CSSR* i, 476 *Reg supp.* 41 fol. 134.
74. *Wig Charters,* 160, no. 131.
75. *Ibid.*
76. *RMS* i app 2 nos 894, 1100.
77. *Ibid.,* app 1 no. 291.
78. *Ibid.* no 910.
79. The lands belonging to him included Lochinvar and other estates in the parishes of Dalry, Kells, Balmaclellan and modern Carsphairn, which he inherited from his father, Sir Adam de Gordon. The latter, who was a Douglas tenant of the barony of Stichill in Roxburghshire, had acquired these lands from Sir John Maxwell, of the Caerlaverock family, who in turn had been granted them by John Comyn, earl of Buchan. Later on, the fourth earl of Douglas granted further lands to William's grandson, Sir Alexander Gordon, in order to establish him as a power in the Ken valley.
80. Brooke, 'The Glenkens' 46.
81. *RMS* i app 2 nos 258, 1556. The grant consisted of 'the whole new forest below the county of Dumfries' (i.e. in modern Kirkcudbrightshire), and conceivably Countess Euphemia may have inherited some right in this from her grandfather, Earl Hugh.
82. *Ibid.* app. 1 no. 912.
83. *Ibid.* no 192.
84. *Ibid.* no 282, app 2, no 1574.
85. *Bower* 7, p 301.
86. *RMS* i no 329.
87. *Ibid.* no 250. This was issued in 1367 confirming Thomas in the earldom.
88. A wadset was an old form of mortgage which entitled the creditor to take possession of the debtor's lands and revenues until such time as the loan was repaid, and if the debtor failed to do so the creditor was entitled to retain possession.

89. These lands would remain in the family until 1629, when they were sold virtually in their entirety to John Gordon of Over Ardwall.

90. This asserts that the last of that family, having sired a string of daughters, celebrated the birth of the longed-for son by holding a skating party on the nearby Black Loch, in the course of which the ice broke and everyone, including the infant son, was drowned. A daughter, who had been left ill at home, was the only survivor, and it was through her marriage to a McCulloch that Cardiness passed into that family.

91. McKerlie refers (iii, 11) to an account written by Colonel William Maxwell of Cardoness in 1699 which mentions a deed allegedly executed by one Margaret Cardincss (perhaps the surviving daughter). This apparently conveyed the lordship of Cardiness to her husband, a McCulloch, who had been a servitor of her family. Although this is merely hearsay evidence and McKerlie's assertions have to be treated with caution it cannot be entirely discounted.

92. Dr Oram rules this out, as there is no evidence from the chamberlains' accounts that Cardiness was ever part of the lordship demesne.

93. McKerlie refers (i, 25) to 'the grievous feuds that had arisen between him [Thomas] and the more powerful . . . inhabitants of the earldom'.

14

THE DOUGLAS SUPREMACY

A NEW REGIME

King David died in 1371. In spite of being twice married (and having a number of mistresses) he had no children, so the succession passed to his nephew, Robert the Steward. Now aged fifty-five, he had spent his entire adult life building up his position as one of the most powerful magnates in the realm, and having acted as guardian during David's absences he already had ample experience of government. However, David had long regarded him as a potential threat to his authority, and this became a reality in 1363 when Robert colluded with William, earl of Douglas, and Patrick, earl of March, in an abortive coup to supplant his principal advisers. After its failure, Robert, fearing for his succession rights, was quick to abandon his fellow conspirators and make his peace with the king, and although he accepted Robert's submission he deliberately marginalised him for the rest of his reign. Meanwhile, his fellow conspirators were justifiably aggrieved at Robert's defection, and this left a legacy of bad blood between them which would dog the opening years of his kingship.

In addition, Robert was opposed by David's supporters and placemen, as well as those whom he had crossed in the course of his career. They amounted to a formidable combination, ranging from members of the nobility, like George Dunbar, the new earl of March, to the lesser baronage, including Sir Walter Leslie and his relatives the Lindsays, who represented a powerful affinity. More challenging still, Robert had to contend with a number of influential regional magnates who were determined to resist his authority, and foremost among them were the Douglases. Earl William,[1] the acknowledged head of the kindred, with whom he was already at odds, had even made a somewhat futile attempt to challenge his succession. And since Archibald the Grim and Sir James Douglas of Dalkeith, who were the other principal leaders of the Douglas faction, owed their political advancement to David they, too, were opposed to Robert.

Therefore, he was forced to buy off their hostility by a combination of bribes and marriage alliances. For example, he secured Earl William's acquiescence by giving one of his daughters to William's son and heir,

James, gilding the match with a handsome pension. He also confirmed Archibald in the lordship of Bothwell, which he claimed in right of his wife, while Sir James Douglas of Dalkeith was given the barony of Preston, in eastern Galloway.[2] The powerful earl of March was also persuaded to abandon his opposition in return for being confirmed in the lordship of Annandale, to which he claimed an inherited right.[3]

The Lindsay clan, too, were won over by grants of land, and this had repercussions in Galloway. Here, Sir James Lindsay of Crawford, the son of Robert's half-sister, had been established by David as a landowner in the Glenkens. Robert now gave him the lands and barony of Wigtown, having prevailed on him to hand over his lands in the Glenkens to his sister, Isabel, and her husband, Sir John Maxwell of Pollok.[4] However, his right to do so was questionable, since these were among the lands which Thomas Fleming had sold to Archibald the Grim, and it was only because Fleming had subsequently resigned them to the crown[5] that Robert assumed the right to make the grant to Lindsay. Archibald promptly challenged it, and the matter came before the general council. It upheld his appeal, so Robert was forced to back down, and shortly afterwards he issued a charter formally confirming 'our dearest cousin' Archibald in possession of the lands which he acquired from Thomas Fleming,[6] Lindsay meantime being palmed off with a pension.[7]

Robert's policy of bartering his way to power was reinforced by a strategy of establishing his sons as influential magnates in their own right. Therefore, through a combination of marriages with well-dowered brides, grants from the royal patrimony, and the devious manipulation of a number of northern lordships, he equipped each of them with a territorial power-base. As he saw it, they would serve as agents for the extension of his own royal authority but, as events would prove, he was unwittingly sowing dragon's teeth. For his sons used their endowments to build up their own power to the extent that they became overmighty subjects, and ultimately posed a threat to Robert himself and his successors.

A case in point was his second son, Robert, who acquired through marriage the earldom of Menteith, while his father secured for him the important earldom of Fife. Not content with that, he acquired still more lands, and at the same time built up his political power to the extent that he became the effective ruler of the kingdom for a period of thirty-two years, from 1388 until his death in 1420. Another was Alexander, who was given the lordship of Badenoch and became the supreme power in the north, while he also acquired lands in the Glenkens in right of his wife, Euphemia, countess of Ross, the widow of Sir Walter Leslie. Inevitably, rivalries developed between these sons, and their vendettas were sustained with even greater animosity by the next generation who would become a seriously disruptive force throughout the next two reigns.

The supreme example was King Robert's eldest son, John. Although his star shone brightly for a time, he was to be edged out of power during his father's lifetime, never regaining it until the last years of his reign. He had been a creature of David II, who sought to detach him from his father by granting him the earldom of Carrick, along with the attaching lands, as well as giving him his wife's niece, Annabella Drummond, in marriage. Nevertheless, King Robert gave John his ancestral Stewart estates in Ayrshire and Renfrewshire, along with a number of important offices, such as the keepership of Edinburgh castle. This was deliberately designed to build up his power in southern Scotland, where Robert's own authority was tenuous, in order to establish him as a counterpoise to the Douglas influence there. However, Robert's plans went badly awry because, instead of being content to act as his father's surrogate, Carrick performed a volte-face by allying himself with the Douglases and other leading magnates in the region, including the Lindsay faction. This was to put him in such a commanding position that, a few years later, he and his allies launched a partially successful coup against his father.

According to Froissart's politically-slanted account, this was because the king was now 'bowed down and blear-eyed with age', and had lost the power to govern effectively. The reality was that, as he was now approaching seventy and looked like going on for ever, Carrick was impatient to edge him aside. The crisis came in 1384 when Robert refused to sanction an invasion of England, and Carrick and his allies took advantage of this to force a confrontation with the object of stripping him of his royal powers. It was successful to the extent that, while the general council appointed Carrick as guardian, it would only agree to the transfer of limited judicial powers to him. Although this was somewhat less than Carrick set out to achieve, it enabled him to secure the passing of a number of statutes which were designed to facilitate the apprehension of criminals. However, Archibald the Grim was determined they should not impinge on his own jurisdictional powers in Galloway. So, using the sanctity of its traditional laws as a pretext, he formally protested 'on behalf of the privilege of his right and of the said law',[8] and he was powerful enough to ensure that his wishes prevailed.

Having been swept to power on a law and order ticket, Carrick proved incapable of delivering, because he was unable to keep his brothers, in particular Robert, earl of Fife, and Alexander, lord of Badenoch, in check. Therefore, he was forced to rely increasingly on Douglas support, and this could only be bought by the time-honoured methods of bribery and matrimonial alliances. Here, Carrick had the advantage of marriageable daughters whom he could use as political pawns, so he gave his daughter, Margaret, to Archibald the Grim's son, the future fourth earl of Douglas, while Elizabeth was married to the heir of Douglas of Dalkeith. Bribery involved granting the royal lordship of Nithsdale to Archibald's illegitimate son, Sir William Douglas ('a dark-skinned giant like his father and grand-father'[9]), and, 'on account of his skill in war', Carrick also gave him his sister, the 'werry beautiful ladye' Egidia,[10] as a bride.

THE GALLOWAY LORDSHIP

The administrative and judicial powers conferred on Archibald the Grim in eastern Galloway superseded the authority of the sheriff of Dumfries, but as Archibald's other commitments precluded him from exercising these in person he delegated them to a steward appointed to act on his behalf. Consequently this region became known as the 'stewartry'. In Wigtown-shire the situation was different. Here, Sir Malcolm Fleming had wielded similar powers during his lifetime, but after his death King David withdrew them, restoring them to the local sheriff, and because they were thereafter retained by his successors, this region has traditionally been referred to as the 'shire'.

Archibald needed to establish a ruling centre in Galloway. While Buittle was the obvious choice, this was not available as it belonged to Douglas of Dalkeith, and therefore he chose the alternative power-centre of Threave, where he built a castle on an island in the river Dee. Much of this stone fortress still stands today, and it is a tribute to its massive construction that it successfully withstood two major sieges during the following centuries. One of the first of its type to be built in Scotland, it represented a signifi-cant advance on the conventional timber donjons of the Galloway baronage, being designed as much as a status symbol as to withstand the firepower of the improved type of cannonry which was being developed at the time.

Available sources indicate that the lands granted to Archibald in eastern Galloway comprised a mosaic of estates, which were mainly concentrated in the Dee valley and extended down river to the coast, and eastwards as far as the barony of Buittle. The remainder were scattered throughout the region, including lands along the Colvend coast, and others at the northern end of Twynholm parish, and in addition there were two outliers beyond the Fleet, namely King's Laggan and Pulchree. To the north lay the rocky wilderness of the forest of Buchan, of which he owned the superiority title. Those in Wigtownshire, which he acquired from Thomas Fleming, consisted mainly of lands in the southern and eastern Machars, with sundry estates to the west, and also in the Rhinns. While his regality title was limited to the lands in eastern Galloway, he had full baronial powers throughout. Therefore, the legend that at Threave the 'knob' (a corbel protruding over the main entrance to the castle[11]) was never without a 'tassle' (a corpse) testifies to the severity with which Archibald and his successors exercised these powers.

THE CHURCH IN TURMOIL

Archibald was responsible for completing a number of projects for the benefit of the local Church which Edward Bruce had embarked on but was unable to complete. One involved building a Poor Hospital on the site of the abbey at Dercungal (Holywood). Papal authority was necessary, so in his petition of 1378 Archibald justified the request by claiming that, although 'places anciently dedicated to the service of Christ's poor as poor hospitals and lazar houses and the like' already existed, they were 'rendered uninhabitable by wars'. Furthermore, the present institution was of no further use because 'the poor pilgrims who visit [it] encounter great difficulty because of the de-population along the border between England and Scotland'.[12] Therefore, he undertook that if sanction was granted he would 'restore the same to usefulness and maintain them and cultivate their lands and defend them against the enemies of the realm'. It was a fair request, so consent was granted, the hospital was built, and Archibald endowed it with lands in the parish of Troqueer.[13]

The pope probably let the plea through on the nod, because he was heavily involved in the Great Schism which was splitting the Church. Pope Gregory XI had recently died and the cardinals had elected the archbishop of Bari as Pope Urban VI in his place. However, he proved such an appalling choice that they deposed him and elected the archbishop of Geneva as Pope Clement VII instead. Urban defied them, and remained at Rome, subsequently torturing and murdering five of the offending cardinals.[14] Therefore, Pope Clement set up a rival court at Avignon, he and his successors being known as the antipopes, and both popes proceeded to excommunicate one another, causing havoc and confusion throughout the Church. Britain too was divided, because when England declared for the Roman Pope Urban, the Scots demonstrated their independence by recognising Pope Clement at Avignon.

This meant that the diocese of Whithorn was torn by conflicting loyalties, and the divisions came to a head following the death of Bishop Adam de Lanark. Taking their lead from York, the prior and chapter elected Abbot Oswald of Glenluce as his successor, his appointment being confirmed by Pope Urban. At this point the Scottish Church intervened, and, using its influence, it ejected Bishop Oswald and replaced him with the prominent Franciscan friar, Thomas de Rossy. Oswald appealed to Pope Clement to overrule the Scottish Church and reinstate him, but when he declined to intervene Oswald abandoned Whithorn in disgust and retired to York, where he remained until his death in 1417. Rossy was duly consecrated, but he became deeply embroiled in the Schism and made what was described as an 'authentic contribution to the controversies of the fourteenth century' by challenging the pugnacious bishop of Norwich to a duel.[15] However, this seems to have been ignored, and Bishop Thomas reigned at Whithorn until his death in 1406.

In 1389, Archibald embarked on an ambitious scheme to convert the nunnery at Lincluden into a resident community of secular priests for the purpose of saying masses for the salvation of his soul. But, first of all the nuns had to be evicted and their institution closed, and this required the consent of Pope Clement at Avignon. With, one would hope, some hyperbole, the petition stated that the nuns 'have now taken to leading dissolute and scandalous lives, allowing the beautiful monastic buildings to fall into disrepair and ruin through neglect, while they dress their daughters, born of incest, in sumptuous clothes with gold ornaments and pearls'.[16] As Pope Clement was clearly anxious not to offend so powerful a Scottish magnate as Archibald, whom he had already described as 'the most devoted and eldest son of the Pope in Scotland',[17] he gave his consent without further ado. Thereafter, the provostry of that institution remained in the gift of Archibald and his successors, who used it for pensioning off their senior clerks.

In 1397, Archibald gave the patronage of the church of St Calmonel of Buittle to Sweetheart Abbey to help defray the cost of repairing the fire damage it had recently suffered. For the monks claimed it was beyond their means to do this themselves, because of 'its poverty and the smallness of its income' resulting from the depopulation of its lands.[18] This was due to the prevailing inflation. Whereas the original abbatial endowments were assumed to be sufficient to maintain them in perpetuity, this was now no longer the case, because war damage had eroded their income, while rising costs increased their expenditure. While the larger abbeys like Dundrennan could subsidise the shortfall from their commercial enterprises, the less well-favoured, smaller ones were forced to economise on essential repair and maintenance work. One example was Soulseat, where in 1393 the abbot Finlay A'Hannay, petitioned for a grant of the church at Kirkmaiden on the grounds that 'the fruits of the abbey could not sustain the abbey and convent in comfort'. Although this was standard monastic pleading, his claim that 'the edifice was in a dilapidated condition on account of wars in those parts'[19] was probably more authentic.

Even Whithorn was a victim of inflation, because in 1434 it was given the church of Longcastle to supplement its income.[20] Earlier, in 1410, Tongland was given the nearby church of Senwick, as well as that of Leswalt, ostensibly to subsidise the cost of entertaining visitors and travellers to the abbey,[21] but in reality to renovate the abbey and build a surrounding wall. Nevertheless, most houses managed to survive, though the small, little-known nunnery of St Evoca the Virgin at Nunton near Kirkcudbright had to be abandoned 'on account of the meagreness of its fruits'. In 1423, John of Inverkeithing, a canon of Holyrood, petitioned the pope to allow him to take it over for a period of ten years to give him the opportunity to resuscitate it, but he was unsuccessful, as all that remains of it is the name Nunton itself, and possibly that of the nearby farm of Kirkeoch.[22]

ARCHIBALD EARL OF DOUGLAS

A fourteen-year truce had been agreed between David II and Edward III in 1369, but as soon as it expired John of Gaunt conducted a raid into Scotland. However King Robert, who was anxious to avoid being drawn into a war with England, refused to retaliate, and this resulted in the coup of 1384. Carrick and his allies had no such inhibitions, and once they had sidelined the old king they embarked on plans for an invasion of England with French help. This took place in 1388, and it consisted of a three-pronged attack. While James, earl of Douglas, led an army into Northumberland, another one under Archibald the Grim and the earl of Fife, which included levies from Galloway, descended on the English west marches. At the same time, a third force was dispatched to Ireland under Douglas of Nithsdale with the object of destabilising the Anglo-Irish lordship there.

The earl of Northumberland dispatched an army from Newcastle under his son, Harry Hotspur, to oppose Douglas, but when it encountered the Scots at Otterburn on 14 August it was heavily defeated. However it was a Pyrrhic victory for the Scots, because Douglas was killed in the battle. Since he had no legitimate issue, this led to a dispute over the succession to the earldom and the entailed Douglas estates. The main contender was Archibald the Grim, but he was opposed by Sir Malcolm Drummond, the husband of the dead earl's sister, Isabella, countess of Mar; and because Carrick was married to Drummond's sister, he naturally supported his candidature. Earl James's illegitimate sons, William Douglas of Drumlanrig[23] and Archibald of Cavers, also staked a claim, but their bastardy ruled them out. In the end, the general council adjudged in Archibald's favour. While perfectly correct as far as the entailed estates were concerned, the decision to award him the earldom was far more controversial, being nothing less than a cave-in to the superior might of Archibald and his allies, Fife and Douglas of Dalkeith, compared with Drummond and Carrick.

The entailed Douglas estates which devolved on Archibald were substantial, being mainly situated in Douglasdale, Eskdale, and Lauderdale, and the forest of Selkirk. The consequent enhancement of his political power was matched by a corresponding wane in Carrick's. The failure of his candidate, Malcolm Drummond, to secure the Douglas succession was a grave setback, while his resulting estrangement from Archibald tore apart his power-base in southern Scotland and left him politically sidelined. He was also the victim of bad luck, because at about this time he was accidentally kicked by a horse belonging to Sir James Douglas of Dalkeith, the effects being aggravated by age, as Carrick was now in his fifties, an elderly man by the standards of the time. This left him with a permanent disability which would seriously hamper his capacity to govern effectively.

His younger brother, Fife, grasped the opportunity to edge him out of power, and the consequent change in their relative positions was officially recognised when, with their father the king's approval, the general council ejected Carrick from the guardianship in favour of Fife. Therefore, with the king living in semi-retirement, and Carrick politically marginalised, Fife and Earl Archibald effectively controlled the country between them, and while the former ruled the regions beyond the Forth, Archibald dominated those to the south. This meant that he had little time to devote to the affairs of Galloway, and to underscore his advanced status he transferred his administrative headquarters from Threave to his stronghold of Bothwell.

The old king's death in 1390 changed little, since he had been virtually excluded from affairs of state, and although Carrick succeeded as Robert III, he too remained in political eclipse. This was primarily due to Fife's machinations, because although his guardianship automatically lapsed on his father's death he was quick to persuade the general council to re-appoint him. For had this been delayed until after Robert III was crowned he would have been in a position to prevent it. Therefore, living in semi-retirement in his ancestral castle on Bute, the new king concentrated on building up the power of his eldest son David, now earl of Carrick, as his surrogate.

The new earl quickly proved to be an aggressive and ambitious man, while his growing power in the south-west posed a threat to Archibald's authority there. His lands in Carrick, combined with the ancestral Stewart territories to the north, which his father had handed over to him, gave him a strong power-base. From this foundation, he was steadily building up a system of alliances with Archibald's opponents, the Kennedys, who controlled much of Carrick, and the Lindsays, who were entrenched in the regions of the upper Clyde. He also had designs on Nithsdale, which Archibald had been ruling for his grandson, William Douglas, since 1391 when his son, Sir William, was killed on a crusade against the Teutonic knights in Prussia. Therefore, Carrick's sudden appearance in its ruling centre of Dumfries was seen by Archibald as a deliberate challenge to his authority.

There was also every risk of his attempting to extend his influence into Galloway by allying himself with the opposition movement to the Douglases, which appears to have grown up there. This seems to have resulted from a number of high-handed actions on Archibald's part. One example was his confiscation of the Agnew lands of Lochnaw and their re-grant to his relative, and possible illegitimate son, William Douglas,[24] whom he had already established in the barony of Leswalt.[25] Also, he appears to have appropriated lands at Borgue from the McDowells[26] and given them to his ally Douglas of Dalkeith.[27] Most ominous of all were the ties which Carrick – or the duke of Rothesay as he had now become – was developing with his uncle Fife, who had simultaneously been created duke of Albany.

This forced Archibald to change his stance by attempting a reconciliation with Rothesay, and this was sealed with Rothesay's marriage to Archibald's daughter, Mary. However, the negotiations hit a snag, because it transpired that Rothesay had already entered into a form of marriage with the earl of March's daughter, Elizabeth. However, as the necessary papal dispensation had not been obtained this was voidable, so Rothesay had no hesitation in jilting her in favour of Archibald's daughter, and the marriage was duly solemnised in 1400. This was one of the septuagenarian earl's last acts, as he died shortly afterwards on Christmas Eve 1400.

In deference to the Douglas power, contemporary chroniclers were sycophantic. Wyntoun claims 'he yeld [yielded] his sawle till [to] his Creatoure [and] his spirite in till Paradys',[28] while Bower asserts that 'he was called the grim or terrible who surpassed almost all other Scots of his time in wordly wisdom, resolution and daring'.[29] Physically he was a huge man, as Froissart tells us that he 'wielded before him an immense sword . . . which scarcely another could have lifted', and with it 'he gave such strokes that all on whom they fell were struck to the ground'.[30] More to the point, his was a remarkable success story. Having started out as a landless bastard with no prospects, he had, by a combination of good fortune, marrying an extremely wealthy widow, and above all his relentless energy and driving ambition, raised himself to become one of the largest territorial magnates, and a pre-eminent political power in the realm.

ARCHIBALD 'THE TYNEMAN'

His son, Archibald, the fourth earl, was immediately propelled into the position at the forefront of Scottish politics which had previously been occupied by his father. His brother-in-law, Rothesay,[31] was now the dominant figure, having been appointed lieutenant of the realm. However, his increasingly aggressive and unpredictable behaviour so alarmed his uncle, Albany, that he contrived to have him arrested and imprisoned in his stronghold of Falkland. Earl Archibald was probably not involved in this, but because he was persuaded to defect to Albany shortly afterwards he was drawn into the events that followed. For the two earls were now in a quandary; they had burnt their boats and knew full well that if Rothesay were released he would be hell-bent on revenge. Therefore, there was only one solution. In March 1402 Rothesay died in prison, allegedly of dysentery, though few believed it. Reflecting the popular view, Sir Walter Scott claims in his *Tales of a Grandfather* that he was deliberately starved to death, adding the grisly detail that in an extremity of hunger he had been reduced to devouring his own flesh. While these embellishments were no doubt fanciful, the finger of suspicion pointed unwaveringly at Albany and Archibald, but on the king's instructions they were exonerated and granted formal remissions.[32]

Meanwhile, the earl of March was so infuriated at Rothesay's jilting of his daughter that he had defected to the English, and consequently his lands were forfeited,[33] his Annandale lordship being given to Earl Archibald. March retaliated by launching, with the help of the northern earls, a series of raids on the east marches, and in 1402 the Scots responded by invading the lands belonging to these earls. This ended in disaster, because when battle was joined at Homildon Hill the English archers inflicted such a fearsome toll on the Scots that they were 'cut down like fallow deer', and many noblemen, including Earl Archibald, were taken prisoner. He also lost an eye and a testicle in the battle, as well as most of his lands, since the earl of Westmorland appropriated the lordship of Galloway, while the remainder was seized by the earl of Northumberland. However, Hotspur released Archibald shortly afterwards on condition that he assisted his father, Northumberland, and his fellow northern earls in their rebellion against Henry IV. This also proved a fiasco, because when the rebels were defeated at the battle of Shrewsbury Archibald was taken prisoner once again, his double defeat earning him the soubriquet 'the tyneman', or loser.

The death and capture of so many nobles at Homildon Hill meant there were no adult earls left in Scotland, so Albany had virtually untrammelled power. Meanwhile, Henry IV was anxious to end the war, and when he sent emissaries to Albany the latter broke off his campaign in the north to parley with them. However, opposition came from an unexpected quarter. Albany's distractions had allowed the old king to shuffle his way back into power, and at the urging of a number of hawkish barons he broke off negotiations. So the state of war continued, though it amounted to little more than a small-scale naval conflict which broke out in the Irish Sea in 1405. Here, a Wigtownshire magnate, Sir Thomas McCulloch, launched an attack on the English ports in Ulster, but shortly afterwards he was defeated and captured in an engagement in Dublin Bay. The Irish retaliated by mounting an expedition against the Scottish coast, which included an attack on Whithorn and extended to the royal castle of Brodick on Arran, whose captain was taken prisoner and his son killed.

Having recovered a semblance of authority, Robert III began building up the power of his heir, James, creating him duke of Rothesay and giving him the lands which had previously belonged to his brother. However, in 1406, perhaps fearful of Albany's intentions towards the young prince, he

decided to send him off to France for safety. Unfortunately, his ship was
intercepted by an English privateer and he was carried off a prisoner to
England, where he remained for the next eighteen years. The following
month the elderly king died. Although vigorous and forceful in his youth,
he, like his father before him, succumbed to advancing age and infirmity,
and as the sixteenth-century historian, John Mair, put it, 'many Scots are
accustomed . . . to compare the Stewarts to the horses in the district of
Mar, which in youth are good, but in their old age bad'. Albany was now
appointed governor of the realm, and he exercised these powers with undiminished vigour for the next fourteen years until his death in 1420. He
immediately arranged a truce with Henry IV and negotiated the release of
a number of Scottish captives, including Earl Archibald, though at the cost
of a large ransom.[34]

ARCHIBALD, LORD OF GALLOWAY

The opposition to the Douglas rule in Galloway seems to have focused on
Sir Gilbert Kennedy of Dunure who, like Thomas Fleming, had been given
up as a hostage for David II's ransom. He was one of the leading landowners in Wigtownshire, having inherited a number of estates, including
Cruggleton and Kidsdale, from his father, John Kennedy,[35] who had originally acquired them from his confederate, Sir Malcolm Fleming.
Meanwhile, his family's power in Carrick had been greatly enhanced by his
father's marriage to a daughter of Sir Gilbert of Carrick,[36] while it was a
measure of his own influence that his son, James, was married to Mary, the
daughter of Robert III.

In order to counteract the Kennedys' hostile influence, Archibald
established two powerful supporters there, one being Michael Ramsay, the
keeper of Lochmaben castle and chancellor of Annandale,[37] while the
other was William Hay,[38] the sheriff of Peebles. Yet, the Wigtownshire
magnates were by no means uniformly hostile to Archibald, because he was
supported by the heads of the McDowell and the McCulloch kindreds, both
of whom regularly provided him with men and ships for his military
expeditions, besides serving in his administration.[39] For example, in 1414
Archibald appointed Uchtred McDowell sheriff of Wigtown,[40] while also
confirming McDowell's relative, Sir Fergus McDowell, in possession of his
lands of Garthland.[41]

Archibald was at similar pains to entrench his authority in
Kirkcudbrightshire by establishing trusted adherents as landowners there.
First and foremost was his *scutifer*, Alexander Gordon, who was already a
substantial landowner in the Glenkens. In 1403, he granted him a charter
of the lands of Kenmure,[42] and this was followed in 1408 by one of
Balmaclellan,[43] which his father, Archibald the Grim, had bought from

Gilbert McLellan. At the same time, Gordon was given the lands of Ardoch, in the parish of Dalry, and in addition he was confirmed in the ownership of the important barony of Lochinvar. Two years later, Gordon was confirmed in the lordship of the Glenkens and appointed baillie of the barony of Earlston, near Dalry. Notwithstanding previous attempts to rehabilitate the region, a contemporary description of the church of Dalry as being situated in woods 'far from the habitations of other Christian faithful, among men ill-versed in the faith'[44] suggests it still remained a wilderness.

Other beneficiaries included Archibald's relatives, John Cairns, Sir Simon Glendonyng, and Thomas Murray. John Cairns, who was also his *scutifer*, was granted the lands of Cultis (or Cults),[45] which lie mid-way between Garlieston and Whithorn. His clerical brother, Alexander, was appointed the earl's chancellor, chaplain and secretary, and later given the provostship of Lincluden, as well as the livings of Wigtown and Kirkinner, as a pension. At the same time, Alexander acquired the lands of Carsluith, but being childless he left these to his brother John's son, William. The latter's descendants subsequently acquired the estate of Orchardton, near Auchencairn, and continued to be landowners in Galloway until the seventeenth century.[46]

Sir Simon Glendonyng, who is thought to have been Archibald's son-in-law,[47] was given the barony of Parton,[48] which remained in the hands of his descendants until the nineteenth century. Like the Gordons, his family were Douglas tenants in Roxburghshire, while Sir Simon was among the hostages given up to Henry IV in security for Archibald's ransom. Thomas Murray, a long-standing ally of Archibald's, had been given lands of Cockpule, in Annandale, and later the estate of Arbigland, near Kirkbean.[49] Other beneficiaries included Gilbert Grierson of Lag, a tenant of William Douglas of Nithsdale, who was given the lands of Drumjohn, in the Dee valley, while John Stewart was established in the lands of Cally,[50] adjacent to the river Fleet.

As ever, the Church was the key to controlling Galloway, so it was essential for Archibald to have a reliable incumbent at Whithorn, but although he was in a position to exercise the crown's right to nominate a candidate, he could not insist on his appointment, since the final decision rested with the pope. The first time round he was successful, because when the reigning bishop died in 1406 he secured the appointment of his own placeman, Eliseus Adougan,[51] who by special dispensation was allowed to retain his provostship of Lincluden.[52] Nevertheless, it proved a controversial appointment, because Adougan's attempts to generate revenue by selling dispensations to men of illegitimate birth to qualify for the priesthood, and to couples within the forbidden degree of relationship to marry, brought him into conflict with the prior and chapter of Whithorn.

So, when Adougan died in 1415, the pope appointed the local archdeacon, Thomas of Buittle,[53] his successor in preference to Archibald's nominee, Gilbert Cavan, the rector of Kirkinner. Archibald appealed the decision, but withdrew his objections when Cavan was compensated with other valuable benefices. The third time round, Archibald was more successful, because when Bishop Thomas died in 1421 he was in a stronger position to influence the nomination, and therefore he contrived to have his candidate, Alexander Vaus, bishop of Caithness, translated to Whithorn.[54]

THE FRENCH ENTERPRISE

Following his return to Scotland in 1408, Archibald had resumed his former political role, but he also aspired to play a part on the European stage, and this accounted for his participation in the civil war which had broken out in France. The mentally unstable king Charles VI had finally become insane, and a power struggle ensued between his son, the dauphin, and his cousin, the duke of Burgundy, for control of the regency. Seizing the chance to regain the former Angevin possessions in France, the English king, Henry V, intervened on the side of the Burgundians, and the hard-pressed dauphin appealed to Albany for help. He responded by dispatching a force there under the joint leadership of his younger son, the earl of Buchan (also Archibald's son-in-law), and Archibald's own son, the earl of Wigtown. This helped tip the scales – initially at any rate, because in the following year the French and their Scottish allies defeated the English at the battle of Baugé.

Archibald, however, deliberately avoided committing himself until he saw which way the war was likely to go. However, when both Henry V and his father-in-law, Charles VI, died within months of each other in 1422, Archibald was lured by the bribe of a French duchy, and the offer of supreme military command, to intervene on the side of the dauphin, now Charles VII. Therefore, the elderly earl left Scotland for the last time, having handed over control of the lordship of Galloway to his wife, Margaret, and the management of his other estates to his son, the earl of Wigtown. On arriving in France, this 'most renowned giant of a fighting man', as the French called him, pledged himself to Charles VII's service, being rewarded with the duchy of Touraine. But he was not destined to enjoy the honour for long, because he, his second son Sir James Douglas, and his son-in-law Buchan, were all cut down and slain when the Scots army was virtually annihilated at the battle of Verneuil in 1424.

A KING UNLEASHED

Shortly after Archibald's departure for France, James I was released from captivity. An able and energetic man, he was determined to restore the royal authority, and those members of his own family who were an obstacle to his ambitions were marked down for destruction, while others would have their powers curtailed. Among them was his nephew, Archibald, the new fifth earl of Douglas, and in a calculated bid to deprive him of his power-base in Galloway, James confirmed his widowed sister, Margaret, duchess of Touraine, in possession of the lordship.[55] Also, in order to assert his royal authority in Galloway, James declared the see of Whithorn to stand on the same footing as the other Scottish dioceses. Although this was designed to end the fiction that it was subject to York,[56] his declaration was never endorsed by the pope, and so the *status quo* continued – in theory at least, though in practice Whithorn's links with York had become virtually non-existent.

Earl Archibald remained in political limbo for the rest of James's reign, and since he was untainted with James's assassination in 1437 he was appointed lieutenant-general of the kingdom for the six-year-old James II, sharing power with the queen mother, Joan Beaufort, who was the young king's guardian. However, it seems that Archibald attempted to use his position to wrest the lordship of Nithsdale from his cousin, Egidia, the dowager countess of Orkney, the daughter of Sir William Douglas.[57] This would have been a valuable prize, since it formed a wedge between his lands in Annandale and the lordship of Galloway, and would have provided him with the means of extracting the latter from his mother. However, his ambitions were thwarted by his death – possibly from plague – in 1439. According to the Auchinleck chronicler, this epidemic 'began at Dumfres' and was 'callit the pestilens bot [without] mercy, for thai that tuke it nain ever recoverit, bot thai diet within xxiiij houris'.[58] It must have spread to Galloway as well, because contemporary records speak of a famine there, which was probably attributable to a dearth of manpower to harvest the crops.

Archibald's successor was his elder son, William, but as he was only fifteen his elderly great-uncle James 'the gross', earl of Avondale, a younger son of Archibald the Grim, became the effective head of the black Douglases. His soubriquet reflected his physique, as he was candidly described by Bishop Lesley as 'ane man of gryit stature and verrey fat'.[59] He had been at the forefront of Scottish politics ever since the beginning of the century, and was latterly a creature of James I, who had deliberately built up his power with the object of creating a division within the black Douglas faction. Therefore, it was primarily due to his influence that this nobleman had become a political – as well as a physical – heavyweight.

Within months of Earl Archibald's death, he, along with the chancellor, Sir William Crichton, and other members of the council, stripped the queen mother of her guardianship of the king, warding her and her new husband, James Stewart of Lorn, in Stirling castle under the keepership of Sir Alexander Livingstone of Callendar.[60]

Meanwhile, the new Earl William aspired to a prominent political role, being encouraged by his supporters to assert a claim to his father's office of lieutenant-general. Consequently, Avondale and his allies saw him as a potential threat, but whether Avondale himself had a hand in the events that followed can only be conjectured, although he undeniably had much to gain from them. The story has it that Earl William and his brother David were prevailed on, under promises of a safe conduct, to attend what became known as 'the Black Dinner' in Edinburgh castle. At the end of the proceedings, a dish was placed in front of them bearing a black bull's head which, as the chronicler tells us, 'was ane signe and taikin [token] of condemnatour to the death'.[61] The youths were promptly arrested and hauled out to the 'castell hill' where the executioner 'straik their heidis fre them',[62] and with the blows of his axe the senior line of the black Douglases came to an end.

NOTES

1. He had been created earl of Douglas in 1358, and, as his father and Sir James Douglas were half-brothers, he and Archibald the Grim (who incidentally was his protégé having been brought up in his household), were first cousins by the half blood.
2. *RMS* i, no.628.
3. *Ibid.* no. 800. He claimed a half share through his mother, who was a daughter of Thomas Randolph, earl of Moray, while the other half came to him through his predecessor, Earl Patrick, who had married his mother's sister, 'Black Agnes'.
4. *Ibid.* no. 576.
5. *Ibid.* nos. 414, 527.
6. *Ibid.* no. 507.
7. Boardman, *The Early Stewart kings*, 66 (note 36).
8. *APS* i, 550: Nicholson, *The Later Middle Ages*, 190.
9. Brown, *Black Douglases*, 131.
10. All the king's daughters were renowned for their good looks, being described in a papal dispensation concerning their parents' marriage as 'fair to behold' (Nicholson, *The later Middle Ages*, 186).
11. In fact, this is the one remaining support of a box machicolation which originally provided a wall-head defence for the entrance.
12. *CPS.*
13. *RMS* i no. 483.
14. Nicholson, *The later Middle Ages*, 237.

15. McEwan, 'A Theolog Solempne', 28–9.
16. CPS.
17. CSSR.
18. McKerlie iii, 234, and v, 5.
19. Wig Charters, 92.
20. Ibid., 22.
21. Ibid., 21.
22. Easson, 'The nunneries of Galloway' 196 et seq.
23. His descendants became the earls, marquesses and dukes of Queensberry, and are now represented by the duke of Buccleuch and the marquess of Queensberry.
24. Agnew refers to this in Hereditary Sheriffs (i, 234–5), but the information he vouchsafes is extremely sketchy, while its accuracy is debateable. Boardman also refers to it in The early Stewart kings, 198–9.
25. William Douglas apparently styled himself lord of Leswalt, and he and his immediate descendants continued to be influential magnates in Wigtownshire for much of the rest of the century.
26. Brown, Black Douglases, 63.
27. Reg Morton, nos 83, 99, 100, 124. The barony eventually passed to Douglas's second son, the ambitious and unscrupulous Henry Douglas, who later married a daughter of Archibald the Grim's younger son, James, the seventh earl.
28. Wyntoun, XXI, 77.
29. Bower 8, p 35.
30. Froissart ii, 225.
31. In fact he was doubly Archibald's brother-in-law, since Archibald was married to his sister Margaret (the future duchess of Touraine), while Rothesay was married to (but had now abandoned) Archibald's sister.
32. APS i, 582–3.
33. The forfeiture did not include the Mochrum estate, as this seems to have passed to March's younger brother, David Dunbar, the ancestor of the Dunbars of Mochrum.
34. Nicholson, The later Middle Ages, 232.
35. Gilbert Kennedy's right in them was confirmed by a charter issued in 1366 (RMS i, no. 223 and app 2, no 1531), which describes them as consisting of 'Crogiltoun and Poulltoun, the two Broughtons and Kythreull' (Cruggleton, Poulton, the two Broughtons and Kidsdale).
36. McKerlie ii, 213, 362.
37. Brown, The Black Douglases, 165.
38. Ibid., 171. He was the ancestor of the marquises of Tweeddale.
39. Ibid., 162, 173.
40. Ibid., 173.
41. McKerlie i, 55 and ii, 166.
42. Ibid. iv, 53.
43. Ibid.
44. CSSR ii.
45. Wig Charters, 161.
46. Lawlor, History of the Cairns. Orchardton was sold to Sir Robert Maxwell in the sixteenth century, while Carsluith passed to an heiress, Margaret Cairns, who married James Lindsay of Fairgirth, and their son, Michael Lindsay, was confirmed in the ownership of both these estates in 1506 (RMS iii no. 1664).

When his grandson, John Lindsay, died childless in 1527, Carsluith went to his sister, Elizabeth, who married Richard Broun, while Fairgirth passed to his uncle, James Lindsay, and his descendants.

47. Reid asserts in 'The family of Glendonyng' that he was the husband of Earl Archibald's daughter Mary, and so does McKerlie (v, 35), but there is no mention of this in the *Scots Peerage*.

48. Brown states in *Black Douglases* (p.171) that he probably acquired this in the 1390s, in which case the granter would have been Archibald the Grim.

49. McKerlie ii, 428–9. Thomas Murray's great-grandson, Mungo Murray, subsequently acquired the lands of Broughton near Whithorn, and his descendants ultimately inherited the Cally estate at Gatehouse through marriage with the heiress of the Lennox (Levenax) family. Arbigland, on the other hand, passed to his senior descendants, the earls of Annandale, who owned it until the mid-1600s, when it was sold to the earl of Southesk.

50. Agnew refers in *Hereditary Sheriffs* (i, 238) to John Stewart and his daughter, Elizabeth, receiving a charter of confirmation of these lands in 1411.

51. *CPPS* ii, 151.

52. *Ibid.*, 153.

53. *Ibid.*, 317–8.

54. Oram, 'Heirs to Ninian', 71–3.

55. *RMS* ii no 47. Margaret habitually used her husband's grander ducal title in preference to that of countess of Douglas.

56. Oram, 'Heirs to Ninian', 73.

57. Earl Archibald's raid into Nithsdale, and the probable reasons for it, are discussed by Brown in *Black Douglases*, 249.

58. *Chron. Auchinleck*, fol. 1092.

59. *Lesley, History*, 16.

60. Livingstone, who subsequently acquired supreme political power, was a man with Galloway connections. His cousin, Thomas Livingstone, was abbot of Dundrennan until deprived by Pope Eugenius IV, though this did not prevent him from trying to appropriate the revenues of Kirkinner as a pension. Another relative, Alexander Livingstone, was the owner of the lands of Duchra near Mossdale, the name being preserved in the local estate there.

61. *Pitscottie*, chap IX, 45.

62. *Ibid.*

15

THE FALL OF THE DOUGLASES

THE RULE OF DUCHESS MARGARET

Margaret, duchess of Touraine, had been in control of Galloway since 1424, and although she seems eventually to have imposed her authority on the province, the opening years of her rule were dogged by controversy. Possibly there was some aversion to the principle of a female ruler, while the fact that she had been imposed by James I in preference to her son Archibald, the rightful heir, could have provoked some resentment. Nevertheless, she inherited a generally loyal *corpus* of servants from her husband, the fourth earl, while those whose allegiance was suspect were replaced by her own relatives and placemen. However, there was continuing opposition to the Douglas rule among certain sections of the Wigtownshire baronage, though Sir John Kennedy was more amenable than his grandfather Gilbert had been, since he was Margaret's nephew.

The main opposition came from William Douglas of Leswalt, so in 1426 Margaret dismissed him from the sheriffship of Wigtown, replacing him with her *scutifer*, Andrew Agnew,[1] whom she had already appointed constable of Lochnaw castle. Then, somewhat surprisingly – at least on the face of it – Douglas himself gave Agnew the lands of Lochnaw,[2] but the transfer, confirmed by a royal charter of 1431,[3] was made under duress. Initially, Margaret tried to coax Douglas into it by using Cruggleton as the bait. Although this belonged to Kennedy she had secured his agreement to part with it in exchange for the office of chamberlain of Leswalt. This meant she could now offer it to Douglas in place of Lochnaw.[4] However, when she put the proposal to him he rejected it out of hand and threatened to defend Lochnaw by force if necessary.

Margaret was now compelled to seek the assistance of her son, Earl Archibald. He responded enthusiastically to this opportunity to intervene in the affairs of Galloway, and seizing the excuse to parade his power there and remind the people of his contingent rights in the lordship, he arrived at Threave in October 1426 at the head of a large force recruited from the west march.[5] As this was designed essentially as a political demonstration it was far in excess of what was needed for the comparatively simple task of enforcing Douglas's co-operation, so the result was a foregone conclusion. Douglas duly surrendered Lochnaw[6] in return for Cruggleton, while Kennedy obtained the prestigious office of chamberlain of Leswalt, which was thereafter held by successive generations of his family. This was to be the foundation of their growing power in the region which they consolidated through a network of marriage alliances with the leading local families.[7]

Margaret's appointees to the principal offices of state in Galloway included her cousin, Alexander Mure, a native of Ayrshire, who was appointed steward of Kirkcudbright and justiciar of Galloway.[8] Another was her ally and kinsman, Sir William Stewart of Dalswinton and Garlies. In 1426 he was given the lands of Glasserton in the southern Machars,[9] and this became the nucleus of the huge landholding which his descendants, the earls of Galloway, eventually built up in Wigtownshire. The McCulloch kindred were consistent supporters of the Douglases, and as evidence of this Margaret appointed a member of the family, John McCulloch, her chancellor,[10] later giving him the provostship of Lincluden.

In contrast to her husband and Archibald the Grim, who ruled Galloway from their main administrative centre of Bothwell, Margaret established hers at Threave, and this meant she was in closer touch with her Gallovidian subjects. So it may have reflected a concern for them that she was responsible for replacing Dervorguilla's bridge over the Nith with the existing stone one. The Church could have been instrumental in this, since it was constantly agitating for better facilities to reduce the hazards of travel, and would even subsidise the cost of building bridges. It is known to have done so in the case of the bridge over the Bladnoch which Margaret commissioned in 1441,[11] so it may well have defrayed the cost of the bridge at Dumfries as well. Margaret seems to have been a considerable benefactor to the Church, having endowed a chapel within the cathedral church at Whithorn, as well as being instrumental in having the lands belonging to Glenluce erected into a regality.[12] In addition, she granted seven separate properties, including 'Maynys of Southwick', to Lincluden in memory of her husband and her son James who fell with him at Verneuil.[13]

Regrettably, Duchess Margaret was forced out of the lordship in her old age. The process began with the marriage of her granddaughter Margaret, the 'fair maid of Galloway', who had inherited the Galloway and Bothwell lordships from her brother the murdered earl, to her cousin William, the eighth earl – a union forced on her against her own wishes and those of her immediate family for the purpose of reuniting these lordships with the earldom. Having secured possession of Galloway, William proceeded to edge the old duchess aside, and it seems that by 1447 she was forced into resigning the lordship (though this was not formalised until 1450[14]), because William thereafter took possession of Threave and proceeded to grant lands in Galloway without reference to either his wife or her grand-mother.[15] Meantime, the aged Margaret was warded at Lincluden where she remained until her death in 1450,[16] and it was there that in accordance with her wishes she was buried.[17] Clearly inheriting the longevity of those of her race who survived to their full term, she must by then have been about eighty.

THE AVONDALE DOUGLASES

James the Gross succeeded his murdered great-nephew as seventh earl of Douglas, although his inheritance was limited to those Douglas estates which had been entailed in 1342. Because Archibald the Grim had acquired the Galloway lordship before inheriting the Douglas earldom this was not covered by the entail, and it was for this reason that it passed to Margaret. Although Earl James used his political influence to secure her marriage to his son William, papal dispensation was needed, as they were within the forbidden degrees of relationship. Inevitably this involved a delay, so it was not until after James's death in 1443[18] that consent was granted and the marriage took place.

Since Earl James did not marry until about 1421 (his bride, Beatrix St Clair, being his own great-niece[19]), the new Earl William would only have been in his early twenties when he succeeded. Nevertheless he, like his predecessors, aspired to a leading role in government. The political scene was dominated by the rival Crichton and Livingstone factions, and since the latter were now in the ascendant William naturally allied himself with them. They were joined by a group of powerful nobles, including the Kennedys, under the leadership of Bishop James Kennedy, a younger brother of Gilbert of Dunure and the now-dead Sir John. Earl William contrived to have himself appointed lieutenant-general of the kingdom, and armed with these powers he engineered an attack on the Crichtons, besieging Sir William Crichton in his tower house at Barnton near Edinburgh. However, Crichton managed to escape to the safety of Edinburgh castle and from there he organised a raid into Earl William's own lands at Linlithgow; but by this time the council, yielding to pressure from the Livingstones and their allies, had denounced the Crichtons as rebels and put them to the horn.

The Livingstones now had custody of the young king, and although he was only fourteen they declared him of age to rule so that they could exercise power in his name. Therefore, one of their first acts was to secure retrospective approval of their actions against the Crichtons. Yet their victory was incomplete, because Bishop Kennedy had defected to the Crichtons, and so too did the earl of Angus, William's rival for the headship of the house of Douglas.[20] However, they were forced to pay a price for their switch of loyalties, because their lands were singled out for attack when war broke out shortly afterwards between the rival factions. The Douglas Livingstone alliance rapidly gained the upper hand, and when Crichton and Angus capitulated their ascendancy was complete, their triumph being consolidated by the parliament of July 1445.

A USURPING LORD

The Douglas Livingstone success greatly enhanced William's political standing, and it was this which enabled him to force Duchess Margaret out of the Galloway lordship and take it over himself. Nevertheless, he was the target of considerable hostility in Galloway. While some of the baronage were opposed to the Douglases in principle, others saw him as the head of a usurping dynasty tarred with suspected implication in the murder of their rightful lord, while the old duchess's unceremonious ejection from power must have evoked a good deal of sympathy. To their discredit some of Margaret's placemen were prepared to switch their allegiance to Earl William, among them being Sir Thomas Murray of Cockpule, Sir Simon Glendonyng,[21] and Alexander Mure whom William appointed his justiciar in 1448.[22] William's own appointees included James Lindsay of Covington, who became his secretary and was later rewarded with the provostship of Lincluden.[23] Clearly a man with an eye to the main chance, he subsequently defected to James II and became an important player on the national stage during James III's minority.[24]

Although William was powerful enough to ignore local Gallovidian opposition, he does seem to have made some attempt to win over the local Church. Particularly so the bishop, Alexander Vaus, an appointee of the fourth earl, since William gave the lands of Barnbarroch near Whauphill in the Machars to his nephew Robert Vaus.[25] The ageing bishop resigned his see in 1451,[26] and although his successor Thomas Spens was a Douglas placeman, having been provost of Lincluden, he seems to have gone over to the king the following year.[27] One example of William's benefaction to the Church was the grant to Whithorn priory of a number of rights pertaining to the local burgh, as well as the customs from the Isle of Whithorn.[28] Perhaps he had further plans in mind, but fate was to deny him the chance to implement them.

Earl William's appropriation of the Galloway lordship was part of a wider strategy to secure control of the entire south-west. He was already well entrenched in Carrick, since he had inherited the lordships of Dunlop and Stewarton from his father, as well as a network of alliances among the lairds of central Ayrshire. His main opponents were the Kennedys, but because they were locked in a power struggle he was able to exploit this to his advantage. The dispute had broken out some years before between Sir

John and his uncle Thomas Kennedy, and after Sir John's death his cause was taken up by his brother Gilbert of Dunure. William took Gilbert's part and proceeded to lay siege to the key fortress of Loch Doon which was held by Thomas's supporters, including 'men of the name McLellan',[29] which suggests they were his principal opponents in Kirkcudbrightshire. Once William captured the stronghold it gave him a commanding position in southern Carrick; so much so that Gilbert Kennedy took fright and secretly defected to William's opponents.

Having gained control of Carrick, William's next step was to consolidate his position in Annandale. However, his plans were interrupted by a renewal of hostilities with the English, when a Scottish raid provoked the earl of Northumberland into carrying out a retaliatory invasion across the Solway. Establishing his camp at Clochmabenstone, his plan was to launch a raid into Annandale, but the following day he was attacked by a force from the 'westlands' under the joint leadership of Earl William's brother, Hugh, earl of Ormonde, and lord Maxwell. Unable to fall back because of the incoming tide, his army was cut to pieces and a large number of knights taken prisoner. Consequently, the haul of plunder taken and the ransoms exacted were such that, according to Pitscottie, 'thair was sic abundance of riches silluer and gold . . . that never was the lyke sene in na man's tyme befoir'.[30]

AN OVERMIGHTY SUBJECT

King James's minority officially ended with his marriage to Mary of Gueldres in 1449.[31] He immediately grasped the opportunity to turn on his Livingstone masters, and acting with a suddenness which caught them offguard he arrested Sir Alexander and members of his family. Details of the charges brought against them are not known, but they are likely to have involved peculation and the misappropriation of crown revenues. Certainly, the state of the royal finances was so parlous that James was barely able to meet his financial obligations to his wife under their marriage settlement. This could have serious repercussions, because her wealthy uncle, Philip, duke of Burgundy, had undertaken to provide her dowry, but it was conditional on James fulfilling his obligations under the contract. Therefore, if James defaulted there was every chance of further payments being suspended, so the prospect of acquiring the Livingstones' possessions would have given him an additional incentive to break their power.

The Livingstone allies were quick to defect, among them being Earl William, so when victory was finally achieved James rewarded him by confirming him in possession of Galloway[32] and sanctioning his marriage to Margaret. William's position now seemed impregnable, and therefore he decided he could afford to set off on a pilgrimage. So, with the king's 'licence and blessing' he and his brother James, along with a large retinue, set out for Rome in October 1450 in order to attend a papal jubilee. As the last antipope Felix V had submitted to the pontiff Nicholas V in 1449 and the schism was at an end the celebrations promised to be spectacular, and William appears to have matched the occasion, being 'commended by the supreme pontiff above all pilgrims'[33] for his display of magnificence. But while he was flaunting himself at the papal court his enemies were conspiring to undermine his position at home. They included Sir William Crichton, whose fortunes had recovered after the downfall of his Livingstone rivals, and by playing on King James's own apprehensions he cajoled him into launching an attack on the Douglas lands. Therefore, as the chronicler put it, 'by their counsel King James II besieged all the castles of the earl and slew many free tenants of the said earl and received the rest to his peace upon oath'.[34]

James also revived an eighty-year-old claim, first asserted by Robert II, that the Douglases' title to the Wigtown earldom was defective and that it properly belonged to the crown. Its legality was dubious, but it was enough to serve as a pretext for annexing the earldom and giving it to the queen in part settlement of his obligation under their marriage contract. As a further step, James appointed his *scutifer*, Andrew Agnew of Lochnaw, sheriff of Wigtown, and by entailing it on his heirs made it hereditary.[35] This was highly provocative since Agnew was one of Earl William's leading opponents in Wigtownshire. Equally challenging was James's appointment of Gilbert Kennedy, now a declared enemy of William, as keeper of Loch Doon castle.[36] However, the gauntlet was finally cast when James began to style himself lord of Galloway,[37] though it was an unconvincing assertion since he had already confirmed William in possession of the lordship.[38]

These high-handed actions provoked Earl William's youngest brother, John Douglas of Balvenie, whom he had left in charge of his estates, to retaliate. Therefore, when the earl of Orkney[39] was commissioned by the king to collect the rents due to the queen from her Wigtownshire estates Douglas's men forcibly prevented him from doing so. This prompted the king to intervene, and mustering a force he descended on Galloway, where he was joined by a number of disaffected local magnates. Together they drove John Douglas and his adherents out of the province and imprisoned them in the strongholds of Douglas and Lochmaben where they had taken refuge.[40]

Earl William's return in April 1451 threatened to lead to a showdown, but James, realising he had underestimated the power of the Douglases, was compelled to back down. Therefore, a compromise was agreed whereby James abandoned his claims on Galloway in return for the queen being allowed to keep her Wigtownshire lands, this being formally ratified by parliament. However, this was merely postponing the inevitable, as James well knew that if his authority were to carry any credibility the

Douglases would have to be crushed, so he concentrated on building up his power in anticipation of a showdown.

Meanwhile William, confident of his supremacy, is alleged to have been responsible for a number of high-handed actions which were seen as a deliberate challenge to the king's authority. Pitscottie gives some lurid examples, but as they were designed for propaganda purposes their veracity is dubious. One concerned Sir John Herries, a younger brother of Herries of Terregles, who was 'a faithful subject to the Kingis majestie at all tymes'. Apparently 'sum theiffes of Douglasdaill' who were the earl's vassals had been harrying his lands, but as the earl consistently refused to intervene Herries was forced to take the law into his own hands. Therefore he arrested them and had them summarily executed. The earl retaliated by having Herries 'castin in yrrones and hangit schamefullie as [if] he had bene ane thief nochtwithstanding the king commandit in the contrair'.

Another example concerned Earl William's alleged imprisonment of McLellan the tutor of Bombie, who out of loyalty to the king had refused to answer the earl's call to arms, or as Pitscottie put it, 'he wald on na wayis . . . ryd with the erle of Douglas'. He goes on to assert that the king sent McLellan's uncle, Sir Patrick Gray, as an envoy to Earl William demanding his release. The earl gave him a courteous welcome and proceeded to entertain him to dinner and 'maid him guid cheir', but before doing so he gave orders for McLellan to be executed. So, when dinner was over the earl escorted his guest out into the courtyard remarking to him, 'Schir Patrick ye ar come a litill to leit; bot yondar is your sistir sone lyand; bot he wantis [lacks] the heid; tak his bodie and do with it quhat ye will'.[41]

More ominously, Earl William proceeded to enter into a bond with the earls of Crawford and Ross. While such bonds were commonplace among the nobility, this was rendered particularly sinister by the fact that both Crawford and Ross were at odds with the king. Therefore, in February 1452 James issued a summons to Earl William to attend his court at Stirling to account for his entering into the bond. But suspecting treachery the earl demanded a safe conduct, and this was duly given. No doubt the fiery James had every intention of honouring it, but when king and earl finally encountered each other the meeting did not go according to plan.

The Auchinleck chronicler gives a graphic account of what followed. After they had 'dynit and sowpit [dined and supped]' the king charged Earl William to break the bond. He replied that 'he mycht not nor wald not'. 'Fals traitour', cried the king losing his temper, 'sen [seeing] yow will nocht I sall', whereupon he 'stert sodanly till him with ane knyf and straik him in at the colere and down in the bodie'. This was the signal for a bloodthirsty free-for-all which the chronicler describes with such vividness as to suggest he was among the witnesses. According to his account, 'Patrick Gray strak him nixt [after] the king with ane poll ax on the hed and strak out his branes and syne [then] the gentillis [courtiers] that war with the king gaf thaim ilkane [each one] a straik or twa with knyffis'. By the time the courtiers had finished their gory work the corpse of the murdered earl is alleged to have borne the marks of no less than twenty-six wounds.[42]

THE FINAL SHOWDOWN

This was slaughter under trust, since the breaching of Earl William's safe conduct constituted a violation of the medieval code of honour which probably outraged contemporary opinion far more than the murder itself. Moreover, it showed James's word as king to be totally worthless. Yet, even if morally compromised, James was now in a far stronger position than before, because William's murder resulted in the break-up of a number of important alliances on which his power was based. Also, as he left no issue the Galloway and Bothwell lordships became separated from the earldom, since they now reverted to his widow Countess Margaret, though she was firmly kept in Douglas custody.

Undeterred by the storm of indignation, James moved quickly to press home his advantage by launching an attack on the Douglas lands in the Borders. This extended as far as Galloway[43] where he and his Crichton allies sought to dismember the Douglas lordship and secure part of the lands for themselves.[44] The new Earl James retaliated by sacking the burgh of Stirling, and at the same time he engaged in a war of words by 'blowing out xxiij hornis attanis the king . . . for the foule slauchter of his brother'[45] and speaking 'rycht sclanderfully' of him.[46] Manifestos appeared in Edinburgh declaiming that 'the king was bot ane blodie murtherar' and 'ane fallis [false] ungodlie thrister [thirster] of innocent bloode'.[47] However, it soon became apparent that march, counter march and propaganda were not going to achieve anything and that some accommodation would have to be reached between the two Jameses.

Accordingly the king entered into an 'appoyntement' with Earl James and his ally Lord Hamilton, whereby the earl forgave the king for 'arte and parte of the slaughter' of his brother and undertook to repair the damage he had committed in Galloway, while renouncing all 'treasonable leagues contrare' the king.[48] In return James gave up his claim to the earldom of Wigtown (much to the queen's disgust), and received him into his peace. This was followed by a second agreement in which the king undertook to help Earl James obtain papal dispensation for his marriage to his brother's widow Margaret. As this was forthcoming the earl duly forced the 'ungodlie and wickit marrieage'[49] on the luckless Margaret, and the Galloway lordship was again reunited with the earldom.

Both king and earl were well aware that the 'appoyntement' was merely a fig-leaf that did no more than stave off a final confrontation which now looked inevitable. Therefore, perceiving control of Galloway as vital to his plans to build up his strength, Earl James visited the province on three separate occasions between November 1452 and October 1453[50] in order to build up his authority in the region. There were many possible sources of friction between him and the king, but the clash which brought matters to a head was a dispute over the control of the Dalkeith estates following Sir James Douglas's final relapse into insanity. King James claimed the right to administer his lands, but this was challenged by Douglas's brother, Henry of Borgue, who was a brother-in-law and ally of Earl James. An undeclared state of war broke out as king and earl jockeyed for position, while the latter's partisans in Galloway murdered the sheriff, Andrew Agnew, and burnt his lands.[51]

King James took the initiative and laid siege to the earl's castle of Abercorn on the Forth. However, instead of marching to its relief Earl James dithered, and during the stand-off many of his adherents drifted away. Among them was his principal supporter, Lord Hamilton. His attachment to the Avondale Douglases was motivated purely by political considerations; he had no personal loyalty to them,[52] so when he saw their cause in jeopardy he was quick to defect to the king. His switch of allegiance was enough to turn the scales; Abercorn was taken, and this marked the end of the Douglas supremacy. Earl James fled to England, while his three brothers carried out a series of plundering raids in the Borders. Here they encountered a group of local lairds, including Lord Maxwell and the heads of the Johnstones and the Scotts, and in the course of an engagement at Arkinholm near Langholm the Douglas brothers were routed. John of Balvenie escaped, but the earl of Ormond was captured, tried and executed, while the corpse of the earl of Moray who was killed in the battle was decapitated and his head sent to the king as a trophy.[53]

THE AFTERMATH

The triumphant king issued summonses to Earl James and his relatives to appear before him to answer charges of treason. This was purely a formality, since there was no possibility of any of them returning to defend the charges, knowing full well that they would face certain death. So they were pronounced guilty in their absence, their estates were forfeited, and later that year an Act of Parliament was passed abolishing the earldom and barring any member of the family from laying claim to the black Douglas possessions in Scotland.[54]

Forfeiture of the Douglas lands necessarily involved physical possession, and as the stronghold of Threave was the key to the Galloway lordship, strategic considerations demanded its capture. In a desperate attempt to obtain help from the duke of York's government in England, Earl James had agreed to surrender Threave to him in return for the 'succour, victualling, relief and rescue' of the castle.[55] But it was too late, as the castle was already under siege. Its walls were so massive that they could only be breached by the 'great bombard', a new type of cannon recently imported from the Low Countries where the Burgundians had used it to good effect. It was a crude device and the barrel was made of strips of wrought iron bound together with metal hoops and tightened with wedges. While its range could exceed two miles, its accuracy was poor and gunners compensated for this by using large quantities of shot amounting to as much as half a tonne. Metal shot was expensive, however, and although stone was cheaper it was liable to cause the cannon to blow up and could be as hazardous to the gun crew as the enemy.

Transporting this heavy contrivance across country from Linlithgow to Threave proved a major undertaking, particularly when one of its wheels broke while it was being hauled across Crawford Moor. Attempts to pull it out merely forced it deeper into the mire, so troops had to be summoned from Edinburgh to give assistance. As King James took a particular interest in cannonry he was present throughout most of the siege, staying alternately at Dundrennan and Tongland abbeys. In the end it was bribery and a loss of morale rather than firepower which induced the garrison to surrender. For the custodian, Sir John Fraser, was prevailed on to hand over the keys in return for a sum of money and a promise that he could keep his lands. So, once they were delivered up and the king formally took possession all further resistance in Galloway was at an end.

Notwithstanding the decree of forfeiture against the black Douglases members of the family continued to be landholders in Galloway, George Douglas remaining in possession of Leswalt until his death in about 1463.[56] Since he had no lawful issue this reverted to the crown and was appropriated by the queen mother Mary of Gueldres.[57] Meanwhile Gilbert Kennedy of Dunure, now Lord Kennedy, claimed the barony for his own son John on the grounds that he was George Douglas's half-brother.[58] It seems the Kennedy claim was conceded, because sometime after the queen mother's death the barony was given to John's younger son, Alexander Kennedy, who subsequently transferred it to his brother David, third Lord Kennedy,[59] and thereafter it remained in the hands of his descendants the earls of Cassilis. Surprisingly, since he was an ally of Earl James, married to his sister Margaret, and was the king's rival for control of the Dalkeith estates, it seems Henry Douglas was allowed to retain his lands of Borgue as these remained in his family for well over a century, until they were sold in 1588.

Another black Douglas survivor was William prior of Whithorn, an illegitimate son of the fifth earl,[60] and evidently a somewhat controversial character. He attempted to appropriate the teinds from the neighbouring lands of Biskeby which belonged to Dundrennan, and this became the subject of a long-standing dispute between the two houses.[61] He also appears to have fallen somewhat short of the Christian ideal, as he was accused by the influential Sir Fergus McDowell of Garthland of having 'committed fornication with his married sister [i.e. sister-in-law]', and 'committed dilapidations and converted to damnable uses a number of goods belonging to the priory which he had obtained simonaically [by bribery]'. However, a subsequent enquiry cleared him of these charges, and in 1467 in recognition of his 'pure life, good counsel, and honorable service'[62] – which sounds suspiciously like a whitewash – the pope granted him a full remission. As Douglas had already been suspended from office, he was compensated with the lands of Poulton and Cruggleton, along with a large annual allowance of meal which was levied on the principal churches in the diocese.[63]

ROYAL GOVERNMENT

Once Threave was taken, James and his queen made a royal progress through the province in a public demonstration of his new-found authority. This included a state visit to Kirkcudbright, when he confirmed the town's status as a royal burgh and granted it a monopoly of all trade from the Nith as far as the Cree. This right was vested in an official known as a custumar, the first recorded holder of the office being William McLellan of Bombie. At the same time, the king erected the Franciscan friary there into a conventual friary of the Scottish Grey Friars,[64] from which the present church takes its name. During their visit to Kirkcudbright the royal couple would almost certainly have stayed at the priory of Trail, and from there they took ship to Wigtown where the queen received in person the tribute due to her from her Wigtownshire lands.

They revisited that centre in 1458, accompanied this time by the king's cousin Andrew Stewart, lord Avondale, the prospective chancellor, the local secretary Thomas Vaus, Bishop Thomas Spens, and Abbot William of Dundrennan, the chamberlain of Galloway. The big names were obviously designed to impress, because they were there to attend to the formalities connected with leasing out the former Douglas lands which had now reverted to the crown. William Douglas, the prior of Whithorn, was among those commanded to attend. However, when he failed to appear Thomas Vaus was dispatched with a body of men to fetch him, or in a literal translation of the Latin to abduct him,[65] since James was determined to ensure a full turn-out to impress upon the local people his undisputed mastery of the region.

The reversion of the vast Douglas possessions to the crown finally relieved James of his financial difficulties, since the revenues now went into the royal treasury. So, too, did the fines imposed on malefactors within these domains, and this was no mean consideration, since in Galloway they amounted to almost as much as the revenues themselves.[66] This coincided with James attaining the age of twenty-five when parliament, setting a precedent for the future, passed an Act of Annexation entitling him to revoke all gifts of crown lands and revenues made to his possible prejudice during his minority. It also stipulated that certain former Douglas possessions were to remain the inalienable property of the crown, including 'the haille lordschipe of Galloway with sick fefdomes and commoditeis as it has . . . togidder with the castell of the Treife'.[67] Since this was designed to assure the king and his successors the wherewithal to meet the costs of government a sanction was imposed prohibiting the alienation of these lands,[68] though it seems to have rapidly become a dead letter.

For administrative purposes the Douglas lands in Galloway were divided between those 'above the Cree', i.e. Wigtownshire, which came within the jurisdiction of the king's chamberlain for Carrick, and those 'under the Cree'. The latter comprised the Kirkcudbrightshire estates, and these were controlled by a chamberlain specifically appointed for the purpose. The first was Abbot William of Dundrennan, and his successors, who were mostly local magnates, continued to hold that office until 1609, when it was abolished. It was a demanding task since it involved managing the tenantry, ensuring the punctual payment of their rents, and submitting regular accounts of their income and expenditure to the king, all of which are preserved in the Exchequer Rolls.[69]

The tenantry embraced a wide range of classes, while its composition was constantly changing. It came to include members of the nobility like Patrick Hepburn, earl of Bothwell, who acquired a lease of most of the lands and sub-let them to his own tenants,[70] while other tacksmen included William Lennox of Cally who leased the lands of Kirkandrews.[71] At the other end of the scale came the kindly tenants, referred to as the 'auld kindly possessors', who seem to have been given preferential treatment, as did those who held their lands under steelbow.[72]

The fall of the black Douglases allowed other families to rise to positions of influence, the most obvious example being the Maxwells.[73] Although they would become key players on the national stage they never exercised the same authority over the province as the Douglases, and it was because there was no one to fill their place that the ensuing period witnessed an outbreak of feuding in the former Douglas-controlled territories which was unsurpassed in their entire previous history. Although these inter-family disputes were later romanticised in ballads, they were in reality squalid and unedifying disputes where the participants were primarily motivated by a hankering to settle old scores and the prospect of booty.

THE MANX THREAT

Scottish relations with England continued to be unsettled, and the uneasy peace between them was regularly broken by cross-Border raids and piracy. One such incident involved the hijacking of a vessel with a cargo of iron and wine belonging to Bishop Thomas Spens of Whithorn. As such a blatant act of aggression could not be overlooked King James sent Rothesay herald to the English court in October 1457 to demand redress,[74] though there is no record of whether his mission was successful. Incidents like these highlighted the constant threat of invasion, and as the west marches were seen as the most likely point of attack, a constant watch was maintained there. In 1455 parliament passed a series of measures specifying how this was to be done; sentinels were to keep watch on the Solway fords, and beacons set on the principal hills of Annandale and Nithsdale ready to be lit in the event of an attack. Evidently the possibility of a seaborne invasion was not discounted, since another chain of beacons was set on the principal hills dominating the Kirkcudbrightshire coastline – Criffel, Bengairn, Cairnsmore of Fleet, and also the Knock of Luce.[75]

The choice of that western outpost suggests a threat of invasion from the Isle of Man in retaliation for King James's provocative attack on the island earlier that year. Although formerly belonging to the kings of Scots, it was annexed by the English in the aftermath of Nevill's Cross in 1346, and in 1405 Henry IV granted the lordship to Sir John Stanley, whose grandson Thomas, Lord Stanley, was now in control. Successive Scots kings had their sights firmly fixed on recovering the island, but James II was the first to take positive action. The pretext was the appointment of an English bishop to the see of Man in 1455, which James saw as a direct challenge, since he claimed it was part of the diocese of Sodor and Man, and as this was a Scottish bishopric it followed that he had the sole right to appoint the incumbent. Determined to impose his own nominee by force, he dispatched an army there (probably the besiegers of Threave) in a fleet of Gallovidian ships from Kirkcudbright,[76] while conferring the empty title of lord of Man on his second son Alexander. This provoked Lord Stanley to retaliate by descending on Kirkcudbright in company with James, the exiled earl of Douglas. Having reduced the town to a heap of smouldering ruins, they continued up the Solway to plunder the west marches.

Not long afterwards, in July 1460, the English king Henry VI was defeated and captured by his Yorkist opponents at Northampton, but his queen, Margaret of Anjou, and their son Edward, prince of Wales, were still at large and a focal point for a revival of the Lancastrian cause. At their urging King James summoned an army to invade England, but before doing so he laid siege to the strategically important Roxburgh castle which had been in English hands since Edward Balliol delivered it up to Edward III in 1332. Artillery was mustered to breach the walls, but unfortunately James's fascination with these engines of war caused him to stand too close to one of the cannons, and when it accidentally exploded he suffered injuries which proved fatal. The untimely death of this able king at the early age of twenty-nine was a disaster for Scotland, since it deprived the country of the able and forceful ruler it so desperately needed, and instead it was confronted once again with a long royal minority.

NOTES

1. This can be inferred from Agnew's assertion that there is documentary evidence of William Douglas styling himself as *vice comes de Wigtoun* up to 1424 and thereafter dropping the title (Agnew i, 243).
2. Agnew claims Lochnaw already belonged to his family and had been filched from them by Archibald the Grim and given to Douglas of Leswalt (i, 234–5), but there is no absolute certainty about this.
3. *RMS* ii no 183.
4. Agnew i, 243.
5. Brown, *Black Douglases*, 241.
6. Including, it would seem, those of Lochryan, since they passed to Agnew's second son William (McKerlie i, 140), an ancestor of the present owner.
7. This could have included the Agnews, since Andrew Agnew of Lochnaw was allegedly married to Kennedy's sister, while their mother was a sister of both Duchess Margaret and the king.
8. *Wig Charters*, 171. Alexander Mure belonged to the Rowallan family, to whom Duchess Margaret was related through her paternal grandmother, who was the first wife of Robert II. His descendants subsequently acquired land in Galloway and continue to be represented there.
9. This was confirmed by a royal charter of 1479 (*Wig Charters*, 173–4).
10. Assuming this is a correct rendering of the name Macgilhauche, which appears as a witness to a number of charters (*RMS* ii no 87 and others).
11. Cowan, 'Church and Society', 134.
12. *Wig Charters*, 57–8.
13. *RMS* ii no 133.
14. *Ibid.* 309.
15. Brown, *Black Douglases*, 275.
16. This can be inferred from the fact that James II first asserted his claim to the Galloway lordship in January 1451.
17. Brown refers to Duchess Margaret's deposition and her subsequent confinement at Lincluden in *Black Douglases*, 275.
18. By this time the venerable earl had become so corpulent that the Auchinleck chronicler tells us when his body was opened up after his death 'he had in him four stane of talch (fat or tallow) and maire' (*Auchinleck Chron* f. 109 v).
19. This is on the evidence of the *Scottish Peerage* which asserts that his wife was a daughter of Henry, earl of Orkney, while her mother Egidia was the daughter of Archibald the Grim's illegitimate son, Sir William Douglas of Nithsdale.

20. James Douglas of Dalkeith, the head of the other main branch of the house of Douglas, was insane and therefore of no political account.
21. He was one of the courtiers who participated in Earl William's assassination (*Chron. Auchinleck*, 115r).
22. Brown, *Black Douglases*, 275.
23. *RMS* ii 1705.
24. Following his defection Lindsay became a member of the council, and in 1453 he was appointed to the important office of keeper of the privy seal. Yet the king does not appear to have trusted him, perhaps because of his connection with Earl William and the fact that he was tainted with his family relationship with the hostile earl of Crawford. This is evident from the fact that after the fall of the Douglases he was 'excludit fra the counsall' and only escaped being put to death on payment of a heavy fine (Auchinleck Chron. f. 120v: Brown, *Black Douglases*, 314).
25. *Wig Charters*, 163–5: McKerlie i, 360. The Vauses continued to maintain their links with the Church, as Robert's descendants included George Vaus bishop of Whithorn, while another became prior of Whithorn, and two more were successively abbots of Soulseat.
26. Oram, 'Heirs to Ninian', 73–4.
27. *RMS* ii nos. 606–11 etc.
28. *Ibid.* no. 383.
29. Brown, *Black Douglases*, 276.
30. *Pitscottie* i, 76.
31. This link with this Dutch ducal family was a reflection of Scotland's increasing importance on the European stage, as is evident from the marriages of James I's daughters to a number of foreign princelings, including the French dauphin. While Mary of Gueldres' own family were of minor importance, her powerful uncle Philip, duke of Burgundy, was able to foster Scotland's valuable trading links with the Low Countries.
32. *RMS* ii no 309. The rubric states that the charter was granted 'after mature deliberation' and with the consent of the three estates (of parliament). Picturesquely, the *reddendo* was one red rose to be handed over to the king or his representative annually at the bridge of Dumfries on the feast of St John the Baptist.
33. J Law, *De Cronicis Scotorum brevia*, 1521, Edinburgh University library DC7, 63f, 1282.
34. Brown, *Black Douglases*, 287.
35. *RMS* ii no 447. In consequence, his descendants held the sheriffship almost continuously until 1747 when hereditary jurisdictions were abolished.
36. *Ibid.* 412.
37. *RMS* ii no 383. This charter confirmed Earl William's grants to Whithorn priory.
38. *Ibid.* 309.
39. He was the uncle of Earl William and Douglas of Balvenie, and although formerly an ally of their father, James the seventh earl, he defected to the king, being rewarded with the earldom of Caithness.
40. *Pitscottie* i, 83.
41. These incidents are described in *ibid.* i, 90–2, though neither Sir Patrick Gray nor the tutor of Bombie can be positively identified.
42. *Chron. Auchinleck* f. 114v, 115r, though one wonders why Gray should come to a dinner party armed with a poleaxe!

43. Brown, *Black Douglases*, 295.
44. Sir William Crichton's cousin, George earl of Caithness, had already acquired the baronies of Buittle and Preston through his marriage to the widow of Sir James Douglas of Dalkeith.
45. *Pitscottie* i, 95.
46. Brown, *Black Douglases*, 297.
47. *Pitscottie* i, 100.
48. Brown, *Black Douglases*, pp 298–9.
49. So Countess Margaret described it to the king after her divorce from Earl James (Pitscottie i, 125). King James seems to have had some sympathy for her since he arranged for her to marry his half-brother, John, earl of Atholl, while endowing her with the forfeited Douglas lands of Balvenie. She had two daughters by him, one of whom married the powerful earl of Huntly and the other lord Forbes, both of them leaving numerous descendants.
50. Brown, *Black Douglases*, 302.
51. *Ibid.*, 306.
52. Hamilton's loyalties lay firmly with the senior branch of the black Douglases since he was married to the fifth earl's widow.
53. Nicholson, *The Later Middle Ages*, 370.
54. *APS* ii, 42, C2 abd 43–4, C14.
55. Brown, *Black Douglases*, 308.
56. Agnew i, 273.
57. *RMS* ii no 762.
58. Their mother Katherine, a daughter of the first lord Maxwell, was married first to William Douglas of Leswalt and after his death to Gilbert, lord Kennedy.
59. *RMS* ii no 2954. *Wig Charters*, 162.
60. Brooke argues for this in *Wild Men*, 178.
61. *Wig Charters*, 8.
62. Brooke, *Wild Men*, 177–8.
63. *Wig Charters*, 9–10.
64. *CSSR* ii, 663.
65. *ER* vi, 456.
66. It has been calculated that the gross money rents assessed on these lands came to £751 3/4 (*ER* vi, 557–8: McGladdery, *James II*, 93), while a justice-ayre held at Kirkcudbright in 1455 or 1456 yielded up a further £600 6/8 (*ER* vi, 195, 206). It later transpired that the rents were set at too high a level, and by 1460 they were reduced to a total of £470 (*ER* vi, cx).
67. *APS* ii, 42.
68. *Ibid.*
69. *ER* vi, 344–54.
70. *ER* x, 701–5. Bothwell was a leading supporter of James IV in his rebellion against his father, and this was doubtless part of his reward.
71. Murray, 'Crown lands in Galloway', 11.
72. Disc. *ibid.*
73. Although they were subordinate to the Douglases, the Maxwells of Caerlaverock were a politically-important family long before the Douglases rose to power, Aymer Maxwell having been chamberlain, justiciar of Galloway and sheriff of Dumfries during the 1250s and 1260s (Young, *The Comyns*, 68, 69).
74. Brown, *Black Douglases*, 312.
75. Agnew i, 256.

76. *ER* vi, 204. There are a number of references to this expedition in the records, and the exchequer rolls for 1456 refer to the sending of a ship to the Isle of Man 'while the King's army was there' (*ER* vi, 204). Those for 1457 refer to compensation being paid 'for the wreck of a ship while at the Isle of Man on the King's service' and the payment of 5/- for carrying letters from Dundrennan to the king 'with news of the ships' (*Ibid*, 309).

16

CONTEMPORARY SOCIETY

PREVAILING CONDITIONS

The wars of the fourteenth century left much of Scotland devastated, while Galloway probably suffered worst of all, having been one of the main battle-grounds in the war of independence, as well as the target of repeated plundering raids during Edward Balliol's campaign. The result was that, when peace was restored following Balliol's retirement to England in 1356, it took the region all the longer to recover, and even twenty years later the rental for the demesne estate of Buittle indicates a reduced acreage under cultivation.[1] The plight of the Glenkens was far worse, for it had ceased to be a rural deanery,[2] and in spite of David II's attempts to rehabilitate it the region was reduced to a state of dereliction.

Nature contributed to the general hardship, because contemporary records speak of a deterioration in the climate, with more frequent storms and a higher rainfall. The winter of 1431/2 was particularly hard, and Bower refers to 'ice and gales' causing 'widespread losses of sheep and cattle',[3] while 1435 was a year of 'great food-shortage'.[4] The year 1484 seems to have been bad too, as we are told that meteors 'filled the country with dread as harbingers of calamity', while Sir James Balfour records that on 25 September 'three moons appeared in the firmament . . . with much fyre, thunder and raine'. The worsening weather was endemic throughout the whole northern hemisphere; alpine glaciers were on the advance, while closer to home there was a virtual cessation of cropping in Ireland and vines came close to dying out in southern England.

Recurrent outbreaks of bubonic plague took their toll, the most devastating being those of 1349 and 1362. The first of these had already swept through much of England and by early summer it reached the northern counties, where people were dying in large numbers. The Scots were quick to take advantage of their plight, and an army was summoned to assemble in the forest of Selkirk in readiness for a raid on the sickly English. Although the troops had been assured that this evidence of divine wrath was reserved for the sinful English alone they were clearly taking no chances, and invoking 'God and Sen Mungo, Sen Ninian and Seynt

Andrew' they prayed for their help to 'scheld us this day and ilka [each] day fro Goddis grace and the foule deth that Ynglessh men dyene upon'.[5] In the event they never marched, for within a few weeks their worst fears were realised when they themselves fell victim to the pestilence. The army quickly disintegrated and the terrified men carried the dreaded disease home with them.

Describing its effects in gruesome detail, Fordun observed that it 'led to a strange and unwonted kind of death, insomuch that the flesh of the sick was somehow puffed out and swollen and they dragged out their earthly life for barely two days'. He went on to claim that 'nearly a third of mankind were thereby made to pay the full debt of nature', the disease attacking 'especially the meaner sort and common people'.[6] Wyntoun tells much the same story, and referring to southern Scotland in particular he observed that 'off lywand [living] men the thryd part of it [is] destroyid'.[7]

This was known as the first pestilence, to distinguish it from the second outbreak of 1362. According to Bower, the latter spread 'as much among the nobles and magnates as among the common people [and] nearly a third of the human race that remained after the first pestilence were forced to render their debt to nature'.[8] There were further outbreaks in 1379 and 1417, and also in 1439. The last of these originally appeared in the west marches and, as already mentioned, it struck Dumfries with particular virulence,[9] the fifth earl of Douglas being supposedly among the victims. A complete mystification as to the cause of these outbreaks added to the terror they inspired in the people. Unaware that the rat-borne flea was the culprit, they attributed them to a poisonous state of the atmosphere which could result from any number of factors, ranging from a malignant combination of the stars, to malodorous vapours emanating from the bowels of the earth. Another theory had it that they arose from some local source of putrefaction such as stagnant water, foul-smelling marshes, or unburned carrion.

A particularly serious outbreak in 1455 caused parliament to pass an Act decreeing that the wealthier people within the burghs were to be 'quarintined' in their houses, but unlike the dwellings of the less privileged they were not to be burnt in the drive to stem the disease. The infected poor, on the other hand, were to be 'put furth of the toun', which meant banishment to isolation camps on the burgh muir, where they were con-signed to the mercies of the 'foul clenzers'. Drawn from the lowest ranks of society, these people represented the dregs of humanity, and their principal task was to force the victims to dig their own graves and make sure none of them escaped.[10] In an attempt to invoke divine assistance the Act also ordered prelates 'to mak generale processiounis throu out thair dyoceis twyss in the wolk [week] for stanching of the pestilence'.[11]

A CHANGING SOCIETY

The combined effects of war, recurrent spells of bad weather, famine, and pestilence accounted for a drastic decline in the population, and a consequent shortage of manpower. This gave added impetus to the changes which were already occurring among the lower ranks of society, and most important of all it led to the final disappearance of serfdom – 'that great, peaceful, silent revolution which has never found its way into the pages of our histories', as Innes described it.[12] Former serfs now graduated to become landless labourers and in many cases small-time tenants or cottars, and while in some respects it represented an improvement in their lot, it meant they were now denied the protection traditionally extended by landowners to their serfs.

As there was also a shortage of tenants available to farm the land, they were now in a stronger bargaining position, and this led to changes in the landlord–tenant relationship to the advantage of the latter. They could obtain better leasehold terms, often increasing the size of their holdings, as well as extending the period of their leases and securing lower rents, and the last of these accounted for the reduction in landowners' incomes which is apparent from the fourteenth century onwards. Three-year leases seem to have been customary in Galloway,[13] and the estate rental of Buittle for 1376–8 shows a mix of annual and three-year leases.[14] The sixteenth-century historian, John Mair, mentions periods of four and five years as the norm,[15] while the exchequer rolls indicate this as being current practice on the former Douglas lands there,[16] though in some cases they were longer still.[17]

The rental of the Dalkeith estates of 1376–8, a valuable source of information, confirms the trend towards leasing out larger holdings, since these show husbandmen farming up to fifty acres and cottars anything from five to ten. This was probably a fairly typical example, particularly in the case of the husbandmen who were now substantial tenants or 'tacksmen' and generally sublet much of their land to groups of small tenants.[18] As a class they were comparatively well-to-do, and significantly there was a growing practice among fifteenth-century landowners of establishing younger sons as tacksmen by endowing them with leases of holdings on their estates. The abbeys followed suit, though in their case it was frequently a means of distributing favours – often to relatives of church dignitaries.

Yet, tenants were still liable to eviction at the whim of their lord, nor was there any guarantee of renewal when their leases came to an end – the 'ish',[19] to use the contemporary term – and this frequently resulted in severe hardship. In fact, a statute of 1469 refers to the uproar that invariably accompanied the evictions which regularly occurred at the terms of Whitsunday and Martinmas.[20] Alternatively, tenants might be given an opportunity to renew their leases, but only on extortionate terms, and there was an instance of this in Galloway when Bishop Ninian Spot attempted to extract a penal rent from Andrew Agnew, the hereditary sheriff, as a condition of renewing his lease of the episcopal lands of Sheuchan, near Castle Kennedy. However, Agnew not only declined to pay but refused to remove himself and appealed to the general council, and perhaps reflecting his local influence it found in his favour. So he remained in possession and the bishop was forced to accept the situation.[21]

One class of tenant who seem to have been privileged were 'kindly' tenants – a term derived from 'kin' rather than connoting benevolence. They were tenants whose forbears had farmed the same holding before them and whose association with it was tacitly acknowledged by the landowner,[22] and that they existed on the former Douglas lands in Galloway is evident from James II's insistence that they be given preferential treatment.[23] Another local example was Robert I's grant of fishing rights in the river Annan to his kindly tenants of Lochmaben, the *caput* of his Annandale lordship. Military service was still a requisite, and all tenants whose annual income exceeded £10 were statutorily obliged to keep themselves armed and horsed and ready to turn out for their lord whenever a summons was issued. As John Mair observed, 'the farmers rent their land from the lord [and] keep a horse and weapons of war, and are ready to take part in his quarrel, be it just or unjust, with any powerful lord, [and] if need be to fight to the death'.[24]

Parliament passed a number of measures for the purpose of protecting tenants' interests – not so much out of concern for the tenants themselves, but to encourage greater productivity to feed a population that was beginning to expand again. An early Act of 1366 forbade horsemen from riding through growing crops,[25] while another of 1400 abolished a tenant's liability for his landlord's debts.[26] Other measures, which were designed for the protection of crops and the regulation of farming practices generally, included two Acts passed in 1424, one being concerned with the destruction of predatory birds and animals (later re-enacted in 1457),[27] while the other revived the Act of 1214 which stipulated that ploughing was to begin no later than fifteen days before the feast of the Purification.[28] Similarly, James I issued a decree in 1429 ordering his barons to refrain from summarily evicting their tenant husbandmen.[29]

The spate of legislation continued throughout the reigns of James II and James III. One Act which was passed in 1449 protected the leasehold rights of the tenants in the event of a change in the underlying ownership of their land,[30] while another of 1452 specified the date by which corn had to be threshed, and there are also references to larger farmers (i.e. those with eight oxen or more) being required to sow a specified quantity of peas and beans.[31] Temporary food shortages accounted for the Acts passed in 1449 and 1482 against the hoarding of grain in order to sell it into a dearer market,[32] and further legislation was introduced in 1468 to ban the export of cattle and sheep.[33] It was for the protection of the latter in particular that an Act was passed in 1427 requiring barons and their tenants to 'chase and seek quelpes of the woolf, and gar slaie them', stipulating a reward of two shillings for each man responsible for a kill.[34]

There was evident concern at the dearth of trees resulting from the systematic felling of woodland to provide timber for building and charcoal production, and the failure to replant. John Mair attributed this to the insecurity of tenants who had no incentive to 'plant trees or hedges' which, as he observed, was 'no small damage to the whole realm'.[35] Consequently, an Act was passed in 1454 requiring all freeholders to cause their tenants to plant woods and trees, and to make hedges and sow broom.[36] This seems to have been widely ignored, since an Act of 1504 declared 'the wod of Scotland is uterlie destroyit' as a preamble to ordering landowners to plant hedges and orchards, and at least one acre of timber.

FERME-TOUNS

The ferme-toun was the basic social and economic unit of medieval Scotland. While their size, shape and organisation varied according to local conditions they were essentially small, clustered settlements which were farmed communally under a multiple tenancy arrangement.[37] Although not necessarily conforming to any standard pattern they did have certain features in common, the most important being the infield/outfield system of farming. Therefore most medieval touns were divided into the 'infield' land, which was capable of being regularly cultivated and was adjacent to the toun itself, the 'outfield', and the common land.

The infield was generally divided into two or three breaks, being cropped in turn on a two- to three-year rotation. While the emphasis continued to be on growing oats, there is evidence of a greater abundance of peas and beans, and although this may have been in response to statutory requirement, farmers are more likely to have associated it with an improved yield from the subsequent cereal crop. There is little evidence to show whether these leguminous crops were grown to any extent in Galloway, but if so it was probably the exception rather than the rule.[38] The fertility of the infield was maintained by a constant application of manure, to the extent that this was generally referred to in the south-west as the 'mukitland'.[39]

The outfield consisted of poorer quality land which was farmed less intensively. In contrast to the infield, it was divided into a larger number of breaks, each being cultivated in turn for anything up to five years at a time, while the remainder was left as pasture for livestock in order to build up its fertility. These animals were corralled within the turf-built dykes, but as they are unlikely to have been stockproof the chances are the cattle constantly breached them and went on a rampage through the growing crops. Beyond the outfield were the common grazings which were generally used for summering the livestock. 'Common' was an elastic term since it could mean that it was common to the tenants of one particular toun or else shared between a number of different ones.

The conventional method of farming the infield was the 'runrig' system which involved dividing it up into strips or parcels of ground. These were allocated among the tenants according to their respective shares in the tenancy – and provision for this, and the number of livestock each of them was allowed to keep, would normally be set out in the lease. As the plots of ground allocated to any one tenant were not necessarily contiguous it made for inefficiency and was undoubtedly a frequent source of neighbourly disputes. However, these would have been severely dealt with since close co-operation between all the tenants was essential if the system was to work properly. It was for this reason that birlaw courts were established to adjudicate on such matters and punish those offending against the canons of neighbourly behaviour.

The system was constantly evolving as the pressure to increase productivity led to parts of the outfield being brought into permanent cultivation. Even by the fifteenth century some ferme-touns had expanded to the point where they could no longer be managed as a single entity, and consequently the original touns spawned new ones. This was a gradual process which took place over a matter of centuries, so it was not until later, when an expanding population put additional pressure on the land, that the fragmentation of these 'touns' gathered pace.

These split touns are still recognisable today in the place-names prefixed by words like 'nether', 'meikle', or 'laigh' [low]. The more fertile parts of Galloway would have supported a large number of ferme-touns, and the 1376 rental of Buittle for example shows no less than fifteen on that estate alone,[40] while the physical remains of others are still detectable on the former estates of Galtway and Dunrod which were part of the priory lands of Traill.[41] The multiple tenancy system survived in parts of Galloway until as late as the nineteenth century before finally disappearing under the impact of enclosures, advances in farming techniques, and land improvement.

FEU-FERME

An alternative type of tenure, which became increasingly popular from the late fifteenth century onwards, was feu-ferme. This was essentially a sale in exchange for an up-front capital payment known as a *grassum* and a fixed annual feuduty payable in perpetuity. In effect, the granter made a permanent alienation of the land, since it was only in cases where the feuing conditions were breached that he could recover it. It was not a new concept, as ecclesiastical institutions had been raising money in this way since the thirteenth century, mainly to pay their papal taxes, but it was James II who popularised it when he extended the practice to crown lands. Successive parliaments willingly co-operated in this, since it relieved them of the need to subsidise his expenditure through taxation, and the initial authorisation was given in an Act of 1458, while an earlier one had extended a similar concession to the Church and baronage. This ordained that the king would ratify and approve the actions of 'quhat prelate, barone or frehaldare [freeholder] that can accorde [come to an agreement] with his tenande upone setting of feuferme of his awin lande in all or in part'.

This set the trend for the future, as landowners increasingly took advantage of the licence, to the extent that feu-ferme would become the basis for the whole system of landholding in Scotland. It differed from the old feudal grants in that it was essentially a financial transaction and there was only a limited emphasis on the superior-vassal relationship which was integral to the latter. For example, no obligations of military service were involved, the feudal superior had no right of wardship of a vassal during minority, nor in the marriage of a female vassal, while the feuar was spared the uncertain and frequently crippling imposition of feudal casualties.

For the granter the benefits were obvious, since the *grassum* gave him an immediate cash payment, while the feuduty, which was invariably higher than the former rent, was a useful provision for the future. The main attraction for the feuar, on the other hand, was that he now had full security of tenure of his holding, and therefore it meant he could improve his land in the confidence that his descendants would reap the benefit. It was a gradual process, because initially only relatively few tenants could afford to buy their holdings, while not all landowners were willing to sell. However, those tenants who did acquire possession of their holdings benefited from the subsequent rise in land values, and as inflation eroded the value of the annual feuduty, this became progressively less onerous. Conversely it operated to the detriment of the sellers, because the purchasing power of their feuduties was correspondingly diminished.

There were a number of instances of the religious institutions in Galloway disposing of land in this way. For example, McKerlie asserts that in 1437 Dundrennan feued off the lands of Orroland to Henry Cutlar,[42] whose name he suggests was derived from the trade of an ancestor employed to sharpen the tools of the masons who were responsible for building the abbey.[43] Also, in 1448 Bishop Alexander Vaus made a grant of land in the parish of Kirkcolm to McDowell of Garthland,[44] while in 1485 Quentin Agnew of Lochnaw's lease of Sheuchan was converted into a right of feu-ferme.[45] McKerlie also asserts that at much the same time Thomas McLellan of Bombie acquired Lochfergus and other properties in the parish of Kirkcudbright,[46] which formerly belonged to the priory of Traill.

On occasion prelates provided for their bastard offspring in this way, a case in point being Bishop George Vaus's gift of the property of Portincalzie in the Rhinns[47] to his illegitimate son, Abraham Vaus,[48] while crown lands were hived off to royal favourites. For example, in 1472 James III rewarded William, Lord Monypenny, for 'his praiseworthy and loyal service' with the gift of the barony of Kirkandrews,[49] followed by a further grant of lands at Buittle.[50] It seems these rewards were well merited, since Monypenny had a long and distinguished career, first as a member of James II's household, and later as a diplomat at the court of the French king, Louis XI, where he was assiduous in pursuing the interests of both James II and James III. Although the former Douglas lands were sacrosanct, James III gave his queen, Margaret of Denmark, the rents and customs of Kirkcudbright and Wigtown, along with Threave castle, in part payment of her dowry, but to ensure conformity with the 1455 Act this had the express consent of parliament.[51]

Many landowners granted holdings on their estates in feu-ferme as a means of providing for their younger sons, or alternatively they converted their existing leases into feus. This was particularly common in Galloway, and the descendants of these younger sons were among the class of 'bonnet' lairds who occupied the lowest rung of the landowning hierarchy. Sometimes landowners bought estates elsewhere as a portion for them, and one example was Sir John Gordon's purchase of part of the former barony of Craichlaw in 1500 as an endowment for his younger son William,[52] whose descendants would become prominent landowners in Wigtownshire.

TOWER HOUSES

The earliest tower houses in Galloway date from the fifteenth century, but reflecting the inferior status of the builders, these were constructed on a much more modest scale than Archibald the Grim's massive creation at Threave. Nearly all of them have been abandoned to become quarries for building material, and though some remain as ruins the majority have disappeared altogether. Among the earliest in Galloway is the original keep at Lochnaw which was completed in 1426,[53] while Garlies castle and the round tower at Orchardton date from the latter part of the century.

Among the survivors is Cardiness castle, near Gatehouse of Fleet, and though it was abandoned by its Gordon owners at the beginning of the eighteenth century, it was restored in the 1920s by the former Ministry of Works and is now maintained to a high standard by Historic Scotland. Others include nearby Rusco, which is believed to have been designed by the architect of Cardiness, and Old Place of Mochrum, both of which have been restored and are now occupied as private houses. Sixteenth-century towers, on the other hand, reflect a changing fashion and perhaps a modest concession to domestic comfort. The walls are less thick, and some have machicolations or slots formed by corbelling out a parapet walkway through which missiles could be dropped on intruders, an example being Hills tower, near Lochfoot, which was built in about 1520.

Cardiness, which dates from some sixty years earlier, is a typical example of its time, and the thickness of its outside walls indicates defence as the paramount consideration. A rectangular structure perched on a knoll overlooking the Fleet estuary, it is six storeys high and the floors are interconnected by a spiral stairway within a corner of the building. Underneath were the storehouses and cellarage and a purpose-built prison,[54] while the sleeping quarters were confined to the upper floors and the attics within the roof space. Adjacent to the castle were a number of outhouses comprising the court where baronial justice was dispensed, as well as kitchens, bake- and brew-houses and stabling, the whole complex being surrounded by a defensive wall or barmkin. While other contemporary tower houses may have had certain individual characteristics, they would all have conformed to the same basic design.

Parliament gave added impetus to castle-building with the passing of a statute in 1535 which required all landowners dwelling 'in the inland or upon the borders' whose land was valued at £100 or more to build a barmkin or enclosure for the 'defens of him, his tennentis and their gudis in trublous tyme' with 'ane tour in the samen for himself' if necessary.[55] This could have inspired the building of tower houses like Dunskey and Myretoun, whose ruins stand in the grounds of Monreith House, which date from later in the century. And perhaps also Castle Kennedy, though this was built sometime around 1600.[56]

While the earlier tower houses were essentially defensive fortifications, their principal function was to serve as the baron's administrative headquarters, while at the same time symbolising his status. Although their stark and forbidding appearance suggests a bleak, comfortless existence, the reality would have been very different, since wood was used extensively in the construction of the interior. The main rooms were lined with lathe and plaster and hung with tapestries, while the stone floors were covered with heather, straw or bracken. In winter time the heat from the fires in the main appartments, combined with the animal warmth generated by the large number of people living there, must have rendered the whole atmosphere almost unbearably stuffy, particularly as the glazed windows would have remained hermetically sealed throughout. It must have been extremely rank and fetid as well, since personal hygiene was minimal, most people being permanently lice-ridden and verminous, and sanitation was rudimentary, though most towers were equipped with privies of a sort. Only the higher nobility and royalty had a predilection for washing themselves in a barrel of water, and there are frequent references in the exchequer rolls to 'baith fatts' (bath vats). In the lesser lords' establishments, on the other hand, the description of medieval times as 'a thousand years without a bath' must have been noisomely apparent.

The leisure pursuits of the barons were many and varied, and sport played an important part in medieval life, hawking being a particularly popular pastime. The birds were highly prized and hence liable to be stolen, and there is a record in 1494 of the theft of hawks from Dundrennan, when their keepers were found tied up. Hunting with hounds was equally popular, Scotland being renowned for breeding hunting greyhounds, and churchmen participated in the sport as enthusiastically as secular lords. Towards the middle of the sixteenth century the chase frequently involved using guns, but this was severely frowned on, and an Act of 1551 prohibited on pain of death and forfeiture those who insisted on 'schutting with the halfehag, culverine and Pistolett at Deare, Rae [roe], wilde-beastes, or wilde-fowles'. The alleged justification for such draconian measures was that it was because of this that 'all sik [such] wilde-beastes and wilde-fowles ar exiled and banished', meaning they had been frightened away.

A SLUGGISH ECONOMY

In the eyes of his inferiors the lifestyle of a baron must have appeared enviable, for he lived well, had plenty to eat, entertained on a lavish scale, and had ample opportunity to devote himself to the chase. But outward appearances could deceive, since his baronial duties were time-consuming and demanding, as they involved the administration of local justice as well as the management of his estates. Moreover, he belonged to a highly competitive and militaristic society which meant he was in constant rivalry with his neighbours, and this frequently erupted into mutual plundering raids and even open warfare. Financial concerns beset the barons as well, for besides the omnipresent risk of crippling feudal casualties they all had to contend with periodic tax levies. In addition, they had to cope with the insidiously destructive effects of inflation and the consequent depreciation of their incomes, which had already been affected by falling rents.

The inflationary process was started by David II, who systematically debased the currency as a means of paying off his ransom, while James III gave it a further twist by adulterating the coinage with copper. This was primarily designed to repay the national debt, but it soon became an addiction, and as a result the country was flooded with worthless coinage known as 'black money'.[57] However, it proved a self-defeating exercise, because it drove sound money out of circulation and was rapidly 'cryit doun' (devalued), causing widespead hardship. As a contemporary chronicler put it, 'thir was blak cunzhe [coinage] in the realme strikken [struck] and ordinyt [ordained] by King James the thred', adding that this was one of the factors that 'causit baith hunger and derth and mony pure folk deit of hunger'.[58] The effect of this manipulation of the currency, combined with subsequent devaluations, was such that from 1368 to 1603 the value of the Scots currency fell from parity with the English to a level where the Scots pound was worth a mere twelfth of the pound sterling.

The combined effects of inflation and intermittent war with England had a severe impact on trade. The war resulted in Scottish ships being denied access to the Irish ports, and as these were the principal markets for Galloway's exports the embargo was particularly detrimental to its seaport burghs. Details of Galloway's exports were recorded in the custumars' accounts preserved in the exchequer rolls, the custumars being the royal officers responsible for collecting the export duties known as the 'great custom'. While it was normal practice for each burgh to have its own custumar this was not universally the case, for in the regions where trade was small it was usual to give him responsibility for several burghs, as well as an extensive length of coastline. Generally speaking, the jurisdiction of the custumar for Kirkcudbright extended from the Nith to the Cree, while his counterpart at Wigtown controlled the remainder of the Galloway coastline as far as the Ayrshire border, and this included the burgh of Whithorn.[59]

Traditionally Galloway's exports consisted of horses, cattle and sheep, and their by-products of hides and wool, though a minor variation was the export of herrings. For some reason these had migrated en masse into Scottish waters during the later fifteenth century, and from 1479 onwards they were among the principal exports of the west-coast burghs,[60] though this was apparently less evident at Kirkcudbright and Wigtown.[61] Hides were exported, either in their natural state or as leather, which was mainly processed in the burghs. Records reveal a lively trade in these during the mid-fifteenth century when some 2,700 hides were exported from Kirkcudbright, but this later declined to a fraction of its former total.[62]

Demand for wool was also a mere shadow of the heady days of the thirteenth century. Although it staged a dramatic recovery in the four-teenth century, and even as late as 1471 it accounted for three-quarters of the whole customs of Scotland,[63] it too fell away to the extent that by the early 1500s it was no longer of any significance.[64] This was mainly because the wool was being woven into cloth or plaiding, for the records show an explosive growth in their export during the fifteenth century.[65] Also, an act was passed in about 1456 empowering sheriffs to forbid the export of wool if they considered this to be detrimental to the home market, and it is possible that this provision was invoked by the local sheriffs in Galloway. Equally, the fall-off in demand may have been attributable – at least in part

– to the practice of smearing the sheep with a mixture of tar and butter[66] to protect them against blowfly strike and maggot infestation, which made the fleeces difficult to clean.

Galloway's external trade, however, was tiny compared with other parts of Scotland, and even that was small enough. It was a measure of this that whereas in 1434/5 five ships landed at Kirkcudbright, this had dwindled to about two a year by the end of the century, and the same applied at Wigtown.[67] The exchequer rolls tell the same story, as these show a fall-off in exports from these burghs compared with elsewhere in Scotland,[68] and as this was occurring against the background of a decline in Scottish exports as a whole, the stagnation in Galloway's external trade is starkly evident.

THE BURGHS

Galloway's seaport burghs were protected from the decline in exports by their status as important local markets, while their monopoly of trade within their localities assured them a continuing prosperity. So too did the grants of lands and other rights which they had acquired through course of time. In the case of Wigtown, these were set out in a charter of confirmation issued by James II in 1457.[69] This shows the community as owning a considerable amount of land locally, as well as grain mills and their attaching thirlage rights, along with fishings, and perhaps most important of all a right to levy tolls on all traffic crossing the Cree.[70]

The organisation of these communities was substantially the same as in the past, with the burgh councils continuing to be controlled by the merchant guilds. This was keenly resented by the second-class citizens, the craft guilds, who were continually pressing for a more meaningful role in the conduct of burgh affairs, and it was a reflection of their enhanced status that an Act was passed in 1469 giving them a limited say in elections to the burgh councils.[71] Another of 1487 went further by permitting craftsmen to pursue mercantile activities, while stipulating that they were to 'desist and cease from all trade and occupation in their own person that is not comely and decent for a gild brother'. Similarly, they were to abjure 'the personal exercise of a craft which soiled their hands'.[72] Clearly these did not go far enough to satisfy the craftsmen, and there were occasions when their resentment erupted into outbreaks of violence, such as occurred at Kirkcudbright in the following century.[73] On the other hand, the craftsmen may have been cautious about pushing their demands too far, since parity with the merchants could render them liable to a comparable share of the fermes or rents due by the burgh to the crown.

Although burghs were independent entities, there was nevertheless a tendency among all classes within the community to look to a member of the local baronage for leadership as well as protection.[74] Consequently these landowners tended to dominate the affairs of the burgh under their control, and normally they would have a town house to enable them to do so more effectively. For example, the McLellans of Bombie controlled Kirkcudbright, where successive generations of the family had occupied the post of custumar, while the Hannays of Sorbie exercised a similar authority over Wigtown in conjunction with the Mures of Craichlaw and the Mundwells of Eggerness. Whithorn, on the other hand, remained firmly under the control of the priory, which effectively treated the burgh as its own private property.

The layout of the burghs tended to conform to a standard pattern. At its heart stood the mercat cross, symbol of the king's peace which protected the trade of the town, while the market place itself was frequently defined by a widening of the main street, and both Wigtown and Whithorn are good examples. Public proclamations were made there, and it was also the place where the most important of all events – the fair – was held. Adjacent to it were the public buildings, including the tolbooth, where the burgh council met, the court sat, tolls were collected, and the prison was housed. Despite its extensive jurisdictional powers, the records show the burgh court as dealing mainly with petty offences like backbiting, slander and 'outspokenness'.

The Wigtown court books give some examples. John Ahostane is charged with 'wrongously witholding George Henglis's steel bonnet from him', and 'Isbell McGathyne's dotir [daughter]' is arrested for causing 'stroublans [a disturbance]' and calling down 'blasfemacioune' on Jonet Mwris. There are squabbles over the use of the town's communal oven, and in one case the accused is charged with throwing dogs down his neighbour's well.[75] Punishment for the more venial offences could entail fines or loss of burghal privileges, while in more serious cases it extended to the pillory and the stocks, as well as flogging, branding, or nailing by the ear to the tron (the public weighbeam). In the most extreme cases it could involve banishment or even the death penalty.

It is not hard to imagine the squalor that must have pervaded these communities, and how it was rendered incomparably worse by the practice of dumping piles of rubbish and human excrement in the streets outside the houses. From their booths in the streets farriers and skinners hung out what the records aptly term 'their stynking goods', while fleshers and fish dealers threw out their trimmings to be scavenged by the dogs and swine that habitually roamed the burgh. In the market place conditions were even worse, since there was more space for dumping refuse, and this frequently overflowed into the churchyard, which was generally used as a public convenience as well as a trysting place for lovers. Cattle which grazed the burgh lands by day were driven into the sanctuary of its walls at night, and there they were allowed to roam at will and add to the general filth.

Sporadic attempts were made to clean up the burgh by carting away the refuse to dung the burgh land, and tanners, whose practice of soaking hides in stale urine and treating them with dog dung was deemed offensive even by these standards, were banished to the sea-front.

Inevitably the burghs were spawning grounds for diseases, and therefore it was no coincidence that the recurrent outbreaks of plague raged with particular virulence in these communities. The victims were carted away to be buried in mass graves known as 'pest knowes' which were situated well away from the burghs in order to reduce the risk of further infection. Other diseases included 'le Quhew' – 'this sickness by which not only magnates but also numberless men of the people were snuffed out', as Bower put it.[76] It usually meant whooping cough, but it could be applied indiscriminately to any pulmonary complaint, and was attributed to 'dampness and the resulting putrefaction [which] generates acute fevers and brings on many other diseases'.[77] Among these was 'wame-ill' which covered a multitude of afflictions, ranging from diarrhoea to dysentery to abdominal cancer.

Worst of all was syphilis, which went under a variety of names, the most common being 'grandgore'.[78] One particular outbreak which occurred towards the end of the fifteenth century originated in Italy and was brought back by English soldiers serving in the French wars. This spread like wildfire and eventually penetrated as far as Scotland, where the records speak of brothels being closed 'for eschewing the infirmity that comes out of France and strange partes', and in the pious hope that 'their sinful inmates would turn to honest work'.[79]

Altogether the evidence suggests the general state of health was poor, that disease was endemic, and few people reached middle age, while fewer still survived beyond it. In fact Scotland altogether was an uncomfortable and inhospitable country even by medieval standards – so much so that Froissart observed that 'when the English invade [Scotland] they have to take their provisions with them as there is nothing to be found in the country'. Expectations were correspondingly low, and for the mass of people 'happiness depended above all on safety of the person, safety in possessions, a tolerable winter and a kindly summer'.[80]

NOTES

1. *Reg Morton*, 155.
2. Brooke, 'The Glenkens'.
3. *Bower* 8, p 267.
4. *Ibid.* 299.
5. Nicholson, *The Later Middle Ages*, 148: *Chron. Knighton* II, 62.

6. *Fordun*, 359.
7. *Wyntoun*, 482.
8. *Bower* 7, p 319.
9. Ritchie, 'Plague in Dumfries'.
10. *Ibid.*
11. *APS* ii, 46.
12. Innes, *Scottish Legal Antiquities*, 159.
13. Grant, *Social and Economic Development*, 255.
14. Nicholson, *Scotland*, 262: *Reg Morton*, l, xlvii–lxxvi.
15. Mair, *History of Greater Britain*, 31.
16. Nicholson, *Scotland*, 456: Grant, *Social Development*, 254: *ER* ix, xii (introdn).
17. Symon, *Scottish Farming*.
18. Disc. *Ibid.*, 66.
19. This was symbolised by the breaking of a wand.
20. Grant, *Social Development*, 255.
21. Agnew i, 283.
22. For a discussion of the subject of kindly tenants see Grant, *Social Development*, 248–52, and Dodgshon, *Land and Society*, 100–101.
23. Murray, 'Crown lands in Galloway'.
24. Nicholson, *Later Middle Ages*, 261: Mair, *History*, 47.
25. Symon, *Scottish Farming*, 79.
26. *APS* i, 213.
27. *Ibid.*
28. *Ibid.*
29. *Ibid.* ii, 17.
30. *Ibid.* ii, 35.
31. Grant, *Social Development*, 293.
32. Symon, *Scottish Farming*, 78: *APS* ii, 36, 144.
33. *Ibid.*: *APS* ii, 41.
34. Lythe, 'Economic Life', 81: Agnew i, 247.
35. Mair, *History*, 31.
36. Grant, *Social Development*, 291: *APS* ii, 51.
37. Dodgshon, *Land and Society*, 141.
38. This is apparent from accounts drawn up in connection with the 'thirds of benefices' in 1561 to 1572 for purposes of determining the crop levy on Church lands. These show that western benefices like those in Wigtownshire had 'rather sparse regimens of oats, barley and meal' (*Ibid.*, 158–9).
39. *Ibid.*, 255: *Archaelogical and Historical Collections relating to Ayrshire and Galloway*, 6.
40. *Reg Morton*. It is possible to identify from this where almost all these ferme-touns were located.
41. Dodgshon, *Land and Society*, 173.
42. This marked the start of a long tenure of these lands by his descendants the Laurie-Cutlars, and latterly the Laurie-Fergusons, who continued to own the property until the twentieth century.
43. McKerlie v, 104.
44. *Wig Charters*, 4, 163.
45. *Ibid.* 3, 176.
46. McKerlie iv, 197.
47. *Wig Charters*, 189 no. 201.
48. *RMS* ii no. 2956. Abraham Vaus was subsequently a contender for the priorship

of Whithorn.
49. This previously belonged to James lord Hamilton but he resigned it in exchange for lands at Bothwell (*Ibid.* no 1055).
50. *Ibid.* no 1043.
51. *Ibid.* no. 1143.
52. *Wig Charters*, 171.
53. This is according to the plaque on the outside wall which bears that date.
54. In fact, in this case there were two prisons, one on top of the other, being separated by a grating. While prisoners of higher rank were confined in the upper cell, the lower one, which must have quickly become a cesspit, was reserved for those of lesser consequence.
55. *APS* ii, 346.
56. See Roberts, *Towers of Stone*.
57. Disc. Macdougall, *James III*, 158–161.
58. *Ibid.*, 158.
59. Disc. Murray, 'The Customs Accounts of Kirkcudbright etc. 1434–1560', 136.
60. *Ibid.*, 149. The herring industry is discussed in Grant, *Social Development*, 312–5.
61. Murray, 'Customs Accounts', 155.
62. *Ibid.*, 143.
63. *Ibid.*, 142.
64. *Ibid.*, 142–3.
65. *Ibid.*, 143–4.
66. This was still practised in Galloway in the 1920s.
67. Murray, 'Customs Accounts', 146.
68. Grant, *Social Development*, 353–5.
69. *Wig Charters*, 123.
70. This right had to be bought out in the 1860s when the railway was extended from Castle Douglas to Portpatrick.
71. *APS* ii, 95.
72. *APS* ii, 178.
73. Grant, *Social Development*, 427.
74. Nicholson, *Later Middle Ages*, 449.
75. Truckell, 'Wigtown Burgh Court Book'.
76. *Bower* 8, p 117.
77. *Ibid.*
78. Nicholson, *Later Middle Ages*, 564.
79. *Froissart*, 265.
80. Lythe, 'Economic Life', 84.

17

THE ROAD TO FLODDEN

A REGENCY

James II was succeeded by his eldest son, James III, but because of his youth
– he was only eight at the time – custody of the new king was given to his
mother, Mary of Gueldres, and the lords of her council.[1] A capable and
determined woman, she proceeded to consolidate her position by
appointing her own placemen to the principal offices of state, the most
controversial being James Lindsay, who became keeper of the privy seal. A
protégé of William, eighth earl of Douglas, he subsequently defected to
James II, who appointed him to that office but dismissed him shortly
afterwards.[2] This time his tenure lasted longer, and as he proved a capable
administrator he was eventually rewarded with the treasurership. Another
of Mary's placemen was Ninian Spot, formerly James II's comptroller, who
had been given the bishopric of Whithorn in 1458, which was a significant
appointment since it set a precedent for using the see to reward faithful
royal servants.

The powerful Bishop James Kennedy, on the other hand, was excluded,
and because of this he and his ally, George Douglas, fourth earl of Angus,
became the leaders of the opposition movement. As Kennedy was primate
of Scotland subsequent chroniclers, being ecclesiastics themselves, were
naturally biased towards him, so they sought to blacken Mary's reputation
by imputing a number of amorous affairs to her. One of her alleged lovers
was the Lancastrian duke of Somerset, and this has been cited as the reason
why she initially supported the Lancastrian cause in the Wars of the Roses
which had broken out in England in 1455. By the same token, they suggest
that her subsequent switch to the Yorkists was prompted by sour grapes
when he abandoned her.

These are simply examples of history being distorted for the sake of
propaganda, because her support for the Lancastrians was dictated by
political considerations. In August 1460, a truce was arranged between the
two sides when the Lancastrian, Henry VI, designated the duke of York his
successor, to the exclusion of his own son Edward, prince of Wales.
However, Henry's forceful and energetic wife, Margaret of Anjou, would

have none of this and she was determined to continue the war for the sake of protecting her son's succession rights; but she needed foreign help, so she sent emissaries to Mary of Gueldres suggesting they enter into an alliance. Mary's response was positive enough to encourage the English queen to travel to Scotland to negotiate with her. So in December of that year she and her son sailed for Kirkcudbright, and landing there they continued their journey to confer with Mary at Lincluden, where the provost, James Lindsay, would doubtless have acted as host.

At this point news reached them of a resounding Lancastrian success at Wakefield and the death of the duke of York in the battle. This could hardly have come at a more propitious time for Margaret, as it was enough to persuade Mary to contribute a Scottish force to her war effort, and her decision seemed well justified when, two months later, the Lancastrians scored another success at St Albans. However, the situation was reversed in March 1461 when the Lancastrians were routed at the battle of Towton. The duke of York's son, Edward, proclaimed himself king as Edward IV, and Henry VI was forced to flee to Scotland with his wife and son, landing once more at Kirkcudbright.

Undaunted, Margaret redoubled her efforts to secure foreign help, so in April 1462 she set sail from Kirkcudbright for the Continent with the intention of raising a force of Burgundian levies, leaving her feeble-minded husband and her son Edward behind in Scotland. Promises were given but only a small number of troops materialised, and as most of them were drowned in a storm while crossing the Channel she was forced once again to seek help from Mary. Reluctantly the latter gave her a token force, and although it was enough to capture Alnwick castle this was retaken shortly afterwards by the earl of Warwick, and this time Margaret was compelled to seek refuge in Scotland. By now she had become a political embarrassment to Queen Mary, so the latter was forced to cut her losses by ordering Margaret and her son to leave the country, though Henry was allowed to remain there.

Queen Mary died shortly afterwards, in 1463, and as the earl of Angus predeceased her by a few months, political power, and with it custody of the king, passed to Bishop Kennedy. When he died two years later, in 1465, his brother Gilbert of Dunure, now Lord Kennedy, became the king's custodian, sharing power with the Boyds. They were a prominent Ayrshire family who owed their advancement to Robert Bruce and latterly James I, but now they aspired to political supremacy. Therefore, when in 1466 Lord Boyd and his brother Sir Alexander succeeded in kidnapping the king, they were in a position to edge Kennedy aside. However, they in their turn were driven from office by the king when he assumed full ruling powers on his marriage to Margaret of Denmark in 1469.

A DOOMED KING

James III shared the autocratic aspirations of his father and grandfather, but because he lacked their ability his kingship was a failure. For a variety of reasons, such as his pro-English foreign policy and his choice of low-born favourites, he incurred the hostility of a powerful group of nobles who were joined by his brothers, the duke of Albany and the earl of Mar. Matters came to a head in 1479 when James had his brothers arrested and their lands confiscated. Mar died in captivity, allegedly bled to death by his physician, but Albany managed to escape to France, where the king, Louis XI, welcomed him as an ally against James III. Three years later a diplomatic revolution occurred when Edward IV demanded the cession of Berwick, threatening to take it by force if necessary, and this caused James to abandon his league with the English and seek a renewal of the Franco-Scottish alliance. This meant that Albany was now *persona non grata* in France, so he moved to England where Edward undertook to support him in his efforts to overthrow James and usurp the throne.

An English army was mustered to invade Scotland under the duke of Gloucester (the future Richard III), with Albany acting as his principal lieutenant, and James responded by mustering the Scottish host at Lauder. Once it became evident that resistance would be useless, Archibald, fifth earl of Angus, instigated a mutiny, and many of the nobles defected to the king's hostile half-uncles, the earls of Atholl and Buchan. They proceeded to arrest James and took him back to Edinburgh, where they locked him up in the castle. When the English army arrived there Gloucester agreed a truce with the Scottish representatives, and Albany was restored to his former honours and estates on condition that he remained at peace with the king.

The accommodation soon broke down, because Albany, still with his eye on the throne, returned to his treasonable alliance with Edward IV. So with English help he launched another invasion of Scotland in 1484, joined this time by the exiled James, former earl of Douglas, but when they were defeated by a hastily summoned force at Lochmaben the ex-earl was taken prisoner. His life was spared, but he was confined to the monastery of Lindores in Fife, where he remained until his death in 1491, latterly becoming a pensioner of the Scottish crown. Albany himself escaped to France, being killed shortly afterwards in a jousting match against the future king, Louis XII.

Albany's flight left his supporters marginalised, and consequently the king was restored to power. However, he was now pathologically mistrustful of his immediate family – he had good cause to be – and his suspicions focused in particular on his eldest son James, duke of Rothesay, who remained a virtual captive, and in mounting fear for his life, at Stirling castle. When in early 1488 it began to look as though his apprehensions were about to be realised,[3] Rothesay escaped, and as he was forced to rely on his father's opponents for support he was unwittingly thrust into the leadership of the rebellion which now broke out. The main instigators included the earl of Angus, who had remained rebellious ever since the crisis of 1482, his mutiny having cost him the offices of steward of Kirkcudbright and keeper of Threave, and lord Maxwell. Although Maxwell's father was killed fighting for the king at Lochmaben he himself had been alienated by a number of overtly hostile acts on the king's part. Therefore, when the rebellion broke out he raised a contingent from the south-west, including levies from Galloway, to serve in the rebel army.

When news of the rising reached the king he mustered his host, and the two armies finally encountered each other at Sauchieburn, near Stirling, on 11 June 1488. The royal forces were defeated, and according to Agnew the Gallovidian levies made a significant contribution to the rebels' victory. With characteristically colourful imagination, he asserts that when the vanguard of the rebel army broke under the onslaught of the king's claymore-brandishing Highlanders, it was they who saved the day by going 'into action mounted on small but hardy steeds, wielding their long spears, and charging into the Highland host with terrific cries [as they] drove back all before them'.[4] Once it became clear the battle was lost, the king escaped from the field and attempted to make for the sanctuary of a ship lying in the Forth, but he never got there as he was ambushed and murdered on the way, and his assassins escaped.

Rothesay now succeeded as James IV, but his reign began inauspiciously since he was inevitably tainted with his father's assassination, and although not directly implicated, it caused him severe remorse. This compelled him to make confession to his confidant, Bishop George Vaus of Whithorn, and in token of his penance he is reputed to have worn an iron belt for the rest of his life.[5] Moreover, being a usurper he was at a grave disadvantage politically, and therefore to legitimise his essentially illegal régime he was crowned at Scone within a fortnight of his father's death. This was crucially important as there was still strong support for James III, particularly in the north, where a rebellion broke out under the master of Huntly, who was later joined by the earl of Lennox. James suffered the additional disadvantage of having to rely on the support of his father's enemies – men of dubious loyalty like Angus, and the leading members of the Home and Hepburn families, who were instrumental in propelling him into the kingship. So it was not until 1494/5 that he became master of his own house.

FACTION AND FEUD

James and his council regarded it as imperative to show that a new and forceful government had replaced that of James III, so in the spring of 1489 he and the leading members of the council[6] set out on a justice-ayre throughout the southern counties. This involved spending nearly a month in Galloway, making a leisurely progress through the region by way of Tongland to Kirkcudbright and Wigtown, eventually reaching Ayr about 21 March,[7] and from there they returned to Edinburgh. The purpose of his lengthy stay in Galloway in the company of these powerful magnates was to demonstrate his determination to stamp his authority on that region which had become as notorious for its lawlessness as for its traditional separatism.

The causes dealt with in the course of the circuit included the trial of two local men, Thomas Hutchison and James Carruthers, who were indicted on a charge of arson for having taken part in the burning of Thomas McLellan of Bombie's manor of Lochfergus.[8] A lenient view seems to have been taken and remissions were granted to both men on payment of a fine, which was hardly surprising since McLellan had been a leading supporter of James III in the south-west.[9] In fact, Lochfergus seems to have been a regular target for attack, as another band of raiders, including McLellan's neighbour, John Cairns, burned it again in 1498, and once again justice was settled with the purchase of a respite.

These acts of wanton destruction were symptomatic of the prevailing lawlessness in Galloway, for it is highly likely that the reported incidents were merely the tip of the iceberg, and the vast majority of such incidents were settled extrajudicially by recourse to arms. One of the earliest instances mentioned by Agnew occurred in 1466, this being a comparatively minor affray which was recorded in a complaint by Bishop Ninian Spot against Finlay McCulloch of Torhouse and his sons 'for having wrongously spulzeit his corn, cattle and goods'.[10] After a long delay McCulloch was ordered to make restitution, though whether he did so is not recorded. In the following year, a fierce encounter took place 'between many Galloway gentlemen' at Sinniness near Glenluce, in the course of which a McDowell was killed and fines were imposed on his assassins, including members of the Adair and Agnew families.[11]

In spite of being the hereditary sheriffs, the Agnews seem to have played a leading part in these disputes, perhaps because their records are better preserved than those of other families. On one occasion, Sheriff Quentin Agnew was the subject of a claim for the 'wrongous withholding' of a quantity of 'clene breddit oats',[12] while on another the complaint concerned the theft of cattle in the course of a plundering raid into Ayrshire.[13] A similar foray down the Rhinns, which occurred in 1488, included an attack on his brother-in-law William Adair's fortress of Kilhilt, when Agnew and his men drove off a number of cattle – probably in retaliation for an unrecorded raid on his own lands. On their return journey they attacked Archibald McCulloch's stronghold of Ardwell, stripped it of its contents and added to their booty by appropriating the owner's cattle. The victims appealed to the lords auditor who ordered Agnew to make restitution, but as they were unable to enforce it he simply ignored the command.[14]

In spite of parliament's passing an Act empowering fiscals to call on sheriffs and their deputes for assistance in apprehending wanted men,[15] this was unlikely to be forthcoming when the person in question happened to be one of the deputes, and still less so that the sheriff would be impartial. This occurred on one occasion when Agnew's depute, John Muirhead, was among those charged with the 'masterful spoliation' of the parson of Wigtown's 'whole lamb teinds, cheese and dues of kirk since the feast of Pasch', and for the 'wrangous occupation and manuring of his kirkland and glebe'.[16] Predictably, the sheriff dismissed the case and Muirhead and his accomplices went unpunished.

The Agnews were involved in a long-running dispute with the Kennedys over the right to exercise jurisdiction within the barony of Leswalt. This led to a series of clashes which culminated in a pitched battle near Stranraer between Patrick Agnew of Lochnaw, assisted by the abbot of Soulseat and a number of local lairds, and Sir David Kennedy, the future earl of Cassilis. The Agnews triumphed, and when Kennedy appealed to the council for redress it imposed a token fine of ten merks on Agnew's supporters. Still, it was a moral victory for Kennedy, so Agnew's brother retaliated by mustering a band of henchmen to make a physical assault on him, an outrage which resulted in charges of 'oppression' being laid against them, though how they were disposed of is not disclosed.[17] This was not the end of the matter, because when Kennedy was later appointed to the council he took the opportunity to level a whole series of charges against Agnew, ranging from minor thefts to the ill-treatment of a horse.[18]

BISHOP VAUS

The appointment of George Vaus to the see of Whithorn in succession to Ninian Spot in 1482 added an ecclesiastical dimension to the feuding. His involvement may have stemmed from his being a local man – he was a brother of Vaus of Barnbarroch, though his previous appointment as parson of Wigtown could have drawn him into a number of disputes. Since his elevation took place during James III's imprisonment in Edinburgh castle he was not one of his placemen; therefore James IV could trust him as his confidant and confessor, and when he founded the Chapel Royal at Stirling in 1501[19] he appointed Vaus its dean. This was a well-endowed institution whose possessions in Galloway included the provostry of Lincluden and the church of Kells, and as Bishop Vaus was anxious to secure it for his successors he persuaded the king to petition the pope to have it annexed to the bishopric. Consent was eventually granted in 1503, and this greatly enhanced Whithorn's value as a benefice.

However, the bishop was less successful in his squabbles with his neighbours. Vaunting the regality jurisdiction which attached to his office, he attempted to interfere with the administration of local shrieval justice. As Sheriff Agnew was incapacitated, the bishop's pretensions brought him into conflict with his depute, Alexander McCulloch of Myretoun. The first of a series of brushes between them occurred when McCulloch issued a decree of distraint of the lands of one Mitchell McBriare for payment of a debt. McBriare appealed to the bishop, who overturned the decree and forbade the sheriff officers to touch his goods on pain of excommunication. McCulloch countered with the threat of force if his decree was ignored, which was clearly much the more daunting prospect, as the sheriff officers duly obeyed him. The bishop responded by solemnly cursing Sir Alexander 'Knycht of Myrton'; he cursed the sheriff clerk; he cursed the sergeants and other officers indiscriminately; and he cursed them all 'by bell, book and candle'. Then, committing his curses to writing, he ordered letters of cursing to be served on his opponents, but as ecclesiastical thunder failed to impress either the sheriff or his depute the bishop appealed to the council. It overruled him, so the prelate was firmly put in his place.[20]

On another occasion John Dunbar, younger, of Mochrum, was charged with stealing the sum of £43 and 'uther small gere' from the bishop.[21] While the latter no doubt roundly cursed Dunbar he was probably glad this time to rely on the civil authorities to bring him to book, though in the event Dunbar was pardoned with the purchase of a respite.[22] In 1502 Dunbar's father, Sir John of Mochrum, was appointed steward of Kirkcudbright and keeper of Threave, but he was murdered the following year by Sir Alexander Gordon, younger, of Lochinvar. The sequel demonstrates how a comparatively minor matter could escalate through the operation of the ubiquitous bonds of manrent. The murdered Dunbar was a brother-in-law of William McLellan of Bombie, and because the Agnews were bound in manrent to the Gordons, Patrick Agnew of Lochnaw being the son-in-law of Sir John Gordon of Lochinvar, McLellan proceeded to plunder Agnew's lands. Obviously he could not judge his own case, so it was passed to a higher court which ordered McLellan to have 'his hede stricken fra his body', though he was reprieved at Agnew's intercession. However, as his descendant drily observed, 'society had little reason to thank the sheriff for his clemency'.[23]

Another flagrant breach of the law by its own officers occurred in 1497, when Alexander McCulloch, who was deputising for the sheriff, decided to take the law into his own hands against William Adair of Kilhilt and his kinsman McCulloch of Ardwell. They were popularly supposed to have been responsible for the murder of one Dionysius Hamilton at Wigtown, and notwithstanding their protestations of innocence and the fact that they had neither been tried nor convicted, McCulloch, in company with McDowell of Garthland and a large following, descended on Adair's fortress of Dunskey. Having burnt and ravaged it, they moved on to Ardwell where they pillaged the contents and made off with a drove of livestock. The victims immediately posted to Edinburgh where they appeared before the lords auditor demanding redress, and although restoration was decreed[24] there is no record of it ever being made. Quite the reverse in fact, as it seems suspiciously likely that McCulloch took revenge on the laird of Ardwell, since the latter was murdered 'under silence of nycht' the following year by one Patrick McCulloch. However, in an act of rough justice, the said Patrick was himself murdered by a Dunbar shortly afterwards.[25]

These outrages were judicially disposed of by the purchase of a respite for a large sum of money. Justice in those days was by no means even-handed, and there was clearly one law for the rich and another for the poor, in the sense that while the former could buy respites or pardons those unable to do so had to face the full rigour of the law.[26] There was a practical aspect too, because in spite of the practice being regularly condemned by parliament and the council, pardons were a valuable source of revenue to the king. In any case, he was hardly likely to risk antagonising a powerful magnate like Alexander McCulloch, particularly in a region where he needed all the allies he could get, merely for the sake of applying even-handed justice.

Sir Alexander (he was knighted in 1506) is usually identified with Cutlar McCulloch who launched a predatory raid on the Isle of Man in retaliation for a descent by Thomas, Lord Stanley, on Kirkcudbright in 1507. According to Agnew, the visit was repaid with interest, as McCulloch and his men carried away with them everything that was not 'too hot or too heavy'. In a flight of fancy, he goes on to say that repeated descents on the island so terrorised the Manxmen that they are alleged to have made a practice of eating their meat before their soup, to make sure of something substantial in case the meal was interrupted by this ubiquitous pirate.[27] However, a certificate signed by an official at Peel castle listing the articles alleged to have been plundered paints a more modest picture. Claiming it had been 'taken by Collard McCulloch and his men by wrangous spoliation', it describes the booty as including 'xl knowtes [forty cattle], a cote mailzie [a coat of mail], and twa kystes [chests] with a quantity of malt and corn, twa box beddes, and a feder bouster [feather bolster]'.[28]

In spite of his misdemeanours Sir Alexander was clearly a favourite of James IV, since he appointed him one of his falconers and later installed him as captain of Linlithgow palace.[29] Sir Alexander's support was recognised in the king's charter of 1499, confirming him and his wife in possession of lands in Wigtownshire which they had originally been given by James III, as this specifically stated that it was in recognition of 'the gude service done be him till [to] oure said faidir and us'.[30] In 1504 James IV granted him a further charter erecting Myretoun into a burgh of barony, which Agnew alleges was in reward for his hospitality to the king during his pilgrimages to Whithorn.[31] He goes on to claim that there was a room in the old tower of Myretoun, latterly used as a pigeon house, which was traditionally known as the 'King's chalmer' since it was reputedly set aside for his use during his visits there.[32]

Judging from the contemporary criminal records, James IV's attempts to impose his authority on Galloway seem to have been less than successful. 'Slaughter' appears with distressing frequency, while 'burning' was a common offence. The Adair stronghold of Dunskey appears to have been a regular casualty, since not only did it suffer at the hands of the McCullochs, MacDowalls and McKies in 1498 but the McKies burned it again in 1502, and yet again in 1513.[33] William Lennox of Cally combined fireraising with predatory activities, for in 1508 he was charged with 'besieging Thomas McKie in the kirk of Girthon, poaching salmon in the Fleet, and burning the wood at Rusco'. Three years later he appeared on another charge – this time for 'striking the sheriff and destroying the woods at Lochinvar'. The second offence was in retaliation for an earlier incident when Sir John Gordon of Lochinvar was convicted of 'oppression of Mr. Lennox of Cally', and because it was settled with the purchase of a remission[34] Lennox doubtless considered he had got off too lightly.

Other offences were more venial. John McLellan was fined three merks for 'stealing two hogsheads of Gascony wine' and a further ten for pulling a monk of Dundrennan off his horse.[35] Patrick Mure, a frequent law-breaker, was charged with a whole litany of offences, including 'casting the vicar's servant over his own stair', unlawfully releasing a victim from the stocks, and pursuing the sheriff-depute with a drawn 'quhinzear',[36] while Ninian McCulloch of Cardiness was charged somewhat quaintly with 'taking and tearing up the King's letters'.

BURGH RIVALRIES

The rivalries among the leading families were reflected in the dissensions between the principal burghs, and while the element of physical violence may have been lacking, the competition between them was equally intense. Kirkcudbright and Wigtown were the main contestants, principally because they were trying to capture each other's seaborne trade. Initially Kirkcudbright had the edge, but during the fifteenth century the bulk of the trade, such as it was, shifted to Wigtown. Geography had much to do with it, since Wigtown was more accessible, besides being the main port of entry to the increasingly productive region of the Machars. On the other hand, Wigtown was finding it progressively more difficult to police the long stretch of coastline under its jurisdiction; in fact Reid suggests that in 1500 the king was forced to take matters in hand by appointing the influential James Lindsay as its custumar. Evidently this was resented as Lindsay was 'deforced' by the provost and burgesses, so the king appointed John McKie of Merton in his place.[37]

Wigtown's difficulties stemmed mainly from the activities of the chapmen, and because of this crown letters were issued in 1503 to the sheriff and provost, prohibiting all chapmen from buying and selling 'wax, iron, tar, skins or victuals under pain of confiscation of their goods'.[38] Clearly these measures cannot have been successful, as further letters were issued in 1517 empowering the sheriff and baillies to confiscate the goods of those who infringed the 'liberty of the community of Wigtown'. These were specifically directed against 'chapmen and other unfree traders who buy and sell in landwart places and do not bring their goods to the burgh mercats thus defrauding the customs and the rights of burgesses'.[39]

Meanwhile, it was coming under increasing competition from Whithorn, whose fortunes had risen sharply in consequence of the large number of pilgrims who were now flocking to St Ninian's shrine in emulation of the king. Also, reflecting his close association with Whithorn, King James issued a number of charters which were designed to promote the interests of both the priory itself and the burgh. While the priory was given a grant of the customs of all skins, hides, fish, cloth, wool and other goods 'transported in their own ships',[40] the burgh was issued with a charter in 1511 confirming the privileges granted to it in the reigns of Robert I and David II.[41] But these concessions were not enough to satisfy the prior and burgesses, as they aspired to the same trading rights as Wigtown. So they are alleged to have hijacked a vessel bound there and seized its cargo which they proceeded to sell off – or so Wigtown claimed in an action it raised against Whithorn. The litigation was prolonged and eventually the issue hung on whichever of the two burghs was the older. Whithorn could produce King Robert's charter of 1325, but as Wigtown's earlier records had been destroyed – allegedly by rats – the best it could manage was James II's one of 1457, so judgment was given in favour of Whithorn and the claim dismissed.[42]

JAMES IV AND WHITHORN

James's associations with Whithorn stemmed from the pilgrimages he regularly made there. The first took place in the autumn of 1491,[43] and he was back there two years later in 1493. As this was part of a royal progress through the outlying parts of the realm to underscore his authority and to meet and be seen by the people, and was therefore a more formal visit, James was accompanied by members of his council.[44] The itinerary was a demanding one, since it involved travelling via Dingwall to the Western Isles and back to Dunstaffnage castle on the Firth of Lorn where the royal party arrived on 18 August. Eleven days later they were at Durisdeer on their way to Galloway, and ultimately Whithorn, from where they travelled by sea to Ayr, and so back to Edinburgh.[45]

James's next recorded visit was in 1501 when his journey took him via Dumfries and Kirkcudbright,[46] where he stayed at the friary, making a donation to it of eight French crowns.[47] He was back again in 1503, but this time the pilgrimage combined piety with pleasure, as it included a detour by Bothwell castle to visit his current mistress, Janet Kennedy[48] – or Janet 'bair ars' as she was unchivalrously dubbed – who had recently taken up residence there. On another occasion, in 1505, James arrived in Galloway from the opposite direction, having travelled by way of Ayr. The first night was spent at Glenluce abbey, where he and his fellow guests took part in a skittles match, his betting losses apparently amounting to 17s.[49]

Although it would be unjust to deny James the penitential and devotional aspects of these pilgrimages, he clearly enjoyed the opportunities they provided for entertainment, and it would doubtless have been a relief for him to get away from the stuffy atmosphere of his court and its intrigues. Sometimes he travelled incognito with only a small retinue, but usually his progresses were more elaborate, being graced by a large number of courtiers and a travelling circus of Italian minstrels, whose appearance in the wilds of Galloway must have been a source of amazement to the local inhabitants. James habitually maintained an impressive style, and as he aspired to rival his fellow renaissance princes in Europe his court was one of his main extravagances. A man of wide learning himself, he attracted to it men of letters and others skilled in music and the arts, and in consequence it achieved a level of sophistication hitherto undreamt of in Scotland. Yet for all their entertainment value his visits to Whithorn – and the other shrines he regularly visited – were essentially pilgrimages, and to emphasise the fact he would dismiss his minstrels before reaching his destination to allow himself to spend long hours in prayer uninterrupted by their serenades.

James IV was a man who enjoyed life to the full. Gregarious and good company, his formidable charm combined with his kingly status ensured him a succession of mistresses and many casual amours, so it was not until 1503, by which time he was nearly thirty, that he finally married. His bride was Margaret Tudor, the elder daughter of the English king, Henry VII. Like all royal marriages this was dictated by political considerations, since it was designed to cement an alliance – optimistically known as the Treaty of Perpetual Peace – which he had recently entered into with his prospective father-in-law.

Their first two children died at birth, and therefore it was not until 1508 that the queen produced a child that looked likely to survive. However, it had been a difficult birth, the queen was gravely ill, and James 'grevit him sa sair that he wald not be comforted'.[50] So in a quest for divine help he embarked on another pilgrimage to Whithorn, and as self-mortification was thought to improve the chances of success he undertook the journey on foot. This took him by way of West Linton and Leadhills, from where the royal party crossed the Lowther Hills to Durisdeer and down the Carron valley to the Nith. By this time James's shoes had worn out, so they had to be re-soled by a cobbler at nearby Penpont before the party could continue on their way, past Dalry and Penninghame, and finally to Wigtown. From there James was escorted by a guide for the rest of the way to Whithorn, arriving at the cathedral in time to attend the first service of 'prime' after a journey which lasted eight days.[51]

The object of the exercise seems to have been achieved – temporarily at any rate – as both mother and child survived, so later that year James made another pilgrimage there, accompanied this time by the queen, 'to give thanks to the saints and to God' for her recovery. This was a much grander affair, and if Agnew's imagery is anything to go by it must have been an impressive spectacle. With obvious hyperbole he tells us that 'as the royal procession advanced, from every tower and manor-place martial groups of gaily dressed horsemen presented themselves to swell the gorgeous train'. Led by 'the white canons of Whithorn, black friars from Wigtown and parti-coloured Cistercians from Glenluce', they processed through the burgh where 'the lairds of Garthland and Myretoun asserted the privileges of their ancient houses by carrying the Host'. Behind them came the king and queen in their robes of state, followed by the royal household, the sheriff and his brother lairds. The imagery continues with a description of how 'fair ladies graced the scene apparelled in their gayest attire', while the queen employed seventeen horses to 'carry the necessaries for the royal toilet'. Asserting it was also an occasion for celebration, he conjures up a picture of how 'the solemn services being concluded, all was revelry and mirth; and the barons having duly assisted to do justice to the feast, to which their good ladies had contributed, were in full humour to conclude the revels with a daunce in the Queen's chalmer'.[52]

On their return journey the royal couple stayed at Glenluce abbey, donating four shillings to the gardener[53] – an appropriate token, since the fame of its garden and orchard was widespread, this being long before such amenities became fashionable among the gentry. From there the royal party's progress took them by way of Soulseat and Innermessan to Ayr before finally returning to Edinburgh. Unfortunately, the infant prince, whose birth was the occasion for these festivities, died the following February. It is sad, too, to reflect that within a couple of centuries Whithorn, formerly the scene of such magnificence, was described as a place where 'dunghills lay before almost every door and swine fed on the luxuriant herbage in the street'.[54]

THE CHURCH IN DISREPUTE

While James's visits to Whithorn and other shrines reflected a genuine religious fervour, his reorganisation of the church, which involved Whithorn, was dictated entirely by political and financial considerations. Although James I had declared Whithorn to stand on the same footing as the other Scottish dioceses, this was not endorsed by the pope until 1472, when Whithorn became a suffragan of the newly-created archbishopric of St Andrews.[55] In 1492 the archbishop was William Scheves, but because he was a placeman of his father's, James IV attempted to downgrade his authority by obtaining papal consent to the elevation of Glasgow as a rival archbishopric, and Whithorn was transferred to it as one of its suffragan sees. Robert Blacader, a prominent supporter of James in the rebellion against his father, was appointed archbishop, but Scheves tried to block the changes, and consequently much of the revenues of both archbishoprics were dissipated in claim and counterclaim at the papal court[56]; but it was a fruitless exercise, as the pope had already sanctioned them.

When Scheves died in 1497 James IV arranged for his twenty-year-old brother, the duke of Ross, to succeed him as archbishop, as this meant the archiepiscopal revenues would accrue to the crown until he reached the consecrable age of twenty-seven. In fact it gave the king a double advantage, because he made his brother's appointment conditional on his surrendering the duchy of Ross to the crown, and this meant he became entitled to its revenues as well.[57] As events turned out, Ross died in 1504 before reaching full canonical age, but as James was determined to retain this lucrative source of revenue he deliberately kept the see vacant until his eleven-year-old illegitimate son, Alexander Stewart, was of an age to become the archbishop.[61]

Notwithstanding this, James was permanently on the hunt for new sources of income to finance his extravagances. So when Archbishop Blacader died in 1508 James detached the now-valuable see of Whithorn from Glasgow and returned it to St Andrews, so that its revenues would accrue to him. This arrangement lasted until the chancellor Gavin Dunbar's appointment to Glasgow in 1525, when he persuaded the pope to return Whithorn to his archiepiscopal see, and this time the arrangement was permanent. Four years later, Whithorn effectively acquired control of Tongland abbey when the latter was annexed to the Chapel Royal,[59] and later still the diocese was enlarged to include the whole region as far as the Nith, when it became the bishopric of Galloway.

James's appointment of James Beaton as Blacader's successor was part of an elaborate scheme to augment the royal revenues still further. The scion of a family of Fifeshire lairds and the first of a dynasty of clerics who would exercise supreme power in the Church and State, Beaton was already prior of the wealthy house of Coldingham on the merse of Tweed and had recently been nominated bishop of Whithorn. While he was quick to abandon the latter for the sake of his unexpected preferment he was less willing to sacrifice the priorship of Coldingham. However, James insisted on it as a condition of his appointment so that he in turn could give it to his son Alexander[60] and thus secure the revenues for himself, in addition to those accruing from St Andrews.

James's cynical appropriation of these ecclesiastical revenues was merely a foretaste of what would become virtually standard practice. Nevertheless, the abuses that were already rampant within the Church had encouraged the emergence in the 1490s of a faction known as the Lollards of Kyle who were openly critical of them. Consisting of a small group of influential Ayrshire families,[61] they followed the teachings of John Wycliffe, a fourteenth-century English preacher who denied the Church's right to temporal possessions and challenged the validity of papal decrees, while his criticisms of certain aspects of the mass caused him to be branded a heretic. When the Lollards of Kyle began to proclaim similar doctrines Archbishop Blacader proceeded against them, and in 1494 thirty adherents were duly arraigned before him and found guilty of heresy.

Since they refused to recant, Blacader invoked the secular arm of the law by appealing to the council. Thirty-four charges were laid, accusing them of claiming the pope as 'head of the Kirk of Antichrist', that 'he and his ministers were murderers', and that 'they which are called principals in the Church are thieves and robbers'. It was enough to burn them at the stake, but the Lollards of Kyle were fortunate, as the charges were dropped, and as Knox put it, 'the Bischop and his band war so dashed out of countenance that the greatest part of the accusatioun was turned to lawchter'.[62] While Knox's obvious sympathy for the Lollards is understandable, the king's dismissal of such serious charges and the implied snub to his ally Blacader is harder to fathom. Conceivably, it stemmed from the Lollards' close associations with the Boyds, who were still a powerful Ayrshire family besides being closely related to the king. Moreover, the chancellor Angus's wife was a daughter of the first Lord Boyd, and perhaps more to the point, her niece, Marion Boyd, was the king's current mistress. It is significant, however, that Ayrshire would become one of the main centres of reformism during the following century.

THE FINAL CHAPTER

The Treaty of Perpetual Peace with England was not destined to last. It was already being breached during the reign of Henry VII, and while he was careful not to allow these infringements to lead to war, Henry VIII, who was fired with ambition to achieve military glory, was less so, and after his accession in 1509 the situation became increasingly unstable. Although the treaty was renewed this amounted to little more than a nod to protocol, so when in 1512 Henry was drawn into a hostile league against Louis XII of France the latter began to make overtures to James. Lavish promises of assistance were made towards the crusade he was planning, and in return James renounced the English treaty and entered into a Franco-Scottish alliance. This was essentially a mutual assistance pact, in that if either of them were drawn into hostilities against England the other would automatically follow suit.

Therefore, when in June 1513 Henry embarked on an invasion of France, Louis called on James to honour his pledge by launching a diversionary raid into England. The Scottish host was duly summoned to assemble at Ellem in Berwickshire, and in August the entire army, probably the largest ever to invade England, crossed the Tweed. After scoring some initial successes, it encountered the English under the earl of Surrey at Branxton Hill, near Cornhill-on-Tweed in Northumberland, where battle was joined. In the long, hard-fought engagement which ensued, known as the battle of Flodden, the English archers cut down the Scots in their thousands, and this, combined with James's inferior generalship, resulted in a catastrophic defeat. Scarcely a noble family emerged unscathed, and many of the gentry, including a large representation from Galloway,[63] were among the fallen.

Worst of all, they included the king, whose attempts to set up decoys to mislead the enemy proved in vain. For Pitscottie describes how, in the aftermath of the battle, the English picked their way through the piles of corpses in search of his body, and how they failed to identify it because he 'caussit ten to be clad in his leifray [livery], clad witht his cott airmour'.[67] News of the disaster and the king's death was greeted with such appalled disbelief throughout the country that many preferred to believe he had somehow escaped from the field. Pitscottie subscribed to the popular illusion by recounting how there were found among the corpses 'tuo of his gaird the ane callit Alexander Makcullouck[65] and the uther the Squyer of

Clesche, quilk was men of makdome [build] baitht allyke to the king', and how the English, believing one of them to be the king, 'caist him in ane cairt and had him away to Ingland'.[66] Finally, he claims that four mounted rescuers, appearing from nowhere, like the four horsemen of the apocalypse, spirited him away to safety.[67] In fact his body was found with the head transfixed by an arrow and the skull cleaved by an English halberd within a spear's length of Surrey's command post. Thus perished the forty-year-old king, leaving a seventeen-month-old son, the sole survivor of his five legitimate children,[68] to succeed him, and once again the country was faced with a long royal minority.

NOTES

1. Armstrong, C. A. J., 'A Letter of James III to the Duke of Burgundy' *SHS Misc.*, viii, 19–32.
2. This was on account of his opposition to James II's 'appoyntment' with the ninth earl of Douglas, since it involved restoring him to the comital lands of Wigtown at the queen's expense. So her reinstatement of Lindsay was clearly a reward for his support.
3. Pitscottie suggests this was because news reached him that the king was marching on Stirling with an army to seize him (i, 201 et seq.).
4. Agnew i, 293. He claims this to be on Pitscottie's authority, but it is a highly tendentious interpretation of that chronicler's terse comment that 'nixt thame [i.e. the men of the Merse, Teviotdale and Lothian] in battel [stood those from] Liddisdaill and Annerdaill, and money [many] of Galloway' (i, 207).
5. *Pitscottie* i, 218.
6. They included the earl of Argyll, Patrick Hepburn earl of Bothwell, the justiciar lord Drummond, treasurer Knollis, Alexander Inglis who served as both comptroller and clerk register, and master Richard Lawson the justice clerk (McDougall, *James IV*, 62). Bothwell was already a man with strong Galloway connections, as he was keeper of Threave and was tenant of much of the former Douglas lands in the Stewartry (*ER* x).
7. *TA*, i, lxxvi–lxxviii, 104–6.
8. *RSS* i, nos. 3, 4.
9. Young, *Protocol Bk.*, 22–3.
10. Agnew i, 282.
11. *Ibid.*, 281.
12. *Ibid.*, 283.
13. *Ibid.*, 284.
14. *Ibid.*, 284–5: *ADC*, 1200.
15. *Ibid.*, 292.
16. *Ibid.*, 293.
17. The whole unedifying saga is described in *ibid.*, 322–5..
18. *Ibid.*, 328–9.
19. Cowan, *Medieval Churches in Scotland*, 179.
20. Agnew i, 298.

21. *Ibid.*, 305.
22. *Ibid.*
23. *Ibid.*, 332.
24. McKerlie ii, 265: *ADC,* 1496/1501.
25. *Ibid,* 172 (quoting Pitcairn's *Criminal Trials*): *RSS* i, 163
26. Disc. Brown, *Scottish Society,* 63–4.
27. Agnew i, 320.
28. *Ibid.*, 321.
29. *ER* xiii, 538.
30. *Ibid.* xi, 191–2.
31. Agnew i, 303. *RMS* ii no. 2974. The rubric merely states that this was a favour to the king's familiar, Alexander McCulloch of Myretoun, the rest being Agnew's embellishment.
32. *Ibid.*, 303.
33. Reid, 'Dunskey Castle', 241–2.
34. McKerlie iv, 54.
35. *Ibid.* iii, 197–8: Agnew i, 332.
36. Agnew i, 333.
37. *Wig Charters,* 137.
38. *Ibid.*, 138: *RRS* i, 927, 928.
39. *Ibid. RRS* i, 2924.
40. *RMS* ii, no. 3569.
41. The original grant was dated 1491/2 (*RMS* ii no. 2075), but as James was then under age he confirmed it in 1499 (*Ibid.* no. 2486).
42. Disc. *Wig Charters,* 138–9.
43. Macdougall, *James IV,* 197.
44. The party included the earl of Angus the chancellor, the justiciars Bishop Elphinstone and the earl of Bothwell, lords Lyle, Gray and Glamis, lord Home the chamberlain, Treasurer Arnot, Secretary Whitelaw, and John Fresell the clerk register.
45. Macdougall, *James IV,* 102.
46. McKerlie iv, 167.
47. Agnew i, 308.
48. The heroine of Pamela Hill's novel *Flaming Janet,* she was a half-sister of the first earl of Cassilis and had a somewhat colourful career, having originally been the mistress of Archibald, earl of Angus, before James IV took her over. She eventually married Sir Alexander Gordon, younger of Lochinvar, and after he was killed at Flodden she was married at least once if not twice more.
49. Agnew i, 309.
50. *Lesley, History* ii, 123.
51. Agnew i, 309–10: Macdougall, *James IV,* 198.
52. Agnew i, 309–10. While the description is fanciful it nevertheless gives a good flavour of the occasion, and being based on informed guesswork is probably not all that far-fetched.
53. *Ibid.*, 311.
54. TSA xiv, 422.
55. Stephen, *Church History* i, 484.
56. Macdougall, *James IV,* 212.
57. Nicholson, *Later Middle Ages,* 558.
58. Stephen, *Church History* i, 490.
59. *The letters of James V,* (ed) R. K. Hannay and D. Hay, (Edinburgh, 1954), 162.

60. Stephen, *Church History* i, 490.
61. They were evidently a tightly-knit group, their spokesman being Adam Reid of Barskimming, while others were drawn from the Mures of Rowallan, the Campbells of Cessnock, and the family of Chalmers of Gadgirth, among whom was Mariota, the wife of Sir William Dalrymple of Stair (Macdougall, *James IV*, 106–7).
62. Knox, *Historie* (Thomasson and Pullen) lib. i, 4: Easson, 'The Lollards of Kyle', 123–8
63. Agnew gives their names as Sir Alexander Gordon, Stewart of Garlies, the McDowells of Garthland, Freuch and Logan, Alexander McCulloch, McLellan of Bombie, the earl of Cassilis, the lords Maxwell and Herries, and Sir William Douglas of Drumlanrig (i, 335).
64. *Pitscottie* i, 273.
65. Son-in-law and namesake of Sir Alexander McCulloch of Myretoun.
66. *Pitscottie* i, 273.
67. *Ibid.*, 272.
68. In fact another son, the duke of Ross, was born posthumously but he only survived for two years.

18

A ROYAL AUTOCRAT

THE RED DOUGLAS ASCENDANCY

James IV willed the appointment of his widow, Queen Margaret, as guardian of their son James V for as long as she remained unmarried, and although it gave her extensive political powers she was never formally appointed regent. This was mainly on account of the opposition of a powerful faction of the nobility who were suspicious of her close ties with her brother Henry VIII. Her sex told against her as well, because in a male-dominated society there was a deep-rooted aversion to being ruled by a woman, despite the precedent set by Mary of Gueldres forty years before – not that this prevented a number of women from wielding power in Europe later in the century. These nobles inclined instead to John, duke of Albany, son of the rebel Duke Alexander, and the young king's nearest adult male relative, so there was a move to edge Margaret aside and offer him the regency instead.

However, the issue was resolved the following year when Margaret sealed her political fate by contracting an ill-considered and quickly-repented marriage with Archibald Douglas, sixth earl of Angus, who had recently succeeded his grandfather, the chancellor, as head of the red Douglases.[1] She intended this to reinforce her authority, but far from doing so it automatically deprived her of the guardianship, and hence political power. This opened the way for the council to offer the regency to Albany, but he was unenthusiastic and it was only under considerable pressure that he was persuaded to accept it. Nor was it a choice calculated to inspire, since he had been brought up in France (was in fact half-French), could barely speak a word of Scots, and had scant affinity with his native land. Yet in spite of this unpromising start he proved a capable and respected ruler.

Angus, however, remained on the council, but it was now split between a pro-English faction, in which he was the key figure, and those like his arch-rival James Hamilton, earl of Arran,[2] and Albany himself, who supported the French alliance. Meanwhile relations between him and the queen mother had deteriorated into such mutual loathing that she defected to the Albany-Arran faction, and together they succeeded in banishing him to England. In 1524 Albany left for France, promising to return later that year under pain of forfeiting the regency, but by this time he was weary of Scottish politics and their constant intrigues, so he decided to remain there and thus lost it by default. This gave the queen mother an opportunity to regain power, and following a time-honoured precedent she and Arran declared the twelve-year-old James's minority at an end, and having invested him with full ruling powers they proceeded to exercise these in his name.

Angus returned to Scotland in 1525, determined to regain his authority, but he was astute enough to proceed with caution. Therefore, by making a show of reconciliation with the queen mother he contrived to have himself reappointed to the council, where he rapidly became the dominant influence. He now proposed that custody of the king be rotated between each of the four main factions within the council, and that he should take first turn. Unsuspecting, his fellow members fell in with the plan, but when they perceived his true intentions it was too late, for when Angus's custodial period came to an end he refused to give up the king, and instead consolidated his power by appointing his relatives and allies to the key positions in the royal household. Finally, the same charade performed by Arran and the queen mother two years earlier was re-enacted when Angus and his supporters declared the king of age to rule, though more convincingly this time, since James was now fourteen.

However, Angus had overreached himself, and his monopolising of the principal offices of state for his friends and relatives cost him the support of a number of powerful nobles like the earls of Arran and Lennox, though Arran's political affiliations were to prove marketable. However, there was little they and their fellow opponents could do in the meantime, since Angus kept the king in a virtual state of captivity and exercised power in his name, while their efforts to challenge him were consistently unsuccessful. Two years later, James is alleged to have escaped from his clutches, and while this may be fanciful it is clear that from then on he began to act more independently of Angus. This culminated in a breach between them, when charges of treason were laid against Angus for having detained the king against his will.

At a meeting of the council, which was held in July 1528, all the members of the Douglas family were ejected from office and replaced by James's supporters, the chancellorship being restored to his tutor, Archbishop Gavin Dunbar,[3] who had previously been dismissed by Angus. Meantime, Angus himself was effectively exiled to the region beyond the Spey – well away from his power base in southern Scotland. As he refused to comply with the order, a parliament which was held in the following September drew up a lengthy indictment against him and his supporters which was served on him in person at Dalkeith castle, along with a demand that he give up his principal strongholds. Predictably, this earned a dusty reply, so the entire red Douglas faction were formally put to the horn and declared rebels.

To invoke the law against them was easy enough, but to enforce it by taking possession of their strongholds proved well-nigh impossible. As James was under no illusions about this, letters were issued to all sheriffs instructing them to raise local levies and dispatch them to Edinburgh in readiness to march against the Douglases.[4] The campaign was only partially successful, and although some castles were captured, Angus's own stronghold of Tantallon near North Berwick held out against all attempts to take it. Eventually Henry VIII intervened and mediated a truce whereby Angus gave up Tantallon in return for being allowed a safe haven across the Border, but once he was safely out of the way all the Douglas lands were declared forfeit.

GALLOVIDIAN OPPOSITION

There appears to have been some support for the red Douglases in Galloway, because no less than seventy-one local lairds, including Sheriff Andrew Agnew, refused to answer the summons.[5] Most were outlawed by the justice-ayre held at Wigtown the following January, though in most cases justice was settled by the purchase of remissions.[6] The reasons for their support for the Douglases are hard to fathom because the family had virtually no links whatever with Galloway. True, the fifth earl was formerly keeper of Threave and steward of Kirkcudbright until deprived of these offices by James III, but these were essentially titular appointments and hardly likely to draw him into close association with the Gallovidians. Therefore, the mutiny may have reflected a continuing undercurrent of separatism and a consequent automatic support for anyone who was prepared to challenge the royal authority.

Equally, it could have resulted from the knock-on effects of a feud between the Kennedys, who were politically aligned with the Douglases, and the royalist Campbells of Loudoun. This stemmed from a dispute between Hugh Campbell of Loudon, the sheriff of Ayr and one of the king's advisers, and Gilbert, second earl of Cassilis, over the lands of Turnberry. In 1528 Campbell, having failed to obtain satisfaction from the privy council, took matters into his own hands and murdered Cassilis. This was a serious crime, but the ever-needy James V turned it to his advantage by absolving Campbell on payment of a substantial remission. This incensed the Kennedys, who considered Campbell had got off far too lightly, and in retaliation the murdered earl's cousin, Hugh Kennedy of Girvanmains, along with a band of retainers, killed a Campbell relative who was the tenant of Lochfergus.

Now it so happened that the new earl of Cassilis and Campbell of

Loudoun were neighbouring landowners in Wigtownshire, since the Kennedy lands of Leswalt were adjacent to Campbell's barony of Corsewall, so the feud must have spread there as well. The local landowners who were drawn into it would automatically have sided with the Kennedys, since they were much the more powerful of the two contestants, and therefore it may have been because of the Kennedys' association with the Douglases that these lairds refused to answer the royal summons.[7] Evidently the carl of Arran was suspected of being implicated in Cassilis' murder, for his stronghold of Brodick on the island of Arran was burned and its keeper murdered by the dead earl's son-in-law, Fergus McDowell of Freuch, assisted by his kinsman, Thomas McDowell of Mindork, and two sons of the sheriff of Bute. Eventually they were all apprehended, and while the sheriff of Bute's sons were outlawed the McDowells compounded for their part in the felony by purchasing remissions.[8]

These incidents were symptomatic of the feuding which, because it had been allowed to go unchecked – and in some cases actively encouraged – throughout James's minority, had reduced the country to a state of virtual anarchy. As Tytler observed, many of the nobility 'traversed the country at the head of large bodies of armed vassals and waged private war against each other with a ferocity which defied all interference'. Consequently the realm was, to quote Bishop Lesley, 'in sic deformitie [state of unrest] that justice appeirit rugett up be the rutes [torn up by the roots]', and English travellers in Scotland described it as a land where there were 'continual murders, theft and robbery'.

That Galloway was no exception is evident from two affrays which broke out in the streets of Edinburgh in 1526, when a number of local lairds had gathered there to attend parliament. The first occurred when the earl of Cassilis and a number of adherents, including McDowell of Freuch, Hannay of Sorbie and McKie of Merton, rode into Edinburgh at the head of a band of retainers. As they approached the city centre they encountered a party of rival lairds and a pitched battle broke out, in the course of which some two hundred and fifty men were killed. Another fracas occurred a few days later when James Gordon of Lochinvar was walking down the High Street, accompanied by his relatives, Agnew of Lochnaw and Sir James Douglas of Drumlanrig, along with a number of other lairds and their retainers, and they encountered a rival group led by Sir Thomas McLellan of Bombie. Now it so happened that McLellan and Gordon were already at loggerheads, as McLellan had recently married Gordon's widowed mother and was attempting to assert her rights of terce in Gordon's lands. This was already the subject of a litigation between them, and in fact the case had been heard that very morning, though judgment was reserved. However, the matter quickly became academic, because neither party would yield the 'crown of the causeway' to the other, so a skirmish ensued, and among the casualties was McLellan himself who was killed at the door of St Giles' church.[9]

Incidents like these provoked James into exercising his judicial powers in person by going on a progress through the south to hold justice-ayres in the principal towns there. These included Kirkcudbright, and also Wigtown, since it was there that the charges against the seventy-one recusant landowners were dealt with. To emphasise his authority the king was accompanied by the leading members of his council, including lord Maxwell, Bishop Henry Wemyss, and David Beaton, the future cardinal and then keeper of the privy seal.[10] In Galloway he would have been attended by Gordon of Lochinvar, as he had recently been appointed chamberlain – somewhat surprisingly considering his recent involvement in the murder of his step-father – but it was clearly a measure of his local power.

James was determined to suppress feuding, come what may, and for what it was worth he invoked the moral authority of the church by causing Archbishop Dunbar to issue letters of cursing against the 'common tratouris, revaris and theiffis duelland [dwelling] in the south part of the realm'. Starting with 'thair heid and all the haris of thair heid', he proceeded systematically to curse each and every part of their anatomy before cursing generally 'everilk part of thair body, fra the top of thair heid to the soill of thair feet, befoir and behind, within and without'. Their families, servants, friends and everybody connected with them were included in the anathema, which wound up with an awesome peroration condemning them perpetually to the 'deip pit of hell, to remain with Lucifer and all his fallowis, and their bodeis first to be hangit, syne [then] revin and ruggit [torn apart] with doggis, swyne and utheris wylde beistis abhominable to all the warld'.[11]

A fine farrago, but archiepiscopal thunder was no substitute for punitive action, and in 1530 James mustered an army to march on the Borders with the object of bringing the principal troublemakers to book. Summonses were issued to all local sheriffs to raise levies to participate in the campaign, all men between the ages of sixteen and sixty being ordered to mobilise.[12] Many of the lairds however, perhaps fearing to leave their lands a prey to others, managed to produce plausible excuses – certificates of sickness, licences from the king and his lieutenant, and river flooding which prevented their passage – to avoid the draft, so the turnout was disappointingly small. Nevertheless, James was undeterred, and no holds were barred in his single-minded resolve to achieve his objective.

The most notorious of the Border reivers was Armstrong of Staplegordon (popularly known as 'Johnnie' Armstrong of Gilnockie), and James was prepared to breach all conventions of contemporary warfare in his efforts to capture him. Under pretence of a parley, Armstrong and his followers were induced to come to his camp unarmed, but once there they were promptly seized and hanged on the nearest trees. Treacherous though this may have been, James was determined to demonstrate beyond all doubt his insistence on obedience to the law. Brutally put and in language the offenders understood, it had its intended effect. Although this did not put an end to feuding, it was a successful start to a campaign which James extended to other parts of the realm, but it was to take him some years to reduce it to manageable proportions.

A KING IN PENURY

James's efforts to establish his authority cost money, but the extravagances of his father and the depredations on the treasury during his minority had left it so depleted that he could barely afford the costs of government. Worse still, many of the traditional sources of revenue to the crown, such as feuduties and customs, had been remitted or improvidently given away, or burdened with 'pensions' by his predecessors. In other cases they were simply diverted into the pockets of those responsible for collecting them. In fact, James's financial situation was such that he was reduced to farming much of the crown lands himself – a step which so appalled his royal uncle, Henry VIII, that he instructed his ambassador, Sir Ralph Sadler, to rebuke him for lowering his kingly dignity by 'gathering into his hands numbers of sheep and other such vile and mean things'. Instead, he advised him to take a leaf out of his own book by enriching himself at the expense of the monasteries[13] – a course which James would unhesitatingly have followed had it been possible for him to do so.

His act of revocation of all grants of land made in his name during his minority was also turned to advantage. Normally it was the custom to regrant them to their rightful owners, but because there was no obligation on a king to do so James made them pay heavily for the privilege. Feuing off crown lands was another source of revenue, but there is little evidence of this happening in Galloway. An exception seems to have been made in the case of Robert, fifth lord Maxwell, who was given the keepership of Threave and appointed steward of Kirkcudbright.[14] Having acquired the lands of Spottes near Haugh of Urr in 1529,[15] he was granted the barony of Buittle in 1535,[16] after it had been forfeited by the third earl of Morton.[17] While Buittle itself passed to lord Maxwell's successors, the adjoining estate of Logan became the portion of his illegitimate son, John Maxwell, whose descendants, the Maxwells of Munches, continued to own it until the twentieth century. Spottes, on the other hand, passed to Maxwell's second son, Sir John Maxwell, subsequently the fourth lord Herries, and a key player in Gallovidian affairs later in the century.[18] The only other recorded disposal of crown lands in Galloway was the grant in 1533 of a feu of the king's grange of Baldoon to the sitting tenant, Archibald Dunbar,[19] presumably at the behest of his brother, Archbishop Gavin Dunbar, the chancellor.[20]

A marriage with a well-dowered bride offered the prospect of a lucrative windfall to the treasury, and James's ambitions were realised when in 1536 he secured the hand of Francis I of France's daughter, Madeleine. However, his plans were in danger of being shipwrecked (literally) when he set out on a voyage to inspect his future bride. This included a detour round the north of Scotland and down the west coast for the purpose of demonstrating his authority in the lordship of the Isles, but when he reached the North Channel his fleet was forced by 'contrare wyndis and extreme stormis' to seek refuge at the Isle of Whithorn.[21] So the trip was abandoned and James and his party returned overland through Galloway back to Edinburgh.

Shortly afterwards he made another attempt, sailing this time down the east coast of England, and successfully eluding the English merchantmen which were patrolling the area he landed safely in France. However, his bride proved a delicate child who survived her arrival in Scotland by only a few weeks, though James contrived to keep her dowry. His next venture into the marriage market in 1539 proved more successful (and equally lucrative), his bride this time being Mary of Guise, the mother of his only surviving child, the future queen Mary. Ironically, Henry VIII also had designs on her as a possible bride, but as he had already executed one wife she claimed to have too slender a neck for such an undertaking.

DISPOSAL OF CHURCH LANDS

James's cupidity extended to the Church, as this represented a potentially huge source of revenue, but papal consent was necessary before there could be any question of imposing an ecclesiastical tax. In normal circumstances any such petition would have been rejected out of hand, but reformism was spreading so rapidly that Pope Clement VII was susceptible to blackmail – all the more so since there was every prospect of England going schismatic over his refusal to grant Henry VIII a divorce from his wife, Catherine of Aragon. The Scots, on the other hand, had already given ample proof of their adherence to the old faith. For example, an act had been passed in 1525 against 'the dampnable opunyeounis of hcrcsy [which] are spred in diverse cuntries be the heretik Luther and his discipillis' which banned the importing of reformist literature into the country under pain of confiscation of the offending merchants' ships.[22] More recently James had written to the pope assuring him of his continuing support and promising to do all he could to 'banish this foul Lutheran sect'. Therefore, as the pope was particularly anxious to retain Scotland in the Catholic fold he was in no position to quibble over James's request.

The upshot was that he consented to the levying of a permanent tax of £10,000 a year, known as the 'great tax', on the Scottish Church, as well as a charge of a tenth of the income of all benefices worth more than £20 a year. The ostensible reason was to pay for the cost of establishing a college of justice – a perfectly legitimate excuse, since a reform of the administration of the law was essential to restoring the royal authority. Justice-ayres had proved highly unreliable instruments, because their effectiveness depended on the co-operation of local magnates, and this was unlikely to be forthcoming if they, their friends or supporters, were among the accused. However, as the costs of establishing and maintaining the college of justice represented only a fraction of the proceeds of the tax, the balance simply went into the royal treasury.

The clergy, however, were not prepared to remain supine, and some senior Church dignitaries attempted to resist James's efforts to impose the tax. The prime mover was Archbishop Beaton, but James had a short way of dealing with them, and when he arrested Beaton for 'treasonable intercourse with England' the clergy became more amenable. Although the great tax was eventually commuted to a capital sum of £72,000, and as a further concession James allowed it to be paid in four annual instalments, it was nonetheless a crippling burden on the Church.[23] It came at a bad time too, since a growing disregard for ecclesiastical censure was making it increasingly difficult to collect Church revenues.[24]

This meant that the only way the Church could raise the money to pay the tax was by feuing off more land, and the pope co-operated by simplifying the procedure for this. Whereas in the past his predecessors had insisted on ratifying every charter disposing of Church property, he now delegated the task to the two Scottish archbishops, which meant that land sales could be dealt with more expeditiously.[25] However James, seeing it as a means of raising additional revenue, usurped the right by insisting on granting the necessary confirmatory charters himself and charging extortionate feudal casualties for doing so.

There is ample evidence of the impact of the tax in Galloway, where Bishop Wemyss, for example, was compelled to feu off his *mensa* lands in the parish of Twynholm. While most were sold to William McLellan, a younger brother of the laird of Bombie,[26] Kirkchrist went to James Kennedy of Blairquhan, who was the proprietor of the neighbouring estate of Twynholm.[27] Thereafter, they held these lands in feu of the church, and later on they became part of the St Mary's Isle estate. The bishop also disposed of the nearby lands of Barcaple. Although it belonged to Tongland abbey he was *ex officio* its commendator, and therefore he would have been instrumental in feuing it to his predecessor, Bishop David Arnot's son, Henry.[28] Similarly, the *mensa* lands in the Rhinns were sold off to members of the McDowell kindred.

Dundrennan, being under similar pressure, sold off its outlying estates in the parish of Kirkpatrick Durham. In 1537 it granted a feu charter of the lands of Barncailzie to Gilbert Neilson of Craigcaffie,[29] and shortly afterwards the remainder, which comprised Marquhirn and Crofts (including present-day Brooklands), went to Edward Maxwell of Drumcoltran.[30] In 1543 its lands at Kirkmabreck went the same way, though ostensibly this was to pay for repairs to the abbey buildings. The purchaser was James Makgill, an expatriate Gallovidian[31] who had moved to Edinburgh, where he became its provost. He bequeathed them to his son, James Makgill of Nether Rankeillor, in Fife, the clerk register, who seems to have combined his official duties with the private role of a land speculator, since he had already bought up lands belonging to Lindores abbey in Fife and sold off parts of them for a profit. He also cashed in on the rise in land values by selling off the Kirkmabreck lands[32] to his neighbour, John Broun of Carsluith, in 1583.

There is no evidence of the other institutions in Galloway, such as Sweetheart, Glenluce, Whithorn, Lincluden, and Trail, following suit, though they may have made some minor disposals where the records have been lost. Glenluce in fact had already sold off the Dunragit estate earlier in the century to its commendator, Cuthbert Baillie, who was the king's chamberlain for Galloway and later the royal treasurer.[33] He left it to his illegitimate son William, whose descendants continued to own it until the 1680s, when it was acquired by the Dalrymples and thereafter became part of the Stair estates.

Gilbert, third earl of Cassilis, was poised to acquire the lands belonging to Soulseat, and may in fact have already obtained some, but the canons put a stop to it by securing the appointment of James Johnstone, a younger brother of Johnstone of Lockerbie, as their commendator.[34] He was apparently well known in the Border country as 'a shifty and unreliable character who was treacherous to everyone, especially the English'. Notwithstanding this, when he was released as an assured Scot after Solway Moss, Sir Thomas Wharton allegedly bought his support with a bribe of a hundred crowns, referring to him as one 'whom I have found the best sort of Scots since they were won'.[35] Once installed as commendator, James Johnstone proceeded to sell off parcels of the abbey lands – but not, it would appear, to Cassilis.

However, when the commendator married his mistress in 1545 Cassilis seized the opportunity to strike back, so he cajoled the earl of Arran into petitioning Pope Paul III to have him removed from office. This was successful, and all the more so since the former commendator was charged with treason.[36] However, any hopes Cassilis may have had of replacing him with his own son, James Kennedy, the future laird of Ochtrelure, were scotched when the appointment went instead to Johnstone's kinsman, John

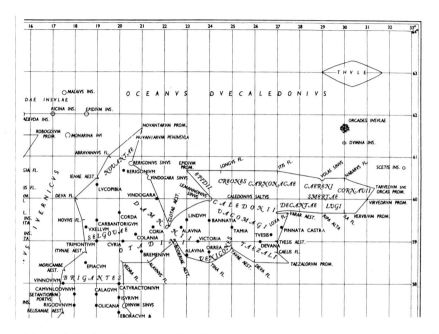

1. Map of Scotland drawn up by the second-century Alexandrian geographer, Ptolemy. *Courtesy of Dr D. J. Breeze.*

2. Roman camp at Glenlochar with the River Dee to the right; its geometrical design is clearly visible from the crop discolourations. *Courtesy of the Ewart Library.*

3. The remains of Dervorguilla's creation of Sweetheart Abbey. Founded for the Cistercians in 1273, it was the last new abbey to be built by that Order in Scotland. *Courtesy of the Ewart Library.*

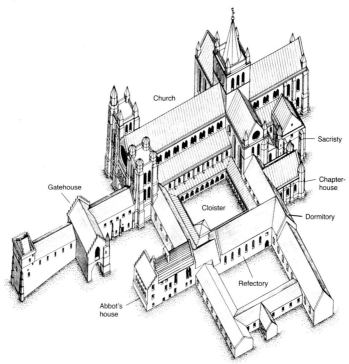

4. The standard layout of a medieval abbey; special quarters were set aside for those second-class citizens, the lay-brothers. *Courtesy of Historic Scotland.*

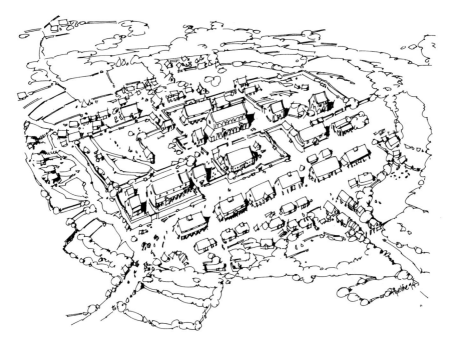

5. Whithorn: reconstruction of the Northumbrian minster as it was *c*. 800. Note the large church in the centre which served as the focal point of the community. *Courtesy of Historic Scotland.*

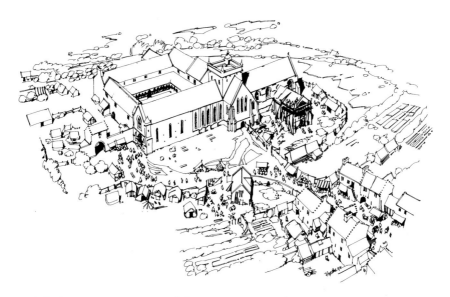

6. Whithorn: reconstruction of the priory as it would have existed at the time of James IV. *Courtesy of Historic Scotland.*

7. Aerial view of the Mote of Urr, near Dalbeattie. The largest of its type in Scotland, the earthwork, along with its former motte-and-bailey castle, was built by Walter de Berkeley in the 1160s, while the settlement which grew up round it was constituted a burgh of barony. *Courtesy of the Ewart Library.*

8. Artist's impression of the type of motte-and-bailey castle which Walter de Berkeley and his peers were building during the latter half of the twelfth century.

9. Threave Castle, on the River Dee. One of the earliest of its type, it was built by Archibald the Grim, primarily as a status symbol, in the 1370s. *Courtesy of Air Images.*

10. Cardiness Castle, Gatehouse. This was built by its McCulloch owner in about 1460, when the baronage were beginning to replace their timber-built donjons with stone-built strongholds. *Courtesy of Air Images.*

11. Kirkdale House, near Carsluith. This fine architectural masterpiece was built by Sir Samuel Hannay, bart., between 1780 and 1787 to a design by Robert Adam, which was subsequently much modified. *Courtesy of the Ewart Library.*

12. Cardoness House, Gatehouse. A prime example of the Victorian Gothic baronial style, and a standing justification for the fact that this and many others like it have been the victims of fire and dynamite. *Courtesy of the Ewart Library.*

13. The oldest house in Wigtownshire. Even this represented an improvement on the type of accommodation traditionally occupied by agricultural labourers. *Courtesy of the Ewart Library.*

14. Barnie McGhie's cottage, Kirkcolm. Although it incorporates accommodation for livestock, it was still an improvement on the type of dwelling traditionally occupied by the poorer people in earlier times. *Courtesy of the Ewart Library.*

15. Water colour drawn in about 1847 of the cotton mills which were established at Gatehouse by James Murray.

16. The former bobbin mill at Gatehouse, which has recently been restored and is now a popular tourist attraction.

17. Transport: brigs at Dub o' Hass, the port of Dalbeattie, in about 1880. Traditionally, the sea was Galloway's main link with the outside world, but the development of roads and railways spelt the demise of the shipping trade and Galloway's consequent relegation to a backwater. *Courtesy of the Ewart Library.*

18. Aerial view of Gatehouse. Its layout is a classic example of an eighteenth-century 'planned village'. *Courtesy of the Ewart Library.*

19. Life behind the green baize door: the domestic staff at Terregles House. Taking their tone from their employer, the maids would consider themselves socially superior to the agricultural labourers on the estate. *Courtesy of the Ewart Library.*

20. Country life in the early twentieth century: a shooting party at Knockbrex, on the Carrick coast, near Borgue. The light-coloured clothing worn by the guns seems calculated to scare off the game. *Courtesy of the Ewart Library.*

21. Steam engine at Kirkcudbright station in 1960. This branch line was subsequently closed in June 1965. *Courtesy of C. J. Gammell.*

22. Early twentieth-century agriculture: steam threshing mill owned by J. Derby & Son, Castle Douglas. Note each individual sheaf of corn being forked up on to the mill. *Courtesy of the Ewart Library.*

23. Early twentieth-century agriculture: a drove of sheep in the main street of Carsphairn. Sheep farming was the traditional form of husbandry in the hills of northern Kirkcudbrightshire, until they fell victim to the ubiquitous conifers. *Courtesy of the Ewart Library.*

24. Dry-stone dyking competition on the Cally estate at Gatehouse. A worthy attempt to revive a traditional craft which is in danger of dying out. *Courtesy of the Ewart Library.*

25. James Stewart, earl of Moray. Illegitimate son of James V, counsellor to Queen Mary, and regent for his nephew, James VI, he secured for himself virtually all lands belonging to Whithorn Priory in the Machars.

26. James Douglas, fourth earl of Morton, and a landowner in Galloway. A successful regent, he was equally so at feathering his own nest – and those of his illegitimate sons – and execution on the 'maiden' was his forfeit.

27. John Knox, the architect of the Reformation in Scotland. Far from being a religious fanatic, he was a shrewd statesman with a pleasantly human side to him.

28. Andrew Melville. The stormy petrel of the early Reformed Church, he was responsible for the rise of presbyterianism, though not the extreme fanaticism into which it degenerated.

29. James Graham, marquis of Montrose. A man of high principle, he was originally a covenanter but abandoned the extremists to support the royal cause, though Charles II made little effort to save him from the gallows.

30. Samuel Rutherford, one-time minister of Anworth. Eulogised as 'the saint of the Covenant', he was described as combining personal piety with 'a warmth of language which was hardly compatible with decency'.

31. James Graham of Claverhouse, later viscount Dundee. In spite of his deceptively effeminate appearance, he was the chief enforcer of the privy council's campaign against the extremist covenanters in the south-west.

32. Sir James Dalrymple, first viscount Stair. A former soldier in the covenanting army, he was later a noted jurist and became lord president of the Court of Session, as well as a leading politician of his day. He was a man of higher principle than his son, the first earl, though that is not saying much.

33. John Dalrymple, second earl of Stair. Soldier, diplomat and finally agriculturalist, he was promoted field-marshal late in life. His twenty years of political eclipse were devoted to pioneering new farming methods.

34. Admiral the Hon. Keith Stewart, son of the sixth earl of Galloway. Having inherited the Glasserton estate, near Whithorn, which comprises some of the richest land in Galloway, he was pre-eminent among the eighteenth-century improvers.

35. James Murray of Cally. Having inherited the estates of Broughton and Cally, he became a noted cattle-breeder, and the processing of their carcases provided the initial stimulus to the setting up of his industrial enterprises.

36. Lady Catherine Stewart, daughter of the sixth earl of Galloway, and wife of James Murray. A broad-minded lady, she was much concerned with the upbringing of her husband's illegitimate children. Her name is preserved in Catherine Street, Gatehouse.

37. Sir William Douglas, bart. Through his own efforts, he rose from humble origins to become a leading entrepreneur in Galloway, and the founder of Castle Douglas.

38. The Rev. Professor Alexander Murray. The traditional 'lad o' pairts', he started life as a shepherd's boy from Talnotrie, was later called to the ministry, and ultimately held the chair of Oriental languages at Edinburgh University.

39. Sir Andrew Agnew of Lochnaw, 8th bart. Author of *The Hereditary Sheriffs of Galloway*, he tells a good story and, unlike his contemporary, McKerlie, clearly had a good sense of humour.

40. The Rt Hon. Sir Herbert Maxwell of Monreith, 7th bart KT, FRS. A noted politician of his day, he was a recognised authority on a wide range of subjects, on which he was author of a prodigious literary output, dying in 1937 at the age of ninety-two.

Johnstone. He proceeded to feu off a substantial portion of the abbey lands to his predecessor[37] – perhaps in consideration for engineering his appointment as commendator – but was careful to ensure that Cassilis remained excluded.

A CHURCH IN DISREPUTE

These cynical manoeuvres to acquire the revenues and assets of the ecclesiastical benefices were symptomatic of the general malaise that was becoming evident within the Church, and it proved a valuable source of ammunition to the agitators for reform. The movement was already taking hold in the east coast burghs where, in defiance of the law and the heavy penalties involved, merchants were importing banned Lutheran tracts from the Continent. As the seeds of this new faith fell on the fertile soil of a widespread discontent with the well-publicised abuses of the Church, it rapidly spread to other parts of the country where the lairds and lesser gentry were among the principal converts.

By this time some 85 per cent of all churches in Scotland were appropriated to religious institutions, and this applied in the case of all but five out of the forty-five churches in Galloway west of the Urr.[39] Therefore, invidious comparisons were inevitably drawn between the ostentatious wealth of the Church, which was derived from its teind income, and the contrasting poverty of those who were forced to contribute to it. Equally inevitably, this access to wealth meant the Church had become essentially secular in its outlook, and this was particularly apparent in the appropriation of its revenues in the form of pensions by an increasingly laicised senior clergy. Unsurprisingly, teind payers were becoming recalcitrant, and as the task of collecting them became increasingly difficult many institutions resorted to farming them out to private individuals. This meant that in return for an annual rent they were assigned the right to collect them and retain the proceeds – a practice which applied in the case of nearly a third of all the churches in Galloway.[39]

The quality of spiritual service had also declined, accelerated by the long-standing practice of underpaying the vicars who were responsible for looking after the parishes. In many cases they held a number of parishes, farming out the pastoral work to curates, but their pay was so bad that only men of inferior calibre could be persuaded to undertake the task. So, however diligent they may have been, they were not qualified to minister properly to the spiritual needs of the people, and it was for this reason that the reformers laid particular emphasis on providing for the education of a suitably qualified clergy. Moreover, there was a growing impatience with the practice of conducting worship in Latin, since it was unintelligible to the vast majority of the people, though it was not until 1543 that an Act was passed at the instance of lord Maxwell which authorised the circulation of the Bible in the vernacular.[40]

The increasing secularisation of the Church led to a widespread disregard of the Gregorian ideals of poverty, chastity and obedience, so it was frequently the custom for clergymen to take a woman who was a wife in all but name and to have a tacitly acknowledged family. Records show that during the thirty years preceding the Reformation 350 male and 50 female children of priests were legitimised, one example being John Vaus, the parson of Wigtown, who was granted legitimation for his son and daughter in 1543.[41] As petitions were only made where an inheritance was involved, the number of bastards fathered by men in holy orders must have been far higher. While the majority of churchmen doubtless pursued their calling with care and diligence it was these kind of abuses which caught the attention of the public, and consequently the Church lost both respect and credibility. Therefore, pamphlets imported from abroad inveighing against 'the corruption of morals and the profane lewdness of life' of 'incontinent, intemperate and negligent' churchmen struck a chord with a wide section of the population.

The heads of most religious houses were now commendators, and the holding of these benefices *in commendam*, as it was known, was a device for appointing non-monks to these positions. Since they were disqualified from exercising the spiritual functions of abbots and priors, their responsibilities were confined to administering the secular interests of these institutions. This gave them control over the disposal of their revenues, with a consequent temptation to apply them for the benefit of themselves and their families. Historically, the right of appointing the heads of religious institutions was vested in the papacy, but as the Scottish kings could not countenance Church lands being effectively controlled by Rome, laws were enacted to prevent churchmen from seeking provision – or commendation – by the pope. As this put them in an impossible position a compromise was agreed between James III and Pope Innocent VIII in 1487, whereby the latter conceded to James and his successors the right to nominate a candidate to a benefice within eight months of its becoming vacant, provided it was worth more than two hundred gold florins.[42] James IV later secured a concession extending this to twelve months, though in practice his nominations received automatic papal approval, while James V was virtually able to dictate these appointments himself.

Pluralism – the holding of more than one benefice by the same person – had also become a scandal. James IV was guilty of it in the case of his son Alexander Stewart, but James V carried it to excess. Notwithstanding their defect of birth, he persuaded Pope Clement VII to allow his five illegitimate sons to hold benefices, and consequently he provided them to six of the wealthiest abbeys and priories in the country, the eldest James becoming commendator of Kelso at the ripe age of five.[43] Another was given the priory of Coldingham, whose incumbent, Adam Blacadder, was transferred to Dundrennan to make way for him. As his sons were all minors at the time of their appointment James was entitled to the revenues from their benefices, and according to the Catholic propagandist John Lesley, the combined income from them amounted to 'greitar profitt to him nor [than] the whole revenues of the Crown'.

There were occasions when the pope attempted to claw back the right of appointment to a vacant benefice, and an instance occurred at Whithorn following the death of its prior, Henry McDowell, in about 1516. Albany appointed his illegitimate half-brother, Alexander Stewart, to the post, but the pope, Leo X, refused to confirm it, putting forward his own nominee, Silvio, cardinal of Cortona instead, and offering to buy off Alexander Stewart with the commendatorship of Scone – a valuable prize. Stewart fell for the bait and withdrew his candidature, giving place to the cardinal.

However, Albany refused to accept Cardinal Silvio on the grounds that, being an absentee prior, he would not be able to entertain visitors, nor could he protect the pilgrims from pirates. Therefore, he froze the revenues to prevent them from being remitted to the cardinal. The pope retaliated by holding up the bull confirming Alexander Stewart's appointment to Scone, so deadlock ensued. Eventually a compromise was agreed whereby the cardinal gave up the priorship in return for a pension and the pope undertook to accept Albany's choice of Gavin Dunbar, a native Gallovidian, who was at that time dean of Moray, and his appointment was duly confirmed in 1519.

A sequel occurred in 1524 when Dunbar was appointed archbishop of Glasgow. The chapter elected John Maxwell, abbot of Holywood, a younger brother of the fifth lord Maxwell, but he was transferred to Dundrennan instead. Once again the cardinal threw his hat into the ring, but this time the offer of the revenues from the benefice was enough to persuade him to cede his claim to the priorship to the fifteen-year-old Ninian Fleming, a younger brother of the powerful lord Fleming.[44] Ninian was exceptional in that he became a monk of his own volition and got into trouble for doing so because it was against the terms of his appointment.[45] However his tenure was short-lived, and when he died some five years later he was succeeded by his staunchly Catholic brother Malcolm, who held the priorship until his death in 1568.

These disputes pale into insignificance compared with the shenanigans which were going on at Glenluce. When Cuthbert Baillie died in 1513 Arran secured the appointment of his illegitimate half-brother, David Hamilton, bishop of Argyll, as commendator. The pope refused to sanction it and appointed his own nominee, the cardinal of Eusebius, instead.[46] At this point the monks intervened by electing one of their number,

Alexander Cunningham, principally because he had the support of his powerful relative, the earl of Glencairn. He proceeded to barricade the abbey buildings before hurrying off to Rome to have his appointment confirmed, and while there he contrived to have his opponent, David Hamilton, excommunicated. However, no sooner had he returned to Glenluce than Arran had him evicted from the abbey by force, his hand being mutilated in the process, and thereafter he was confined in the tolbooth in Edinburgh. David Hamilton was then bribed to resign the commendatorship of Glenluce in exchange for the much wealthier abbey of Dryburgh, while the cardinal agreed to stand down in favour of the duke of Albany's secretary, Walter Mallyn.

Bishop David Arnot, a somewhat controversial prelate with a proneness to litigation, had meantime been looking after Glenluce, and as he had presumably been helping himself to the revenues he did not take kindly to Mallyn's appointment. Matters came to a head when he issued letters of cursing against Mallyn personally and the monks in general, and followed this up with a visitation in 1524. Quite apart from the irregularity of the proceeding, this proved to be no ordinary visitation, because the bishop arrived in force with James Gordon of Lochinvar and a number of other local lairds.[47] They and their retainers occupied the abbey for five days, causing extensive damage and looting much of its contents; in fact it was nothing short of a spoiling raid deliberately engineered by Gordon who had forced the pliant bishop to organise the visitation as a pretext. Abbot Mallyn duly complained to the council, and while Gordon was ordered to make restitution[48] the bishop was excommunicated and removed from office, though it seems that he was pensioned off with half the episcopal revenues as a golden handshake.[49]

AN INGLORIOUS END

James had consistently maintained an uneasy peace with his uncle, Henry VIII, but this finally broke down in 1542 when Henry was induced by the Emperor Charles V to join the pope's inaptly-named Holy League against France, to whom the Scots were bound by the auld alliance. The Scots now came out in support of the French by launching a series of raids into northern England, so Henry retaliated by threatening to invade Scotland unless James formally undertook not to support the French. James demurred, and a meeting was arranged between the two kings at York, but when James failed to appear Henry, who had waited there for eight days in vain, returned to London in a vengeful rage. He ordered his wardens of the northern marches to launch a punitive raid into Teviotdale, but the Scots managed to intercept the invaders and defeated them in an engagement at Haddon Rig in August 1542. On the same day, Henry VIII issued instructions to the duke of Norfolk to prepare for war, but when news of the defeat reached him he agreed to a parley. Negotiations dragged on throughout the next two months, and when they finally broke down Norfolk was ordered to march, but his invasion petered out through lack of food, beer and transport.[50]

Meanwhile the Scots were planning a counter invasion, and local sheriffs were ordered to enlist recruits, the sheriffs of Dumfries and Wigtown being instructed to muster the local landowners and their retainers to serve under lord Maxwell.[51] This was to be a two-pronged attack, with one army advancing on the east march while the other, which was commanded by lord Maxwell and Sir Oliver Sinclair, was to concentrate on the west. In the course of a probing operation towards Carlisle the latter found itself trapped by an English force under the deputy warden, Sir Thomas Wharton, between the river Esk and the Solway Moss. In spite of their numerical superiority the Scots were defeated, and a large number of local lairds and nobles, including lord Maxwell, taken prisoner.

Three weeks later the thirty-year-old James died at Falkland, and while contemporary chroniclers ascribe this to his disappointment at the defeat he was more likely the victim of typhus or cholera.[52] As his two legitimate sons predeceased him the crown passed to his six-day-old daughter, Mary. His premature death was a tragedy for the country, as he had proved a capable and effective king, and while he clearly lacked the charisma of his father, James IV, earlier historians gave him a good press, portraying him as 'the king of the commons' and 'the poor man's king'. Later scholars tended to place greater emphasis on the avarice and increasingly vindictive cruelty of this enigmatic and even sinister monarch, though it is now considered this is carrying revisionism too far.[53] But deliberately vengeful or not, there is no denying the ruthlessness with which this able monarch restored the royal authority and thereafter maintained it throughout his reign.

NOTES

1. There was one child of this marriage, namely Margaret, who married Matthew Stewart earl of Lennox, and became the mother of Henry, lord Darnley, the second husband of Queen Mary and father of James VI.
2. Formerly lord Hamilton, he was created earl of Arran in 1504. As his mother was a daughter of James II he was a first cousin of James IV and Albany, and he and his son, the second earl, were successively the heirs presumptive to the throne until the birth of James VI in 1566.
3. The son of a former crown tenant of Baldoon, his mother was a daughter of Alexander Stewart, 3rd of Garlies.
4. Cameron, *James V*, 42–3.
5. *Ibid.*, 53.

6. *Ibid.*, 56: Pitcairn's *Criminal Trials* i, pt. i, 140.
7. Disc. Cameron, *James V*, 115.
8. *Ibid.*, 35: Agnew i, 348.
9. These incidents are described by Agnew (i, 339–41). He claims that shortly afterwards, in a somewhat Gilbertian situation, McLellan's son fell in love with Gordon's daughter and the principal participants in the affray buried the hatchet at their wedding. A romantic story, but a fabrication, because McLellan's son was still a boy at the time of his father's death and he subsequently married a daughter of the second earl of Cassilis. In fact, it was McLellan's grandson, Thomas of Bombie, who married Gordon's daughter, but this did not occur until some forty years later, by which time the main participants in the affray were long since dead.
10. Cameron, *James V*, 74: *TA* v, 354, 387.
11. Maxwell, *History of Dumfries and Galloway*, 187.
12. Cameron, *James V*, 78: *ADCP*, 328–9.
13. *Ibid.*, 262.
14. *RMS* iii no. 1402.
15. Lord Maxwell was much in favour with King James, and during the latter's visit to France in 1536–7 he was appointed vice-regent, so this grant could well have been his reward.
16. This grant was held to be invalidated by the subsequent act of revocation, so it was confirmed in 1541 (*RMS* iii nos. 2277, 2368).
17. Married to an illegitimate daughter of James IV, he was associated with his kinsman Angus in keeping James V in protective custody. Thereafter, James waged a remorseless vendetta against him, eventually forcing him to resign his earldom along with the comital lands. Coincidentally, Buittle passed to his descendants, since his eldest daughter was married to Maxwell's eldest son the future sixth lord. Preston, on the other hand, was acquired along with the earldom by the future regent Morton, the husband of the youngest daughter.
18. Lord Herries in turn left Spottes to his second son, Sir Robert Maxwell, who subsequently acquired the estate of Orchardton, which his descendants continued to own until the end of the eighteenth century.
19. *RMS* iii, no. 1365.
20. So asserts McKerlie i, 385.
21. Cameron, *James V*, quoting correspondence between the queen mother and Henry VIII
22. *APS* ii, 295, c.4.
23. Donaldson, *James V – James VII*, 47.
24. *Ibid.*, 46.
25. *Ibid.*, 136.
26. Specifically they included Nunton, Bishopton, Kirkeoch and Auchengassel.
27. He subsequently exchanged these with Thomas McLellan (iii) of Bombie for the barony of Itoun near Eggerness, which the latter had acquired from the priory of Traill.
28. McKerlie v, 197.
29. *Ibid.* iv, 309.
30. *Ibid.*, 323.
31. *Ibid.* ii, 215.
32. These consisted of Glenquicken, Larg and Bagbie (McKerlie iv, 271–2), and therefore they comprised much of the original parish of Kirkmabreck.
33. McKerlie i, 177.

34. *Wig Charters*, 95. Papal consent to his appointment was given sometime before 1539.
35. Reid, 'Soulseat', 175.
36. *APS* ii, 481.
37. *Wig Charters*, 112 (no. 85).
38. Donaldson, 'Galloway clergy at the Reformation', 38.
39. McKerlie makes frequent reference to the letting of teinds.
40. *APS* ii, 415, c.12.
41. McKerlie ii, 326.
42. *CPR.* XIV, 4.
43. Cameron, *James V*, 205: *RMS* ii no. 1620.
44. Cowan, *Medieval Church in Scotland*, 198: The episode is described in *Wig Charters*, 11–13.
45. Dilworth, *Scottish Monasteries*, 22.
46. Ibid., 198: James V *Letters*, 3, 13, 31, 71–2.
47. According to Agnew, they included Alexander Stewart of Garlies, Thomas McLellan of Bombie and Uchtred McDowell of Garthland.
48. Details of the booty taken are given in *Wig Charters*, 62–5 (no 45), quoting *Brev. Lateranensis* vol. 7, fol. 206.
49. The saga is desc. in *Wig Charters*, 43–8.
50. Ridley, *Henry VIII*, 368: Cameron, *James V*, 291.
51. Cameron, *James V*, 314.
52. *Ibid.*, 325.
53. *Ibid.*, 328 et seq.; see also Macdougall, *James IV*, ix–xi.

19

THE REFORMATION

THE ENGLISH THREAT

James V left the direction of affairs in the hands of Arran, Cardinal David Beaton, his illegitimate half-brother, the earl of Moray, and the earls of Huntly and Argyll. It was a fractious partnership because it was split between those like Arran who favoured closer co-operation with England, and others who were determined to maintain the auld alliance with the French. During the next few months Arran managed to gain enough support to launch a successful coup against his rivals, and their leader, Beaton, was arrested and imprisoned in Blackness castle. Henry VIII seized the opportunity to release a number of prisoners taken at Solway Moss[1] on condition that they would actively pursue his interests in Scotland and give up hostages as an earnest of their co-operation, and this gave added strength to the pro-English faction.

Consequently, Arran entered into negotiations with Henry for the marriage of the infant queen Mary to his son Edward, prince of Wales, these being concluded by the treaty of Greenwich in July 1543. Henry's high-handed approach to the Scots now became insultingly evident, and when he demanded the surrender of the principal castles in southern Scotland it provoked such an outcry that Arran was forced to abandon his pro-English policy and seek closer ties with France instead. As a result, the rump of the pro-English faction, whose leaders included the earl of Lennox and the recently-returned earl of Angus, went into eclipse. With the French party now in the ascendant, Beaton was released from prison and reinstated as chancellor, while his ally, John Hamilton, Arran's illegitimate half-brother and abbot of Paisley, was appointed treasurer. At their dictation, parliament revoked the treaty of Greenwich and renewed the auld alliance with France.

An infuriated Henry retaliated by ordering his brother-in-law, the earl of Hertford, to invade Scotland. His brutally uncompromising instructions embraced the systematic destruction of the principal towns, and the mass slaughter of their inhabitants, in a deliberate attempt to terrorise the Scots into submission. One force was dispatched by sea, and disembarking near

Leith it sacked Edinburgh before burning and looting its way southwards with the intention of joining forces with the other army which was invading the east marches; but before it could do so it was intercepted and defeated by the Scots at Ancrum Moor, near Jedburgh. Undaunted, Hertford launched another equally destructive invasion the following year, and the devastation resulting from these campaigns was so extensive that they came to be known with grim humour as the 'rough wooing'. In the end they proved counter productive, because they merely stiffened Scottish resistance and drove them into closer co-operation with the French.

This would have been expected to lead to a strengthening of the bonds with Rome, but in fact the contrary was the case, because the church's authority was being steadily undermined by the spread of reformism under the impetus of the preaching of George Wishart. Formerly an expatriate Scot living in England, he returned to Scotland in 1543 and thereafter embarked on an evangelising mission, in which he was ably assisted by John Knox. However, the authorities regarded his preaching as dangerously seditious, and three years later he was arrested and taken to St Andrews. There he underwent a charade of a trial as a preliminary to being convicted of heresy and sentenced to burning at the stake – a spectacle witnessed by Cardinal Beaton himself.

Six weeks later the cardinal was assassinated there when a group of Fifeshire lairds broke into his castle, and having stabbed him to death they slung his corpse over the battlements in a public demonstration of English power. While Henry almost certainly connived at this, the chief instigator was the Protestant third earl of Cassilis, who had already offered to carry out a contract on the cardinal two years previously.[2] He and his fellow conspirators proceeded to occupy the castle, and in April 1547 they were joined by Knox who served as chaplain to the garrison. Three months later, the castle was captured by a French expeditionary force, and, in contravention of the terms of surrender, they took Knox prisoner, consigning him and his fellow preachers to slavery in their galleys. Meanwhile, Beaton's death left the primacy vacant, and this was eventually filled by John Hamilton, while James Hamilton, another of Arran's illegitimate half-brothers, was appointed to Glasgow in succession to Archbishop Dunbar who had recently died.

Henry VIII died in January 1547 and Hertford, now duke of Somerset, was appointed Protector of the realm for the new king Edward VI. He was determined to force the marriage between Edward and Mary on the Scots, so in a repetition of the rough wooing he launched another invasion of Scotland. Crossing the Border with a force of 16,000 men equipped with artillery and heavy cavalry, he finally encountered the Scots army under Arran at Pinkie near Musselburgh. When battle was joined the latter found itself caught between the river Esk and the sea, and their casualties were such that, according to one eye-witness, 'the dead bodies lay as thick as a man may notte cattle grazing in a full plenished pasture'.[3] The victims included six Galloway lairds[4] who were among those ordered to raise levies to take part in the campaign.

Meanwhile Lennox and lord Wharton (as he had now become) opened up a second front by invading the south-west with a force of 2,000 men, including a detachment of Scots soldiers in the English service. Their advance was virtually unopposed, since the Maxwells and their dependants, in common with other local lairds who were equally fearful for the safety of their hostages in England, quickly capitulated. Accordingly, the invaders took possession of the principal strongholds of Caerlaverock and Lochmaben. The Kirkcudbrightshire people, on the other hand, proved less tractable, and when Lennox issued orders for 'the gentlemen of the west part of Scotland' to muster at Dumfries[5] only 300 out of the expected 2,000 did so, most of them being simply freebooters.[6] This caused him to make an example of Sir James Douglas by attacking his stronghold of Drumlanrig, in the course of which he relieved 'the poor tenants of his lands' of five thousand oxen, cows and sheep with other goods to the value of £5,000.[7] The lesson struck home, and two days later an assortment of Galloway lairds, including the prior of Whithorn, as well as other compliant magnates from Annandale and Nithsdale, assembled in Dumfries.[8]

A notable absentee was lord Maxwell's younger brother, Sir John Maxwell. Still a bachelor at the age of thirty-five, he was bought off by Arran with the offer of marriage to Agnes Herries, the eldest of the three co-heiresses of the third lord Herries. However there was a price to pay, as fourteen of his hostages were hanged at Carlisle, but presumably he bore their fate with equanimity for the sake of such a valuable prize.[9] In consequence, Maxwell acquired his wife's share of the extensive Herries patrimony, and when he eventually bought out her sisters' shares he became the most influential magnate in Kirkcudbrightshire. Although he became closely involved with the reformers he eventually made his peace with Queen Mary in 1565, being rewarded with the revival of the Herries barony in his favour, so it is as the fourth lord Herries that he is best known in the annals of the south-west.

Lord Wharton ordered his lieutenant, Sir Thomas Carleton, to advance across the Nith into Galloway, where his immediate objective was the capture of Kirkcudbright to serve as a port of entry for supplies coming by sea from England, and also as a base from which to cut off communications between Scotland and France. However, his troops failed to take the town because the burghers, assisted by Thomas McLellan of Bombie and a contingent of local levies, beat them off. So in their frustration they turned to reiving instead, rounding up some 2,000 sheep as well as a large number of cattle and horses. However when they were intercepted by a force of

'Galloway folk from beyond the Water of Dee'[10] they abandoned the sheep and drove the cattle and horses off to Dumfries.[11] Nevertheless, their defeat encouraged many of the defecting Dumfriesshire lairds to revoke their pledges of loyalty, so Wharton's control of the south-west rapidly collapsed and he was compelled to fall back on Carlisle.

The duke of Somerset had been unable to follow up his success at Pinkie because rumours of a French invasion forced him to return to England. However, this did not spell the abandonment of his plans to force the projected marriage between Edward and Mary on the Scots, and in the following year he issued a proclamation setting out the terms of the proposed union – an action which so infuriated them that it stiffened their resistance and drove them still further into the arms of the French. This encouraged the latter to send more gold to Scotland to help their war effort, and to bribe the leading nobles to support the auld alliance. Among them was Cassilis, who appears to have had few scruples about swallowing his Protestant principles for the sake of French gold, while the gift of 2,000 francs was enough to induce lord Maxwell to abandon his allegiance to the English. As the unusually severe winter of 1548 prevented supplies and reinforcements from reaching the English army in Scotland, Wharton was left virtually stranded, so when he suffered a minor reverse in February 1549 he abandoned his campaign and returned to England.

This opened the way for Arran to conclude a treaty with Henry II of France, in terms of which he undertook to deliver up a number of castles to the French, and this was sealed with the promise of a marriage between Mary and Henry's eldest son, the dauphin. As a pay-off for his part in the negotiations, Arran was given the valuable French duchy of Châtelherault to help restore his sagging prestige at home. In late July, the six-year-old queen was smuggled away by ship to France where she would remain for the next thirteen years. French influence in Scotland was now paramount, but its identification with Catholicism and the indiscipline of its occupying troops rendered it increasingly unpopular, and this was largely responsible for the comparative ease with which the Reformation would be established in Scotland.

PRELUDE TO THE REFORMATION

Reformism was rapidly gaining ground, particularly among the ranks of the gentry and minor lairds, and this seems to have been particularly apparent in Ayrshire and the south-west. Foremost among the reformist lairds in Galloway was Sir Alexander Stewart of Garlies, who was among the prisoners taken at Solway Moss and subsequently released as an assured Scot. As his son was married to one of the co-heiresses of the third lord Herries, the family tie with Sir John Maxwell, who was already closely associated with the reformers, undoubtedly strengthened his links with them. The Gordons, too, were united in their support for them, Sir John of Lochinvar being a signatory of the First Book of Discipline, while his cousin, William Gordon of Craichlaw, was another,[12] and their kinsman, Alexander Gordon of Airds, was well known for his adherence to the new religion.[13]

A colourful character by all accounts, it was a tribute to Gordon of Airds' immense size and strength that he was popularly known as 'Sannie rough'. In his youth he had visited England, and during his time there he came under the influence of Wycliffe's followers. So, when he returned to Scotland he brought with him a copy of Wycliffe's Bible, widely proclaiming the fact despite the official ban on it and the risk of incurring severe penalties for possessing it. Tradition has it that when an act of parliament was passed stipulating that every beast of burden made to work on Church festivals was liable to forfeiture, Gordon deliberately flouted it. Yoking his ten sons to a plough and guiding it himself he tilled a rig of land, while challenging the clerical bystanders to do their worst. This, along with other similarly provocative acts, led to the confiscation of his estate of Airds, though it was later restored to him. By this time advancing years and an expanding family had earned him the more respectful soubriquet of 'the patriarch', and it was there that he died in 1580 having reputedly achieved the great age of a hundred and one.[14]

The reformers also benefited from a number of political changes which occurred during the 1550s. In 1554 the queen was declared of age, and in exercise of her new-found authority she appointed her mother, Mary of Guise, as regent in place of Châtelherault, who went into temporary eclipse. Mary's approach to the reformers was conciliatory, and although some popular plays were banned for being politically unacceptable she carefully avoided adding to the number of Protestant martyrs, even allowing Knox to return to Scotland – to marry – in 1555. In the following year, when he was arraigned by the Catholic hierarchy on charges of heresy she quashed the trial, though he left shortly afterwards for Geneva. There he issued a series of propaganda pamphlets, including the famous *First Blast of the Trumpet against the Monstrous Regiment of Women*, which argued that women in authority represented a detestable offence against religion and natural law.

Meanwhile reformism continued to gain ground, and a number of influential nobles, perceiving it to be in their interests, were pursuaded to join them. In 1557, the leading Protestant lords, including Lord James Stewart, an illegitimate son of James V and future earl of Moray, the earl of Glencairn, and the future regent Morton, entered into a band. Calling themselves 'the lords and barons professing Christ Jesus' and known as the lords of the congregation, they dedicated themselves to the cause of establishing the Protestant religion in Scotland. In April 1558, Mary of

Guise achieved her abiding ambition when her daughter, the fifteen-year-old queen, was married to the dauphin Francis, but in spite of all her efforts to win support for the match it was highly unpopular and consequently it gave a valuable fillip to the reformers. So too did the death in the following December of the Catholic Mary I, and the accession of the Protestant Elizabeth to the English throne.

The growing strength of reformism in Scotland so alarmed Henry II of France that he decided to send additional troops to Scotland, but his plans were thwarted by his unexpected death in July 1559 from injuries he received in a jousting match. The dauphin now succeeded as Francis II, with Mary becoming his queen consort, and this heralded the rise of Mary of Guise's brothers to power in France. They poured further troops into Scotland, and at the same time put pressure on their sister to take a firmer line with the reformers, or as Knox put it 'sche began to spew furth and disclose the latent venom of her double heart'.[15] Meantime, she cajoled the Church into making a final attempt to put its house in order, and at her urging Archbishop Hamilton convened another Church council in 1559 to consider further reforms. But it was too late and events moved relentlessly on.

Knox had returned to Scotland in May of that year, and so electrifying was his preaching that it was said of him that he was 'able in one hour to put more life into us than five hundred trumpeters continually blustering in our ears'. In a series of sermons he issued a torrent of invective against the practices of the Church, thundering in particular against the 'diabolical, rotten and stinking' ritual of the mass which he castigated as 'more odious in God's sight than murder'. So the scene was set for a confrontation. When he reached Perth in the course of his evangelising mission, he delivered a sermon 'vehement against idolatry' in the presence of a 'multitude' of burgesses and lairds.[16] After he left the church a priest began to say mass, and when a boy tried to interrupt him he was given a well-deserved cuff. Retaliating, the youth threw a stone at the priest but it missed him, shattering an image instead, and this provoked an instant reaction from the congregation, who proceeded to smash every sacred ornament in the church. The disorder spread to the people outside, and soon a rabble – or the 'rascall Multitude' as Knox called them[17] – embarked on an orgy of destruction of other religious houses in the town.

When news of the outrage reached Mary of Guise she summoned a force to Stirling, but on hearing that the earl of Glencairn had come to the aid of the reformers with reinforcements from the west she was forced to temporise. Lord James Stewart and the earl of Argyll were ordered to parley with them, and an armistice was declared in return for the promise of a general amnesty, liberty of worship, and an undertaking by Mary not to garrison Perth with French mercenaries. But when she effectively breached this by using Scottish troops in French pay instead, Stewart and Argyll defected to the reformers. This spurred them into further acts of wanton destruction, and having sacked the religious house at nearby Scone they went on to vandalise those at St Andrews, Stirling and Linlithgow, before finally reaching Edinburgh. By this time they were short of money and unable to pay their troops, and many of them 'maid Mutiny becaus they lacked Part of their Wages'.[18] Therefore they were forced to agree to a truce, in terms of which they undertook to give up Edinburgh provided the indwellers were allowed freedom of worship.

This was purely a temporary concession on Mary's part, since there was no chance of a permanent accommodation with the reformers so long as she remained at the helm; but her days were numbered, as she was already dying of dropsy. In April 1560 an English army invaded Scotland, and in the following month it laid siege to Leith, while an English fleet blockaded it from the sea. As the French were unable to send a relief force it surrendered on 11 June, the very day that Mary of Guise died. This opened the way for a truce, and French and English commissioners were appointed to negotiate a peace which was concluded by the treaty of Edinburgh in July 1560. Its terms included a general amnesty for the reformers, the removal of all French troops from Scotland, and an abandonment by Mary of her claim to the English throne. It also gave the lords of the congregation, now calling themselves the lords deputy, the right to summon a parliament.

Consequently the Reformation parliament, as it was known, was convened. This proceeded to adopt without amendment the Protestant Confession of Faith, while denouncing the old Church as 'the Roman harlot' and its clergy 'a rabble of thieves and murderers, traitors, rebels and adulterers'.[19] It also abolished the jurisdiction of the pope, as well as the authority of bishops and priests to act in his name. No one was allowed to administer the sacraments except those admitted by 'the congregation', while the saying or hearing of mass was made a criminal offence. These measures provoked little opposition, since the bishops remained cravenly silent throughout the proceedings. A committee consisting of Protestant nobles and lairds was now instructed to supervise the drawing up of a Book of Discipline, which was to serve as the blueprint for the reformed Church in Scotland. Mary, however, never gave her assent to the treaty of Edinburgh, and this meant the Reformation parliament was illegal, and consequently all the legislation flowing from it was invalid. Disregarding such technical niceties, the reformers embarked on the challenging task of establishing their religion throughout the country, though political and financial constraints were to impose a moderation on them which was unique in Protestant Europe.

THE BOOK OF DISCIPLINE

In December 1560, Queen Mary's weakly and ill-favoured husband Francis died from the agonising effects of a purulent inflammation of the ear. This heralded the fall of her Guise uncles and the assumption of power by her formidable mother-in-law, Catherine de Medici, who lost no time in edging her aside. Consequently, there was every prospect of her returning to Scotland, and as she was known to be a devout Catholic this filled the reformers with alarm. Moreover, they assumed that her consistent refusal to ratify the treaty of Edinburgh indicated a determination on her part to use its fundamental illegality as a lever for toppling the Reformation. So her half-brother, Lord James Stewart, was sent to visit her in an attempt to find out what her intentions were and to offer her counsel. In particular he is reported to warned her, 'abuiff all things, madame, for the luiff of God presse na [not] matters of religion'. This was sound advice and as events would show Mary had the good sense to heed it.

Nevertheless, the expectation of Mary's return gave added urgency to the work of completing the Book of Discipline, and in January 1561 it was ready to be submitted to parliament. Reflecting the influence of Knox, it called for the suppression of all existing religious institutions, apart from parish churches and schools, and the ejection of all clergy from their charges. Provision was made for the election, examination and admission of ministers and other officials, including the superintendents who would replace the bishops as the administrators of the dioceses. Presiding over the whole reformed Church was to be a governing body – 'the Council of the whole Kirk' or, as it came to be known, the general assembly.[20]

Pastoral discipline at parish level was to be exercised by kirk sessions consisting of the minister himself, assisted by elders and deacons. They had power to reprove, correct and punish misbehaviour such as drunkenness, brawling, swearing, and sexual misdemeanours which brought disgrace on the Church. Punishment was to be administered by private rebuke, public admonition or, as a last resort, excommunication for the more heinous or persistent crimes. The penalties following rebuke or admonition were as severe as those imposed by the old Church, though expiation and forgiveness were still available to the penitent. Elders were to be publicly nominated from among those 'of best knowledge in God's word, of cleanest life, faithful men, and of the most honest conversation that can be found in the Kirk'. If a minister failed in his duty or was merely 'light in his conversation' he would be admonished, and once a year his elders were required to report on his 'life, manners, study and diligence' to the superintendent.[21]

As the reformers were determined to raise the standard of education, the Book of Discipline set out detailed plans for compulsory education to instil 'wisdom, learning and virtue' into 'the youth of the land', while stipulating that each church should have its own school. Ministers were to be paid adequate stipends on the grounds that 'it is not expected that men will dedicate themselves to God to serve his Kirk so wholeheartedly as to work for no worldly commodity'. As the authors of the Book were under no illusions about the cost of these proposals they stipulated that teinds, supplemented by rents from Church lands, should be used for paying ministers' stipends and schoolmasters' salaries, while the excess was to go to the deserving poor. It also provided that the revenues from appropriated Church benefices should be applied towards the cost of maintaining the universities and making proper provision for the superintendents.[22]

The Book was now put before parliament, but this time the bishops were less supine. Although willing to accept most of its provisions they rejected the proposal to appropriate the teinds and revenues of the old Church, but as these were essential for implementing the reformers' proposals this effectively sabotaged their whole agenda. However, a compromise was agreed whereby bishops, abbots, priors and other beneficed people were allowed to retain their ecclesiastical revenues for life on condition that they paid over a third of them – known as the 'thirds of benefice' – to the reformed Church to finance ministers' stipends, and for the 'support of the Queen's Majesty above her own proper rents'. Knox however, disapproved of this, castigating it as an arrangement where 'two parts [are] freely given to the Devil, and the third must be divided betwixt God and the Devil',[23] but he was overruled. He was right to oppose it because it sounded better in theory than it would prove in practice, in that the 'thirds of benefice' were difficult to collect, and those responsible for doing so were frequently the victims of physical violence. Moreover, as the revenues had in many cases been remitted or burdened with pensions the total fell far short of expectation.

The result was that some ministers were forced to subsist on charity, and as this made it difficult for the reformed Church to attract suitably qualified men it was forced to accept beneficed clergy from the old Church as ministers. To induce them to make the changeover their obligation to give up their 'third of benefice' was waived, and this meant that in addition to receiving their stipend they also retained the revenues they had previously enjoyed. The reformers merely intended this as an interim arrangement until their finances were put on a sound footing, but it was to be a long time before this was achieved.

Other principles had to be relaxed or sacrificed altogether. For example, the reformers had intended to pull down the abbeys, which they regarded as objectionable symbols of the wealth and other abuses associated with the old Church. Although the general assembly of 1561 successfully petitioned parliament for the necessary authority, citing fears that 'the pestilent

generation of anti-Christ were again rearing their monuments of idolatry'
as their justification, local vested interests prevented them from doing so.
In Galloway, Sir John Maxwell was instrumental in saving Dundrennan,[24]
and also Sweetheart where he deliberately defied the orders of his fellow
lords of the congregation to pull down an abbey 'quhair he was maist part
brocht up in his youth'. In token of his gratitude Abbot Gilbert Broun gave
Maxwell a charter of the 'Yle of Lochkindelocht with all the fowlis that sall
abyde and big [build nests] thair'.[25]

Churches too were to be destroyed, but again the reformers were forced
to compromise, as they lacked the means to build new ones. So they econ-
omised by converting existing churches to their own uses by stripping them
of their 'monuments of idolatry'. This could be done quite cheaply, since
the Book of Discipline merely required that 'everie church must have
durris [doors], cloise wyndoes of glass, thak or sclait able to withold raine,
a bell to convocat the pepil together, a pulpite, a basyn for baptisme, and
tables for the ministratioune of the Lordis supper'.[26]

Reformism was slow to take hold in those regions where Catholicism was
strongly entrenched, and in certain enclaves in the south-west mass continued to be said in spite of it being a punishable offence. Those magnates
who continued to adhere to the old faith included Gilbert, fourth earl of
Cassilis (though his religious principles were to prove just as marketable as
his father's), his uncle Quintin Kennedy, abbot of Crossraguel, and
Malcolm Fleming, prior of Whithorn. They seem to have represented a
small minority, since the local baronage were almost solidly Protestant, Sir
Alexander Stewart of Garlies, Sir John Gordon of Lochinvar, and Sir John
Maxwell being among the signatories to the Book of Discipline, while
Maxwell in particular earned a complimentary remark from Knox in his
Historie of the Reformation. This occurred in connection with his description
of a visit to Dumfries in 1562 when he refers to a discussion he had on
'divers matters' with 'the Master of Maxwell, a man of great judgement and
experience'.[27] He might perhaps have been less fulsome had he known that
Maxwell would become one of Queen Mary's most loyal supporters.

BISHOP ALEXANDER GORDON

According to the minutes of the fifth general assembly, Knox's visit was
undertaken for the purpose of 'the planting of kirks in the Sheriffdoms of
Dumfries, Galloway and Nithisdaill and the rest of the Western daills'.[28]
This assembly also agreed to 'nominat for the superintendentship [of
Galloway] Master Alexander Gordon entitled Bishop of Galloway'. The son
of an illegitimate daughter of James IV, and brother of George, fourth earl
of Huntly, he clearly carried his religious principles lightly, while his
previous career had been devoted to pursuing his preferment in the

Church with a single-mindedness matched only by his failure to achieve it.
He was admittedly a victim of the system in that most of the bishoprics were
under the control of an exclusive coterie of magnates, while others were
filled by political appointees. Although a prelate of flexible principles he
was tarred with the Huntly Catholicism, and as this meant his wagon was
automatically hitched to Mary of Guise's star it followed that the regent
Arran consistently blocked every attempt on her part to advance his career.

An example occurred in 1544 when Mary persuaded the recently
appointed chancellor, Cardinal Beaton, to have Gordon appointed bishop
of Caithness, but when Arran regained power following the cardinal's
murder he engineered Gordon's ejection from the see. He encountered a
similar disappointment in 1550, when Mary of Guise managed to have him
presented to the archbishopric of Glasgow, and it was only after he had
departed for Rome to be consecrated that Arran succeeded in blocking his
appointment. In consolation the pope appointed him to the honorific
office of bishop of Athens, and as a further solace Gordon managed to
secure the commendatorship of the abbey of Inchaffray. However
promotion came at last in 1558 when the ineffectual Bishop Andrew Durie
of Galloway[29] died from shock after witnessing a Protestant riot in
Edinburgh (or so Knox alleges), and Mary of Guise succeeded in having
Gordon appointed as his successor – though this was mainly a sop to the
Huntly faction to gain their political support. But by this time Scotland was
on the verge of Reformation and as papal consecration was out of the
question he remained bishop-elect.

Galloway was small consolation for an ambitious prelate from whom the
plum appointment of Glasgow had been snatched away at the last minute,
and perceiving that the reformed Church offered better prospects of
promotion he had no hesitation in defecting to it. Consequently, he was
one of the signatories of the First Book of Discipline, while his conversion
meant he could now openly acknowledge the existence of his 'wife' of
seventeen years and their family of seven children. As the reformers were
short of suitably qualified clergy they were prepared to accept him, and
thus he became the first bishop in the old Church to be appointed a
superintendent in the new one. This created an anomalous situation,
which was reflected in the ambivalent title accorded him of 'Bishop of
Galloway and Commendator of Towngland, owirsear [overseer] there'.[30]

According to Knox, when Bishop Gordon's name came up in the course
of one of his meetings with Queen Mary it was evident she was under no
illusions about him. 'I hear that the Bishop of Caithness would be
superintendent [of Galloway]?', she enquired. 'He is one, madam, that is
put in election' came the guarded reply. 'If you knew him as well as I do',
rejoined the queen, 'you would never promote him to that office, nor yet
to any other within your kirk'. Prevaricating, Knox replied, 'I am assured

God will not suffer His Church to be so far deceived as that an unworthy man shall be elected'. 'Well', said Mary dismissing the matter, 'do as ye will, but that man is a dangerous man'. In a rare tribute to his royal adversary Knox went on to observe that, 'therein was the Queen not deceived: for he had corrupted most part of the Gentlemen not only to nominate him, but also to elect him'.[31] In other words, he is suggesting that Gordon had secured his appointment through bribery, though it should be remembered that by the time Knox was writing his *Historie* he had fallen out with Gordon, following the latter's appointment to the council.

The task of imposing the reformed religion involved replacing existing vicars and priests with Protestant ministers, or persuading them to change over to the new Church. In Galloway this was facilitated by sympathetic landowners who put pressure on their local incumbents to do so.[32] Nevertheless, Bishop Gordon's commission to 'admit ministers, exhorters and readers and to do such other things as were before accustomed in planting of kirks'[33] was a challenging one, and it was a measure of his success that as early as 1563 he had filled about nineteen out of the forty-five parishes beyond the Urr with Protestant clergy. All the more so since it was achieved in the face of the implacable opposition of Malcolm Fleming, the prior of Whithorn, who controlled nineteen of them. In addition, he established Protestant clergy in a further eleven parishes in the remainder of the diocese which lay to the east of the Urr.[34]

The aristocratic Gordon soon found himself at odds with the new men of the reformed Church who were generally speaking men of humbler birth. The differences between them were exacerbated by Gordon's consistent refusal to give up a share of the benefits he derived from his offices of bishop of Galloway, dean of the Chapel Royal, and commendator of Inchaffray, and the consequent withholding by the reformers of the stipend due to him as superintendent. He was also widely criticised for his continuing support for Queen Mary after her deposition, and eventually the general assembly of 1575 insisted he do penance in sackcloth, though as a concession he was allowed to compound with a single act of penance at Holyrood. This was duly carried out within a few months of his death which occurred later that year.[35]

Notwithstanding the substantial emoluments he earned from his ecclesiastical appointments, Gordon died a comparatively poor man, but this may have been because of the handsome provisions he made for his family. Although he resigned the commmendatorship of Inchaffray under pressure from his reformist colleagues, he nevertheless secured substantial pensions from it for the benefit of his sons, John and Laurence. In 1568 he handed over the temporalities of his Galloway bishopric to his other son, George, while his daughter Barbara was given an endowment on her marriage to Anthony Stewart, a younger son of Sir Alexander of Garlies, the reformer, and their descendants are still represented among the Galloway landowners today.

NOTES

1. Those from the south-west included lord Maxwell, his brother Sir John Maxwell, Alexander Stewart of Garlies, James Gordon of Lochinvar, and James McLellan, the tutor of Bombie (Agnew, *Hereditary Sheriffs* i, 352).
2. *Scots Peerage* II, 468.
3. Agnew i, 367.
4. Specifically, they were James Gordon of Lochinvar, Agnew of Lochnaw, McDowell of Freuch and his kinsman of Garthland, Vaus of Barnbarroch, and Thomas McLellan of Bombie (Agnew i, 367: McKerlie i, 105, 364, v, 56).
5. Smith, 'Alexander Stewart, younger, of Garlies', 103.
6. *Ibid.*
7. Pitcairn's *Criminal Trials* i, 348.
8. Smith, 'Alexander Stewart', 104–8.
9. *Ibid.*, 102.
10. Maxwell, *History of Dumfries and Galloway*, 177.
11. Agnew i, 370.
12. This can be assumed from the fact that his mother was a Chalmers of Gadgirth, an Ayrshire family who were among the Lollards of Kyle.
13. Ancestor of the Gordons of Earlston.
14. His career is described in Agnew i, 345–7 and McKerlie iv, 74.
15. Knox, *Historie* (Walker), 37.
16. *Ibid.*, 41.
17. *Ibid.*, 42.
18. *Ibid.*, 51.
19. *APS* ii, 525–34.
20. *Scot. Hist. Docs.*, 126–34.
21. *Ibid.*
22. *Ibid.*
23. Shirley, 'Greyfriars', 318 (quoting *Knox Hist.* ii, 310–1).
24. Fraser, *Carlaverock* i, 568.
25. TSA xiv, 282. This cites Lesley's *Historie* which was written in 1578 and refers to Dundrennan as being among those religious houses that 'standis zit [yet] haill'.
26. *Scot. Hist. Docs.*, 127.
27. Knox, *Historie* (Thomasson and Pullen) lib. I, 343.
28. *Ibid.*, 342.
29. He was a nephew of Archbishop James Beaton and formerly abbot of Melrose.
30. This account of Bishop Gordon's career is based on Donaldson, 'Alexander Gordon, Bishop of Galloway', 111 et seq.
31. Knox *Hist.* lib. I, 353.
32. Donaldson, 'The Galloway clergy at the Reformation', 40.
33. Donaldson, 'Alexander Gordon', 119.
34. Donaldson, 'The Galloway clergy', 45.
35. Donaldson, 'Alexander Gordon', 127–8.

20

EPISCOPACY VERSUS PRESBYTERY

Queen Mary's personal rule

Queen Mary returned to Scotland in August 1561. She was well informed about the situation there, had been advised to accept the Reformation as a *fait accompli* and not to make any attempt to dismantle it. Therefore, she adopted a conciliatory policy towards the reformers by choosing her half-brother, Lord James Stewart, and Maitland of Lethington, as her principal counsellors. Both represented the moderate wing of the movement, and on their advice she allowed her subjects freedom of worship, insisting only that she be permitted to hear mass in her private chapel. Moreover, they proved capable men, and because Mary delegated much of her governmental responsibilities to them, the first few years of her personal rule witnessed a degree of peace and stability which exceeded all expectation.

A major threat to her authority was the mighty earl of Huntly, who wielded almost sovereign powers in the north, and since 1549 had been allowed to hold the large and profitable earldom of Moray under the crown. As members of his family had already shown a propensity to rebel, Mary attempted to curtail his influence by secretly giving the earldom to Lord James. In the following month she went further by investing him with the earldom of Mar, in which Huntly also had an interest. Later that year, in the course of a royal progress in the north-east, she effectively defied Huntly by publicly proclaiming James as earl of Moray. Huntly rose to the challenge by coming out in open rebellion, but it soon became apparent that he had underrated the strength of the reformist influence in the north-east as he had difficulty in mustering support. The result was that when he finally encountered a royalist force at Corrichie his troops were routed. Huntly himself died of apoplexy, but his corpse was taken to Edinburgh, where it remained unburied for over a year until an act of attainder was passed authorising the forfeiture of his estates.

Mary now felt sufficiently confident of her position to leave the government in the hands of Moray and Maitland of Lethington, while she went on a royal progress through the south-west for the purpose of being seen by her subjects and indulging her passion for hunting. Details of her itinerary can be gleaned from the record of expenses maintained by her French equerry throughout the tour. This tells us that she reached Ayr at the beginning of August 1563 and was entertained to dinner by the fourth earl of Cassilis at his stronghold of Dunure. From there she travelled down to Glenluce, where she stayed briefly before continuing her journey to Whithorn. Her visit to that centre was equally short, since she spent only one night at the priory before progressing through the Machars to Clary, where she was the guest of Alexander Stewart, younger of Garlies.

Resuming her journey she travelled up the Cree, fording it at Minnigaff, from where she followed the pilgrims' way through some of the wildest country in Galloway as far as Kenmure at the northern end of Loch Ken, where her host was Sir John Gordon of Lochinvar. From there she travelled down the Dee to Kirkcudbright, staying the night at the nearby priory of Traill as the guest of its commendator, Robert Richardson. Next day she set out for Terregles, where she was the guest of Sir John Maxwell, and so to the Douglas stronghold of Drumlanrig where she arrived on 21 August.[1] Clearly she covered a great deal of country in the course of these three weeks, but being young and energetic it must have been an extremely exhilarating experience for her.

Among the problems confronting her on her return to Edinburgh was the question of finding a suitable husband, since it was imperative that she should marry and produce an heir. This had been a live issue ever since she became a widow, but as Scotland was a poor country she counted for little on the international marriage market compared with her royal counterpart, Queen Elizabeth, who was constantly beset by suitors. She, for her part, took a particular interest in the question of Mary's marriage, because unless she herself married and produced an heir, which looked increasingly unlikely, there was every chance that a child of Mary's would ultimately succeed to the English throne.[2] Her own preference was the earl of Arran, whose father, Châtelherault, was the heir presumptive to the throne, but he held no attraction for Mary, and in any case he was rapidly going insane. Other candidates from as far afield as Spain and Sweden were proposed, but they were all controversial and none of them met with Elizabeth's approval, while the choice of her own favourite, Robert Dudley, earl of Leicester, was unacceptable to Mary. Moreover, she rebelled against the idea of marrying for political reasons; these had dictated the choice of a sickly unattractive boy as her first husband and she was determined this time to marry according to her own wishes.

Her choice finally fell on her cousin, Henry Stewart, Lord Darnley – the 'lustiest and best proportionit lang man that sche had seen', as she described him. It was a love-match on her side at least, but politically it proved a disaster. Darnley's nearness to the English throne, derived through his mother, the countess of Lennox, rekindled Elizabeth's apprehensions about Mary's claim to it which had never been formally renounced, and consequently she broke off diplomatic relations with her. As friendship with England had been the main plank of Moray's foreign policy, and as he was adamantly opposed to Darnley in any case, he considered his position no longer tenable and withdrew from the council. Moreover, he now turned against Mary, and this led to a breakdown of the co-operation which had hitherto existed between her and the moderate reformers.

It was a disastrous choice in other ways, because Darnley proved a weak, vain and callow youth whose vaulting ambitions far exceeded his very limited capabilities. Mary's passion for him was soon spent, and perceiving him in his true colours she not only denied him the crown matrimonial, on which he had set his heart, but began to exclude him from her counsels altogether. Instead, she chose as her confidants members of her household, and in particular her Italian secretary, David Rizzio. Resenting this, Darnley was readily inveigled with promises of the crown into making common cause with Moray and the other defecting lords in a bid to overthrow Mary, though it was his complicity in Rizzio's murder which led to a final and irreparable breach between the royal pair.

John Knox, who did not shrink from countenancing murder, compounded Mary's anger and distress by warmly applauding the assassination of 'that poltroon and vile knave Davie', which he described as 'a just act most worthy of all praise'.[3] His outspokeness prompted suspicions that he himself was implicated in it, and to avoid the risk of arrest he was prevailed on to escape to the west country, where he 'buried himself in the friendly recesses of Kyle'.[4] His wanderings are believed to have taken him to Galloway, as there is an old tradition that he found refuge for a time at the McCulloch stronghold of Barholm, near Creetown.[5] However, his self-imposed exile was short-lived, as he was back in Edinburgh again in 1567.

DISINTEGRATION

Shortly afterwards Darnley was assassinated. He had fallen victim to a syphilitic infection contracted from his regular frequenting of brothels, and the house where he was recuperating mysteriously blew up. As his apparently unmarked body was found some distance from the scene of the blast it was widely believed that he had been smothered while trying to escape. Many suspected Mary as an accessory to his murder, and when in an act of incredible folly she married almost immediately afterwards the ruffianly earl of Bothwell, who was known to have been one of the instigators, she sealed her political doom. A powerful faction of the nobility considered that by entering into this *mésalliance* she had forfeited her right to rule and were prepared to oppose her, and forming themselves into a confederate band they raised an army and marched on Edinburgh.

Mary and Bothwell escaped to his castle at Dunbar where they scraped together a token force, but when it encountered the confederate lords at Carberry, near Musselburgh, on 15 June 1567, it was put to flight. Abandoning Mary, Bothwell fled to Denmark where he had the ill-luck to fall into the vengeful hands of the family of a discarded mistress. They quickly consigned him to prison where he survived for ten years in such appalling conditions that he finally went mad. Mary, on the other hand, surrendered to the confederate lords, who took her prisoner and escorted her to Edinburgh, where she had to endure the humiliating insults of the mob before being taken away to captivity in the Douglas stronghold of Lochleven. The following month she was forced to abdicate in favour of her infant son, James VI, and, in fear of her life, she was blackmailed into proclaiming her 'dearest brother' Moray as regent.

Ten months later, she escaped from Lochleven and headed for the friendly Hamilton territory in the west. Her adherents raised an army, and Sir John Maxwell (now lord Herries) contributed levies from the south, including a contingent of Gallovidian foot soldiers who had been recruited by a number of local lairds.[6] The following month, Mary's supporters encountered the regent Moray's army at Langside where, according to Agnew, the Gallovidian levies hurled themselves into the fray with such lack of discipline that they were heavily defeated. He goes on to assert that, realising the day was lost, they turned tail, and appropriating the best horses they could find, galloped from the field with both the enemy and the owners of the stolen horses in full pursuit.[7]

Mary also fled. On Herries's advice she headed for the south-west, her journey taking her across the barren wilderness of the upper Glenkens and down the Dee valley towards Tongland, and tradition has it that she paused briefly to rest at nearby Queenshill. Cutting across country past Corra, near Kirkgunzeon, where she is believed to have spent the night, she finally reached the Herries stronghold of Terregles, and during her stay there she made the fateful decision to flee to England in the forlorn hope that Queen Elizabeth would help her regain the throne. Joined now by Herries's nephew, John, eighth lord Maxwell, the small group headed for Dundrennan, where Herries's son, Edward Maxwell, was commendator, and there she spent her last night on Scottish soil. The following day, accompanied by Herries and Maxwell, she set sail from nearby Abbey Burnfoot[8] for England, from where she would never return.

A ROYAL MINORITY

The regent Moray has been described as one of the best kings Scotland never had. He possessed all the ability of his father and his Stewart forbears, and would have been king had James V been allowed to marry his mother, Mary Erskine, as he had wanted to do, but she was already betrothed to Douglas of Lochleven, so bastardy was Moray's lot, and he resented it. While the regency may have been some consolation, it was a flawed prize, because the régime he represented was widely regarded as illegal, and therefore it commanded only limited support. Most of it came from the Church and members of the protestant nobility, but as many of the latter were notoriously unreliable their support was of questionable value.

Mary still had many adherents, particularly in the south-west, where Sir John Gordon of Lochinvar and others of his kin were among her staunchest supporters. Although a signatory of the Book of Discipline, Gordon subsequently went over to Mary's side and was instrumental in forming a 'band' of adherents among his fellow lairds. Moray must have seen them as a potential threat, because one of his first acts as regent was to launch a punitive raid into Galloway. According to a contemporary account, his troops penetrated 'ane valley callit barbarusle the holm of Dawhernyn [Dalquhairn]'[9] and destroyed the Gordon-owned keeps of Airds[10] (where the octogenarian 'patriarch' was still living) and Shirmers.[11] However, by the time they reached Lochinvar's stronghold of Kenmure he had escaped, so all they could do was burn it as an act of retribution. Other supporters[12] were ordered to appear before the regent to answer for their conduct, but by the time the summonses were issued Mary's chances of regaining the throne had receded, so they followed the line of least resistance and submitted.[13] Herries himself was imprisoned, and although his stronghold of Terregles was earmarked for destruction it was spared at the intercession of his uncle, Sir James Douglas of Drumlanrig, who was a close associate of Moray's.[14]

As a staunch Protestant, Moray was concerned for the welfare of the Church, so the first parliament of his regency formally ratified the treaty of Edinburgh, thus legalising the Reformation. It also attempted to solve the problem of ministerial stipends because, to quote from the Act, the clergy had been reduced 'to such great poverty that unless speedily relieved they would be obliged to abandon their ministry'. It therefore enacted that these were henceforth to be a first charge on the 'thirds of benefices', and all existing remissions and pensions to third parties were statutorily revoked.[15] This was intended as a temporary measure until the Church came into possession of its teinds, but Moray was denied the chance to pursue the matter as he was assassinated by a Hamilton adherent at Linlithgow in January 1570.

With Moray's removal from the scene there was a strong possibility of civil war breaking out between Mary's supporters – known as the Marians – and the king's party; so Queen Elizabeth intervened by dispatching an army of 5,000 men under the earl of Sussex to invade Scotland in support of the latter. At the same time, Lord Scrope, the warden of the English marches, descended on Dumfriesshire and devastated the lands of known Marian supporters before reaching Dumfries, which he is reported to have reduced to 'a blackness of ashes'.[16] Although he stopped short at the Nith, an invasion of Galloway was clearly on the cards, as spies had already been sent into the region. Specifically, they were required to report on castles of strategic importance, their accessibility, how many men it would take to capture them, and the numbers needed for garrison purposes. Among those surveyed were Cruggleton and Cardiness castles, and the report on the latter – a meticulous and comprehensive document – still survives,[17] while another was made on the port of Kirkcudbright.[18]

Meanwhile, the earl of Lennox appeared with a force at Ayr, where he issued a summons to the Wigtownshire landowners to attend in person and guarantee their support for his grandson the king, those failing to do so being threatened with having their lands destroyed and their castles burnt. As there is no evidence of his taking punitive action it would seem that they must have complied, and certainly the threat was enough to persuade the earl of Cassilis to abandon his support for Mary.[19]

Shortly afterwards Lennox was appointed regent at the dictation of the victorious Elizabeth. He already had a long and less-than-distinguished career at the forefront of Scottish politics, but he proved unable to bring an end to the civil war which had now broken out between the Marians and the king's party. In April 1571, his forces took the fortress of Dunbarton, where they captured Archbishop John Hamilton. He was taken to Stirling where he underwent a mock trial and, pronounced guilty of complicity in the murders of Darnley and Moray, he was hanged on the common gibbet dressed in the full panoply of his ecclesiastical vestments. Ironically, Lennox himself was killed there six months later in the course of an attempted coup on parliament – the scene being witnessed by his five-year-old grandson, the king.

He was succeeded as regent by the king's guardian, the earl of Mar. A more emollient character than his predecessor, his regency marked a determined attempt on the part of the Church and council to agree on the role of bishops in the reformed Church. The issue was brought to a head over the choice of a successor to Hamilton as archbishop of St Andrews, when Mar's unilateral appointment of the aged John Douglas had raised a storm of protest. The compromise agreed upon, which was enshrined in the Concordat of Leith, allowed bishops and archbishops to serve in the reformed Church, but their title was to have no ecclesiastical significance;

they were to be under the control of the general assembly, and all new appointments were to be drawn from ministers qualified to serve in that Church. This arrangement was enthusiastically endorsed by Knox who, an old man now, and partially paralysed as the result of a stroke, was no longer able to play an active role in the affairs of the Church. It was said that on the last day he could sit at table he called for a hogshead of wine to be broached for a visitor, telling him to finish it as he would not survive for long enough to drink it all himself.[20] Coincidentally, he and Mar both died on the same day – 24 November 1572, the latter under suspicious circumstances, when he was succeeded by James Douglas fourth earl of Morton.[21]

THE REGENT MORTON

Now in his mid-fifties, Morton was formerly one of the lords of the congregation, and later chancellor, though he was dismissed from office for his implication in Rizzio's murder and a suspected complicity in Darnley's as well. An arch-schemer with a habitually callous disregard for human life, he is described as 'a man of the most boorish calibre, the small greedy eyes in his florid face betraying the essential cruelty of his nature, [while his] pudgy hands grasped avariciously at all the rewards and benefits which were his for the taking'.[22] Nevertheless he proved a capable regent, and under his harsh rule law and order – and even a semblance of prosperity – were restored to the realm. He was also a strong upholder of the English alliance, and when, with the aid of artillery and engineers supplied to him by Elizabeth, he succeeded in capturing Edinburgh castle, the last Marian stronghold, his position was unassailable.

His regency witnessed the return from Geneva in 1574 of that stormy petrel, Andrew Melville, who was to become a highly controversial figure in the annals of the Church. More than anyone else he was responsible for the baleful influence which it was to have over the life of the people during the following centuries. Educated in the traditions of Calvin, it was his conviction that the Church and State were two separate kingdoms, of which the former was the dominant while the temporal authority of princes was subservient to it. He was implacably opposed to the hierarchical structure of the Church and what he perceived as the corrupting presence of bishops. Instead, he adhered dogmatically to the view that all ministers were of equal status and that the Church should be governed by committees of ministers, known as presbyteries, under the control of the general assembly.

There is no certainty that he was ever ordained, but he claimed the right to sit in the general assembly by virtue of holding a number of important teaching posts in the Church; and, being the forceful and influential man he was, he acquired an ascendancy over it which lasted for some twenty years. At his instigation the compromise over the question of bishops in the Church, enshrined in the Concordat of Leith, was overturned, but more importantly he was primarily responsible for the split within the Church between the episcopalians and the presbyterians. Whereas the former were intent on retaining the existing hierarchical structure, with its bishops and superintendents, Melville's presbyterian adherents were equally determined to replace them with their preferred form of government. Eventually, the issues between the two factions became so rancorous that they led to a civil war which was conducted by its protagonists with a ferocity only equalled by their bigotry, and was infinitely more sanguinary than the Reformation itself.

In 1578 the reformed Church issued a second Book of Discipline. Reflecting Melville's influence, this provided for a Church structure consisting of kirk sessions, presbyteries and synods, broadly similar to the Church of Scotland's present constitution, while calling for the abolition of bishops and superintendents. It also demanded the transfer of the patrimony of the old Church to the reformed Church and the vesting of landowners' rights of patronage in elders and congregations.[23] Unfortunately, most of the patrimony had already been disposed of and more was continuing to be alienated, so there was little the Church could do other than to fulminate against the practice. One example was a minute of the general assembly which stated that 'to tak ony of this patrimonie be unlawfull meinis and convert it to the particular and profane use of ony person we hald it ane detestable sacriledge befoir God'.

This found little favour with Morton, who had consistently manipulated the Church's patronage for the sake of rewarding his supporters and endowing his illegitimate sons. His policies had already alienated the Church, while his systematic trampling on vested interests provoked a powerful opposition movement which eventually secured his deposition in 1578. A resourceful man, however, he contrived by devious means to secure custody of the king, and thus regained power, though not the regency. Nevertheless, his fate was eventually sealed in 1582 when, through the machinations of his favourite, Esmé Stewart, James lost confidence in him. So, when the sixty-five-year-old former regent was arrested on a charge of complicity in Darnley's murder, James deliberately refrained from intervening on his behalf, nor when Morton was consigned to the scaffold did he make any attempt to have the sentence quashed. During his regency he had been responsible for introducing into Scotland a crude form of guillotine, known as the 'maiden', and ironically it was on this that he was dispatched to his doom.[24]

THE RISE OF PRESBYTERY

The Church's financial position was now much improved, and as this allowed stipends to be set at more realistic levels it meant that people from a higher social background, like the sons of minor lairds and burgesses, were attracted to the ministry. In fact, it was a measure of the clergy's increasing affluence that the assembly of 1575 specifically forbade ministers and their wives from decking themselves out in fine clothing, adorning themselves with jewellery, and wearing a silk hat. Instead it recommended that 'thair haill habit be of grave colour, as black, russet, sad gray, sad browne or sicklyke', though the wearing of black gowns for conducting worship did not become compulsory until 1609. These measures were symptomatic of the régime of cheerlessness and austerity which has traditionally been associated with the presbyterians, and would become the hallmark of the Church of Scotland for centuries to come.

On the same theme, the general assembly abolished certain long-established religious festivals such as the 'superstitious time of Yule' which were 'usit before in tyme of ignorance and Papistrie'.[25] As evidence of their grim censure of any attempt to celebrate these festivals, the records of the same year tell of a group of convivial Aberdonians being charged with 'playin, dansin and singin of fylthie carroles on Yuell Day at evin'.[26] In Dumfries some enterprising burghers attempted to evade the ban by thronging to the collegiate church at Lincluden to celebrate Christmas there instead,[27] while lord Maxwell was temporarily warded in Edinburgh castle for marking the occasion by celebrating mass there.[28]

Lamenting 'the universall corruptions of the hail estates of the bodie of this realm' and 'the daily increase of all kind of fearful sinnes and enormities',[29] the general assembly also regulated, and in some cases suppressed, other forms of innocent amusement. At the same time a strict code of morality was imposed and, supported by the civil authorities, the Church cracked down on a whole range of misdemeanours. Adultery was regarded as particularly serious, and offenders were forced to stand dressed in sackcloth, barefooted, with shaven heads, first at the kirk door and then on the public stool of repentance in front of the congregation every Sunday for six months. In cases of sodomy or incest (the latter probably being quite common) the punishment could last for several years, and involved whipping and fining as well, the offender being obliged to submit to these ordeals under threat of the dread sentence of excommunication.

Drunkenness too was regarded as a sin, though the records tell of a phenomenal amount of wine – usually claret – being drunk at communion. For example, the Edinburgh burgh records reveal that, at Knox's three communions there in 1561, the participants consumed no less than twenty-three gallons of wine, while on another occasion in 1578 the same quantity was drunk on a single sacrament Sunday alone![30] However, there was no apparent connection between the quantity of wine drunk and the incidence of riotous behaviour that sometimes occurred at these sacraments – or so it has been asserted. On one occasion at Stirling in 1597 the session took the congregation to task for the 'great misorder amongis the pepill of this congregatione at the last ministratione of the Lord's Supper, in rash and sudden cuming to the tabill, in spilling of the wyne, and in thrusting and shouting in thair passage out at the Kirk dur aftir the ministratione'.[31] The provision of communion cups was frequently a problem, since much of the Church plate had been melted down at the time of the Reformation, and it was the need to provide makeshift vessels that prompted Winzet's jibe that the reformers were forced to use 'basins and cups furth of any prophane taveroun'.[32]

THE NEGATIVE CONFESSION OF FAITH

Morton's downfall led to the emergence of Esmé Stewart, now earl of Lennox, as the king's principal adviser. Although a Catholic, his adherence to the Roman Church was tepid, so he had few scruples in professing the reformed faith when he found it expedient to do so. Nevertheless, this failed to convince the Presbyterians who suspected him of being a covert supporter of Mary and having treasonable dealings with Spain. Their distrust of him was heightened as the result of the Jesuit scare which occurred at this time, because it prompted fears of a plot involving a Spanish invasion to restore Mary to the throne and the re-establishment of popery in Scotland.

Both Lennox and the king did their utmost to allay their misgivings, even going to the length of putting their signatures to the comprehensively anti-papist Negative Confession of Faith as a demonstration of their adherence to the reformed faith. Furthermore, in 1581 they prevailed on parliament to give statutory force to an act of the general assembly of 1568 banning pilgrimages to religious shrines, as these were regarded as relics of papistry. Local sheriffs were ordered to 'search and seek out the persons passing in pilgrimages to any kirks, chapels, wells, crosses or sick [such] other monuments of idolatry . . . and to hold them in prison'. As this rendered pilgrimages to St Ninian's shrine a punishable offence, Whithorn's importance as a religious centre was extinguished. Therefore, shorn of its former prosperity, it was allowed to deteriorate into the impoverished rural backwater which it would remain for centuries to come.

These measures failed to convince the presbyterian-dominated Church, for it continued to regard the king and Lennox with suspicion. Particularly so the latter, since he had attempted to appropriate the revenues of the archbishopric of Glasgow by imposing an acquiescent accomplice to that see in preference to the Church's nominee. This led to a deplorable scene in which the rival candidates struggled for possession of the pulpit. Other members of the cloth were drawn into the fray and beards were pulled and teeth knocked out until the law intervened and the presbytery moderator was locked up in the tolbooth.[33] When Lennox eventually fell from power he was replaced as the king's favourite by another cousin, James Stewart, who was created earl of Arran.[34] However, his tenure was brief as he was replaced some two years later by the equally unprincipled master of Gray.

ROYAL AUTHORITY ESTABLISHED

By this time James was of an age to assume full ruling powers. His overriding ambition was to impose his authority on the Church, but it was to prove a long, hard struggle and would take him over twenty years to achieve. He had been particularly incensed at the way the general assembly had applauded the actions of the Ruthven raiders in kidnapping him. So, after he escaped from his captors he summoned Melville to stand trial for sedition, but knowing full well what this would entail the latter fled to England. Two months later, James passed a series of measures known as the Black Acts. Although their provisions were wide-ranging they were specifically directed against the Church, for they declared his authority over it, revoked all statutes passed by the general assembly without his consent, and banned it from doing so in the future. Finally they suppressed presbytery, for which James had conceived a lasting hatred,[35] these measures being supplemented by a further Act forbidding ministers from slandering him either from their pulpits or in the general assembly.[36]

In spite of their differences, James and the Church were at one in their opposition to popery and their determination to resist the ever-present threat of a Spanish invasion. In fact, there was now little support for Catholicism among the Scottish nobility and only a handful were actively in league with Spain. They included lord Maxwell,[37] but he was now in prison and deservedly so. In the previous year he had been allowed to go abroad on condition that he refrained from doing anything publicly or privately which was likely to be prejudicial to 'the new religion' (presbyterianism), and that he would obtain James's permission before returning to Scotland. His pledge was broken on all counts, as his immediate destination was Spain, where he gave an undertaking to Philip II that if his Armada were to land in south-west Scotland preparatory to launching an invasion of England he would give it his full support.[38]

Returning to Scotland, without the king's permission, he landed at Kirkcudbright and raised a local force in readiness to assist the Armada should it land on the Galloway coast. This treasonable act provoked James into making a lightning strike on Dumfries where Maxwell was known to be lurking, but as soon as he got wind of this he galloped off to Kirkcudbright. James followed, but by the time he arrived there Maxwell was on the high seas.[39] However, James remained at Kirkcudbright for a few days, and while there he presented the burgh with the famous 'siller gun' as a prize to be shot for, as a means of encouraging firearms practice.[40] Maxwell landed on the Ayrshire coast shortly afterwards, and when James heard of this he had him arrested and imprisoned in Edinburgh castle.[41] Nevertheless, he was released shortly afterwards and made his peace with the king by renouncing his Catholicism and subscribing to the Negative Confession of Faith.

Maxwell now became the king's principal law enforcer in the south-west, and when some years later the Johnstones raided the lands belonging to Crichton of Sanquhar he was ordered to drive them out and restore the king's peace. As there was already a long-standing feud between his family and the Johnstones, Maxwell seized the chance to raid the Johnstone lands, and for good measure, promised a reward for the head of Sir James Johnstone, the family chieftain. The latter responded by offering a reward for Maxwell's head or his hand, and the opportunity came when the rival forces encountered each other at Dryfe Sands in December 1598. The story has it that Maxwell was thrown from his horse and as he lay helpless a Johnstone, seizing the chance of a reward, chopped his hand off and took it away with him. Later, Maxwell was found hiding under a thorn bush by the wife of Johnstone of Kirkton who had come to tend the wounded, and without further ado she dashed his brains out with the castle keys she was carrying with her.[42]

A sequel occurred fifteen years later when Maxwell's son, the ninth lord, shot and killed Johnstone in the course of a parley. He escaped to the Continent, but when he returned in 1612 he was betrayed and handed over to the king, who made an example of him by ordering him to be executed.[43] His lands were forfeited, though most of them were subsequently restored to his brother, the tenth lord and future earl of Nithsdale, who was a favourite of Charles I.

In 1592 a rebellion broke out in the north under the earl of Huntly, and James appealed to the Church for help in stamping it out. Aid was forthcoming but the pay-off was reflected in an Act of Parliament passed later that year which partially repealed the Black Acts by allowing the establishment of a presbyterian system of Church government. However, as these Acts had already been modified and their effects eroded through time, this Act merely gave statutory recognition to a *fait accompli*, so its benefits to the Church were more apparent than real.[44] Nevertheless the presbyterians hailed it as a victory, dubbing it the 'Golden Act', and to some extent their triumphalism was justified since it marked the eclipse of episcopacy and the high point of presbytery during James's reign.

He was now faced with the daunting task of reasserting his authority, and the way he did so, and his success in achieving it, was a masterpiece of political astuteness. He did, however, have one important weapon in his armoury. This was a seemingly innocuous provision in the Golden Act which stipulated that while a general assembly had to be convened once a year, the date and place of its meetings were to be named by the king or his commissioner at the previous assembly. Consequently, James could ensure that they were held at centres where the moderates were in control, and that places like Edinburgh and St Andrews, where the extremist influence was strongest, were avoided. By paying the travelling expenses of reliable ministers he could to some extent 'pack' the assemblies and thus influence their proceedings.

The assembly of 1597 conceded him the right to introduce for debate any matter affecting relations between Church and State, while the next one appointed a commission of ministers to consult with James on a range of ecclesiastical issues. Melville tried to block it, but when he was overruled he contrived to have himself appointed to the commission. However, James succeeded in outmanoeuvring him, and in the following year he managed to have Melville ejected from the assembly. Although James's accession to the English throne in 1603 prevented him from attending any further assemblies in person, he was still able to influence them through his commissioner, and by 1606 he secured the right to prorogue it and appoint titular bishops to vacant sees.[45]

In that year Melville was summoned to Whitehall, where he became involved in a fracas with Archbishop Bancroft of Canterbury when, with characteristic temerity, he denounced the latter's vestments as 'Romish rags'. The ensuing quarrel resulted in Melville being imprisoned in the Tower, and thereafter he was banished to France where he died an old man wracked by gout in 1622. With his removal James's ultimate success was assured, as there was nothing the presbyterians could do to stop him. Episcopacy was finally restored in 1610 when three Scottish bishops – Spottiswoode, Lamb of Brechin and Gavin Hamilton of Galloway – were formally consecrated by four English bishops, and they in turn consecrated their fellow bishops in Scotland. Finally, in 1618, James's ascendancy over the general assembly was so well entrenched that he was able to prorogue it indefinitely. Twenty years would elapse before it met again, but by then the political situation had changed beyond all recognition.

NOTES

1. Her itinerary is described in Maxwell, 'Tour of Mary Queen of Scots', 84 et seq.
2. Henry VIII had stipulated in his Will that the English throne was not to pass to a foreigner, thus impliedly reserving it for the descendants of his younger sister Mary duchess of Suffolk, though he had no power to do so.
3. Stephen, *Church History* ii, 59.
4. *Ibid.*
5. NSA (Kirkcud, 328) confirms on the authority of John McCulloch, the owner of Barholm, that he was told by a former footman of the family that the latter recalled seeing Knox's signature in a small upper chamber in the tower.
6. They included the earl of Cassilis, the Gordons, Agnew of Lochnaw and McLellan of Bombie, as well as the commendators of Soulseat and Glenluce, and also Bishop Gordon.
7. Agnew i, 387–8. An unlikely story!
8. So asserts McKerlie v, 71, and this makes more sense than the traditional notion that she set sail from Port Mary.
9. *Scots Peerage* v, 110.
10. McKerlie iv, 75.
11. *Ibid.* iii, 83.
12. The terms of the summons, as set out in Agnew (i, 388), lists the principal supporters in Wigtownshire as Agnew of Lochnaw, Kennedy of Chappel, Vaus of Barnbarroch, Baillie of Dunragit, Gordon of Craichlaw, the commendator of Glenluce, and the McCullochs of Killasser and Ardwell.
13. Agnew i, 388–90.
14. Fraser, *Carlaverock* i, 529.
15. *APS* iii, 37.
16. McDowall, *History of Dumfries*, 271.
17. A copy can be seen at Cardiness castle.
18. Robison, 'The Greyfriars and the Moat Brae', 14.
19. Fraser, *Carlaverock* i, 564.
20. Stephen, *Church History* ii, 95. This reveals a pleasantly human side to Knox's character in sharp contrast to the popular perception of him as a grim religious fanatic. In fact, it was said that he generally enjoyed a game of bowls after conducting a Sunday service, strict sabbatarianism being a later development in the church.
21. He was a scion of the red Douglases, his father being Sir George Douglas of Pittendreich, a younger brother and close associate of the sixth earl of Angus.
22. Fraser, *Mary Queen of Scots*, 148–9.
23. *Scot. Hist. Docs*, 143–53.
24. As he had no legitimate sons the earldom, along with its possessions, including the superiorities of Borgue and Preston, devolved on lord Maxwell as the son of his wife's eldest sister (*APS* iii, 262). Maxwell was thereafter officially styled earl of Morton until deprived by an Act of Revocation of 1585. The title then reverted to the third earl's kinsman, Douglas of Lochleven, who represented a junior branch of the Douglases of Dalkeith.
25. Stephen, *Church History* ii, 105.
26. Cowan, *The Scottish Reformation*, 156.
27. Stephen, *Church History* ii, 105–6.

28. Agnew i, 419.
29. Stephen, *Church History* ii, 112.
30. Cowan, *The Scottish Reformation*, 147.
31. *Ibid.*
32. Winzet, *Certain Tractates* i, 84.
33. Stephen, *Church History* ii, 127.
34. This was in spite of there already being an earldom of Arran in existence whose holder, the third earl, had long since become insane.
35. *APS* iii, 292–303.
36. *APS* iii, 375.
37. Donaldson, *James V – James VII*, 185.
38. His exploits are described in McKerlie v, 167 and Agnew i, 420.
39. Fraser, *Carlaverock* i, 277.
40. McKerlie iv, 69.
41. Fraser, *Carlaverock* i, 278.
42. *Ibid.*
43. *Ibid*, 282–313.
44. Donaldson, *James V – James VII*, 199.
45. Disc *ibid.*, 200–207.

21

THE CHURCH PATRIMONY PRIVATISED

BACKGROUND

The taxation of the 1530s, and war damage in the 1540s, accelerated the process of feuing off Church lands, while the difficulty in collecting teinds, combined with the collapse in the price of wool, formerly a major source of income to the religious houses, gave it added impetus. So, too, in the 1550s did fears of an impending reformation and a possible confiscation of Church property. Although land disposals were less evident among the houses in Galloway during this period, once the Reformation was established the process gathered pace. Most of the lands passed into the hands of local magnates, and the lengths they went to in their efforts to secure them – almost certainly on discounted terms – constitutes one of the most deplorable episodes of the entire Middle Ages.

In most cases, they acted as bailie of the abbey, an appointment which reflected the general lawlessness of the times, as this compelled the monks to put themselves under the protection of a local noble. Bailie was the term used to give him official status, and his responsibilities embraced the safeguarding of the abbey's possessions and the management of its lands, which involved controlling its tenants and ensuring their rents were regularly and punctually paid. In return he was usually given a parcel of land or a pension, though much more important from the magnate's point of view was the fact that it gave him a measure of control over the institution, as well as the opportunity to impose his own nominee as the abbot or commendator. This in turn gave him the means to influence the disposal of its lands.

DUNDRENNAN

An outstanding example in south-west Scotland were the lords Maxwell who held the hereditary bailiaries of Sweetheart, Dundrennan, Holywood and Lincluden.[1] Following the premature death of his brother, the sixth

lord Maxwell, the office was exercised by Sir John Maxwell, the future lord
Herries, as tutor successively to his nephews, the seventh and eighth lords.
The extent of his control over Dundrennan in particular is apparent from
the fact that, on the death of Abbot Adam Blacadder in 1566, he secured
the commendatorship for his third son, Edward, and was thereafter
instrumental in disposing of the abbey lands to members of his family.

For example, Newlaw was acquired by his younger son James, apparently
as an outright gift, since the charter states that it was 'in return for
protection, money and other benefits received by Dundrennan from John
lord Herries'.[2] Judging from the names of the properties mentioned in the
charter, the grant included a swathe of fertile land extending eastwards
along the coast from Dundrennan itself as far as Auchencairn.[3] Meanwhile
Herries's second son, Robert, acquired the lands of Netherlaw to the west
of the abbey,[4] and as he also inherited Spottes and subsequently purchased
Orchardton from his kinsman, Edward Maxwell of Drumcoltran, the representative of the Cairns family, he and his descendants became prominent
landowners in Galloway.

When James Maxwell of Newlaw died in 1576, his father lord Herries
directed that 'the feus of Dundrennan wherein his brother James was put'
should go to his youngest son, John.[5] The latter was subsequently given the
provostship of Dumfries by his cousin, the eighth lord Maxwell, and as this
was deliberately intended to deny it to Maxwell's rival, Sir James Johnstone,
it led to a reopening of the feud between the two families. As this focused
on Provost John Maxwell he ended up a victim of Johnstone's allies, the
Irvines, in the course of a street fight in Dumfries in 1598.[6] The privy
council records contain a gruesome account of the incident. Apparently
the provost was struck to the ground, and in consequence of 'dyverse
crewall and deidlie woundis given to him with suordis, quhingeris
[whingers] and utheris forbiddin wappones', he lay 'bullerand in his blood
[with blood gushing out of him]'. And 'they [the Irvines] believing him to
be deid woosche thair handis in his bloode, feeding thair cruell hairtis with
the abominable spectacle [and] schortlie thaireftir he depairtit this lyfe'.

The provostship now passed to John's eldest brother, William, fifth lord
Herries,[7] while his lands at Dundrennan went to Commendator Edward's
second son, another John Maxwell.[8] These remained in the hands of his
descendants until the eighteenth century when they were mostly bought up
by Thomas Cairns, a London merchant who claimed kinship with the
Orchardton family.[9] Almost all the lands of Netherlaw passed into the
hands of the McLellans, and when the fourth lord Kirkcudbright sold them
to Sir David Dunbar at the end of the seventeenth century they became the
nucleus of the St Mary's Isle estate. Dundrennan still owned the lands of
Biskeby, near the Isle of Whithorn, where Abbot Adam had already feued
off the 10-merklands of Tornageich (Tonderghie) and Boyoch to Sir John

Maxwell in 1560.[10] Shortly afterwards, the latter resold them to John Stewart, a relative of Stewart of Garlies and ancestor of the Barclye family.[11]

When Commendator Edward died in 1598 he was succeeded by the king's favourite, Sir John Murray of Lochmaben, and in 1606 the abbey was dissolved. Its assets, which consisted of the abbey buildings, the superiorities of its former lands, and possibly some property in the parish of Kirkmabreck, automatically passed to the crown under the Annexation Act of 1587, and King James converted them into a temporal lordship which he gave to Murray, now earl of Annandale.

LINCLUDEN

Lord Herries also exercised the office of bailie of this institution as tutor to his nephews, though it was controlled by his uncle, Sir James Douglas of Drumlanrig, who had secured the appointment of his illegitimate son, Robert Douglas, as provost in the late 1540s. Douglas's tenure was a long one, as it lasted for over sixty years until his death in 1609, and during that time he presided over the dispersal of virtually all the collegiate lands. While the properties near Southwick, originally given to it by Margaret, duchess of Touraine, were sold off to the neighbouring landowner, James Lindsay of Fairgirth, it seems the remainder, which consisted of lands in the parishes of Crossmichael and Troqueer, went to members of his immediate family.

Sometime after the Reformation, Douglas feued off a block of land at the southern end of Crossmichael parish, and a few bits and pieces at Drumsleet on the south-western edge of Dumfries, to his legitimate half-brother, William Douglas, younger of Drumlanrig.[12] Most of the rest was disposed of to his nephew, Sir James Douglas of Pinzearie,[13] who bequeathed them to his son William. Unfortunately, this William proved a reprobate, and following his conviction of a number of serious offences he was sentenced to be taken to the Mercat Cross in Edinburgh. There his right hand was to be 'stricken from his body' before he was hanged 'upon ane gibet quhill [until] he be deid', and his lands were forfeited to the crown.

King James then re-granted them jointly to Sir John Murray of Lochmaben and Sir Robert Gordon of Lochinvar, both gentlemen of his bedchamber.[14] As this proved a wholly impractical arrangement, they agreed to split them, with Murray taking the lands near Dumfries, which he had erected into the barony of Drumsleet, and subsequently sold to Robert Maxwell, first earl of Nithsdale. Gordon, on the other hand, took those at Crossmichael and then bought back much of the land which had been sold off to William Douglas, younger of Drumlanrig. Finally, in 1621 he had the complete holding constituted a barony and this passed to his successors the viscounts Kenmure.[15]

SWEETHEART

The Maxwell influence is also apparent in the disposal of the lands belonging to Sweetheart, as it seems that lord Maxwell appropriated most of those in the parish of Kirkpatrick Durham.[16] The abbots Broun, on the other hand, appear to have been given a free hand in the disposal of the lands at New Abbey, so they were mostly distributed among members of their own family who were already tenants there. These abbots, John and Gilbert, were the respective sons of Thomas and Richard Broun who arrived in Galloway sometime in the early 1500s, and while the elder, Thomas, became a tenant of the abbey,[17] Richard married Elizabeth Lindsay the heiress of Carsluith, and Abbot Gilbert was their second son.

John Broun was appointed abbot sometime in the 1550s, and during his tenure he granted a number of leases of the abbey lands to his family, including his father, Thomas. After the Reformation he fortified their rights in these holdings against a possible confiscation of Church property by converting their leases into feus. When Abbot Gilbert succeeded him in 1565 he continued the process, to the extent that by the time he was forced from office in 1586 'the whole countryside stretching out from the abbey in every direction for a mile or more belonged to one member of the Broun family or another'.[18] Among the beneficiaries was Gilbert's brother, Thomas, whose holding included the 4-merk lands of Shambellie. This was later sold by his daughter to John Stewart of Auchinleck (whose wife was reputedly an illegitimate descendant of Abbot Gilbert[19]), and this, along with the other parcels of land he acquired from members of the Broun family, was the foundation of the Shambellie estate which now belongs to his descendant.

Abbot Gilbert was one of the leading opponents of reformism in the south-west, and by all accounts he sounds one of the most colourful. Even after he was forced from office for allegedly 'enticing his people to papistry', he stayed on in the district 'saying Masses, baptizing sundry bairns and preaching the Catholic religion'. Having avoided a number of attempts to arrest him he escaped to France, but before long he was back again in New Abbey continuing his work as 'a busy trafficker for Rome', and even as late as 1608 there was 'a daylie and frequent resort of people unto him with qhome he intertenys the exercise of his popische and fals religioun'.

When the king's guard attempted to arrest him, they were beaten off by 'a grite nowmer of rude and ignorant people of the New Abbay who armed with staves, muskets and hagbuts . . . resisted his apprehension'. The next time they were more successful, and on this occasion John Spottiswoode, the future archbishop,[20] was thanked for 'going to the toun of New Abbay, and thair breaking up the chamber door of Mr Gilbert Broun'. Having found 'a grite nomber of bookis, copes, imageis and such uther popische trasche', he proceeeded 'most worthelie and dewtiffulie' to burn them in the presence of 'a grite confluence of people in the hie street of the Burgh of Dumfries'.[21] Broun was then warded in Blackness castle, but on his release he left Scotland for good, dying in Paris in about 1612, at the reputed age of a hundred.[22]

KENNEDY RAPACITY (1): SOULSEAT

Unlike the Maxwells, who did at least obtain their lands by legitimate means even if their tactics were questionable, the grasping Kennedys had no such inhibitions; and their efforts to obtain the lands belonging to Soulseat are a case in point. Notwithstanding that they had already acquired some of the abbey lands, they had looked on with mounting anger as Commendator John Johnstone feued away others to his relatives. Finally, they decided to put a stop to it before the entire patrimony was placed beyond their reach. So Gilbert, fourth earl of Cassilis, induced his cousin, Ninian Adair of Kinhilt, to withhold payment of his teinds to the abbey, and when Commendator John quite properly took out Letters of Horning against Adair, Earl Gilbert retaliated on his behalf by refusing to pay feuduty for his share of the abbey lands. Undaunted, the commendator raised an action against him as well, and the account of what followed comes to us from his executors.

Cassilis had him kidnapped and spirited away to Adair's stronghold of Dunskey. There he was subjected to the kind of treatment that had recently been applied to the abbot of Crossraguel in a successful attempt to persuade him to sign a charter of his abbey lands to Cassilis. The only difference was that whereas the abbot of Crossraguel had been slowly roasted over a fire, maiming him for life, commendator John's ordeal was by water. This involved tying him by the ankles to the end of a rope which was suspended from a beam projecting from the castle battlements over the sea, where he was left dangling head downwards just above the waves. By paying out the rope he would be submerged, and by pulling on it he could be lifted out again. So one can readily imagine the scene where each time the abbot responded to a request to sign the charter with a spluttering curse he was simply lowered into the sea again. The outcome was inevitable. The commendator was not prepared to die a martyr's death for the sake of the abbey lands, so he finally consented to sign.[23]

However, no sooner had the luckless commendator been returned to the safety of the abbey than he moved heaven and earth to have the charter revoked on the grounds that his signature had been obtained under duress. The abbot of Crossraguel managed to have his charter reduced, and it seems Commendator John did so as well, because he was hounded remorselessly by the Kennedys for the rest of his days. However, this time they used the law as an instrument of vengeance. It so happened that, many years before, the commendator had stood cautioner for a debt due by the head of his family, but he had long since been formally discharged. However, the Kennedys managed to get hold of the deed of discharge which they destroyed and then bribed John Johnstone, the parson of Kirkmahoe, one of the creditors, to sue Commendator John for the debt. As he was unable to pay, his lands of Courance in Dumfriesshire were devastated, while he was bankrupted and flung into the Edinburgh tolbooth, where he languished until the debt was finally redeemed by his nephew.[24]

When he died an old and broken man in 1600, the Kennedys contrived to have one of their number, John Kennedy of Baltersan, appointed as commendator, and one of his first acts was to make a large payment out of the abbey revenues to John Johnstone, the parson of Kirkmahoe, 'in respect of a favour done'.[25] Although the Kennedys were thwarted in their attempts to secure the abbey lands by force, they did succeed in acquiring the remainder of the lands with the co-operation of Commendator John Kennedy and his successor William Adair. As they also managed through time to buy back most of the lands which had been feued off to the Johnstone relatives, they were ultimately successful, but by then Earl Gilbert was long since dead.

KENNEDY RAPACITY (2): GLENLUCE

According to the anonymous author of the *Historie of the Kennedyis*, Earl Gilbert used much the same tactics to secure the lands belonging to Glenluce, and here he had the advantage of being the bailie[26] – an appointment which was tantamount to inviting a wolf into a sheepfold. Prefacing his account with a description of the earl as 'ane particular manne and ane verry greidy manne who cairrit nocht how he gatt land so [long as] he culd cum be the samin', the author narrates how Gilbert entered into a 'bloking' (an arrangement) with the commendator to feu the abbey lands to him. But no sooner had the charter been drawn up than the commendator died, and therefore it remained unsigned. However, the earl was undaunted, and he prevailed on one of the monks to forge the commendator's signature. Fearing the monk might blab, he hired a hit man to kill him, or as the writer puts it 'he caussit ane cairill [churl] quhilk thai calt Carnochaine to stik [him]'. And stick him he did, but, apprehensive that Carnochan might reveal his share in the conspiracy, Earl Gilbert arranged for his uncle, Hugh Kennedy of Bargany, to arrest him for murdering the monk, and he was duly hanged at Crossraguel. 'And sa', as the author of the account laconically observes, 'the lands of Glenluse was conqueist'.[27]

A good story, and as it was entirely in character with the Kennedys it was widely believed. In fact, although the result was the same, in that Earl Gilbert managed to secure the abbey lands, it was John (later Sir John) Gordon of Lochinvar, and not he, who was the villain of the piece. Lochinvar's chicanery was the culmination of a series of events which started with Gilbert's father, the third earl's, appointment as bailie in 1543. His attempts to assert his jurisdictional rights within the abbey lands brought him into conflict with Sheriff Andrew Agnew of Lochnaw. This was because Agnew had been instructed by Mary of Guise, who was well aware of Cassilis' designs on its lands, to occupy Glenluce to prevent him from holding a court there.[28]

Cassilis duly complained to the council, and after a delay of some two years it ordered Agnew to remove his men, while securing an undertaking from Cassilis that he would 'hald na maner of Court there'. No sooner had Agnew and his men departed than Cassilis broke his promise by forcibly attempting to hold a court there – an enterprise in which he was assisted by his nephew, Ninian Adair of Kilhilt, and the MacDowells of Garthland and Freuch, and for good measure they stripped the abbey of its contents and drove off a large number of sheep and cattle.[29] Consequently, Abbot Walter Mallyn was forced to appeal for help to his neighbour, William Gordon of Craichlaw, and he in turn enlisted the support of his cousin, James of Lochinvar (the participant in the street brawl in Edinburgh) who had continued to cast predatory eyes on the abbey lands ever since the failure of his attempt to use Bishop Arnot's visitation as a pretext some twenty years previously. However, he was denied the chance to exploit his advantage as he was killed at Pinkie shortly afterwards, when his claim was taken up by his son John. However, it seems that the latter was not in a position to pursue it as vigorously as his father – for the time being at any rate, so he seems to have come to some sort of accommodation with Cassilis, and this was eventually formalised in 1555 by a decree of arbitration by the council.[30]

However, when Abbot Walter Mallyn died later that year, John Gordon contrived to have his brother James appointed as his successor – doubtless on the understanding that he would arrange to feu him the abbey lands. Although one can hardly imagine that this was much to Cassilis' liking, he was unable to do much about it because he died shortly afterwards from poisoning,[31] when he was succeeded by his son Gilbert as fourth earl. This gave John Gordon the opportunity to proceed with his plans, so a charter was duly drawn up conveying the abbey lands to him. Then suddenly his carefully-laid scheme went awry, because Abbot James died unexpectedly before he had a chance to sign it. Therefore, contrary to the account given in the *Historie of the Kennedyis*, it was John Gordon who was reduced to pressurising one of the monks into forging his brother's signature, but in a fit of conscience the monk confessed, whereupon the new Earl Gilbert promptly challenged the deed and had it reduced.

Meanwhile, John Gordon had occupied the abbey buildings, and when Earl Gilbert, using his bailiary powers, secured the appointment of his nominee, Thomas Hay, as abbot,[32] the latter found himself locked out. So he and his monks were forced to seek shelter as Earl Gilbert's guests at Crossraguel, and in return for undertaking to feu him the abbey lands they were allowed to remain there until such time as the matter came before the council. Both parties were allowed to present their case, and the council, deciding in Gilbert's favour, ordered Gordon to remove himself and his men from 'the abbey and the yards of Glenluce' and to hand over the contents and the keys to Gilbert. As a fiat from this source was not to be defied, Lochinvar had no alternative but to comply.

Once installed as commendator, Thomas Hay proceeded to honour his pledge to Earl Gilbert by granting him a charter of the abbey lands. The consideration was £2,000, apparently the sum needed to make good the damage caused by Lochinvar's men during their occupation of the premises. But this was not the end of the matter, as it transpired that the deed was defective in that it omitted to convey the teind rights. So an amended charter was issued in 1572,[33] and thus the abbey lands were indeed 'conqueist'. Thomas Hay was given the lands of Park as a reward for his co-operation, and these remained in the hands of his Dalrymple-Hay descendants until the twentieth century. James Ross, who acted as Earl Gilbert's legal adviser throughout the negotiations, was another beneficiary, as he was given the lands of Balneil. He later acquired Carscreugh castle, and some seventy years later his descendant, Margaret Ross, married James Dalrymple, the future viscount Stair. Thereafter these lands became the nucleus of the extensive estates which Dalrymple and his descendants, the earls of Stair, subsequently built up in the district, mainly at the expense of the Kennedys.

When Thomas Hay died in 1581 he was succeeded by Laurence Gordon, a son of Bishop Alexander Gordon, who was simultaneously constituted the pensionary bishop of Whithorn in succession to his elder brother John.[34] However, he was ejected from Glenluce almost immediately afterwards, and tantalisingly, the relevant charter refers to the king as being *egritudine vexatus est*[35] which is pretty strong language, so it would be intriguing to know how he came to incur the king's displeasure. Back into the ring, now, came Sir John Gordon of Lochinvar who contrived to have his younger son William appointed as commendator. But it seems to have been a pointless exercise, because by this time the abbey's possessions were reduced to the buildings themselves, their immediate surroundings, a handful of appropriated churches, and the superiorities of the lands feued off to Earl Gilbert; and in any case these passed to the crown under the Annexation Act of 1587. James VI then erected them into a temporal lordship, and in

1602 he gave it to Laurence Gordon,[36] clearly now forgiven for his past misdemeanour. When he died in 1610 he left it to his elder brother John the former bishop, now dean of Salisbury, and he in turn gave it to his daughter and her husband, Sir Robert Gordon. In 1613 they sold it back to James VI who proceeded to annex it to the bishopric of Galloway.

WHITHORN PRIORY

The Kennedy family tentacles extended to the Whithorn priory lands as well, because the principal beneficiary, Sir Patrick Vaus of Barnbarroch, was married to Earl Gilbert's sister, Katherine. His acquisition of these marked the culmination of a train of events which started with the death of its prior, Malcolm Fleming, in 1568. The regent Moray arranged to have his half-brother, Lord Robert Stewart, another of James V's illegitimate sons, appointed as Fleming's successor. However, he was challenged by Fleming's nephew William, an illegitimate son of his brother, lord Fleming, who was killed at Pinkie. According to Agnew, William's half-brother, the present lord Fleming, planned to make a descent on the priory with the intention of occupying it in order to enforce William's claim. Meanwhile, Sheriff Patrick Agnew had been deputed to safeguard Lord Robert's interest, so when he got wind of Fleming's intentions he forestalled him by occupying the priory himself, and for good measure he raided its lands of Cruggleton, making off with 'xvij score yowes and xvij tupes [rams]'.[37]

As William Fleming had been thwarted in his efforts to establish his claim to the priorship by force, he fell back on the law, asserting that he had been issued with a deed under the privy seal giving him the reversion of the commendatorship in the event of his uncle Malcolm's death or resignation. Lord Robert Stewart countered by arguing that the deed was a sham, that it contained blanks at the time it was executed, and that they had been filled in afterwards to show Malcolm Fleming as the beneficiary. The dispute was protracted, and although Lord Robert was the successful candidate he was prevented from gaining entry until 1573, and even then it dragged on into the 1590s, by which time he was long since dead.[38]

It is quite obvious that the regent Moray had organised his brother's appointment for the sole purpose of acquiring the priory lands for himself. For immediately on his appointment, and notwithstanding Malcolm Fleming's challenge, Lord Robert proceeded to feu away most of the priory lands to Moray.[39] The relevant charter lists over twenty-five separate holdings in the southern Machars alone, not counting the Glenswinton estate in the parish of Parton and the priory lands in Argyllshire which he also acquired. As almost all the place-names are easily identifiable, it is evident that Moray acquired virtually all the priory lands in the southern Machars, with the exception of those of Broughton which had already been acquired by the Murray family.

The Church was at pains to ensure that the alienation of their lands did not interfere with the rights of their 'kindly' tenants. In fact, the Church council of 1559 formally minuted its disapproval of the practice of feuing its lands to others than the 'ancient, native tenants, occupiers and tillers of the land'.[40] The civil authorities were equally concerned for their well-being, and a number of measures were passed for the purpose of protecting their interests,[41] so one can assume the safeguard applied in Galloway as much as elsewhere.[42] Prominent among the priory tenants was the Hathorn family who farmed the holding of Meikle Airies to the west of Sorbie, and whose tenancy was ultimately converted into a feu.[43] While some of the family became small-time landholders one of them, John Hathorn, eventually acquired the estate of Physgill through his marriage to the heiress Agnes Stewart.[44]

When the regent Moray was assassinated in 1570 his lands passed to his three daughters, but when the younger two died without issue they fell into the lap of his eldest daughter Elizabeth, countess of Moray. By this time the commendator Lord Robert Stewart had died, having been succeeded by Patrick Stewart, the son of his half-brother Robert, earl of Orkney, who was the youngest of James V's bastards. As Patrick was a minor, Sir Patrick Vaus used his position as a favourite of James VI to obtain the appointment of administrator of the priory lands. He clearly used his office to good effect – at least as far as his own interests were concerned – because he appears to have prevailed on Countess Elizabeth to sell him most of her lands,[45] though others went to sitting tenants.

Not long afterwards Sir Patrick's successors fell on hard times, so they in turn were forced to sell these lands, most of them being acquired by the Stewarts of Garlies. Therefore, these combined with other former Church lands which the Stewarts had already secured in the vicinity of Whithorn comprised the bulk of the huge landholding which they and their descendants, the earls of Galloway, eventually built up in the eastern Machars. The priory was now left with the superiorities of its former lands, the priory buildings themselves and their appropriated churches, of which there were nineteen in Galloway alone.[46] These passed to the crown under the Annexation Act of 1587, and James VI subsequently granted them to the bishopric of Galloway.[47]

THE MINOR HOUSES

Sir Alexander Stewart of Garlies, the reformist, also acquired, for the sum of £1,000 Scots, the assets belonging to Dervorguilla's friary of Wigtown.[48] Reflecting the friars' rule of poverty, the crown confirmation of the relevant feu charter shows these as being limited to a few parcels of land, some salmon fishings on the Bladnoch, and rents payable in the form of meal from a number of properties in the neighbourhood.[49] Its sister institution at Kirkcudbright was virtually controlled by the local council, but if it had designs on acquiring its assets for the burgh these were thwarted by the provost, Sir Thomas McLellan of Bombie, who secured a charter of them in 1569.[50] Later, the council came to an arrangement with McLellan whereby it acquired the site of the present church in exchange for giving him the nearby 'peithouse'. McLellan insisted on a *douceur* of 500 marks and 100 bolls of lime as part of the bargain, and it was on the site of the 'peithouse' that he proceeded to build his castle which was completed in 1582.[51]

Further down the Dee estuary was the priory of Traill, where the avaricious Robert Richardson had been the commendator since about 1558. Scion of a family of Edinburgh burgesses, his speciality was land speculation and the amassing of properties for his bastard children. For example, in 1563 he bought up much of the lands belonging to Dunfermline abbey which he resold to the sitting tenants,[52] presumably at a profit, and by the time of his death in 1578 he had endowed his illegitimate son James[53] with the baronies of Smeaton and Pencaitland, in East Lothian. James was the eldest of his many natural children, and he continued to procreate bastards during his commendatorship of Traill, because in January 1564 he was ordered to do penance before the whole congregation in Edinburgh for 'getting a woman with child'. This was a considerable disgrace, particularly as he was now a leading politician, having been appointed treasurer by Queen Mary in the previous year.

He clearly turned his control of Traill to his pecuniary advantage, for when he finally resigned office he retained a pension for the enormous sum of £500, thus amply justifying the epithet applied to him of 'the usufructuary of St Mary's Isle'.[54] Since he had no legitimate children, his heir was his niece Kathleen Charteris, the wife of James Lidderdale,[55] and between them Richardson and his successor, William Rutherford, disposed of virtually all the priory lands, consisting of Grange, Torrs and Galtway, to the couple with a destination to their son Thomas.[56] According to the 1630 tax-roll for the priory, Thomas himself eventually became prior, while James Lidderdale was the baillie.[57] Although most of the lands were subsequently acquired by the McLellans of Bombie, eventually becoming part of the St Mary's Isle estate, members of the Lidderdale family continued to own the Torrs estate until the eighteenth century.[58] Under an arrangement which was presumably to Richardson's advantage, the priory sold off the barony of Itoun, near Eggerness, to his neighbour Sir Thomas McLellan of Bombie,[59] while much of the remaining lands there went to John Dunbar of Mochrum.[60]

THE EPISCOPAL LANDS

The bishops' *mensa* lands were originally extensive, but they were widely dispersed throughout the region so that the incumbents could be adequately provided for during their travels in the course of their episcopal duties. This meant that the lands ended up in the hands of a number of different families. There had already been a steady trickle of disposals during the fifteenth century, but the imposition of the great tax hastened the process, since it forced Bishop Henry Wemyss to dispose of the remainder of the *mensa* lands in the present-day parish of Twynholm, as well as others in the Rhinns.

Later, however, there was a flood of disposals, much of the lands in the parish of Inch, for example, going to Sheriff Patrick Agnew,[61] thus adding to those of Sheuchan which his forbear Quentin Agnew acquired from Bishop Vaus back in the 1490s.[62] Most of the remaining episcopal lands there eventually fell into the hands of Earl Gilbert's son, John, fifth earl of Cassilis.[63] Meantime, Bishop Alexander Gordon continued the process by feuing away virtually all the lands in the parish of Penninghame. The lion's share, which consisted of the bishop's principal residence of Clary and the neighbouring lands, were feued to Sir Alexander Stewart of Garlies, the reformer,[64] and thereafter he and his descendants continued to use Clary as their main residence. Some went to Vaus of Barnbarroch, and others to the rapacious Sir John Gordon of Lochinvar,[65] while his brother William, a son-in-law of Stewart of Garlies and ancestor of the later viscounts Kenmure, acquired the £5 lands of Bordland of Penninghame.[66] Most of the *mensa* lands at Whithorn passed into the hands of the Stewarts of Garlies as well,[67] while the bulk of those in the parish of Kirkcolm were divided between members of the McDowell kindred.[68]

Tongland abbey had been appropriated to the Chapel Royal of Stirling in 1529, and as that institution was under the control of the bishopric of Whithorn, its lands can arguably be counted as part of the episcopal patrimony. Therefore, it would have been at the instance of Bishop Alexander Gordon, as *ex officio* commendator, that its lands were feued off – in their entirety it would seem – to Sir John Gordon of Lochinvar for the sum of £2,000.[69] Nevertheless, it still retained the teinds from its appropriated churches of Senwick, Tongland and Leswalt, because some years later the last two became the subject of a somewhat incestuous deal between the bishop's two sons, when the elder John, who was himself the bishop by this time, disposed of them to his brother Laurence. Those of Senwick, on the other hand, were given away as a pension to William Melville, the last incumbent of Tongland, and when he died in 1613 they reverted under an assignation to the bishopric of Galloway.[70]

THE RISE OF THE GORDONS

Sir John Gordon's acquisition of the lands belonging to Tongland, and the parcels of *mensa* lands, represented only a fraction of those which his family had been amassing since their ancestor William Gordon was established as a prominent landowner in the Ken valley by the fourth earl of Douglas. With the marriage of William's grandson, Sir Robert Gordon, to Marion Accarsone at the end of the fifteenth century, the family acquired the barony of Glenskyreburne (later known as Rusco) which comprised an expanse of rough hill ground extending from the upper Fleet across to the Skyreburn. When he died in 1525, his widow made an ill-judged match with Thomas McLellan of Bombie, who promptly packed her off to the gloomy Scott keep of Tushielaw. He then proceeded to help himself to her own lands, as well as claiming her terce rights in those belonging to the Gordons, until his death at the hands of her son James in the street brawl in Edinburgh in the following year put paid to his designs. James's son, Sir John Gordon, married Elizabeth Maxwell, a daughter of John Lord Herries, his fellow adherent of Queen Mary, and it was because of this that his stronghold of Kenmure was singled out for destruction in the course of the earl of Moray's spoiling raid into Galloway.

Although Sir John failed to secure the lands belonging to Glenluce, he consoled himself by amassing a considerable amount of property in Kirkcudbrightshire. According to a charter of 1593, he appears to have purchased a number of former Douglas estates in the parishes of Balmaghie, Kelton and Buittle[71] from the crown, and later on the barony of Kirkandrews.[72] By that time he had already acquired the abbey lands of Tongland,[73] as well as the feu of a number of former Sweetheart lands in the parish of Kirkpatrick Durham from lord Maxwell.[74] In addition, he secured the lands of Enrick near Gatehouse, which were formerly part of the bishop's *mensa*,[75] so altogether he was able to pass on a princely inheritance to his son.

This son – Sir Robert Gordon of Lochinvar – became a favourite of James VI, who appointed him a gentleman of his bedchamber, besides conferring on him the justiciarship of the Border shires in 1609, and the provostship of Lincluden in 1617.[76] Yet it is hard to equate this cascade of honours with his distinctly murky track record. For example, he was in competition with Kennedy of Bargany for the office of Admiral of the south-west coast, and sour grapes at his failure to secure it would have accounted for his raid on Kennedy's house, in the course of which his men carried off Kennedy's wife and children. Not content with that, he seized a valuable cargo of salt from Portugal belonging to Kennedy while it lay at anchor in Loch Ryan – an exploit which earned him a spell of imprisonment in Blackness castle. He is also alleged to have murdered his servant, James Gordon, 'of whom', says Balfour, 'he was jealous as being too familiar with his lady'. 'This', he adds, 'was esteemed by all a wicked calumny and only forged by him [Gordon] to stain her honour, with a view of taking [ridding himself of] her and getting another'.

In 1609 he was involved in a minor contretemps with William McLellan of Auchlane, which ended up in court. The official account is inevitably somewhat biassed, since only McLellan's version of the story has survived, and this contains a distinct whiff of injured innocence. It arose as a result of a social call which McLellan paid on Gordon and his mother 'who was lykewayse in the said toun [Kirkcudbright]'. While McLellan was 'begynning to entir in familiar and friendlie discours with thame' Gordon 'begouth [began] to utter outragious and dispytfull speitches against the said complenair, calling him a coseyner'. So, one can readily picture the obsequious McLellan ingratiating himself with the old lady to the hot-tempered Gordon's mounting irritation. Anyway, he goes on to aver that Gordon drew out his 'neve [knife]' and 'presit [threatened] to have strickin him upon the face'. McLellan escaped but was run to earth by a posse of Gordons who 'with drawin swordis boisted [raised] and minassit [menaced] the said complenair, bidding him pack – knave!' Gordon's defence, if any, does not survive, but it cannot have been convincing, since he was warded in Edinburgh castle until he could find surety.[77]

Yet the king not only granted him a general remission for all these offences, as well as other equally serious ones, but loaded him with honours, as well as giving him half the collegiate lands of Lincluden which had been forfeited by William Douglas.[78] Therefore, once he had traded his interest in the Drumsleet lands with Murray of Lochmaben for those at Crossmichael and bought up Douglas of Drumlanrig's property there, his already substantial inheritance was greatly increased. In fact, his land-holdings would have been comparable with the Kirkcudbrightshire estates of his contemporary, the sixth lord Herries. Thus the formidable power and prestige of the Gordons rose to new heights, and they would be boosted even further when Robert's son, John, was created viscount Kenmure in 1633.

The Gordon ramifications included a number of cadet branches who were themselves substantial landowners in Galloway. The most important were the Gordons of Earlston, whose stronghold was situated on the Ken immediately upstream from Dalry, and whose lands extended as far as the upper reaches of the Ken and the Deugh. The other main cadet branch were the Gordons of Craichlaw, an estate comprising much of the parish of Kirkcowan, and having acquired it in 1500 the family remained there until the eighteenth century. Other members of the Gordon kindred were established as small-time landholders in the Ken valley, though one of them, William Gordon, said to be an illegitimate half-brother of Sir John of Lochinvar,[79] was already in the process of amassing properties in Girthon and the neighbouring parish of Anwoth, where he and his descendants eventually acquired much of the former Cardiness barony.[80]

CONCLUSION

By the 1580s the ecclesiastical institutions had feued away virtually all their lands, while their remaining assets reverted to the crown under the Annexation Act of 1587.[81] Smacking strongly of special pleading, the preamble to the Act claimed 'the greitest part of [the king's] proper rent to haif bene gevin and disponit of auld to abbayis, monasteries and utheris personis of clergy quhairby the Crown hes bene sa greitly hurte', and that because of this 'his maist noble progenitouris had not sufficient meanis to beir furth the honour of thair estait as thai had befoir'. Then, in a public relations exercise worthy of any modern politician, it goes on to assert that the appropriation of these assets was preferable to the other alternative of raising taxes which 'for the grite luif and favour quilk [the king] beiris to his subjects [he is] nawayes myndit to greve thame'.

The Act went on to categorise the assets belonging to these institutions which now devolved on the crown. This was effectively a blanket clause which was designed to cover everything they possessed, though it made a specific exception in the case of the teinds payable from their appropriated churches,[82] and the dwellinghouses occupied by their incumbents and other church dignitaries. The most valuable assets were the feuduties, as these represented a huge source of revenue. Although the Act stipulated that they were to remain the inalienable property of the crown, King James was quick to perceive them as a useful means of buying the support of influential people. For example, Archbishop John Spottiswoode, the persecutor of Abbot Gilbert Broun, was given the superiority of the former Sweetheart lands, while his son Sir Robert, the lord president of the Court of Session and favourite of Charles I, was given much of the remainder.[83] However, these all eventually reverted to the crown.

In her paper, 'The Feuars of Kirklands', Dr Sanderson concludes that, generally speaking, the break-up of the monastic lands resulted in a wide distribution of land among the tenant class and incomers from the burghs, though her supporting evidence does not include the religious houses in Galloway.[84] In fact, her only reference to them is to suggest that in some instances the dispersal of their lands 'frequently reinforced the long record of tenure enjoyed by many small families who were neither descended from nor closely related to substantial, long-established lairds'. Although she goes on to cite the Browns as feuars of Sweetheart, and the Welshes and Edgars as feuars of Dundrennan, the evidence points firmly to the Maxwells and the Herries Maxwells, the Kennedys, the Lochinvar Gordons and the Stewarts of Garlies as being the principal beneficiaries of the break-up of the church lands in Galloway.

NOTES

1. Fraser asserts (*Carlaverock* i, 224) that John eighth lord Maxwell was infeft in these bailiaries as heir of his predecessors, while referring (p 165) to John, the fourth lord, and his heir Robert being constituted bailies of Sweetheart, and (p 175) to the latter acting as bailie of Dundrennan, Tongland and Lincluden as well.
2. Herries, 'John Maxwell of Newlaw', 96.
3. Christie, *Dundrennan*, 79.
4. Fraser, *Carlaverock*, 590 (genealogical tree): Christie, *Dundrennan*, 85.
5. Christie, *Dundrennan*, 96.
6. Herries 'John Maxwell of Newlaw', 97–102.
7. *Ibid.*, 102.
8. Fraser, *Carlaverock*, 592.
9. He left them to his niece, who was the wife of Adam Maitland of Castlecreavie (Lawler, *History of the Cairns*, 250–1), and part of them still belongs to their descendant.
10. *Wig Charters*, 251–2 (no. 355).
11. *Ibid.* (no. 355a).
12. *RMS* iv no. 1653.
13. Present-day Baitford near Penpont. Incidentally, he does not feature in the *Scots Peerage*.
14. *RMS* vii no. 501.
15. Most of the farms were disposed of to sitting tenants, while the Greenlaw estate was sold by the eighth viscount in 1745 – allegedly in settlement of a bad debt – to his cousin, William Gordon of Culvennan, whose descendant eventually disposed of it in 1879.
16. This conclusion is based on the uncertain account in McKerlie iv, 295–331. It seems the Maxwells feued away all the properties, some of them going to Sir John Gordon of Lochinvar, so their successors the earls of Nithsdale would have been left with the mid-superiorities.
17. Stewart and Reid, 'Early Browns in New Abbey', 94.
18. Stewart, 'Sweetheart Abbey', 60.
19. Stewart, *The Early Stewarts of Shambellie*, 28–9.
20. He was a leading member of the reformed Church who became archbishop of Glasgow and later St Andrews, as well as chancellor, during the reign of Charles I.
21. The exploits of this former abbot are described in Stewart, 'Sweetheart Abbey', 61.
22. While it would be churlish to question this impressive feat the theory has been advanced that there were two Gilbert Brouns, and that it was the later one who suffered for his adherence to the Roman faith and died in about 1612, having achieved the more modest age of eighty.
23. Disc. Reid, 'Soulseat', 177–8, and 'Dunskey Castle', 245: Reid describes him as

'commendator, but really abbot' (*Wig Charters*, 97).

24. Reid, 'Soulseat', 178–9.
25. *Ibid.*, 178.
26. *Scots Peerage* II, 471.
27. Morton, 'Glenluce Abbey', 233–4.
28. Reid, 'Dunskey Castle', 243.
29. Morton, 'Glenluce Abbey', which refers to a Deed of Remission and Discharge granted to the fourth earl for the spoliation of the abbey by his father and the lairds of Kinhilt, Garthland and Freugh.
30. *Wig Charters*, 75–76, no. 59.
31. He was one of the commissioners sent to Paris to negotiate the marriage treaty between Queen Mary and the dauphin. This contained a number of secret provisions, the most controversial of which was an undertaking that if Mary were to die childless her kingdom would pass to the French crown. Clearly the fewer people who knew of this the better, so an attempt was made to poison the commissioners at Dieppe on their return journey, and in Cassilis' case it was successful.
32. This was the subject of a petition by Queen Mary and her husband Francis to Pope Pius IV who issued the necessary Bull in 1559 (Morton, 'Carscreugh Castle', 136)
33. This lists all the eighty-one properties belonging to Glenluce, which comprised broadly the present-day parishes of Old and New Luce.
34. *RMS* v no. 335.
35. *Ibid.*, 336.
36. *Ibid.* vi no. 1338.
37. Agnew i, 394.
38. Donaldson, 'Bishops and priors of Whithorn', 147.
39. *RMS* iv no. 2823.
40. Sanderson, 'The Feuars of Kirklands', 125.
41. *APS* ii, 539–40, 545, 606.
42. This is the conclusion drawn by Sanderson in 'The Feuars of Kirklands', 117–136.
43. Gillon, 'The Hathorns of Meikle Airies', 69 et seq.
44. *Ibid.*: Reid, 'Physgill', 100.
45. McKerlie i, 370, 376, 402, 501, all references to deeds pointing to the sale to Vaus of most of the properties mentioned in the charter to the earl of Moray (*RMS* iv no. 2823).
46. Donaldson, 'Bishops and priors of Whithorn', 147–8.
47. McKerlie i 469.
48. *Wig Charters*, 118, 132–3.
49. *Ibid.*, 133 (no. 107).
50. Robison, 'Greyfriars and Moat Brae, Kirkcudbright', 14.
51. *Ibid.*
52. Sanderson, 'The Feuars of Kirklands', 124.
53. He subsequently married a daughter of the regent Morton and acquired a baronetcy which still exists.
54. Reid, 'The Priory of St. Mary's Isle', 21.
55. Lidderdale, 'A tax-roll for the priory of St. Mary's Isle', 172. McKerlie wrongly asserts (iv, 178) that he was the husband of Richardson's legitimate daughter Katherine.
56. *RMS* iv no. 2155 (dated 1573).

57. Lidderdale,'A tax-roll'.
58. McKerlie iv, 181–2.
59. *Ibid.* i, 458. He subsequently exchanged this with Kennedy of Blairquhan for Kirkchrist which was closer to home.
60. *Wig Charters*, 251 (no. 353) and 'The Priory of St Mary's Isle', 21.
61. *RMS* v no. 1231.
62. *Wig Charters*, 3.
63. *RMS* vi no. 1633.
64. *Wig Charters*, 3.
65. *Ibid.*, 4.
66. *RMS* v no. 187.
67. *Wig Charters*, 4–5.
68. *Ibid.*, 4.
69. *RMS* iv no. 1719.
70. McKerlie v, 190.
71. *RMS* v no. 2278, which confirmed Sir John in the ownership of these properties.
72. *RMS* vi no. 646. This was granted in 1598 and confirmed the gift of these properties (seven in number) to his son and heir Robert.
73. *RMS* iv no. 1719.
74. *RMS* v no. 2278 which confirmed Sir John in the ownership of these properties as well.
75. *Wig Charters*, 6.
76. *Scots Peerage* v, 110 et seq.
77. The incident is described in Torrance, *The McClellans in Galloway*, 38.
78. *RMS* vii no. 501. That this was a gift seems evident from the fact that no consideration is mentioned in the rubric.
79. McKerlie iv, 288–9.
80. McCulloch, *Galloway McCullochs*, 144–54.
81. *APS* iii, 431.
82. On the very day the act came into force (29 July) Sir John Murray, as commendator of Dundrennan, granted himself a number of rights belonging to that house, including the teind sheaves of Kirkmabreck (*APS* iv, 326). Obviously he was rushing to beat the deadline and cutting it pretty fine.
83. Stewart, 'Sweetheart Abbey', 61–2.
84. Sanderson, 'The Feuars of Kirklands', 118 et seq.

22

REVOLUTION

THE GATHERING CRISIS

James VI died in 1625, having reigned for nearly sixty years. He was succeeded by his only surviving son Charles I, who in sharp contrast to his father was a sober, principled and deeply committed family man. Also a man of strongly-held religious convictions, he was never prepared to sacrifice them in the interests of political expediency, and when finally compelled to do so it was invariably too late and the damage was done. This was symptomatic of his lack of the guile and political astuteness with which his father had been so well endowed, and nowhere was this unfortunate combination of political incompetence and religious dogmatism more apparent than in his dealings with the Scots.

His concern for the Church, and his efforts to secure a better remuneration for the bishops in particular, accounted for the passing of the Revocation Act of 1625,[1] which proved the first major blunder of his reign. Although he was merely following the example of his predecessors, its scope was far wider, in that it cancelled all grants of crown property, and by implication abbey lands with their attaching teinds,[2] as well as all heritable jurisdictions, made since 1540. This entailed potentially devastating results for those who had benefited from the land revolution of the previous century, and would account for the defection of many of the nobility to the covenanters. The Act was also designed to protect the interests of the minor lairds and feuars by curbing the powers of the magnates, of whom they held their lands, but, as many of these people stood to be affected by the revocation as well, it earned Charles little support from that section of the community.

Compensation was available to the owners of teinds, and commissioners were appointed to determine their value in consultation with representatives from each shire.[3] Those for Wigtownshire included Sir Patrick Agnew the hereditary sheriff, but the sixth earl of Cassilis, who had much to lose by the arrangement, took keen exception to his willingness to co-operate. Therefore, emulating his predecessors' exploits, he drove Agnew's bailiffs out of his estates of Leswalt and Menybrig and installed his own men with orders to uplift the teinds.[4] He also prevented Agnew from holding his court there by setting up an encampment of 300 wild Irishmen armed with 'musketts, hagbutts, pistolls, lances, and other such invasive weapons' round the building, and they began provocatively to 'shoot off their pieces . . . to the great terror and disquieting of the country'. In desperation Agnew appealed to the council, and the chancellor, lord Dupplin, sent a contingent of soldiery to Wigtownshire who eventually forced Cassilis to withdraw.[5] Nevertheless, his actions were symptomatic of the widespread hostility to the Revocation Act; and, although Charles was driven to moderate its terms, it left a legacy of suspicion and mistrust which would dog his relations with the Scottish nobility for the rest of his reign.

These were equivocal from the outset, because those who occupied the principal offices of state were placemen of his father's, and as they had established their own political fiefdoms during his absence in England they naturally resented Charles's attempts to upset this cosy arrangement by intruding his authority. In fact, there were very few magnates on whom Charles could rely, all the more so since his principal supporters, the earls of Nithsdale and Stirling, were unable to set foot in Scotland, the one because of the numerous debt actions pending against him, while the other was on a murder charge. Consequently, Charles was constrained to look to the clergy for support, and this accounted for his appointing time-servers like Thomas Sydserf and the elderly Archbishop John Spottiswoode to high office, the latter becoming chancellor in 1634. Being Charles's placemen, their presence on the council was widely resented, particularly because the statute compelling them to wear vestments similar to those of the Anglican clergy[7] was seen as a nod to popish rites.

Equally unpopular was Charles's fiscal policy and the imposition of taxes. This was forced on him by the dramatic fall in real terms of the crown feuduties which were formerly the staple of the royal revenues, as this left him unable to meet the costs of government. King James had been in much the same position, and it was only by considerable financial juggling with an occasional resort to taxation that he was able to make ends meet. Now inflation had bitten deeper and the situation was worse, so further taxation was the only answer and this effectively became an annual levy from 1630 onwards.[8] The Scots, however, regarded it as an English fiscal measure passed by an 'English' king, because it was not until 1633 that Charles first visited Scotland in order to be crowned. That this delay was attributable to his inability to pay for the refurbishment of the royal residences failed to register with them, and instead they saw it as indicating a lack of interest in them.

His coronation in the abbey church of Holyrood in 1633 was a scene of considerable magnificence, but at the same time much resented, as its show of ecclesiastical splendour greatly offended the susceptibilities of the onlookers. Charles took the opportunity to hold a parliament which passed a number of measures which were designed to consolidate the bishops' power, and he also founded the bishopric of Edinburgh. This led to a readjustment of the episcopal bench, as a result of which Sydserf, then dean of Edinburgh, was promoted to the see of Brechin and almost immediately afterwards translated to Galloway. A number of honours were showered on lesser magnates as a means of buying their support, though when the crisis came the majority deserted him to join the covenanters. Among the magnates in the south-west, John Gordon of Lochinvar became viscount Kenmure, Robert McLellan of Bombie lord Kirkcudbright, and William Douglas of Drumlanrig was created earl of Queensberry,[9] while Sir Alexander Stewart of Garlies had already been created earl of Galloway by James VI in 1623.[10]

THE STORM BREAKS

The simmering discontent erupted into open protest when Charles attempted to impose his new liturgy on the Scottish Church in 1637. This was primarily the work of Archbishop Laud, and although he canvassed the views of the Scottish bishops scant attention was paid to them, so it was seen by the Scots as a blatant attempt to foist an English, neo-catholic form of worship on them. Opposition was widespread, and petitions for the withdrawal of both the liturgy itself and the Book of Common Prayer came pouring in to the council, while crowds of protesters from Fife and the Lothians streamed into Edinburgh.

To emphasise their point, they organised demonstrations in a number of churches in the city, including the interruption of a special service to mark the introduction of the Prayer Book, which was held in St Giles' cathedral in Edinburgh in July 1637. To underline the importance of the occasion it was attended by all the senior ecclesiastics, the lords of the privy council, members of the judiciary, and the city magistrates. No sooner had the dean begun to recite the new liturgy than pandemonium broke out and books and other missiles were hurled at him. When the bishop of Edinburgh went into the pulpit to rebuke the demonstrators and restore order, he was assailed by a stool which narrowly missed his head. At this point the magistrates intervened to clear the church of the rioters, and thereafter the service proceeded without further interruption. However, the mob was waiting for the bishop outside, and his carriage was stoned for most of the way back to the palace of Holyrood.[11]

Within a week the new prayer book was abandoned, but a royal proclamation ordering the rioters to leave Edinburgh was ignored, and the whole ecclesiastical establishment came under attack, with abuse being hurled in particular at their representatives on the council. The situation became so serious that the whole council was forced to take refuge at Linlithgow, virtually abandoning Edinburgh to the mob. Bishop Sydserf was a particular target of attack, mainly because he was suspected of wearing a crucifix,[12] and on one occasion he only just managed to reach the sanctuary of the council chamber in time to avoid being lynched by the mob.[13] Slated by his religious opponent, Drummond of Hawthornden, as 'Galloway Tam, that squint-eyed stridling asse',[14] Sydserf was destined to be the last surviving bishop of the pre-Covenant era. However, in Galloway he is chiefly remembered for being the principal adversary of Samuel Rutherford,[15] whom he ejected from his charge of Anwoth and banished to internal exile in Aberdeen.

Eventually the authorities were forced to temporise, and a committee, consisting of representatives of the lords, gentry, ministers and burgesses, who were generally sympathetic towards the dissidents, was appointed to receive petitions from them. Representations were drawn up and submitted to the king in London, but blindly unaware that the country was on the verge of revolution he refused to make any concessions and ordered the Prayer Book to remain in use. The Scots responded by appointing a steering committee to undertake the task of drawing up a National Covenant for mass signature, and among its authors was Archibald Johnston of Wariston who would become a principal leader of the extremist wing of the covenanting movement.

The document was published in 1638[16] and, taking its stand on the Negative Confession of Faith of 1581, it systematically denounced all subsequent Acts of Parliament deemed prejudicial to presbyterianism, while binding its subscribers to maintain what it described as 'the true religion'. Although it was by no means an extremist manifesto and was careful to pledge loyalty to the king, it would become the principal article of faith of the whole covenanting movement, while the radicals who were loudest in their protests against royal despotism were the very people who would turn it into an instrument of tyranny. John Livingstone, the minister of Stranraer, was commissioned to deliver a copy to the English presbyterians in London, but he was forced to leave the capital in a hurry when Charles heard of his presence there and threatened to have fetters put on his feet.[17]

At last Charles began to appreciate the seriousness of the situation, so he sent the marquis of Hamilton as an emissary to treat with the supporters of the Covenant. His official instructions were to promise them that if they repudiated the Covenant the Prayer Book would be withdrawn and a general assembly summoned, although Charles privately told him to 'flatter them with what hopes you please . . . until I be ready to suppress them'. The mission was a complete failure. The covenanters were in no mood to compromise, and since they refused to give way Charles was forced to waive his condition that the Covenant be repudiated, and summoned an assembly. This was convened at Glasgow in November 1638 – the first time it had met since 1618. The covenanters moved fast, and by securing control of the election of its commissioners they made sure the assembly was packed with their own supporters, and as the bishops dared not attend for fear of their lives, some of them having already taken refuge in England, they effectively controlled the proceedings.

Hamilton was appointed the king's commissioner, but when the assembly attempted to pass judgement on the bishops he declared the proceedings unconstitutional and dissolved it. Defying his orders, the members continued to sit as an illegal body, and almost without debate they denounced as unlawful all assemblies held since 1608. They also condemned the Book of Common Prayer in the strongest terms, tried, deposed and excommunicated the bishops in their absence for a whole litany of alleged offences – which was designed purely for propaganda purposes – and called for the restoration of presbytery.

THE BISHOPS' WAR

This was tantamount to treason, and as civil war began to look inevitable both sides spent the following winter preparing for it. The committee of estates, which was dominated by adherents of the Covenant, commissioned sympathetic noblemen like the earls of Cassilis and Glencairn, and lord Kirkcudbright, to raise regiments and encouraged younger members of the baronage to enlist as junior officers. Among them was James Dalrymple, the future viscount Stair, who became a captain in Glencairn's regiment. Support from the gentry in the south-west was crucial as an invasion from Ireland was imminently expected, and that these fears were well-founded is evident from a letter Charles received at this time advising him about the possibility of landing 'flat-bottomed boats from Ireland' at Loch Ryan and Kirkcudbright.[18]

In fact, Charles decided to launch the invasion on the coast of Argyllshire instead, but when the covenanters heard of this they forestalled him by capturing the key fortress of Dunbarton. As this effectively nullified his plans for an attack on the west coast, his hopes were now pinned on the other arms of his strategy. These involved sending the fleet under Hamilton with a force of 5,000 men to Aberdeen to link up with his supporter, the marquis of Huntly, while he himself would lead the main army across the Border. They both failed dismally. Only one of Hamilton's ships managed to land at Aberdeen, and though the town was taken it was recaptured shortly afterwards by the covenanters under the earl of Montrose, who had successfully decoyed Huntly to Edinburgh.[19] Charles was equally unsuccessful, because no sooner had his army crossed the Tweed than it encountered the main covenanting army under the veteran Alexander Leslie at nearby Duns Law. Consequently, he was forced to withdraw and a truce was declared, with both sides agreeing to disband their armies, while Charles undertook to summon parliament and a general assembly.

When the assembly met in August 1639 its members were in defiant mood. All the Acts of the previous assembly were confirmed, episcopacy was condemned, and the office of bishop was declared contrary to the law of God.[20] Moreover, it insisted that every individual should be compelled to subscribe to the Covenant under pain of civil penalty, which meant that instead of being a bond of defence it became an instrument of oppression. It also stipulated that the principal academic appointments within the Church would henceforth be monopolised by adherents of the Covenant. Among them was Samuel Rutherford who was appointed principal of St Mary's College at St Andrews, and during his time there he wrote a number of controversial works, the best known being his *Lex Rex, a Plea for the Peoples' Rights* which was subsequently banned by the Restoration régime. However, when parliament, which was now controlled by the covenanters, endorsed the assembly's Acts, the king refused to give his assent,[21] and this led to a renewed outbreak of war.

Anticipating this, the covenanters had not only forborne to disband their army but instead they appointed local war committees for the purpose of enlisting recruits. As they had no legal powers to conscript they had to rely on exhorting the gentry and coercing the peasantry. Therefore, a summons was issued declaring that 'barrones and gentilmen of good soirt are the greatest and maist pouerful pairt of the kingdome, by quas valure the kingdom hath evir been defendit' and urged them to 'come to the armie in their own persones . . . and considder that now or never is the tyme to gaine honour and eternal reputatioun, and to saive or lose thair countrie'.[22] The peasantry, on the other hand, were compelled to volunteer under threat of reprisals against those attempting to evade the draft. A quota was imposed on each committee, the one for Kirkcudbright being instructed to contribute eighty horsemen. At its first meeting, which was held at Cullenoch (Laurieston) on 27 June 1640, it resolved that its contribution should be raised on a parish basis, and that 'ilk horseman have for arms at the leist ane steill cape and sworde, ane paire of pistolles, and ane lance'.[23]

Money was raised from men of substance, who were individually summoned to appear before the committees to give a declaration of their means on oath as a basis for assessing their contributions. At the same time, the committees were authorised to 'plunder ony persone that shall happen no to mak thankful payment of the sogers' pay'.[24] All 'silverworke and goldworke' belonging 'as weill [to] noblemen, barrones and burgesses as utheris of whatsumevir degrie or qualitie they be'[25] was to be handed over to them to be melted down into coin for paying the troops, and the minute book of the war committee for Kirkcudbright lists in comprehensive detail the articles delivered up to them.

Charles was also making preparations, and he instructed his supporter, the earl of Nithsdale, to garrison the castles of Caerlaverock and Threave against possible attack. However, when news of this reached the local war committee it pre-empted him by sending a force under Colonel Hume to besiege the castles. Threave held out for thirteen weeks until, bowing to the inevitable, Charles wrote to Nithsdale authorising him to surrender. As soon as it was delivered up, the committee of estates ordered the local war committee to dismantle it. Therefore, the latter issued a warrant directing that 'the sklate roof of the hows [house] and battlement thairof be taken downe, with the lofting thairof, dores and windows of the samen, and to stop the vault of the said hows'.[26] Sir John McGhie of Balmaghie, a local landowner, was instructed to supervise the work, but its massive construction defied all the efforts of the demolishers, and so this stronghold still remains a prominent feature of the surrounding countryside.

War broke out in August 1640, when Montrose invaded England at the head of a covenanting army, and defeating a royalist army at Newburn on Tyne he occupied Newcastle. Charles was forced to agree to a truce, and in terms of the treaty of Ripon, which was concluded in June 1641, the covenanters were permitted to occupy the six northern counties of England in return for a payment of £850 a day, while Charles undertook to ratify all the Acts of the previous parliament. This put the covenanters in a commanding position, and they proceeded to entrench their authority by systematically purging the assembly of all non-covenanting clergy. Thus the revolution was complete, and the covenanters now set their sights on exporting it to England and Ireland.

Nevertheless, a minority took the view that as the object of the revolt had been achieved, there was nothing to be gained by pursuing it for its own sake. They included Montrose, but when he publicly declared for the king his former colleagues committed him to prison. When Charles came to Scotland in August 1641 he attempted to placate the leading covenanters with gifts of honours and titles, to the exclusion of his friends, for whom he did nothing except to secure Montrose's release. However, when news reached him that the Roman Catholics in Ireland had rebelled and were inflicting a series of atrocities on the local Protestant population, he was forced to cut short his visit and hurry back to London.

THE SOLEMN LEAGUE

Meanwhile events in England were moving towards a crisis, and on 22 August 1642 Charles raised his standard at Nottingham and called on his loyal subjects to come to his aid against the parliamentarians. This marked the outbreak of civil war between king and parliament, and both sides now attempted to solicit the support of the Scottish privy council and the general assembly. The parliamentarians made their pitch to the assembly on the basis of their common commitment to presbytery, while gilding it with an invitation to attend an assembly of Protestant representatives from Europe, which was to be convened at Westminster for the purpose of achieving uniformity of doctrine, government and worship. This was enough to win over the assembly, but not the privy council, who voted by a majority of one against taking sides against the king in a foreign war. However, under pressure from the assembly, they reversed their decision and reluctantly agreed to follow suit.

A convention of the estates was summoned without the king's authority, and offers of help were sent to the parliamentarians. This came at an opportune moment, as the war was going badly for them and they were in desperate need of reinforcements. So they sent commissioners to the general assembly to negotiate an alliance and obtain military assistance. However, the assembly was divided, and while a moderate element was opposed to the idea, the majority saw this as a golden opportunity to export their brand of presbyterianism, and hence their revolution, to England. Also, they hoped it would give them the means to influence the Westminster Assembly which was now in session, in order, as they saw it, to achieve 'nearer agreement with the Church of Scotland and other reformed churches abroad'.

Consequently, the general assembly drew up the document known as the Solemn League and Covenant for approval by the English parliamentarians. Its specific aims were to reform the religion in England and Ireland in doctrine, worship, discipline and government 'according to the Word of God and the example of the best reformed Churches', the assimilation of the Churches in the three countries, 'the extirpation of popery and prelacy', and 'the firm peace and union' of England and Scotland.[27] Representatives consisting mainly of extremists like Johnston of Wariston and Samuel Rutherford, the former minister of Anwoth, were appointed to attend the Westminster Assembly. Rutherford in particular seems to have impressed his fellow divines, since he was described as 'a fair little man' and eulogised as 'the flower of the Church' and 'the saint of the Covenant', though as his biographer put it 'he combined a personal piety with a warmth of language which was sometimes hardly compatible with decency'.[28] Interestingly, considering his future role as a leading opponent of the extremist covenanters, they included lord Maitland, the future earl of Lauderdale.

As acceptance of the Solemn League and Covenant was the price of military assistance, the English parliamentarians had no alternative but to go along with it, but they never paid it more than lip service. In Scotland, on the other hand, all opposition to it was suppressed, and copies were ordered to be circulated throughout every burgh and parish for mass signature, those refusing to do so being liable to confiscation of their goods. Thus the choice lay between subscribing to this instrument of oppression or facing the prospect of beggary.[29] Notwithstanding, some moderates stuck to their principles and refused to do so, one being John Glendonyng of Parton who in consequence forfeited his estate, though it was subsequently purchased by a relative and restored to him.[30] The moderates now formally disassociated themselves from the main body of the covenanters and joined Montrose. However, their former colleagues regarded them as heretics – counter revolutionaries in fact, branding them 'malignants', and thereafter the divisions between these factions continued to widen and their mutual rancour grew as the main body of the covenanters veered ever further towards intolerance and tyranny.

Once the war began to go their way, the parliamentarians quietly abandoned the Solemn League, but this was not before they had obtained permission to establish a series of staging posts on the route between Carlisle and Portpatrick for the purpose of maintaining contact with their army in Ireland. There were four of these in Galloway. Going westwards from Dumfries, the first covered the section as far as 'Steps of Or' (Haugh of Urr), while the next was responsible for the stretch as far as the Fleet. Another one at 'Pethous' (near Blackcraig) supervised the section traversing the high ground across Glenquicken moor as far as the Cree, while the fourth covered the final stretch as far as Portpatrick. At each staging post an official, generally 'an innkeeper of approved honesty', was given responsibility for ensuring the safe transmission of the dispatches along his particular section of the route.[31]

The Westminster Assembly continued to sit until 1645, and the Scottish representatives achieved their ambition by exercising an influence over its proceedings which was quite disproportionate to their number. After considerable debate, a Directory of the Public Worship of God was drawn up to replace the Book of Common Prayer, and this was followed by a Confession of Faith and two Catechisms, a Shorter and a Larger version. These were approved by the general assembly, and all parish ministers throughout the country were ordered to use them. Consequently, the Westminster Confession of Faith, as it is known, became one of the tenets of the covenanters and has remained the official standard of the Church of Scotland ever since.

MONTROSE'S CAMPAIGN

In January 1644, Alexander Leslie, now earl of Leven, was instructed to lead an army of 20,000 men into England to reinforce the parliamentarians. Meanwhile, Charles appointed Montrose lieutenant-general of his forces in

Scotland, and having equipped him with a 1,000-strong force consisting mainly of Englishmen, he ordered him to march across the Border against the covenanters. They were particularly strong in southern Scotland, so when Montrose encountered a force at Dumfries he was forced to withdraw to Carlisle.[32] Worse still, he was now left virtually stranded, because Charles's plans to send him English reinforcements were negated by the parliamentarians' victory at Marston Moor. Similarly, Huntly had been expected to deliver the north-east into royalist hands, but when he was defeated by the marquis of Argyll that strategically important region fell into the hands of the covenanters. Therefore, Montrose's one remaining hope was to link up with an Irish force which had landed in the west of Scotland, and it was only by slipping through covenanting-held territory dressed in disguise and accompanied by a few companions that he managed to do so.

His first major success came with the defeat of a covenanting force at Tippermuir in September 1644. This was the prelude to a series of brilliant tactical victories, in the course of which he defeated all the covenanting armies, but when in September 1645 he continued his advance into southern Scotland his Highland troops began to melt away. The covenanters, on the other hand, had been steadily attracting recruits, and a second regiment was raised from Kirkcudbrightshire under the fourth viscount Kenmure.[33] Therefore, when later that month a covenanting army under the earl of Leven encountered the remnants of Montrose's army at Philiphaugh near Selkirk, it scored an overwhelming victory. In the sanguinary aftermath the triumphalist covenanters, goaded by their chaplains into believing it was the will of their old testament God, ran amok and butchered their prisoners – including the women and children who had followed Montrose's army – to the bloodthirsty yells of 'Jesus and no quarter'. More exalted prisoners, like Sir Robert Spottiswoode, the former lord president, were spared in order to undergo the formality of a 'show' trial before a pre-determined sentence of execution was passed on them, although Montrose himself managed to escape.

A KING AT BAY

Charles was now in dire straits. His campaign in Scotland had ended in disaster and he was beleaguered by the English parliamentarians in Oxford; but, optimistic as ever, he hoped that by playing on the growing disenchantment of the Scots with their English allies he could win them over to his side. Therefore, in May 1646 he managed to slip out of Oxford and surrendered to the Scots army at Newark. When the troops withdrew to besiege Newcastle they took Charles with them, but his adamant refusal to subscribe to the Solemn League and Covenant put them in a quandary.

The general assembly had forbidden him to set foot in Scotland unless he did so, and in any case they feared his presence there would pose a threat to their régime. Yet they were reluctant to hand him over to the parliamentarians for fear it would put his life at risk. Nevertheless this was the course they decided on, encouraged by the payment of arrears of expenses due to them under the treaty of Ripon. So Charles was handed over to the parliamentary commissioners who arrived inopportunely while their prospective captive was enjoying a game of golf with the earl of Leven.[34]

The siege of Newcastle had disastrous consequences for the Scots, as their troops became infected by the plague which had broken out among the garrison, and when they brought it back home with them it spread with a virulence which far exceeded the previous outbreaks in 1637 and 1644. This affected the south-west as well, and the burgh council of Kirkcudbright was compelled to issue draconian measures in order to protect the community. Indwellers were forbidden to travel beyond the Urr 'because the pest was in Dumfries', and the town gates were closed against all itinerants such as beggars and gypsies, as well as the inhabitants of the neighbouring parishes of Tongland and Kelton.

Meanwhile events in England were taking a sinister turn, and it began to look as though the covenanters' fears might be realised. Having won the war the parliamentarians decided to scale down the army, but as the troops were owed substantial arrears of pay they refused to disband, and because parliament declined to consider their grievances the disgruntled soldiery turned instead to their generals, Cromwell, Ireton and Fairfax. Unlike the parliamentarians, who were prepared to accept a monarchy with limited powers, these men were hardline republicans, so when they succeeded in kidnapping the king and threatened to put him on trial his prospects began to look distinctly ominous. This caused the Scottish committee of estates, who were more sympathetic than the extremist-dominated general assembly, to send commissioners to visit him at Carisbrooke castle on the Isle of Wight for the purpose of negotiating a settlement. The outcome was an engagement, concluded in December 1647, in terms of which Charles made a number of far-reaching concessions, including an undertaking to ratify the Solemn League and Covenant.[35]

ECCLESIASTICAL DESPOTISM

The engagement proved highly controversial, and it led to a split within the covenanting movement between the moderates – or the engagers, as they were known – and the extremists who were implacably opposed to it. Moreover, it drove a wedge between the extremist-dominated general assembly and the committee of estates, where the moderately-inclined nobility were in control. Under pressure from the extremists – or the protesters, as they now called themselves – the general assembly ordered every parish minister to preach against it, and defying the committee of estates, it issued a call to arms. A number of ministers in the south-west responded by raising an army of some 2,000 'slashing communicants of Mauchline', as they styled themselves, who mustered on the moor above that town in readiness to march on Edinburgh. When news of this reached the committee of estates they dispatched a force under General Middleton, who put them to flight before they had even set out on their march. This success encouraged the committee of estates to attempt to consolidate its supremacy over the general assembly, so it raised an army of some 20,000 men and dispatched it under the command of Hamilton, now a duke, to the aid of the English royalists.

This proved a disastrous venture. Hamilton was no general; the army was poorly disciplined and he was constantly distracted by conflicting advice from his subordinates, so when they encountered the English army under Cromwell at Preston they suffered a shattering defeat. This gave the protesters new heart; the slashing communicants reassembled and, along with a horde of covenanters, they converged on Edinburgh in what became known as the 'Whiggamores' Raid'. This so alarmed the engagers, whose morale was already shaken by the defeat at Preston, that they fled the city, abandoning control of the committee of estates to the protesters.

Political power now passed to the extremist Argyll and his colleagues, but their lack of popular support meant they had no alternative but to appeal to Cromwell to help shore up their régime. As events would prove, this was tantamount to supping with the Devil, and it was certainly an unlikely alliance considering that the only common ground between them was their mutual detestation of the engagers. Cromwell agreed to help, but he demanded that the protesters purify their revolution by purging the Church of all heretical elements. With the backing of the committee of estates, the general assembly dutifully complied by ejecting from their charges not only those ministers in any way tainted – or even suspected of being tainted – with support for the engagement, but also those who either refused or omitted to preach against it.

When Cromwell reached Edinburgh on 4 October he demanded that the purge be extended to the civil administration as well, and at his insistence the committee of estates passed the notorious Act of the Classes in January 1649.[36] This was aimed specifically at 'the cheff actoris and pryme promotters of the horrid rebellioun of James Grahame [Montrose]', as well as those who were active in the 'unlaufull engagement', and others 'censured for malignancie'. Not only were they banned from holding any public office at national and local level, but so too was anyone suspected of having deviated from the strictest interpretation of the Solemn League and Covenant. It was also tainted with a bias against the nobility, since they were regarded as being generally sympathetic towards the engagement, and reflecting this the Act abolished lay patronage. The army was also purged, and local committees, such as the military association of the western shires, which included Kirkcudbright and Wigtown, were set up for the purpose of eradicating 'all Engagers, Malignants and other backsliders'.[37] The effect this had on its military capability soon became disastrously apparent.

These measures resulted in the establishment of a clerical oligarchy, but, as so many natural leaders had been purged, the positions of power were now filled by second-raters who were as notorious for their extremism as their incompetence. So too were ministerial charges, and it was the upstart clerics who replaced the ejected ministers that provoked the odium of the nobles and lairds in particular. As Sir Ewen Cameron observed: 'every parish had a tyrant who made the greatest Lord in the district stoop to his authority. The kirk was the place where he kept his court; the pulpit his throne or tribunal from where he issued out his terrible decrees; and twelve or fourteen soure, ignorant enthusiasts, under the title of elders, composed his councill'. Thus was the dictatorship of the extremist covenanters consolidated, but it was to prove transient, because it was to be overthrown two years later and ultimately replaced by a far more effective one under the commonwealth.

NOTES

1. *RPC*, sec ser i, 352.
2. The implications are discussed in Donaldson, *James V to James VII*, 296 and Lynch, *Scotland: A New History*, 266–7.
3. *RPC*, sec. ser. i, 510–2.
4. Agnew i, 456–6.
5. *Ibid.*, 466–7.
6. Confirmed by the parliament of 1633 (*APS* v, 27).
7. *APS* v, 21. I am grateful to Dr Oram for pointing this out to me.
8. Donaldson, *James V to James VII*, 302.
9. *RMS* viii no 2163.
10. *Ibid.* no 524 .
11. Stephen, *Church History* ii, 253.
12. *Ibid.*, 257.
13. *Ibid.*
14. On the other hand, when Bishop Sydserf was subsequently excommunicated by the general assembly, Robert Burnet of Crimond, the father of Gilbert Burnet the historian, complained about this unprecedently 'unjust sentence', and in a letter to his brother-in-law, Johnston of Wariston, he remarked 'I have known him these twenty-nine years, and I have never known any wickedness or unconscientious dealing in him' (Stephen ii, 277).
15. He was an extreme presbyterian whom subsequent writers, taking their cue from the Church of Scotland, have elevated to a position of importance in the

annals of Galloway. Nevertheless, he was an exceptionally gifted scholar, as well as being a notably conscientious pastor, and for many years after his ejection from Anwoth in 1636 he maintained a voluminous correspondence on religious matters with a number of local people.

16. *Nat. MSS Scot*, iii, no. xcvii.
17. *Life of Livingstone* (Wodrow Society) i, 156–60.
18. Agnew ii, 15.
19. Donaldson, *James V to James VII*, 323.
20. *Ibid.*, 324.
21. *Ibid.*
22. Minute Book kept by the War Committee of the Covenanters in the Stewartry of Kirkcudbright in the years 1640 and 1641, (Kirkcudbright, 1855), 50–1.
23. *Ibid.*, 2.
24. *Ibid.*, 24.
25. *Ibid.*, 21–2.
26. *Ibid.*, 66–7.
27. *APS* vi, pt. i, 41.
28. Stephen, *Church History* ii, 297.
29. *Ibid.*, 297.
30. McKerlie v, 37.
31. These staging posts are referred to by Anderson in 'The development of the road system', 205.
32. *Hewison* i, 404.
33. Agnew ii, 28.
34. *Hewison* i, 441.
35. *Scot. Hist. Docs.*, 214–8.
36. *APS* vi, pt. ii, 143–7.
37. Stevenson, *Revolution and Counter Revolution*, 125.

23

THE COMMONWEALTH

THE ENGLISH CONQUEST

In 1648 Cromwell, supported by a triumphant, radicalised, new model army, established himself as dictator in England, and on 30 January 1649 he staged the ultimate coup by executing Charles I. This appalled Scots of all shades of religious persuasion, for they still retained a deep-seated loyalty to a dynasty which had ruled their country for nearly three hundred years. Even the protesters disapproved, and it was a measure of their concern for Charles's plight that they sent a delegation (which included William Glendinning, the minister of Kirkcudbright) to London on a vain mission to plead for his life. Putting the king to death had never been part of their agenda, since all they wanted was to coerce him into subscribing the Solemn League and Covenant and accepting the whole paraphernalia of presbytery, including the Westminster Confession of Faith.

In token of their condemnation, the committee of estates tacitly repudiated their alliance with Cromwell and his regicides by proclaiming the prince of Wales king as Charles II. Nevertheless, it was impressed upon him that his crowning would be conditional on his clear and unambiguous acceptance of presbytery. Charles demurred, not so much from scruple but because Montrose was campaigning for the royalist cause in the north, and if he were successful the conditions would automatically lapse. This was not to be, as Montrose was routed at Carbisdale and handed over to his former colleagues. They took him to Edinburgh where he was subjected to a mock trial before sentence of death was passed and, paraded in a cart through the city streets when his bearing inspired the sympathy of the crowd, he was taken to the gallows where he was ceremonially hanged.

Charles now had no alternative but to meet the protesters' demands, and salving a conscience which he would seldom allow to interfere with political expediency he duly subscribed the Covenant, the Solemn League and the Westminster Confession of Faith.[1] Notwithstanding this, the protesters demanded that he sign a humiliating declaration denouncing his parents, and at the same time they subjected him to a series of such insultingly personal harangues touching on his private life as to colour forever his attitude towards them. This was primarily accountable for the ruthlessness which this essentially tolerant man would display towards the extremist covenanters in the future.

The presence of a king in Scotland, and the threat it posed to his political settlement in England, were quite unacceptable to Cromwell; besides, he and his supporters had no brief for presbytery, which they saw as a threat to their own religious establishment. So, in July 1650, he led an army across the Tweed with the intention of driving out the king and overthrowing the protesters' régime. The committee of estates sent an army under David Leslie to oppose him, but the purge had left it so debilitated that, in spite of his numerical inferiority, Cromwell inflicted a crushing defeat on it two months later at the battle of Dunbar. Shortly afterwards he arrived in Edinburgh, but, whereas two years before he had been welcomed as a deliverer, this time he came as an aspiring conqueror.

Their humiliation at Dunbar caused a split among the protesters between the realists, who considered the purge had gone too far, and the fanatics, who saw it as divine retribution for doctrinal impurity within the army. This view was shared by the covenanters in the south-west, where the local military association was reconstituted for the avowed purpose of opposing the 'malignant' Scots, as well as the 'sectarian' English. The revived association was now ordered to raise an army – the 'holy' army, as it came to be known to underscore its doctrinal purity – and this was placed under the command of Colonel Gilbert Kerr. To emphasise their commitment to religious extremism, the covenanters of the south-west also drew up a document known as the Western Remonstrance. Contending that the Act of Classes had not been properly enforced, this declared that the 'holy' army would not fight for Charles 'until he had given satisfactory evidence of sincere repentance and of honest intention to abandon the company of malignants'.[2]

Even the protesters considered this was too extreme, and after a heated debate the Remonstrance was denounced by the committee of estates and the general assembly.[3] Consequently its supporters – or the 'remonstrants', as they called themselves – split off from the main body of the protesters to form an extremist group. However, the ground was cut from under their feet when the 'holy' army was routed by an English force under Major-General Lambert at Hamilton.[4] It was now abundantly clear that the Act of the Classes was impractical and the restrictions would have to be relaxed if an effective fighting force was to be raised. Therefore, the general assembly passed by a majority vote the 'first public resolution' which allowed anyone who was not 'excommunicated, forfeited, notoriously wicked or an obstinate enemy of the Covenant', and who appeared in church as a penitent dressed in sackcloth, to enlist.[5] Nevertheless, the minority refused to accept the decision, branding its proponents 'resolutioners', but their fulminations were in vain, because the Act of the Classes was finally repealed in June 1651.

Charles was crowned at Scone on 1 January 1651, the ceremony being performed by the extremist leader Argyll. But it was an empty title since Cromwell's army was in control of the south-east and ready to advance across the Forth, while General Lambert's army was in occupation of the south-west, with his headquarters at Dumfries. So Charles's authority was confined to the north, and even that was precarious. This remained the situation for the next eight months, because Cromwell's advance was delayed on account of his recurrent bouts of illness, so it was not until August that he finally captured Perth. Charles now gambled everything on marching the bulk of his army into England with the intention of drawing Cromwell away from Scotland.[6] In the short term this was successful, in that Cromwell was lured into following him there, leaving General Monck in charge of the campaign in Scotland. In the end it proved a fatal misjudgement, for when Cromwell eventually caught up with Charles at Worcester he cut his army to pieces, and Charles was lucky to escape with his life to France. But even that proved unsafe, because three years later, following a rapprochement between the English and French, he was compelled to move to Holland.

UNION WITH ENGLAND

Meanwhile Monck had taken Stirling on 14 August, and with its surrender the Scottish public records fell into English hands, and it was only by spiriting away the regalia and burying them under the church floor at Kinneff in Kincardineshire that they were saved for the nation. In the following month he arrested the members of the committee of estates who had taken refuge at Alyth in Perthshire, and with their capture and the destruction of their army at Worcester in the previous week Scotland's political and military independence was destroyed. Pockets of resistance still remained in the Highlands, but by October these had been wiped out and the conquest of Scotland was complete. Cromwell was now in a position to proceed with his plans to merge the country into a single commonwealth with England and Ireland, and as an interim measure commissioners were appointed to govern Scotland.

On 4 February 1652 a Tender of Union was proclaimed to the accompaniment of a fanfare of trumpets at the Mercat Cross in Edinburgh. Generally speaking it was a moderate, statesmanlike and practical document whose terms were designed to serve as a blueprint for the future government of Scotland. Parliament was to be dissolved, though the fabric of local government would be retained, while the monarchy was to be abolished and the crown's patrimony confiscated in order to compensate for the damage caused during the campaigns which culminated in the defeats at Preston and Worcester. There was nevertheless a bias against the nobility and gentry, since they were perceived as 'the chief Actors in these invasions', while those who took part in them forfeited their estates.[7] On the other hand, their tenants and vassals were pardoned and allowed to remain in occupation of their holdings provided they acknowledged the commonwealth.[8]

As toleration was the keynote as far as religious matters were concerned, it was proposed that those ministers 'of pious life' who were 'well affected to Parliament' and 'most fitted to preach the gospel and instruct the people' should be licensed to do so.[9] Since this indulgence extended to episcopal ministers, it provoked a storm of protest from covenanters of all shades – malignants, resolutioners, protesters and remonstrants – as they were at one in their conviction that only those who were pure in doctrine should be entitled to preach. It even caused the resolutioners to make overtures to the protesters in an effort to sink their differences and present a united front against the Tender, but they were rejected out of hand and relations between them continued to deteriorate. Matters came to a head at the general assembly later that year when twenty protesting ministers, including Samuel Rutherford, withdrew to set up their own assembly, and thereafter they continued to challenge one another's authority.

Meanwhile, all burghs and shires were required to elect representatives to attend a meeting with the commissioners at Dalkeith castle on 12 February, where the terms of the Tender would be explained to them. Most complied, but some refused to do so, and oddly enough Kirkcudbrightshire and Wigtownshire seem to have adopted opposing stances. Whereas the former was among the three counties which lodged a formal dissent to the Tender, the latter[10] evidently signed up without demur, merely asking that 'ye protestant religion as it is preferred in Scotland in Doctrine Worshipp and Discipline bee in noe sort Innovated or altered'.[11] Once the terms of the Union had been read out to them, the representatives were required to sign it as evidence that the 'happy union' reflected the popular will. Although seventy-three out of the eighty-nine present did so,[12] this was certainly not representative of the country as a whole, as there was widespread opposition to it. Notwithstanding this the commissioners proceeded to implement their proposals, and in August twenty-one deputies, including Sir James McDowell of Garthland[13] who represented Galloway, attended parliament at Westminster as the Scottish representatives.

However, it would be some years before Scotland was fully incorporated into the commonwealth, because Cromwell's quarrels with successive English parliaments meant the union did not receive legislative sanction until 1657. Meantime, Scotland continued to be governed by the commissioners on an interim basis, and on the whole their rule was both fair and moderate. The diarist, John Nicoll, was particularly complimentary about the impartiality of those appointed to supervise the administration of justice. 'To speak treuth', he wrote, 'the Englisches wer moir indulgent and merciful to the Scottis nor [than] wes the Scottis to their awin cuntriemen and nychtbouris', adding that 'they also filled up the roumes of justice courtes with very honest clerkis and memberis of that judicatory'.[14]

THE GLENCAIRN RISING

After his arrival in Holland Charles set up an embryonic and penurious court at Middleburg. This became a haven for royalist refugees who fed him reports of the disturbances which had broken out in the Highlands during the early months of 1653, though their accounts of the strength of the opposition to the commonwealth proved wildly exaggerated. Nevertheless, taking them at their face value, Charles sent the earl of Glencairn to Scotland to rally the dissidents, and the subsequent campaign became known as the Glencairn rising.

Landing on the West Highland coast later that year, Glencairn was joined by a number of local chiefs, and with their help he raised a force of some 5,000 men. A number of lowland lairds also came out in his support, among them being the fourth viscount Kenmure, who contributed a force of 100 local horsemen. Clearly a man in the image of his turbulent Gordon forbears, he was renowned for using as his standard 'a rundlet of strong waters'. In plain terms, this was a barrel of brandy which was popularly known as 'Kenmore's drum', though his habit of broaching the contents too freely was to lead to an irreparable breach with his commander, General Middleton. Initially, Charles's supporters focused their efforts on extorting men, money and supplies from the local population, but by autumn they were conducting a series of lightning raids on the south, in the course of which they penetrated as far as Galloway.[15] Colonel Lilburne, the acting commander-in-chief, responded by ordering the formation of an armed guard of twenty-four men to apprehend 'all Moss Troopers, Tories, or other disturbers of the public peace' there,[16] and later he authorised the local gentry to raise armed bands from among their tenantry as a local defence force.

It soon became evident that perpetrating a series of spoiling raids on the south was not going to achieve anything, and that a more experienced general was needed if the campaign was to stand any chance of success. So, in early 1654, Charles sent General Middleton to take over command. A tough, hard-drinking ex-ranker who had started out as a pikeman in the covenanting army, Middleton was essentially a man of the sword, and, as diplomacy was clearly not his strong suit, he soon fell out with Glencairn. Nevertheless, it was a tribute to his energy and ability that he turned the rising into a serious threat to the commonwealth régime in Scotland, and by the end of March it had spread to Dumfries and Galloway.[17] This seems somewhat surprising (and Lilburne admitted as much in his dispatches to Cromwell), since it was a stronghold of the anti-royalist protesters, and one can only conclude that it was a measure of the strength of the local opposition to the commonwealth.

Lilburne had been placed in temporary charge of the English army in Scotland while Monck was conducting the Anglo-Dutch war, but once peace was declared the latter returned to resume command. He immediately went on the offensive against Charles's supporters, whose campaign was already faltering as a result of disputes between its leaders – a state of affairs which caused Charles to complain that he 'could never hope to prevail against enemies so united with friends who cannot agree among themselves'.[18] Throughout the summer of 1654 Monck scored a number of tactical successes, steadily wearing down the royalists' resistance, so that by the end of September most of their leaders had submitted. However, news of Penruddock's rebellion in south-west England in early 1655 gave them new heart and, as Monck reported, it caused the Scots to 'prick upp theire eares, and have thoughts of riseing againe', adding that 'a party of twenty-four Tories' had been formed in Galloway.[19] A few months later Penruddock's rebellion was crushed, and with it further resistance in Scotland came to an end.

Monck was statesman enough to realise that punitive reprisals could be counter productive, so his surrender terms were on the whole lenient. These were incorporated in the Act of Pardon and Grace, which stipulated that if the participants laid down their arms and gave bonds for their future good behaviour they would be granted an amnesty. Harsher treatment was reserved for the principal actors, and while some incurred swingeing fines others had their estates forfeited. Kenmure was deprived of his, while the earl of Galloway was heavily fined, and McDowell of Freuch had his house burnt down,[20] he himself being consigned to imprisonment in England. In many cases, fines were tantamount to forfeiture because the victims had to borrow money on the security of their estates to pay them, and if unable to repay they were forced into sequestration. However the government, concerned as ever to dilute the landowning class, introduced a measure which allowed – or rather compelled – lenders to accept land instead of money in satisfaction of their debts.

THE COMMONWEALTH

An Ordinance of Union had already been published in April 1654. This declared the merging of Scotland with England and Ireland to form a single commonwealth which would be administered by a centralised parliament consisting of 430 seats at Westminster. These were distributed between the three countries according to their respective contributions towards the total revenue of the commonwealth. Therefore, reflecting its comparative poverty, Scotland was allotted thirty seats; twenty representing the shires and ten the burghs. Galloway formed one constituency, the sitting member being McDowell of Garthland, while another seat represented the principal burghs in Dumfries and Galloway. This was held by Major Jeremiah Tollhurst, one of the English officers to whom half the Scottish seats were allotted.

The reprisals taken against the magnates and other landowners following the collapse of the Glencairn rising were symptomatic of the commonwealth's discrimination against their class in general, since they were perceived as sympathetic to Charles and therefore a potentially disruptive force. So, in order to reduce their capacity for causing further trouble, a measure was passed abolishing tenure by military service, whereby vassals and tenants could be called out to fight for them. Other relics of a past age disappeared too, such as the feudal casualties of ward and relief, while the barons' courts were suppressed by an ordinance of 1654.

Similarly, hereditary jurisdictions were abolished, and Sir Patrick Agnew was suspended from office as sheriff of Wigtown, as was his opposite number, the third lord Kirkcudbright, both being replaced by Colonel Matthew Alured, who now became sheriff of Galloway. His commission gave him full powers to 'hold Sheriff Courts for doing of Justice to those who are inhabitants of the late Stewartry within the tolbooth of the Burgh of Kirkcudbright . . . and to the whole remnant of the Shire of Galloway within the tolbooth of our Burgh of Wigtoun and other places where they used to sit'. He was later recalled in 1656 when, in conformity with a change of policy which involved appointing Scotsmen to positions of authority, both Agnew and lord Kirkcudbright were reinstated.[21]

The appointment of serving officers to represent half the Scottish seats in the new parliament reflected the military character of the commonwealth régime. It was strict in that the country was heavily policed by the occupying army, which was never less than 10,000 strong, while personal liberties were severely curtailed. For example, there was a restriction on the use of firearms, and permits were needed to travel from one part of the country to another. On the other hand, the régime was not gratuitously oppressive, because the troops were under strict discipline and the records of the courts martial show that crimes like robbery and horse-stealing were severely dealt with, and so too was the delicately-termed offence of 'illicit relations with Scottish women' – in plain terms rape. The result was that by 1655 it was boasted – perhaps with slight exaggeration – that 'a man may ride all Scotland over with a switch in his hand and £100 in his pocket which he could not have done these five hundred years'.[22]

The fundamental weakness of the régime was the cost of maintaining the whole apparatus of military occupation and civil administration. Initially this was assessed at a monthly total of £10,000, which was an enormous imposition for a poverty-stricken country like Scotland, and predictably the target was never met. At the same time, the method of apportioning this among freeholders, which was done in rough-and-ready fashion with the co-operation of local presbyteries and kirk sessions,[23] could result in flagrant injustices. Eventually the commissioners introduced a more efficient and equitable method of tax collection by levying assessments on the burghs and shires. Thus Kirkcudbrightshire and Wigtownshire were required to contribute £377 15s 6d between them, while the proportion levied on the local burghs ranged from £12 and £10 10s for Kirkcudbright and Wigtown respectively, to 15s for New Galloway.

Each burgh and shire was required to draw up a Roll of Heritors in order to determine the contribution from each individual, and the roll for Wigtownshire, which still survives,[24] casts an interesting light on the structure of contemporary landownership there. These assessments were later scaled down in line with the reduction of the monthly levy to £6,000, following the withdrawal of part of the occupying army. However, this did not come into effect until 1657, and even then it was only grudgingly conceded, at Monck's repeated insistence, that it placed an intolerable burden on the country's economy.

The appointment of a ruling council under the thirty-four-year-old lord Broghill to take over the civil administration of the country in September 1655 marked a change of policy. Although the army was still retained, with its network of spies and informers, its role was reduced to a peacekeeping force and the new régime tried to achieve more general public acceptance by involving Scotsmen in the administration of their country. As this required the support and co-operation of the nobility and lesser magnates, the discriminatory attitude towards them was abandoned. An example of this was the introduction of a rule which forbade the army from quartering its troops on 'gentlemen's houses', those disobeying the order being severely reprimanded.[25] At the same time, the restrictions on firearms were lifted to the extent that the gentry were allowed to keep them for purposes of maintaining law and order within the bounds of their estates. In some cases, compositions were agreed over the unpaid fines levied on those who had taken part in the Glencairn rising.

THE CHURCH IN CONFLICT

After the protesting ministers withdrew from the general assembly in 1652, they appealed to the commonwealth government for support on the grounds of their common hatred of 'Charles Stuart styled king'.[26] The resolutioner-controlled general assembly countered by threatening them with excommunication, and so the bickering continued. Finally, Cromwell decided to suppress a body which had degenerated from a spiritual court into a political conclave, and was becoming a threat to civil and religious liberty alike. Therefore, when the general assembly convened at Edinburgh in July 1653, a detachment of cavalry and musketeers was ordered to surround the church where they sat in session. A body of troops forced their way inside, and the commanding officer interrupted the proceedings to order the members to leave the building. Their furious protests at this unheard-of treatment were quickly muted when loaded guns were turned on them, and one by one they were herded out into the street and escorted to the Bruntsfield links on the edge of the town. There the colonel took a note of their names, forbidding them ever to reassemble on pain of death,[27] and thirty-seven years would pass before the assembly met again.

The emasculation of the Church, and the fact that it no longer posed a threat to the commonwealth régime, meant that Monck could eventually afford to relax the restrictions imposed on it. Although the ban on general assemblies remained in force, presbyteries and synods were allowed to reconvene once more, and one of the first to do so was the protester-dominated synod of Galloway.

When lord Broghill took over the civil administration he tried to secure the co-operation of both sides in order to establish an ecclesiastical polity. As the protesters had consistently supported the commonwealth during the Glencairn rising, in contrast to the resolutioners who had ordered prayers to be said for 'Charles Stuart', it was natural that he should turn to them in the first instance. But they were so divided that when a possible solution was finally hammered out the extremists, under Wariston, fearing it would compromise their principles, vetoed it. In fact, it was doomed in any case because the resolutioners had already intimated that it was unacceptable to them, but it did at least demonstrate the utter impossibility of trying to work with the protesters.[28]

As an Irishman (and in private life a noted dramatist), Broghill was not remotely concerned with the narrow doctrinal differences between the two factions whom he regarded with equal disdain, remarking that whereas the former 'love Charles Stuart and hate us', the latter 'love neither him nor us'.[29] Nevertheless, he was genuinely concerned to achieve a settlement in the interests of political stability. Since he had found it impossible to deal with the protesters he was forced to turn to the resolutioners instead. They responded positively, and, once they had formally renounced their loyalty to Charles in return for a general pardon, the way was open to reach an accommodation with them. The result – as Broghill had anticipated – was that the protesters took fright at the prospect of being sidelined and suddenly became more amenable and indicated a willingness to co-operate.

Although Wariston and his extremists still remained obdurate, Broghill ignored them and concentrated his efforts on bridging the differences between the moderate majority of the protesters and the main body of the resolutioners, whose leaders included the arch-conciliator James Sharp. Not to be outdone, the extremists sent representatives, including Wariston, to London to intercede with Cromwell, whereupon the resolutioners dispatched James Sharp there to put the contrary view. Thereafter the contending representatives continued to badger an increasingly indifferent English government, and stalemate prevailed until after the Restoration.

DISINTEGRATION

Cromwell died in September 1658, having bequeathed his office of lord protector to his son Richard. It soon became apparent that he lacked his father's authority, and his inability to reconcile the competing political factions in England resulted in a military coup and his enforced resignation the following May. Political power passed to General Fleetwood who abolished the protectorate, thus automatically dissolving the union, and restored the Rump Parliament. This too was unable to cope with the rapidly deteriorating situation, so in October Fleetwood and his fellow general Lambert expelled it and set up a Committee of Safety instead. As the two men were bitter rivals this was doomed from the start, and when they lost the support of the army they were forced to resign and the Rump Parliament was reinstated. As it proved no more effective than before, it began to look as if the only man capable of restoring order was General Monck with his army in Scotland behind him.

Notwithstanding the dissolution of the union, he had continued to govern Scotland on an *ad hoc* basis with the support of the army, while systematically purging it of politically unreliable officers and establishing his trusted supporters as the principal garrison commanders. In December, when it had become obvious that the Rump Parliament was losing control, he set up his headquarters at Coldstream in readiness to march on London. Three weeks later he decided to act, and on 1 January he ordered his army to cross the Tweed into England, though at this stage it seems likely that his immediate objective was to shore up the Rump Parliament rather than to restore the monarchy. In the course of his advance southwards he defeated an army under General Lambert, taking him prisoner, and as this persuaded the disaffected units to join him there was no one left to oppose his victorious entry into London.

Once he arrived there it was evident that the Rump Parliament was beyond redemption and that salvation lay in broadening its representation by re-admitting those members who had been the victims of Colonel Pride's purge ten years before. As most were pro-monarchist, a restoration became inevitable and on 8 May Charles was proclaimed king. This was a signal for Sharp and his colleagues to pay court to him at Breda in the hopes of obtaining promises of support for the presbyterian cause, and the resolutioners in particular. But Charles was far too astute to commit himself at this stage, and in any case he was in no position to decide how to deal with the thorny question of the ecclesiastical polity in Scotland. So, while blandly assuring Sharp of 'a great affection for our country and kirk' and that he had no desire 'to wrong the settled government of our church', he told him that 'he would reserve a full communing about that till his coming to England'.[30]

THE RESTORATION

Charles's formal restoration on 29 May 1660 was celebrated riotously in Edinburgh. Bells were rung, cannons roared, trumpets were sounded, and there was dancing in the streets. However, apprehensive of what it might bode for presbytery, Wariston saw it as a 'great ryot, excess, extravagancy, superfluity, vanity, naughtinesse, profanetye, drinking of healths', praying that 'the Lord be merciful to us'.[31] His fears proved abundantly justified – at least from his point of view, though it was not until later that Charles was able to assess the strength of his own position and form a judgement as to the shape of the religious settlement to be imposed on Scotland. In the meantime its government was administered on an interim basis by four commissioners, and this remained the situation until August 1660 when they were replaced by a committee of estates.

By this time Charles was able to gauge the political situation, and although he enjoyed overwhelming public support he was shrewd enough to realise that this was unlikely to last, and that the best way of consolidating his authority in Scotland was to appoint a broad based administration comprising former adherents of the Covenant. Therefore, his choice of ministers included Glencairn as chancellor, while the earl of Lauderdale, who had atoned for his covenanting past by fighting for Charles at Worcester and spending the intervening period in a succession of English gaols,[32] was appointed secretary of state. Others with a covenanting past included the earl of Rothes, who was appointed lord president of the council, and Cassilis who became justice general, though he was dismissed the following year for his refusal to abandon his adherence to the Covenant.

The Scottish parliament was summoned in October 1660, and Charles capitalised on his continuing popularity by arranging for the elections to be rigged so as to ensure it would be packed with his own supporters. This meant that once it was convened on 1 January 1661 he could rely on Middleton, whom he appointed as his commissioner, to dismantle the revolution of the 1640s and consolidate his counter revolution. Like every revolution this needed a martyr, so Montrose's remains were disinterred and his skull removed from the spike on the Edinburgh tolbooth where it had remained since 1650, and these relics formed the centrepiece of the magnificent state funeral which was organised in his honour. He deserved no less, but it is ironic that this was ordered by a king who had signed the Covenant within days of his execution and arranged by Middleton who had fought against him at Philiphaugh.

Similarly, every revolution needs its enemies, and inevitably the protesters found themselves cast in that role. Although Charles had a personal grudge against them stemming from his treatment at their hands ten years previously, the decision to abolish presbytery, which, as Charles remarked to Lauderdale, 'was not a religion for gentlemen',[33] was entirely political. These people had been instrumental in toppling his father; they had been a consistently disruptive force throughout the commonwealth, and Charles was not going to risk them undermining his régime. They had already obligingly compromised themselves when a number of protesting ministers had assembled in Edinburgh to present a petition to him reminding him of his obligation to observe the Covenant – a piece of temerity which resulted in their summary arrest.

Even before parliament had assembled the committee of estates issued a series of discriminatory measures. All unlawful meetings and conventicles were banned; so too was the publication of seditious petitions and remonstrances, while those who had been associated with the Western Remonstrance of 1650 were discriminated against in particular. This provided a pretext for arresting Wariston and his fellow extremist, James Guthrie, both of whom were subsequently executed, while Argyll followed them to the block shortly afterwards.

Samuel Rutherford was also summoned before parliament to answer charges of treason on account of his seditious *Lex Rex*, but a timely death saved him from a similar fate. His spiritual descendants, the Church of Scotland, have established him as one of the heroes of the covenanting movement, and it was in tribute to this that the monument on the hill behind his former parish church at Anwoth was erected. While there can be no denying the sincerity of his religious convictions, and his other attributes as a man of learning and a conscientious pastor, he has to be viewed in perspective as one of the leaders of a faction which was dedicated to imposing an ecclesiastical tyranny to the forcible exclusion of all other forms of church government, doctrine or worship.

Once the new parliament was assembled it ratified the measures passed by the committee of estates, and at Charles's behest it passed the Act Rescissory of 1661.[34] This declared the parliaments held between 1641 and 1648 invalid, and consequently all the legislation flowing from them was abolished, including the Covenant, the Solemn League and the Westminster Confession of Faith which were now expunged from the statute book. This meant that the whole political and religious revolution of the 1640s, and the entire apparatus of presbytery, were systematically dismantled. When parliament adjourned in July 1661 the task of carrying on the government devolved on the privy council, and this body became the main instrument of Charles's authority in Scotland throughout the rest of his reign.

On his instructions, it introduced a series of measures which were designed to impose his chosen form of ecclesiastical polity on Scotland. These included the the restoration of episcopacy and the repeal of all the Acts, including the 'Golden Act' of 1592, which established the presbyterian form of Church government. It was a bold move on Charles's part, and the decision to do so was the outcome of a prolonged debate within the privy council; but, as he rightly judged, his popularity made it politically feasible. When this was ratified by parliament in the following year[35] bishops were appointed to all the former dioceses, and James Sharp, who was largely responsible for paving the way for the restoration of episcopacy, was appointed archbishop of St Andrews and primate of Scotland. Thomas Sydserf, the only survivor of the old order of bishops, was not restored to Galloway and instead he was given the wealthier diocese of Orkney, but as he was over eighty it was beyond his failing powers to travel there to be consecrated. Galloway went instead to James Hamilton, a prelate of flexible principles and a former adherent of the Covenant who probably owed his preferment to the influence of his royalist brother, lord Belhaven.[36]

The elevation of the bishops was keenly resented by the hardline protesters, and equally so the reimposition of the Apostles' Creed and the Lord's Prayer which they denounced as 'rotten wheelbarrows to carry souls to Hell'. But they were merely crying in the wilderness, because by September 1662 the counter revolution was complete; the church was in the hands of bishops once more, presbytery was swept away, and moreover these measures seem to have commanded wide popular support. Having achieved their initial objective, Glencairn and Middleton, who now exercised supreme power in Scotland, embarked on a campaign to impose the new ecclesiastical polity on the hard-core of extremists who are habitually but inaccurately known as the covenanters.[37]

NOTES

1. Gardiner, *Commonwealth* i, 256, 263–5.
2. *Ibid.*, 378.
3. Dow, *Cromwellian Scotland*, 9.
4. Gardiner, *Commonwealth* i, 381.
5. Stephen, *Church History* ii, 319.
6. Gardiner, *Commonwealth* i, 131.

7. Dow, *Cromwellian Scotland*, 31.
8. *Ibid.*
9. *Ibid.*, 33.
10. *Ibid.*, 40, 42.
11. Terry, 'The Commonwealth Union', 38.
12. Dow, *Cromwellian Scotland*, 38.
13. He was responsible for raising a regiment from Wigtownshire to fight for the covenanters in 1639 and later became a member of the commonwealth administration in Scotland.
14. C. J. Nicholl, 'A Diary of Public Transactions' (*Bannatyne Club*, 1836), 95.
15. Dow, *Cromwellian Scotland*, 83–4.
16. *Ibid.*, 299 (note 4).
17. Gardiner, *Commonwealth* ii, 404.
18. This resulted in a series of duels between the commanders, and in one case Middleton's deputy Sir George Monro and McDonnell of Glengarry even quarrelled over the choice of weapons with which to fight their duel!
19. Dow, *Commonwealth*, 139.
20. Agnew ii, 63.
21. *Ibid.*, 66–7.
22. Donaldson, *James V to James VII*, 349.
23. Dow, *Commonwealth*, 24.
24. Agnew ii, 75–7.
25. Dow, *Commonwealth*, 138.
26. Stephen, *Church History* 2, 238.
27. The episode is described in *ibid.*, 323–4.
28. Dow, *Commonwealth*, 147.
29. *Ibid.*, 199.
30. *Ibid.*, 263.
31. *Ibid.*, 265.
32. *Ibid.*, 269.
33. Hewison, *Covenanters* ii, 70.
34. *APS* vii, 86–7.
35. *Ibid.*, 372–4.
36. Stephen, *Church History* ii, 341.
37. They were covenanters in that they had subscribed the Covenant, but they were merely the radical element and therefore unrepresentative of the movement as a whole.

24

THE RADICAL COVENANTERS

THE OFFENSIVE

In January 1662, the privy council opened its campaign against the extremist covenanters by issuing an an edict banning all meetings of synods, presbyteries and kirk sessions. In June, an Act of Presentation and Collation[1] was passed requiring all clergy who had been admitted to their charges after 1649 to have their appointments confirmed by their diocesan bishop. As few complied, a further decree was issued ordering all recusants to remove themselves from their parishes by the end of October. This provoked a storm of protest, but it was quickly stifled, and when the synod of Dumfries threatened to depose all ministers who conformed with the edict it was immediately suspended. Similarly, when the synod of Galloway protested against 'this violation of our liberties' its proceedings were abruptly terminated in the the king's name by the earl of Galloway.[2]

Although the deadline was extended to February 1663, some 270 ministers in the dioceses of Glasgow and Galloway remained contumacious, so the privy council issued a decree 'charging and commanding them to remove themselves, their wives, bairns, servants, goods and gear from their manses, and out of the bounds of their presbytery' within four weeks. In all, thirteen ministers in the presbytery of Kirkcudbright and a further six in Stranraer and Wigtown were deprived of their livings,[3] and by 1666 the number had risen to thirty-four out of a total of thirty-seven in the synod of Galloway alone.[4] John Welsh, a great-grandson of Knox, who would become a principal opponent of the ultra-extremists, was ejected from his parish of Irongray, while another, Alexander Peden, preached at New Luce for the last time in February 1663.

The men appointed to replace the ejected ministers were in general ill-trained and ill-educated, their principal qualification being a willingness to accept episcopacy, and popular resentment against them flared into outbreaks of violence. Welsh's replacement at Irongray was forced to flee for safety, pursued by a hail of stones flung at him by the women of the parish, while a similar riot prevented the induction of a replacement minister at Kirkcudbright.[5] Eventually the pulpits of the deprived ministers were filled, but in some cases troops had to be called in to protect the new incumbents. This was hardly surprising, since according to Professor Gilbert Burnet they were 'the worst preachers he had ever heard . . . ignorant to a reproach and many of them [were] openly vicious. They were a disgrace to orders and the sacred function, and were indeed the dregs and refuse of the northern parts'.[6]

In many cases, they found themselves preaching to depleted congregations as their parishioners deserted them for the conventicles held by the deprived ministers in private houses or out in the fields and hills. The earl of Rothes, who had succeeded Middleton as parliamentary commissioner, retaliated by passing an Act which banned these conventicles and made preaching at them a punishable offence.[7] This was followed by another Act of July 1663, dubbed the 'bishops' drag net', which made attendance at church compulsory under pain of a heavy fine – a quarter of their annual rent in the case of heritors, while farmers stood to forfeit a like share of their moveable goods.[8] Finally, in August the privy council issued an edict known as 'the Mile Act'. This required all deprived ministers to remove themselves and their households to a distance not less than twenty miles from their former churches in order to prevent them from associating with their former parishioners.

Some remained defiant, so the military had to be called in to remove them by force. In September 1663 Sir James Turner, a rough soldier of fortune, nicknamed 'bloody bite-the-sheep', was ordered to Kirkcudbright after a local contingent of foot guards had failed to prevent a non-conforming minister, Alexander Robertson, from preaching at Samuel Rutherford's former church of Anwoth. Incidents such as these caused the hardliner, Alexander Burnet, the recently appointed archbishop of Glasgow, to urge the council to send in more troops, but James Sharp persuaded it to resurrect the court of high commission instead. This instrument of quasi-legal tyranny was equipped with arbitrary powers to fine or arrest those brought before it, even for the most trivial offences; no corroborative evidence was required, nor was the accused given any opportunity to state a defence. However, it had no effect as far as the dioceses of Glasgow and Galloway were concerned, as the deprived ministers continued to hold conventicles, and many of their former parishioners consistently refused to attend church.

Once the ineffectiveness of the court of high commission became apparent, the council was forced to accept Archbishop Burnet's advice and call in the military. The covenanters responded by protecting their conventicles with armed guards who were under orders to retaliate in the event of attack, so the chances of an outbreak of rebellion began to look increasingly likely. As a precautionary measure, the council poured additional troops into the main covenanting strongholds, giving overall command to Sir

Thomas Dalycll, onc of the most experienced generals of the time, whose
service in Russia had earned him the nickname 'the Muscovy beast'. It also
declared conventicles to be 'seminaries of separation and rebellion', and
those attending them traitors,[9] meaning in effect that they were automatically guilty of treason and hence liable to the death penalty.

The covenanters for their part resorted to propaganda by publishing a
pamphlet printed in Holland and ponderously entitled *An Apologeticall
Relation of the particular sufferings of the faithful ministers and professours of the
Church of Scotland since 1660*. Its purpose was to justify their actions by
describing the injustices they claimed to have suffered, but as far as the
council was concerned this merely compounded their guilt as traitors.
Meantime, the troops were ordered to remain on the alert for any sign of
disturbance, which proved a wise precaution as this was not long in coming.
Sir James Turner's repressive rule in Galloway provided the catalyst. He had
been dispatched there again in March 1666, this time with a force of 160
foot guards, for the purpose of fining those who failed to attend church,
the curates being under orders to furnish him with lists of defaulters.
Interpreting his instructions with the maximum rigour, he extorted fines
which far exceeded the stipulated amount, much of them finding their way
into his own pocket. At the same time, his troops were quartered on
suspected delinquents whom they treated so roughly that even the bishop
of Galloway was constrained to appeal for leniency.

THE PENTLAND RISING

In November 1666, a party of four covenanting fugitives, including
McLellan of Barscobe, received word that a troop of soldiers were about to
roast a local farmer on a griddle as a punishment for non-payment of a
fine. They rushed to his rescue, and in the ensuing fracas one of the
soldiers was shot and wounded before escaping. Normally this would have
been treated as an untoward incident meriting appropriate punishment,
but the situation had become so inflammatory that it sparked off a revolt.
A call went out to all who were ready to 'come in companie to Irongray kirk
that they might enter Dumfries by daybreak', and this drew an immediate
response.[10] On hearing of this, Turner ordered his troops to assemble in
Dumfries at nine o'clock the next morning to 'rassave [receive] powder,
match and ball'[11] before marching on Dalry; but before he could do so he
himself was taken prisoner.

During the night his lodgings in Dumfries were attacked, and when the
raiders reached him they found him hanging outside his window in his
'nightgown, nightcap, drawers and socks', shouting 'Quarters, gentlemen,
for Christ's sake, quarters, there shall be no resistance'.[12] He had good
cause to be alarmed, as a move to shoot him out of hand was only dropped

at the insistence of Neilson of Corsock. Instead, the insurgents ransacked his house, impounding a quantity of money before proceeding to the town cross where, with seeming incongruity (though in accordance with the Covenant), they drank the king's health as a mark of loyalty.

They now embarked on a recruiting campaign throughout the south-west, in the course of which they were joined by 'neere one hundreth ill armed foot', as well as 'some fifteene or sixteene horse' raised from Galloway by John Welsh.[13] Finally, a motley army consisting of 'a few above one thousand' men,[14] some armed only with scythes, pitchforks and staves, assembled at Lanark in readiness to march on Edinburgh. They claimed it was a peaceful demonstration for the sole purpose of petitioning the king and council to redress their grievances. However, the fact they were armed belied this, so the council, already anticipating an outbreak of rebellion, naturally assumed the worst and ordered General Dalyell to march against them.

Encountering the rebels at Rullion Green, on the edge of the Pentlands outside Edinburgh, he quickly put them to flight, killing some forty of them and taking about twice as many prisoner. Reprisals were exemplary; ten were hanged on one gibbet, thirty-five were sentenced to be hanged in batches in their own localities, while others were subjected to torture by the bone-crushing iron boot. Consignments of severed heads and hands were dispatched to a number of towns throughout the south-west to be prominently displayed as a warning. Among the victims was Neilson of Corsock. His story was poignant; he had been fined and persecuted and eventually forced to leave his home to take up arms. In his absence troops were quartered on his house, his wife and children turned out, and his tenants ruined as a result of having to provide for them.[15] Following his capture, his lands were confiscated[16] and he was hanged, having been subjected to the excruciating agony of being 'tortured and examined in the bootes',[17] though to do Sir James Turner justice he tried unsuccessfully to intercede on his behalf.

Another victim was the elderly John McCulloch of Barholm who had already been fined and nearly bankrupted in 1660. This time he was indicted before the justiciary court in Edinburgh which sentenced him to be hanged and ordered that his head and right arm 'be cut off and erected at Kirkcudbright . . . the corpse to be buried where traitors are usually buried'.[18] In fact, he was spared this final indignity and decently buried in Greyfriars churchyard in Edinburgh instead. Maxwell of Monreith's son, John, on the other hand, had a lucky escape. He had taken refuge in Edinburgh, but when his whereabouts became known a detachment of soldiery was sent to arrest him. As they broke into the house where he was hiding, the landlady crammed him into the empty meal cask and derisively told the intruders they were 'welcome to search the meal ark an' see if ony o' ye can hide in't wi'oot giein' a hoast [cough]'. Nobody doubted her and so they left empty-handed.[19]

Having disposed of the prisoners, the authorities appointed justiciary commissions to apprehend, try and condemn all those suspected of being implicated in the rising. A number were eventually tracked down and consigned to the gallows, though in some cases it proved easier to pass sentence than to execute it. At Irvine the official hangman refused point blank to carry out his orders, while the same happened at nearby Ayr, and it was only by offering an amnesty to one of the intended victims that he was persuaded to hang his comrades.[20] Turner and his colleague Sir William Bannatyne were appointed the commissioners for Galloway. Since the covenanters were particularly active in the Glenkens they established their headquarters at Dalry, from where they systematically terrorised the local population in their efforts to ferret out the dissidents.

The commissioners' powers were extended by two edicts of the privy council; the first being an order issued in March 1667 requiring all persons in the south-western counties to surrender their arms and ammunition to the authorities, while non-jurors and non-churchgoers were required to give up their horses as well.[21] Two months later, another proclamation was issued rendering heritors and parishioners liable for fines and compensation for assaults perpetrated on their intruded minister, irrespective of whether they were personally involved or not – a measure which merely gave unscrupulous people like Turner and Bannatyne further scope for embezzlement.

COVENANTING INTRANSIGENCE

As it was rapidly becoming apparent that repression was not working and merely driving the moderates towards extremism, Lauderdale decided on a change of policy. As a former covenanter he had some sympathy for their cause, though he had no brief for the extremists whom he castigated as 'damnd fules' cursed with 'unparalelled obdurness'.[22] So he concluded that a more emollient approach might encourage the moderates to conform, and thus isolate these hardliners. To emphasise the change of policy, Rothes, who was the principal architect of repression, was given the chancellorship, thus removing him from direct responsibility for dealing with the dissidents, and promotion was given to men like Sir Robert Murray and the earls of Tweeddale and Kincardine, who had little zest for his brand of extremism. The army was disbanded, and while those dissidents who were willing to take a bond of peace were granted a pardon and an indemnity, the more obdurate were faced with possible transportation to the plantations of the West Indies. Meanwhile, evidence of Turner and Bannatyne's peculation had come to light, and while the former was dismissed from the king's service, the latter was sentenced to imprisonment.

The new approach succeeded in weeding out a number of moderates, but the hardliners merely took advantage of this to hold more conventicles than ever. This led to the emergence of an opposition group within the privy council headed by Archbishop Burnet who urged a return to repression, but they were in a minority, as it decided to persevere with its policy of moderation. In June 1669, following negotiations with two of the leading moderates, it issued an Indulgence[23] which allowed deprived ministers who had 'lived peaceably and orderly in the places where they resided' to reoccupy their former manses and glebes and receive a small allowance. Furthermore, those who were prepared to have their appointments confirmed by their bishop were to be reinstated in their former churches, or in other vacant charges.

The hardliners, however, remained obdurate and launched a series of vitriolic attacks on the Indulgence. Archbishop Burnet also criticised it, setting out his objections in a remonstrance – 'this damned paper', as King Charles called it – and this led to his enforced resignation some months later.[24] Nevertheless, his objections were justified by events, because by March 1670 only forty-three ministers had accepted the terms of the Indulgence, of whom twenty-four were returned to parishes in the southwest. The radical majority, however, branded them as 'dumb dogs who had ceased to bark', and incited attacks on their persons and property, forcing some to abandon their charges.

As appeasement proved a manifest failure, the council reverted to sterner measures. In February 1670, the edicts against field conventicles were renewed, and those responsible for organising and conducting them became liable to the death penalty. In August, these measures were extended to include house conventicles which had now become alarmingly numerous. Notwithstanding this, conventicles continued to be held with increasing regularity, particularly in Ayrshire and Galloway, though the organisers were careful to avoid direct confrontation with government troops. This drove even the moderate Lauderdale to declare in a fit of frustrated rage: 'I would to God they might rebel that I might import Irish papists to cut their throats'.

Nevertheless the council persevered in its attempts to detach the waverers, and a second Indulgence was issued in 1672. As this proved even less successful than the first its attitude began to harden again, and reflecting this, Burnet was restored to Glasgow in 1674 following the death of Archbishop Robert Leighton. Yet the door was still open to those deprived ministers who were prepared to concede – even to a limited extent – the relatively modest demands now required as the price of reinstatement. This encouraged a number of moderates to try and broker a compromise solution which would be acceptable to both the council and the covenanting majority. Although it might have contained the seeds of a possible settlement, their efforts were vitiated by the uncompromising attitude of the extremists who refused to have anything to do with it and continued to defy the authorities by holding conventicles as frequently as ever.

As quartering troops on suspected delinquents had proved an effective measure in the past, Lauderdale arranged for a large number of men from the north to be billeted on known covenanting sympathisers during the winter of 1667/8. This 'Highland host', as it is known in the covenanting annals, has been depicted as consisting of a rabble of 8,000 savages who remained there for the winter, looting and pillaging to such effect that, according to Wodrow, when they went home 'one would have thought they had been at the sacking of a besieged city'.[25] As Wodrow is the arch-apologist for the covenanters it is only natural that his account should overstate the more prosaic fact that they amounted to some 5,000 men and that they came from the more civilised southern and eastern parts of the Highlands rather than the Gaelic heartland in the west. Moreover, they remained for only a matter of weeks, encountered no active resistance, while the plunder taken by the few who did go on the rampage consisted of little more than horses, shoes and money,[26] so unsurpisingly the episode achieved nothing.

As the threat of armed rebellion continued to loom, Lauderdale took the precaution of sending more troops to the south-west to reinforce the garrisons in the principal towns, including Dumfries and Kirkcudbright. At the same time, Graham of Claverhouse was given responsibility for rooting out dissent in the region, being given authority to hold weekly courts and arbitrarily arrest or fine those brought before them – a task in which he was ably assisted by Robert Grierson of Lag. Although this failed to deter the extremists from continuing to hold conventicles, they were forced to take increasingly stringent precautions.

For example, a three-day conventicle held on Skeoch hill in the parish of Irongray, which was attended by some 14,000 people drawn from all parts of the country, was guarded by a regiment of Galloway Horse under the command of Gordon of Earlston, who were ready to meet force with force.[27] Although the turnout sounds impressive, they were unrepresentative of the population as a whole, and it is significant that a number of people, otherwise generally supportive of their cause, were becoming openly critical of the extremists' activities. A case in point was a group of otherwise sympathetically-inclined Ayrshire lairds who sent a deputation to the privy council expressing their detestation of the conventiclers, whom they described as 'a few unsound turbulent and hot-headed preachers, most part whereof were never ministers of the Church of Scotland'.[28] Nevertheless, as these hardliners were in control of events rebellion was unavoidable.

INSURRECTION

It was triggered off by the murder of Archbishop Sharp on 3 May 1679, while on his way from Edinburgh to St Andrews. As he was crossing Magus Moor on the final stage of the journey, his coach was held up at gunpoint by a group of local covenanters who dragged him outside and proceeded to hack him to death with gross brutality in front of his terrified daughter. True, he was a time-server, in that as a former resolutioner he had embraced episcopacy with unseemly haste and was therefore regarded as a Judas by all shades of covenanting opinion. But that was no justification for his murder, and the council, regarding it as a blatant attack on their authority, issued a Hue and Cry and ordered the government troops to pursue his murderers, who had by this time escaped into the west country.[29]

It also drove a wedge between the moderates, who regarded the action as indefensible, and the extremists who applauded it. Endorsing it, their leaders, Richard Cameron, Donald Cargill and Robert Hamilton, issued a manifesto known as the Rutherglen Declaration which was first read out to the assembled populace and then nailed to the market cross in the town centre. It denounced all the statutes which established episcopacy, renounced the Covenants, ousted the ministry, set up royal supremacy and authorised the Indulgences,[30] and it also condemned as illegal all Acts of the privy council. In fact, it was tantamount to a declaration of civil war, and Cameron and his confederates drove the point home by issuing a call to arms; but having learned their lesson from the fiasco at Rullion Green they set about training their recruits into an effective fighting force.

The government responded by sending a force under Claverhouse to Ayrshire to crush them. On receiving reports that a large conventicle was about to be held near Darvel in Ayrshire, he marched there with the intention of dispersing it and arresting the ringleaders. But when he encountered the conventiclers on the marshy moorland of Drumclog he found that, far from being engaged in an open-air service, they were drawn up in readiness for battle. In the ensuing skirmish Claverhouse's troops were worsted, while he himself only managed to escape from the field on a wounded horse. Seeing the government troops in full flight, Robert Hamilton is alleged to have strangled one of the prisoners with his bare hands in his fury that they had been allowed to escape, despite his express orders that no quarter was to be given to 'Babel's brats', as he called them.

Inspired by this success recruits flocked to the covenanting army, and their numbers rose to some 5,000 well-armed men, all eager to fight. But at this point divisions between the moderate and extremist factions came to a head. Whereas the former, led by John Welsh and supported by the overwhelming majority of his fellow ministers, acknowledged the king's supremacy in all civil matters, demanding only freedom of conscience in religion, the latter denied it under any circumstances. Despite three weeks of incessant wrangling, in which portable pulpits were used to enable the rival spokesmen to outshout each other, they were unable to reconcile their differences. Consequently, the army became hopelessly divided as the extremists refused to serve under moderate officers and vice versa, so commanders had to be chosen for their religious persuasion rather than military experience.

It was a recipe for disaster, and this became apparent when they were attacked by a 10,000-strong government army under Charles II's illegitimate son, the duke of Monmouth, at Bothwell Bridge near Hamilton, for they suffered an ignominious defeat. Pulverised by cannonry their army was hopelessly outmanoeuvred and some 1,200 prisoners were taken, while the remainder tried to make for the safety of the hills, many being cut down in the process. One victim was the veteran William Gordon of Earlston, who had been heavily fined for taking part in the Glencairn rising, but was now under sentence for refusing to sanction the appointment of a curate who had been intruded into a living of which he was the patron. His son, Alexander,[31] had a narrow escape when the house where he was hiding was searched, and it was only by dressing up as a woman and rocking a cradle with a sleeping infant inside that he managed to avoid detection.[32] In the aftermath of victory Claverhouse urged Monmouth to order the slaughter of every rebel prisoner, but wiser counsels prevailed and he was forced to abandon his bloodthirsty intentions.

RADICAL DEFIANCE

Following his triumph, Monmouth was put in effective charge of the government of Scotland, Lauderdale, who was still secretary of state, being incapacitated as the result of a stroke. He embarked on a policy of moderation in the hope of isolating the extremists and, having obtained the necessary sanction from his father the king, he issued a Third Indulgence. This relaxed the ban on conventicles by allowing them to be held in private houses, though not out in the open. All fines for ecclesiastical offences other than treason were remitted, while imprisoned ministers were conditionally released, though the amnesty did not extend to those involved in the rebellion. Consequently, a number of leading participants forfeited their estates, including thirty-five in Dumfries and Galloway, one being Patrick McDowell, whose estate of Freugh was given to Claverhouse. Another was Alexander Gordon, whose Earlston estate was given to Major Theophilus Oglethorpe, one of Claverhouse's cavalry commanders.

The policy of moderation extended to the prisoners taken at Bothwell Bridge, whose numbers were swollen by further arrests to some 1,400, as they were treated relatively leniently. Instead of being consigned to the revolting squalor of a prison, they were accommodated in huts in a walled-up section of the Greyfriars' kirkyard in Edinburgh, and most were released within a few weeks on signing an undertaking never to take up arms again. Some remained defiant, but as the saying went 'they expressed themselves more naturally when settled on the ladder'[33]; in other words, the prospect of the gibbet encouraged the more stubborn to relent. As the behaviour of a hard core of some 300 prisoners could not be guaranteed they were sentenced to transportation to the West Indies, but they never got there as their ship went down in a storm off the Orkney Islands.

Monmouth's conciliatory policy might have achieved a settlement had he been allowed to pursue it, but unfortunately he was recalled in November 1679 and replaced by his uncle, the duke of York. The moderates, who now represented the great majority of the covenanters, had shown willingness to compromise, while the extremists were reduced to an insignificant remnant without an ordained minister. However, the return of Richard Cameron from Holland put new heart into their campaign, and in a series of manifestos these extremists – or the Cameronians as they now called themselves – publicly disassociated themselves from the Indulgences, declaring that 'they would sheathe their swords as soon in them that owned the Indulgence as they would do in any of the Malignants'.[34]

This, combined with the discovery of documents known as the Queensferry Papers, which revealed a conspiracy to overthrow the king and government, caused James to abandon Monmouth's conciliatory policy. His decision was vindicated when the Cameronians published their manifesto, known as the Sanquhar Declaration. Defiantly, it specifically repudiated the authority of 'Charles Stewart that has been reigning (or rather tyrannising) on the throne of Britain these years bygone' and declared 'war with such a tyrant and usurper . . . as enemies to our Lord Jesus Christ and his cause and covenants'.[35] This deliberate act of treason resulted in a price being put on the heads of Cameron and Cargill and their principal associates, and when Cameron was killed shortly afterwards in a skirmish at Airds Moss in Ayrshire Cargill became sole leader of these extremists. He proceeded publicly to 'excommunicate' the king, the dukes of York and Monmouth, and also the leading Scottish politicians, so the search for him and his leading associates was intensified. Pursued by bloodhounds he had several hairsbreadth escapes until he was eventually tracked down, convicted of high treason and sentenced to the gibbet in July 1681.

Although these dangerous firebrands had been eliminated, the damage was done as it confirmed the duke of York in his belief that repression was the only answer. This caused him to issue a number of ill-conceived measures which simply drove the moderate covenanters, who could legitimately claim to be the defenders of presbytery, towards extremism. A prime example was the Test Act of 1681.[36] A maladroit piece of legislation, this required all ministers and holders of public office to swear adherence to the Protestant Confession of Faith of 1560, to acknowledge the king as supreme authority and head of the Church, and to disown the Covenants of 1638 and 1643. Commissions were set up in each of the western counties for the purpose of 'tendering the Test to the Gentry and Commons', those appointed for Wigtownshire including Grierson of Lag, Sir Godfrey McCulloch of Myretoun and Sir David Dunbar of Baldoon.

As the Test oath itself contained a number of inconsistencies, as well as an implicit acceptance of the Catholic duke of York as Charles's successor, many moderate presbyterians could not in conscience subscribe to it. These included members of the council such as Sir James Dalrymple, the lord president of the Court of Session, as well as leading members of the nobility like the duke of Hamilton and the earls of Cassilis and Nithsdale, and also lesser ones, of whom the fifth viscount Kenmure was an example. Not only that, but some fifty indulged ministers who refused the Test were ejected from their charges, and most of them threw in their lot with the dissenting covenanters. Therefore, all the Act did was to raise new recruits for the extremists' cause and encourage the Cameronians to continue their insurrection.

In January 1682 they issued their Declaration of Lanark which, confirming those of Rutherglen and Sanquhar, repudiated all allegedly unconstitutional Acts of the king. This blatant challenge to the royal authority resulted in further acts of repression. A principal instrument of this policy was Claverhouse, and to provide him with the necessary powers he was given a number of important judicial offices. These included the sheriffship of Wigtown, Sir Andrew Agnew having been dismissed for refusing the Test, while he was also appointed sheriff-depute of Kirkcudbright, Annandale and Dumfries. In addition, he was given full statutory powers to prosecute those implicated in the 1679 rebellion who had refused the bond of indemnity – a task in which he was zealously assisted, as before, by Robert Grierson of Lag.

Those refusing to take the bond were harried relentlessly, soldiers were quartered on their land, and their families reduced to near starvation. As Claverhouse himself admitted, he 'rifled so their houses, ruined their goods . . . that their wyfes and schildring were broght to sterving',[37] and his force of specially enlisted rough-riders scoured the countryside day and night in their efforts to hunt down recusants. Those apprehended were cast into prison, and contemporary petitions paint an appalling picture of the prevailing conditions. A minister lies in freezing cold in a vault with the clothes rotted off his back, icy water dripping from the roof and his legs eaten to the bone by iron chains. Another begs to have his cell-mate removed as the man is not only verminous but mad. A shopkeeper beneath the Dumfries prison complains that 'a furious madd person' had been kept for some months in the 'Theaves' Hole' above his shop, and as 'he has no tub in which to ease nature' urine and faeces are soaking through the ceiling of his shop and making it 'somewhat noisome' and the goods 'damnified' to the detriment of his business.

DEFEAT

The duke of York was recalled in May 1682, and reflecting the changed political complexion of the council his policy of repression was intensified. This was a direct result of the Test Act, as those whose consciences forbade them from taking the Test represented almost by definition the moderate element, so hardliners like the earls of Perth and Queensberry and Sir George Gordon were now in control. The latter two were eventually pushed aside (the one being compensated with a dukedom and the other with the earldom of Aberdeen), and replaced by Perth's equally uncompromising brother, the earl of Melfort. Perth himself was the justice-general, and under his influence the judiciary, whose integrity had been suspect ever since 1676, when judges were declared to hold office at the king's pleasure, was reduced to an organ of the state.

The discovery in 1683 of the Rye-house plot to kill the king and the duke of York, and the fact that a number of Scotsmen were implicated in it, alerted the council to the possibility of a further outbreak of rebellion. Their fears were heightened when Alexander Gordon was captured at Newcastle on his way to Holland in June of that year, as papers found in his possession revealed the treasonable activities of the Cameronians and their contacts with malcontents in the Low Countries.[38] A worthy descendant of the old patriarch, the story goes that when Gordon was about to be subjected to torture by the boot 'he rose in fury, roared out like a bull and, being in his prime, like a shaggy Galloway he tossed macers and soldiers about the chamber to the dismay of his tormentors'.[39] Nevertheless a prison cell in Blackness castle was his fate, and there he remained until 1689, when a general amnesty was granted and all forfeited estates were restored to their previous owners.

The return of the Cameronian leader, James Renwick, from Holland in September 1683 provoked the council into streamlining its judicial procedures, and a circuit court was established to dispense justice wherever required. This was essentially a 'kangaroo' court, because its president, lord Perth, was widely suspected of colluding with the lord advocate, Sir George Mackenzie ('bluidy Mackenzie') of Rosehaugh. Since the prisons were full to bursting point with people who had refused the Test, the judiciary ordered that 'the gallowes stand for the better instruction of the great number of rebells who are cited to appeir',[40] so convictions by the court automatically carried the death penalty. Justice was also speeded up at local level, and in January 1684 new commissions were granted to all sheriffs in the south-west, giving them full judicial powers to 'cause sentence [to] be pronounced' on all offenders 'and justice done on them accordingly'.[41]

Renwick and his fellow Cameronians responded by hurling renewed defiance at the king and government, and on 8 November they published their *Apologetical Declaration and Admonitory Vindication of the True Presbyterians of the Church of Scotland*.[42] This reiterated their determination to maintain the Covenants, while branding the 'viperous and malicious bishops and curates' as 'enemies of God and the covenanted work of the Reformation'.[43] This was tantamount to a declaration of war, and even Renwick hesitated before accepting it.[44] Nevertheless, copies were affixed to market crosses and parish churches throughout the south-west. The council retaliated by issuing an edict proclaiming that 'whoever owned or refused to disown the late treasonable document (the Declaration) shall be executed to death' by anyone authorised to do so, provided two witnesses were present. This meant summary execution. Undaunted, the Cameronians were ready to meet violence with violence, and later that month they attacked the prison at Kirkcudbright, killing a sentry and releasing the prisoners. Shortly afterwards the minister of Carsphairn was murdered, though Renwick and his associates disowned the action and expelled the perpetrators from their communion on the grounds that it was done 'in a rash and not in a Christian manner'.[45]

The council now imposed a general clampdown. Whereas previously it had concentrated its efforts against the Cameronians, it now embarked on a systematic persecution of all supporters of the Covenant – moderates and extremists alike. In May 1684 it proscribed some 2,000 people whom it had marked down for punishment, including 221 people of substance in Galloway. Local garrisons were increased, and the troops were ordered to harrass the relatives of known dissidents to force them to give themselves up. Undeniably draconian though these measures were, the council considered them warranted in the circumstances, and moreover they were successful. The moderates, who represented the overwhelming majority of the covenanters, resented the actions of the extremists, whom they blamed for their plight, and publicly disowned Renwick by denouncing him as 'the great cause and occasion of all the troubles of the country'.[46] Therefore, to avoid being identified with these fanatics they abandoned the conventicles and began returning to their parish churches.

Having successfully isolated the extremists, the council now embarked on a campaign of attrition which was deliberately aimed at grinding them into submission. As a preliminary, it issued a further proclamation denouncing the Apologetical Declaration and demanded that its supporters be 'executed to death'.[47] To identify them, a roll-call of the inhabitants of every single parish south of the Tay was taken, and each person was required to swear an oath of allegiance to the king. Those who refused were either executed out of hand or tracked down and killed, and it is for this reason that the years from 1684 to 1686 have been pejoratively dubbed by Wodrow as 'the killing times'. But this has to be seen in perspective, for it is reckoned that in all about a hundred extremists were executed during the 1680s with perhaps eighty more being cut down by troops in the field.[48] Moreover, the government regarded these people as more of a nuisance than a threat, as its attention was focused primarily on the Highlands where a reign of terror was being instituted in the aftermath of Argyll's abortive rising.

There are a number of memorials to the victims in Galloway. One in particular concerned Grierson's shooting of John Bell, whose massive tombstone in Anwoth old kirkyard, near Gatehouse, gives a graphic account of the incident. The story has it that shortly afterwards Bell's stepfather, lord Kenmure, encountered Grierson in Kirkcudbright and upbraided him for his barbarity, and especially for refusing to allow his victim a decent burial. 'Take him if you will and salt him in your own beef barrel' was the callous rejoinder. Tradition asserts that Kenmure tried to run Grierson through with his sword but was restrained from doing so by Claverhouse.[49]

Some of these executions have become the stuff of folklore, a notable example being the 'Wigtown Martyrs'. Although there is evidence of two local females being condemned to death by drowning, it has never been conclusively proved that the sentence was carried out.[50] According to tradition, the women concerned were Margaret McLachlan, a widow in her sixties, and the eighteen-year-old Margaret Wilson. Their crime was to have attended conventicles, while the older woman had pointedly absented herself from church in order to hold private prayer meetings at home instead. Allegedly betrayed by a friend, they were apprehended, and as they refused the oath of abjuration the council was compelled to pass sentence of death on them, though it subsequently appealed to the king to exercise his prerogative of mercy. The story has it that he was prepared to extend his clemency and a stay of execution was granted, but it arrived too late to stop it from taking place.

Tradition asserts that the older woman, Margaret McLachlan, was tied to a stake further out from the shore, where the incoming tide would reach her first, but Margaret Wilson's was placed within earshot of the spectators, as it was hoped that the sight of the older woman drowning might shake her resolve and persuade her to recant. As the waves lapped against the nostrils of Margaret McLachlan, one of the soldiers coarsely remarked 'tis needless to speak to that old damn'd bitch, let her go to hell',[51] but her death made no impression on the younger woman who continued to pray as the water began to engulf her. Despite desperate pleas from sympathisers in the crowd, from soldiers, and even their commander, she remained steadfast to the end. 'I will not', she replied to their entreaties, 'I am one of God's children. Let me go'.[52] When the waters rose higher, a soldier was ordered to hold up her head in a last-minute attempt to make her change her mind, but her resolution remained unshaken as the incoming tide swept over her. She has been portrayed as one of the most famous of the covenanting martyrs, but if there is any truth in the story she was arguably much more a martyr to the terrifyingly insidious brain-washing and indoctrination by her fanatical elders, to which her youth and innocence would have rendered her particularly susceptible.

    In the liberal climate of three centuries later it is hard to comprehend the fanaticism of these extremists, though their unshakeable faith in the rightness of their convictions, and their readiness to accept oppression, torture and death for them, compels admiration. Yet, one might legitimately question what they achieved by it. The Church of Scotland, as spiritual descendants of the covenanters, has sedulously fostered the notion that they above all were responsible for the survival of presbytery, hallowing the victims of government policy as martyrs, and even saints. So they may have been, according to their lights, just as those who are regarded by the established authorities as dangerous revolutionaries see themselves as freedom fighters. But the freedom these people aspired to was an unchallengeable right to impose their tyrannical brand of religion on the people to the exclusion of all other forms of church government, doctrine and worship. For in the end it was not these fanatics, but the acquiescing majority who were able to take advantage of an unexpectedly favourable turn of events, that were responsible for securing the establishment of a free, independent, presbyterian Church of Scotland.

NOTES

1. *APS* vii, 376.
2. Agnew ii, 87.
3. Cowan, *Scottish Covenanters*, 52.
4. *Ibid.*, 54.
5. *Ibid.*, 57.
6. Burnet, *History of his Own Time* i, 269.
7. *APS* vii, 379.
8. *APS* vii, 455, c. 9.
9. RPS, 3rd series, ii, 109.
10. *Memoirs of Rev. John Blackadder*, (ed) A Crichton (Edinburgh, 1823), 137.
11. *Ibid.*, 145.
12. *Ibid.*, 138.
13. Cowan, *Scottish Covenanters*, 67.

14. Sir James Turner, *Memoir of his Own Life and Times* (Bannatyne Club, 1829), 176.
15. Hewison, *Covenanter*, 205–6.
16. These were subsequently bought back by his uncle and restored to his family who continued to own them for another century. (McKerlie v, 44).
17. *RPS*, ii, 231.
18. *Calendar of Kirkcudbright Records.*
19. Agnew ii, 101.
20. Cowan, *Scottish Covenanters*, 70.
21. *Ibid.*, 71.
22. *Lauderdale Papers*, ed. O Airy (Camden Society, 1884–5) i, 254.
23. *RPC* iii, 38–40.
24. *Lauderdale Papers* ii, lxviii.
25. Stephen, *Church History* ii, 380.
26. Disc. Lynch, *A New History*, 294.
27. Hewison, *Covenanters* ii, 276.
28. Wodrow, *Sufferings* iii, 37–8.
29. Reid alleges ('The Culvennan Writs', 23) that the Galloway laird, William Gordon of Culvennan, was implicated in Sharp's murder. This is hard to believe, but coming from such a respected source it requires mentioning.
30. Wodrow, *Sufferings* iii, 66–7.
31. Gordon was a brother-in-law of Robert Hamilton, having married his sister Janet.
32. Hewison, *Covenanters* ii, 312.
33. *Ibid.*, 318.
34. Wodrow, *Sufferings* iii, 104.
35. *Ibid.*, ii, app. xlvii.
36. *APS* viii, 244–5.
37. Hewison, *Covenanters* ii, 371.
38. *RPC* xii, 435.
39. Hewison, *Covenanters* ii, 406–7.
40. *Source Book* iii, 181–2.
41. *Ibid.* 196.
42. Wodrow, *Sufferings* ii, app. xcix.
43. *Source Book* iii, 181–2.
44. Cowan, *The Scottish Covenanters*, 120.
45. Hewison, *Covenanters* ii, 446–7.
46. A Shields, *The Life and Death of . . . J. Renwick* (Edinburgh, 1724), 52–3.
47. *RPC* x, 84.
48. This point is made by Lynch, *A New History*, 295.
49. Hewison refers to this meeting in *Covenanters* (ii, 468). It makes a good story but highly unlikely considering Kenmure was a fervent supporter of the Covenant, and had Grierson and Claverhouse encountered him in the streets of Kirkcudbright they would have had him arrested on the spot.
50. Donaldson, *James V to James VII*, 372 (note 44). Much has been written for and against the martyrdom of the two women. For example, see M. Napier, 'The Case for the Crown' in *re the Wigtown Martyrs* (Edinburgh, 1863): A. Stewart, *History Vindicated in the Case of the Wigtown Martyrs* (Edinburgh, 1867): *History Rescued* (in answer to *History Vindicated*) (Edinburgh, 1870).
51. Hewison, *Covenanters*, ii, 476.
52. *Ibid.*

25

PRESBYTERY TRIUMPHANT

Charles II died in February 1685, being succeeded by his brother, the duke of York, as James VII. Initially, his policy towards the covenanters was as uncompromising as ever, and his first parliament declared it treason to own the National Covenant 'as explained in the year 1638', while imposing the death penalty on all those attending conventicles. Defiant as ever, the Cameronians retorted by publishing their Sanquhar Protestation on 28 May,[1] in which they described themselves as 'the contending and suffering remnant of the true presbyterians of the Church', branding James a 'murderer . . . who hath shed the blood of the saints of God', and concluded with an appeal for comfort to a 'poor wasted, wronged, wounded, reproached, despised and bleeding remnant'. The council retaliated by redoubling its efforts to apprehend Renwick, and in the following year he was discovered purely by chance in the course of a routine search for smuggled goods. At his trial he was offered every inducement to acknowledge the king's supremacy, but steadfastly refusing to do so he was sentenced to be executed – a fate he bore with a fortitude which earned him the accolade of 'dying like a ripe Christian'.[2]

James was concerned above all to help his fellow Catholics, so in 1686 he offered the Scottish parliament free trade with England in return for removing the statutory restrictions against them. This was refused, so after it was dissolved he turned to the more amenable privy council, which he had packed with time-servers like Sir James Dalrymple's son, Sir John, now the lord advocate, and the Drummond brothers, the earls of Perth and Melfort, who had recently changed their religion for the sake of political preferment. It duly complied by issuing an edict in August 1686 allowing Catholics to worship in private houses. Six months later they were given greater latitude, but in order to render it politically acceptable, the concession was extended to allow presbyterians to meet for worship in private houses, provided the officiating minister was indulged.[3] In the following June, the council issued a further proclamation allowing all the king's subjects 'to meet and serve God in their own way, be it in private houses, chapels, or places purposely built or hired for that use'.[4] This meant that imprisoned ministers could now be released, while others who had taken refuge in Holland could return to resume their ministry, and as a result presbyterianism became a cause with a future.

Within three years James's policies, including in particular his attempts to override parliament and the preferment given to his fellow Catholics, alienated all shades of public opinion. Therefore, at the invitation of the English protestants, his son-in-law, William of Orange, landed at Torbay on the coast of Devon on 5 November 1688, with a multinational force of 14,000 men. James greeted the news with complacency; he could raise an army of almost three times that number, so he anticipated little difficulty in repelling the invasion. Orders were issued to his troops who were scattered throughout the kingdom, including his 4,000-strong army in Scotland, to assemble at Salisbury to pin William down in the west country. It soon became evident that James's strength was illusory, as his officers began to defect and revolts flared up throughout the country, and seven weeks later, on 23 December, he fled to France.

The revolts spread to Scotland and outbreaks of unrest occurred in the Highlands. As there were no troops available to suppress them, they spread to other parts of the region, eventually leading to a general uprising. The same happened in the south-west, and as the privy council was powerless to maintain order, the diehard covenanters took the opportunity to revenge themselves on the intruded ministers in a disgraceful episode known as the 'rabbling of the curates'. Deliberately timed to start on Christmas Day, an important event in the episcopal calendar, this was mainly the work of roving bands of Cameronians assisted by a sympathetic peasantry.[5] Arming themselves with pitchforks, staves and clubs, they attacked the manses and dragged the occupants outside to shouts of 'strip the curate'. In some instances this was literally done, the unfortunate clerics suffering the indignity of having their vestments cut off and burned in front of them. Their manses were ransacked and the contents set on fire, while the victims were driven off into the cold to make shift for themselves as best they could. These outrages were so widespread that during the course of the winter more than 200 curates were forcibly evicted.[6]

THE REVOLUTION SETTLEMENT

In the aftermath of James's flight, the English parliament formally deprived him of the throne and declared his daughter Mary and her husband William as joint king and queen. As the committee of estates declined to follow suit, James remained king of Scotland for the time being, but because of the mounting opposition to him a convention of the estates was summoned in March 1689 to determine the issue once and for all. The outcome hinged primarily on the tenor of two letters received from the rival kings. Whereas James's was a hastily-drafted missive consisting of a combination of threats and vague promises which offered nothing to the presbyterians, William's was moderate and conciliatory, inviting the convention to settle the religion of the country on a broad and liberal basis. This was enough to swing the majority of representatives in his favour, and when a number of James's supporters, including Claverhouse (now viscount Dundee), withdrew in protest it left William's presbyterian supporters in control.

As a result, the convention voted by an overwhelming majority to deprive James of the crown and offer it jointly to William and Mary.[7] However, this was conditional on their acceptance of two important constitutional measures passed by the estates, one being the Claim of Right which laid down certain fundamental constitutional principles concerning the independence of the judiciary and the summoning of parliament. Reflecting the views of the presbyterian majority, this included a condemnation of prelacy as 'a great and insupportable grievance and trouble to this Nation', and decreed that no papist could be sovereign or bear office in the kingdom. The other measure was the Articles of Grievance which dealt mainly with relations between the executive and the legislature.

A delegation, which included the veteran Sir James Dalrymple, was sent to London to tender the crown formally to the royal couple. At first William had reservations about accepting it, as he objected to a clause in the traditional coronation oath requiring him to 'extirpate from his dominions all heresies and enemies to the true worship of God that shall be convicted by the Kirk of God'. However, when the earl of Argyll blandly assured him that this was merely a matter of form, William accepted his assertion – and the crown – in good faith, though it is doubtful whether he specifically accepted the Articles of Grievance and the Claim of Right.[8]

Unfortunately, it later transpired that by accepting the oath in that form he had given the presbyterians a valuable hostage to fortune, in that he was powerless to prevent them from turning the offending clause to their advantage. Not only that, but he was obliged to concede a number of measures which were designed to consolidate their supremacy, and this involved abandoning his own preference for a broad-based church embracing episcopacy.[9] Nevertheless, the issue over the succession was now resolved, and although William was denied a free hand in the choice of his principal advisers, his supporters the Dalrymples were marked out for high office, Sir James (now viscount Stair) being reappointed lord president, while his son, Sir John, was confirmed in office as lord advocate. Once he accepted the crown William declared the convention a parliament, and two days later it passed a measure requiring all ministers to proclaim the new sovereigns and to pray for them under pain of deprivation.[10] Many episcopal clergy refused to do so, and this was used as a pretext for ejecting them from their charges.

Meanwhile, Claverhouse was enlisting support for James in the north, and in early April he raised the standard of rebellion on Dundee Law. The turnout was disappointingly small, but with the aid of reinforcements sent to him by James from Ireland he defeated the government troops in the pass of Killiecrankie in July 1689, though he himself was killed by a stray bullet in the aftermath of the battle. The following month, the remnant of his army was compelled to withdraw after an unsuccessful encounter with a government force consisting mainly of Cameronian levies at Dunkeld,[11] though it was not until the following May that the rebellion was finally crushed. It seems almost perverse that the Cameronian extremists should have come out in support of the government, and that they did so was a measure of their overwhelming hatred of the Stuart dynasty. In fact the decision was the outcome of a prolonged debate, and was vehemently opposed by a minority who protested in the strongest terms against such a 'sinful association'[12] with 'presbyterian malignants'.[13]

William and Mary's acceptance of the crown led to the emergence of the moderate presbyterians as the dominant political faction, and accordingly parliament passed a number of measures for the purpose of re-establishing presbytery. On 11 April 1689 it adopted the Claim of Right,[14] and this was followed by an Act which abolished prelacy and enjoined the king and queen to settle a form of Church government which 'is most agreeable to the inclinationes of the people'.[15] The next parliament of April 1690 went further and passed an Act adopting the Westminster Confession of Faith as the creed of the church.[16] Presbyterian ministers who had been ejected from their charges in 1662, of whom there were about sixty survivors, were restored to their former charges, while the episcopalian incumbents were ordered to remove themselves to make way for them. In June, another Act was passed[17] restoring presbyterian government to the Church as it existed at the time of the 'Golden Act' of 1592. It also partially revived the right of patronage, to the extent that heritors and elders were given the right to nominate candidates to fill vacant charges subject to the approval of the congregations,[18] and finally it convened a general assembly for the follow-ing October.

This was attended by 180 ministers and elders, all representing parishes south of the Tay, and inevitably the proceedings were dominated by the survivors of the pre-1662 era, known as the 'antediluvians', while three Cameronian ministers from the west were invited to attend. The assembly consolidated the new-found authority of presbytery by systematically eliminating all episcopal ministers, and even those suspected of being in sympathy with episcopalianism. Two commissions of visitation were appointed, one for the presbyteries to the north of the Tay and the other for the south, their remit being to purge all 'inefficient, negligent scandalous and erroneous ministers'.[19] Accordingly, they charged these ministers with a string of alleged offences as a pretext for bringing them before their presbyteries who, assuming the roles of prosecutor and judge, automatically deprived them of their livings. The purge extended to the universities, where those suspected of being similarly tainted were systematically weeded out. William repeatedly tried to impose moderation and urged indulgence of episcopal ministers, but as he was constrained by his coronation oath he was powerless to prevent it. So these commissions continued their work with unrelenting vigour until almost all the charges were filled by presbyterian conformists.

Presbyterian despotism

These ministers now represented the established Church, but to consolidate their authority against a possible Jacobite revival, and a consequent reimposition of episcopacy, they imposed a tyranny on the people which far exceeded that of the pre-reformed Church. The abject misery of man, the vengeful wrath of their old testament God, the dreadful power and the permanently insidious presence of Satan in all the guises in which he appeared on earth, and the agonies of Hell which awaited the transgressors, was the constant theme of their excoriating tirades from the pulpit. The people cowered in helpless subjection before them as kirk sessions arrogated the right to control and pry into the most intimate details of their private lives. Nothing could be concealed from them, and their rigid social discipline cast a pall over the most innocent amusements. Card games were regarded as dangerously secular, the theatre the devil's playground, while the popular pastime of 'promisky' dancing was seen as nothing more than an incentive to sensuality, and dancing assemblies the recruiting sergeants for Satan.

Kirk sessions seem to have been obsessed above all with the sins of the flesh. For example 'penny weddings', where everyone contributed a penny – and later food and drink – towards these festivities, were regarded with particular disapproval. For these were the few occasions when the people could really enjoy themselves and when, as an Act of the assembly put it, 'delicacy and decency were alike discarded'.[20] No doubt they were frequently an excuse for orgies of drinking, roistering and debauchery, but the Church made no distinction between youthful high spirits and more serious dissipations, castigating both indiscriminately. These weddings were the target for a concerted blast, and punishment was meted out to participants, musicians and dancers alike. Merely to have played at gatherings where there had been 'promiscuous dancing' entailed a fine of £20, while those found to have participated in them were liable to be denied communion.[21]

Typical of their attitude was the minute of a kirk session in 1715, which in an extraordinary farrago of bigotry described 'the great abuse that is committed at wedding dinners, and in particular by promiscuous dancing betwixt young men and young women' as 'most abominable . . . and condemned in former times by presbytery as not only unnecessary but sensuall'. Expanding on the theme, it described these celebrations as 'an inlet of lust and provocation to uncleanness through the corruption of man and woman in their loose and degenerate age'. Inevitably the hand of Satan was seen in this 'uncleanness and profanity', 'the tempting of the flesh', and the consequent 'drawing [of] men and women to dishonour God, ruine their souls, and cast reproach on the holy ways of religion'. Finally it ordained that 'the persons so dancing shall be rebuked before the congregation'.

In spite of all efforts on the part of Church and State to suppress it, immorality was rampant. Offenders were compelled to 'stand at the pillory' (a raised platform or stool) dressed in sackcloth for ten, fifteen or even twenty-six Sundays in succession. Here they were subjected to the smirks and whispers of the self-righteous congregation as denunciations were thundered at them from the pulpit, and it was probably small comfort to them that the earlier practice of standing delinquents bare-legged in a tub of water had been abandoned. Rather than face the social humiliation, many offenders fled the country or committed suicide, while girls in their terror killed their bastard offspring in the hopes of concealing their 'sins', and infanticide became a crime of terrible frequency. Hanging was the invariable outcome, and where the presumed father denied paternity he was forced to swear his innocence before the congregation. Although some did so with a lie on their lips, the awesome consequence of perpetual hellfire, which they believed awaited them, was enough to extort confessions from the most obdurate.

Contumacy, or the refusal to obey the order to stand rebuke, incurred the dread sentence of 'greater excommunication', which involved being 'delivered over to Satan', banishment from the church and the denial of the sacraments. Such a judgement, enforceable as it was by the civil authorities, was so potent as to cause the most obstinate sooner or later to submit themselves to whatever 'satisfaction' was demanded. However, there were occasions where people of higher rank refused to tolerate such presumption on the part of upstart ministers. For example, Agnew tells the story of how on one occasion the laird of Dunskey took such exception to being publicly reproved that he incited his retainers to seize the communion plate in order to prevent the celebration of the sacrament.

Strict sabbatarianism was integral to the doctrine of the reformed

Church since the days of Andrew Melville. This was reinforced by the commonwealth government in 1656 when Broghill, perhaps as a sop to the protesters, introduced a measure forbidding anyone to 'frequent taverns, dance, hear profane music, wash, brew ale, bake bread, profanely walk', or travel, or do any other worldly business on the Sabbath. The strictness with which this was observed was the subject of comment by an English traveller during a visit to Kirkcudbright, when he noted that 'Certainly no Nation on Earth observes the Sabbath with that strictness of Devotion and Resignation to the Will of God'.[22] In fact it became so deeply entrenched that the tradition of sabbatarianism would persist in Scotland until well into the twentieth century.

WITCHCRAFT

Witchcraft was regarded as the most dangerous and therefore the most heinous crime of all, and the lengths that ministers and kirk sessions went to in their efforts to detect and stamp it out reflected some of the worst aspects of the insensate bigotry of the early presbyterian Church. The persecution of witches originally burst on the north European scene in the 1500s. It stemmed from a belief, originating in Germany, that all local superstitions (which were legion) formed part of a vast organised conspiracy by the Devil and his witches to suborn individual people as their instruments for undermining the Church. This warping of the collective mind came in three or four terrible epidemics which occurred during the sixteenth and seventeenth centuries. However, it was not until the middle of the sixteenth century that it spread to Scotland, where the first statute against witchcraft was passed in 1563.[23] Another Act against 'Conjuration, Witchcraft, and dealing with Evil and Witched Spirits' was passed at the beginning of James VI's reign, and, reflecting the influence of the covenanters, further legislation was introduced during the 1640s.

In an age when credulity was universal and no rational explanation could be given for a number of untoward events, ministers readily persuaded their flocks to believe they were the work of Satan and evidence of his insidious presence on earth. This induced a state of mindless panic with all the ugly consequences of which a deluded and frenzied people are capable, and in particular it involved a series of witch-hunts to ferret out those suspected of being his accomplices. Almost invariably they were hapless old crones whose declining mental powers were manifested in a number of eccentricities, and who were incapable of defending themselves against the charges brought against them. As soon as a suspect was identified, neighbours were quick to come forward with the most bizarre allegations, which kirk sessions seem to have accepted without demur or requirement of any corroborative evidence. If the case was sufficiently serious it was remitted to a commission of the privy council. This happened only rarely, but when it did the matter was examined in exhaustive detail, though in all cases sentence seems to have been passed on the strength of unsubstantiated evidence.[24]

A particularly unpleasant method of detecting followers of the Evil-one was through 'witch pricking' by professional witch finders. Since they were paid a fee for each witch unmasked, there was every incentive to maximise the number of convictions. As a preliminary all the hair was shaved off the victim's body, and with the aid of needles fitted into wooden handles the 'prickers' would try to discover some part which was insensitive to pain. This was known as the 'devil's mark' and if found it was regarded as proof that the victim was a follower of Satan. The terror inspired by the arrival of a witchpricker within a community can readily be imagined, particularly when it was suspected that some resorted to the use of retractable needles in their efforts to secure a conviction.

Death was the inevitable outcome, and in extreme cases the victims were burned at the stake, though they were almost invariably strangled before the fire took hold. Tradition has it that an even more terrible fate was the lot of an elderly widow living in the parish of Irongray during the reign of James VI. She seems to have been a fairly harmless old creature who was addicted to certain minor idiosyncrasies such as sitting on a certain rock of a summer's evening. However, the fact that she could occasionally foretell the weather and 'her lips were sometimes seen to be moving when she was in church' seems to have aroused the suspicions of her neighbours that she was a witch, so when she was convicted and sentenced to drowning in a local river (the Cluden), the people clamoured for a more extreme penalty. This had to be authorised by the bishop, and so with his reluctant consent she was nailed up in a tar barrel which was then set alight and rolled down the hill into the river.[25]

The best-known case of witch-burning in Galloway was that of Elspeth McEwen. She was arraigned before her local kirk session at Dalry in 1696 on a charge of having a removable pin in her 'kipple foot' (the end of a rafter in her house), which enabled her to draw an inexhaustible supply of milk from her neighbours' cows. Other accusations were levelled against her, including a supposed mystic power to interfere with the egg-laying powers of their hens. When the beadle was dispatched with the minister's mare to haul this wretched woman before the kirk session, he testified that on mounting it she caused the animal to panic and 'sweat great drops of blood' as it carried her up the hill to the village.[26] The kirk session decided the allegations were so serious as to warrant trial by a commission of the privy council, and in the meantime she was lodged in the tolbooth at Kirkcudbright, where the conditions were so appalling that she regularly implored her gaolers to end her life. After a delay of more than two years she was brought before the commission, who found her guilty of 'a compact and correspondence with the devil' and sentenced her to burning at the stake. The local treasurer's accounts shed a macabre light on the proceedings, as these reveal that twenty-four shillings were spent on a tar barrel, and £1 'for peits [peats] to burn Elspet wt', while two shillings was paid for 'ane pint of aill' to William Kirk the executioner 'qn [when] she was burning'.[27]

Most of the charges levelled at suspected witches related to matters concerning everyday life in rural communities: illness and death, mortality among livestock, and alleged interference with butter-making and milking, the last being almost certainly due to mastitis. Some, on the other hand, sound more esoteric. The February 1701 minute book of the Kirkcudbright kirk session refers to an allegation made by a neighbour that on going to the accused Janet McRobert's house in the Millburn she saw a spinning wheel apparently going round of its own accord, and when she tried to stop it she was beaten back to the door by an unseen force.[28] Another neighbour claimed that, on visiting the same house 'at about cock-crow', she saw a candle moving around without anyone holding it.[29]

A third witness, the wife of a local farmer, testified that the accused had voluntarily helped her winnow some corn, though she seemed displeased by the meagreness of her reward. The same witness went on to claim that on the following day her breast 'swelled to a great height which continued for about five weeks so that the young child who was sucking decayed and vanished away to a shadow',[30] while another claimed the accused had caused his dog to go mad 'to the beholding of many'.[31]

The parish records of nearby Twynholm reveal another case which occurred shortly afterwards, in 1703. This time the accused was Jean McMurrie, a destitute old woman who was reduced to beggary. Apparently she solicited alms at the local farm of Mark, but was turned away, and the following day the farmer's wife found their milk 'was made useless having a loathsome smell', while she herself fell sick 'and was like a daft bodie for eight days'.[32] Others were quick to make equally preposterous accusations. One claimed it was through Jean McMurrie's intercession with the devil that 'his horse did sweat until he died', while another suspected 'his horse was killed with divelrie'. A third alleged that after Jean had threatened him with misfortune he 'lost a quey [heifer] by drowning'. The upshot was that she was banished from the stewartry under pain of death should she ever set foot there again.[33]

So deeply ingrained were these superstitions, and so universal the belief in fairies, brownies and goblins, that the statutes against witchcraft were not abolished until 1736,[34] by which time advances in medical science provided a rational explanation for the behaviour of those who were formerly seen as 'possessed of the devil'. Yet the minister of Kirkpatrick Durham, writing in 1791, claimed that 'the belief in witches, fairies, brownies and other superstitions once universal in Galloway, has not entirely been laid aside'. However he did add that 'the Kirk Session no longer indulges a spirit of inquisitorial investigation on a train of idle and vexatious processes', and 'the wildness of superstition and the bigotry of fanaticism are giving place to liberal sentiment and rational religion'.[35]

Nevertheless, a trial connected with witchcraft took place at Kirkcudbright as late as 1805 where the accused, Jean Maxwell, was charged with 'pretending to exercise witchcraft, sorcery, enchantment, and conjuration, and undertaking to tell fortunes', though she was arraigned for possessing witching power rather than being a witch.[36] Specifically, she was alleged to have told a servant girl with the aid of 'Tea cups and the grounds of Tea' the name of the father of her prospective bastard child, adding that she was able to intercede with the Devil to prevent the birth from taking place. Having gained the servant girl's confidence, she proceeded to blackmail her into handing over sums of money and the occasional joint of meat to her until the girl grew suspicious of her *bona fides* and reported her to the local constable. As a result, Jean Maxwell was sentenced to a year's imprisonment, during which time she was to stand 'openly' on four separate occasions 'upon a Market day in the Jugs or Pillory at the Market Cross of the Burgh of Kirkcudbright for the space of One Hour'.[37]

A CARING MINISTRY

Unlikely though it may seem, the excoriations from the pulpit and the retribution exacted on backsliders reflected the caring face of the ministry, because they were motivated by a genuine concern for the salvation of the souls of the offenders. A more obvious aspect of this, however, was the arduous and unremitting labour which a minister's calling entailed. Many had large parishes, and their pastoral work involved extensive travelling to visit their parishioners, particularly those living in the outlying districts, to examine and catechise them, as well as to visit the sick, the dying and the bereaved. The austerity and self-denial which were integral to much of their preaching are equally evident in the frugality of their lifestyle. For their standard of living, while perhaps marginally better than the majority of their parishioners, was comparable with that of the tenant farmers. The minister's manse would normally consist of a low-roofed, heather-thatched building, with perhaps a primitive outhouse for stabling his horse, while his heterogenous collection of livestock was pastured on the surrounding glebe land.

Sundays were particularly arduous, as he was required to conduct two lengthy services and preach a sermon of suitable length at each. Prayers had to be extempore, for it was believed that the Almighty was speaking

through the minister and 'showing him the light', and therefore to prepare
them in advance was regarded as a sin. At the same time histrionics were
permissible, because a minister stood to gain great credit with his parishioners if he was adjudged a 'mighty wrestler in prayer'. Meetings of the kirk
session also placed considerable demands on him as they could continue at
interminable length, dealing as they frequently did with matters of the
utmost triviality. Every rumour of misdemeanour and every suspicion of
scandal was raised and discussed, with parties summoned and interrogated
and witnesses called, and an inordinate amount of time was spent exam-
ining charges of 'horrid swearing', cursing, brawling and fighting, and
uttering 'terrible imprecations' in the genuine belief that they might
literally be carried out through the agency of the Devil.

There was a charitable side to the Church too, and following the precept
enshrined in the First Book of Discipline that 'every kirk must provide for
the poor',[38] kirk sessions were responsible for dispensing alms to the deserving 'impotent' poor among their parishioners. However, the laws of both
Church and State drew a distinction between the genuinely needy and the
able-bodied mendicants, so that whereas the former were objects of charity,
the latter were the target of discriminatory legislation. The First Book of
Discipline set the tone when it stated that 'we are not patrons for stubborn
and idle beggars . . . but for the widow and fatherless, the aged, impotent
or lamed, who neither can nor may travail for their sustenation'.[39] The Act
anent the Poor of 1574[40] confirmed this, since its declared purpose was
'alsweill [as well] for the utter suppressing of the strang and ydill beggaris
sa outragious enemeis to the commoun weill, as for the cheritibill releving
of the aigit and impotent puyr people'. Therefore, whereas the 'impotent'
poor who acquired a 'settlement' of seven years' residence in a parish were
entitled to relief, 'ydill personis' were to be 'scurgeit and burnt throw the
girssel [gristle] of the rycht eare with ane het irne of the compass
[circumference] of ane inch'.[41]

Discrimination against the able-bodied poor was a blunt instrument
since it made no allowance for those reduced to beggary through harvest
failure, eviction, redundancy, or other adversity. Therefore, an Act was
passed in 1672[42] which made some concessions towards them. This
imposed an obligation on kirk sessions to draw up a poor's roll for each
parish, while stipulating that where there was no employment available for
those 'who are of age and capacity to werke', they were to be sent to
establishments known as 'correcting houses'. These were maintained at the
expense of the heritors, and there they would be provided with 'cloathes
. . . to cover their nakedness'.[43]

The parish records of New Abbey,[44] for example, show the needy poor
being supplied with food in the form of meal for porridge, and on occasion
a load of peats for fuel, while pensioners were given a half-yearly allowance

of ten shillings (50p). Charity also extended to orphaned or abandoned children who had no-one to take them in, and this could include paying someone to look after them, clothing them, and equipping them for school until they reached working age. The main sources of parish relief came from fines levied on defaulters (mainly for immorality) and the proceeds of hiring out seats in church, and these were supplemented by the poor box to which parishioners were invited to make voluntary contributions. Other incidental sources included fees for proclamations of marriage and baptisms, which were assessed according to the means of the parties involved; also the hire of a mortcloth to cover coffins while they were being transported from the church to the graveyard. A parish coffin however was available for the destitute. This was a re-usable 'slip coffin' which was so constructed that when lowered part of the way bolts were released causing the bottom to fall open and allow the corpse to drop into the grave.[41]

The First Book of Discipline imposed an obligation on the Church to provide an education for the youth on a parochial basis. Affirming its desire 'for the virtuous education and godly upbringing of the youth of this Realm', it stipulated that in rural parishes the reader or the minister was to instruct 'the children and youth of the parish . . . in their first rudiments, and especially in the Catechism'.[46] Although this amounted to no more than the provision of a Sunday school education, most parishes expanded it into a more comprehensive course of instruction. This became a statutory requirement when the Education Act of 1616[47] imposed a duty on every parish to establish a school 'whair the youthe may be taught at the least to write and reid, and to be catechised and instructed in ther groundis of religioun', while stipulating that 'a fitte persone [be] appointit to teache the same'. Subsequent legislation[48] provided that where there was no parish school, the heritors and their tenants were to be responsible for establishing one, and thereafter to maintain it and pay the schoolmaster's salary.

These early schools must have been cold, bleak and grim institutions, and while in some parishes the church itself was used as a schoolroom, in most cases a byre or stable, or any dilapidated hovel, had to suffice. Teaching was entirely by rote, and the pupils were goaded into learning by a frequent application of the tawse or cane – in fact insufficient chastisement was generally noted with disapproval by kirk sessions. However, judging from the *Statistical Account* of the 1790s, truancy appears to have been frequent, while attendance declined sharply during the summer when the children were needed to help with the farm work at home. Later, a wider range of subjects became available in some schools, and particularly in those benefiting from private endowment. There were a number of these in Galloway: a grammar school was founded at Kirkcudbright sometime before 1576, while a free grammar school was constituted by private endowment at Dalry in 1668, and another school was established at

Minnigaff sometime before 1696. Nevertheless, the Church continued to exercise overall responsibility for education until their teaching institutions were taken over by the school boards which were established under the Education Act of 1872.

The revolution settlement and the actions of subsequent general assemblies consolidated the supremacy of the presbyterian Church, and it has remained the established Church of Scotland ever since. Nevertheless, the spectre of a Jacobite counter-revolution was never far away, while the presbyterians' fears were compounded by the Union; for, notwithstanding the settlement of their Church being guaranteed by statute, they saw themselves under threat from prelatical England. These fears were realised to some extent by the passing of the Toleration and Patronage Acts of 1712. The Toleration Act was primarily designed to secure the right of episcopalians to use their preferred form of worship, but it led to a loosening of ecclesiastical discipline, and the consequent secession of the small Cameronian element who now found a leader in James Hepburn, the minister of Urr. The Patronage Act restored the rights of patronage to heritors, and this became an increasingly divisive issue within the Church and culminated in the first major secession, which occurred in 1733. This set a precedent for further secessions which would lead eventually to the Disruption of 1843.

NOTES

1. *An Informatory Vindication* (Edinburgh, 1744), 102–6.
2. Hewison, *Covenanters*, ii, 510.
3. *Source Book* iii, 196.
4. *Ibid.*: RPC xiii, 156–8.
5. Lynch, *A New History*, 300: Cowan, *Covenanters*, 135.
6. Stephen, *Church History* ii, 407.
7. *APS* ix, 33–4.
8. Ferguson, *Scotland 1689 to the Present*, 6.
9. Stephen, *Church History* ii, 411–2.
10. Burleigh, *Church History*, 253.
11. These levies formed the nucleus of the Cameronian regiment which was raised for the specific purpose of resisting 'Popery and Prelacy and arbitrary power, and to recover and establish the work of the Reformation in Scotland'. For some three centuries they would distinguish themselves in the annals of British warfare until they fell victim to cutbacks in government expenditure.
12. Hewison, *Covenanters* ii, 524.
13. The Cameronians survived as a small fissiparous sect, John McMillan, who became the minister of Balmaghie in 1701, emerging as the leader of the main body. He was deposed in 1703, but, in defiance of presbytery, and with the enthusiastic support of his parishioners, he continued to occupy the pulpit and

manse until he retired voluntarily in 1727. Thereafter he spent the rest of his long life carrying out an itinerant ministry for the Reformed Presbyterian Church, as the Cameronians now called themselves.

14. *APS* ix, 37.
15. *Ibid.*, 104.
16. Stephen, *Church History* 2, 416.
17. *APS* ix, 133–4.
18. *Ibid.*, 196–7.
19. Stephen, *Church History* 2, 426.
20. *Ibid.*, 461.
21. Laws had already been passed against them in the reign of Charles II and these were revived by the assemblies of 1701 and 1706.
22. Macky, *Journey through Scotland* iii, 3.
23. Act 73 of the 9th parlt. of Queen Mary.
24. Truckell, 'Unpublished witchcraft trials'.
25. Maxwell-Wood, *Witchcraft in south-west Scotland*, 122–4.
26. An account of her trial is given in *ibid.*, 72–9.
27. *Ibid.*, 79.
28. *Ibid.*, 82–3.
29. *Ibid.*, 87.
30. *Ibid.*, 83–4.
31. *Ibid.*, 84.
32. *Ibid.*, 89.
33. *Ibid.*, 89–91.
34. Acts Geo II, cap. 5.
35. *OSA* 2, p 249.
36. The proceedings are narrated in Maxwell Wood, *Witchcraft*, 98–110.
37. *Ibid.*, 110.
38. *Scot. Hist. Docs.*, 128.
39. *Ibid.*
40. *APS* iii, 86–8.
41. *Ibid.*
42. *APS* viii, 89–91.
43. *Ibid.*
44. This information is based on Holland, 'The New Abbey Poor's fund'.
45. This device was apparently the brainchild of a Galloway minister (see Edgar, *Old Church Life in Scotland* (second series, 1886), 249).
46. *Scot. Hist. Docs.*, 128.
47. *RPC* x, 671–2.
48. Education Acts 1633 (*APS* v, 21, c. 5), 1646 (*APS* v, pt. I, 554, c. 171) and 1696 (*APS* x, 63, c. 26).

26

THE 1600s: REGRESSION

A BRIGHT PROSPECT

The dawn of the seventeenth century augured well for the country's economy. James VI had been on the throne for upwards of thirty years, and it was a tribute to the harsh but effective regency of Morton, and latterly the firm rule of James himself, that the later 1500s was a time of peace and relative tranquillity. The devastating English invasions of the 1540s were a mere echo of the past, Morton had stamped out the civil war between the Marians and the king's party, while James was responsible for the final suppression of feuding. This meant that merchants could ply their trade in peace, and farmers were able to sow their crops in the confidence of being able to harvest them without human interference. Consequently, there was evidence of a growing prosperity throughout much of the country and, as Burnet put it, 'mass famine and mass destruction were slipping into the mists of memory'.

Judging from the observations of the well-travelled observer, William Lithgow, in the course of his journey through Scotland in the early 1600s, this relative prosperity was also evident in Galloway. 'I found here', he wrote, 'in divers road way innes as good cheere, hospitality and serviceable attendance as though I had been engrafted in Lombardy or Naples. Likewise their Nobility and Gentry are as courteous and everie way generously disposed as either discretion could wish or honour command. Certainly Galloway is become more civil of late than any maritime country bordering the western sea'. Commenting on the quality of the livestock, he went on to say 'the wool of this country is nothing inferior to that of Biscay in Spain, nay the Calabrian silk had never a finer lustre and softer gripe than I have seen, and touched this growing wool there on sheep's backs. The mutton thereof excellent in sweetness. So this country aboundeth in bestiall especially in little horses, which for metal and riding might be termed bastard barbes than Gallwegian nagges'.[1]

Hand-in-hand with the improving conditions went a corresponding rise in the population, and this was particularly evident in the more fertile parts of the country, such as the coastal regions of the Solway Firth. It had already become apparent in the 1580s, when an English commentator observed that 'the Scots have children without number', while two decades later a Scottish writer attributed their fertility to the fact that 'our women do not indulge themselves with wine, exotic foodstuffs and spices from distant lands so harmful to the womb, hence the more readily do they conceive'. On the other hand, periodic increases in grain imports during the later 1500s – and the bans imposed on the export of corn in 1621/2 and 1629/30 – suggest occasional bad harvests, and a consequent check on the population growth, and so too did the intermittent outbreaks of plague.[2]

Nevertheless, the evidence from hearth tax returns points to a continuing population growth until the 1640s when the wars of the Covenant, the consequent devastation of the countryside, and the resulting deaths of many able-bodied men, checked it, and numbers declined sharply. This continued until the 1650s, and it was only after the English conquest and the imposition of peace under the commonwealth that the trend began to be reversed.[3] Natural disasters played a part as well, since the outbreak of plague brought back by the infected soldiery from Newcastle in 1648 coincided with a poor harvest, while the excessively hot summer of 1652 was accompanied 'ane extraordinary great drought throwout the whole kingdom' when 'the cornes [were] generallie both short and thin'. Although peace was restored under the commonwealth, this did not herald a return to prosperity, as the cost of maintaining it was such that even Cromwell was forced to concede that Scotland was 'a very ruined Nation'.[4]

ASPIRING BURGESSES

The prosperity of the earlier years of the century is evident from the number of well-to-do merchant burgesses who were establishing themselves as landed proprietors. While some would have bought their estates in the open market, the indications are that most acquired them through wadset, since the setting out of money on loan on the security of land was one of the few forms of investment available to a merchant with surplus money available, and defaults must have been frequent. The lure of becoming a landowner has always beckoned those who have made money in other fields, and that this was as true in the early seventeenth century as later is clear from the comments of a contemporary writer. 'So soon as a Merchant hath scraped together a piece of money, perhaps to the value of 4,000 or 5,000 lib. ster.', he wrote, 'instead of employing it for promoting Trade, or by projecting any new thing that may be serviceable to his Country, and to the augmenting of his Stock, nothing will satisfy him but the laying of it out upon a Land Estate, for having the Honour to make his Son a Laird, that is, an Idle Person, who can find as many Methods in spreading his Father's Money as he had of gaining it'.

The burghs were the main centres of wealth, and that Dumfries was no exception is evident from the account of James VI's visit in 1617, when it was reported as being 'in a prosperous state . . . its trade [having] greatly increased since the Union of the Crowns and the settlement of the Debatable Land'.[5] Among its burgesses who aspired to landed status was Stephen Laurie,[6] who acquired the Maxwellton estate in the Cairn valley from Sir Robert Gordon of Lochinvar, and this remained in the hands of his descendants until the 1960s. Similarly his brother-in-law John Corsane, provost of Dumfries, acquired the property of Meikleknox near Castle Douglas, which remained in his family until the end of the following century. A third was William Craik, who purchased the more distant property of Duchra (now Hensol) near Mossdale, and later the fertile estate of Arbigland near Kirkbean from the earl of Southesk. The latter eventually passed to his grandson and namesake who was one of the foremost agriculturalists of the following century. The same was happening in smaller burghs like Kirkcudbright, and in the early 1600s William Fullerton, a burgess of the town, purchased the property of Carleton[7] in the parish of Borgue, from William McLellan of Senwick.

Although the prosperity of the early 1600s gave added stimulus to the process, merchant burgesses had been buying up neighbouring properties long before then, and in the previous century the thriving burgh of Wigtown spawned a number of aspiring landowners. This was under the control of the Hannays of Sorbie,[8] and in 1532 Alexander, a burgess of the town and younger brother of Robert Hannay of Sorbie, purchased the estate of Kirkdale, between Gatehouse and Creetown. Having no children, he bequeathed it to his nephew John whose descendant is the present proprietor. Another example in the following century was Provost William Coltrane who acquired a number of properties in the neighbouring parish of Kirkinner.[9]

The early seventeenth century was the heyday of the merchant burgesses, but it also proved their Indian summer since the wars of the Covenant and the resulting dearth of trade heralded a decline in their wealth and status. Thereafter, they became the target of discriminatory legislation which was aimed at eroding their traditional rights and privileges, one example being the Act anent Trade of the Burghs of 1672.[10] This abolished their monopoly of foreign trade, and as it meant people could now export their own produce it gave an important fillip to the cattle trade in Galloway. It was also designed to encourage the establishment of new burghs, a notable example being the recently-founded settlement of Newton Stewart, adjacent to Minnigaff, which was created a burgh of barony by Major-General William Stewart[11] in 1667. Although burghs of barony were being created in the twelfth and thirteenth centuries in Galloway, no new ones seem to have been erected, apart from the burgh of Myretoun, until the seventeenth century, when Stranraer was constituted one in 1617, while New Galloway became a royal burgh at the instigation of Sir Robert Gordon of Lochinvar in 1612.

The decline in the external trade of the burghs, which began in the 1640s and was accelerated by the trade war with England in the 1660s, is evident from the records. Those for Kirkcudbright, for example, show that whereas a total of sixty ships landed there between 1606 and 1629, this tailed off until 1692 when there were none, a trend repeated at Wigtown[13] and Whithorn.[14] Even during the commonwealth Kirkcudbright was described as a port where there were only 'very poor merchants, or pedlars rather, tradeing for Ireland',[15] but by 1692 its trade seems to have come to a virtual standstill since a report of that year tells us that its 'inland trade is verie inconsiderable',[16] and all it had was one small boat of 8 tons 'for carreing their coals [which] hath never as yet been imployed'.[17] Daniel Defoe endorsed this bleak picture when he described the town in his *Tour Through The Whole of Britain* as 'a harbour without ships, a port without trade, a fishery without nets [and] a people without business'.

The re-erection of trade barriers following the dissolution of the commonwealth led to a revival of smuggling, for which Galloway, with over two hundred miles of coastline facing England and Ireland, is conveniently situated. It seems that waiters and other government officials were bribed to turn a blind eye to the trade, as a contemporary writer speaks of 'the practice of Manadgers . . . who hinder all except their own dear friends and relations in Goods forbidden'. The ban imposed on the import of Irish cattle in 1672 gave a further fillip to the smuggling trade. This prompted parliament to pass an Act in the following year which compelled all landowners and heritors in the western counties, including Kirkcudbrightshire and Wigtownshire, to 'give bonds that they, or their tenants, or any dwelling on their lands, shall not import or resett any sort of victual from Ireland under pain of twelve hundred pounds', while magistrates in the seaport burghs were bound in a similar obligation. It also appointed commissioners to seize any vessel suspected of carrying them 'betwixt the head of Kintyre and Loch Ryan, or any port, loch, river or creek from Loch Ryan to Dumfries'.

OVERLAND TRADE

The virtual extinction of Galloway's seaborne trade was compensated for by a thriving inland trade and the development of overland commercial links with England. Wigtown, for example, benefited very substantially from the trade in the Machars, and its quarterly fairs appear to have been a hive of activity. According to Symson, people from the neighbouring regions, as well as merchants from Edinburgh, Glasgow and Ayr, 'come and buy in great numbers . . . great quantities of raw broad cloth', and 'eighteen score of packs of cloath have been sold thereat'.[18] Horses were sold as well, and in the run-up to Christmas there was a market 'for fat kine [which] is frequented by butchers and others from Dumfries, and other places thereabout'.[19] Also at Minnigaff, where a market held there every Saturday was 'frequented by the moormen of Carrick . . . who buy there great quantities of meal and malt'.[20] Another, known as the St Laurence fair, was held annually on 9 August within the kirkyard of Kirkandrews where 'all sorts of merchant wares' were sold, and 'the people who flock thither in great companies, drink and debauch, and commonly great lewdness is committed'.[21]

Traditionally, most of Galloway's surplus produce was sold to itinerant merchants who resold them in the east coast burghs, which constituted the main consumer markets. However, with the settlement of the debateable lands of the Border following the union of the crowns it became possible to transport goods safely to England, and this opened up a whole new market. As Galloway's economy was almost exclusively agricultural, her exports were limited to primary products such as salted meat, some fish, livestock and unprocessed goods like hides and skins – including those of hares, polecats and foxes.[22] The region also established a reputation for its cottage-manufactured woollen cloth or 'pladding' and the rough, white version known as 'Galloway whites'.

The main export however was cattle, and the growth of the trade during the seventeenth century is apparent from the records. Whereas the customs accounts of Dumfries and Kirkcudbright for 1621 show some 2,500 animals being exported to England, the records at Gretna reveal that by the 1680s numbers had increased by more than threefold.[23] Its buoyancy in the south-west, compared with other parts of the country, was attributable to the combination of the beneficial climate and consequent abundance of grass, the availability of cheap Irish cattle, its accessibility to the principal English markets, and above all improved management practices. Traditionally, cattle were simply turned out on to the grazing land to run wild and mate at random, and as it was unenclosed they regularly strayed on to neighbouring land, particularly in winter time when there was a shortage of grass. It was in an effort to control this that parliament passed the Winter Herding Act of 1686[24] which stipulated that 'because of uncontrolled, promiscuous grazing, stock must be tended, particularly at night'.

However, innovative landowners were now building enclosures to enable them to carry out more sophisticated management practices, and the best known of the early pioneers was Sir David Dunbar (c.1610–1686). Having inherited the family estate of Baldoon, a former royal grange consisting of a large, flat coastal plain adjacent to the lower reaches of the Bladnoch, in about 1640, he built a large park where he experimented with improving his stock. This extended to 'about two miles and an halfe in length and a mile and an halfe in breadth', and he could 'keep in it, winter and summer, about a thousand bestiall'.[25] Most of them were bought in as stores and sold the following summer, either to drovers or direct to the southern graziers for fattening off.

Dunbar's original breeding stock, which consisted of some 200 cows, are thought to have been mainly small, black, brindled and dun, horned animals with a shaggy coat.[26] These were orginally crossed with bulls import-ed from Ireland, but when this was banned he is believed to have used hornless bulls of an unknown breed from Cumberland instead, and their surplus progeny were sold as four-year-old stores. Eventually he developed a far superior – and much larger – type of animal which was highly prized for its meat quality; so much so that English cattle rearers became envious of his success, and on at least one occasion they tried to sabotage his efforts. This occurred when a drove of his cattle was impounded by the authori-ties on the pretext that they were suspected of being contraband Irish cattle. Unfortunately there was no-one available to testify to their true origin, so in spite of knowing perfectly well that they came from Scotland the local justices ordered them to be 'knockt on the head and kill'd', which, as Symson justly observed, was 'an act unworthy of persons of that quality and station'.[27]

Dunbar's successes encouraged others to follow suit. Among them was the third earl of Galloway, who established an enclosure on his Wigtown-shire estates, and likewise Sir James Dalrymple, as well as other lairds, such as Maxwell of Monreith, McDowell of Logan, and McCulloch of Myretoun.[28] The market was buoyant, since the rapidly expanding population of south-ern England, and the mushroom-like growth of London which occurred after the Restoration, led to a huge increase in demand for beef. The trade received a further fillip in 1666 when the English government banned the import of Irish cattle, and when the Scottish parliament followed suit in 1672 competition from that source was eliminated altogether. Above all, it was the Act anent Trade of the Burghs, which was passed in the same year, that was responsible for the upsurge in the trade, since it meant that cattle rearers could deal direct with the English markets.

Most hired drovers to take them there, and the growth in the cattle trade led to a corresponding expansion of the droving trade. However, the passage of ever-larger herds of cattle through Galloway, and the damage caused to neighbouring farmers' crops, which frequently led to ugly inci-dents, prompted demands for an officially recognised drove road.[30] So, in 1697, the privy council appointed a commission to mark out a route between New Galloway and Dumfries to link up with the existing drove road at Annan. The course decided on was described as 'the line of passage taken by immense herds of cattle which were continually passing from the green pastures of the Galloway hills into England – a branch of the economy held to be the main support of the inhabitants of the district and the grand source of its rents'. Legislation was also passed requiring drove roads to be fenced where they crossed cultivable land so as to avoid damage to crops, while the occupiers of the land could benefit from charging the drovers for overnight 'stance' rights for their cattle.

The majority of these drovers were self-employed contractors, though some were employees of the cattle-breeding landowners who expanded into droving as an ancillary to their farming activities. For example, Sir Alexander Maxwell of Monreith built up a large cattle-droving business in the following century, while Patrick Heron, younger of Kirroughtree, who was Sir David Dunbar's manager and sometimes took his cattle down to England, also went into business on his own account. Some landowners went into partnership with a drover, while others stood surety for his bank borrowing in return for a share in the profits. Many drovers were dealers on their own account, and Symson mentions Sir David Dunbar as selling his stock to drovers.[31] While the rewards could be handsome, this was a risky business, since it frequently involved having to borrow money to buy the stock, and if trade was slack and the drover failed to cover his costs he stood to be ruined.

A CHANGING LANDOWNERSHIP

The seventeenth century was a time of sharp swings in the fortunes of the Galloway landowners, and nowhere was this more apparent than in the rise of the Dalrymples: Sir James, the future viscount Stair,[32] and his son Sir John who became the first earl of Stair.[33] Scion of an old-established landowning family from Stair in Ayrshire, Sir James was an incomer to Wigtownshire, having married Margaret Ross, the heiress of the Balneil estate near New Luce. Using the money he had amassed in the course of his career he acquired a number of wadsets over lands in the neighbourhood – to the extent that the Roll of Heritors for 1657[34] shows his rental income as being among the highest of any in Wigtownshire. In fact it was only exceeded by the earls of Galloway and Cassilis, and John McCulloch of Myretoun.

In the 1680s Sir James Dalrymple acquired the Dunragit estate, near Glenluce, which had belonged to the Baillie family since Commendator Cuthbert acquired it from Glenluce abbey some two centuries previously. At this time it belonged to Thomas Baillie, who was a minor, besides being a great-nephew of Sir James's wife, while Sir James himself not only held a wadset over the property but was also one of the young laird's guardians. Apparently, he pretended to take much interest in the welfare of his ward to the extent of borrowing the estate title deeds on the pretext of checking them, but they were never returned. It was only after Thomas Baillie reached his majority that it transpired that his estate had been filched from him and was 'in the possession of others'. Although he attempted to recover it by due process of law, his efforts were doomed from the start for, as McKerlie says, 'how could he succeed when four sons of Viscount Stair were the leading lawyers of the day and some of them sitting on the bench?'[35]

Meanwhile Sir John, the future earl, was building up a landholding in Wigtownshire independently of his father. This comprised the lands formerly belonging to the earls of Cassilis, and the lengths he is alleged to have gone to in his efforts to secure them make a still more unedifying story. The last of the Kennedy owners was the seventh earl who inherited them on his father's death in 1668. Like his father before him, he was a man of strong covenanting sympathies and was consequently forced to pay a heavy fine, besides having the Highland Host quartered on him. This so pauperised him that he was eventually forced to sell his Wigtownshire estates. The purchaser was John Hamilton, lord Bargany, but he too was suspected of being a covenanting supporter, and in consequence he was imprisoned and his lands forfeited.

After his release, Bargany discovered he had been convicted on the perjured evidence of two witnesses who had been suborned by Sir John Dalrymple for the express purpose of giving him the opportunity to acquire his Wigtownshire estates.[36] Bargany therefore demanded an enquiry, but at Sir John's instigation the duke of York refused it, for had Bargany been acquitted he would have been entitled to recover his lands.[37] Consequently he never did, so Sir John remained in possession of virtually all the lands formerly belonging to Glenluce and Soulseat abbeys, as well as much of the barony of Leswalt. His successors continued to build on this during the following centuries, to the extent that their landholdings in the region eventually matched those of the earls of Galloway, while they wielded virtually supreme political power in Wigtownshire.

The McCullochs, on the other hand, went into almost total eclipse. John McCulloch's appearance in the roll of heritors as among the largest landholders in the county represented the climax of a long career of land acquisition. Having inherited his family estate of Ardwell in the Rhinns, he married Elizabeth McCulloch,[38] the daughter of his kinsman, William McCulloch of Myretoun, and his wife Marie, the heiress of the Cardiness McCullochs. However, Myretoun was sold in the early 1620s, Cardiness going the same way at the end of the decade, and while John subsequently re-acquired Myretoun the task of attempting to recover Cardiness was left to his son and grandson.

John McCulloch was succeeded by his son Alexander. A man of some pretensions, he bought a Nova Scotia baronetcy in 1664 (thus keeping up with his brother-in-law Sir David Dunbar who acquired one the same year), and as he was then forced to pay a swingeing fine of £1,200 for his adherence to the Covenant he was left almost bankrupt. However, this did not prevent him from trying to recover the Cardiness estate from John Gordon.[39] He too was in financial difficulties as a result of crippling fines imposed on him for opposing the commonwealth, so Sir Alexander McCulloch attempted to exploit his predicament in order to filch his lands from him. Although he was partially successful, in that he acquired a portion of the barony, the costs were ruinous, and it resulted in his son Godfrey being fined 2,000 merks and incarcerated in the Tolbooth in Edinburgh.

Godfrey succeeded to the baronetcy and the family estates in 1675, but by that time much of them had been disposed of, and as he too was financially embarrassed he was forced to sell off virtually all the rest. In 1683 he sold Myretoun to his cousin Sir William Maxwell, and when Ardwell went the same way six years later he removed himself to Bardarroch, the site of the present-day Cardoness House, near Gatehouse. As he was now a near neighbour of William Gordon, who had succeeded his brother John, it was only a matter of time before the dispute between the two families flared up again. This occurred in October 1690 when some of Sir Godfrey's cattle happened to stray on to the Cardiness lands and William Gordon seized them. When Sir Godfrey and his henchmen attempted to recover them by force, Gordon resisted, and in the ensuing fracas Sir Godfrey shot him, allegedly remarking as he gloated over his victim writhing in his death agonies, 'now dog I have got myself avenged of you'. Thereafter he fled the country, but returning six years later he was apprehended, tried, found guilty and had the dubious distinction of being the last person to be executed on the maiden.[40]

Although the original McCullochs of Myretoun disposed of their family estates in the early 1620s they left numerous descendants, all of whom live in the United States. Other families of the same name, though not necessarily connected with the house of Myretoun, continued to be small landholders or 'bonnet' lairds in Galloway, the only exception being the McCullochs of Barholm who were more substantial landowners, though at this time they were under a cloud in consequence of their adherence to the Covenant. The tower overlooking Wigtown Bay, which they built in the sixteenth century, was abandoned some two centuries later when the family removed itself to a new house erected on the outskirts of Creetown, and there they remained until the 1950s.

Another family which went into eclipse were the Dunbars of Mochrum. They had been prominent in Wigtownshire ever since the barony was granted to their predecessor, the earl of March, in 1342, and they were still adding to their estates in the sixteenth century with the acquisition of the lands of Pankill from the priory of Traill. The owner at this time was Sir

James Dunbar who was famed alike for his partiality to claret, his general conviviality and his gigantic size.[41] In fact so huge was he that legend has it that, when he died in 1718, his coffin could not be manoeuvred down the staircase, nor even out of a window, so a hole had to be knocked through the outside wall of his house, the Old Place of Mochrum, in order to extricate it.[42] It is possible that, like Sir Alexander McCulloch, he over-extended himself with the purchase of a baronetcy, because his son Sir George was forced to sell the family property. While a portion was bought by Maxwell of Monreith the remainder went to Colonel William Dalrymple, a younger son of the first earl of Stair and husband of Penelope, countess of Dumfries.[43]

The Maxwells of Monreith, on the other hand, were steadily adding to their estates at the expense of their neighbouring landowners. Having acquired a baronetcy in 1681, Sir William Maxwell bought the former McCulloch baronies of Myretoun and Ardwell, and while the former became part of the expanding Monreith estate the latter went to his younger son John. His descendants continued to own it until the end of the following century, when it was sold to John McTaggart,[44] an ancestor of the present owner. Later, Sir William acquired the barony of Longcastle from Vaus of Barnbarroch, while it was his son Sir Alexander who continued the family tradition of land acquisition by acquiring part of the former Mochrum barony.[45] Thereafter, they remained one of the foremost families in Wigtownshire until the twentieth century, when the estate was progressively sold off, leaving the house itself and the surrounding grounds in the hands of the present baronet.

Sir David Dunbar appears to have invested the profits from his cattle breeding enterprise in the purchase of lands in the vicinity of Kirkcudbright, including in particular those of Dunrod.[46] This previously belonged to the McLellans, but they had become impoverished as a result of the extravagances of the third lord Kirkcudbright in raising a regiment to serve in the army of the Covenant. His financial difficulties were compounded still further by the crippling fines imposed on him for his adherence to the Covenant, and it was on this account that he and his successors were forced to sell off the family estates.[47] Most were purchased by Dunbar and his immediate successors,[48] who continued to add to them to the extent that by the 1870s they were among the largest landowners in the county.

Sir David's only son David married as his first wife the eldest daughter of Sir James Dalrymple, and her tragic death shortly afterwards in mysterious circumstances was the inspiration of Sir Walter Scott's novel *The Bride of Lammermoor*. The younger David subsequently remarried and had a daughter Mary, and as he was killed in a riding accident during his father's lifetime she inherited her grandfather's estates on his death in 1686. She subsequently married Lord Basil Hamilton,[49] a younger son of the duke of Hamilton, and on her death in 1760 the Dunbar family estates devolved on their grandson Dunbar who had by that time succeeded his great-uncle as fourth earl of Selkirk.[50]

The decline of the lords Kirkcudbright was mirrored by a similar down-turn in the fortunes of the Kenmure Gordons. Its extent is evident from the fact that, whereas at the beginning of the 1600s they were among the largest landowners in Galloway, some two centuries later their lands were reduced to a tract of hill ground in the parish of Kells. This was mainly because of the uncanny ability of successive holders of the title to back the wrong side at the wrong time. Whereas the fourth viscount was an ardent royalist who paid heavily for his participation in the Glencairn rising, the fifth viscount suffered similar penalties for supporting the covenanters, and for good measure his son, the sixth viscount, was a leading player in the 1715 rebellion, which would cost him his head.

Among the first of the Gordon properties to go was the Penninghame estate, which the fifth viscount's forbear, William Gordon, had acquired from the bishopric of Galloway during Alexander Gordon's episcopacy. This was bought by Colonel William Stewart (coincidentally a descendant of the bishop), and it formed the nucleus of his Castle Stewart estate which was centred on the old keep adjacent to Penninghame itself. The former Lincluden lands at Crossmichael were acquired by the Gordons of Culvennan, who were an offshoot of the Craichlaw family, while those in the parish of Tongland were ultimately acquired by the Murrays of Broughton and Cally.

Whereas most of the remaining Gordon properties appear to have been sold off piecemeal during the 1700s, those in the parishes of Borgue, Kirkmabreck, Girthon and Anwoth, including the old castle of Rusco, were acquired by William McGuffog, whose family had long been small land-holders at Alticry in the parish of Mochrum.[51] These passed to his daughter Grizel who was married to Hugh Blair.[52] He was a younger son of the Rev. Hugh Blair, the purchaser of the former Adair lands of Dunskey, and became the member of parliament for Kirkcudbrightshire after the Union. While the family's star shone brightly for a time it proved transitory, as their son, William Blair-McGuffog, got into financial difficulties, and in 1727 he was forced to sell the estate. Although Rusco itself was retained, the remainder of the lands were sold – almost in their entirety – to John Murray,[53] thus adding substantially to the Cally estate.

Another family which rose to prominence during the seventeenth century were the Herons, an old-established family whose lands at the head of Wigtown Bay were granted by Robert Bruce to their supposed ancestor, Martin McGech. This was mainly due to the success of Patrick Heron's cattle-breeding enterprise which proved so lucrative that he eventually went into parliament, being the first of three generations of his family to do so. His son married the heiress of the Mackies who owned the neighbouring lands of Largs, and the combined estate was formally constituted a barony. His grandson, however, aspired to the world of commerce and was a co-founder of the ill-fated Douglas, Heron & Co. Bank, whose collapse in 1772 resulted in his bankruptcy. Nevertheless, he managed to retain the Kirroughtree estate, and this passed to his daughter, whose Heron-Maxwell descendants continued to own it until the 1930s.

The constructive interest taken by the more enlightened landowners in their estates was reflected in the new type of houses which were being built at the time. No longer geared primarily to defence, as in the past, they now reflected a modest concession to amenity and domestic comfort. Kenmure castle at New Galloway, and Ravenstone near Sorbie, are typical examples, while the contemporary additions made to Lochnaw were designed exclusively for amenity. The best example is Balsarroch house near Corsewall in the Rhinns, which dates from the last quarter of the seventeenth century. This was built for a middle-ranking laird, and epitomises the transitional phase between the medieval towers and the houses of the eighteenth century,[54] where architectural symmetry was the paramount consideration.

The growing interest in estate management, combined with the buoyancy of the cattle trade, accounted for the fashion of building enclosures, which would become increasingly common during the following century. As it was not until the early 1700s that drystone dyking was introduced into Galloway (apparently on the initiative of Lord Basil Hamilton), these walls were built of turf with a cope of whins secured by short stakes to give them added stability. This enabled grassland to be used more productively and, as Samuel Smith put it, grass 'which had before been an object of no value became valuable on its own account',[55] while going on to say that 'it could not fail to strike farmers as a lesson in husbandry'.

THE ILL-YEARS

Charles II's reign saw a return to a semblance of prosperity, though spells of bad weather were responsible for periodic setbacks. For example, the winter of 1674 was so severe that it was preserved in local folklore for long afterwards, and even two centuries later stories were still told of shepherds frantically trying to protect their sheep with the aid of shelters built from the carcases of those which had perished. The following year the harvest failed, and the resulting food shortage forced the government to exempt the western counties from the ban on imported grain for a period of three months, in order to relieve 'death and scarcity'. A further reprieve was granted the following December, when the concession was extended to oatmeal and beans as well.

Worse was to come in the 1690s, when a succession of harvest failures caused such unremitting hardship that they were known for long afterwards as 'the Ill-years of King William's reign'. The decade started reasonably well, but the poor harvests of 1693 and 1694 marked a sharp reverse, while the effects were aggravated by the government's policy of allowing surplus grain to be exported from other regions, and the re-imposition of the ban on imports from Ireland. In 1695 the harvest failed again and rocketing grain prices encouraged a revival of smuggling, though it was not until December, when there was 'a scarcity nixt to a famine', that the government finally relented, first by allowing grain to be imported from Ireland, and later by suspending import duties on food. Another poor harvest the following year forced it to extend these concessions, though they were later repealed following a better harvest in 1697. This proved exceptional, because 1698 brought even worse calamities when 'the harvest became altogether disastrous, first by great winds and thereafter by rains, yea and storms',[56] while the severe winter that followed caused widespread stock losses.

At last the government confronted reality. Old Acts against profiteers were revived, local authorities were ordered to fix prices, the movement of grain was restricted, malting prohibited, and the duty on imported grain was removed once again. Unfortunately, grain was so scarce that the price rocketed, and it was only thanks to the better harvests of 1699 and 1700 that it fell back to an affordable level. Although spells of bad weather were a regular occurrence, the introduction of improved farming practices during the following century meant that people were never again so critically exposed to them as in the past. Altogether, the cost in human lives was such that a contemporary estimate put it at something approaching a third of the entire population of the worst affected areas. Notwithstanding this the Church consistently attributed the famine to 'God's wrath' for the sins and backslidings of the nation, and as a propitiation it recommended the statutory introduction of fast days![57]

Contemporary accounts of this appalling episode are legion, but few are as poignant as that of Sir Robert Sibbald. 'The Bad seasons these several Years past', he wrote, 'hath made so much scarcity and so great a Dearth, that for Want some Die in the Way-side, some drop down in the Streets, the poor sucking Babs are Starving for want of Milk, which the empty Breasts of their Mother cannot furnish them'. Elaborating on the theme, he went on to say that 'Every one may see Death in the Face of the Poor that abound every where; the Thinness of their Visage, their Ghostly Looks, their Feebleness, their Agues and their Fluxes threaten them with sudden Death; if Care be not taken of them'.[58]

That the victims were not confined to the lowest ranks of society is evident from Sibbald's observation that 'it is not only common wandering

Beggars that are in this Case: but many House Keepers who lived well by their Labour and their Industrie are now by want forced to abandon their Dwellings, and they and their little ones must Beg, and in their Necessity they take what they can get of Spoiled Victual'. In their desperation we are told that 'some eat these Beasts which have died of some Disease, which may occasion a Plague among them'. There are also harrowing descriptions of how the living were so undernourished that they could scarcely carry the dead to the churchyard, or feeling the approach of death they literally crawled towards the nearest churchyard in a frantic effort to ensure a decent burial. Even allowing for a touch of hyperbole this must undoubtedly have been an extremely grim episode indeed.

Its effect on the country's economy was equally dire, because precious bullion was needed to pay for imported grain. This meant it was in such short supply that when Scotland was drawn into the War of the Spanish Succession in 1702 the economy came to a virtual standstill, as we are told that it 'occasioned ane entire surcease of the circulation of money or even so much as credit for a great while'. Evidently the cattle trade suffered as well, as it was reported that 'for thir severall years by-past the Scots cattle sold verie ill in England so that trade cam now to be of no account'. In fact, it was a measure of the seriousness of the situation that, according to the records of the English customs for 1704 and 1706, not a single beast was driven across the Border, and while many were doubtless being smuggled into England the trade was clearly at a very low ebb.

Most insidiously of all, however, the combined effect of these calamities, and the consequent elimination of all scope for self-betterment, induced a general spirit of lassitude among the people which it would take them many years to shake off. Yet the potential was there, and that perceptive observer, Daniel Defoe, was aware of it when he commented on the situation at Kirkcudbright. 'People tell us that slothfulness begets poverty, and it is true', he wrote, 'but I must add too that poverty begets slothfulness, and I doubt not were two or three brisk merchants to settle at Kirkcubry, who had stocks to furnish out ships and boats for these things, they would soon find the people as industrious and laborious as in other places'. This was prophetic, for once the opportunities became available people were quick to grasp them, but as these took time to materialise, grinding poverty continued to be their lot for many years to come.

NOTES

1. Agnew (1864), 265.
2. Flinn, *Population History*, 116–26.
3. *Ibid.*, 150 *et seq.*

4. Donaldson, *James V to James VII*, 352.
5. McDowall, *History of Dumfries*, 338.
6. He was the great-grandfather of Annie Laurie, in whose honour the well-known local song was composed.
7. This property passed by inheritance to the Gordons of Earlston, and as they had already disposed of the original Earlston estate, the name was transferred to it. It continued to belong to the family until the 1920s, when it was broken up following the death of the sixth baronet's widow.
8. The name Hannay or A'Hannay features from time to time in the Galloway records, though it was not until the fifteenth century that they acquired the barony of Sorbie. That they were landowners in Wigtownshire during the thirteenth century is evident from the appearance of Gilbert de Hannethe in the Ragman Roll, though the indications are that the kindred was already long established there.
9. Valuation Roll for Wigtownshire 1667
10. *APS* viii, 63, c.5.
11. He was a younger son of the second earl of Galloway and had married a well-dowered heiress, Elizabeth Gordon. In addition to inheriting the lands of Cardiness from her father's family, she was the sole beneficiary of her maternal grandfather, Colonel William Stewart of Castle Stewart, who amassed a fortune in the service of King Gustavus Adolphus of Sweden during the Thirty Years' War. Cardiness passed to William and Elizabeth Stewart's daughter, Nicholas, who married Colonel William Maxwell, and it now belongs to their descendant.
12. McKerlie i, 130.
13. Writing in 1684, Symson observed that 'ships of two hundred tun may come neer to it at a spring-tide, with a good pilot; but yet it hath but little trading by sea' (*Large Description of Galloway*, 34).
14. *Report on the State and Condition of the Burghs of Scotland* 1692.
15. Murray, 'Customs Accounts of Dumfries and Kirkcudbright' 124.
16. *Report on the State and Conditions of the Burghs of Scotland* 1692, 107.
17. *Ibid.*
18. Symson, *Large Description of Galloway*, 35.
19. *Ibid.*
20. *Ibid.*, 30.
21. *Ibid.*, 25.
22. Smout, 'Foreign trade in Dumfries and Galloway', 38–9.
23. Admittedly this is not an entirely fair comparison since the latter figure included cattle from the regions beyond Dumfries and Galloway, while it is highly likely that many more were being smuggled across the Border to evade export duties.
24. *APS* viii, 595 c.21.
25. Symson, *Large Description of Galloway*, 41.
26. Agnew ii, 198.
27. Symson, *Large Description of Galloway*, 42.
28. *Ibid.*, 81.
29. *APS* viii, 63 c.5.
30. Anderson, 'The Development of the Road System', 208: Agnew (1864), 464.
31. Symson, *Large Description of Galloway*, 41.
32. He was one of the most prominent Scotsmen of his day and famed above all as a jurist who codified the law in his treatise the *Institutions of the Law of Scotland*.
33. Credited with responsibility for the massacre of Glencoe, which has been much

inflated by Jacobite propagandists, he was one of the principal architects of the Union.

34. As detailed in Agnew ii, 75–7.

35. McKerlie i, 182–3, and Agnew (1864), 499. Although the story has the ring of fantasy I mention it for what it is worth.

36. Based on McKerlie i, 150–2. The facts, as far as the earl of Cassilis and lord Bargany are concerned, are vouched for by the *DNB*, though not of course the means by which Dalrymple allegedly secured the lands.

37. Ironically, Bargany's granddaughter and heiress of his Ayrshire estate married Dalrymple's nephew, their descendants taking the name Dalrymple-Hamilton, and the two families were reunited in the nineteenth century.

38. One of their daughters, Elizabeth, was married to Sir David Dunbar of Baldoon, while another, Agnes, was the wife of William Maxwell of Monreith, whose son, Sir William, acquired most of the McCulloch family estates.

39. He was the father of Elizabeth Gordon, who married Major-General William Stewart.

40. The fall of the McCullochs is described in McCulloch, *Galloway McCullochs*.

41. Agnew ii, 124.

42. *Ibid.*, 237: McKerlie i, 269–70.

43. McKerlie i, 270. She was his first cousin, as her mother was a daughter of Sir James Dalrymple. Their ultimate heiress subsequently married the eldest son of the first marquis of Bute, and Mochrum itself passed to a junior branch of the family who continues to own it. The Dunbars subsequently bought another property on the Bladnoch which they re-named Mochrum Park, and although this too has been sold the baronetcy still exists.

44. *Ibid.* ii, 79.

45. *Ibid.*, 270.

46. Symson, *Large Description of Galloway*, 13.

47. Although the family eventually became landless the Kirkcudbright barony survived until the death of the ninth lord in 1832 when the title became dormant.

48. McKerlie is not helpful here, so it is difficult to distinguish between the properties in the neighbourhood of Kirkcudbright which were acquired by Sir David Dunbar and those purchased by his successors.

49. He too became a noted cattle breeder, having obtained special permission from the privy council 'to import six score young cows from Ireland for the park at Baldoon' (Agnew (1864), 463). However his promising career was cut short by his accidental drowning in the Minnoch in 1701 while rescuing his brother, the earl of Selkirk.

50. In 1744 when he changed the family name back to Douglas.

51. They would almost certainly have been of the same kin as – and perhaps even descendants of – the Richard McGuffog, to whom Robert Bruce made a grant of the lands of Kilsture adjacent to the Moss of Cree.

52. He married as his second wife Margaret, the daughter of Sir David Dunbar, and their three sons were all landholders in the parish of Borgue, the second one, Hugh, having acquired the lands of Dunrod which his son ultimately disposed of to William Corrie, an incomer from Northamptonshire whose family continues to be represented in the district.

53. He had inherited the lands of Broughton from his father Richard Murray, and those of Cally from his mother Anna Lennox, while his nephew James Murray became a leading Galloway entrepreneur.

54. Smith, 'Balsarroch House, Wigtownshire', 71–81.
55. Smith, *Agricultural Survey*, 43.
56. Flinn, *Population History*, 169.
57. *Ibid.*, 168: Ferguson, *Scotland: 1689 to the Present*, 79.
58. Sir Robert Sibbald, *Provision for the Poor in Time of Dearth and Scarcity* (1699), 2–3.

27

THE EARLY 1700s: DESTITUTION

The Treaty of Union

King William died in 1702[1] and was succeeded by James VII's Protestant daughter, Queen Anne. She had already produced a large family but none of them survived, and, although still only thirty-seven, the chances of her having any more children seemed remote. Anticipating this, the English parliament passed the Act of Supremacy in 1701 which excluded Catholics from the succession and formally recognised the claim of James VI's Lutheran granddaughter, the Electress Sophia of Hanover,[2] to the reversion of the throne. The Scottish parliament pointedly declined to follow suit, and as there was strong support for Anne's half-brother, the Catholic Prince James,[3] it looked as though her death could result in a separation of the crowns.

Of more immediate concern to the English was that they were now at war with France over the issue of the Spanish succession, and unless there was full political union with Scotland there was a distinct possibility that the Scots would revive their auld alliance with the French, in which case they would find themselves fighting the war on two fronts. The Scots, on the other hand, were generally hostile to the idea. They attributed the recent failure of the Darien scheme to English machinations,[4] and besides they feared that they would remain the junior partner and simply become absorbed into England, with a consequent loss of their national identity.

Meanwhile, Queen Anne was statutorily obliged to summon a Scottish parliament within twenty days of her accession, but on the advice of her English ministers she delayed doing so in order to allow the more compliant privy council to declare war on France. Therefore, when parliament assembled the duke of Hamilton claimed that the council had acted beyond its powers, and as parliament had been summoned outwith the twenty-day period it was an illegal body and therefore lacked the competence to endorse the council's actions. However, when he failed to carry his point, he and his supporters withdrew in protest, leaving

parliament in control of the pro-Union duke of Queensberry. Responding
to English demands, the latter appointed commissioners to negotiate an
incorporating Union with representatives of the English parliament, but
their deliberations were so fraught with difficulty and ill-will, as well as
bedevilled by political intriguing at home, that they eventually broke down.

This was attributable in the first instance to the actions of the Scottish
parliament which, in a demonstration of its independence, passed an Act
of Security which affirmed its right to appoint a successor to Queen Anne.
It also asserted its power to declare peace or war, which was a highly
provocative step since it raised the possibility of the Scots changing sides in
the War of the Spanish Succession and fighting against the English. The
latter responded by passing the Alien Act of 1705. This threatened to treat
the Scots as aliens and ban all trade between the two countries unless the
Act of Security was withdrawn and the Scots accepted the Hanoverian
succession. It was deliberately aimed at those leading anti-Unionists like the
duke of Hamilton who owned estates in England, since these stood to be
forfeited, while the banning of trade would kill off the market for Scottish-
bred cattle. Predictably, this provoked a storm of indignation, but cooler
heads, tempted in a number of cases by English bribes, accepted the reality
of the situation, and a ministry was appointed under Argyll for the purpose
of working positively for 'ane entire union'.[5]

New commissioners were appointed to negotiate the Articles of Union,
and within three months a set of twenty-five articles was agreed, including
freedom of trade, exemption from the English malt tax, and the
preservation of the law of Scotland and its judiciary. The treaty was now put
to the vote in both parliaments. In Scotland the opposition mounted a
strenuous campaign, though they had the ground cut from under their feet
when the general assembly, which still had a powerful voice in political
affairs and had hitherto been vehemently opposed to the Union, changed
its stance after the passing of a bill guaranteeing the presbyterian settlement. Other former opponents were suborned by a combination of English
bribes and titles, with the result that the treaty was finally ratified by the
Scottish parliament in January 1707, and in May it passed both houses of
the English parliament.

This set out the framework for the combined parliament and, reflecting
the disparate wealth and populations of the two countries, Scotland was
given 16 of the 206 seats in the House of Lords and 45 of the 558 in the
Commons. Of these 45, 30 represented the counties (Kirkcudbrightshire
and Wigtownshire being separate constituencies), and the remaining 15
the burghs. The method of apportioning the latter was complex; in the
south-west, one seat represented the Wigtownshire burghs, and another
those in Dumfriesshire. The two royal burghs in Kirkcudbrightshire were
split between them, with New Galloway being included with Stranraer,

Wigtown and Whithorn. Kirkcudbright, on the other hand, was incorporated with those in Dumfriesshire, while the parliamentary representatives were chosen by commissioners from each burgh.

Notwithstanding that the Act of Union was passed by a majority in the Scottish parliament it was widely unpopular. The Edinburgh mob went on the rampage and pro-union politicians hesitated to venture out into the streets for fear of their lives. Riots also broke out in Dumfries where, in an unlikely alliance, some 300 armed Cameronians and Jacobites entered the town. Here they ceremoniously burned the Articles of Union, claiming them to be 'utterly destructive of the nation's independence, crown rights and our constitute laws both civil and sacred'. They also publicly condemned the actions of parliament who, as they put it, 'shall presume to carry on the said Union by a supream power over the belly of the generality of the nation'.[6] With a few exceptions, such as the fifth earl of Galloway, who was Queensberry's nephew, and his other uncle, Major-General William Stewart, whose support was secured with a bribe of £500, the Galloway landowners were equally opposed to it. Although the attitude of the majority softened through time, men like Colonel William Maxwell of Cardoness, the local member of the Scottish parliament, and McKie of Palgowan remained obdurate.

In the short term the union did not augur well, and many Scots felt their opposition to it was fully justified. It brought no immediate benefits apart from giving a stimulus to the cattle trade, while the English-dominated parliament betrayed an arrogant high-handedness, amounting to a breach of good faith, in its dealings with the Scots. A notable example was the abolition of the Scottish privy council, despite English assurances that it would be retained, while another was its attempt to extend the malt tax to Scotland. This flagrant breach of the terms of the treaty provoked such an outcry that it was abandoned, so all it did was to give an added fillip to the Jacobite cause.

The new electoral arrangments lent themselves to abuse as well, mainly because the Court of Session, as the supreme court in Scotland, was powerless to control them. Although suffrage was limited to property owners with lands valued at £400 or more, local magnates could artificially extend this by making temporary grants of land – 'trust conveyances' as they were known – to their supporters, one of the worst offenders being Queensberry, whose influence extended into Kirkcudbrightshire. Similarly, the costs of attending parliament were so prohibitive that only those who could obtain the financial backing of these magnates could afford a career in politics. This meant that in Galloway control of the local parliamentary seats was virtually delivered into the hands of the earls of Galloway and Stair, as the two wealthiest magnates in the region, and it was to be a constant source of rivalry between the two families.[8]

THE 1715 REBELLION

When Queen Anne died in 1714, the succession passed to her nearest Protestant relative, the Electress Sophia's son who ascended the throne as George I. A somewhat bovine character, whose principal claim to fame was to have locked his wife up for thirty years after she had been caught out in an adulterous affair, he was scarcely calculated to inspire the loyalty, let alone the affection, of his new subjects. While the English grudgingly accepted the situation, many Scots continued to favour Prince James, in spite of his Catholicism disqualifying him from the succession. Nevertheless, the earl of Mar, a failed politician who harboured a personal grudge against King George, took the initiative, and in an act of uncharacteristic decisiveness he raised his banner for 'James VIII' on the Braes of Mar in September 1715.

There was little support for Prince James's cause in Galloway, since this was traditionally a stronghold of Protestant extremism, while memories of the oppressive rule of his father and uncle, Charles II, still ran deep. Most of the landowners were Whigs who supported the Hanoverian succession, though there were some exceptions, such as the staunchly catholic Maxwells who were naturally inclined to the Jacobites, the most active being the fifth earl of Nithsdale and George Maxwell of Munches, whose two sons fought for them and were taken prisoner. Others included the strongly anti-unionist sixth viscount Kenmure, Colonel William Maxwell, and Ferguson of Craigdarroch, near Moniaive, while the only Jacobite-supporting landowner in Wigtownshire was Basil Hamilton, the heir to the Dunbar estate of Baldoon.[9]

On Ferguson's initiative, a meeting of Jacobite sympathisers was convened at Dalmellington to enlist support among 'the well-affected nobility, gentry and citizens within the Shires of Clydesdale, Renfrew, Ayr, Galloway, Nithsdale and the Stewartries and bailiaries thereof'. Most of the leading Jacobite supporters attended, as well as McLellan of Barscobe and Grierson of Lag who had not so far declared for Prince James; so in a flush of optimism plans were drawn up to raise an army in the south-west. This was put under the command of Kenmure, with Basil Hamilton acting as one of his principal lieutenants.[10] It was also arranged that once the standard of rebellion was raised, he would join forces with the earl of Mar in his planned advance into England.

This failed to materialise because, when Mar encountered the government troops under the duke of Argyll at Sheriffmuir, the result was a drawn battle in which the left wing of each army was defeated. Nevertheless, Argyll managed to prevent Mar from marching southwards to join up with other

Jacobite supporters, so they were left to take the initiative themselves. Therefore a ramshackle army, which included Kenmure's contingent, marched across the Border in the hopes of attracting Jacobites in northern England in a concerted invasion of the south. However, their hopes proved illusory because very few English Jacobites materialised, so they were left to conduct the campaign on their own. Ill-trained and ill-equipped, the invading army was nothing more than an undisciplined rabble commanded by inexperienced leaders with no clearly defined objective apart from the prospect of English loot. When it finally encountered the government troops at Preston it was routed and many of the leaders taken prisoner, the chilly and uncharismatic Prince James having by that time made his way back to France.

Severe reprisals were taken, and the estates – and titles – of the leading rebels were forfeited, many of them, including Kenmure, being executed, though in his case the title was eventually restored to his family. Nithsdale was also under sentence of death, but thanks to the efforts of his resourceful wife he contrived to escape from prison in disguise almost on the eve of his execution. Thereafter he escaped to France where he remained for the rest of his life, his title being forfeited.[11] Basil Hamilton was also sentenced to death, and although he was subsequently reprieved at the intercession of his cousin, the duke of Hamilton, his estates were also confiscated.[12]

THE LEVELLERS' REVOLT

Meanwhile, the principal landowners in Galloway were pursuing the prevailing fashion of enclosing their estates. This involved evicting many small tenants and amalgamating their holdings into larger units, so that they could be enclosed with stone dykes and re-let for a substantially higher rent. A noted dyke-builder was the veteran Sir Alexander Gordon of Earlston, of covenanting fame, and in the early 1720s he was responsible for building a four-mile wall to enclose 'a substantial grazing park', while Quintin McAdam of Craigengillan (a large moorland estate straddling the northern reaches of Kirkcudbrightshire) is reported to have 'built perhaps more stone dykes and of better quality than any man in Scotland at that period'.[13] Another was the anti-Unionist Alexander McKie of Palgowan,[14] whose lands embraced another large tract of moorland on the western slopes of the Merrick range. In all, 'thousands of miles of drystone dykes' were built in Galloway alone.[15]

The dispossessed farmers were put to extreme hardship, and the resulting discontent created a highly volatile situation. Matters came to a head when a large number of tenant farmers, hit by a run of bad harvests and in arrears with their rent, were faced with eviction at the term of Whitsunday 1723, many of them, according to John Maxwell of Munches, being 'utterly destitute from age and poverty'.[16] Some of the less tractable stood their ground, and it was the refusal of two tenants on the Earlston estate to remove themselves that sparked off what became known as the 'levellers' revolt'. A protest meeting of tenants, mostly drawn from the lower Dee valley and adjacent parishes, was held at Kelton Hill near Castle Douglas in June 1723 – an event which was deliberately timed to coincide with the annual fair.

Some had already entered into a bond with each other not to quit their holdings, but it was here that the idea of razing dykes to the ground, or levelling them, was first mooted. Therefore it was decided to split up into gangs, and with the aid of 'pitchforks, gravellocks and spades' systematically to level all dykes in the neighbouring parishes and to target the Earlston estate in particular. Also, because Basil Hamilton was widely unpopular on account of his support for the rebellion, his St Mary's Isle estate was singled out as well,[17] notwithstanding his attempt to appease the levellers by offering them lands at Cumstoun.[18] According to one account, another proprietor was more successful in escaping their attentions when he offered the levellers a drink before embarking on the work of demolishing his dykes, because the upshot was 'they drank his ale and spared his dikes'.

Since the local Church was initially sympathetic to their cause, the levellers fixed manifestos setting out their grievances to the church doors of Twynholm and Borgue, whose minister, James Monteith, was particularly vociferous in his support for them.[19] However, as the rising gathered momentum and the levellers' campaign became increasingly destructive, the Church changed its stance and a minute of the Kirkcudbright presbytery denounced them as striking 'against the institution of Heaven' and 'overthrowing magistracy contrair to the word of God'.[20]

The levellers' depredations extended into Wigtownshire, where the earl of Galloway's estates were the main object of attack. This caused him to send an anguished plea for help to his influential brother-in-law, Sir John Clerk,[21] and in a letter dated 2 May 1724 he describes how they had 'destroyed the whole encloasures in the Stewartrie' and were planning to demolish 'all parks upon the Watter of Cree', at consequent risk to his livestock. Finally, he warned that 'if we have not the protection of the Govert by allowing troops to march into the countrie for our assistance I do relie [really] believe the whole gentlemen of Galloway will be ruined'.[22]

However, Sir John Clerk was already being kept abreast of events by his brother James, who was the collector of customs at Kirkcudbright. So it was probably at his instigation that the steward depute ordered all landholders to assemble at the steps of Tarff 'with their best horses, arms, and ammunition to proceed against the levellers'.[23] Some fifty horsemen turned up, mainly with the intention of parleying with them, but after several hours of fruitless discussion the levellers threatened to abandon negotiations and resume their work of destruction. At this point Heron of Kirroughtree[24] intervened and persuaded them to agree to resume negotiations a few days later on Bombie Moor. When the appointed time came the levellers turned up in force, but as no landowners appeared, apart from some representatives of Basil Hamilton, they immediately dispersed to continue their work.[25] Less defensibly this included houghing cattle, while they deliberately slaughtered fifty-three animals belonging to Blair of Dunrod, claiming that they were suspected of being illegally imported from Ireland.[26]

This impelled the earl of Stair to dispatch four troops of dragoons to restore order. After an initial success, in which they captured a number of the ringleaders, a skirmish took place at the steps of Tarff when further prisoners were taken. Shortly afterwards, a more serious engagement took place at Duchrae in the parish of Balmaghie in October 1724[27] where some 200 prisoners were captured, although a number of them were tacitly allowed to escape while being taken to the Kirkcudbright gaol.[28] Sporadic acts of destruction continued for some months afterwards until the situation was brought under control, though the authorities wisely decided against adding more recruits to the mythology of Galloway martyrdom and released most of the prisoners. Nevertheless, this was small comfort to them when there was no other employment available, and in common with others who were equally frustrated by the lack of opportunity for self-advancement, they emigrated to England, or further afield to America and the West Indies. In fact the exodus was such that the Wigtown customs officer is recorded as complaining of 'a spirit of emigration . . . in this country next to madness'.

Some turned to a life of crime and threw in their lot with the bands of gypsies, who roamed the Galloway uplands and lived chiefly by stealing and predation. Still more profitable were their protection rackets, since farmers living in isolated locations were readily persuaded to part with blood-money as an insurance against having their stock stolen, their crops and even their houses burnt. Unsurprisingly these people were universally regarded as the curse of the countryside, and Heron castigates them as being 'among those savage animals which increasing population and order expel or exterminate'.[29] Warming to the theme, he goes on to describe how 'they devour carrion with wolfish rapacity – they steal poultry, and tear them in pieces almost raw', and as to their morals, he tells us that 'the intercourse of the sexes among them, is promiscuous, as among the brutes: no laws of marriage are faithfully observed: no relation of affinity or consanguinity imposes any restraints upon lust'.[30]

The most famous of the Galloway gypsy 'kings' was Billy Marshall, who reputedly served as a trooper in the Scots Greys in the War of the Spanish Succession until he deserted to take up a life of brigandage. He was also a prominent participant in the levellers' revolt, where his military experience would have been put to good use in drilling and training them in the art of warfare.[31] Tradition gives him sixteen or seventeen wives and a host of children which he continued to sire into his eleventh decade, and when he died in 1792 he is believed to have reached the ripe old age of a hundred and twenty. Even as late as the 1790s he would recall seeing King William's fleet lying storm-bound in Kirkcudbright Bay during its passage to Ireland more than a century before. Despite Heron's tirade that 'hardly could a crime, or a species of dissipation be named, of which he had not, at one time or another, been guilty; murder, robbery, incest',[32] he ended his days a pillar of respectability with the earl of Selkirk acting as chief mourner at his funeral.

CONTEMPORARY GALLOWAY

For those who remained in Galloway the prospects were as bleak as the contemporary descriptions of the region itself, for poverty was endemic and life for the mass of the people a constant struggle against hardship and adversity. An English visitor paints a doleful picture. 'If the traveller entered [Scotland] by Dumfriesshire and the moors of Galloway', he wrote, 'he was at once filled with dismay by the dismal change from his own country – the landscape a bleak and bare solitude, destitute of trees, abounding in heather and morass and barren hills'. Cultivation was minimal and 'found only in dirty patches of crops on ground surrounded by heather and bog . . . the inhabitants spoke an uncouth dialect, were dressed in rags, lived in hovels and fed on the grain which the Englishman would feed to his horses'. Describing the abysmal standard of accommodation available to the traveller, he goes on to say that 'when night fell, and he reached a town of dirty, thatched huts, and gained refuge in a miserable abode which passed for an inn, only to get a bed he could not sleep in, and fare he could not eat, his disgust was inexpressible'.

The reference to the dearth of trees is significant, as this was characteristic of much of Scotland and, as is evident from recurrent legislation on the subject, it had long been the case. It was also the subject of comment by other English travellers to Scotland, and one of them, Sir Anthony Weldon, who had visited the country in 1617, wrote in a picturesque turn of phrase that 'if Christ had been betrayed in Scotland Judas would sooner have found the grace of repentance than a tree on which to hang himself'. Dr Johnson also observed in the course of his tour of the Highlands during the mid-eighteenth century that 'a tree in Scotland is as rare as a horse in Venice'.

On the other hand, a number of landowners were establishing plantations on their estates, and Sir John Clerk makes a number of references to this in the course of his journey through Galloway in 1721,[33] when he expatiated in particular on Andrew Heron's estate of Bargaly near Creetown. And well he might, since he describes it as including gardens, orchards, orangeries, waterworks, fishponds, bagnios (hothouses), enclosures, arbours and woods with 'a fine collection of various sorts of shrubs and evergreens'.[34] Others had to overcome the resistance of their tenants, and the earl of Stair's factor wrote to him in 1731 complaining that 'the people will not let the plantations grow'.[35] Similar objections were raised against their attempts to plant hedges, because the tenant farmers were concerned that their roots spoiled the ground, their shade prevented growth, and they attracted birds to the detriment of their crops.

Poverty was endemic throughout the region and, according to a contemporary observer, this 'was evident from the dirt-stained natives, the horses [being] dwarfish, lean and hungry, the cattle emaciated and stunted, the miserable hovels of turf and stone and the poor patches of tilled land abounding in thistles and nettles in the ridges'. As a result, the people themselves became 'shiftless, apathetic and sluggish, seeming to dignify dirt and consecrate laziness'. The Church was primarily responsible for encouraging this, since it was integral to its teaching that crop failure – and indeed all adversity – was an act of God and to do anything to hinder the workings of Providence was sinful. Consequently, their apathy and shiftlessness became proverbial and the physical appearance of the people a source of ridicule to contemporary writers. Typical of this was the observation of one commentator that, 'the common people are such in outward appearance as you would not take them at first to be of the human species, and in their lives they differ little from the brutes, except in their love of spirituous liquors . . . the nastiness of the lower people is really greater than can be reported'.

Their diet was unremittingly poor and monotonous, for they had nothing to eat apart from the ubiquitous oatmeal, 'knockit bere', or kail. Writing in 1793, the minister of Tongland recalled how 'they ate of the meanest and coarsest food [which] consisted of brose, pottage, oat-meal flummery, and greens boiled in water with a little salt. The dishes out of which they fed were seldom washed after meals, and of course, were often thick with dirt'.[36] Although the potato was first introduced as an experiment in Galloway in 1725 the people were convinced it was an inferior substitute for meal, regarding it with angry suspicion, and it was not until much later that they came to accept the potato as part of their staple diet. Contemporary commentators are unanimous in stressing the importance of oats, how crop after crop was grown until the ground was exhausted and had to be left fallow and a prey to weeds. The only exception was a small patch of in-bye land known as the *bere-lay* which was kept permanently under cultivation, received the whole dung of the farm, and was regularly sown with bere or barley.[37]

Farms were invariably overstocked, and whereas in summer constant supervision of livestock was necessary to prevent them from straying on to the growing crops, in winter they were allowed to forage for themselves. Some were accidentally drowned in the boggy flows which were prevalent throughout Galloway, and by springtime the survivors were frequently so weak that it was customary for neighbours to co-operate in lifting them on to the new grass.[38] The carcases of those which had perished were the only source of meat available[39] though, according to Maxwell, this could extend to 'a crock [diseased] ewe now and then about Martinmas'.[40]

The milk yielded by their undernourished cows was invariably in short supply and frequently rendered sour from being kept in filthy containers. In fact cleanliness was regarded as a positive disadvantage, while the glorification of dirt was reflected in a number of superstitions. For example, it was widely believed that if a frog was put into a milk tub it would help the milk to churn better, and the quality of butter was rated according to the number of hairs it contained, while such aphorisms as 'muck makes luck' and 'the clartier the cosier' were widely accepted. Fish was available for those living near the coast, but it was regarded in some quarters with suspicion, since it was popularly supposed to be responsible for some unpleasant bowel diseases. Those living near rivers benefited from salmon, trout and coarse fish, though eels were apparently less popular, as it was claimed that the people had 'an insuperable prejudice against feeding on an animal which so strongly resembles the serpent'![41]

Clothing for both men and women consisted entirely of home-made plaiding. While the older women wore shawls the girls went bareheaded, but the men wore their headgear permanently, even in bed. In fact, the only time they ever removed it was in church and then only during prayers, the singing of the psalm, and the pronouncing of the blessing.[42] Outwardly there was little to distinguish the bonnet laird from his tenantry, for they too wore home-made clothing woven by their family or servants, or perhaps the village 'wabster', and the only sartorial difference was that, as his name implied, he wore a bonnet. According to Maxwell, 'they thought themselves very well dressed for going to church on Sunday with a black kelt-coat of their wife's making', since only the wealthier gentry could afford to buy their clothes elsewhere.[43]

Living conditions had changed little over the centuries. The peasants' accommodation is described as consisting of 'wretched, dirty hovels built with stones and mud, thatched with fern and turf, without chimneys, filled with smoke and black with soot, having low doors and small holes for windows [which are] often stopped with turf, straw, or fragments of old clothes'.[44] Ventilation seems to have been minimal, as one commentator describes how 'the people lived in a constant cloud of smoke, enough to suffocate them had they not been habituated to it from infancy'.[45] Usually the fire itself was in the centre of the floor, though in some cases a fireplace was built against the gable wall. The only part of the building which was of any value was the timber frame supporting the roof, and a householder would normally try and remove it at the end of his tenancy to use it in the construction of another dwelling.

The interior consisted of a single room, while a layer of straw, and sometimes heather or bracken, covering the bare earth sufficed for a floor. In winter time it was customary for the house cows to be accommodated in the dwelling, where they constituted an additional source of warmth, and as there was no intervening wall or partition[46] they were simply 'tied to stakes on one end of the house'[47] Their presence must have been noisomely apparent, and a contemporary Gallovidian writer describes how his mother always knew it was time to warm the porridge when she heard the family cow pass water for the second time.[48] Plagued as they were by flies and other insects which flourished in the rank humidity of a Galloway summer, those who objected to these fetid conditions were told that 'dirt was wholesome and never killed swine'!

The condition of the tenant farmer was only marginally better, since his house was larger, and generally consisted of two rooms which comprised the traditional 'but and ben'. The 'but' was used as the kitchen, as well as the sleeping quarters for the maidservants and the daughters of the house. As beds were still a rarity, people generally wrapped themselves in plaids and slept on piles of straw or heather on the floor. A large table stood in the kitchen at which everyone ate, while the other main feature was the chimney – the 'ingle nook' – which was built over a cradle grate and surrounded by a wooden bench. The 'ben' was the private apartment of the householder and his wife, and here they entertained their guests, and also slept with their younger children. The boys of the house were accommo- dated either in a loft up in the rafters, or in an outside shed known as a 'bothy', which they shared with the menservants – or the 'hinds', as they were generally known. Immediately outside the front door was the com- munal midden on which all the human and animal excrement was dumped, and which the women would carry away in creels on their backs to the infield, where it was used to dung the barley crop.[49]

MORTALITY

Unsurprisingly, disease in all the forms which lack of ventilation and general filth could engender was rampant, and smallpox – frequently the result of living in close proximity to the cows – was a particularly vicious killer. Its appearance, however, was accepted with the same fatalism as any other adversity, reflecting the common belief that it was ordained of God and that to take precautionary measures was seen as thwarting His will and therefore tantamount to sin. Once a disease struck, the close proximity of the dwellings would ensure its rapid spread through a community, and nothing could be more calculated to assist the process than the prevailing custom of 'helpful' neighbours crowding into the patient's hovel and inhaling an atmosphere already saturated with germs and foul air.

Other common ailments included ague – a generic term for all types of fevers – and the flux, or diarrhoea, caused by dysentery, from which many people were regularly prostrated. Rheumatism, too, was the inevitable result of incessant exposure to cold and wet, and reflecting the general debility of the people was their practice of drawing blood from the cows to mix with meal to make black puddings, or simply sucking this form of protein straight out of the animals themselves. Infant mortality was appallingly high – a reflection alike of the prevailing social conditions and the primitive state of medical science. Typical of this were the instructions given in a popular medical guide for the care of newborn babies. 'Do not', it enjoins, 'give babies wine or whisky as soon as they are born; they prefer milk, and it is much better for them. Do not drop them straight into a basin of cold water; it is better to bathe them in warm water'.[50] The universal panacea was bloodletting with the aid of leeches, to the extent that it was customary for upperclass people to undergo this at regular intervals in the belief that it was good for their constitution, and boys sometimes earned a pittance by standing in a stagnant pond to attract leeches to sell to the local apothecary.

As recovery from disease was rare, death was almost invariably the outcome. Here, tradition dictated the funeral to be as lavish as the family could afford, since it was the ambition of everyone to have 'a decent funeral', to be properly clad as a corpse, and buried respectably. Therefore, it was customary for a woman as soon as she was married to spin her own winding sheet, and this was reverentially kept until the time came for it to be used. When death came – and it was generally sooner rather than later – the body clad in its winding sheet was laid out to view so that friends could come and pay their last respects. On the day of the funeral, friends and neighbours would gather at the cottage to escort the body to the kirkyard where the burial took place. This was followed by the 'wake' which was generally an occasion for excessive drinking – a practice which applied to all classes, for a man who enjoyed his fill during his lifetime was anxious that his friends should enjoy equally unstinted hospitality at his death. 'For God's sake', one dying laird abjured his son, 'give them a hearty dram' .

THE SMUGGLING TRADE

Smuggling was a traditional activity in Galloway, and the regular upsurges in the trade coincided with the imposition of duty on imports and the creation of an artificial market for contraband goods at discounted prices. The revival which occurred during the eighteenth century was triggered off initially by the extension of the malt tax to Scotland, while a later Act of 1726,[51] raising the level of duty, gave it added impetus. However, it was not until the latter half of the century, when growing prosperity led to an escalating demand for contraband goods, that it blossomed into a major industry in which a large number of local people participated.

Almost all the goods landed on the south-west coast of Scotland – principally from the vicinity of Ayr as far round as the Urr estuary – and were dispersed to other parts of the country. They consisted mainly of tobacco, wines and spirits, including in particular rum, brandy and geneva (gin), and to a lesser extent textiles such as silk, cloth and lace, while tea, spices and salt were also included in the cargoes brought ashore. Many of these commodities came from the East Indies, and the British East India Company, which had a local monopoly in these goods, set up subsidiary companies in Europe for the specific purpose of organising their freight-age to the British mainland. Ostend, and to a lesser extent the island of Guernsey, were the main entrepôts, and the goods were generally shipped to temporary staging posts, such as the Isle of Man, the island of Rathlin, or Sanda, an island adjacent to the Mull of Kintyre, where they would be held until conditions were right for a run ashore.

Once landed, the goods were stowed away in caves or remote farm-houses equipped with concealed cellars known as 'brandy holes', or they were simply buried in the ground. Local crofters and farmers would transport them to the main collecting points; and, according to Webster, some of the leading participants went to the lengths of buying coastal farms as a cloak for their activities,[52] while the local gypsies were also ready to assist in return for a share of the proceeds. Minnigaff was the main collecting point in western Galloway, while the goods landed further up the Solway were taken to New Galloway, and there they were loaded on to pack horses and taken out of the region to be dispersed to their markets.

Legislation was passed giving customs officers additional powers to put a stop to this, and an Act of 1753 decreed that any ship found with contra-band goods aboard was liable to be broken up and burnt. However, these appear to have had little or no effect, for an exciseman is reported as complaining in 1761 that 'the insolence and audacity of smugglers is much increased . . . and now they ride openly thro' the country with their goods' in troops of up to fifty horses 'suffering no officers to come near'.[53] The excisemen were fighting a losing battle, because too many people were involved in the trade for the legislation to bite; in fact, there were instances of customs officers being forcibly restrained while cargoes were landed, and even when the goods were impounded in the king's warehouses they were seldom safe from attack.

The government responded by increasing the number of excisemen (Robert Burns being one of them), and an Act of 1784, known as the 'Hovering Act',[54] decreed that any vessel found at anchor, or hovering within four leagues of the coast, was liable to be boarded. Yet, the following year the collector of customs at Dumfries was reporting to his superiors that 'adventurers from the Isle of Man had landed from their sloop a small quantity of tobacco and brandy in open day in the neighbourhood of the Water of Urr'.[55] In fact, smuggling was so rampant that it became a divisive political issue, and while some politicians were opposed to the trade on principle, others were more concerned to appease the government at Westminster, which was highly critical of the apparent laxity of the Scottish authorities in enforcing the anti-smuggling laws.

Profitable though the trade may have been, there was an obverse side to it, for according to Agnew 'the whole tone of country life became thoroughly demoralised'. 'The thrifty toiler', he went on, 'degenerated into a dissolute, lazy loafer. All honest work on the land was abandoned, and strife and intemperance went hand-in-hand with even less desirable failings'. Certainly drunkenness seems to have been on the increase and, as Sir Robert Chambers observed, 'it was nothing unusual for the whole family – men, women and children – to continue in a state of intoxication for three days and nights without intermission'. Nevertheless, the minister of Mochrum, writing in 1794, admits that 'the illicit trade, for which this place was, till of late, so noted, however reprehensible in itself, and generally hurtful, has contributed considerably, both to the increase of population, and the improvement of agriculture here'.[56]

This view was not shared by his superiors, since the Church naturally adopted a high moral stand, and ministers constantly railed and the general assembly thundered against smuggling. But clerical denunciations were no deterrent to those practitioners of free trade who had so much to gain from it, particularly when some members of the cloth were suspected of receiving contraband goods themselves. However, it was a change in the law rather than government intervention or clerical fulmination which accounted for its decline. Prime Minister William Pitt's reduction in the duty on tea from 119 per cent to 12 per cent in favour of an increase in the window tax, introduced in 1785, was one example,[57] but it was the long overdue relaxation in excise duties in the 1830s which finally killed off the trade.

THE 1745 REBELLION

By early 1745 plans were well advanced to raise another Jacobite rebellion, and this time the initiative was taken by Prince James's son, Charles Edward, who had received promises of French help. His intention was to land on the west coast of Scotland, where a number of Highland chiefs had pledged their support, and then make a lightning dash for the south. This was to synchronise with a French invasion across the Channel, though the latter was abandoned at an early stage when their fleet ran into a violent storm and had to put about. Notwithstanding, Prince Charles persevered with his plans, and on 3 August he landed with a small force on the coast of Moidart. However, when he raised his standard at Glenfinnan a fortnight later local support proved disappointingly meagre.

Undeterred, Charles proceeded to march southwards and a few minor successes encouraged more clansmen to join him. Perth was taken, and eventually his army entered Edinburgh almost unopposed. On 21 September he defeated a government force under Sir John Cope at Prestonpans, which opened the way for an advance into England. By this time it had become apparent that there was little support for his cause in the lowlands, so Charles's advisers had misgivings about crossing the Border, and it was only by a narrow majority that his war council approved it. The decision was justified, as opposition proved minimal and within a month Charles's army reached Derby; but here fortune began to turn against him. Many of his Highland troops were deserting, and unless he retreated north immediately there was a risk of the government troops cutting him off; so, much against his will, he was prevailed on to abandon his intention of marching on London and order a withdrawal. By late December his army was back in Scotland. Although it defeated an English force at Falkirk the following month, its fate was sealed in April, when it encountered a numerically superior force under the duke of Cumberland on Culloden moor, near Inverness. The Jacobite army was cut to pieces, and after a number of adventures Charles escaped back to France.

The rising had little impact on Galloway, where there was no more sympathy for the Jacobite cause than in 1715, the only local landowner to come out in support being the Catholic James Maxwell of Kirkconnel. Yet, the Gallovidians had no particular wish to identify themselves with the Hanoverians either. For, when the duke of Cumberland ordered the northern counties to raise a militia to cut off Prince Charles's retreat from Derby, only a token force could be raised, and this included twelve men from Lochrutton parish who volunteered to guard Annan bridge.[58] Not surprisingly, the local defence force failed to prevent Charles and his soldiery from reaching Dumfries, where they commandeered arms and gunpowder from the officials, as well as a large supply of footgear.[59] Or, as a local minister put it, 'they were most rude in the town – pillaged some shops – pulled shoes off from gentlemen's feet in the street' and extorted money from the leading citizens.[60] Sir Walter Scott adds a human touch by describing how Provost Corsane's six-year-old daughter saved her father's house from being looted and burnt by agreeing to address Charles Edward as 'prince'.[61]

LOCAL JUSTICE

In the aftermath of the rebellion the government systematically dismantled all the paraphernalia of Highland society, and consequently the Heritable Jurisdictions Act was passed in 1747, which abolished all hereditary tenures, including sheriffships. Nevertheless, consolatory golden handshakes were paid, and Sir Andrew Agnew, for example, was compensated with the substantial sum of £4,000.[62] These changes must unquestionably have led to an improvement in the quality of local justice, since this appears by all accounts to have been highly arbitrary and capricious. It often happened that the hereditary sheriffs were ill-educated in the law and unaware of its finer points, or merely bored by the whole procedure. Trials could descend to macabre farce, and the last of them, Sir Andrew Agnew, had a short way with lawyers and their involved pleas, castigating them as 'schoondrels' and 'blethering loons'.[63]

Curiously enough the changeover did not go unmourned by local people who claimed they 'aye liked gentlemen's law', meaning they preferred to be tried by people to whom they owed instinctive deference rather than the upstart professional lawyers who replaced them.[64] Even the arbitrary justice of those like the fifth earl of Galloway who could hold his court and sentence in a trice those criminals caught 'red-hand' was viewed with nostalgia, and as one admirer observed 'Yerl James was the man; he'd hang them up just o' his ain hand: nane o' your law'![65]

However, the days of such rough-and-ready application of the law were past, and the new breed of lawyers who now occupied the seats of local justice could be relied on to take their duties more seriously. Those appointed to judicial office in Galloway included James Boswell, the future lord Auchinleck and father of Dr Johnson's biographer, who became the first sheriff of Galloway under the new régime, while his steward-depute was Thomas Miller,[66] an Ayrshire laird who inherited the estate of Glenlee near New Galloway. These improvements in the system of administering local justice were symptomatic of the far-reaching changes that were already occurring in other parts of Scotland, and would become increasingly apparent in Galloway from the middle of the eighteenth century onwards.

NOTES

1. He died as a result of a fall from his horse when it stumbled over a molehill – hence the Jacobite toast to the gentleman in the black velvet coat.
2. Her mother was Elizabeth, the 'winter' queen of Bohemia, and James VI's only daughter, while she herself was the mother of George I.

3. The son of James VII by his second wife, Mary of Modena; he claimed the throne on his father's death in 1701, and in consequence was dubbed by Queen Anne as 'the pretender'.

4. This was an ambitious project which involved the establishment of a Scottish trading entrepôt in central America to open up trade with America, Africa and the Pacific rim, and Scots of all classes invested a huge amount of money in it. Unfortunately it came into conflict with local Spanish interests, and as the English government was concerned to maintain diplomatic relations with Spain it prohibited the English colonies in North America from trading with it. This was largely responsible for its collapse, the consequent ruination of many of the investors, and a serious shortage of capital in Scotland.

5. Lynch, *A New History*, 312.

6. McDowall, *History of Dumfries*, 508–9.

7. Ferguson, *Scotland: 1689 to the Present*, 135.

8. Agnew ii, 266–8.

9. *Ibid.*, 230.

10. Agnew (1864), 505.

11. Notwithstanding that his son William styled himself earl of Nithsdale the title was never revived. His Herries barony, on the other hand, was successfully claimed by his descendant, William Constable-Maxwell, as the result of a House of Lords decision in 1858.

12. He subsequently became the member of parliament for Kirkcudbright in 1741 until his death the following year. The forfeiture was rescinded by an act of parliament of 1732 when the family estates were restored to his mother, the former Mary Dunbar, and on her death in 1760 they passed to his son Dunbar, fourth earl of Selkirk.

13. Smith, *Agricultural Survey*, 86.

14. *Ibid.*, 91.

15. Lenman, *Economic History*, 69.

16. This was stated in a letter dated 8 February 1811 to W. M. Herries of Spottes, a copy of which is preserved in the National Library of Scotland, Abbotsford Collection, *MS* 874, *f* 158, and is quoted in full in *OSA* 17 (Buittle). Maxwell acquired Munches through his marriage to Agnes Maxwell, the heiress of that estate, and as he died in 1814 at the age of ninety-four he was writing from first-hand knowledge of the levellers' activities.

17. Prevost, 'Letters re the levellers', 197.

18. So asserts Morton in 'The levellers of Galloway' 234, though it is difficult to see how he could have done this given that the estate was under forfeiture.

19. It may have been because of this that the dykes on Roberton in the parish of Borgue were spared (Smith, *Agricultural Survey*, 91).

20. Wodrow *MS*, folio xl, no. 77.

21. He was a baron of the exchequer, having been one of the commissioners appointed to negotiate the Articles of Union, and has left valuable accounts of his visits to Galloway in 1721 and 1735.

22. As quoted by Prevost in 'Letters etc.', 197–8.

23. Morton 'The levellers', 236.

24. Patrick Heron was the local member of parliament, and as a prominent cattle breeder he was particularly vulnerable to the levellers' actions.

25. Prevost, 'Letters etc.', 200.

26. *Ibid.*, 201: Morton, 'The levellers', 236.

27. Prevost, 'Letters etc.', 203.

28. Morton, 'The levellers', 257.
29. Heron, *Observations* ii, 257.
30. *Ibid.*, 257–8.
31. Prevost, 'Letters etc.', 197: Agnew ii, 251.
32. Heron, *Observations* ii, 255.
33. Prevost, 'Sir John Clerk's journie to Galloway in 1721', 186 et seq.
34. *Ibid.*, 196.
35. The second earl of Stair was planting 20,000 trees annually, most being Scots firs (*OSA* 3, p 135).
36. *OSA* 9, p 326.
37. Webster, *Agriculture*, 12.
38. *OSA* 9, p 327.
39. *Ibid.*, 326.
40. Letter to W. M. Herries 1811.
41. *OSA* 1, p 171.
42. *Ibid.* 9, p 324.
43. The minister of Tongland confirms (*OSA* 9, p 325) that 'the men wore kelt coats, made of a mixture of black and white wool, as it came off the sheep, in its natural state'.
44. Smith, *Agricultural Survey*, 39.
45. *OSA* 9, p 324.
46. Smith, *Agricultural Survey*, 39.
47. *OSA* 9, p 324.
48. Robinson, *Reminiscences*, 43.
49. *OSA* 9, p 327.
50. Buchan, *Domestic Medicine*, 126.
51. Act 12 Geo. I, 20 Jan 1726.
52. Webster, *Agriculture*, 9.
53. Prevost, 'Solway smugglers', 59.
54. Act 24 Geo. III, cap. 47.
55. Prevost, 'Solway smugglers', 61.
56. *OSA* 17, p 563.
57. Prevost, 'Solway smugglers', 60.
58. McDowall, *History of Dumfries*, 585.
59. *Ibid.*, 589.
60. Agnew ii, 303.
61. This is recounted in his *Tales of a Grandfather*, but according to McDowall's *History of Dumfries* (p 589) the chief magistrate at the time was George Bell. Scott, however, asserts that this was told him by the girl herself who was the mother-in-law of his brother, Capt. Thomas Scott, but as she was then over eighty the facts may have been distorted in the re-telling.
62. Agnew ii, 333.
63. *Ibid.*, 263.
64. *Ibid.*, 335.
65. *Ibid.*, 337, 'law' in this context implying the antithesis of equity and justice.
66. He subsequently became lord president of the court of session, while his son William, who was also raised to the bench, took the name Glenlee as his judicial title.

28

THE 1700s: UPTURN

A DAWNING RECOVERY

The latter half of the eighteenth century saw a recovery in Galloway that was nothing short of miraculous. It was due initially to the knock-on effects of the upturn which was already occurring elsewhere in Scotland, particularly in the Lothians, and was subsequently fuelled by the rising price of grain and other commodities – a trend which began in the mid-1700s and would continue into the following century. However, men of vision and enterprise were needed to develop these advantages, and it was fortunate that the principal landowners in Galloway at the time included people with the initiative to introduce new farming techniques, the motivation to force them on a generally recalcitrant tenantry, and the means to carry out comprehensive improvements to their estates. Once the benefits became apparent in terms of higher output, greater profitability, and hence increased rents, other landowners began to follow suit.

During the late seventeenth and early eighteenth centuries land improvement was limited to building enclosures for purposes of rearing beef cattle, but later on they became more ambitious. This was attributable to the introduction of new farming techniques and the consequent expansion of agriculture, as well as rising prices, for the resulting escalation in their rental incomes meant that landowners could afford to bring more land into cultivation. Much of the work was done by those tenants who were given sufficiently long leases to encourage them to do so, while the landowners carried out the more comprehensive schemes with the aid of contract labour. As many of these were expensive, and could not be financed out of rents, they had to borrow on the security of their estates, and this was one example of the vital contribution which the early eighteenth-century development of a banking system in Scotland made to the growth of the country's economy.

Improvement schemes and the expansion in farming created a growing demand for labour, and as this began to outstrip the available supply it acquired a scarcity value which was reflected in higher wages. As growing farm profits rendered these affordable, agricultural workers' wages increased steadily throughout the second half of the century, although this occurred unevenly depending on local conditions. However, it was enough for the recovery to feed through into the lower ranks of society and galvanise them out of the poverty-induced torpor which had hitherto been so dismally apparent.

THE PIONEERS

The introduction of new farming techniques into Scotland was an incidental result of the Union because, in the course of their journeys to attend parliament at Westminster, Scottish members and representative peers saw the advances in crop husbandry which were being practised in the south and were encouraged to emulate them at home. Although these experiments were by no means always successful, the potential was enough to capture the interest of other enterprising landowners, and symptomatic of this was the founding of the Society of Improvers in the Knowledge of Agriculture in Scotland in 1723. The secretary was Robert Maxwell, the laird of Arkland, near Kirkpatrick Durham,[1] who 'devoted himself to the improvement of agriculture and probably did more than any other to intro-duce or encourage the practice of new methods'.[2] Unfortunately, the same source tells us that 'he appears to have paid more attention to experiment than to making a profit',[3] with the result that he eventually went bankrupt and his estate had to be sold, though his interest in the subject continued unabated until his death in 1765.

Foremost among the early pioneers in Galloway were the second earl of Stair,[4] the fifth earl of Galloway,[5] and William Craik,[6] whose Arbigland estate comprised a stretch of low-lying, fertile land adjacent to the coast near Kirkbean. Linguist, architect, hard drinker and 'sower of wild oats' who was regularly out before dawn bludgeoning his tenants into following his example,[7] he was described by Maxwell of Munches as 'a man of many accomplishments'.[8] At a time when most of his fellow proprietors were primarily concerned with cattle-rearing he was 'among the first that under-took to improve the soil', and in the course of a career that spanned much of the century (he died in 1798 at the age of ninety-five) he 'raised the value of his land fourfold',[9] while we are told that 'his example was soon followed by other proprietors and a new system of agriculture began to be understood'.[10]

He is credited above all with introducing the concept of crop rotation to maintain the fertility of the soil, in contrast to the traditional monocultur-al system of growing successive crops of bere or oats until the land was exhausted. Sir John Clerk commented on the practice during his visit to Galloway in 1721. 'Their grain is nigh bear and oats black and white', he noted, 'barley they have none[11] [and] their bear sets as they call them are never changed. That ground which I saw carrying bear has produced nothing else in the memory of man'.[12] Endorsing this, another commentator described how 'they sow their Bear in the same place every year, and without intermission'. The reluctance of the local farmers to adapt to change is evident from the fact that, even by the end of the century, the majority 'were still growing crop after crop of oats upon the fields till both the fertility of the ground and the strength of the manure are exhausted'.[13]

Craik, on the other hand, forbade his tenants to grow more than two cereal crops in succession before allowing the ground to rest. Instead of letting weeds take over, as was the universal practice, he encouraged them to grow green crops such as turnips and cabbages, and to undersow the cereal crop with ryegrass or clover[14] in order to restore fertility to the soil. At the same time, he attempted to break with tradition by growing wheat on the land he farmed himself, but his efforts were thwarted by the ignorance and downright resistance on the part of his own farm servants, because we are told they 'were too imperfect for executing . . . it with the care and attention which the system required'.[15]

With his inventive turn of mind, Craik was passionately interested in the development of farm implements, being inspired in particular by the English agriculturalist and inventor Jethro Tull's recently published work *The Horse-Hoeing Husbandry*. The type of plough traditionally used in Galloway could barely scratch as much as half an acre of land a day and, as lord Kames put it, was 'more fit to raise laughter than raise soil'. Craik, however, perfected a technique of tearing up the soil in one direction and then ripping it again crossways in order to produce a proper seedbed.[16] He was also responsible for introducing a granite roller as a substitute for the laborious work of breaking up clods of earth with mallets. Similarly, he was instrumental in pioneering a rudimentary threshing machine to replace the traditional flail, though it was not until 1786 that Andrew Meikle produced the first successful machine.[17]

The efforts of Craik and his fellow pioneers like the earl of Stair to persuade their tenants to adapt to modern farming methods were continually hampered by their blinkered conservatism. Equally obstructive was their slavish adherence to all the traditional notions in which they had been reared, such as the belief that weeds should not be removed, as they kept the corn warm, and that musty hay helped cows come in season. As Webster justly observed, 'the backwardness of the people to new methods threw many difficulties in the way of his [Craik's] first essays'.[18] Stair encountered similar difficulties when he attempted to grow turnips in the field,[19] since not only did most of his tenants refuse to grow them but when they saw the size his turnip-fed bullocks grew to compared with their own stunted creatures, they refused to have anything to do with such monsters.[20]

In fact, opposition to growing turnips was so universal that they were still only grown in limited quantities in Galloway half a century later, and this in spite of their demonstrable superiority over hay as a source of winter feed. The same applied in the case of potatoes, and although they were first introduced into Galloway in 1725[21] it was not until much later that people came to accept them as an integral part of their diet. However, his tenants' automatic opposition to anything remotely innovative did not deter lord Stair from growing lucerne and sanfoin, as well as cabbages and carrots in the field,[22] in spite of their scornful dismissal of his efforts as 'the dilettante ways of a gentleman farmer'.

Livestock improvement

The introduction of new farming techniques extended to attempts to produce a superior quality of livestock – a process which, as we have seen, began in the previous century. As cattle rearing was the principal form of husbandry it followed that experimentation was initally confined to these animals. The early pioneers included the earls of Galloway and Stair, and William Craik, who in addition to his other activities built up a large cattle-rearing enterprise – to the extent that by 1748 he was exporting 1,700 black cattle annually to England. At the same time, he attempted to increase their size by crossing them with the products of Robert Bakewell's animal breeding experiments at Dishley Grange in Leicestershire.[23]

Breeding for improvement is a long and costly exercise, since it is only through trial and error, combined with good stocksmanship, that an animal can be developed which not only has a high meat-quality but is also a good converter of food into liveweight gain, particularly in the parts of the carcase from which the best cuts of meat are taken. The rewards, however, could be handsome because, apart from the fact that a successful breeder could obtain a better price for his stock, he could also hire out bulls with a proven record of siring good quality stock to other farmers, thus diffusing the improved strain throughout the local cattle population. Advances were also being made in management techniques, and it was now the practice to in-winter store cattle in straw-filled yards or under cover, where they could be fed a regular diet of hay and turnips. Judging from the observations of one contributor to the *Old Statistical Account*, a century of experimentation seems to have produced results, as he stated that 'the true Galloway breed of cattle, in proportion to their size, is the handsomest and best in Britain and draws the best price in every market in the kingdom where they are exposed'.[24]

The buoyant cattle trade provided the key to the development of Galloway's economy and the initial spur to land improvement, and as it continued to thrive for much of the century it was the foundation of a number of fortunes. By 1765, 20,000 beasts were, 'according to very accurate information', being exported annually,[25] but the lifting of the ban on Irish cattle that year[26] raised the spectre of a downturn. However, to begin with, they were not imported in sufficiently large numbers to depress the market, but later they were and towards the end of the century prices began to slide. Most of the cattle exported from Galloway were taken to the centre at St Faiths and other markets in Norfolk, where they were bought by local farmers for fattening off in readiness for sale at the main cattle market at Smithfield. Some went to Brough, on the main route between the Eden valley and Yorkshire, while there was also a long-established cattle tryst at Falkirk. But wherever they went they were bound to lose weight in the course of the journey, and this invariably affected the selling price.

Drovers were needed to take the cattle there, which was expensive since their charges could amount to as much as an eighth of the proceeds of sale, and besides there was always the risk of accidents or cattle being lost in the course of the journey. Much depended on the quality of the drovers, and while some established a reputation for reliability others were less trustworthy and attempted to undercut them by offering a lower price to tempt farmers into a false economy. Commenting on this, Webster expressed amazement that people were prepared to trust a huge value of stock to drovers who had hardly any capital or were former bankrupts who had not paid their creditors in full,[27] while Smith reckoned that nine out of ten of them had 'in the course of their dealings become once or oftener insolvent'.[28]

Smaller farmers, on the other hand, generally sold their cattle to drovers who acted as dealers, and were known as jobbers. The minister of Colvend was particularly scathing about them, slating them as 'young fellows who dislike labour and scour the country infesting the cattle markets to pick up cattle and intercept a profit between the breeder and the grazier to the prejudice of both'.[29] If, as often happened, the jobber could only pay for the cattle after he had sold them, the farmer was compelled to accept a promissory note which was negotiable at some future date, and if it proved worthless he risked losing the entire proceeds.[30] Yet, in spite of their frequently dubious provenance, these notes were widely accepted as currency and on occasion farmers used them to pay their rent.[31]

While stock rearers in Galloway concentrated on producing beef cattle, some Ayrshire farmers were developing a milk-producing cow. The Ayrshire, as the animal came to be known, was traditionally regarded as the poor man's cow and attempts to introduce it into Galloway were unsuccessful because it was found to 'milk no better than the native breed'.[32] Also, unlike the Galloway, which is a polled animal, these were horned which meant they could be dangerous to handle, and as the bulls tended to be fiercer than the Galloways they were not popular with farmers.[33] Nevertheless, this did not deter people from trying to introduce them, though it was not until the late nineteenth century, when changing conditions put a premium on milk production, that the Ayrshire finally came into its own.

The late 1700s witnessed a steady rise in the price of sheep. This was attributable to an increased demand for mutton from the growing population of central Scotland, and also to the wool requirements of the expanding textile industry in the north of England. Consequently, a number of Galloway farmers and landowners were encouraged to exploit the market by improving the quality of the native sheep. The stock seems to have deteriorated greatly since the late Middle Ages when the collapse of the wool market led to an abandonment of sheep farming, and by the eighteenth century they had reverted to small animals with a black or sometimes grey face, black legs, and wool of very poor quality[34] – 'not worth the cutting' as one contributor to the *Old Statistical Account* put it. Breeding for improvement in sheep is, if anything, more complicated than cattle because there is the additional factor of producing an animal whose fleece quality meets market demand. Altogether this was a tall order, and unsurprisingly the eighteenth-century breeders do not seem to have been particularly successful.

A leading experimenter was the earl of Selkirk's son, lord Daer, who took over the management of the family estates in 1786. He tried importing Spanish sheep to cross with a selection of local animals, while others introduced long-woolled sheep from Lincolnshire called 'muggs' – an unlikely choice, since they are described as 'large, scraggy animals, voracious eaters, very slow in fattening, and of a bad quality of meat'.[35] Many other breeds were tried with equal lack of success, though as Smith presciently observed 'the species which bids fairest . . . to come into general use is the small Leicestershire'.[36] As to the native sheep, he asserted that the Blackface was 'considered by all the principal storemasters in Galloway as superior to every other', since they were 'an active, hardy race and peculiarly adapted for the wild mountains and barren moors of Galloway'[37] – a view which has stood the test of time.

These innovators, however, were limited to 'a few enlightened and public-spirited gentlemen, [and] some of the more opulent farmers guided and encouraged by their example',[38] because contemporary sheep husbandry practices in Galloway were slated by Webster as 'the most wretched that can well be conceived'.[39] He went on to say that 'the farmers have no regular bred shepherds, nor any system of management; and the tups [rams] are permitted to go with the ewes the whole year round, the lambs come at a very improper season and generally far too early, and [are] therefore stunted in their growth before the Spring food gets up'.[40] It seems they were constantly menaced by wild dogs as well, since he tells us that 'everyone [labourers and beggars] must have their dogs, and the hordes of these half-starved animals roaming the countryside are a menace to travellers and stock alike'.[41] The result was that 'the loss sustained to lambs by these vermin is so great that people consider themselves fortunate if they can save half, three fourths oftener [from being] destroyed'.[42]

Horse-breeding was a fashionable pastime. Earlier in the century, the second earl of Stair had attempted – apparently with some success – to increase the size of the traditional lightweight Galloways by crossing them with larger imported stallions. Now, a new generation of landowners like the seventh earl of Galloway and his brother, Admiral Keith Stewart, were attempting to build on his efforts. While some improvers bred horses for hunting or for show purposes, the majority were concerned with developing a heavier and more robust type of animal which was capable of being used for draft purposes in place of the traditional oxen. Their success is evident from the comments of the minister of Glasserton that 'the variety of horse now prevalent . . . has been gradually produced by the continual crossing of the small old Galloway breed with foreign stallions',[43] though, according to another source, they virtually extinguished the old native breed in the process.[44]

Pig-keeping became a popular form of husbandry, particularly among the labouring classes, because their meat formed 'a great proportion of the food of the poorer inhabitants' and therefore 'every family kept one or more of them'.[45] The late eighteenth century saw a dramatic increase in their number, because Webster writing in 1794 tells us that it had risen from 150 to some 10,000 'in the space of the last twelve to fourteen years',[46] while he describes the villages as 'swarming with them'.[47] Not only were they prized for their meat, but being virtually omniverous they were a useful – as well as a productive – means of disposing of household garbage, though it was the expansion of potato-growing that accounted above all for the dramatic increase in their number.

IMPROVEMENTS

Land improvement during the second half of the eighteenth century expanded from the building of enclosures into a much wider range of activities, which included the application of lime to raise the general level of fertility, the provision of better housing, upgrading farm steadings, and building fences and dykes to mark out fields. They also included comprehensive schemes to bring marginal land into cultivation, as well as afforestation, and – to a limited extent – reclaiming marshy land. There was ample scope for this, since we are told that roughly a tenth of the entire region consisted of boggy flows,[48] some of them extending 'with little interruption [for] eight or ten miles'.[49] Yet, by the end of the century Samuel Smith noted that there was 'still a great deal to be done in that direction',[50] as it was not until the early nineteenth century that the major drainage schemes were undertaken.

Liming was an essential preliminary to land improvement, since this counteracts the natural acidity of the soil. That it was already being practised during the previous century is evident from Symson's (probably exaggerated) observation that 'the whole shire' used lime processed in rudimentary peat-fired kilns from 'the incredible quantities of cockle shells' washed up on the shore at Baldoon.[51] Otherwise lime is in short supply in Galloway, being limited to a few pockets in western Wigtownshire and a stratum of carboniferous limestone further up the Solway coast, although farmers in eastern Galloway had access to the limeworks at Barjarg in the Cairn valley and at Closeburn. This meant that much of the lime used in Galloway was imported, and Sir James Agnew, for example, used Irish lime to improve the fertility of his Lochnaw estate.[52]

Lime was also available from Cumberland, but export duty rendered the cost prohibitive to most farmers. Craik developed the deposits underlying the district round Arbigland by establishing two limekilns there, one at Torrorie[53] and the other about a mile west of Arbigland, both being fired by coal imported from Cumberland,[54] though this too was subject to export duty. An inferior and cheaper substitute for lime was shell marl. This was first discovered in Galloway in about 1730,[55] and although small pockets of the material are scattered throughout the region, Carlingwark loch outside Castle Douglas proved much the most prolific source. However, as in the case of lime, transport costs could render it uneconomic, and therefore only those farmers living in the vicinity of these deposits could afford to use it.

Afforestation was a popular form of improvement, and judging from previous complaints about the dearth of trees it was necessary as well. The example set by people like the second earl of Stair and William Agnew of Castlewigg near Whithorn[56] was followed by succeeding generations of landowners. Prominent among them was the seventh earl of Galloway, who embarked on a programme of planting some 200,000 trees a year, while others included the fifth earl of Stair and Admiral Keith Stewart, who was planting up his Glasserton estate. The earl of Selkirk is also recorded as establishing trees on 'several hundred acres of his St Mary's Isle Estate', while Samuel Smith described his plantations as extending 'from Tongland to the sea on both sides of the river', adding that 'they are laid out with the most exquisite taste' and 'cover upwards of 800 acres'.[57] James Murray was establishing woodlands on his Cally estate,[58] while Craik's brother-in-law Charles Stewart was responsible for the magnificent coniferous woodlands on his estate of Shambellie near New Abbey, which are still a feature of the locality.

MANSION BUILDING

The current rage for improvement was reflected in the growing fashion among the gentry to build superior mansion houses where architectural symmetry was the paramount consideration. This was already evident in the wealthier parts of Scotland during the late 1600s, but it was not until the following century that it spread to Galloway because the prevailing poverty there meant that only relatively few landowners could afford to build them. Among the earliest was Lochryan, which was built by Andrew Agnew[59] in 1701, while Robert McDowell's creation of Logan dates from the following year. In 1719 Patrick Heron, the member of parliament for Kirkcudbrightshire, was responsible for Kirroughtree to underscore his enhanced social status, while Argrennan,[60] the creation of William Cutler, dates from roughly the same time. The 1740s saw the building of Cairnsmore House near Palnure by David Maxwell, a younger son of Colonel William Maxwell of Cardoness,[61] and also Greenlaw near Castle Douglas, where the work was begun by Robert Gordon, a younger son of the sixth viscount Kenmure, though he died before it was completed.[62]

The growing affluence of the second half of the century accounted for a corresponding increase in mansion-building. For example, Galloway House near Garlieston which dates from around the 1750s was the creation of the sixth earl of Galloway, but it was so added to by his successors as to spoil the original. Later in the century, his son, Admiral Keith Stewart, applied part of the prize money he amassed in the course of his career towards the building of Glasserton. Arbigland, which William Craik is credited with having designed himself, dates from the 1760s, and also the Lindsays' creation of Southwick, though it was sold along with the estate shortly afterwards. Contemporary with them was James Murray's original house of Cally, the brainchild of Robert Mylne and subsequently spoilt by the additions of the later Murray Stewart owners who succumbed to the Victorian habit of embellishing their houses to reflect their social notions. The result was that while it 'was clearly intended to stun the visitor it just fails to deliver the knock-out blow'.[63]

Other mansions dating from this period include Barnbarroch (destroyed by a fire in 1941),[64] Terregles (now demolished), which was built by William Maxwell, the son of the forfeited earl of Nithsdale, and also Monreith and Spottes near Haugh of Urr. Monreith was the creation of Sir William Maxwell, while Spottes was built by Michael Herries, and both continue to be occupied by their descendants. Probably the best known architects of the time are the Adam brothers, and it was Robert who designed for Sir Samuel Hannay in 1787 that fine architectural masterpiece of Kirkdale which commands an impressive view over Wigtown Bay from its elevated position above the main road from Gatehouse to Creetown. Although a substantial house, it represents a considerable modification of the original design which envisaged a truly palatial mansion of at least twice its present size.

As the rent rolls of the bonnet lairds and minor gentry increased, they too launched out into building the more modest creations of the period. Among them is Robert Mure of Glenquicken's house at Livingstone on the lower reaches of Loch Ken. Also the original part of Ardwall near Gatehouse, which was the creation of David McCulloch, and subsequently added to by his descendant in the 1890s, though atypically this enhanced the house. Fortunately, a higher proportion of the mansions dating from this time survive compared with the less appealing creations of the Victorian age, many of which have been victims of fire and dynamite.

The ornamental grounds and formal gardens surrounding these establishments reflected the prevailing fashion for elevating a garden from a utility to an object of colour and beauty, and Heron's creation at Bargaly was one of the earliest of its type. Among the best-known landscape architects of the time was John Loudon (1783–1843), an early pioneer in the field, whose creations in Galloway include the gardens at Castle Kennedy and Barnbarroch. While the former, which were restored in the 1840s, continue to be maintained to a high standard and are a justifiably popular tourist attraction, Barnbarroch fell on hard times. After the house was burnt down, the decaying remnants of the once magnificent grounds passed into the hands of the Forestry Commission which, in a less environmentally sensitive age, destroyed a number of rare tree species by ring-barking them before planting up much of the former demesne with conifers.

The grounds of Cally were another example, being described by the local minister as 'amongst the largest, and most princely, in the south of Scotland'. He goes on to tell us that 'the place is laid out on an extensive scale [and] about 1,000 acres are in planting, gardens, orchards and pleasure grounds'.[65] The gardens themselves are described as being made 'at great expense, and have equalled the proprietor's expectations, [and] besides the common fruits, they yield apricots, figs, grapes, nectarines equal to any in the hot-houses of this country'.[66] Scarcely less impressive were those established by the earl of Selkirk at St Mary's Isle, where we are told that 'there are 6 hothouses besides forcing frames all upon a new construction which contain various sorts of fruits and exotics'.[67] In fact, according to Smith, the establishment of orchards producing 'all kinds of fruit . . . in great perfection' appears to have been the rule among contemporary landowners.[68]

NEW LAIRDS

Meanwhile, a number of people who had made money in other fields were buying up land in Galloway – a practice which would become increasingly common during the nineteenth century. Land was seen as a sound investment, rising rents meant the return on it would continue to grow, and the potential was further enhanced where there was scope for improvement. Moreover, the ownership of land has always been regarded as a status symbol and therefore a prize continually sought after by the socially motivated. Prominent among the newcomers was William Forbes, the younger son of an old Aberdeenshire family, who made his fortune by cornering the market in copper which was in keen demand for strengthening the hulls of naval vessels. Towards the end of the century he purchased much of the former Gordon barony of Earlston,[69] and he and his descendants added to it with the acquisition of further lands in the Glenkens,[70] including those belonging to the earls of Galloway.

At much the same time, Sir William Douglas and his brothers James and Samuel were buying up properties in the neighbourhood of Castle Douglas. A remarkable man by all accounts, Sir William rose from relatively humble origins in the parish of Penninghame to become a leading entrepreneur in Galloway. He is reputed to have started life as a country pedlar, and later he 'entered extensively into the American trade'. He must have made a great deal of money out of this because in 1785, while still only forty, he decided 'to retire from business and reside on his Estates in Galloway'[71] – or retire in the sense that he devoted the remainder of his life to expanding his wide range of interests there. Although he acquired a number of properties, Gelston was his flagship, while his brother James acquired Orchardton and Almorness adjacent to the Urr estuary, and Samuel settled at Netherlaw near Dundrennan.[72]

Another newcomer to Galloway at this time was Richard Oswald who made his fortune in the highly lucrative tobacco trade.[73] He had already acquired the Auchincruive estate near Ayr, and in about 1773 he bought the Cavens estate near Kirkbean[74] as well as acquiring other properties in the Stewartry.[75] Although these were subsequently disposed of, Cavens itself remained in the hands of his family until the 1950s. Using the wealth he amassed as one of the Glasgow 'tobacco lords', he and his son were responsible for carrying out comprehensive improvements to their lands in Kirkcudbrightshire, as well as those in Ayrshire.

A REVERSE

The escalating scale of improvements meant that landowners were increasingly resorting to bank borrowings to finance them, and this led to the establishment of a number of small banks to meet the demand. One of them was Douglas, Heron & Co. which was based in Ayr. This was founded in 1769 by Patrick Heron of Kirroughtree in partnership with a Dumfriesshire laird, whose relative, the duke of Queensberry, was appointed chairman. As its main purpose was to assist in the financing of improvement schemes, many landowners in the south-west subscribed to its initial capital, and by so doing they incurred unlimited liability for its debts. The whole enterprise seems to have been conducted on somewhat amateurish lines and the managers employed to run it were clearly not properly qualified, for according to one account they 'acted as fools to a major degree and as knaves to a lesser'. It seems that loans were advanced without a proper investigation into the projects they were intended to finance, because it apparently encouraged 'a number of speculative individuals to engage rashly in extensive agricultural operations'. Not only that, but Douglas, Heron & Co. was ill-advised enough to take over the ailing Ayr Bank, and in consequence became liable for its debts. When it found itself unable to meet them it was forced to stop payment, and in June 1772 it collapsed.

The shareholders became personally liable for its debts, while the liquidators foreclosed on the outstanding loans. Consequently, 'many of those who had most distinguished themselves by their active exertions to ameliorate the state of husbandry were deeply involved in its failure',[76] and no less than 140 Scottish lairds were ruined.[77] In Galloway we are told that 'a great change of property ensued, and a series of years elapsed before either the capital, credit or improvements of the country would be replaced in their former situation',[78] while others claim that it came near to killing off the whole process of land improvement.

The Old Statistical Account contains a number of allusions to it, the minister of Buittle, for example, referring to 'the prodigious alteration [which] took place in landed property' in his parish on account of 'the fatal American War and the scarce less deplorable concern of the Douglas and Heron Bank'.[79] Similarly, his colleague at Kells reported that 'a part of the landed property [in his parish] has been of late years exchanged, owing partly to the failure of the Douglas and Heron Bank, which has much distressed this part of the country'.[80]

It seems the victims were mainly smaller landowners, though the only example cited by McKerlie was Patrick Brown of Gaitgil near Twynholm,[81] while the laird of King's Grange near Castle Douglas was another. It is difficult to gauge how far the major landowners in Galloway were affected, though it is known that a number of them were left with worthless bonds of cash credit,[82] and it could have been responsible for the sale of Sir Robert Maxwell's estate of Orchardton. McKerlie asserts that Sir Robert 'spent much time in farming which we think caused his ruin, as he became a shareholder in the Ayr Bank [Douglas, Heron & Co.]',[83] so it is equally possible that this was the result of over-extending himself in improvement schemes. Whatever the reasons may have been, the estate was sold after his death, when the purchaser was Sir William Douglas's brother, James.

The bank's failure led to the dissolution of the 'Society comprehending the greater part of the Noblemen and Gentlemen of property and know-ledge in Galloway and Dumfriesshire'. This was founded for the purpose of educating farmers in modern farming techiques and teaching them the value of a proper system of crop rotation. Consequently, it was a valuable agent for disseminating new ideas, and its cessation was all the more regrettable since it came at a time when the collapse of the bank put a temporary brake on the whole process of land improvement. Nevertheless, it was resuscitated under a new name[84] in 1776 on the initiative of William Craik who became its first president.[85]

The failure came at a particularly unfortunate time for a number of landowners whose estates were entailed, and who had taken advantage of a recent Act of 1770 which enabled them to borrow on the security of them. The entailing of an estate was a legal device which was introduced in 1685[86] to enable landowners to protect their estates from creditors and thus pre-serve them for their family. Many landowners took advantage of this, and, according to Samuel Smith, more than half the estates in Galloway were encumbered by an entail.[87] On the other hand, because an entailed estate was effectively held in trust, the owner – or the 'heir of entail', as he was known – was unable to give a valid security over it and was therefore prevented from borrowing on it to finance improvements.

The 1770 Act, known as the Montgomery Act,[88] went some way towards removing the impediment by making it possible, within certain limits, for an heir of entail to borrow on the security of his lands, and some of those who did were victims of the bank's collapse. One result of the practice of entailing estates was that, because of the legal complexities involved, there was a tendency to delegate their management to lawyers rather than factors. After the passing of the Act it increasingly became the practice to employ Edinburgh agents, since they had more access to loan finance,[89] and this set a not altogether happy precedent for the future.

LANDLORD AND TENANT

Unlike their predecessors whose tenants tried to obstruct their efforts to modernise farming practices, the landowners of the later 1700s were finding them more co-operative. This was not so much because the tenants were abandoning their traditional ways, though doubtless some were coerced into doing so, but more because they were being replaced by incomers to Galloway who already had experience of the new techniques and were prepared to apply them there. As they reckoned on being able to make higher profits they generally outbid the traditionalists for the lease of vacant farms, and consequently the latter were edged out and forced to become landless labourers. However, it could happen – and by all accounts frequently did – that some of these incomers found to their cost that local conditions were unsuited to the new techniques and were compelled to give up their leases, a number of them even going bankrupt.[90]

Generally speaking, there was a higher proportion of incomers on the better managed estates, because the majority of landowners, perhaps through apathy or a reluctance to upset the *status quo*, were prepared to be more indulgent towards these traditionally-minded farmers and their antiquated farming practices. For Smith, writing at the end of the century, observed that 'the same wretched plans of husbandry which prevailed forty or fifty years ago are still continued there', blaming the proprietors who failed to move with the times.[91] In fact, it is evident from the *New Statistical Account* that the old multiple tenancy system was still tolerated on some estates until well into the following century.

The more forward-looking landowners, on the other hand, adopted a policy of amalgamating smaller holdings into larger units and carrying out comprehensive improvements before reletting them. A notable example was the seventh earl of Galloway, who would systematically renovate the farm buildings, the farmhouse itself and the workers' cottages, as well as repairing fences and dykes, and if necessary building new ones, and at the same time giving the holding a comprehensive application of lime.[92] Unfortunately there was another side to the coin, because these improvements had to be funded by borrowings, and this saddled future owners with a heavy interest burden. In the case of the Galloway estates – and others as well – it became insupportable and was a contributory factor to their ultimate break-up.[93]

This lay in the future, but in the meantime the continuing escalation in prices was mainly responsible for the explosion in rents which occurred during the later 1700s, and this was the subject of widespread comment by the contributors to the *Old Statistical Account*. Writing in 1792, the minister of Twynholm noted that 'since 1763 the arable land yields four times the rent it drew then, and one farm belonging to the Earl of Selkirk yields fourteen times the rent it paid in the year 1761'.[94] On the Stair estates the increase was even greater, and whereas in the case of one particular farm the rent jumped from £7 2s 6d to £195, on another it rose from £48 4s 8d to £245.[95] That these were by no means exceptional is evident from the comments of the minister of Urr who observed that 'it is not quite 100 years, since farms in this neighbourhood that now pay a rent of above 200 lib. per annum, were offered at the church doors to any tenant who would pay the land tax, minister's stipend and other public burdens'.[96]

Another contributory factor was the almost panicky rush of farmers to cash in on the boom, and their willingness to pay over the odds to secure a tenancy. This was particularly apparent when the farms on the Baldoon estate were advertised for let by public roup in 1787, following its sale to the seventh earl of Galloway. Evidently this attracted farmers from all over Scotland and 'rents were offered then that never had been dreamed of by a Galloway farmer'. There was a curious twist to the transaction because the sale agreement allowed Selkirk's son, lord Daer, to continue managing the estate for the next ten years, while the earl of Galloway undertook to increase the sale price by a sum equivalent to twenty-five years' purchase of the total rental in excess of £7,000 at the end of that period. As an increase of £5,000 was achieved the earl had to pay an additional £125,000.[97]

Unfortunately, some landowners were tempted to become too greedy and concentrated their efforts on maximising their rental income to the detriment of the long-term benefit of the land. This led to a practice of granting shorter leases and, as Smith says, 'a great many of them impressed with the idea that rents will always rise, as they have done, shorten the terms of leases to fifteen, twelve, or even six years'.[98] While this enabled the landowners to take advantage of the rising rental market, it naturally discouraged tenants from carrying out improvements which, as Smith goes on to say, 'cannot fail to obstruct the progress of good husbandry'.[99] Still more short-sighted was the growing practice of letting out good arable farms from year to year as grass parks, which was merely, as he put it, 'for the accommodation and encouragement of jobbers'.[100] Elaborating on this, he goes on to say that 'there are many landlords who lay out no money on their farms and whose management consists wholly of receiving rents [and] the mischief is sometimes aggravated when the management of estates is committed to gentlemen of the law'.[101]

Responsible landowners, on the other hand, appreciating that 'short leases make thriftless tenants',[102] continued to grant them sufficiently long leases – nineteen years being the norm – to encourage them to carry out improvements to their holdings. In other cases – particularly where more ambitious schemes were involved – the landlord provided the materials, leaving the tenant to do the work, or he might contract out the work and charge the tenant interest on the cost.[103] The difficulty was that where improvements were carried out on the landlord's initiative they were naturally geared to the long-term interests of the estate rather than to the immediate advantage of the tenant,[104] and this could be a source of contention. Nevertheless, in a time of rising prices the landlord–tenant system appears to have worked reasonably well, and it was not until the onset of the depression in the following century that its drawbacks became apparent.

NOTES

1. Although an uncle of John Maxwell of Munches, the latter omits any mention of his contribution in his letter to W. M. Herries of 1811.
2. *DNB.*
3. *Ibid.*
4. Born in 1673, he was the second surviving son of the first earl, having accidentally shot his elder brother while they were boys. A professional soldier turned politician, he was appointed ambassador to Paris in 1714, and after his recall in 1720 he devoted the rest of his life to improving his estates. Later promoted field-marshal, he died in 1747.
5. This is evident from his brother-in-law Sir John Clerk's observations during his visit to Galloway in 1735, when he refers to 'several good improvements' as a result of draining the Moss of Cree and 'many more [being] made in time'. Another comment about 'planting going well' refers to the earl's programme for establishing woodlands on his estate (Prevost, 'Sir John Clerk's journie to Galloway in 1735', 135).
6. He was rumoured, though without foundation, to be the father of John Paul Jones who was born in a cottage on the Arbigland estate. Although the latter subsequently became famous as the founder of the American navy, he was evidently a somewhat disreputable fellow in his early days, the local minister observing of him that 'of this person's character the parish cannot boast' (*OSA* 15, p 132).
7. Cowan, 'Agricultural improvement', 160.
8. Letter to W. M. Herries.
9. Webster, *Agriculture*, 13.
10. *Ibid.*
11. Apparently the soil in Galloway was too acid to grow the crop.
12. Prevost, 'Sir John Clerk's journie to Galloway in 1721', 10.
13. Heron, *Observations* ii.
14. Shirley, 'Two pioneer Galloway agriculturalists', 152.
15. *Ibid.*, 151.
16. *Ibid.*, 154–5.
17. Donnachie, *Industrial Archaeology*, 41.
18. Webster, *Agriculture*, 13.
19. Shirley, 'Two pioneer Galloway agriculturalists', 136.
20. It was Stair's ambition to show that better cattle could be raised on the Galloway hills than in the Lothians (Shirley, 136), so it looks as if he proved his point.

21. Agnew (1864), 519.
22. He was also responsible for setting up a linen manufactory to process the flax which was grown in parts of western Wigtownshire, and this must have been the first of its kind to be established in the region (Shirley, 136).
23. Shirley, 'Two pioneer Galloway agriculturalists', 153.
24. This incidentally was about the first time the Galloway was recognised as a distinctive breed of cattle.
25. Smith, *Agricultural Survey*, 249.
26. 5 Geo III, cap. 10, 1. This was only for a limited period, but it was regularly renewed until 1776 when the ban was lifted permanently (16 Geo III, cap. 8).
27. Webster, *Agriculture*, 24.
28. Smith, *Agricultural Survey*, 251–3. He also asserts that many arable farmers were similarly exposed when they sold their grain to itinerant corn dealers in return for a less than gilt-edged promissory note.
29. *OSA* 17, p 12.
30. Disc. *ibid.* 113, and in the *NSA* (Wig), 221–2.
31. Lenman, *Economic History*, 89.
32. *OSA* 17, p 568.
33. *Ibid.*
34. *Ibid.*, p 56.
35. Smith, *Agricultural Survey*, 272.
36. *Ibid.*, 273.
37. *Ibid.*, 274.
38. Heron, *Observations* ii, 85.
39. Webster, *Agriculture*, 31.
40. *Ibid.*
41. *Ibid.*, 38.
42. *Ibid.*, 39.
43. *OSA* 17, p 587.
44. *Ibid.*, p 118.
45. Webster, *Agriculture*, 39.
46. *Ibid.*
47. Smith, *Agricultural Survey*, 185.
48. *Ibid.*, 295.
49. *Ibid.*, 18.
50. *Ibid.*, 204.
51. Symson, *Large Description of Galloway*, 42.
52. Agnew ii, 208.
53. This was still operating in 1855, but by that time changes in farming practices had led to a decline in the demand for lime.
54. Donnachie, 'The lime industry in south-west Scotland', 150–1.
55. Smith, *Agricultural Survey*, 45.
56. He was one of the twenty-one children of Sir James Agnew of Lochnaw.
57. Smith, *Agricultural Survey*, 175–6.
58. *Ibid.*, 180.
59. Agnew ii, 238. He was a kinsman, as well as a son-in-law, of Sir James Agnew of Lochnaw.
60. Apparently when this was put up for sale in the following century the agent complained of difficulty in finding a buyer because it frightened people!
61. McKerlie iv, 455.
62. *Ibid.* iii, 367.

63. Gifford, *Buildings in Dumfries and Galloway*.
64. This occurred in 1941 and was caused by a candle left burning by the elderly Mrs Vans Agnew, which set alight to a curtain, and the fire spread throughout the whole house, she herself perishing in the blaze.
65. The writer also refers to a 'well stocked deer park' there. This was latterly home to a herd of wild white cattle which was acquired from the duke of Hamilton's herd at Cadzow in Lanarkshire. When Cally was sold in the 1920s the herd was dispersed, some of the purchasers putting the animals to their own stock, and it was from these matings that the White Galloways of today have sprung.
66. *OSA*, 310.
67. *Ibid*, 8.
68. Smith, *Agricultural Survey*, 165.
69. McKerlie iii, 428, 431, iv, 81, 84, 100.
70. *Ibid.* iii, 69, 104, iv, 121.
71. Donnachie, *Industrial Archaeology*, 91.
72. Sir William never married, so when he died in 1809 his estates were divided between his nieces and nephews, but by mid-century two separate branches of the family had emerged as the principal heirs of the Douglas estates, both being descended from his brother James. One was the Robinson Douglases whose forbear was James's daughter Mary, and who continued to be the principal landowners in Buittle parish until the 1950s, while the other was the Maitland-Kirwans of Gelston. Their ancestor was James Douglas's youngest daughter, Matilda, who married William Maitland, a son of David Maitland of Barcaple and a member of the Dundrennan family. Another branch were the Abercrombys of Forglen in Banffshire, whose name is preserved in a street name in Castle Douglas.
73. This was the pre-eminent trade in Scotland throughout much of the eighteenth century until it was effectively killed off by the American War of the 1770s. It was the foundation of a number of fortunes, as well as the modern city of Glasgow.
74. McKerlie iv, 148.
75. *Ibid.* iii, 337, 345, iv, 2, 20, 477, 479, v, 2.
76. Smith, *Agricultural Survey*, 352.
77. Fergusson, *Lowland Lairds*, 22.
78. Smith, *Agricultural Survey*.
79. *OSA* 17, p 126.
80. *Ibid.* 4, p 271.
81. McKerlie iii, 221.
82. They included lord Garlies (the future seventh earl of Galloway), his brother Keith Stewart of Glasserton, Agnew of Sheuchan, McDowell of Logan, James Murray of Broughton and Cally, and Blair of Dunrod.
83. McKerlie v, 91.
84. This was the Society for the Encouragement of Agriculture within the Counties of Dumfries, Wigtown and Kirkcudbright (Cowan, 'Agricultural improvement', 161).
85. *Ibid.*
86. *APS* viii, 477.
87. Smith, *Agricultural Survey*, 36.
88. So-called after the lord advocate, Sir James Montgomery of Stanhope, who was responsible for piloting it through parliament. As a matter of local interest his son, also Sir James, married a daughter of the fourth earl of Selkirk, she being

given land in the parish of Rerrick as a dowry.

89. Campbell, *Owners and Occupiers*, 112.
90. It is noteworthy that nineteen years after the sale of the Baldoon estate in 1787 only three of the original tenants of the farms leased out on that occasion were left, and they were all Galloway men (Smout, *History of the Scottish People*, 311).
91. Smith, *Agricultural Survey*, 33.
92. In the case of his estates in the parishes of Penninghame and Minnigaff this was ferried up the Cree in barges at a considerable saving in transport costs.
93. Campbell, *Owners and Occupiers*, 160–80.
94. *OSA* 15, p 81.
95. *Ibid.* 3, p 135.
96. *OSA.* 11, p 64.
97. Campbell, *Owners and Occupiers*, 161.
98. Smith, *Agricultural Survey*, 77–8.
99. *Ibid.*, 360.
100. *Ibid.*
101. *Ibid.*, 35.
102. *NSA* (Wigtown), 213.
103. Smith, *Agricultural Survey*, 35.
104. Campbell, *Owners and Occupiers*, 135.

29

THE LATE 1700s:
INDUSTRIALISATION

IMPROVING COMMUNICATIONS

The growth of the local economy led to pressure for better communications, as these were vital to its further expansion. Hitherto, they consisted of a few rough, ill-defined tracks whose existence can be gleaned from old place-names and the location of the bridges shown on Timothy Pont's map of 1590. In 1642, a lateral route was established through the province as part of the system for enabling the English parliamentarians to make contact with their troops in Ireland. This amounted to little more than marking out a line of existing tracks and persuading certain local residents to allow their premises to be used as staging posts, although it was subsequently dignified with the name of the Great Western.

Legislation was passed from time to time to ensure that these routes were maintained to a usable standard, though in practice it seems to have amounted to little more than a pious hope. Two acts of 1617 and 1661 gave justices of the peace powers to mend highways to and from the market towns,[1] while a later one of 1669 introduced a system of statute labour. This required all tenants to give six days' labour on the roads each year, and a further Act of 1686 made local commissioners of supply jointly responsible with the justices of the peace for maintaining them. However it was not a particularly effective arrangement, since it proved impossible to co-ordinate an overall plan for the maintenance work, so it was necessarily haphazard, while the statutory labour contributed by tenants was both grudging and ineffective. Its shortcomings became so apparent that in 1751 parliament introduced changes to the system by giving the commissioners of supply powers to levy a charge on landowners of £1 10s (£1.50) per £100 of rents received, and a *per capitum* charge of 2s 6d (12.5p) on all householders and 'mechanics' (small businessmen). This meant the commissioners now had the wherewithal to carry out improvements on a contract basis. Nevertheless, the legislation providing for statute labour still remained in force, and it was not until 1779 that the commissioners of supply obtained

444

a local Act of Parliament which allowed them to commute the liability into a monetary payment.[2]

Sir John Clerk's account of his second visit to Galloway in 1735 is eloquent of the deplorable state of the old pilgrims' way from New Galloway to Minnigaff in particular. 'I mounted at the Water of Ken [near New Galloway]', he writes, 'and had a monstrous bad road to the Brig of Dee [at Clatteringshaws] and from there to Minnigaff'. He goes on to say, 'all the way is full of precipices and rocks. The pass called Sadle Loup is here about four miles from Minnigaff. Nothing in the Alps is worse'.[3] On the other hand, he did concede that the road from Kirkcudbright to Dumfries (via Carlingwark) was 'very fine'.[4] The marquess of Downshire had an unfortunate experience when he attempted to travel through Galloway on his way from Ireland to London in the same year. Prepared for the worst, 'he took with him a squad of labourers to heave his coach out of the ruts, mend axles, replace wheels, and so on; but he still ended up stuck and benighted with his family in his coach near Creetown'.[5]

The first positive step towards road improvement came in 1757, when the commissioners of supply for Dumfries and Galloway petitioned for the establishment of a road between the Sark bridge, near Carlisle, and Portpatrick.[6] This was evidently in line with government thinking, because the initial survey stated that its main object was 'to open a speedy, and certain communication between Great Britain and Ireland; especially with regard to the passage of the Troops from one kingdom to the other, whenever the Exigency of Affairs may require it'.[7] Because army engineers were responsible for carrying out the work this became known as the military road. Although stated to have been completed in 1763,[8] the minister of New Luce was complaining thirty years later that 'it was in such a state as to be almost impassable with carriages of any kind . . . and only a small part of it yet being formed'.[9]

This was the prelude to the construction of a number of other roads. In 1768, work was started on a new coach road from Rhonehouse via the head of the Dee estuary at Cumstoun to Twynholm. It was completed in 1772,[10] while at much the same time the road leading south from Dumfries was upgraded as far as Cargen. The 1770s also saw the completion of a road up the Urr valley from Dub o' Hass, which was the port of Dalbeattie, as far as Kirkpatrick Durham[11] to link up with an existing route from Dumfries to the northern end of Loch Ken. At the same time, another road was constructed along the western edge of the loch to connect Kenmure with Clachanpluck (Laurieston). Although allegedly completed in 1785 the minister of Balmaghie, writing some ten years later, complained that the section in his parish was 'not so completely made up as it ought to be',[12] while Heron describes the roads there as 'universally miry and unsolid'.[13]

In 1786, in response to local demand, work was started on a coast road from the Fleet as far as Ferrytown of Cree (Creetown). This was done in stages, the first section being the westernmost portion from Newton moss, at the entrance to Fleet Bay, as far as Creetown, which was finished in 1788. As there was already a track between Newton moss and the Skyreburn, all that was needed to complete the project was to build the section from there to the Fleet. This became a reality two years later,[14] and the completed road followed broadly the line of the present-day A75.

In 1794, another road was established along the line of the old Roman road leading northwards from Carlingwark for some three miles as far as Greenlaw.[15] Other sections of road were built or upgraded at the same time, but it appears that this marked the end of the first flurry of activity. However, the passing of the Turnpike Road Act for Kirkcudbrightshire in 1796,[16] which authorised the setting up of turnpike road trusts with powers to levy tolls to fund improvements, led to a further burst of road-building in the following century.

There was clearly a considerable amount of private road-building as well, as Smith observed that 'there is no species of rural improvement which . . . has more attracted the gentlemen of Galloway, than planning, making and keeping in repair the parochial roads'.[17] For example, lord Daer, who perceived 'good roads as a preliminary step to every species of agricultural improvement',[18] was responsible for building at his own expense a road from the lower Dee into the parish of Borgue to serve his farms there. Therefore, it was in order to link these with the port of Kirkcudbright that he was one of the main proponents of a plan to build a bridge over the Dee there.[19] Also, we are told that 'many of the most important roads' in the parish of Buittle were made 'at great expense by the heritors, through whose lands they passed, advancing money without interest, to be repaid when the road funds from the parish would admit'.[20]

The provision of adequate bridges was essential to the establishment of a road network. Pont's map shows twelve bridges in Kirkcudbrightshire, including those at Dumfries, Cargenbridge, the old bridge of Urr and the original bridge across the Fleet. The latter two were subsequently washed away, and in 1661 Richard Murray, the proprietor of Cally, secured an Act of Parliament authorising him to replace the bridge across the Fleet with a timber construction, and to levy a toll on livestock crossing it[21] in order to recoup his outlays. However, this too was washed away in 1721 and not replaced until 1729 when another one was built at the site of the present bridge at Gatehouse. Traditionally the Church was responsible for building bridges, or at least subsidising the construction costs, and therefore the synod of Dumfries undertook the building of a bridge over the Dee at Clatteringshaws in 1703,[22] while the local kirk session was responsible for constructing one at Twynholm in 1740.[23]

The first half of the eighteenth century saw the establishment of bridges across all the major rivers, the earliest being the one spanning the Urr at Buittle. Later, a bridge was built across the Palnure Burn, and although comparatively small it was an important one, as this was the point where the former pilgrims' way converged with the military road. Therefore, when it was washed away in a flood it was replaced by another one almost immediately afterwards in 1739–40.[24] Two bridges were built across the Dee in 1729; one near its mouth at Tongland[25] and the other at Bridge of Dee, while a third was built at Mossdale in 1737–40 though it has since disappeared.

Some twenty years later, between 1745 and 1748, a bridge was built over the Cree to link the ancient market at Minnigaff with the burgh of Newton Stewart, but this was swept away in 1806, the bridge at nearby Creetown having already collapsed in 1769.[26] This seems to have been the fate of most of the earlier bridges in Galloway, doubtless because their timber construction rendered them incapable of withstanding the flash floods associated with the high rainfall in the Galloway uplands. Among the last of the bridges dating from this period is the now-redundant one at the mouth of the Skyreburn which was built in 1772[27] and subsequently incorporated into the road from Gatehouse to Creetown.

CANALS

Canal-building was the rage in England since the original one was cut to link Manchester with Runcorn at the head of the Mersey estuary in 1759. The first to be dug in Galloway was a channel linking the Carlingwark loch with the river Dee,[28] which was done on the initiative of the local landowner, Sir Alexander Gordon of Culvennan, in 1765. This was designed to assist the process of land improvement in the district by enabling shell marl to be ferried in flat-bottomed barges to farmers in the Dee valley. As Carlingwark is slightly higher than the Dee, the cutting of the channel lowered the level of the loch by some ten feet, and by exposing some eighty acres of marl[29] it greatly facilitated the work of extracting it. Labourers were hired to carry out the digging and dredging work, and Sir Alexander Gordon provided accommodation for them by establishing a settlement at the head of the loch. Known as Causewayend and later renamed Carlingwark, it was the forerunner of Castle Douglas. In 1780, he extended the accessibility to these marl deposits by cutting another channel below Glenlochar bridge to allow supplies to be ferried further upstream to farmers in the Glenkens.

At about this time, William Douglas commissioned an investigation into the feasibility of linking Carlingwark with the sea via the river Urr,[30] though this was pronounced impracticable. Meanwhile he, along with Sir Alexander Gordon and a number of other interested parties, was co-ordinating plans for a more ambitious scheme. This involved extending the

navigability of the Dee by cutting a canal with a series of locks to bypass the
rapids at Tongland in order to give boats access up river as far as Dalry, so
that landowners and farmers in the district could export their agricultural
produce direct to the English markets. Although Sir Alexander obtained an
Act of Parliament authorising its construction in 1802,[31] the estimated costs
proved prohibitive, so the project was abandoned.

This was linked to a still more ambitious project which involved
extending the canal up the Ken and across the watershed into the Doon
valley, to give access to the coalfields at Dalmellington. The promoters
included an impressive roll-call of local landowners and industrialists, and
the initial report was positive enough to encourage them to form a
company with the somewhat pretentious name of The Company of the
Proprietors of the Glenkens Canal Navigation to carry out the work.
Unfortunately this too proved impracticable, so it was abandoned as well
and the company put into liquidation. The unpaid creditors included a
number of disgruntled lawyers who dismissed the whole project as 'the ill-
digested fancy of a moment, wild in its conception, impracticable in its
execution, not desired by the country or thought of or talked of but in
jest'[32] – which makes one wonder why they were willing to become involved
in the first place. Yet, the scheme deserves a better press because, although
it may have proved impractical, its concept was admirable in that it
embraced a visionary and imaginative plan to bring coal into Galloway in
sufficient quantity to generate industrial development there.

INDUSTRIAL DEVELOPMENT

The beginnings of an industrial revolution were becoming apparent in
Scotland during the second half of the century, but because Galloway lacks
a readily available source of coal it remained peripheral to the main thrust
of industrial development. True, there are coalfields on the fringes of the
region at Dalmellington and in upper Nithsdale, but as transport costs
rendered it uneconomic to carry coal more than twelve miles from the pit
this ruled it out as a source of power. There are also coalfields in
Cumberland, but the cost was inflated by export duty, and when this was
lifted in 1792 the local coalmasters hiked the price up[33] to a level where it
became uneconomic for the entrepreneurs in Galloway to use it. Efforts
were made to find local coal deposits, but to no avail, and although Smith
tells us that 'the most promising indications . . . appeared on the estate of
Mr Craik of Arbigland'[34] these hopes never materialised. Therefore, the
only source of power available to Galloway industrialists was water, and
while this is available in unlimited quantity it meant that only light industry
was capable of being developed in the region.

Initially, industrial development in Galloway constituted an extra dimension to farming, and particularly cattle-rearing because, instead of dispatching their animals to market, enterprising landowners found it more profitable to process them instead. First they had to be slaughtered and the carcases skinned, so rudimentary slaughterhouses and skinning works were established. While the meat was exported, the hides were processed into leather, and this led to the establishment of tanneries, while other enterprises were set up to manufacture leather goods such as saddles, shoes and clogs. The fat was rendered down and made into soap, and this accounted for the existence of soapworks in the larger towns. Similarly with sheep, as their wool was used for the processing and manufacture of cloth and other woollen goods, and centres like Kirkcudbright and Minnigaff had already established a reputation for their manufacture of blankets and plaiding as early as the 1730s.[34]

The rationalisation of the local woollen industry included the setting up of a number of 'wauk' mills equipped with water-driven machinery to streamline the process of spinning, carding and weaving. From 1790 onwards a number of mills were established in Galloway, one of the earliest being at Waukmill on the Bladnoch. Others were built at Twynholm and Kirkpatrick Durham, the latter being at the instigation of the local land-owner, the Rev. Dr David Lamont[35] – a man who appears to have served God and mammon with equal success. Ordained at a young age, he inherited an estate in the parish of Kirkpatrick Durham, became the minister there in 1774, and continued to occupy the charge until his death in 1832, having been appointed moderator of the general assembly of 1822. At the same time, he was one of Galloway's leading entrepreneurs, being described as a man 'who with great ingenuity, spirit, and success, laboured to improve his own fortune, and to set a laudable example to other landholders in the neighbourhood'.[36]

The mill at Twynholm was established under the aegis of lord Daer.[37] A remarkable man by all accounts, he is described as paying 'uncommon attention to every species of improvement that can be useful to the country both in agriculture, manufactures and roads',[38] and according to Smith he 'showed talents of the highest order'. 'The ardour with which he turned his powerful mind, to the investigation of every subject connected with rural economy', he went on, 'was only equalled by the perseverence and ability which he displayed in the practical execution of his plans'.[39] A fine tribute, but tragically his life was cut short by his death from consumption in 1794 at the early age of thirty-one. The Twynholm mill was originally designed to be a distillery, but we are told that 'an alteration in the distillery laws, and other circumstances' forced the tenant to change it into a woollen mill and encourage other entrepreneurs to join him.[40]

The man who probably did more than anyone to promote industrial development in Galloway was James Murray, a man of many parts who pursued a wide range of interests throughout his career, which spanned the second half of the century until his death in 1799.[41] An aristocrat and a prominent landowner, he inherited the family estates of Broughton and Cally, and in addition he purchased Killybegs in Co. Donegal from his kinsman, the earl of Annandale. However, his interests were primarily focused on developing the small settlement of Gatehouse, which lay at the edge of his Cally demesne, into a substantial industrial centre, and it was to give added status to the township it had now become that he was responsible for having it erected into a burgh of barony in 1795.

As a preliminary, he embarked on an ambitious scheme to draw water from Loch Whinyeon, which lies some three miles (5 km) away in the hills above Gatehouse. This included tunnelling some 230m through a section of hill to the loch, and constructing a series of small canals to channel the water across two minor river systems to a reservoir at the head of the village, from where it could be diverted to his factories by means of sluices.[42] As he was primarily a cattle breeder, it was logical that a tannery was among the first of the enterprises to be established at Gatehouse. This was completed and ready to be put into operation in about 1768,[43] and the tanpits where the skins were treated are still preserved in the local nomenclature. Although he supplied the initial capital, he ran the business in partnership with two tanners brought in from elsewhere, and when he eventually bought out their interests he employed another tanner, James Davitts, to run it. This prospered, and in 1797 Murray sold it to Davitts under a feu, and thereafter the latter ran it himself making a substantial fortune in the process.[44] Its success encouraged other aspiring industrialists to follow suit, and by the end of the century the demand for hides had expanded to the point where they exceeeded the local supply and had to be imported, most of them coming from Ireland.[45]

James Murray also established a brewery, allegedly for the purpose of weaning the local people away from their habit of drinking whisky, which was now the popular tipple.[46] True or not, the increasing demand for beer associated with the expanding population made brewing a highly profitable business, and all the more so since Galloway was renowned for the quality of its malting barley.[47] Nevertheless, the progressive increase in beer excise duty rendered whisky cheaper by comparison, and this accounted for its growing popularity and the establishment of a number of distilleries in Galloway – though not at Gatehouse. James Murray's other enterprises included a brass foundry, a soapworks, and a boat-building yard on the Fleet, but these were mere sideshows compared with the cotton mills, which were the most important of all his enterprises.

Cotton was paramount in the late 1700s, and a thriving industry had grown up around Liverpool and in the west of Scotland, where it was centred round Glasgow, replacing the tobacco trade as its main source of wealth. As Galloway had close links with both these centres, it naturally followed that a cotton industry grew up there as well. The initial impetus came from James Murray, who established four mills at Gatehouse, two of them being managed by the Yorkshire firm of Alexander Birtwhistle, the senior partner of which was the founder's son John. Somewhat incongruously, they were originally cattle dealers who came to Galloway at the behest of lord Daer to set up a cotton mill on the Dee near Kirkcudbright, but this was vetoed by his father, the earl of Selkirk, who feared 'his mansion might be disgraced by the vicinity of an establishment of manufacturing industry'.[48] So James Murray lured them to Gatehouse instead, where they established a jointly-owned company to manage his mills. This proved highly successful, and in 1792 Heron reported that they were spinning 300 lbs (136 kg) of cotton wool into yarn each week and employing a labour force of three hundred – 'of whom two hundred are children',[49] adding that 'the success of Gatehouse had roused a passion for cotton manufacture through the whole country'.[50]

Among those who followed his lead was William Douglas. His interest in cotton manufacture was fired in particular by David Dale, the enlightened entrepreneur who was responsible for expanding the New Mills at Lanark, where the conditions of employment were far in advance of his time. In fact, Dale was jointly responsible, with William and his brother Samuel, for setting up the cotton mills at Newton Stewart in about 1793,[51] although William ran those at Carlingwark on his own. In order to attract other entrepreneurs to set up in business there, he expanded this into a small 'planned' town, and in 1792 he was responsible for having it erected into a burgh of barony and renamed Castle Douglas.[52]

Somewhat presumptuously, his association with Newton Stewart caused him to rename it Newton Douglas, a piece of self-advertisement which inspired Burns's acid comment about his 'christening towns far and near'.[53] Although his cotton enterprises succumbed to the recession during the Napoleonic Wars, his other industries at Castle Douglas, which included a soapworks, brewery and tannery, as well as a woollen mill, proved more durable. While they have long since disappeared, it is to him that Castle Douglas owes its existence and its subsequent development as a thriving market town. His interests also embraced banking, being the founder of the Galloway Banking Company, and also land improvement. It was for this purpose that he bought up a number of estates in Galloway, and it is at Gelston that a substantial obelisk was subsequently erected to the memory of this outstanding man.[54]

A linen industry had also been developing in parts of Galloway since the early decades of the century, when the second earl of Stair established a small manufactory near Castle Kennedy. This was traditionally a cottage industry, and as it was confined to those few areas where flax can be grown, linen manufacture remained a comparatively small enterprise in Galloway. The main centre in western Wigtownshire was Stoneykirk, though linen mills were established at Stranraer by the 1790s. There was also a small flax industry in Kirkcudbrightshire, notably at Kelton, Dalbeattie and New Abbey, but most of these were small businesses which were set up for the purpose of processing flax supplied to them by the inhabitants of the surrounding district.[55]

Much more important was the local milling industry, which had expanded in line with the rapid growth in cereal production. By the end of the century numerous small mills were established throughout the region, and the passing of the Thirlage Act in 1799 gave an additional fillip to the industry. This abolished the iniquitous practice of thirlage which had grown increasingly burdensome with the expansion in grain production,[56] although many landowners had voluntarily abandoned it.[57] As tenants were no longer astricted to their landlord's mill, they could sell their corn unground without having to pay multures on it, or have it ground at the mill of their choice. Therefore, the disappearance of their former captive market meant that mills were having to compete with one another for custom, and this led to a rationalisation of the industry with the emergence of larger factories which drove the smaller ones out of business. Many of these old mills are still readily identifiable, and in some cases the huge water wheel which was used for driving the grinding machinery remains intact, as well as the mill lade for conducting water from the nearby stream to drive it.

The success of entrepreneurs like James Murray and William Douglas inspired lesser men, imagining it to be an easy road to riches, to follow suit and set up their own businesses. But lacking the necessary ability, the application, or any conception of the risks involved, few survived. A contemporary commentator was particularly scathing about them, when he wrote:

> Whenever they are induced to try anything like manufacture, they begin with the extravagant hope that it is instantly to enrich themselves without considering the extraordinary industry and attention which is necessary to the success of their hopes. They never reflect that no new attempt can be highly profitable in its very commencement. They make no allowance for their own indolence, extravagance or inexperience [and] relinquish it with despondency and disgust, and again sit down satisfied with their former poverty and with that piddling traffic and loitering labour to which they have become accustomed.

PLANNED VILLAGES

Industrial and economic development led to a growing demand for labour, and the need to provide accommodation for workers was primarily accountable for the development of the 'planned villages'. These were quite different from the traditional villages in Galloway where, according to the minister of Borgue, 'the most worthless and wretched part of society is commonly to be found. Thither the dregs of the community, from all quarters, are poured in. Every incentive to vice is presented, and no proper police is established to give a check to the growing evil'.[58] In contrast, planned villages were strictly controlled by the founder, who exercised an almost intrusive discipline over the lives of the inhabitants. Generally speaking, they ranged from the formal planned villages, of which Gatehouse and Castle Douglas were prime examples, to the less formal settlements like Dalbeattie, Kirkcowan and Sorbie. Others, such as Glenluce, were built along the main turnpike roads or, as in the case of Garlieston and Port William, round harbours or seaports.

The following are the more important planned villages in Galloway with their approximate dates of origin and the founder in each case[59]:

Castle Douglas	1791	Sir William Douglas
Creetown	1791	John McCulloch of Barholm
Dalbeattie	c.1781	{Alexander Copland
		{George Maxwell of Munches
Garlieston	c.1790	Lord Garlies
Gatehouse of Fleet	post1775	James Murray of Broughton
Kirkcowan	post1793	John and Robert Milroy
Kirkpatrick Durham	c.1785	Rev. Dr David Lamont
Newton Douglas	1789	Sir William Douglas
Port Logan	1818	Col. Andrew McDowall
Port William	c.1776	Sir William Maxwell of Monreith
Southerness	c.1790	Richard Oswald of Cavens
Twynholm	c.1795	Lord Daer

In addition, Dalry was founded as a planned village by the earl of Galloway towards the end of the eighteenth century before his family's lands there were sold to the Forbes of Earlston. Therefore, with the sole exception of Port Logan these villages were all founded in the eighteenth century, and it is significant that in almost every case the founder was the local landowner, since it was they above all who provided the impetus for improvement. Other villages were projected but never got beyond the planning stage, and examples included James Murray's proposed creation at Tongland and lord Daer's at Kirkandrews.

Planned villages were essentially speculative developments in that they required a large capital outlay, and because their success was by no means assured they involved a considerable element of risk. First, the founder had to establish a successful commercial enterprise as the nucleus, then houses were needed to accommodate the workforce. If the settlement was large enough to attract shopkeepers and small-time tradesmen, and a sufficiently viable community was established to encourage other entrepeneurs to set up ancillary businesses, the founder could start to recoup his outlays by feuing off plots of land for building purposes. As with any private development, strict conditions were imposed regarding the size, standard, design and layout of the houses in order to ensure that the village conformed with the founder's original plan. If sales went well more industry and more tradespeople were attracted, so the success compounded on itself, and from these beginnings there sprang the flourishing commercial centres of today. Only when one realises this can one appreciate how much these urban centres that grew out of an original planned village owe to their founder.

Gatehouse was a typical example, and Heron, writing in 1792, tells us that 'within the remembrance of several now living, there was only a single house, [and] lying on the great road from Dumfries to Portpatrick . . . it was naturally a proper situation for an inn [which] with the advantage of the well-frequented markets, rendered it promising enough for a shopkeeper or two'. Then he goes on to describe how James Murray expanded it by encouraging 'inhabitants to settle and form a village here, by offering very advantageous terms of feu, [so that] tanners, glovers, weavers, shoemakers, tailors, masons, carpenters, butchers, bakers, alehouse-keepers, day-labourers and smugglers were then brought in'.[60] The result was that by 1794 it consisted of upwards of 160 houses and 1,150 inhabitants.[61]

Regrettably, Heron is less than complimentary about these inhabitants. 'I wish I could honestly add', he writes, 'that the morals of these good people have been improved with their circumstances. But prostitution and breaches of chastity have lately become frequent here. Tippling houses are wonderfully numerous. I was informed by the intelligent exciseman of the place, that not fewer than an hundred and fifty gallons of whisky alone had been consumed here for every week of the last six months. The licentiousness of Gatehouse affords frequent business for the neighbouring Justices.'[62] Commenting on their morals, he goes on to say that 'the pious assiduities' of the clergyman and his assistant 'have proved insufficient to maintain among the manufacturers of Gatehouse, all that purity of morals and decorum of manners which might be wished. Marriages are indeed so frequent that the clergyman has found it occasionally necessary, for the sake of dispatch, to dispense with the ordinary ceremonies of the church'.[63] In sharp contrast, the said clergyman asserts in his contribution to the *Old Statistical Account* that 'much praise is due to their religious and moral conduct',[64] describing the people as 'candid, sober and industrious'[65]; but then ministers are naturally concerned to put the best possible gloss on the state of their parishes.

Castle Douglas is another example of a thriving centre which grew out of a small settlement, and it was a tribute to the enterprise of William Douglas, and Sir Alexander Gordon before him, that in 1792 the local minister was able to report that 'there are now six or seven hundred inhabitants where twenty-six years ago there were not twenty'.[66] Similar trends in the parishes of Kirkinner and Sorbie[67] were the result of improvements carried out there by the earls of Selkirk and Galloway, and in Sorbie in particular the population increase reflected the success of lord Garlies's planned village of Garlieston. The increase in the parish of Mochrum, on the other hand, was attributable to a combination of the improvements carried out by Sir William Maxwell on his estate of Monreith[68] and the growth of his creation of Port William.

Seaport villages like these expanded in line with the growing export trade which was associated with Galloway's expanding economy. Pre-eminent among them was Garlieston which is laid out on classic Georgian lines with some fine architecture of the period. This was primarily designed as an outlet for the hugely increased production in the Machars resulting from the comprehensive improvements carried out by lord Garlies and his father, the earl of Galloway, to the family estates there. It also gave lord Garlies the opportunity to establish a small cargo fleet to carry the produce direct to Galloway's principal grain markets at Whitehaven in Cumberland and Liverpool, as well as Bristol and Dublin. Large quantities were also being shipped to the ports on the Clyde for onward transportation to Glasgow to feed the growing population there.

Portpatrick was another example, and so was Creetown, while the ancient harbour at the Isle of Whithorn was brought back into commission. Creetown was originally the embarkation point for the ferry to Wigtown – hence its old name of Ferrytown of Cree – and John McCulloch of Barholm developed it into a seaport by widening and deepening the tidal creek which connects it with the channel of the river Cree. Also, at his instigation it was erected into a burgh of barony in 1791[69] when its name was changed to Creetown. It was also a small industrial centre in that it could boast a lead shot mill, as well as a cotton mill which was subsequently converted into a carpet factory,[70] though it was not until the following century that the local quarries were opened up. Heron, however, seems to have been unimpressed, as he asserts that it was 'inhabited chiefly by seafaring people, and its manners take their tone from these', adding that it contains 'an abundance of tippling-houses, but no decent or commodious inn. Dram-drinking is the vice of the place and of the neighbourhood'.[71]

IMPROVED LIFESTYLES

Such strictures are exceptional, because Heron and his contemporaries paint a generally fulsome picture of Galloway at this time. The dramatic rise in the standard of living is the subject of frequent comment, this being attributable to wages rising far in excess of the cost of living, and the minister of Parton, writing in 1794, observed that as a general rule the wages paid to a single farm worker had more than trebled over the previous thirty years.[72] That this was the case at Parton is significant, because it is mainly an upland parish where farming would have been relatively less profitable, and therefore one can reasonably assume that the increase was higher in the more prosperous districts. On the other hand, there were parts of Wigtownshire where wages were depressed as a result of competition from 'the continual emigration of a great number of Irish labourers'.[73]

The quality of housing had improved, and the single-roomed bothy which was the standard accommodation of earlier generations, had been replaced by stone-built, slate-roofed cottages. Standards of dress were changing too, and this applied to all classes – lairds, tenants, and labourers alike. We are told that the lairds' wives, who formerly spent most of their time in linen frocks and plaids 'of disgusting slovenliness, waited on by maids without stockings or shoes',[74] now 'live as well as any in Great Britain of their rank'. The men were arraying themselves in 'cotton velvets and corduroys' in place of the 'old kelt coat, blue bonnet and plaiding hose',[75] and even their servants appeared on special occasions dressed in 'coats of broad cloth, cotton vests and breeches, and generally with watches in their pockets'.[76] Gone too were the blue cloth cloaks and the home-made gowns of the women, and even the servant girls would turn themselves out in 'silk cloaks and bonnets . . . thread stockings and cloth shoes'.[77]

The prevailing diet was more varied and, although oatmeal – the 'everlasting oatcake' as one Wigtownshire labourer ruefully put it[78] – continued to be the staple food, there was now ample milk, butter and cheese, and one commentator describes the normal dinner of a working man as consisting of barley broth with beef or mutton and potatoes. There was also a wider choice of green vegetables, as the developing enthusiasm of the upper classes for gardening was being copied on a smaller scale in the kailyards of the peasantry. Standards of cleanliness were higher too, since it was no longer acceptable to have the family midden outside the front door. In the towns, street pumps were beginning to be installed to provide a supply of clean water, while the practice of leaving piles of refuse outside the houses was forbidden, and streets were regularly washed down.

This resulted in a generally higher standard of public health. Nevertheless, it is evident from the *Old Statistical Account* that agues were endemic, and so was rheumatism which, understandably, was ascribed to the prevailing cold and damp conditions in which the poorer people lived. There are also references to intermittent fevers of an unspecified type, for which drovers returning from the south were usually blamed. Strangely, there is no mention of tuberculosis, which was a major killer of the times, though it is possible the contributors, who were ministers with probably only a rudimentary knowledge of medicine, may simply have regarded it as a type of fever. Thanks to innoculation the impact of smallpox – that scourge of earlier times – seems to have greatly diminished, though its introduction appears to have been greeted with a mixture of suspicion and downright hostility, perhaps because it was something new and unfamiliar. In fact, there were occasions when the local minister had to take the initiative and innoculate his parishioners' children himself, while the incumbent of Kirkmabreck draws a harrowing picture of how 'many of these little innocents' are consigned through 'the inattention, stupidity, and superstition of their parents . . . to the ravages of this terrible disorder, or, perhaps to the gloomy mansions of the tomb'.[79]

For all that, the life expectancy of a newborn child was not high and many were saved from smallpox only to succumb to other recognised killers of the time, such as measles, diphtheria or croup. For those who had access to them there are a number of chalybeate springs in Galloway, which were considered good for 'aguish' and 'stomachic' complaints.[80] Despite the fact that the prevailing state of health may have fallen well short of currently accepted standards, most parishes seem to have boasted of some octogenarians, while there is frequent mention of people in their nineties and the occasional few who achieved three figures.

It was perhaps a reflection of the greater opportunities for self-advancement which were now available that two Gallovidians of humble origin who were born during the latter part of the 1700s made their mark in the world. One was Alexander Murray, a shepherd's son from a remote settlement near Talnotry, on the Newton Stewart/New Galloway road, who was born in 1775. Almost entirely self-taught, he became the minister of Urr, and latterly professor of oriental languages at Edinburgh University. Three years his junior was Thomas Brown, the son of the minister of Kirkmabreck, who became a noted metaphysician and philosopher. Unfortunately, both men died at a comparatively early age – Brown in 1820, while Murray succumbed to consumption in 1813 and the memorial erected to his memory near his birthplace is a fitting tribute to his achievements.

CONCLUSION

Reflecting the advances made during that period is the startling comparison drawn by a contemporary observer between the lifestyle of the people
living at the end of the century, and that of their 'wretchedly poor' forefathers where 'want sat upon every brow and hunger was painted on every
face [while] neither their tattered clothes nor their miserable cottages were
a sufficient shelter from the cold'. In sharp contrast, the present generation are described as having 'put off the long clothing, the tardy pace and
the lethargic look of their fathers for the short doublet, the linen trousers
and the quick pace of men who are labouring for their own behoof'. The
prevailing prosperity was reflected in the opulence of the local fairs, the
best known being that at Kelton. Evidently its fame was such that, according
to Heron, it drew horse- and cattle-dealers, 'sellers of sweetmeats and
spirituous liquors, gypsies, pickpockets and smugglers' from as far afield as
England, Ireland and 'the most distant parts of North Britain'. In
consequence the whole fair day was 'one busy tumultuous scene' of
'bargaining, wooing, carousing [and] quarrelling', and even the neighbouring gentry were spectators of 'the rude festivity which it displays'.[81]

While much of the prevailing prosperity can be attributed to the
improvements carried out by the more enterprising landowners, the
majority of lairds seem to have done little to their estates. In many cases,
indolence, apathy or a lack of money were to blame, though in others it was
the result of granting leases for too short a period. In a few instances
competition for labour from local industry was a factor,[82] while Heron tells
us that in Borgue parish it was attributable to a preoccupation with cattle-
rearing to the exclusion of other potentially more profitable types of
farming.[83] Confirming its patchiness throughout the region, Lamont noted
that in his parish of Kirkpatrick Durham 'improvement of the land is only
in its infancy',[84] while Smith remarks on how forcibly he was struck by 'the
very different state of improvement upon estates possessing similar
advantages'.[85] Clearly this was the fault of the landowners, and the minister
of Kirkmabreck drives the point home by asserting that 'there are still
upwards of 1,000 acres [which are] highly capable of cultivation, at present
lying in a state of nature, covered with heath, and almost good for nothing',
claiming this was the fault of 'the landlords, who in that respect are in a
great measure blind to their own interest'.[86]

Nevertheless, Heron gives a glowing description of the countryside he
encountered in the course of his travels through Galloway in 1792.
'Advancing across the ridge which divides the Dee from the Urr', he wrote,
'I found myself in a tract of country that presented every mark of rapid
improvement. The fields are divided by stone-walls of suitable height and

strength. The farm-houses are decently built, and have their roofs commonly covered with slate'.[87] Commenting in particular on the district round Kelton, he goes on to say that 'this tract of country is indeed wonderfully populous. It is a fine proof of the tendency of agriculture to bring wealth to the population . . . the vicinity of the sea-coast affords the farmers sufficient convenience for the exportation of their grain. The highway leading into England gives them considerable advantages for the sale and exportation of their cattle'.[88] Continuing his journey from Kirkcudbright to Gatehouse he described the countryside as 'rich and fertile' and 'either laid out in grass-parks, or in corn-fields'.[89]

Other contemporary writers tell much the same story, while the 50 per cent increase in the population of Galloway that occurred between 1755 and 1801[90] is standing testimony to the success of the efforts and enterprise of the innovative and forward-looking landowners, improvers and industrialists of the time, and the general diffusion of the wealth they created. True, economic trends were working in their favour, and while self-interest laced with a genuinely benevolent paternalism may have been the motive, it was nevertheless fortunate that the owners of the largest estates at this time happened to be men with the far-sightedness to perceive the opportunities, the motivation to grasp them, and the ability to realise their potential. Contemporary commentators are unanimous in emphasising how important a part they played in the recovery, and perhaps none more so than the assertion of the minister of Portpatrick that, 'the progress of improvement is generally owed . . . to the spirit and exertions of particular men who seem born for the purpose of rousing the multitude from the state of ignorance or torpor, from which they are too often unwilling to be emancipated'.[91]

NOTES

1. Anderson, 'The development of the road system', 206.
2. Smith, *Agricultural Survey*, 311.
3. Prevost, 'Sir John Clerk's journie to Galloway in 1735', 135.
4. *Ibid.*
5. Lenman, *Economic History*, 75.
6. Minutes of the Commissioners of Supply 2 August 1757.
7. *General Estimate and Observations on the Proposed Road from the River Sark to Portpatrick: 24 October 1757* (SRO Murray of Broughton and Cally MSS GD 10/546/2).
8. Arnott, 'The military road to Portpatrick', 120: Anderson, 'Road system', 210.
9. *OSA* 13, p 585.
10. Anderson, 'Road system, Part II', 212.
11. Anderson, 'Road system', 210.

12. *OSA*, 13 p 651.
13. Heron, *Observations* ii, 102.
14. Anderson, 'Road system', 210.
15. *Ibid.*
16. A similar act was passed for Wigtownshire in 1802.
17. Smith, *Agricultural Survey*, 310.
18. *Ibid.*, 313.
19. This never in fact materialised, and it was not until 1844, when the local sheriff-substitute was drowned while crossing the river, that the plan was revived, and even then thirty years were to pass before a bridge was built.
20. *NSA* (Kirkcud), 214.
21. Anderson, 'Road system', 206.
22. Dick, *Highways and Byways*, 470–1. The bridge was subsequently washed away and replaced by another one in 1790 (Anderson, 'Road system, Part II', 217), but the site is now submerged by the reservoir.
23. Anderson, 'Road system', 208.
24. *Ibid.*, 209.
25. The building material for this was taken from the ruins of Tongland abbey where, according to Symson, 'the steeple and part of the walls were yet standing'. This bridge was condemned as unsafe in 1800, so work was started on another one, but it was washed away while only half completed, leaving the original one still standing. Eventually a new one was built in 1806, and another in 1832.
26. Anderson, 'Road system', 209–10.
27. Anderson, 'Road system, Part II', 212.
28. This relatively small channel, which is still readily identifiable having recently been cleaned up, extends for some 3 miles (4.5 km). The construction work involved excavating a cutting through the bank close to its inflow (adjacent to present-day Carlingwark House), and thereafter digging a trench as far as its outflow opposite Threave island.
29. *OSA* 8, p 303.
30. Donnachie, *Industrial Archaeology*, 163.
31. 42 Geo III, c 114 Glenkens Canal Bill.
32. Donnachie, *Industrial Archaeology*, 165.
33. Campbell, *Owners and Occupiers*, 6.
34. Smith, *Agricultural Survey*, 24.
35. Heron, *Observations* ii, 107.
36. *Ibid.*
37. Basil Douglas – lord Daer (pronounced Dar) was his courtesy title – was the second of the six sons of the fourth earl of Selkirk, but they all predeceased their father except the youngest, Thomas, who succeeded him as fifth earl in 1799. Lord Daer was also a friend of Robert Burns, and it was in honour of the family that the latter composed the celebrated Selkirk grace while on a visit to Kirkcudbright.
38. *OSA* 9, p 317.
39. Smith, *Agricultural Survey*, 53.
40. *OSA* 15, p 80.
41. For a man who was so successful in the fields of business and commerce his private life was curiously disorganised. In 1752 he married his first cousin Lady Catherine Stewart, a daughter of the sixth earl of Galloway (his mother, Lady Euphemia, being a daughter of the fifth earl) and had a number of children

by her, the last of whom died in 1787. However, in the 1760s, to the consterna-
tion of his friends, he eloped to Cornwall with the daughter of a Dumfriesshire
laird, Johnstone of Carnsalloch, by whom he proceeded to have four children,
including his heir Alexander. One of the daughters, Anne, married William
Stewart of Shambellie, and although they had issue, the present Stewarts are
descended from his second marriage. Yet, in spite of her husband's infidelity,
Lady Catherine was much concerned with the upbringing of his illegitimate
family. At the same time, James himself maintained close links with her family,
the earls of Galloway, because he executed an entail in their favour, with the
result that when his son Alexander died childless in 1845 the family estates
passed to a junior branch of the family who took the name Murray-Stewart.

42. The watercourse is still readily identifiable and the former reservoir which lies
    immediately behind the war memorial at the top of the town has recently been
    cleaned up.
43. Donnachie, *Industrial Archaeology*, 46.
44. *Ibid.*
45. *Ibid.*, 49.
46. It has been asserted that, whereas a labourer in the 1740s might enjoy 'a Scots
    pint of 2d ale or small beer', his counterpart in the 1790s was more likely to
    drink 'a small bottle of unmixed whisky at one sitting'.
47. It is significant that Tennants who dominated the industry in the west of
    Scotland had corn factors in Dumfries, Kirkcudbright and Wigtown.
48. Heron, *Observations* ii, 217–8.
49. *Ibid.*, 220.
50. *Ibid.* The Birtwhistles, incidentally, made a great deal of money out of this, and
    on the strength of it members of the family bought up a number of properties
    in Kirkcudbrightshire.
51. Donnachie, *Industrial Archaeology*, 93.
52. Although its civic coat of arms incorporates the Douglas heart the town has no
    connection with the Black Douglases.
53. Donnachie, *Industrial Archaeology*, 93.
54. In later life he considered it appropriate to round off his career with a title, so
    he went to some pains to cajole Henry Dundas, the dominant power in
    Scotland at the time, to obtain one for him. Evidently Dundas appears to have
    had some difficulty in persuading the prime minister, William Pitt, that
    Douglas's limited political influence was worth a baronetcy, but he must have
    been successful as Douglas finally secured it in 1796.
55. Donnachie, *Industrial Archaeology*, 86.
56. Dr Lamont was particularly critical of the practice, claiming that the multures
    which farmers were obliged to pay the miller could absorb as much as a twelfth
    of their entire grain crop (*OSA* 2, p 252).
57. Webster, *Agriculture*, 58.
58. *OSA* 2, p 42.
59. Donnachie and McLeod, *Old Galloway*, app 3, p 152. I am grateful to both
    authors for allowing me to reproduce the list.
60. Heron, *Observations* ii, 214–7.
61. *OSA* 2, p 312.
62. Heron, *Observations*, ii, 222.
63. *Ibid.*
64. *OSA* ii, p 311.
65. *Ibid.*, 312.

66. *Ibid.* 4, pp 141–2.
67. *Ibid.* 1, p 249.
68. *OSA* 17, p 562.
69. Donnachie, *Industrial Archaeology*, 95.
70. *Ibid*, 75, 77.
71. Heron, *Observations* ii, 246.
72. *Ibid.* 1, p 188. On average these had risen from £2 10s to £8 per half year which was the normal term of engagement.
73. *OSA* 17, p 593.
74. Smout, *History of the Scottish People*, 268.
75. *OSA* 4, p 481.
76. *Ibid.*
77. *Ibid*, 482.
78. Smout, *History*, 317.
79. *OSA* 15, p 549.
80. *Ibid.* 3, p 138 and 13, p 642.
81. Heron, *Observations*, 129–30.
82. *OSA* 11, p 37.
83. Heron, *Observations* ii, 206–7.
84. *OSA* 2, p 259.
85. Smith, *Agricultural Survey*, 33.
86. *OSA* 15, p 547.
87. Heron, *Observations* ii, 122–3.
88. *Ibid.*, 131.
89. *Ibid.*, 201.
90. In round figures, it rose from 37,500 to just over 52,000 (see Donnachie, *Industrial Archaeology*, 13) which is not far short of today's figure of 56,000.
91. *OSA* 1, p 42. While this referred in particular to Sir James Hunter-Blair's development of Portpatrick as a seaport, and the improvements made to his estate of Dunskey, it was intended to apply generally to other similarly-motivated landowners.

30

THE 1800s:
UNEVEN PROSPERITY

IMPROVING COMMUNICATIONS

Galloway's expanding economy highlighted the continuing inadequacy of the local road system, notwithstanding the improvements carried out during the late 1700s. Therefore, the commissioners of supply were forced to make a radical reappraisal of the whole approach to road-building and maintenance. As a result, they obtained two private Acts of Parliament – the Kirkcudbrightshire commissioners in 1796 and those in Wigtownshire in 1802 – which authorised them to set up turnpike road trusts and levy tolls. This marked a complete change, in that the cost of maintaining the roads and building new, turnpiked ones was now shifted from the local residents on to the users.

The first turnpike to be built in Galloway was a new arterial road from Dumfries as far as Castle Douglas, and was the forerunner of the present A75. Work was started in 1797, and when completed in 1805 it replaced the existing military road which thereafter reverted to a minor one connecting Drumsleet, on the outskirts of Dumfries, with Ernespie near Castle Douglas. The extension as far as Gatehouse was finished in 1808, and by that time the work of upgrading the next section to Creetown was already under way. However, it was not until about 1815 that the following section as far as the Cree bridge at Newton Stewart was fully operational.[1]

The north–south route leading from Kirkcudbright towards Dalmellington in Ayrshire, which went up the valleys of the Dee and its tributaries the Ken and the Deugh, was also constituted a turnpike road under the 1796 Act. Trackways had already existed there since time immemorial, so the work which began in 1803 consisted mainly of improving and upgrading them. The lower section crossed the Dee at its mouth by a new bridge at Tongland which was completed in 1807, and from there it followed broadly the line of the present A711 road as far as the main highway from Castle Douglas to Gatehouse, before striking northwards to the bridge over the Dee at Glenlochar. Meanwhile, the Ayrshire road trustees were completing the northern section as far as the county boundary, which lies some five miles beyond Carsphairn. Other sections were built simultaneously or upgraded piecemeal, but it was not until the 1820s that the road was finally completed with a turnpiked link to Castle Douglas.

By this time the road connecting Crocketford with the traditional pilgrims' way between the Ken and the Cree, whose condition so appalled Sir John Clerk, had been upgraded. Lord Daer was responsible for building a new section beyond Clatteringshaws,[2] and later improvements included the entire renovation of the stretch between New Galloway and Clattering-shaws, the whole operation being completed in 1815. However, efforts to build a bridge over the Ken were continually dogged by misfortune as each one was washed away, the last having collapsed in 1806. Work began on a replacement in about 1814, but this was destroyed by a flood while still partially built, and it was only in 1822 that the present one was completed. Lying as it does at the heart of Kirkcudbrightshire, it was integral to the existing byways up the Dee and Ken valleys, besides marking the crossing point of the old pilgrims' way.

A direct link between Kirkcudbright and Gatehouse was established in 1810–11 with the construction of a road from the lower Dee opposite Kirkcudbright, which followed broadly the line of the present A755 as far as Minto (then named Drummore) on the main turnpike through Galloway. At much the same time, a road in the opposite direction was established by upgrading the existing tracks along the eastern side of the Dee past Gelston, and from there to Buittle, crossing the Urr by the present Craignair bridge before continuing to Dalbeattie. From there it followed the course of the existing A711 past Kirkgunzeon and Beeswing (from where a spur road led to New Abbey) to Dumfries. Although further improvements were carried out in the course of the nineteenth century, this provided the framework for the future road system in Kirkcud-brightshire.[3]

The 1820s saw the construction of a road from Portpatrick leading into Ayrshire and eventually connecting with Glasgow. The section from Stranraer to Ballantrae had already been completed in 1782, but the threat to abandon the work of reconstructing Portpatrick harbour if the road between Stranraer and Girvan was left 'in its present barbarous condition'[4] persuaded the local commissioners to extend it to Portpatrick. This had important consequences, for whereas in the past Galloway was seen purely as a conduit for traffic passing between Ireland, Carlisle and the south, it was now a crucial link in the mercantile contacts between Dublin and Glasgow, and hence with other parts of Scotland.[5] The upgrading of this road, as well as the main road through Galloway, was also vital to the mail service between Scotland and Ireland which had been operating on a regular basis since 1804.[6] Initially, the mails were carried on cattle boats plying between Portpatrick[7] and Donaghadee, but because the service was irregular and unreliable special mail boats were introduced. The running costs were defrayed by taking passengers, who understandably preferred them to the cattle boats which had hitherto been the only transport available, since, not surprisingly, they were deemed 'peculiarly offensive'.[8]

Canals were no longer the flavour of the age, and after the stillbirth of the Glenkens Canal Company no further projects were mooted, apart from some minor projects which were designed to improve the accessibility of certain ports. A scheme to dredge the lower Nith to allow larger ships to reach Dumfries received parliamentary approval in 1811.[9] Also in 1824, Alexander Murray completed the work of canalising the lower reaches of the Fleet which had been started by his father in 1792, thus allowing vessels of up to 160 tons access as far as the bridge at Gatehouse.[10] This included building a swing bridge across the river opposite Cardiness castle, as well as an extensive embankment at its mouth to protect the low-lying fields on Cally Mains from flooding. The work was carried out by some 200 Irish peasants from the Murray estates in Donegal, mostly tenants in arrears with their rents who were allowed to commute them into labour.[11]

INDUSTRIAL SLOWDOWN

Ironically, the improvement in communications coincided with a slowing down in the industrialisation of Galloway. The cotton mills were the first to suffer, as the crisis in the industry during the Napoleonic Wars forced the Birtwhistle mills in Gatehouse to cease production in about 1810.[12] However, the subsequent revival of the industry encouraged the firm of James Davidson & Co. to lease them in 1832. The buildings were repaired, new machinery installed, and by 1840 they were employing 174 workers.[13] Some ten years later, however, they ceased production and the mills were taken over by the Dalbeattie firm of Thomas and William Helme. Although they were primarily timber merchants, they converted one of the buildings into a bobbin mill which continued to operate until the 1930s.[14] The cotton factories established by the Douglas brothers at Castle Douglas and Newton Douglas also went out of production, the latter being bought by lord Garlies[15] for a fraction of their original cost in 1826, when he restored the burgh to its original name of Newton Stewart. Nevertheless, the ancillary weaving industry which the Douglases helped promote continued to survive on an agency basis in spite of its being notoriously badly paid.

The tax imposed on leather during the Napoleonic Wars hit the tanning industry, and although a number of small local tanneries survived until the 1830s they had for some time been losing ground to larger concerns such as those in Dumfries which, by operating economies of scale, undercut them and captured their markets. The same was happening in the brewing industry, which had been hit by a further rise in malt duty during the 1780s, and although seventeen breweries were still operating in south-west Scotland in 1825, these all eventually fell victim to the larger breweries that dominated the industry.[16] The brewery at Gatehouse was among the casualties, being symptomatic of the fate of other enterprises which James Murray established there. This was commented on by the local minister who observed that 'Mr. Murray established a wine company, a brewery, and a tannery . . . which were all placed under the management of persons from England: but they did not turn out lucrative speculations . . . and they were eventually dissolved'.[17]

The local woollen industry, on the other hand, was expanding, and the period from 1790 to 1850 saw the establishment of a number of larger mills in the region.[18] One was the waukmill at old Minnigaff, which was built in 1800[19] and continued to operate until the 1920s, while another was the mill at Kirkcowan which had been started by Robert Milroy in 1814. His sons expanded it in 1822, and the business was further enlarged by his grandsons, to the extent that by 1839 it was employing a workforce of thirty-nine and was described as 'a thriving establishment' engaged in manufacturing 'blankets, cloth, plaidings and flannels'.[20] This was logical given the large blackface sheep population in the district, and it was largely because of this that the mills remained in operation until the 1950s. By then the manufacture of woollen products had virtually ceased in Galloway, though the Creebridge Mills at Newton Stewart survived until the following decade. Ancillary to this was carpet-making, and the factory established under the patronage of William Douglas at Newton Douglas in about 1792[21] was the forerunner of a number of others in Galloway, though these eventually went out of production as the local industry became concentrated in Dumfries.

Milling was also an expanding industry, mainly on account of the boom in cereal prices during the Napoleonic Wars and the consequent expansion in corn production. In fact, references to the existence of mills in marginal regions, like the central Machars and the Glenkens, suggest that these were extensively cropped although they have since reverted to pasture and grazing land. The industry continued to flourish until the mid-century, when there were around 140 mills operating in south-west Scotland,[22] but thereafter it began to decline as arable farming gave way to dairying. The trend was accelerated by the depression of the 1880s which forced a number of mills to switch over to producing animal feeds. Most, however, went out of production, so very few of the original mills are now left in Galloway.

The early nineteenth century saw the development of a granite quarrying industry in Galloway in response to a rising demand for building material, for which the toughness of the local stone is particularly well suited. It had already existed in a small way in the previous century, but its subsequent expansion was primarily attributable to the efforts of Andrew Newall, whose family continued to be closely associated with the granite industry at Dalbeattie. The first major quarry was opened at nearby Craignair in 1826 by the Liverpool Dock Trustees under a lease from John Maxwell of Munches.[23] In 1830, they extended their operations by opening a quarry at Kirkmabreck, from where the stone could readily be transported by schooner to Liverpool, but after a promising start production fell away, and by 1844 the workforce, which had peaked out at 450, was reduced to 160.

The same was happening at the Craignair quarries, mainly because the cost of transporting the large blocks which were in demand forced the dock trustees to look for an alternative source.[24] Later, the opening of the Dumfries–Castle Douglas railway, combined with a further upgrading of the local roads, created a demand for granite chips which gave the quarries a new lease of life. At the same time, there was a revival in demand for the high quality granite at Kirkmabreck for building docks, harbours, light-houses and civic and public buildings throughout the world. Consequently, a number of new quarries were opened up there during the 1860s and 1870s to provide stone for the docks at Greenock, Leith, Liverpool, Birken-head, Newport and Swansea, while 'many thousands of tons of material' from the quarry at Craignair went into the construction of the Thames Embankment.[25]

Metal mining enjoyed a brief prosperity on the strength of the deposits of lead, zinc, copper and iron on the fringes of the Cairnsmore of Fleet and Merrick ranges. A small industry had already existed in the previous century when iron ore was mined at Auchinleck on the edge of the Screel and Bengairn range,[26] but this had been abandoned owing to difficulties in smelting it.[27] Lead mining was the most important, and while it enjoyed a boom on the strength of the price-rise from the 1780s onwards, the indus-try was severely hit by imports of cheap Spanish lead after the end of the Napoleonic Wars.[28] However, its partial recovery in the 1830s led to the opening of several new mines, including two in the neighbourhood of Carsphairn where the impact was such that, according to the local minister, 'more money now circulates [there] in a week than a few years ago it did in the course of a year'.[29] Lead, and to a lesser extent copper, was also mined in the hills around Gatehouse, but the ores were soon exhausted, and the abandoned and waterlogged mines which are visible today bear silent testimony to the financial losses incurred by a number of local people who were tempted to invest in these enterprises.

CONTINUING IMPROVEMENTS

The threat of blockade during the Napoleonic War triggered off a boom in cereal prices. These reached their highest level in the years 1812–13, and this was reflected in a rise in livestock prices. Although it spelt prosperity for farmers it drove up prices to the consumer, and the cost of bread in particular escalated to a point where poorer people could no longer afford it. This was a consequence of the Corn Laws. They had been introduced in the 1790s for the purpose of protecting cereal growers from foreign competition by imposing a tariff on imported grain if the price fell below a certain level. Alternatively, if prices remained above that level the tariff was lifted so as to prevent them from escalating to the detriment of the con- sumer. However, as the war cut off grain imports this check ceased to operate, and the resulting hardship led to the formation of the Anti-Corn Law League which was dedicated to their repeal.

From the consumers' point of view the situation was relieved to some extent by the post-war fall in prices. For farmers it was a different story, as their profits shrank, and many who had leased their farms at high rents and had borrowed money to stock them in the expectation of a continuing rise in prices were forced into bankruptcy. Although Galloway farmers, being primarily livestock rearers, were cushioned from the worst effects of the downturn, it was nonetheless evident there as well, because the minister of Borgue tells us that 'for some time after the close of the war agriculture was in a state of stagnation'.[30] While this may have slowed down the process of land improvement, it was clearly only temporary, as the same commentator goes on to say that 'during the last fifteen years [from the mid-1820s onwards] improvements have again advanced rapidly'.[31]

For example, the sixth earl of Selkirk is reported to have 'completely changed the appearance of many of his farms', this being attributed to 'the intelligence and enterprise of his tenantry, but still more to the liberal encouragement given by his Lordship for liming and draining wherever required'.[32] His neighbour, Sir John Gordon of Earlston, was apparently engaged in much the same activities,[33] while Adam Maitland of Dundrennan was praised by the minister of Rerrick for 'turning his zealous attention to every subject connected with rural economy'.[34] He goes on to assert that 'the result of this may now be seen in the admirable roads and bridges, in the extensive plantations, and in the improved agriculture of the district over which his influence and his estates extended'.[35] Similar plaudits were given to Marmaduke Constable-Maxwell of Terregles, where we are told that 'in consequence of the great and judicious improvements which are going on, and the regular employment afforded to the labouring class the residence of this family in the parish is of the utmost benefit'.[36]

The laurels were clearly shared by his tenantry, because the writer adds that, 'the estate can boast of some of the most scientific and enterprising farmers to be found in the south of Scotland'.[37]

Improvements extended to the reclamation of merseland, a case in point being the scheme carried out on the Cavens estate near Kirkbean. Here, the local minister reports that 'a considerable tract of land, called *merse*, has been protected from the inroads of the sea by a very strong and costly embankment, raised by the late Mr. R.A. Oswald for that purpose, whose skill as an agriculturalist is not to be surpassed'.[38] The earl of Galloway was responsible for carrying out a similar scheme, which involved building an embankment along the Cree for the purpose of bringing the best part of 100 acres of flood plain into cultivation.[39] So, too, did the fifth earl of Selkirk[40] who built an embankment along the Dee from Kirkcudbright towards Tongland, and this was equipped with valves which could be shut off at high tide and opened at its ebb to allow the surface water to drain off.[41] Drainage was one of the main features of contemporary improvements – a fact which Lenman asserts is inclined to be overlooked by historians in spite of its being primarily accountable for the buoyant state of farming around 1840.[42]

Being the work of the local ministers, these adulatory reports could arguably smack of obsequiousness towards the local landowners, coupled perhaps with a timely recollection of their right of patronage, and their position as the main financial supporters of the parish church. Nevertheless, others were quite prepared to criticise where the situation warranted, one claiming that improvements such as dyke-building and drainage in his parish had lagged behind those being carried out on lower-lying lands. Some owners seem to have been badly advised, and the minister of Urr noted that 'shell marl was used too copiously which brought the land into a state of consequent sterility',[43] while in other cases landowners were accused of inhibiting progress because they would not grant their tenants long enough leases to encourage them to improve their holdings.[44]

Farmers and landowners continued their efforts to improve the quality of livestock, and Robert McMillan, the tenant of Palgowan on the Galloway estates, is credited with developing a type of sheep which had 'a greater aptitude to fatten, and attain maturity at an earlier period than the old race',[45] though we are not told how he achieved it. Meanwhile, it was discovered that bone manure, which was imported from Liverpool and Ireland, increased the root size of turnips, thus providing additional winter keep for livestock. This virtually revolutionised sheep farming, because the additional scope it offered for fattening off lambs increased the demand for store lambs. Consequently it encouraged hill sheep farmers to expand their flocks of breeding ewes to meet it, and the fact that they were now able to winter their hoggs (young ewes which have not yet produced a lamb) on low ground gave them additional scope for doing so.

On the other hand, it seems by all accounts that many farmers devoted an undue amount of time and attention to cattle-dealing, as this was perceived to be a quicker way of realising profits compared with the slow process of rearing them to maturity. For example, Smith observed that it 'possesses all the fascination of the gaming table', commenting on how the majority of farmers engaged in this were 'constant attendants on fairs and markets' to the detriment of their business. On the same theme, he went on to describe how 'they buy and sell continually without any other object than the prospect of a good bargain [so that] some of them seldom keep a bullock more than a year, or when markets are brisk not more than a few weeks or months in their possession'.[47]

The milk-producing Ayrshire, previously scorned as the poor man's cow, was now becoming more popular, particularly in Wigtownshire, where the minister of Whithorn remarked that 'of late years dairies have been introduced, and the Ayrshire breed is threatening to supplant the Galloway'. This was mainly because of the fall in the price of Galloways which occurred during the 1830s, but such logic was lost on the traditionalists who derided it as a 'sordid commercialisation of agriculture' – a view that prompted the eminently sensible response that 'those who can afford to indulge in luxuries retain the Galloway while those to whom quantity is of importance import the Ayrshire breed of cows'. Attempts seem to have been made to produce a dual-purpose cross to combine the milk-producing capacity of the Ayrshire with the meat quality of the Galloway. However, the minister of Glasserton, echoing the current prejudice against them, opined it would lead to the introduction of a 'spurious, thin-haired, degenerate race of cattle'.[48] In fact the results of these experiments were almost uniformly disappointing, so the two breeds continued to be run separately from one another.

Farmers were now less dependent on drovers to take their livestock to market than formerly. This was because of the advent of steam navigation in about 1830, and the introduction of regular and reliable steamship services between Galloway and the growing conurbations on the Clyde and the Mersey, meant that cattle rearers abandoned their traditional markets and switched to these centres instead. However, this was not destined to last. The extension of the railway system into Galloway during the 1860s provided a cheaper and more rapid means of transporting livestock overland, so the trade was diverted away from the shipping companies and back to its traditional markets. As far as the droving trade was concerned, the introduction of steamships left it tottering, while the railways dealt it a knock-out blow.

PROSPERITY AND PROGRESS

The farming industry soon recovered from the post-war setback, and its renewed prosperity resulted in a continuing population growth and a rise in living standards. This was reflected in the improved diet of the people, and the minister of Kirkinner tells us that their 'ordinary food' consisted of 'porridge and milk to breakfast, broth with bacon and potatoes or oat-cake to dinner, and porridge or beat potatoes to supper'.[49] Hand-in-hand with this went an improvement in manners, and the minister of Girthon refers to the people as being 'more intelligent, refined and cleanly in their habits'. Similarly, the farmer 'instead of sitting in the same apartment with his servants and eating at the same table, has now a snug parlour or dining room appropriated to himself and his family; takes his meals off a covered table; and the horn and pewter spoon has, in most cases, given way to silver'.[50]

The population of Galloway as a whole reached its peak in the 1850s, and the census of 1851 shows a total of 85,510, which was the highest ever recorded. Nevertheless, it was unevenly distributed and becoming increasingly so as people drifted from the remoter areas to the towns, many being displaced as a result of the landowners' practice of amagalmating small holdings into larger units. This trend is known to have been occurring over the past two decades, because the records show the population of certain landward parishes as having peaked out in the 1830s, while employment statistics for subsequent decades indicate that it continued to gain momentum. Yet, even by the end of the 1800s the Galloway uplands were still reasonably well populated, and it was the radical social changes of the twentieth century which were responsible for their final abandonment.

The population growth was heavily slanted towards Wigtownshire, where it was fuelled by a continuing influx of Irish immigrants. This was the source of much adverse comment by the ministers of those western parishes which bore the main brunt of this unwelcome intrusion. The minister of Stranraer remarks on the 'wretchedness among the population . . . who are mostly of the lower orders of the Irish',[51] though perhaps delicacy prevented him from adding that it was probably for this reason that it was one of the few country towns in Scotland which had a prostitution problem. They were also slated by his colleague at Inch who observed that 'they are by no means cleanly in their habits and style of living [while] their habitations are too frequently the scenes of filth'.[52] The extent to which they were swamping the region is evident from the minister of Whithorn's observation that 'the number of Irish families that every year take up their abode in this place is almost incredible'.[53] On the other hand, many seem to have settled only temporarily before moving on to other regions[54] where there was a greater demand for the heavy labour for which they were traditionally renowned.

All sources speak to the extent of Irish penetration in Wigtownshire. The *New Statistical Account* for Wigtownshire states that 'taking an average of the whole county, we have little doubt that a fifth of the aggregate population will consist either of native Irish, or of persons born of Irish parents'.[55] The *Report of the Royal Commission on Scottish Poor Laws* asserts that almost 15 per cent of the population was Irish – four times higher than in Kirkcudbright-shire,[56] but even this pales into insignificance when second or third genera-tion Irish settlers are taken into account. The earl of Stair's factor claimed that by 1844 it amounted to some 80 per cent of the entire population, while going on to say that 'by working at less wages than the natives' they had 'driven them away to other places and have supplied the want of labour so caused'.[57] This is echoed by the minister of Whithorn, who claimed that the influx of Irish exceeded the demand for labour, thus driving down wages to a level where local workers were forced to leave the district.[58] Some took the proverbial high road to England where, according to the minister of Kirkinner, 'they are engaged in the tea trade and other branches of business', while 'many young women go out as servants to Edinburgh, but particularly to Glasgow and Paisley'.[59]

Early population statistics do not reveal the proportion of illegitimate births, since these were not officially recorded until 1855. As they show Galloway as having a higher rate than almost anywhere else in Scotland,[60] the chances are that this had long been the case. The so-called Victorian morality was essentially the preserve of the middle classes, and little stigma attached to a lower-class girl who had lost her virginity before marriage, or to a woman who produced an illegitimate child. Nor does it appear to have prejudiced her chances of finding a husband, since he would have regard-ed the child as a prospective wage-earner for the marital household. Significantly, one contributor to the *Old Statistical Account* claimed there was virtually no evidence of either abortion or infanticide, as 'there was no pressure on a woman to commit such a crime', while another asserted that 'among her own class there was no feeling of indignation aroused in conse-quence of what they would call her "misfortune"'.[62]

Apart from the more obvious inclinations, it was standard practice for couples to test their fertility before marriage for the eminently practical reason that people looked to their children for support in their old age. In fact, the conceiving of a child before marriage was so commonplace that it prompted one minister to complain, 'I really do not remember when I last married a young woman who was not in the family way', while another grumbled that 'I seldom, if indeed ever, perform the service where it should not have been performed long before'. That little changes is evident from the assertion in the *Third Statistical Account* that 'a serious blot on Wigtownshire's reputation is the high rate of illegitimacy [which] has been the source of considerable concern for many years and the subject of grave consideration as well as widespread publicity'.[63]

NEW LANDOWNERS

Early nineteenth century Britain was a predominantly rural society in which the landowners reigned supreme, and their status within that fraternity depended on the length of their pedigree, the amount of land they owned, and for how long it had been in their family. There was nothing new in this, as the upper classes had always been rank-conscious, and Agnew gives an early example when the impoverished Sir James Dunbar of Mochrum attempted to assert precedence over his wealthy neighbour, Sir William Maxwell of Monreith, on the grounds that whereas his family had been established in Wigtownshire since the 1340s, the Maxwells were comparative newcomers, having acquired Monreith in the 1480s. Apparently, the dispute was amicably settled when Maxwell offered his fellow baronet a hogshead of claret on condition of yielding pride of place, which the bibulous Dunbar gratefully accepted.[64]

Until now the landed classes had been the doyens of society and the repository of political power, though this was diluted by the Reform Act of 1832 and subsequent Acts which extended the suffrage. Nevertheless, the lot of the landowner was regarded as an enviable one, so it remained the goal of those who made money in other fields to acquire an estate, as it had been in the past. Moreover, land was still regarded as a sound investment, for rents were rising in line with agricultural prosperity and would continue to do so until the depression of the 1880s, while labour was still cheap by comparison. However, rent levels varied considerably depending on the quality of the land and local conditions. According to the *New Statistical Account*, land round Newton Stewart was fetching up to as much as £3 an acre,[65] as was land in the southern Machars, which has always been renowned for its quality and capacity for cereal growing. This, however, was exceptional, because rents of around £1 an acre were the norm, with proportionately less for marginal or hill ground.

Although wages had risen over the past fifty years they were still low in comparison with rents, and they varied considerably depending on the locality and the type of work involved. The annual wage of a married farm servant increased from about £14 to over £20, though in the parish of Kirkinner it could be as high as £30, mainly because of the improvements being carried out there and the consequent demand for labour. Single farm workers' wages had risen proportionately, while women continued to be paid roughly half the going rate for men. Casual labourers hired by the day fared less well, since their rates only went up by a few pence, but craftsmen such as masons, joiners and dykebuilders commanded premium rates to reflect their more advanced skills.

This meant that, even after meeting the cost of essential repairs, a small-time laird with only a modest rental income could afford to maintain a reasonable style with ample staff, both indoors and out. The attractions of landownership were therefore all the greater, and those establishing themselves in the region during the early nineteenth century included local Gallovidians who had made good elsewhere and returned to settle in their native land. One was David Lenox, who bought the property of Port Mary near Dundrennan, and is described as 'the only son and heir of a native of Kirkcudbright who migrated to America [and] died one of the richest men, and most eminent merchants, in the United States'.[66] Another was Thomas Hughan, the son of a Creetown merchant who made a fortune 'in business in London'. He bought up a number of farms in the neighbourhood of his home town,[67] winding up with the purchase of the former Gordon property of Airds near Parton in the 1830s.[68]

One non-native who bought up a number of properties in Galloway[69] was Robert Carrick, who had started out as a clerk in the Ship Bank in Glasgow in which he eventually became a partner. These included the estate of Corsewall in the Rhinns which he left to his nephew John Carrick-Moore,[70] from whom it passed to the Carrick-Buchanans. The latter was a close relative of Sir John Moore, who was killed at Corunna, and it was in his memory that the woods at Corsewall were laid out on the lines of the formation of the British army at the battle.[71] At much the same time James Beaumont Neilson, an engine wright's son from Govan, who became the manager of the Glasgow Gas Company, bought up a number of properties near Ringford.[70] Famous for having invented the 'hot blast' process which revolutionised the Scottish iron industry – just in time to meet the demands of the developing rail network – the monument to his memory on a local hill is a fitting tribute to his achievement. Meanwhile another family of industrialists, namely the Whighams, who were coal-owners from Kirkconnel in Dumfriesshire, were buying up land in the parish of Irongray.[73]

The new landowners included men like James Blair, who made money by trading and commerce abroad. Although described as a West Indian planter, he is likely to have been involved in the highly profitable slave trade as well, since he amassed enough money to buy the Penninghame estate, which was one of the largest in Galloway, in 1825.[74] On his death in 1841 this passed to his brother-in-law General Edward Stopford, and was ultimately inherited by the latter's daughter, Elizabeth, the wife of Edward Heron-Maxwell of the Kirroughtree family, who subsequently sold it.

Patrick Dudgeon was a successful merchant in China, and presumably it was from opium-derived profits that he bought the Cargen estate on the lower Nith in 1853.[75] This remained in his family for nearly a century until it was sold following the death of his widowed daughter-in-law shortly after the Second World War. Later, William Gordon, a merchant in Brazil (a land of great opportunity at the time) and latterly Liverpool, acquired the Threave estate in the 1870s.[76] This was retained by his family until the mid-twentieth century when a part was acquired by the National Trust for Scotland, who converted its gardens into the showpiece they remain today. Meanwhile, other people of lesser means, mainly from business and the professions, were buying up smaller properties in the more accessible parts of Kirkcudbrightshire – although not, it would seem, in Wigtownshire.[77]

THE CHURCH AND THE DISRUPTION

The Church continued to be responsible for education and the relief of the poor, and this was exercised at parish level by the kirk sessions. However, a number of schools were founded and endowed by private individuals, a prime example being the Borgue Academy. The benefactor was Thomas Rainy, a native of the parish who amassed a fortune in Dominica and set up a fund of £3,000 for the purpose, and it is as much a tribute to him as to those responsible for running it that this was described by the local minister as 'one of the most flourishing and best conducted academies in the south of Scotland'.[78] A bequest by Samuel Douglas paved the way for the founding of the Douglas Ewart Academy in Newton Stewart,[79] while two separately endowed schools and another unendowed one at Kirkcudbright were amalgamated to form the academy there.[80] On the evidence of the *Statistical Accounts*, it seems the standard of education available at these establishments was higher than the parish schools, simply because they could afford to offer a wider range of subjects, and probably a higher standard of tuition.

Relief for the poor was available from a special poor's fund which was administered by kirk sessions, and supplemented to some extent by special collections made at the church door, though more so from the testamentary bequests customarily made by local people of substance. Although alms were distributed sparingly, they did provide help for those beyond working age, or who were disabled through chronic illness or a debilitating accident, and had no family to support them. Each individual application was carefully investigated – in a small community the circumstances of the case would be known – and if the session was satisfied it was warranted the applicant's name would go on the poor's roll. Although the amount of the payments varied between parishes according to the funds available, they were not ungenerous, and in some cases a soup kitchen was provided as well. Often a landowner would take on responsibility for a particular indigent family whom he knew or who lived on his estate, but it was an arbitrary – and even capricious – generosity, and therefore not to be relied on.

Meanwhile, a major split was developing within the Church between the establishment-minded moderates and the evangelicals, who were becoming increasingly concerned at the moderates' growing identification with the middle and upper classes, to the exclusion of the rapidly expanding under-classes in the major industrial centres. However, the immediate cause of the Disruption was the question of patronage, though it was the right of congregations to object to a patron's nominee for a living rather than the principle itself which was the point at issue. The law was unclear, because, although the 1690 Act recognised their right to object, this was not specifi-cally withdrawn by the 1712 Act, which restored the right of nomination to patrons. So, the evangelicals held it was still valid even though it had never been invoked within living memory.

They therefore urged that it be resurrected, but because there were certain practical difficulties a compromise was suggested whereby the Church would assume the parishioners' approval of a nominee unless a majority objected in writing. When this was first put to the general assembly on a motion by the evangelical leader, Dr Thomas Chalmers, it was thrown out, but on a second attempt in 1834, when the evangelicals had a majority in the general assembly, it was approved and the resulting deliverance was known as the Veto Act. The moderates now used a test case to challenge its validity in the Court of Session, but by this time the issue had widened to include the thorny question of the Church's relations with the State and the extent of the latter's jurisdiction over it. After a lengthy hearing the court reached a decision which favoured the moderates, so the evangelicals instigated an appeal to the House of Lords which upheld the decision, only this time the ex-Lord Chancellor Brougham, a Scotsman with strong views on the subject, declared that objections by parishioners were irrelevant and the patrons' rights absolute.

Once it became evident that the government was not going to change the law to accommodate the Veto Act, the general assembly, under the control of the evangelicals, proceeded to defy the courts, and this led to a number of unseemly incidents involving the issuing of interdicts and counter interdicts by Church and courts alike. Matters came to a head at the general assembly of 1843, when the retiring moderator, Dr Welsh, declared it was no longer a free assembly, and forthwith left the chamber. From there he processed down the hill amidst cheering crowds to Canonmills, where he was joined by other seceders who together represented over a third of the entire ministry. They then constituted themselves a general assembly of the Free Church of Scotland and appointed Dr Chalmers its first moderator. The church was now irrevocably split, and so fierce were the passions aroused that in many cases it led to divisions within individual families, while the consequent weakening of the Church's influence set in train a process that would become increasingly apparent throughout the following century.

NOTES

1. Anderson, 'Road system, Part II', 213.
2. In 1795 a payment was made to his father, the earl of Selkirk, for a road made from Clatteringshaws towards Newton Stewart 'by the late Lord Daer' (see *ibid.*, 217).
3. The foregoing information is based on Anderson's two articles on the subject. Unfortunately, no comparable study has been made of the history of the road system in Wigtownshire.
4. Report from the Select Committee on the Glasgow–Port-patrick roads etc., *British Parliamentary papers*, 1824 VII 151, p 5.
5. The point is made in Campbell, *Owners and Occupiers*, 8.
6. *NSA* (Wig), 223.
7. On completion of the military road an attempt was made to build a harbour there as part of the scheme to improve communications with Ireland. However, this was abandoned and not revived until 1801, when fears of an invasion prompted a resumption of the work.
8. *OSA* I, p 41.
9. Donnachie, *Industrial Archaeology*, 175.
10. *Ibid.*, 165.
11. Local tradition has it that their foreman, a huge red-bearded fellow, was responsible for the red-headed element in Gatehouse today.
12. Donnachie, *Industrial Archaeology*, 98.
13. *Ibid.*
14. *Ibid.*
15. He succeeded as ninth earl of Galloway on his father's death in 1834.
16. Donnachie, *Industrial Archaeology*, 50–2.
17. *NSA* (Kirkcud), 304.
18. Donnachie, *Industrial Archaeology*, 70.
19. *Ibid.*
20. *NSA* (Wigtown), 198.
21. Donnachie, *Industrial Archaeology*, 75.
22. *Ibid.*, 30.
23. *Ibid.*, 111.
24. *NSA* (Kirkcud), 210.
25. Donnachie, *Industrial Archaeology*, 113.
26. *OSA* 1, p 48.
27. Smith, *Agricultural Survey*, 24.
28. Donnachie, *Industrial Archaeology*, 127.
29. *NSA* (Kirkcud), 281.
30. *Ibid.*, 58.
31. *Ibid.*
32. *Ibid.*
33. *Ibid.*
34. *Ibid*, 358–9.
35. *Ibid.*
36. *Ibid.*, 231.
37. *Ibid.*
38. *Ibid.*, 236.

39. *NSA* (Wigtown), 184–5.
40. Or 'Selkirk of Red River', as he is better known, on account of his ambitious and public-spirited scheme to establish settlement areas in Canada for the benefit of emigrant Highlanders. The Red River settlement, which he acquired from the Hudson's Bay Company, comprised a vast territory extending from Lake Superior westwards beyond present-day Winnipeg. However, it was seen as a threat to the fur trading activities of the rival North-West Company who set out to destroy it by inciting the local Indians to perpetrate a series of massacres on the settlers and this, combined with the unexpectedly harsh winters and a succession of bad harvests, accounted for its ultimate extinction. This not only left the earl financially embarrassed, but the strain was responsible for his premature death in 1820 (Gray, *Lord Selkirk of Red River*).
41. Smith, *Agricultural Survey*, 229.
42. Lenman, *Economic History*, 194.
43. *NSA* (Kirkcud), 352.
44. *Ibid.*, 58, 213.
45. *Ibid.*, 136.
46. Symon, *Scottish Farming*, 177.
47. Smith, *Agricultural Survey*, 74.
48. *NSA* (Wig), 46.
49. *Ibid.*, 17.
50. *NSA* (Kirkcud), 310.
51. *NSA* (Wig), 97.
52. *Ibid.*, 90.
53. *Ibid.*, 60.
54. Campbell, *Owners and Occupiers*, 35.
55. *NSA* (Wig) iv, 228.
56. Campbell, 'Agricultural Labour in the South-West', 64.
57. Campbell, *Owners and Occupiers*, 40.
58. *NSA* (Wig), 60.
59. *Ibid.*, 17.
60. Flinn, *Population History*, 350–1 (table 5.4.1).
61. *Ibid.*, 362.
62. *TSA* xiv, 387.
63. *Ibid.*
64. Agnew ii, 125.
65. *NSA* (Wig), 182.
66. McKerlie v, 135.
67. *Ibid.* iv, 78, 278, 292.
68. This estate eventually passed to his grandson Admiral Henniker-Hughan, who was briefly the local member of parliament, and now belongs to his descendant.
69. McKerlie v, 17, 209, 244, 315.
70. *Ibid.* i, 124.
71. *TSA* xiv, 479.
72. McKerlie v, 200–3, 210, 282, 384.
73. *Ibid.* iv, 25, 28, 30, 31, 308, 316, 327.
74. *Ibid.* i, 309, 318.
75. *Ibid.* v, 236.
76. *Ibid.* iv, 118.
77. This is evident from the contemporary valuation roll.

78. So states the minister of Borgue (*NSA* (Kirkcud), 56), but Smith asserts (*Agricultural Survey*, 340) that only £2,400 was earmarked for the academy, while the balance was set aside for the benefit of the poor of the parish.
79. *NSA* (Wig), 190–1.
80. *NSA* (Kirkcud), 34.

31

THE LAND IN DECLINE

Agricultural depression

The recovery in farming which followed the post-war setback lasted for upwards of fifty years, until the onset of the depression in the 1880s. The seeds of this were already being sown by mid-century, as large tracts of virgin land in the American Middle West were being opened up to cattle ranching and cereal production, so it was inevitable that sooner or later the growing surplus would hit world markets and depress prices. However, the effects were delayed by the outbreak of the American Civil War of the 1860s and the consequent disruption of trade with Europe. In the meantime, grain prices continued to escalate, reaching an all-time high in 1867, propelled admittedly by a poor harvest and a resulting shortage. This gave farmers a false sense of prosperity and, confident that prices would continue to rise, they were tempted to offer still higher rents to secure a renewal of their leases or take on new ones. Even the end of the Civil War and the consequent resumption of American trade with Europe failed to shatter their illusions, because the wars of 1866 and 1870–71, which led to the unification of Germany, disrupted the European market, so it was not until the late 1870s that prices began to fall.

By this time the situation was aggravated by the rise in exports from other developing countries, such as Canada, the Argentine and Australasia, and this sparked off what became known as the 'Prairie Corn Crisis'. The effects were apparent in the dramatic slide in the price of wheat from its all-time high of 64s 5d (322p) a quarter in 1867 to 45s (225p) in 1882, and finally to 24s (120p) in 1894,[1] and this was the story of grain prices generally. As the corn laws which had protected cereal growers in the past had been repealed in 1846, cereal growers were fully exposed to the effects of the collapsing market. Livestock prices followed suit, because the introduction of refrigerated transport led to an escalation of meat imports, and consequently they dropped by roughly a half, while the price of wool fell by a third. Worse still, the late nineteenth century witnessed the outbreak of a number of diseases, such as pleuro-pneumonia, foot and mouth disease and rinderpest, which affected cattle, while sheep fell victim to scab and liver rot. Spells of bad weather were responsible for a succession of poor harvests, and the situation was exacerbated by a number of particularly cold winters, causing widespread sheep losses.

The fall in grain prices resulted in large tracts of arable land being taken out of production and put down to grass, and probably accounted for the final reversion of the poorer parts of the Machars and the Glenkens, which were previously under cultivation, to permanent pasture. Elsewhere in Galloway it accelerated the changeover to dairying, as this was protected from foreign competition by the perishable nature of its products of milk and butter. At the same time, the extension of the rail network into the region allowed these to reach a wide market in the industrialised central belt of Scotland while still fresh. Cheese was another important by-product, and the growing popularity of dairying led to a revival of the traditional craft of cheesemaking which became evident during the latter half of the century.[2]

The expansion of dairying in Galloway was due less to an abandonment by the local farmers of their traditional prejudice against the Ayrshire cow than to an influx of dairymen from other parts of south-west Scotland. This type of husbandry differs in many ways from the traditional livestock-rearing and crop-growing in that it is unremittingly labour-intensive, and therefore most dairy farms were small, family-run units which seldom exceeded 150 acres (60 ha). As this was generally much more profitable than other types of farming it meant that these incomers could outbid local farmers for the lease of a holding. This is evident from a report published in 1895 which states, 'at least 30 per cent of the farmers in Wigtownshire are Ayrshire men, or their descendants, and any farms becoming vacant in the counties of Wigtown, Kirkcudbright and Dumfries are generally taken by dairymen, most of whom come from Ayrshire, with a few from the counties of Lanark and Renfrew'.[3]

Some incomers leased farms on their own account, but the majority entered into a 'bowing' arrangement with larger dairy farmers or land-owners. Similar in many ways to the old steelbow form of tenure, from which it took its name, this type of contract was essentially a sub-lease where the 'bowers' took on the management of the dairy herd themselves. The farmer or landowner supplied the cows, the fixed equipment and the winter feed, and in return the bower paid him a rent based on the number of cows in the herd. During the 1870s the rate was generally somewhere between £8 and £15 a cow, but by the eve of the First World War it had risen to between £12 and £18.[4] By the late nineteenth century the practice of bowing had caught on to the extent that it was 'the almost universal custom' in Galloway,[5] and it remained common practice until the First World War and even survived in a modified form on some farms until after the Second World War.

Despite the doubling of wages during the latter half of the century, farmwork was becoming progressively less popular – 'a rough, dirty, badly-paid job with long hours and few holidays', as one witness to the Royal Commission on Labour of 1893 described it. A local ploughman put the point still more forcibly. 'To my opinion', he submitted, 'the life of the agricultural labourer is altogether colourless and sordid; his life throughout is sleep, eat and work; no half holiday on Saturday . . . and no holidays as a right, only as a favour'. The lack of prospects for self-advancement was also a drawback, since the best a farm labourer could aspire to was to become a grieve, or foreman. A few might even acquire the lease of a small farm, but this could only be achieved by making careful savings, perhaps marrying a thrifty wife, delaying starting a family, and other sacrifices, and these were enough to deter all but the most ambitious from striving for such a goal. This lack of opportunity for self-advancement accounted, at least in part, for the continuing drift of people to the main urban centres, where there were better prospects, and this in turn led to a continuing decline in the population of Galloway.

THE LANDOWNERS' HEYDAY

The 1870s are generally regarded as the heyday of the landowner, for rents were higher than ever while wages were still low in comparison. The landlord-tenant system was more or less universal, while the owner occupier who farmed his own land was almost unknown in the south-west, and this remained the case until the First World War. Nevertheless his day was to come, and the rise of the owner occupier, which stemmed from the break-up of many landed estates in the post-war period, and was accelerated in the aftermath of the Second World War, changed the whole social and economic pattern of landownership. In fact, its extent would have been inconceivable to the landowners of the 1870s, who saw themselves and their families as securely in possession of their estates for the foreseeable future.

Many landed estates were substantial, and according to the *List of Owners of Land in Scotland*, known as the Doomsday Book, which was published in 1872/3, three-quarters of all the land in Galloway was concentrated in the hands of forty-three owners who possessed estates ranging from 3,500 acres (1,416 ha) upwards.[6] At the top end of the scale came the earls of Galloway and Stair with approximately 80,000 acres (32,000 ha) apiece. But whereas the Stairs were adding to their lands during the century, the Galloway estates had been in decline since 1807, when the eighth earl disposed of all the family estates in the Ken valley to Forbes of Earlston. In the 1840s his son, the ninth earl, sold a large amount of land in the Machars, some going to Maxwell of Monreith, though the major portion was acquired by the earl of Stair.

Some landowners were continuing to carry out improvements, though this was mainly confined to adapting farm buildings to accommodate dairies, providing workmens' cottages, and general upgrading work, as there is less evidence of land reclamation compared with the past. Instead, the emphasis shifted to enjoying the fruits of their predecessors' efforts by following the prevailing fashion of maintaining a high style of living and entertaining on a lavish scale. Large house parties were now the vogue, and to accommodate them, as well as the domestic staff needed to cater for them, houses were enlarged and adorned with an exuberance which frequently spoilt their original appearance.

Other landowners built new houses, but being designed mainly as symbols of wealth and ostentation, and geared to a way of life which disappeared with the First World War, they eventually became redundant and many were demolished. These fashions reflected the increasing anglicisation of the gentry. This had already become apparent among the aristocracy by the beginning of the century, and since then it had been diffusing throughout the landowning fraternity, to the extent that they were now aping English manners and speech, and even such idiosyncrasies as keeping a black servant.[7]

With the shift in social emphasis from the constructive work of husbandry and estate management to the extravagances of leisure, highly organised, large-scale shoots were now the vogue. There was nothing new in this, as field sports had always been a favourite pastime of the baronial landowners, and Smith, writing at the beginning of the century, notes that 'pheasants were some years ago introduced by Lord Galloway into Wigtownshire; and have since, by Lord Selkirk and Mr. Murray, been brought into the Stewartry'. Now, however, there was an opulence about them which was lacking in the past, so great importance was attached to keepering of estates, while the 'bags' were recorded in the game books that were religiously maintained by every estate. The preservation of game involved the systematic elimination of all predators, including birds of prey, and stories are told of keepers, assisted by shepherds who were concerned about their depredations on the lamb population, dangling lighted tar barrels over cliffs in order to burn eagles out of their eyries – a fact which accounted for their virtual extinction in Galloway.

Throughout most of the nineteenth century, the game laws were heavily tilted in favour of the landowners, since they alone had the exclusive right to shoot over their estates. A measure of their influence in parliament was the passing of the Night Poaching Act of 1829 and the Game Act of 1832, both of which imposed harsh penalties on poachers, including transportation to the penal settlement in Australia. However, the Reform Act of 1832, and subsequent Acts extending the suffrage, spelt the political decline of the landed interest, and this was reflected in a gradual change in the game laws to achieve a more realistic balance between the landlord and tenant. One example was the Ground Game Act of 1880, which allowed tenant farmers to kill rabbits and hares on their holdings – a long overdue piece of legislation, because the exploding rabbit population was causing severe damage. Judging from a story told in the 1820s they seem to have been comparatively rare at the time, because this concerned a house party at Munches where the ladies were summoned outside to inspect a strange animal that had just been shot – which proved to be a rabbit![8]

As the century progressed, landowners increasingly disengaged themselves from their estates, delegating their management to agents or factors, and even more so to lawyers. In fact there was a perceived social *cachet* in having one's family estate administered by a leading firm of Edinburgh Writers to the Signet, but quite apart from being an inadequate substitute for personal supervision the practice arguably contributed to the eventual break-up of a number of estates during the following century. Nevertheless, most landowners, cocooned from financial realities and blissfully unaware that in many cases their estates were being indifferently managed, continued to maintain a large staff of domestic servants, keepers, gardeners and estate workers, and consequently they were the largest employers of local labour.

Now that the landowning class generally had more time on their hands, their lives became increasingly dominated by trivia, and particularly the *minutiae* of class distinctions. Although human nature will always dictate a hierarchical society, the Victorian leisured classes carried such shibboleths to extreme lengths, and nowhere was this more apparent than in the attitude of the old-established landowners towards those newcomers to their ranks, who in their eyes were tarred with 'being in trade'. In fact, it is somewhat ironic that those who inherited their estates as a birthright should look down on others who acquired theirs through a combination of energy, enterprise and initiative; but they did. So, not only was there no social contact between them but it would take at least a generation before the barrier was broken.

This narrow outlook was reflected in the limited range of professions which were considered suitable for the sons of gentry.[9] In the past, the law had provided opportunities for self-advancement, but as this was now less fashionable the choice tended to be confined to the army, and to a lesser extent the navy, as well as the imperial and diplomatic services. Commissions in the army could be purchased, and this was almost invariably a prerequisite to a military career. Part-time soldiering in the local militia was also popular, the local units being the Galloway Rifles Militia, the Kirkcudbright Yeomanry Cavalry, and the Galloway Rangers. The first of these was raised in 1803 as part of a local defence force to resist a threatened French invasion, while the latter two were formed shortly afterwards. They were essentially volunteer companies, but if they fell below strength the shortfall was usually made good through conscription by ballot, and these units became a source of recruits for the regular army, eventually being taken over by serving regiments. Thus, the two Kirkcudbrightshire companies of the Galloway Rifles Militia were integrated with the King's Own Scottish Borderers, while those in Wigtownshire came under the wing of the Royal Scots Fusiliers.[10]

Some landowners involved themselves in local government, but this opportunity did not arise until 1889, when county councils were established for the purpose of 'diminishing the excessive and exaggerated power of central government', as the prime minister, lord Salisbury, put it. Hitherto, local government was administered by a fragmented system of councils, boards and committees, which delivered at best an indifferent service. Between them they were responsible for the provision of water and gas, as well as hospital and public health services such as baths, washhouses and laundries, which were designed to cope with the consequences of poverty and poor housing. Under the 1889 Act their responsibilities passed to the new, elective, multi-purpose authorities, which in Scotland were supervised by an office established in Edinburgh under the control of the newly-appointed Secretary of State for Scotland.

LANDLORD AND TENANT

Historically the landlord–tenant relationship was never easy, mainly because their interests were fundamentally opposed, in that an arrangement which suited the one was not necessarily in the best interests of the other. Although it seems to have worked reasonably well in a time of rising prices and general prosperity, the onset of the depression in the 1880s highlighted the drawbacks. Farmers found that the rents they had negotiated in times of plenty were becoming increasingly burdensome, so there was mounting pressure on landowners to grant abatements, but not all were in a position to do so because in many cases the estate rental represented their only source of income.

A study of the records of three of the larger estates in Galloway, namely those of the earl of Galloway, Murray-Stewart of Cally and Agnew of Lochnaw, reveals the extent of the problem. In each case they were heavily burdened with mortgages – a legacy of earlier improvements – and the cost of servicing those encumbering the Galloway estates in particular absorbed more than half the rental income.[11] This may have been exceptional,[12] but it is likely that many other estates – probably the majority – were burdened to a greater or lesser extent. The cost of repairs, improvements and public burdens was a further vexation, and since loan interest was a first charge on the rents these abatements had to come out of the remaining balance.

Moreover, belonging to a society which attached importance to maintaining a high style of living, landowners were reluctant to retrench in order to accommodate a hard-pressed tenantry.

Nevertheless, given the general belief that the recession was temporary and that prices would recover, many did what they could to help. While this did not extend to granting a permanent abatement of rent, allowances were granted to tenants for the improvements carried out to their holdings – thus anticipating the statutory right of tenants to compensation for the unexhausted value of such improvements.[13] In other cases, rental arrears were allowed to accumulate and these were simply written off at the end of the lease,[14] although landowners seem to have earned small thanks for it. This was because many tenants – illogically – considered themselves the victims of an unfair advantage when they signed their leases and agreed a rent which subsequently proved unaffordable.[15] Therefore, in their view, landlords were morally obliged to help them, and even when they did the tenants frequently complained of their stinginess, conveniently forgetting the advantages they had gained in the past from long leases at fixed rents in a time of rapidly rising prices.[16] However, it was from such popular misconceptions that the notion of the rapacious landlord was promoted and would become the stock-in-trade of radical thinking.

An integral part of the law relating to leases which tenant farmers found particularly irksome was the landlord's right of hypothec; a term which was described as one that 'no Englishman can pronounce and few Scotsmen defend'.[17] This gave him a right over his tenant's moveable property for unpaid rent, meaning that in the event of a sequestration he could establish himself as a preferred creditor. Moreover, the right extended to the recovery of agricultural produce, such as grain or livestock, which had already been sold to a third party, or its equivalent value. Although hypothec was rarely invoked, or if so it was generally someone other than the landowner who initiated the sequestration,[18] it deterred merchants from dealing with financially suspect farmers. This meant they were forced to deal in an artificially depressed market, and the lower prices obtained for their produce compounded their difficulties.

However, it would be unjust to see landowners exclusively as absentees pursuing an extravagant lifestyle financed by rents extracted from an oppressed tenantry. For many did live on their estates and almost invariably exercised a genuine concern for the well-being of their tenantry, and within their lights they had a highly developed sense of public and social duty. Illustrative of this were the number of public works executed at their expense, including in particular the building of a number of village halls to serve as centres for the local community. In fact, when landowners were supplanted by owner occupiers they were regarded with some nostalgia, and the minister of Whithorn, writing in 1952, observed that 'the place of lairds and landed proprietors has been taken by the farmers who have not always the same public spirit and have still to learn that material wealth carries responsibilities'.[19]

LANDOWNERSHIP IN DECLINE

Apart from their diminishing incomes, the decline of the landowners was reflected in the erosion of their political power. Formerly, local grandees, perceiving it as their birthright, devoted much time, energy and money to its exercise, motivated in many cases by a genuine sense of public duty. Even if not actively involved in politics themselves, they were prepared to use their influence – and money – to secure the return of a nominee who could be relied upon to pursue their interests. To them the concept of political power reflecting the popular will was no more than a philosophical theory, so a system involving a semi-benevolent paternalism, laced with a degree of self-interest, prevailed.

Political power in the region was traditionally the preserve of the earls of Galloway, though they never entirely monopolised it. In Wigtownshire it was shared with the earls of Stair, while other families, like the McDowells and the Agnews, were frequently involved in the election of members of parliament. In Kirkcudbrightshire, it was operated in conjunction with the dukes of Queensberry (later the dukes of Buccleuch), the earls of Selkirk and the viscounts Kenmure, while the Murrays, the Herons and the Constable-Maxwells played a strong supporting role. Much the same system obtained in the burghs, where the ruling councils became in effect self-perpetuating oligarchies dominated by the local landed interest. Stranraer was traditionally the domain of the earls of Stair, with several members of the family assuming the provostship, while Newton Stewart remained the fiefdom of the earls of Galloway, who produced a number of members of parliament for the Wigtown burghs. Nevertheless, those who wielded political power were forced to pay some attention to local issues for the sake of garnering votes, so to that extent a vestige of democracy prevailed.

The system was radically changed by the Reform Acts of the nineteenth century, the first being the Act of 1832 – a major concession by the Tories who represented the landed interest and only wrung from them in the face of incipient revolution. This opened the way for other interests to achieve political power, including those self-made men who had made their fortunes in commerce and industry, and whose interests and priorities were not necessarily the same as those of their landed counterparts. The succeeding Reform Acts of 1868 and 1884 extended the suffrage still further, leading to a corresponding dilution of the power of the landed interest. Although it continued to control the House of Lords this was eventually minimalised by the Parliament Act of 1911.

Notwithstanding their diminishing political influence, a number of landowners continued to be involved in politics, and generally the members of parliament for the local seats were drawn from their ranks. Although the seat for the Wigtown burghs disappeared with the Reform Act of 1884, the other two survived until 1918 when they were merged to form the single constituency of Galloway.[20] A noted politician of the day was Sir Herbert Maxwell of Monreith who, in the course of his long life – he died in 1937 at the age of ninety-two – combined an interest in politics with a considerable literary output which covered a wide range of subjects. Most landowners took a keen interest in topical issues, identifying themselves fervently with one or other of the main political parties. While the majority were naturally drawn to the Tories who continued to represent the landed interest, others took a broader view by supporting the Liberals in spite of that party's indifference to their own sectional interests.[21]

The introduction of death duties by Gladstone's Liberal Government in 1894 accelerated the decline of the landowner. The concept of a tax arising on death was not new, since probate and legacy duty had been introduced in the previous century, though it was not until the advent of succession duty in 1853 that this was extended to land. But, whereas these taxes had been levied on the inheritors of property, death duties were levied on the assets of the deceased, the rate being graduated according to his net worth. Although the top rate was initially only 8 per cent, it was greeted with alarm by many landowners who anticipated it would lead to the break-up of their estates – justifiably so as it turned out, because the tax was progressively raised until the top rate reached a swingeing 80 per cent. Typical of the reaction was the eleventh earl of Galloway's denunciation of it as 'the most wicked and discreditable invention ever created, and only instituted and kept up by the most degraded and unprincipled men who held the position of Chancellor of the Exchequer'.[22]

THE COMING OF THE RAILWAYS

The construction of a rail network and the consequent speeding up of communications between Galloway and the main population centres of Scotland and the south had a profound impact on the province. This was because it effectively transformed it from a westward-orientated region, whose links with the outside world were mainly seaborne, to a fully integrated part of mainland Britain. Nevertheless it proved a mixed blessing, for while it brought undeniable advantages to the local people the long term result, ironically, was to relegate Galloway to a comparative backwater, and this was particularly true of Wigtownshire whose consequent isolation is underscored by the local saying 'out of the world and into Wigtownshire'.

It was in the 1840s that the Glasgow & South-Western Railway Co. first mooted the idea of extending its railway system into the region in order to provide a link with Ireland. However, the diversion of the Irish mail to Holyhead in 1848, and the discontinuation of the mail service through Portpatrick the following year, persuaded the company not to go 'adventuring in Galloway', as they put it. This prompted a number of local businessmen to take the initiative by inviting members of the public to submit proposals for a rail network in Galloway, and they began to make overtures to the Caledonian Railway Co. instead. Fearing this would give its rival company an advantage, the Glasgow and South-Western Railway Co. changed its mind and decided to co-operate. Therefore, it contributed half the initial share capital to the Castle Douglas and Dumfries Railway Co., which was incorporated for the purpose of building a railway from Dumfries to Castle Douglas via Dalbeattie. The work was put in hand in 1855, and by 1859 the line was fully operational.

Meanwhile, plans were being drawn up to extend the line westwards. The leading proponent was the earl of Stair's son, lord Dalrymple, and on his initiative the grandiloquently-named British-Irish Grand Junction Railway Co. was incorporated to execute the work. Originally it was decided to take the line as far as Glenluce, from where separate branch lines would connect with Stranraer and Portpatrick, though the final plan provided for a single extension to Portpatrick via Stranraer, where a spur would link it with the harbour. This was an ambitious scheme, and the promoters found themselves having to contend with a number of unexpected difficulties before the work could be completed.

The stretch between Mossdale and Creetown needed extensive excavation through tough granite rock, as well as massive embankments, to achieve an acceptable level, and therefore it proved the most difficult section to build. In addition, two viaducts had to be constructed over the upper Fleet and its tributary the Little Water of Fleet, while the remoteness of the line from the nearest public road meant that materials had to be hauled for long distances across country. The directors were also obliged to provide the residents of Gatehouse with a station at Dromore and to subsidise the cost of building the six-mile connecting road up the Fleet valley. Inevitably the final contract price greatly exceeded the original estimate, though it was partially offset by the relative cheapness of the land. Overall, therefore, it proved less expensive than the alternative of taking the railway round the coast. Although seriously considered, that idea was abandoned at an early stage on the grounds of its perceived inability to compete with the local shipping trade.

In spite of the difficulties progress was rapid, and by 1861 the railway was completed as far as Stranraer. However, the extension to Portpatrick took another year to build, mainly because of the engineering problems involved in crossing the Rhinns and the numerous cuttings which were necessary to reduce the gradient. There were financial problems too, because although the government had undertaken to subsidise the costs, its delay in releasing the money led to an acute cash shortage. Then, no sooner was the line completed than it decided to reinstate the Irish mail service from Stranraer to Larne, so almost immediately it became redundant, and the harbour at Portpatrick was abandoned. Meanwhile, the promoters had already drawn up plans to build a feeder line from Castle Douglas to Kirkcudbright, and the necessary Act of Parliament was obtained in 1861. Unfortunately, financial constraints forced them to abandon the project, so it was taken over by the Glasgow & South-Western Railway Co. who completed it in 1864.

Of the other feeder lines mooted, the only one considered financially viable was an extension through the Machars to Whithorn. Therefore, a feasibility study was commissioned from a firm of engineers, but by the time it was completed in 1863 the project had been shelved. However, it was revived in 1871, when a public meeting of 'Gentlemen Favourable to the extension of Railway Communications by Wigtown to Whithorn', which was convened under the chairmanship of lord Garlies, agreed to commission an updated report. This recommended that the line should follow a direct course from Newton Stewart to Wigtown, then take a loop to the west to serve the communities of Kirkinner, Whauphill and Sorbie. From there it would swing back towards the coast at Garlieston, but to avoid impinging on the grounds of Galloway House it was to turn southwards just short of the town, and head for Whithorn.

This was approved and the promoters obtained the necessary Act of Parliament in 1872. As the land is relatively flat the construction work proved easy and progress was rapid. The section from Newton Stewart to Wigtown was completed in 1875, and two months later it reached Sorbie, while another two months saw it completed to within a mile of Garlieston. Then the company ran out of money, so Garlies (now the earl of Galloway) came to the rescue by paying for the cost of a tramway extension to Garlieston harbour, which was duly completed, though it was superseded shortly afterwards by a branch line. Meanwhile, efforts were made to raise the balance of the contract price by public subscription, targeting in particular those merchants, traders, farmers and others who had an interest in extending the line to Whithorn. The promoters were successful, and the work was finally completed in 1876. That year also saw the completion of the rail link from Stranraer to Girvan, which is the only part of the former rail network in the south-west still in operation.

The construction work was mainly carried out by itinerant navvies, many of them Irish, though squads of native labour were drawn from other parts of the country as well. Some were able-bodied poor, while others were suspected fugitives from justice who were taken on with no questions asked. Housed in rough encampments set up near the scene of operations, the men did much of the work by hand, and prodigious feats were achieved with the aid of picks and shovels, assisted by the frequent use of gunpowder to blast through rock. A form of mechanical digger was available, but the navvies saw it as a threat to their jobs and seldom used it, relying on horsepower instead. Where cuttings were excavated horse gins were used to haul cartloads of rock and stones up the sides for transportation to other sections of the line as infill for embankments. Basic rules of safety were consistently ignored, and the navvies increased the hazards by their bravado and recklessness. Some undermined too far and were buried alive by rockfalls, while others were apt to smoke their pipes in dangerous proximity to the gunpowder barrels with predictable results. Well-paid by the standards of the time, they lived hard, and ate and drank in proportion, and the public houses established along the route, notably the 'Buck's Head' near Gatehouse station, which is now a private house, must have done a roaring trade.

Teething troubles continued long after the rail network was completed, as too many companies were involved to allow a smooth operation, and it was only marginally profitable. A series of mergers between the operating companies made for greater efficiency, though financial difficulties persisted. However, when in 1891 the government officially classified the line as a supplementary route for mails, undertaking to pay the company for the service, the additional revenue enabled it to start yielding a commercial profit. After the end of the First World War a spur railway up the Dee valley from Castle Douglas to Dalry to link the Glenkens into the system was considered, and there were even plans to extend it as far as Dalmellington to give access to the coalfields there. However, the growing availability of motorised transport was rightly seen as a threat to its viability and the scheme was abandoned.

Local businessmen promoted the extension of the railway into Galloway in the hopes that it would make the region more accessible, and thus encourage further industrial development. True, it gave a valuable fillip to the local dairying industry by widening the market for its products, but otherwise it brought few commercial benefits. Quite the reverse in fact, because it led to a de-industrialisation of Galloway in that it made it easier for larger businesses operating outside the region to undercut local ones and capture their markets. The resulting decline in the region's economy made it increasingly dependent on farming, though even this was uncertain since the local Galloway cattle were brought into direct competition with the Shorthorn and Aberdeen Angus breeds, as well as beef imports from the American continent and Australasia. Although the extension of the railway into Galloway was not primarily intended to accommodate the travelling public this proved to be its main benefit, and it was because of this that it became predominantly a passenger rather than a goods service.

Its principal victim was the local shipping industry which had thriven on the back of Galloway's growing export trade with the Clyde, Cumberland and the principal markets bordering the Irish Sea. For it meant that trade was diverted away from these centres to the populous regions in Scotland, the Midlands and the south, and therefore the shipping companies had to cut back on their services and scrap or abandon many of their vessels. On the other hand, the coastal shipping trade, which had been largely eclipsed by the advent of steam navigation, continued to survive in a small way, though it too eventually succumbed as its trade was progressively drawn away by motorised transport. So eventually the small Galloway ports became moribund, and formerly echoing to the sounds of their busy prosperity they now fell silent and the lonely cries of the seabirds were all that remained.

APPENDIX

ESTATES IN GALLOWAY

of over 3,500 acres (1,416.45 ha) in order of size
(as given in the return of owners of lands and heritages in Scotland of 1872–3)

		acres
1	The Earl of Galloway	79,184
	The Earl of Stair	79,174
	Horatio Murray Stewart of Broughton and Cally	47,451
	William Forbes of Callendar	40,445
5	Mrs Jean Macadam Cathcart of Craigengillan	39,889
	Edward Stopford-Blair of Penninghame	37,268
	R A Oswald of Cavens	24,160
	The Earl of Selkirk	20,823
	The Marquess of Bute, Mochrum	20,157
10	Sir William Maxwell of Monreith Bart.	16,877
	James McDouall of Logan	16,290
	Frederick Constable-Maxwell of Terregles	15,803
	Trs. of Wellwood Maxwell of Glenlee	15,090
	Hon. Mrs Louisa Bellamy Gordon of Kenmure	14,093
15	Sir Andrew Agnew of Lochnaw Bart.	12,962
	Mrs Murray Dunlop of Corsock	12,774
	Capt. John Maxwell Heron of Heron	12,300
	Trs. of James Mackie of Bargaly	10,850
	David Hunter-Blair of Dunskey	8,255
20	William Maitland of Freugh	7,848
	Adm. Sir John Dalrymple-Hay of Park Bart.	7,400
	John Carrick Moore of Corsewall	6,877
	Robert Vans Agnew of Barnbarroch	6,777
	Thomas Hughan of Airds	6,605
25	William K Laurie of Woodhall	6,569
	Sir William Maxwell of Cardoness Bart.	6,381
	Edward Mackenzie of Auchenskeoch	6,364
	William Hamilton of Craichlaw	6,300
	Mrs Susannah Ommanney McTaggart of Ardwell	5,998
30	Col. Sir William Agnew Wallace of Lochryan	5,785
	James Stewart of Cairnsmore	5,625
	Robert Hathorn Johnston-Stewart of Physgill	5,552
	Mrs Maitland Kirwan of Gelston	5,080
	Wellwood Herries Maxwell of Munches	4,597

		acres
35	Alexander McCulloch of Kirkclaugh	4,348
	Walter McCulloch of Ardwall	4,275
	James Drew of Craigencallie	4,000
	Major F Rainsford Hannay of Kirkdale	3,938
	Alexander Spalding of Holme	3,785
40	Sir William Dunbar Bart., Merton Hall	3,674
	Alexander Clark Kennedy of Knockgray	3,609
	Col. John Fletcher Hathorn of Castlewigg	3,582
	Henry Hilton of Fairgirth	3,551

TOP 24 ESTATES IN GALLOWAY

in order of Gross Annual Value

		£ sterling
1	The Earl of Stair	£40,425 7s
	The Earl of Galloway	£32,197 18s
	The Earl of Selkirk	£19,749 10s
	Horatio Murray Stewart of Broughton and Cally	£16,322 16s
5	R A Oswald of Cavens	£16,184 17s
	Sir William Maxwell of Monreith Bart.	£15,289 10s
	Frederick Constable-Maxwell of Terregles	£12,109 12s
	James McDouall of Logan	£11,785 12s
	Sir Andrew Agnew of Lochnaw Bart.	£9,229 4s
10	Edward Stopford-Blair of Penninghame	£9,035 16s
	William Forbes of Callendar	£7,639 11s
	Robert Hathorn Johnston-Stewart of Physgill	£7,619 5s
	Robert Vans Agnew of Barnbarroch	£6,996 14s
	Mrs Susannah Ommanney McTaggart of Ardwell	£6,616 10s
15	Adm. Sir John Dalrymple-Hay Bart.	£6,601 2s
	William Maitland of Freugh	£5,881 11s
	Mrs Jean Macadam Cathcart of Craigengillan	£5,674 5s
	Mrs Murray Dunlop of Corsock	£5,213 1s
	Col. John Fletcher Hathorn of Castlewigg	£5,169
20	John Carrick Moore of Corsewall	£5,052 15s
	David Hunter-Blair of Dunskey	£4,948 16s
	Wellwood Herries Maxwell of Munches	£4,728 14s
	Alexander Spalding of Holme	£4,259
	Hon. Mrs Louisa Bellamy Gordon of Kenmure	£4,229 18s

NOTES

1. Symon, *Scottish Farming*, 190.
2. Campbell, *Owners and Occupiers*, 71.
3. Royal Commission on Agricultural Depression, *British Parliamentary Papers* 1895, XVII. Report on south-west Scotland by John Speir, para. 18.
4. Campbell, *Owners and Occupiers*, 90, and 'Agricultural Labour', 62.
5. Campbell, *Owners and Occupiers*, 91.
6. See Appendix.
7. There is a portrait of one kept by the Maxwells at Monreith, and it is perhaps not entirely coincidental that there are people living in Wigtownshire today who are distinguished by the negroid characteristic of fuzzy hair, and are named 'Jollies'.
8. *TSA* xiv, 114, though it sounds apocryphal.
9. Reflecting the new spirit of enquiry some turned to intellectual pursuits, among them being the noted physicist, James Clerk-Maxwell, the laird of Glenlair near Parton.
10. Devlin, *Albanach*.
11. The records of these estates have been the subject of a detailed investigation in Campbell, *Owners and Occupiers*, 160–80.
12. This was primarily responsible for the ultimate break-up of the Galloway estates in the following century.
13. This was originally introduced by the Agricultural Holdings Act of 1875, but as it did little to remedy matters more stringent measures followed in 1883. Then came the Agricultural Holdings Amendment Act of 1900 and a subsequent one of 1906, the combined effect of which was to ensure a measure of fairness for tenants.
14. Campbell, *Owners and Occupiers*, 138.
15. *Ibid.*, 148.
16. *Ibid.*, 125.
17. Letter from Sir J. C. Dalrymple Hay to Disraeli, 11 March 1876. Quoted in I. G. C. Hutchison, *A Political History of Scotland, 1832–1924* (Edinburgh, 1986), 104.
18. Campbell, *Owners and Occupiers*, 119.
19. *TSA* xiv, 426.
20. Although Galloway was traditionally a Liberal stronghold it turned Conservative following the collapse of the Liberal party after the First World War. This lasted until 1974 when it was taken by the Scottish National Party, who lost it to the Conservatives in 1979 and subsequently regained it in 1997.
21. Harking back to his youth in the 1880s, my grandfather recalled the depth of feeling that existed, and the continual bickering that went on, between the Tory and Liberal lairds. Locally, the earl of Selkirk, Murray-Stewart of Cally, and Maxwell of Cardoness supported the Tories, while the Liberals included the earl of Stair, Mackie of Ernespie, and Maitland of Cumstoun.
22. So described in a codicil to his trust disposition and settlement dated 17 Sept. 1914 (*SRO, RD* 5/4682/495).

32

MATERIALISTIC PROGRESS

RECOVERY

The dawn of the twentieth century saw a gradual improvement in the price of livestock and cereals, with a consequent easing of the depression, and by the outbreak of the First World War agriculture was restored to a semblance of prosperity. Adversity made farmers more efficient, and this was helped by the increasingly sophisticated types of machinery which were coming on the market. Mechanical reapers[1] were replacing the scythe, and threshing machines the traditional flail, while improved types of plough were being developed, with broader shares which were capable of breaking up the land and burying the turf more effectively. Disc- and spring-toothed harrows appeared, and the design of potato diggers was being constantly improved. Oil-driven engines were now available to operate turnip cutters, potato sorters and the larger threshing mills, while mechanical seeders enabled artificial fertilisers to be spread and seed sown more efficiently. However, it was not until after the war that farming in Galloway became more fully mechanised.

Significant progress was also being made in agricultural education, this being attributable above all to the work of the Highland and Agricultural Society, which was founded in the early nineteenth century for the purpose of instructing farmers in the science of animal and crop husbandry. This included experimenting with new methods of grassland management and developing more prolific strains of cereals, while at the same time disseminating information about pests and diseases, and exposing many of the traditional notions with which farming was riddled. For example, it exploded the idea that cows could be induced to give more milk if they were kept in close, warm, unventilated byres by demonstrating that this merely encouraged the spread of disease. It was also concerned to improve standards of hygiene, so it was primarily responsible for persuading milk retailers to demand higher standards of cleanliness on the part of their suppliers, and the use of milk coolers to improve its keeping quality.

Government support was necessary for the Society to be fully effective, but this was not forthcoming because as long as cheap food could be imported in almost unlimited quantity it was not particularly concerned about the state of farming. Nevertheless, it did establish a Board of Agriculture in 1889, though it was not until 1912 that a similar board was set up for Scotland. Also, money was allocated out of a special fund known as 'whisky money' to local authorities in order to promote technical training, and Kirkcudbrightshire was almost alone in appointing a full-time instructor. Some universities accepted the need to disseminate knowledge of the science of agriculture, and a chair was established at Edinburgh University in the 1880s. Later, at the turn of the century, an agricultural college for south-west Scotland was established in Glasgow, and its acquisition of the Auchencruive estate, near Ayr, two years later enabled it to carry out experimental work and develop practical training. However, it was to be a long time before farmers routinely sent their sons on courses at these institutions.

While these steps were a move in the right direction, their effect was blunted by the government's persistent lack of interest in the farming industry as it continued to adhere to a policy of cheap food and free trade. Nothing – not even the outbreak of war in August 1914 – could shake its conviction that the flow of imports would continue for the foreseeable future. In fact it was not until 1916, when shipping losses mounted alarmingly and it began to look as though the war would last indefinitely, that the government was jolted out of its complacency. Even then it merely appointed committees for each county, instructing them to submit proposals for maintaining and, if possible, increasing current levels of production. No coercion was used because it was thought that rising prices would provide the necessary incentive, so the inertia continued despite further shipping losses and a bad harvest in 1916.

The fall of the government in December 1916, and its replacement by a coalition under Lloyd George, heralded a more dynamic approach to the question of increasing production. Therefore, guaranteed minimum prices were introduced for cereals, these being set at a level which would encourage farmers to take pasture back into cultivation, and as a further incentive they were guaranteed to last until 1922. Compulsory powers were assumed to redirect labour where necessary and to force recalcitrant farmers to raise production. Price controls were imposed on milk and milk products, as well as meat and potatoes, but although they were designed to prevent scarcity from driving up the price to consumers they made no allowance for increases in production costs. Therefore, each resulting problem had to be solved by *ad hoc* measures as it arose, and that the system worked at all was a tribute to the determination of farmers and farm workers to ensure its success.

Conscription left the industry so undermanned that measures were introduced to exempt farm workers from the armed forces, and committees were set up to consider applications for discharge by serving soldiers with farming experience. As horses were commandeered for army transport this led to increasing reliance on tractors. The earlier models had many drawbacks, for apart from using precious imported fuel they were liable to break down at critical moments, but as more reliable versions were developed their advantages over the horse became increasingly apparent. Nevertheless, Galloway farmers were slow to accept them, and even as late as 1939 'only two or three tractors were operating in the whole parish of Kirkcudbright'.[2] In fact, it was not until after the Second World War that they came into general use, and even then horses continued to be used exclusively on some farms until as late as the 1950s.

As food shortages resulting from the war persisted long after it was over, there was no let-up in the drive for production. Land continued to be brought into cultivation, the lifting of price controls on meat encouraged livestock farmers to increase their stock, while the demobilisation of farm workers provided an ample supply of manpower. The war had highlighted the need to maintain a thriving agriculture and, voicing the government's changed approach to the industry, Lloyd George issued a stirring declaration that it would never again be neglected as in the past. This encouraged farmers to increase production, and as profits, and hence rent levels, rose – and land values with them – the future looked bright.

However, some perceptive landowners, realising the days of the great landholdings were numbered, took the opportunity to sell off farms, many of them being disposed of to the sitting tenants. They constituted a ready market because a number of them had profited from the farming boom and could afford to become owner occupiers. There was also the added inducement of being able to buy their farms on discounted terms, depending on the unexpired portion of their leases, while the expectation of a continuing rise in land values provided a further incentive.

An example in Kirkcudbrightshire was the Terregles estate belonging to H. J. Constable-Maxwell-Stuart which was sold in 1920. This comprised some sixty farms, and many of those in the parish of Terregles itself were bought by the Board of Agriculture for subdividing into smallholdings to resettle ex-servicemen, while others were acquired by the sitting tenants. Another was the Craigengillan estate where a number of the component sheep farms were sold off to existing tenants, though the owner, F. A. Cathcart, retained a portion which now belongs to his descendant. These sales were fortuitous because prices were on the verge of a slide as world food production began to outstrip demand, causing a downturn in farming, and a consequent fall in land values.

RETURN TO DEPRESSION

Its extent was reflected in the collapse of the price of wool, which in the course of 1920/1 dropped to almost a quarter of its previous level, and this inevitably affected sheep prices. Cereals followed suit, and in the following year the price of wheat fell by a half, and oats to roughly a third, of the 1919 price, while the doubling of imported dairy products forced the price of milk down to 3d (1.25p) a gallon. The collapse in cereal prices made it financially impossible for the government to maintain its guarantee, and notwithstanding its reaffirmation in the Agriculture Act of 1920 the pledge was revoked. Many farmers who had borrowed money to buy their farms faced ruin as profits fell and land prices declined to a third of their post-war level. No longer able to service their loans, they were reduced to a position of negative equity, and bankruptcies became distressingly common throughout the industry.

This resulted in large tracts of arable land being taken out of cultivation and put down to permanent pasture. At the same time, the fall in beef and sheep prices hit livestock farmers and compelled them to reduce the scale of their enterprises. Eventually prices began to steady and costs, particularly of feeds and fertilisers, settled at reasonable levels; but this proved only a temporary respite. The calamitous year of 1929 ushered in a still more severe recession, when the price of all farm products fell so dramatically that in many areas cereal-growing was abandoned altogether and land was increasingly put down to grass. The situation became so serious that in 1931 the government was forced to abandon its policy of free trade, and in the following year it reintroduced a guaranteed price for wheat, though not for oats and barley which was the main staple of cereal growers in Galloway.

Farm workers were affected by the depression too, as the minimum wage rates introduced during the war were abandoned. Although they were protected to some extent by the Agricultural Wages (Regulation) Act of 1924, which established wage committees to fix a standard rate for each county, the levels set by these bodies were bound to be influenced by what the industry could afford, and therefore wage scales inevitably reflected the prevailing depression. These continued to be fixed on a county basis until the passing of the Agricultural Wages (Regulations) (Scotland) Act in 1937, when a statutory board was created to establish a uniform minimum wage, as well as rates for overtime and a regular annual holiday entitlement.

The need for farmers to co-operate in the face of adversity led to the creation of marketing organisations, which could negotiate from strength to secure a better deal for their members. Although co-operatives had existed in Scotland since the 1880s, and in Galloway the Tarff Valley

Agricultural Co-operative Society had been set up in 1903, the Agricultural Marketing Act of 1931 gave the new boards a virtual monopoly of the sale of their members' products, as well as a say in determining import quotas. One of the first to be established under the Act was the Meat Marketing Board, which was designed to protect the interests of livestock producers by undertaking the collection, slaughter and disposal of their fatstock, and to pay them a fixed rate, depending on the grading of the carcases in terms of weight and quality.

In 1933, the Scottish Milk Marketing Board was set up with a statutory monopoly over the production and distribution of milk for the purposes of protecting the interests of dairy farmers. Although to begin with it encountered considerable opposition on the part of those who resented having to sell their milk to the Board to the exclusion of any other outlet, they soon changed their tune once the advantages became apparent. As a first step, the Board acquired the existing milk marketing agencies in Galloway, such as United Creameries who operated creameries at Dunragit, Sorbie, Tarff, Campbelltown and Colfin in the Rhinns. It also took over a number of independent creameries, including those at Stranraer, Sandhead, Port William, Kirkcudbright, Twynholm and Dalbeattie, and at the same time it established new ones.

Through course of time the Board imposed a series of regulations on its suppliers compelling them to maintain a minimum standard of quality in terms of butterfat content, and a proper standard of hygiene. Whereas the former can be readily measured, a particular type of organism – *bacterium coliformus* – was used as the yardstick for assessing cleanliness, and if found no milk could be accepted from the offending farm until it had been eliminated. Milk testers, usually girls from a dairying background, were employed by the Board to visit each farm in rotation to ensure compliance with these regulations. A determined effort was also made to eradicate tuberculosis, and incentives were given to dairy farmers to have their herds formally designated as attested, though it was not completely eliminated until 1960. Similarly, the Board encouraged the keeping of milk records, as this is an essential tool for breeding to improve the milk-producing capacity of a herd. Most important of all, dairy farmers now had an assured market for their milk, as well as the certainty of receiving a regular monthly payment for the milk sold to the Board, which meant they could realise their profits more quickly and thus maintain a healthy cash flow.

The guaranteed outlet for milk resulted in the abandonment of cheesemaking, since cheeses were less readily marketable. Hitherto, it had been one of the main products of dairy farms, and its importance is evident from the fact that in the early years of the century some 300 farms in Wigtownshire alone were dedicated to cheesemaking. Its by-product of whey was used to feed to pigs, so when cheesemakers turned to milk production it led to a substantial reduction in pig-keeping, and the days when every householder kept a few pigs and 'the drains of Haugh of Urr ran with blood at the annual pig-killing'[3] became an echo of the past.

Nevertheless, commercial pig-keeping was a thriving industry, so boards were established for marketing bacon pigs, as well as wool and potatoes. The last of these had been a staple crop in Galloway since the late 1700s, though it was not until the beginning of the twentieth century that the chancy but potentially highly profitable early potato crop began to be grown. This was confined to the coastal regions of Wigtownshire, where the influence of the Gulf Stream ensured minimal risk of frost damage, while the early spring there made it possible to harvest the crop in time to hit the market at its peak in late May and early June, though it was subsequently killed off by cheap foreign imports.

THE CHANGING COUNTRYSIDE

The depression resulted in a sharp decline in rents, and many landowners who found it increasingly difficult to meet rising repair and maintenance costs were forced to sell land. The Forestry Commission was frequently a buyer, particularly where the estate included marginal or hill ground. This was established as a government-funded body by the Forestry Act of 1919 for the purpose of regenerating woodlands to make good the timber losses sustained during the war. Therefore it systematically bought up land which was suitable for planting with conifers, since these are among the fastest growing of all tree species and, because of the suitability of its climate, Galloway was one of the main spheres of its activities. In 1921 it purchased a large tract of land near Dalbeattie, and later Cairn Edward which consists of an expanse of hill ground extending westwards from Loch Ken. One of the principal sellers of land to the Commission over the years was Mrs Murray Usher, who inherited the heavily-encumbered Cally estate in 1923, while another was the earl of Galloway, and in 1933 it acquired the Kirroughtree estate at the head of Wigtown Bay.

There was a social dimension to the Commission's activities as well, since it was thought that being labour-demanding it would help stem the depopulation of the landward areas – a process that was gaining momentum in consequence of the combined effects of increased mobility and the war. The impact of the latter is grimly apparent on every village war memorial which bears tragic testimony to a whole generation of young men torn from their families, many of them never having left home before, to be consigned to almost certain death in the trenches. Others, for whom the prospects of town life held little appeal, emigrated to the colonies – to the extent that the number of people leaving Scotland during the 1920s was almost equal to the natural increase in the population,[4] though the flow of emigrants would dwindle during the 1930s.[5]

The advent of motorised transport was responsible above all for the disappearance of the small viable communities which formerly existed in the remoter districts. The motor car first appeared on the scene in the early years of the century, but as ownership was limited to the wealthy the great majority of people had to rely on the bus service. However, it was not until after the First World War that this service became widely available, and being much more accessible it eventually displaced the railways as the principal means of public transport. A start had already been made in 1906, when the Portpatrick Railway Co. acquired two steam-driven vehicles capable of carrying thirty passengers, which advertised their readiness to 'stop anywhere to pick up or set down passengers except on steep hills'. This was followed by the introduction of further steam coaches, while small district bus operators ran localised services which later came under the wing of the Caledonian Company. Eventually they were nationalised, becoming part of Western SMT who extended the service to most towns and villages throughout the region.

This gave people living in the landward areas access to shops and other facilities available in the larger towns, and the consequent broadening of their horizons led to a growing reluctance, particularly on the part of younger people, to accept the limitations of life in these regions. Accordingly, the drift away from them gathered pace, and their depopulation is evident from the ruins of many settlements where a thriving and largely self-sufficient community had formerly existed. For as soon as the process starts it tends to become self-fulfilling. As people leave the community diminishing numbers force schools and other local services to close, while the resulting lack of custom drives local shops out of business, and as people are unwilling to accept the inconvenience of travelling further afield by public transport to do their shopping they too eventually move. Changes in agricultural practices gave added impetus to the process as the progressive decultivation of land, combined with an increasing reliance on labour-saving machinery, led to a shrinking demand for farm workers, so they were forced to seek work elsewhere.

To some extent the exodus was stemmed by the demand for labour from the ancillary industries such as creameries and grain mills, which flourished on the back of agriculture. Similarly, the advent of lorries encouraged haulage firms to set up in business, and although initially geared to carrying livestock they soon expanded into transporting general goods. Wool manufacture and carpet making, survivors of the late eighteenth- and early nineteenth-century industrialisation, gave further scope for employment, and forestry, together with its offshoot of sawmilling, provided a growing number of jobs. The work of maintaining and improving the roads was also heavily labour-dependent, particularly as quarrying the necessary materials was done almost entirely by hand. For those landed proprietors who could afford it, habit and status demanded the employment of game-keepers and estate workers, while domestic service was still regarded as an acceptable occupation.

There was also a high proportion of self-employed people who practised the traditional crafts of weaving, leatherworking, shoe- and clog-making, the last being particularly important since clogs continued to be extensively worn. In addition, there was a steady demand for dykers, molecatchers, joiners and plumbers, while there was a particular need for blacksmiths to shoe horses, since they were still widely used. Some traditional smiths were expanding into engineering and setting up their own garage businesses to cater for the growing demands of car owners. A local car manufacturing industry was established at Heathhall in Dumfries, and in 1920 it set up a subsidiary company known as the Galloway Engineering Co. at Tongland. They were the makers of the Arrol-Johnston car known as 'the Galloway', but it seems to have lacked appeal as the factory was closed two years later.

THE CHURCH

Two separate churches, the Free Church and the Church of Scotland, had co-existed in most parishes since the Disruption, the difference between them being epitomised in the nineteenth century jingle:

> The Free kirk, the wee kirk, the kirk without the steeple.
> The auld kirk, the cauld kirk, the kirk without the people.

Although relations between them were inclined to be strained, the increasing secularism of the twentieth century, when religion was no longer the pith and core of Scottish life, encouraged them to sink their differences. The war played a part as well, because the vacancies resulting from the conscription of ministers were frequently filled by their opposite numbers, and as the order of service was the same in both Churches the difference was hardly noticed. Since the question of patronage, on which the church had split, was no longer a live issue, the way was open for a reconciliation. This occurred in 1929, when the main body of the Free Church was reunited with the established Church, and therefore as each Free Church minister retired his charge was amalgamated with that of his opposite number.

The similarity of the services in the two Churches meant that changes introduced into the one soon spread to the other. Originally singing was confined to a single psalm, and while the minister led with the opening lines the congregation followed suit assisted by a tuning fork to set the key. During the nineteenth century hymns came to be sung as a supplement to the psalm, the Free Church being particularly partial to the more evangelical Moody and Sankey-type hymns, though it was not until the 1870s that the Scottish hymnal came into general use.[6] Similarly, the traditional practice of standing to pray and sitting during the singing was abandoned and both Churches adopted the converse.

At much the same time, the organ replaced the tuning fork as an accompaniment to the singing, but because of peoples' innate conservatism regarding matters of worship this was highly contentious and its introduction provoked widespread opposition. For example, the minister of Inch tells us that when his predecessor first introduced it into his church, many of the congregation walked out in protest[7] and he was summoned to defend his action before presbytery. This he did by declaring that he had sought 'to tear the lion's skin from an ass of superstition which has too long terrified and disgraced the Church'.[8] On the same theme, Robert Lee of Greyfriars church in Edinburgh, the stormy petrel of the liturgical movement and a leading advocate of the organ, was accused of 'conducting an American-style service permitting organ music and other innovations'.

The Church's role in the community was steadily diminishing. With the introduction of the statutory old age pension in 1908, and unemployment benefit after the First World War, kirk sessions were relieved of their responsibility for the poor. The Education Act of 1872 had already transferred the obligation to instruct the youth from the Church to the State by inaugurating compulsory education for all children between the ages of five and thirteen – subsequently increased to fourteen by the Education Act of 1883, and fifteen in 1947. The 1872 Act also established publicly-managed, state-funded school boards to administer the new system, which involved giving all children a basic education, while a select few were picked out for instruction in Latin as a preparation for higher education.

Originally primary schools were so sited that no child would have to walk more than three miles to school, and it was because of this that they were formerly so numerous. However, many fell victim to depopulation, while others became redundant following the introduction of a school transport service. Higher education was the privilege of the more promising pupils, though not all those selected necessarily wanted it. Later, the controversial 'eleven plus' exam was introduced as a rough-and-ready means of singling out those regarded as suitable for a secondary education, which was provided by the academies in the main towns of Dumfries, Castle Douglas, Kirkcudbright, Newton Stewart, Stranraer, and Dalry.

Scottish education has traditionally enjoyed a high reputation, mainly on account of the headstart it gave many Scotsmen in making their way in the world, but it was the middle classes who were the principal beneficiaries since they could afford a better education. This remained the case after the introduction of a universal state education, largely because of the indifferent quality of the teaching available in the Board schools. Recognising this, the government introduced legislation in the aftermath of the First World War to improve the situation by replacing the school boards with county education authorities under the overall supervision of the county councils. A further Act was passed in 1933 imposing direct responsibility for education on these councils, and they in turn delegated this function to their education committees which were established for that purpose.

The poor quality of education which was available before 1918 provoked one obviously disgruntled teacher of the time to complain that of those committed to his charge 'the boys are going out to the fields to plough [and] the girls are going to the farms as servants'. Lamenting his fate as their instructor, he went on to say: 'I can teach them to read, and they will read serials in the drivelling weeklies; I can teach them to write, and they will write pathetic notes to me bye and bye; and I can teach them to count, and they will never count more than the miserable sum they receive as a weekly wage'. On a note of despair, he concludes: 'My work is hopeless, for education should aim at bringing up a new generation that will be better than the old. The present system is to produce the same kind of man as we see today'.

LOCAL AUTHORITIES

The county councils were the main instruments of local government, and although lip service was paid to the principles of democracy, in that they were – in theory at least – elective bodies, they tended to be composed of a mix of public-spirited landowners and local people of substance. Their responsibilities were expanded by the Local Government (Scotland) Act of 1929 when they, along with the district councils and the town councils of the main burghs, were given the task of administering a wide range of public services, including the maintenance of classified roads, housing (an important one in view of the shortage after the First World War), town and country planning, public health, water supply, drainage and sewage. Roads were a major expense, for whereas they may have been suitable for horse-drawn vehicles the advent of the car highlighted their deficiencies, and, while heavy rain reduced them to seas of mud, dry weather caused the passing traffic to throw up clouds of dust to the general annoyance of those living in the vicinity, and women passengers almost invariably wore veils as a protection.

The cost of maintaining the roads was subsidised by central government from the proceeds of a hypothecated petrol tax, which gave county councils additional scope for road improvement. There was certainly a need for it, because the roads in Galloway were generally in a poor state and in no condition to cope with the increasing volume of motorised traffic. For example, the main road between Dumfries and Castle Douglas was regarded as sub-standard and in need of extensive realignment, but it was not until 1939 that the work was begun, when the war put a stop to it.

Water was a demanding responsibility too, and during the 1930s an ambitious scheme was put in hand to provide every home with a supply of mains water. A number of reservoirs were constructed to replace the inadequate gravitational supplies which had previously sufficed for the main population centres. Dumfries and Maxwelltown, on the other hand, fared better, as they already had access to a water supply from Lochrutton near Lochfoot since 1851.[9] This was now supplemented by a reservoir built at Glenkiln in 1937, while another one was established at Clatteringshaws. In other cases, existing lochs, such as Lochinvar and Lochenkit, were enlarged by the construction of dams. However, the work of supplying every house with mains water took longer than expected, and even as late as the 1950s the residents in some villages were still having to draw water from street pumps.[10]

A similar delay occurred in the provision of a comprehensive sewage system, and writing in 1951 the minister of Balmaghie could still only say that 'a sewage scheme is planned for each village',[11] though his colleague at Wigtown was praising the advances made in the standard of public health and hygiene compared with earlier in the century. 'About 1910', he writes, 'the burgh's water supply was inadequate and bad, and all but the fortunate few who had private wells had to depend on rainwater from barrels or on water drawn from street pumps, some of which was . . . contaminated from sewers'. He goes on to say that, 'with a new water supply and sewage system, dry closets, germ-laden refuse pits at back doors, and frequently polluted streets became things of the past'.[12] It is somewhat surprising to think that such conditions prevailed in Galloway as late as the twentieth century.

The abundance of water in Galloway accounted for the construction of a major hydro-electric scheme which extended upstream from Tongland to include virtually the entire length of the Dee and its tributaries the Ken and the Deugh. Although the project was originally mooted by Wellwood Maxwell of Kirkennan the convenor of Kirkcudbright County Council in 1923,[13] it was not until 1929 that the Galloway Water Power Act was passed authorising its construction. The work took seven years to complete, which is hardly surprising since it embraced five power stations, nine large dams, four tunnel systems, and no less than seven reservoirs and associated works. Thus, the scheme utilised a catchment area of some 345 square miles of the Ken river system, and a further 50 square miles in the Loch Doon area, from where the water was piped through a tunnel into the Deugh. This was more than ample to provide every home in Galloway with a supply of electricity, but as the installation work was interrupted by the war it was not completed until the 1950s. Notwithstanding that the demand had grown by then, there was still ample surplus power to supplement the national grid at times of peak demand.

Meanwhile, farming remained a beleagured industry throughout the 1930s, or 'the hungry thirties' as they were known. By 1932 the price of beef cattle had fallen so dramatically that the government was compelled to reduce imports from South America by 10 per cent. Yet it was only under extreme pressure and with the greatest reluctance that it did so, because only by exporting their meat could countries like Argentina afford to pay for our manufactured exports. However, this was merely a palliative and the need for further assistance became so compelling that five years later Prime Minister Baldwin's Conservative government introduced a scheme for subsidising beef producers, first as a temporary expedient and later more permanently with the passing of the Livestock Industry Act of 1937.

In the same year, an Agriculture Act was passed which guaranteed a price for oats and barley – a long overdue measure – and set up a land fertility scheme, which was designed to encourage land improvement and prevent the deterioration of grassland. This provided a subsidy of half the cost of liming and 25 per cent of basic slag, and two years later it was supplemented by the Agricultural Development Act of 1939 which introduced a grant of £2 an acre towards the cost of ploughing up and re-seeding old pasture. This was merely tinkering with the problem, as the industry had been ignored for far too long for these measures to have any real effect. Large tracts of arable land still remained under pasture, and former grassland had been allowed to degenerate into rough grazing; therefore it would take nothing short of a national crisis of epic proportions to galvanise the government into taking the far-reaching measures that were necessary to achieve agricultural self-sufficiency. This came with the outbreak of war on 3 September 1939.

NOTES

1. The first reaping machine was invented by John Gladstone, a native of Castle Douglas, who was also responsible for improving the design of the threshing mill.
2. *TSA* xiv, 204.
3. *Ibid.*, 319.
4. Flinn, *Population History*, 447.
5. *Ibid.*, 449 (tab. 6.1.5).
6. For instance it was introduced into Borgue church in 1879 (*TSA* xiv, 106).
7. *TSA* xiv, 446–7.
8. *Ibid.*, 447.
9. *Ibid.*, 245.
10. *Ibid.*, 180.
11. *Ibid.*, 91.
12. *Ibid.*, 394.
13. *Ibid.*, 298.

33

AN UNCERTAIN FUTURE

WARTIME EMERGENCY

The outbreak of war put Britain's entire overseas trade in peril, as the German occupation of north-west Europe and their control of the coastline from Norway to Spain cut her off from the Continent and left her entirely dependent on her lifeline with America. As mounting shipping losses rendered this increasingly hazardous, she was forced to fall back on her own resources and develop a siege economy. This meant that urgent priority had to be given to reviving the agricultural industry – a daunting task since it had been so long neglected, and the local agricultural executive committees, which had been set up during the previous year, set about the challenging task of maximising food production.

As a first step, they carried out a survey of every farm in their area to assess its cropping potential, and where appropriate ordered the necessary work to be put in hand. Priority was given to growing wheat and potatoes, since these are the most productive crops in terms of human energy. Similarly with dairying, since an adequate supply of milk was vital to the nation's health, though less emphasis was placed on livestock production because this is the least efficient method of converting land resources into human energy. The marketing of farm produce was nationalised, and the newly-created Ministry of Food took over the agricultural marketing boards. Plans were drawn up for the introduction of a rationing scheme, and in the meantime price controls were imposed as a temporary measure, but as these failed to make allowance for rising costs they proved no more successful than in the past. Milk producers in particular were badly hit by the escalating price of concentrates, so the government compensated for this by introducing a subsidy, and while not a satisfactory answer it had to suffice until a rationing scheme was ready to be put into operation.

An adequate supply of labour was necessary to work the land, so farming was declared a reserved occupation with those engaged in it being exempted from call-up. Agricultural workers were prohibited from leaving the land for higher paid jobs in industry, though in compensation they were assured a minimum wage which was broadly comparable with that of their industrial counterparts. Women were conscripted for the Land Army, and later prisoners of war were drafted into farm work, while at times of peak labour demand, such as hay and harvest time, workers were drawn from schools, colleges, offices and factories.

Price controls remained in force after the introduction of rationing, though they had to be regularly adjusted in line with production costs. In spite of this, unforeseen problems emerged, one in particular affecting hill sheep farmers, of whom there were a large number in Galloway. Because low ground farmers were being encouraged to crop their land in preference to fat lamb production, this effectively killed off the market for cast ewes and store lambs, on which the hill farmers depended for their livelihood. Therefore they found themselves running their farms at a loss, with a consequent risk that many would be forced to reduce their enter-prises or abandon them altogether, and this raised the spectre of large areas of hill ground going out of production. So, in compensation the government introduced a hill sheep subsidy which was based on the number of ewes kept on each holding, and this was followed shortly afterwards by a hill cattle subsidy.

Although Galloway was spared the bombing raids suffered by the main industrial areas, only thirteen bombs being dropped there without loss of life, the practical impact of hostilities was very much in evidence. For example, a transit camp was established on the outskirts of Stranraer in the summer of 1940, and it is reckoned that over a million men passed through it in the course of the war.[1] In 1942 the harbour at Cairnryan was developed as a base for RAF flying boats, and the first ship to use it after its completion was a destroyer taking King George VI and Queen Elizabeth on a secret visit to Northern Ireland. Later it served as a reception centre for American equipment in transit from the United States to the south of England for the invasion of Europe. After the war the Ministry of Supply took it over as a ship-breaking yard, but by 1959 the work was completed and the base closed down at the cost of some 300 jobs.

Aerodromes were built on the flat, low-lying lands at Baldoon, Castle Kennedy, Corsewall, and also at Dumfries, to serve as operational RAF stations, but these were subsequently closed down, with the exception of West Freuch which continued to be used as an RAF base. Similarly, a seaplane base was established at Wig Bay on the western shores of Loch Ryan, but this too was closed after the war. The only survivor is the Fighting Vehicles Research and Development Establishment at Netherlaw, near Kirkcudbright, which was used as an experimental tank gunnery range, but within the last few years it has been transferred from the army to the civil service who now operate it through private contractors.

POST-WAR MEASURES

The end of the war brought no respite in the drive for production, as the need for food remained acute. Much of Europe was devastated and whole regions remained uncropped, while draught animals and milking cows had been systematically appropriated from the occupied countries. There was also a critical shortage of fertilisers, farm implements and machinery, and the huge death toll left insufficient manpower to work the land. Starvation was rampant and the people had to be fed, but there was a limit to how far Britain could help, as her gold and currency reserves were now so depleted that she could barely afford to pay for essential imports. This meant that the newly-elected Labour government was forced to continue its predecessor's policy of food rationing, and through a generous mix of grants and subsidies to encourage farmers to maintain a high level of production.

Its objective, as set out in the preamble to the Agricultural Holdings Act of 1947, was 'to promote a stable and efficient industry capable of producing such part of the nation's food as in the national interest it is desirable to produce . . . at minimum prices consistently with proper remuneration and living conditions for farmers and workers in agriculture and with an adequate return on capital'. Therefore, measures were introduced to assist specific sectors of the industry, and the Hill Farming Act of 1946 gave hill sheep farmers a 50 per cent grant towards the cost of rehabilitating their farms, while other grants were available to encourage farmers to take land into cultivation. In fact, the level of help given to farmers generally, in the form of grants and subsidies, was such that by the 1960s there was widespread complaint that they were being 'feather bedded'.

Reflecting its political colouring, the government went to great lengths to assist tenant farmers at the expense of landlords, whom a leading member of the administration in a colourful if controversial turn of phrase branded as 'lower than vermin'. Additional obligations were imposed on them by the Agricultural (Holdings) Act of 1948 which compelled them to modernise the cottages occupied by their tenants' farm staff, and to improve other fixed equipment, such as farm buildings, fences and drains, to a specified standard without a compensatory increase in rent. Moreover, tenants were now given full security of tenure, to the extent that not only did their leases remain in force for their lifetime but they were also transmissible to their successors on death.

Rents were no longer a matter for private agreement between landlords and tenants, as there was now a statutory requirement for rents under new leases to be submitted to arbitration, and either party to an existing lease was entitled to do likewise. This sounded better in theory than it proved in practice, because the arbiters were generally drawn from the ranks of the tenant farmers, and as they were naturally biassed towards their peers it was almost invariably the tenants who benefited. Furthermore, the act stipulated that the personal circumstances of the tenant, and his ability to pay, should be taken into account in determining rents, and this was frequently used as a pretext for fixing them at an artificially low level. In fact, it could happen that a prospective tenant might offer a substantial rent in order to secure the lease of a holding and then apply for arbitration once he was safely in possession. True, the Act included a provision enabling a landowner to apply to have a tenant evicted on grounds of bad farming, but only very rarely was this successfully invoked.

In the past tenants had been at a disadvantage, but the wheel had now turned full circle and it was the landlords who were the victims of discriminatory legislation. Therefore, if they were unable to fulfil their statutory obligations to their tenant farmers, there was pressure on them to sell their farms to these tenants at a heavily discounted price, and the families of purchasers at this time are among the most prominent farmers in Galloway today. Although subsequent legislation went some way towards redressing the balance by requiring rents to be fixed in line with open-market values, the damage to the landlord–tenant relationship had been done. Landowners were now unwilling to relet vacant farms, preferring either to take them in hand or sell them. Consequently, the leasehold market virtually dried up, and young aspiring farmers who lacked the means to buy a farm were unable to secure a tenancy. So, while full security of tenure was something that tenant farmers had long aspired to, its realisation proved illusory.

Farm workers had fared reasonably well during the period from the outbreak of war until the 1950s, in that their wages had more than doubled and their working hours were reduced. Although they still lagged behind their counterparts in industry, for those who occupied a tied cottage the gap was narrower than the bare figures suggest, and statutory wage rises became a regular event. Nevertheless, so long as guaranteed prices were linked to production costs there was no pressure on farmers to reduce their workforce, in spite of the availability of casual labour to help with the hay and harvest and other labour-demanding jobs such as turnip-hoeing and potato-lifting. In fact it was traditionally the custom to give children a week off school to help in the potato fields, and the 'tattie holiday' is still an annual event in the school calendar, though potato growing has declined and the operation is entirely mechanised.

Eventually the policy of relating guaranteed prices to production costs became so costly that it had to be abandoned, and therefore farmers were compelled to cut back on labour and invest in farm machinery instead. While a farmworker's right to regular wage rises to keep pace with his counterparts elsewhere is indisputable, the fact was that these steadily priced them out of their market, and as jobs became scarcer the drift away from the land continued to gather pace. As an example, the Rev. John Good used to recall how in the course of his forty-odd years as minister of Twynholm the labour force on one particular farm in his parish was reduced from eighty-five to fifteen.

Dairying, which was traditionally an extremely labour-intensive industry, was a prime example, because the introduction of the milking machine greatly reduced the staffing requirements. Although a milking machine had been successfully pioneered – by a local man, Stewart Nicholson of Bombie – as far back as the turn of the century, it was not until after the Second World War that they came into general use. This enabled a dairyman and his assistant to manage a herd of seventy or eighty cows – and even more with the advent of the milking parlour – in place of the many hand milkers required to perform the same task in the past.

As the successful running of a dairy requires a great deal of hard and unremitting work, as well as a high standard of stocksmanship, a good dairyman generally commanded a high wage compared with other farm workers. It was normally the practice to pay him a proportion of the milk cheque (usually a sixth or a seventh plus a bonus for each calf reared), out of which he would be responsible for paying his assistant. Since his remuneration depended on results, there was every incentive to maximise production by feeding the cows to capacity and making liberal use of bought-in concentrates. As these were still relatively cheap, and milk commanded a high price, dairying was extremely profitable during the immediate post-war years.

This led to a rapid growth in the industry, and while some dairy farmers expanded their herds others whose farms were suited to it put on dairies. Distance from the market and transport costs were irrelevant when assessing the potential profit to be gained from establishing a dairy, because the Milk Marketing Board paid a uniform price for all milk supplied, irrespective of where it was produced. This was of particular benefit to Galloway farmers, because generally speaking they were further removed than most from the principal markets. Inevitably the boom in dairying subsided, and as the supply of milk exceeded demand, profits began to fall. The first indications came in 1954 when the Board imposed a quantity limit and paid a lower price for the excess. At the same time, an escalation in the price of concentrates compelled dairy farmers to make more use of grass and its products of hay, and later silage, and while this reduced the overall milk yield production costs were correspondingly lower. From the 1970s onwards dairying tended to become less profitable, while the compensation offered to those who were prepared to slaughter their cows and go out of dairying accounted for the subsequent decline of the industry.

The farming landowner

As landowners who acquired vacant possession of a farm were now unwilling to relet, they had a choice of either selling up or taking it in hand and farming it themselves. This was something of a challenge because most lacked the requisite knowledge and experience, but there were nevertheless strong financial inducements to do so. For not only did they stand to benefit from the wide range of grants and subsidies available, but they also acquired the means to set estate maintenance costs – as well as much of the expense of keeping up the family home – against their farm profits for tax purposes, which was a valuable concession in a time of punitively high taxation. The rise of the farming landowner was commented on by the minister of Kirkbean who observed that 'the proprietor turned multiple farmer is a new factor in country life. His advent makes one of the most important of the many changes which have taken place in the parish since the Second War'.[2]

It marked an interesting social change too, for landlords returned to their roots after a century or more of losing contact with them. Naturally there were absentees whose other commitments precluded them from a direct supervision of their estates, and who had to rely on factors or farm managers. Others, however, became actively involved in the running of their estates, and with the local community, while their children started their education at the local primary school. As Dr Russell, the Gatehouse schoolmaster, aptly observed in his contribution to the *Third Statistical Account*, 'while it would be untrue to say that there is no awareness of class divisions owing to the survival of the remnant of the aristocracy who have been able to remain on their family estates . . . the absurdity of standing rigidly on these distinctions . . . is freely recognised and there is an easy mingling of people of all classes, occupations and interests'.[3]

The alternative to taking over vacant farms was to sell them, and the resulting break-up of many former landed estates was commented on by several contributors to the *Third Statistical Account*, who ascribed it to a combination of high taxation and death duties.[4] This was true so far as it went, but not the whole story, since it was equally attributable to a combination of rising costs and falling rental incomes. As an example, the earl of Galloway was quoted as saying, on the occasion of the opening of the forestry village at Glentrool, that the rents he was receiving from the lands he had recently sold to the Forestry Commission were only 47 per cent of those his predecessor had received for the same lands in 1870[5] – and this over a period when maintenance costs had multiplied many times. The same source went on to observe that, 'over the past twenty years [up to 1961] there had been a considerable change in the land tenure in the parish [Minnigaff], and that whereas the greater part of it was formerly held by five estates – Cumloden, Kirroughtree, Machermore, Cairnsmore and Bargaly – these had virtually all disappeared'.[6]

This was symptomatic of the changes which were occurring in the pattern of landownership in Galloway. A more detailed picture can be gained by comparing the information contained in the Scottish Doomsday Book of 1872/3 with the statistics given in Wightman's *Who owns Scotland?*,[7] which was published approximately 120 years later. Whereas in the 1870s there were 120 estates consisting of 1,000 acres or more the number had now dropped to 70, and while roughly a third of these continued to belong to the same family the average size of these estates was very much smaller. At present, the two largest privately-owned estates are the Stair Estates, though these are about half their former size, and the Norwegian-owned Forest Lodge estate, near Dalry. Other large landholders include public bodies like Forest Enterprise (the managers of the Forestry Commission), the Electricity Board, the Ministry of Defence, and Scottish Natural Heritage.

The Forestry Commission continued to be an aggressive land-buyer, and its policy of paying a fair market price not only encouraged many impoverished upland owners to sell to it, but it also had a stabilising influence on hill farming generally. This was because it effectively underpinned the value of that type of land, thus rendering it acceptable to banks as security for loans, which in turn enabled many hill farmers to remain in business. A number of larger landowners were also tempted to sell, and, as was aptly observed, 'it is only natural that where a landlord receives a suitable offer for a large block of land from the Forestry Commission it should be accepted in preference to selling isolated farms to tenants'.[8]

This referred in particular to the earl of Galloway's sale of the Bargrennan and Auchinleck estates to the Commission in the 1950s, though it could equally well have applied to the portion of the Cally estate extending from the upper Fleet as far as the Orchars which was sold to the Commission at much the same time. In the late 1960s it extended this holding with the purchase from Cardoness and Kirkdale estates of a large expanse of hill ground comprising much of the Cairnsmore of Fleet range. By 1979 the Commission had acquired 21 per cent of the entire land surface of Galloway, and although it subsequently embarked on a comprehensive land disposal it was still left with nearly 170,000 acres (68,600 ha) of land in the region fifteen years later.

As part of its resettlement strategy in the landward areas, the Forestry Commission planned to create a number of settlements in these regions, and one consisting of fifteen timber-built houses was established at Woodhead, beyond Carsphairn. Its main pilot scheme, however, was the forestry village comprising forty-seven houses, a school and a shop at Glentrool. This was not altogether successful, for while there was ample employment for the men there were few job opportunities for their wives and daughters, and therefore most forestry workers preferred to live in Newton Stewart, where there were shopping facilities and better employment prospects for their womenfolk, and commute to work.

Until the 1980s the government was concerned to promote forestry, and by providing generous grants and tax incentives it encouraged private individuals to plant up land on their own account or as participants in private forestry schemes. So, whereas the costs of establishing woodlands could be set against other sources of income for tax purposes the proceeds of timber sales could, provided the necessary formalities were complied with, be rendered virtually tax-free. This policy was inspired by the fact that forestry makes more productive use of the uplands compared with livestock rearing, because its annual production in terms of timber growth is far higher than running sheep or cattle on the same ground. All the more so on poorer land where it takes up to five acres to support a single Blackface ewe producing on average slightly under one lamb a year.

Changes in the government's policy towards forestry in the 1980s not only led to the removal of the tax concessions available to private owners but it had a devastating impact on the Forestry Commission itself. For, in line with its policy of selling off the national assets, it compelled the Commission to dispose of much of its landholdings, and by denying it sufficient funds for the proper maintenance of its remaining forests these tended to become neglected. Many forestry workers were laid off, reducing the workforce to a quarter of its previous total, and although some were taken on as self-employed contractors, the effect of the rundown on local communities has been continuous. For example, fifteen years ago the Commission maintained seven local headquarters in the region, whereas now there is only one.

Despite the retrenchment and a limited local demand for home-grown timber there is a viable timber processing industry in Galloway, with sawmills at Wigtown, Kirkcudbright, Dalbeattie and New Abbey. Although some 40 per cent of its log requirements have to be brought in from elsewhere, and 60 per cent of locally harvested timber is processed outside the region, a recent study sees scope for further expansion of the industry. But this is perceived more as a means of bringing money into the region rather than a source of local employment, though the study pointedly observes that this could be inhibited by increasingly intrusive health and safety regulations.

LOCAL INDUSTRY

During the past forty years tourism has become a major industry in Galloway. It had existed in a small way since the arrival of the motor car at

the turn of the century, when Captain C. L. Orr-Ewing of Dunskey built the
Portpatrick Hotel in 1905 to cater for the wealthy few who were accustomed
to holiday in style. Mass tourism, however, began in the 1950s with the rise
in private car ownership, as this enabled people to travel further afield for
their holidays, while the expansion of the motorway system has rendered
Galloway increasingly accessible to the large population centres of
Lancashire and the Midlands. With its 200-odd miles of coastline it is an
ideal place for family holidays, and enterprising people began to develop
caravan parks and holiday centres to attract visitors to the region. In fact
caravans were popularly regarded as the farmers' most profitable crop,
while the demand for 'bed and breakfast' accommodation provided those
living near the main tourist routes with the chance to earn a second
income.

The potential benefits to the regional economy soon became apparent,
and this led to the establishment in the late 1950s of the South-West Tourist
Board, which was jointly financed by those involved in the industry and the
local county councils. Following the regionalisation of local government in
1975, the new district councils were placed under a statutory requirement
to promote tourism, and the Dumfries and Galloway Tourist Board was set
up for this purpose. Working in association with the Scottish Tourist Board,
it was also responsible for giving grant assistance, where possible, to
projects which were designed to cater for visitors. The Forestry Commission
made a valuable contribution to the industry by providing signposted walks
and nature trails through much of its land, as well as establishing interpretation centres to acquaint visitors with the lore of the countryside, and the
need for its responsible stewardship.

When local government was reorganised again in 1996 new tourist
boards were established, and these are jointly financed by the Scottish
Office, the local council, and private individuals with an interest in promoting the industry. There is urgent need of this because, although Galloway
has much to offer visitors, its relatively high summer rainfall is undeniably
a disincentive, particularly when it is having to compete with the mass-
produced package holidays to the Mediterranean resorts, where warmth
and sunshine can nearly always be guaranteed. The local tourist industry is
responding to this by encouraging visitors to come for shorter, off-season
breaks. Galloway is also becoming an increasingly popular place for people
to retire to, which is a welcome boon to the local economy since they constitute a valuable market for local shops, services and other suppliers.

Local industry has changed significantly, and one which emerged in the
1960s is fish farming, though this has been adversely affected by acid rain
which is sterilising local lochs by killing off the fish population. Salmon-
netting and deep-sea fishing, on the other hand, have a long tradition in
Galloway, though its native scallop beds have disappeared through over-

fishing, and trawlers are now having to go further afield to the Isle of Man and up the west coast. The growth of small, specialised craft shops and cottage industries is due for the most part to incomers who are attracted to the pleasant way of life which Galloway has to offer. The incomers, whether retired or small entrepreneurs, have helped counteract the number of young people leaving the region, and in consequence population figures have remained at their present level of about 56,000 for the last three decades, though the average age has risen.

The drift away from Galloway is largely due to the lack of job opportunities in the region, and this is particularly apparent in Wigtown-shire. As unemployment is unacceptably high there, the former regional council and its successor, Dumfries and Galloway Council, have consistently tried to attract light industry with the lure of grant facilities and other financial benefits. Efforts are being made to persuade companies based elsewhere to establish subsidiary enterprises in Galloway, and local groups are being urged to set up businesses with a job-creation potential. Through the agency of the European Regional Development Fund, the European Union has set aside a huge amount of money to assist under-developed regions, and Dumfries and Galloway Enterprise was established to tap into this source. Both on its own, and jointly with the local council, as well as the European Union, it has been responsible for setting up a number of projects which are designed to help small businesses by providing training facilities in the relevant skills, and giving specialist advice through its own advisory service.

Local government

The whole structure of local government was radically transformed by the Local Government (Scotland) Act 1974, which abolished the former councils and replaced them with regional and district councils. In the south-west a new regional authority, the Dumfries and Galloway Regional Council, was set up, along with four district authorities, of which Stewartry and Wigtown District Councils covered almost the whole of Galloway. The Act also provided for the establishment of local community councils which, although they had no formal powers, were designed to act as conduits between the people living in their area and the relevant district and regional councils.

Although the former county councils have been jocularly referred to as 'colonels' juntas' on account of the number of retired military men on them, this is to do less than justice to the valuable service they rendered. Their rule may have been paternalistic, but it was not necessarily the worse for that, and it is to their credit that they delivered cheap, disinterested and efficient local government for which they received no financial reward, and in the case of Kirkcudbright County Council no reimbursement for their expenses either. However their day was done, as these councils were not equipped to exercise the hugely increased responsibilities which have been imposed on their successors. Although laudably concerned to keep local rates to a minimum, they achieved this at the cost of failing to create any foundation for the region's future prosperity, which left their successors with a considerable amount of leeway to make up.

Unfortunately regionalisation coincided with a dramatic escalation in the price of oil, and despite the fact that some 85 per cent of the regional councils' costs were funded by central government, the resulting inflation was primarily accountable for the substantial increase in the local rates which was associated with the changeover. Other factors contributed to it as well; extra staff had to be taken on to cope with the additional responsibilities imposed on these authorities, and in addition their administrative structure became top-heavy. In theory, the main object of regionalisation was to improve the efficiency of local government and to render it more responsive to the needs of the people, but in fact the opposite was the case because their hands became increasingly tied through the exercise of a more rigid and direct control by central government. Moreover, the short-comings of a two-tiered administrative structure became increasingly apparent, and this was the main reason why local government underwent a further reorganisation in April 1996, when the regional and district councils were abolished and replaced by unitary authorities. Consequently, the new Dumfries and Galloway Council is now responsible for discharging the administrative functions which were formerly exercised by five separate councils.

Housing continued to be an important responsibility, but it was fraught with difficulties, not least because of the shortage inherited from the former county councils. This was not their fault since it was the result of financial stringency, combined with a lack of materials in the immediate post-war years, and the prevailing fashion for couples to marry younger. Moreover, the problem was compounded by the need to upgrade existing houses to meet the increasingly stringent health and safety regulations. Although some attempt was made to build council housing in remote communities, mainly for the accommodation of farm- and forestry-workers, this policy was discontinued. So, local authority housing has been almost exclusively confined to the peripheries of existing settlements, and in particular the larger towns which have had to extend their boundaries to accommodate it.

Local authorities are also responsible for running a public transport system, but because car-ownership is almost universal, demand is limited, so the service has to be heavily subsidised. The shrinking passenger market, combined with competition from the growing road haulage industry, were primarily responsible for the closing down of the rail network in Galloway. This began in the 1950s with the closure of the branch lines to Portpatrick and Whithorn, but as British Rail's losses continued to escalate the government seconded Dr Beeching from ICI to carry out a supposedly independent survey as a preliminary to taking over its management and turning it into a profit-making organisation. Among the victims were the branch line to Kirkcudbright, and the line between Dumfries and Glenluce which ceased to operate in 1964. But because the decision to close the latter was based on financial considerations to the exclusion of all other criteria, its unwisdom is becoming increasingly apparent with the rising number of Irish heavy goods lorries using the A75.

An uncertain future

To speculate on Galloway's future is a hazardous exercise. At one time there were hopes that the oil reserves which were thought to exist off the Solway coast might encourage the establishment of ancillary industries in the region. However, exploration has so far proved unsuccessful, and even if oil were found it is virtually certain that, because of England's greater accessibility to the principal markets, oil-related industry and development would be drawn there rather than to Galloway. In fact, it is highly unlikely that anything other than light industry will be attracted to the region because it lacks both raw materials and the means of generating industrial power, while its relative distance from the main consumer markets is a further drawback. Even if Scottish industry were to revive under the stimulus of independence within an enlarged European Union, it is more likely to be confined to the central belt with regions like Galloway remaining peripheral to it, though perhaps deriving some spin-off benefit.

Farming has traditionally been the staple of Galloway's economy, as well as the foundation for many ancillary businesses, and in spite of its current parlous state there is every likelihood that agriculture will continue to be its keystone. Unfortunately farmers, and especially livestock rearers, have been the victims of closer integration within the European Union, for whom it has been nothing short of disastrous. As nearly all their qualifying subsidies are paid in euros, the strength of sterling has resulted in a 15 per cent drop in their gross income, yet successive governments have consistently refused to apply for funds set aside to compensate for this in case it should trigger off demands for a higher contribution to the community budget. British agriculture has been virtually surrendered to EU bureaucrats in Brussels, exposing farmers to the constant shifts in official policy and the apparent lack of any controlling direction. This, together with recurrent bouts of scaremongering, makes it impossible for them to plan ahead with either confidence or certainty.

Moreover, farmers are bedevilled by a constant flow of increasingly intrusive regulations issuing from Brussels, many of dubious relevance and all reinterpreted with added rigour by UK government officials. This applies in particular in the case of the rules regarding health and hygiene which place a considerable financial burden on livestock producers, while at the same time they are having to compete with imports from countries, including other EU member states, where lower standards are allowed to prevail. In the long run, these stem from the government's apparent policy of active discrimination against farmers in the interests of discouraging production in order to preserve market stability. However, history demonstrates the essentially cyclical nature of the farming industry, and although at present there is no discernible prospect of it happening, an upturn is bound to occur sooner or later; but when and under what circumstances this will happen is impossible to foretell.

Farmers, therefore, are being progressively reduced to the role of unpaid stewards of the countryside, so they more than anyone stand to be affected by the impact on it of an increasingly urbanised population, though this is less evident in Galloway than in the south. Nevertheless, it is likely to grow in line with an expanding and more mobile society with higher expectations and the wealth to indulge them, so a continuing public education is vital to achieve a responsible use of the countryside and all aspects relating to it. Above all, a realistic balance must be struck between a constructive response to change and the preservation of Galloway's ancient heritage and scenic beauty which constitutes its principal attraction and continues to inspire us today.

NOTES

1. *TSA* xiv, 457.
2. *Ibid.*, 196–7.
3. *Ibid.*, 167.
4. *Ibid.*, 283.
5. *Ibid.*, 256.
6. *Ibid.*, 260.
7. Wightman, *Who Owns Scotland?*
8. *TSA* xiv, 256.

BIBLIOGRAPHY

I. PUBLISHED PRIMARY SOURCES

a. RECORD SOURCES

Accounts of the Lord High Treasurer of Scotland, ed. T. Dickson and J. Balfour-Paul (Edinburgh, 1877–1916). (*TA*)

Acts of the Parliaments of Scotland, eds. T. Thomson and C. Innes, 12 vols. (Edinburgh, 1814–75). (*APS*)

Archaelogical and Historical Collections relating to Ayrshire and Galloway.

Calendar of Close Rolls 1296–1302 (London, 1892–).

Calendar of Documents Relating to Scotland vols i–iv, eds J. Bain and others, (Edinburgh 1881–8); vol. v, eds G G Simpson and J D Galbraith (Edinburgh, 1986). (*CDS*)

Calendar of Entries in the Papal Registers relating to Great Britain and Ireland: Papal Letters, eds. W H Bliss and others, 16 vols., (London, 1893–).

Calendar of the Laing Charters 854–1837, ed. J. Anderson (Edinburgh, 1899).

Calendar of Patent Rolls 1399–1441, 8 vols. (London, 1903–7).

Calendar of Papal letters to Scotland of Clement VII of Avignon 1378–94, eds. C Burns and A. I. Dunlop, *SHS* 1976. (*CPS* i)

Calendar of Papal letters to Scotland of Benedict XIII of Avignon 1399–1419. (*CPS* ii)

Calendar of Scottish Supplications to Rome, vol i, eds. A. I. Cameron and E. R. Lindsay *SHS*, 1934. (*CSSR* i)

Calendar of Scottish Supplications to Rome, vol ii, ed. A. I. Dunlop *SHS*, 1956. (*CSSR* ii).

Documents and Records illustrating the History of Scotland, ed. F. Palgrave (Record Commission, 1827–).

Documents illustrative of the History of Scotland 1286–1306, 2 vols, ed. J. Stevenson (Edinburgh, 1870).

Exchequer Rolls of Scotland, eds, J. Stuart and others, 23 vols. (Edinburgh, 1878–1908). (*ER*)

Feodora, Conventiones, Litterae et Cuiuscunque Generiis Acta Publica, 20 vols, ed. T. Rymer, Record Commission edn. (London, 1816–69).

Liber Cartarum Sancte Crucis (Bannatyne Club, 1840).

Liber Sancte Marie de Dryburgh (Bannatyne Club, 1847).

Liber Sancte Marie de Melros (Bannatyne Club, 1837).

Regesta Regum Scotorum: Acts of Malcolm IV 1153–65, ed. G. W. S. Barrow (Edinburgh, 1960) (*RRS* i).

Regesta Regum Scotorum: Acts of William I 1165–1214, ed. G. W. S. Barrow (Edinburgh, 1971) (*RRS* ii).

Regesta Regum Scotorum handlists: Acts of Alexander II 1214–1249, ed. J. M. Scoular (Edinburgh, 1959) (*RRS* iii.).

Regesta Regum Scotorum handlists: Acts of Alexander III, the Guardians and John 1249–1296, ed G. G. Simpson (Edinburgh, 1960) (*RRS* iv).

Regesta Regum Scotorum: Acts of Robert I 1306–29, ed A. A. M. Duncan (Edinburgh, 1988) (*RRS* v).

Regesta Regum Scotorum: Acts of David II 1329–71, ed B. Webster (Edinburgh, 1982) (*RRS* vi).

Register of the Privy Council of Scotland, eds. J. H. Burton and others (Edinburgh 1877–).(*RPC*).

Register and Records of Holm Cultram, eds. F. Grainger and W. G. Collingwood, in Cumberland and Westmorland Antiquarian and Archaeological Society, Record ser. (1929).

Registrum Magni Sigilli Regum Scotorum, eds. J. M. Thomson and others, 11 vols. (Edinburgh, 1877–1914). (*RMS*)

Registrum Honoris de Morton, (Bannatyne Club, 1853).

Registrum Secreti Sigilli Regum Scotorum, eds. M. Livingstone and others (Edinburgh, 1908–) (*RSS*)

Rotuli Scotiae in Turri Londinensi et in Domo Capitulari Westmonasterii Asservati i–ii, ed. D. Macpherson and others (London, 1814–9).

Scottish Historical Documents, ed. G. Donaldson (Edinburgh, 1970).

b. NARRATIVE AND LITERARY SOURCES

Anderson, A.O., ed, *Early Sources of Scottish History 500 to 1286*, 2 vols (London, 1908, republished Stamford, 1990).

Anderson, A.O., ed. *Scottish Annals from English Chroniclers AD 500–1286* (do.)

Androw of Wyntoun's 'Orygynale Cronykil of Scotland', ed. D.Laing (Edinburgh, 1879).

Auchinleck Chronicle, ane schort Memoriale of the Scottis croniklis for Addicioun, ed. T. Thomson (Edinburgh, 1891–77).

Barbour, 'The Bruce', ed. W.M. Menzie, ed. (London, 1908).

Bede, *Historia Ecclesiastica gentis Anglorum*, eds & trans., B. Colgrave and R. A. B. Mynors (Oxford, 1969).

Brevis Descriptio Regni Scotie (Maitland Club, 1847).

Chronica Magistri Rogeri de Houedon, ed. W. Stubbs (London, 1868–71).

Chronica Regum Mannie et Insularum, trans. G. Broderick (Belfast, 1979).

Chronica Rogeri de Hovedon, ed. W. Stubbs (London, 1869).

Chronicle de Lanercost (Maitland Club, 1839).

Chronicle of Lanercost 1272–1346, trans. H. Maxwell (Glasgow, 1913).

Chronicle of Melrose, ed. A.O. Anderson in Early Sources of Scottish History (London, 1936: republished Stamford, 1990).

Chronicle of Man, ed. A.O. Anderson in Early Sources of Scottish History (do.).

Chronicle of Man, trans. J. Stevenson in Church Historians of England vol. iv (London, 1835–8).

Chronicle of Man and the Sudreys, eds. P. A. Munch and D. Gross (Manx Society, Douglas, 1874).

Chronicle of Pierre de Langtoft, 2 vols, ed. T. Wright, Rolls Series 47 (London, 1866–8).

Chronicle of Walter of Guisborough, ed. H. Rothwell (Camden Society, 1957).

Criminal Trials in Scotland from 1488 to 1624, ed. R. Pitcairn, (Edinburgh, 1833).

Froissart 'Chroniques', ed. J. Joliffe, (London, 1948).

Gesta regis Henrici Secundi Benedicti abbatis (Benedict of Peterborough) in The chronicle of the reigns of Henry II and Richard I, A D 1169–1192), ed. W. Stubbs, rolls series, 2 vols. 1867.

Historie and Cronicles of Scotland by Robert Lindsay of Pitscottie, ed A. J. G. Mackay (Edinburgh, 1899).

Historie of the Reformatioun of Religioun in the Realme of Scotland by John Knox, eds Thomasson and Pullen (Edinburgh, 1732).

Historie of the Reformatioun of Religioun within the Realm of Scotland by John Knox, ed. R. S. Walker (Edinburgh, 1940).

John of Fordoun's Chronicle of The Scottish Nation, Historians of Scotland series, ed. W. F. Skene, (Edinburgh, 1871).

Jordan Fantosme's chronicle, ed. R.C. Johnston, (Oxford, 1981).

Lawrie, A. C., ed. *Annals of the reigns of Malcolm and William, kings of Scotland* (Glasgow, 1905).

Lawrie, A. C., ed. *Early Scottish Charters prior to 1153* (Glasgow, 1905).

Legends of SS Ninian and Machor, ed. W. M. Metcalfe, (Paisley, 1904).

Lesley, History of Scotland from the Death of King James I in the Year 1436 to the Year 1561, (Bannatyne Club, 1830).

Mair, John, *History of Greater Britain* (Scottish History Society, 1892).

Matthew Paris in A. O. Anderson, Early Sources of Scottish History (London, 1936: republished Stamford, 1990).

Minute Book kept by the War Committee of the Covenanters in the Stewartry of Kirkcudbright for the years 1640 and 1641, (Kirkcudbright, 1855).

Orygynale Cronikil of Androw of Wyntoun, ed. F. J. Amours (Edinburgh, 1907).

Protocol Book of James Young 1485–1515, ed. G. Donaldson, Scottish Records Society (1952).

Reginald Monachi Dunelmensis Libellus de Admirandis Beati Cuthberti Virtutibus (Surtees Society, 1835).

Register of the Priory of St Bees, ed. J. Wilson (Surtees Society, 1915).

Reid, R. C., *Wigtownshire Charters*, SHS third series vol. li (Edinburgh, 1960).

Relatio Venerabilis Aelredi Abbatis Rievallensis de Standardo, ed. R. Howlett.

Richard of Hexham, De Gestis Regis Stephani et de Bello Standardii, in R. Howlett, ed., Chronicles of Stephen etc. (London, 1884–89).

Robert Lindsay of Pitscottie, 'The Historie and Cronicles of Scotland', Scottish Text Society, 3 vols. (Edinburgh, 1899–1911).

Saga of Hacon in Icelandic Sagas, ed. G. W. Dasent, Rolls series, 1894.

St Bernard de Clairvaux, 'Life of St Malachy', ed. H. J. Lawler SPCK, (1920).

Scalachronica by Sir Thomas Grey of Heton, Knight, J. Stevenson, ed. (Maitland Club, 1836).

Scottish Chronicle known as the Chronicle of Holyrood, ed. M. O. Anderson (SHS, 1938).

Symeonis Monachi opera, ed. T. Arnold, (London, 1882–5).

Walter Bower, Scottichronicon, ed. D. E. R. Watt, 9 vols. (Aberdeen, 1996).

Walter Daniel, The Life of Ailred of Rievaulx, ed. F. M. Powicke, (London, 1950).

Willelmi Malmesbiriensis Monachi, 'de Gestis Pontificum Anglorum', Libri Quinque in J. Stevenson, ed., Church Historians of England (London, 1854).

Willelmi Rishanger, Chronica et Annales, ed. H. T. Riley , Rolls series, 1865.

William of Newburgh, Historiam Rerum Anglicarum, in Chronicles of Stephen etc., ed. R. Howlett (London, 1884–9).

II. REFERENCE WORKS

The Scots Peerage, ed. Sir J. Balfour-Paul, 8 vols. (Edinburgh, 1904–11).

The Complete Peerage, eds H. A. Doubleday and Lord Howard de Walden, 13 vols. (London, 1940).

Burke's Peerage, 105th edn. (London, 1970).

Burke's Landed Gentry, 15th edn. (London, 1937).

Burke's Landed Gentry, 18th edn. 3 vols. (London, 1969).
Europaïschen Stammtafeln, eds. Isenburg and others (Marburg, 1989).

III. SECONDARY SOURCES

a. BOOKS

Agnew, A., *The Hereditary Sheriffs of Galloway*, (Edinburgh, 1864).
Agnew, A., *The Hereditary Sheriffs of Galloway*, 2 vols. (Edinburgh, 1893).
Anderson, M. O., *Kings and Kingship in Early Ireland* (Edinburgh, 1978).
Armit, I., *Celtic Scotland*, Historic Scotland series (Edinburgh,1997).
Ashley, M., *The Life and Times of King John* (London, 1972).
Ashmore, P. J., *Neolithic and Bronze Age Scotland*, Historic Scotland series (London, 1996).
Barrow, G. W. S., *The Anglo-Norman Era in Scottish History* (Oxford, 1980).
Barrow, G. W. S., *Kingship and Unity: Scotland 1000–1306* (London, 1981).
Barrow, G. W. S., *Robert Bruce and the Community of the Realm of Scotland* (Edinburgh, 1988).
Barrow, G. W. S., *Kingdom of the Scots, 'The Justiciar', Government, Church and Society, from the Eleventh Century to the Fourteenth Century* (Edinburgh, 1973).
Bartlett, R., *The Making of Europe, Conquest, Colonisation and Cultural Change 950–1350* (London, 1993).
Boardman, S., *The Early Stewart kings: Robert II and Robert III 1371–1406*, the Stewart dynasty in Scotland series (East Linton, 1996).
Breeze, D. J., *Roman Scotland*, Historic Scotland series (London, 1996).
Brooke, D., *Wild Men and Holy Places* (Edinburgh, 1994).
Brown, J. M., *Scottish Society in the Fifteenth Century* (London, 1977).
Brown, M., *James I*, Stewart dynasty in Scotland series (Edinburgh, 1994).
Brown, M., *The Black Douglases: War and Lordship in Late Medieval Scotland 1300–1455*, (East Linton, 1998).
Buchan, W., *Domestic Medicine* (London, 1772).
Burleigh, J. H. S., *A Church History of Scotland* (Oxford, 1961).
Cameron, J., *James V: The Personal Rule 1528–1542*, Stewart Dynasty in Scotland series (East Linton, 1998).
Campbell, R. H., *Owners and Occupiers: Changes in Rural Society in South-West Scotland before 1914* (Aberdeen, 1991).
Christie, A. H., *The Abbey of Dundrennan* (Dalbeattie, 1914).
Cowan, I. B., *The Scottish Reformation: Church and Society in Sixteenth-century Scotland* (London, 1982).
Cowan, I. B., *The Medieval Church in Scotland*, ed. J Kirk (Edinburgh, 1995).
Cowan, I. B., *The Scottish Covenanters 1660–88* (London, 1976).
Cowan, I. B. and Easson, D. E., *Medieval Religious Houses in Scotland* (New York, 1976).
Croft Dickinson, W., *Scotland from the Earliest Times to 1603* (Oxford, 1977).
Delaney, F., *The Celts* (London, 1989).
Devlin, I., *Albanach: History of the Galloway Rifle Volunteers* ed. J. Carter (Wigtown, 1996).
Dick, C. H., *Highways and Byways in Galloway and Carrick* (London 1916: republished Wakefield, 1972).

Dilworth, M., *Scottish Monasteries in the Late Middle Ages* (Edinburgh, 1995).

Dodghson, R. A., *Land and Society in Early Scotland* (London, 1981).

Donaldson, G., *Scotland: James V – James VII*, Edinburgh History of Scotland series (Edinburgh, 1965).

Donnachie, I., *Industrial Archaeology of South West Scotland* (Newton Abbot, 1971).

Donnachie, I. and McLeod, I., *Old Galloway* (Newton Abbot, 1974).

Dow, F. D., *Cromwellian Scotland 1651–1660* (Edinburgh, 1979).

Duncan, A. A. M., *Scotland: the Making of a Kingdom*, Edinburgh History of Scotland series (Edinburgh, 1975).

Ekwall, E., *Concise Oxford Dictionary of English Place-names* (Oxford, 1960).

Ferguson, W., *Scotland 1689 to the Present*, Edinburgh History of Scotland series (Edinburgh, 1968).

Fergusson, J., *Lowland Lairds* (London, 1949).

Flinn, M., ed., *Scottish Population History from the Seventeenth century to the 1930s* (Cambridge, 1977).

Foster, S. M., *Picts Gaels and Scots*, Historic Scotland series (Edinburgh, 1996).

Fraser, A., *Mary Queen of Scots* (London, 1969).

Fraser, W., *The Book of Carlaverock* (Edinburgh, 1873).

Gardiner, S. R., *History of the Commonwealth and the Protectorate* (London, 1877–1901).

Gifford, J., *Buildings in Dumfries and Galloway* (London, 1996).

Grant, I. F., *Social and Economic Development of Scotland before 1603* (Edinburgh, 1930).

Gray A., *White Gold?* (Wigtown, 1995).

Gray, J. M., *Lord Selkirk of Red River* (London 1963).

Haldane, A. R. B., *The Drove Roads of Scotland* (Edinburgh, 1952).

Heron, R., *Observations made in a journey through the western counties of Scotland in the Autumn of 1792*, 2 vols. (Perth, 1793).

Hewison, J. K., *The Covenanters: A History of the Church in Scotland from the Reformation to the Revolution*, 2 vols. (Edinburgh, 1908).

Higham, N. J., *The Kingdom of Northumbria AD 230–1100* (Stroud, 1993).

Hill, P. H., *Whithorn & St Ninian* (Stroud, 1997).

Hutchison, I. G. C., *A Political History of Scotland, 1832–1924* (Edinburgh, 1986).

Innes, C., *Lectures on Scottish Legal Antiquities* (Edinburgh, 1872).

Kapelle, W. E., *The Norman Conquest of the North, The Region and its Transformation* (U.S.A., 1979).

Lamb, H. H., *Climate – Present, Past and Future* (London, 1977).

Lawlor, H. C., *A History of the Family of Cairnes or Cairns and its Connections* (London, 1906).

Lenman, B., *An Economic History of Modern Scotland 1660–1976* (London, 1977).

Lynch, M., *Scotland: A New History* (London, 1991).

Macdougall, N., *James III: a Political Study* (Edinburgh, 1982).

Macdougall, N., *James IV*, Stewart dynasty of Scotland series (Edinburgh, 1997).

McDowall, W., *History of Dumfries* (Dumfries, 1906: republished Wakefield, 1972).

McGladdery, C., *James II*, Stewart Dynasty of Scotland series (Edinburgh, 1990).

McKerlie, P. H., *Lands and their Owners in Galloway* (Edinburgh, 1877: republished Wigtown, 1994).

Macky, J., *A Journey Through Scotland*, 3 vols. (London, 1723).

McNamee, C., *The Wars of the Bruces – Scotland, England and Ireland 1306–1328* (East Linton, 1997).

Macquarrie, A., *The Saints of Scotland: Essays in Scottish Church History AD 450–1093* (Edinburgh, 1997).

Maxwell, H., *A History of Dumfries and Galloway* (Edinburgh, 1896).

Maxwell-Wood, J., *Witchcraft in South-West Scotland* (Edinburgh, 1975).

Montgomery, B. G. de, *Origin and History of the Montgomerys* (Edinburgh, 1948).

Nicholson, R., *The Later Middle Ages*, Edinburgh History of Scotland series (Edinburgh, 1974).

Oram, R. D., *Scottish Prehistory* (Edinburgh, 1997).

Oram, R. D., *The Lordship of Galloway c.900 to c.1300* (forthcoming, 2000).

Poole, A. L., *Doomsday Book to Magna Carta 1087–1216*, Oxford History of England series (Oxford, 1955).

Powicke, F. M., *King Henry III and the Lord Edward* (Oxford, 1947).

Prestwich, M., *Edward I* (Los Angeles, 1988).

Ridley, J., *Henry VIII* (London, 1984).

Rivet, A. L. F. and Smith, C.C., *The Place-names of Roman Britain* (London, 1979).

Roberts, I. G., *Towers of Stone – The Fortified Buildings of Dumfries and Galloway* (Dumfries & Galloway Regional Council, 1993).

Robinson, S., *Reminiscences of Wigtownshire* (Hamilton, 1872).

Ross, A., *The Pagan Celts* (Chichester, 1986).

Saltway, P., *Roman Britain*, Oxford History of England series (Oxford, 1982).

Skene, W. F., *Celtic Scotland*, 2 vols. (Edinburgh, 1890).

Smith, S., *Agricultural Survey of Galloway* (London, 1810).

Smout, T. C., *A History of the Scottish People 1560–1830* (London, 1969).

Stephen, W., *History of the Scottish Church*, 2 vols. (Edinburgh, 1894).

Stevenson, C. D., *Revolution and Counter Revolution in Scotland 1644–1651* (London, 1977).

Stewart, F. J., *The Early Stewarts of Shambellie 1550–1700* (Edinburgh, 1997).

Stenton, F., *Anglo-Saxon England*, Oxford History of England series (Oxford, 1968).

Symon, J. A., *Scottish Farming Past and Present* (Edinburgh, 1959).

Symson, A., *A Large Description of Galloway* (1684), (Edinburgh, 1823).

Torrance, D. R., *The McClellans in Galloway* (the Genealogy Society, 1993).

Thomas, A. C., *Britain and Ireland in Early Christian Times AD 400–800* (London, 1971).

Thomas, A. C., *Celtic Britain* (London, 1986).

Thomas, A. C., *Christianity in Roman Britain to AD 500* (London, 1981).

Thomas, A. C., in *The Early Christian Archaeology of Northern Britain* (Oxford, 1971).

Trotter, R. de B., *Galloway Gossip* (Dumfries, 1901).

Watson, F., *Under the Hammer: Edward I and Scotland 1286–1307* (East Linton, 1998).

Watson, W. J., *History of the Celtic Place-names of Scotland* (Edinburgh, 1926).

Webster, J., *General View of the Agriculture of Galloway* (Edinburgh, 1794).

Wickham-Jones, C. R., *Scotland's First Settlers*, Historic Scotland series (Edinburgh, 1994).

Wightman, A., *Who Owns Scotland?* (Aberdeen, 1996).

Wodrow, R., *History of the Sufferings of the Church of Scotland* (1721).

Young, A, *Robert the Bruce's Rivals: The Comyns, 1212–1314* (East Linton, 1997).

b. Unpublished book

McCulloch, W. J., *A History of the Galloway families of McCulloch* (1964) (available in the Ewart Library, Dumfries)

c. Statistical accounts

The Statistical Account of Scotland, ed. Sir J. Sinclair, 21 vols. (Edinburgh, 1791–9). (*OSA*).

The New Statistical Account, 15 vols. (Edinburgh, 1845). (*NSA*).
The Third Statistical Account of Scotland, eds. M. C. Arnott and others. (Glasgow, 1951–92). (*TSA*)

d. ARTICLES

Abbreviations:

PSAS	Proceedings of the Society of Antiquaries of Scotland (1851–)
RCAHMS	Royal Commission on the Ancient and Historic Monuments of Scotland
SHR	Scottish Historical Review
SHS	Scottish History Society
TDGNHAS	Transactions of the Dumfries and Galloway Natural History and Antiquarian Society (third series)

Anderson, A. D., 'The development of the road system in the Stewartry of Kirkcudbright 1590–1890' *TDGNHAS,* lxiv (1967).

Anderson, A. D., 'The development of the road system in the Stewartry of Kirkcudbright, 1590–1890' part II *TDGNHAS,* xlv (1968).

Arnott, M. C., 'The military road to Portpatrick 1763' *TDGNHAS,* xxviii (1949–50).

Ash, M., 'The Church in the Reign of Alexander III' in Reid ed., *Scotland in the Reign of Alexander III.*

Ashley, A., 'Odo, elect of Whithorn 1235' *TDGNHAS,* xxxvii (1958–9).

Backmund, N., 'The Premonstratensian order in Scotland', *Innes Review* (1953).

Birks, H. H., 'Studies in the vegetational history of Scotland: two pollen diagrams from the Galloway hills, Kirkcudbrightshire', *Journal of Ecology* lx (1972).

Bishop, W. W. and Coope, G. R., 'Stratigraphical and faunal evidence for the late-glacial and early Flandrian environments in south-west Scotland' in Gray, J. M. and Lowe, J. J., eds, *Studies in the Scottish Late-glacial Environment* (London, 1977).

Brooke, D., 'The Northumbrian settlements in Galloway and Carrick: an historical assessment' *PSAS,* 121 (1991).

Brooke, D., 'The deanery of the Desnes Cro and the church of Edingham' *TDGNHAS,* lxiii (1987).

Brooke, D., 'Fergus of Galloway: miscellaneous notes for a revised portrait' *TDGNHAS,* lxvi (1993).

Brooke, D., 'Gall-gaidhil and Galloway' in Oram, R. D. and Stell, G. P., eds, *Galloway: Land and Lordship* (Edinburgh, 1991).

Brooke, D., 'The Glenkens 1275–1456: snapshots of a medieval countryside' *TDGNHAS,* lix (1984).

Cameron, S. and Ross, A., 'The Treaty of Edinburgh and the Disinherited (1328–1332)' *History,* vol. 84 (1999).

Cameron Smith, A., 'Wallace's capture of Sanquhar and the rising in the south-west' *TDGNHAS,* xi (1923–4).

Campbell, R. H., 'Agricultural Labour in the South-West' in Devine, T. M., ed., *Farm Servants and Labour in Lowland Scotland 1770–1914* (Edinburgh, 1984).

Cessford, C., 'Pictish raiders at Trusty's Hill' *TDGNHAS,* lxix (1994).

Clancy J., 'Taliesin, The Battle of Gwen Ystrad' in Clancy, T O, ed., *The Triumph Tree: Scotland's Earliest Poetry AD 550–1350* (Edinburgh, 1998).

Corcoran, J. X. W. P., 'Excavation of a chambered cairn at Mid Gleniron Farm, Wigtownshire: Interim Report *TGDHNAS,* xli (1962/3).

Corcoran, J. X. W. P., 'Excavation of a chambered cairn at Mid Gleniron Farm,

Wigtownshire: Second Interim Report *TDGNHAS*, xlv (1968).

Cormack, W. F., 'A mesolithic site at Barsalloch, Wigtownshire' *TDGNHAS*, xlvii (1970).

Cormack, W. F. and Coles J.M., 'A mesolithic site at Low Clone, Wigtownshire' *TDGNHAS*, xlv (1968).

Cormack, W. F. and others, 'Barhobble, Mochrum – excavations of a forgotten church site in Galloway' *TDGNHAS*, lxx (1995).

Cowan, E. J., 'The Vikings in Galloway: a review of the evidence' in Oram, R. D. and Stell, G. P., eds, *Galloway, Land and Lordship* (Edinburgh, 1991).

Cowan, E. J., 'Agricultural improvement and the formation of early agricultural societies in Dumfries and Galloway' *TDGNHAS*, liii (1977–8).

Cowan, I. B., 'Church and Society' in Brown, J. M., ed., *Scottish Society in the Fifteenth Century* (London, 1977).

Cowie, T. G. and others, 'Torrs Warren, Luce Sands, Galloway: a report on archaeological and palaeoecological investigations undertaken in 1977 and 1979' *TDGNHAS*, lxxi (1996).

Craig, D. J., 'Pre-Norman sculpture in Galloway: some territorial implications' in Oram, R. D. and Stell, G. P., eds, *Galloway, Land and Lordship* (Edinburgh, 1991).

Donaldson, G., 'The Galloway Clergy at the Reformation' *TDGNHAS*, xxx (1951–2).

Donaldson, G., 'Alexander Gordon, Bishop of Galloway (1559–1575) and his work in the Reformed Church' *TDGNHAS*, xxiv (1945–6).

Donaldson, G., 'The bishops and priors of Whithorn' *TDGNHAS*, xxvii (1948–9)

Donnachie, I., 'The lime industry in south-west Scotland' *TDGNHAS*, xlviii (1971).

Duncan, A. A. M. and Brown, A. L., 'Argyll and the Isles in the Later Middle Ages' *PSAS*, xc (1956–7).

Easson, D.E., 'The nunneries of Galloway' *TDGNHAS*, xxiii (1940–44).

Easson, D.E., 'The Lollards of Kyle' *Juridical Review*, xlviii (1936).

Edwards, K. and others 'New mesolithic sites in south-west Scotland and their importance as indicators of inland penetration' *TDGNHAS*, lviii (1983).

Feacham, R., 'Ancient agriculture in the high land of Britain' *PSAS*, xxxviii (1972).

Fellows-Jensen, G., 'Scandinavians in Dumfriesshire and Galloway: the place-name evidence' in Oram, R. D. and Stell, G. P., eds, *Galloway, Land and Lordship* (Edinburgh, 1991).

Gillon, S. A., 'The Hathorns of Meikle Airies' *TDGNHAS*, xiv (1926–8).

Gough Cooper, H., 'Some notes on the name Ninian' *TDGNHAS*, lxxii (1997).

Haggarty, A. and G., 'Excavations at Rispain camp, Whithorn' *TDGNHAS*, lviii (1983).

Hawkins, J., 'Numismatic Report' in *Interim Report on Botel bailey* (1995).

Henshall, A. S., 'Report on cloth associated with a socketed axe from Luce Sands' in Penney, S. H., 'Unpublished finds from Luce Sands *TDGNHAS*, li (1975).

Herries, D. C., 'John Maxwell of Newlaw, sometime Provost of Dumfries' *TDGNHAS*, x (1922–3).

Hill, P. H. and Kucharski, 'Early medieval ploughing at Whithorn and the chronology of plough pebbles' *TDGNHAS*, lxiv (1989).

Hingley, R., 'Society in Scotland from 700 BC to 200 AD' *PSAS*, vol 122 (1992).

Holland, W., 'The New Abbey Poor's fund' *TDGNHAS*, lxiv (1989).

Hoek, M. A. M. van, 'Prehistoric rock art of Galloway', *TDGNHAS*, lxi (1986).

Hope-Taylor, B., 'Excavations at Mote of Urr: Interim Report 1951' *TDGNHAS*, xxix (1951–2).

Hunter, F., 'Dowalton loch re-considered' *TDGNHAS*, lxix (1994).

Jardine, G., 'Holocene raised coastal settlements and former shorelines in

Dumfriesshire and eastern Galloway' *TDGNHAS*, lv (1980).

Laing, L., 'The Angles in Scotland and the Mote of Mark' *TDGNHAS*, l (1973).

Lidderdale, J. D., 'A tax-roll for the priory of St. Mary's Isle' *TDGNHAS*, lii (1976).

Lythe, S. G. E, 'Economic Life' in Brown, J M, ed., *Scottish Society in the Fifteenth Century* (London, 1977).

McEwan, H., 'A Theolog Solempne: Thomas de Rossy, Bishop of Galloway' *Innes Review*, viii (1910).

McKerrow, M. H., 'Sweetheart abbey' *TDGNHAS*, xviii (1931–3).

McMichael, T., 'The feudal family of de Soulis' *TDGNHAS*, xxvi (1947–8).

Macquarrie, A., 'The Kings of Strathclyde' in Grant, A. and Stringer, K. J., eds *Medieval Scotland: Crown, Lordship and Community* (Edinburgh, 1993).

MacQueen, H. L., 'The Kin of Kennedy, 'Kenkynnol', and the common law' in Grant, A. and Stringer, K. J., eds, *Medieval Scotland: Crown, Lordship and Community* (Edinburgh, 1993).

MacQueen, J., 'Yvain, Ewen and Owein ap Urien' *TDGNHAS*, xxxiii (1954/5).

Maxwell, Sir H., 'The Tour of Mary Queen of Scots in the south-west of Scotland, August 1563' *TDGNHAS*, x (1922–3).

Maxwell-Irving, A. M. T., Kenmure Castle' *TDGNHAS*, lxvi (1991).

Mayewski, P. A. and others, 'Climate change events as seen in the Greenland ice core: Implications for the Mesolithic in Scotland' in Pollard, T. and Morrison, A., eds *The Early Prehistory of Scotland* (Edinburgh, 1996).

Maynard, D. and others, 'The dune system at Brighouse Bay' *TGNHAS*, lxix (1994).

Miller, D., 'Interim Report on lithic assemblies from Botel bailey 1992–4'.

Morrison, A., 'Cinerary urns and pygmy vessels in south-west Scotland' *TDGNHAS*, xlv (1968).

Morrison, I. A., 'Galloway: locality and landscape evolution' in Oram, R. D. and Stell, G. P., eds *Galloway, Land and Lordship* (Edinburgh, 1991).

Morton, A. S., 'Glenluce Abbey' *TDGNHAS*, xxi (1936–8).

Morton, A. S., 'Craichlaw: its history and its owners' *TDGNHAS*, xxi (1936–8).

Morton, A. S., 'Carscreugh Castle' *TDGNHAS*, xix (1934–5).

Morton, A. S., 'The levellers of Galloway' *TDGNHAS*, xix (1933–5).

Murray, A., 'The Crown lands in Galloway 1456–1543' *TDGNHAS*, xxxvii (1958–9).

Murray, A., 'The Customs Accounts of Kirkcudbright, Wigtown and Dumfries 1434–1560' *TDGNHAS*, xl (1961–2).

Murray, A., 'The Customs Accounts of Dumfries and Kirkcudbright 1560–1660' *TDGNHAS*, xlii (1965).

Murray, J., 'The stone circles of Wigtownshire' *TDGNHAS*, lvi (1981).

Nicholson, R., 'A sequel to Edward Bruce's invasion of Ireland' *SHR*, xlii (1963).

Oram, R. D., 'The mythical Picts and the monastic pedant: the origin of the legend of the Galloway Picts' *Pictish Arts Society Journal* 4, Autumn 1993 edn.

Oram, R. D., 'Scandinavian settlement in south-west Scotland with a special study of Bysbie' in Crawford, B. E., ed. *Scandinavian Settlement in Northern Britain* (Leicester, 1995).

Oram, R. D., 'In obedience and reverence: Whithorn and York c.1128 – c.1250' *The Innes Review* xlii, no 2 (1991).

Oram, R. D., 'Fergus, Galloway and the Scots', in Oram, R.D. and Stell, G.P., eds *Galloway, Land and Lordship* (Edinburgh, 1991).

Oram, R. D., 'A family business? Colonisation and Settlement in twelfth- and thirteenth-century Galloway' *SHS*, lxxxii (1993).

Oram, R. D., 'Heirs to Ninian: The medieval bishops of Whithorn (c.1100–1560) in McCluskey, R., ed. *A History of the Medieval Diocese of Whithorn and the Diocese of*

Galloway in Modern Times (Ayr, 1997).

Oram, R. D., 'Dervorgilla, the Balliols and Buittle' *TDGNHAS,* lxxiii (1999).

Oram, R. D., 'Bruce, Balliol and the lordship of Galloway' *TDGNHAS,* lxvii (1992).

Piggott, S., 'Three metal-work hoards from the Roman period in southern Scotland' *PSAS,* vol 57 (1952).

Prevost, W. A. J., 'The Solway smugglers and the customs port of Dumfries' *TDGNHAS,* li (1975).

Prevost, W. A. J., ed., 'Letters reporting the rising of the levellers in 1724' *TGNHAS,* xliv (1967).

Prevost, W. A. J., ed., 'Sir John Clerk's journie to Galloway in 1721' *TDGNHAS,* xli (1962/3).

Prevost, W. A. J., ed., 'Sir John Clerk's journie to Galloway in 1735' *TDGNHAS,* xlii (1965).

Radford, C. A. R., 'Excavations at Whithorn: final report' *TDGNHAS,* xxxiv (1955–6).

Reid, N. H., 'Crown and Community under Robert I' in Grant, A. and Stringer, K.J., eds *Medieval Scotland: Crown, Lordship and Community* (Edinburgh, 1993).

Reid, R. C., 'The Ventidius stone, Kirkmaiden' *TDGNHAS,* xxxvi (1957–8).

Reid, R. C., 'The Mote of Urr' *TDGNHAS,* xxi (1936–8).

Reid, R. C., 'Myrton castle' *TDGNHAS* , xxi (1936/8).

Reid, R. C., 'The family of Glendonyng' *TDGNHAS,* xxii (1938–40).

Reid, R. C., 'Dunskey Castle' *TDGNHAS,* xxi (1936–8).

Reid, R. C., 'Soulseat' *TDGNHAS,* xvii (1930–1).

Reid, R. C., 'Physgill' *TDGNHAS,* xxviii (1949–50).

Reid, R. C., 'The Priory of St. Mary's Isle' *TDGNHAS,* xxxvi (1957–8).

Reid, R. C., 'The Culvennan Writs' *TDGNHAS,* x (1922–3).

Richmond, I. A. and St Joseph, J. K., 'The Roman fort at Glenlochar, Kirkcudbrightshire', *TDGNHAS,* xxx (1951–2).

Ritchie, J., 'Plague in Dumfries' *TDGNHAS,* xxi (1936–8).

Ritchie, J. N. G., 'Beaker pottery in south-west Scotland' *TDGNHAS,* xlvii (1970).

Ritchie, J. N. G. and Shepherd, A. G., 'Beaker pottery and associated artefacts in south-west Scotland' *TDGNHAS,* xlx (1973).

Robison, J., 'The Greyfriars and the Moat Brae' *TDGNHAS,* iv (1915–6).

St. Joseph, J. K., 'The Roman fortlet at Gatehouse of Fleet' in Hartley and Wacher, eds *Rome and her Northern Provinces.*

Sanderson, M. H. B., 'The Feuars of Kirklands' *SHS,* vol. 52 (1973):

Scott, J. G., 'The partition of Strathclyde 1092–1153' *TDGNHAS,* lxxii (1997).

Scott, J. G., 'The origins of Dundrennan and Soulseat abbeys' *TDGNHAS,* lxiii (1988).

Scott, J. G., 'An early sheriff of Dumfries?' *TDGNHAS,* lvii (1982).

Scott-Elliot, J., 'McCulloch's castle, Arbigland' *TDGNHAS,* xli (1962–3).

Shirley, G. W., 'Two pioneer Galloway agriculturalists – Robert Maxwell of Arkland and William Craik of Arbigland' *TDGNHAS,* xiii (1925–6).

Shirley, W. G., 'The End of the Greyfriars' Convent of Dumfries and the last of the Friars' *TDGNHAS,* i (1912–3).

Smith, A. C., 'Alexander Stewart, younger of Garlies and Dalswinton, the Reformer' *TDGNHAS,* xiv (1926–8).

Smith, I. M., 'Balsarroch House, Wigtownshire' *TDGNHAS,* lx (1985).

Smout, T. C., 'Foreign trade in Dumfries and Galloway' *TDGNHAS,* xxxvii (1958/9).

Spikins, P., 'Rivers, boundaries and change: A hypothesis of changing settlement patterns in the Mesolithic of northern England' in Pollard, T. and Morrison, A., eds *The Early Prehistory of Scotland* (Edinburgh, 1996).

Stewart, F. J., 'Sweetheart Abbey and its owners over the centuries' *TDGNHAS*, lxiv (1989).

Stewart, F. J. and Reid, R. C., 'The Early Browns in New Abbey' *TDGNHAS*, xxxvii (1958–9).

Stewart, O. M. & Cormack, W. F., 'The present botany of a former medieval site: a checklist of plants at Barhobble, Mochrum' in 'Barhobble, Mochrum – excavations of a forgotten church site in Galloway' *TDGNHAS*, lxx (1995).

Stringer, K. J., 'Periphery and core in thirteenth-century Scotland: Alan son of Roland, lord of Galloway in Grant, A. and Stringer, K. J., eds *Medieval Scotland: Crown, Lordship and Community* (Edinburgh, 1993).

Stringer, K. J., 'A new wife for Alan of Galloway' *TDGNHAS*, xlix (1972).

Tabraham, C. J., 'Norman settlement in Galloway' in Breeze, D. J., ed. *Studies in Scottish Antiquity* (Edinburgh, 1984).

Terry, C. S., ed., 'The Commonwealth Union' *Scottish History Society*, 1902.

Thomas, A. C., 'Excavations at Trusty's hill, Anwoth' *TDGNHAS*, xxxix (1960/1).

Thomas, A. C., 'Ardwall isle: the excavation of an early Christian site of Irish type' *TDGNHAS*, xliii (1966).

Truckell, A. E., 'A photo-history of Galloway' *TDGNHAS*, lxiv (1989).

Truckell, A. E., 'Wigtown Burgh Court Book' *TDGNHAS*, lxii (1987).

Truckell, A. E., 'Unpublished witchcraft trials' *TDGNHAS*, li (1975).

Truckell, A. E., 'Unpublished witchcraft trials (part II)' *TDGNHAS*, lii (1976).

Truckell, A. E. and Williams, J., 'Medieval Pottery in Dumfriesshire and Galloway' *TDGNHAS*, xliv (1966–7).

Wickham-Jones, C. R., 'Rhum, mesolithic and later sites at Kinloch: excavations 1984–6' *PSAS* monograph series no 7, 1990.

Williams, D., 'The frontier policies of Antoninus Pius in Scotland and Germany' *TDGNHAS*, lvi (1981).

Williams, J., 'Neolithic axes in Dumfries and Galloway' *TDGNHAS*, xlvii (1970).

Wilson, A., 'Roman penetration in west Dumfries and Galloway: a field survey *TDGNHAS*, lxiv (1989).

e. THESES

Emond, W. K., *The Minority of King James V 1513–1528* (St Andrews).

Oram, R. D., *The Lordship of Galloway c.1000 to c.1250* (St Andrews, 1988).

Smith, I., *The Archaeological Background to the Emergent Kingdoms of the Tweed Basin in the Early Historic Period* (RCAHMS).

IV. LECTURES

Daphne Brooke, 'Saints and Goddesses: the interface with Celtic paganism' (seventh Whithorn lecture, 1998).

Rosemary Cramp, 'Whithorn and the Northumbrian expansion westwards' (third Whithorn lecture, 1994).

D. N. Dumville, 'The churches of north Britain in the first Viking age' (fifth Whithorn lecture 1996).

A. C. Thomas, 'Whithorn's Christian beginnings' (first Whithorn lecture, 1992).

Genealogical Tables

EARLIER KINGS of SCOTLAND

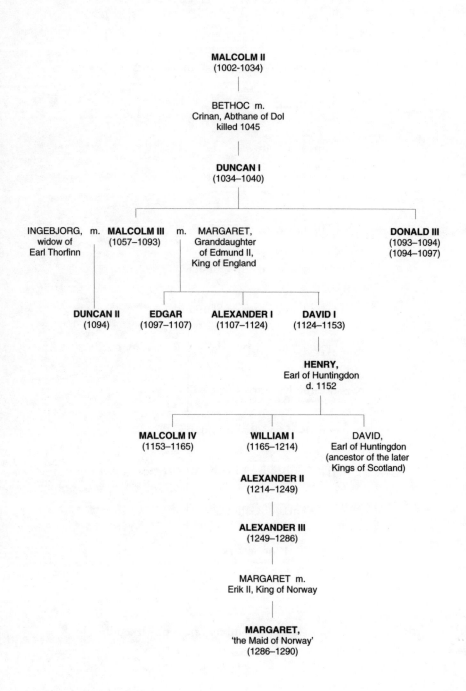

MALCOLM II
(1002-1034)

BETHOC m.
Crinan, Abthane of Dol
killed 1045

DUNCAN I
(1034–1040)

INGEBJORG, m.   **MALCOLM III**   m.   MARGARET,   **DONALD III**
widow of   (1057–1093)   Granddaughter   (1093–1094)
Earl Thorfinn   of Edmund II,   (1094–1097)
                                   King of England

DUNCAN II   **EDGAR**   **ALEXANDER I**   **DAVID I**
(1094)   (1097–1107)   (1107–1124)   (1124–1153)

HENRY,
Earl of Huntingdon
d. 1152

MALCOLM IV   **WILLIAM I**   DAVID,
(1153–1165)   (1165–1214)   Earl of Huntingdon
                                      (ancestor of the later
                                      Kings of Scotland)

ALEXANDER II
(1214–1249)

ALEXANDER III
(1249–1286)

MARGARET m.
Erik II, King of Norway

MARGARET,
'the Maid of Norway'
(1286–1290)

LORDS of GALLOWAY

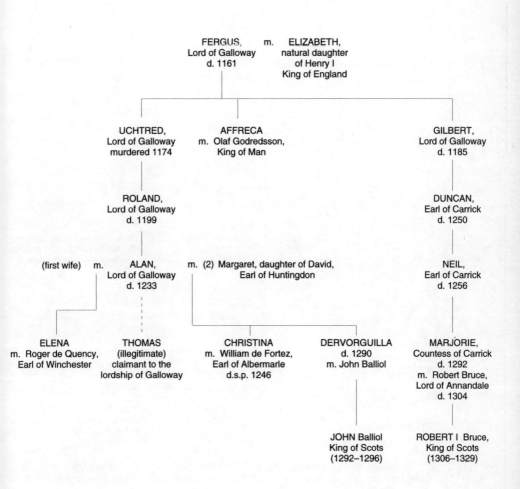

FERGUS, m. ELIZABETH,
Lord of Galloway   natural daughter
d. 1161   of Henry I
King of England

UCHTRED,   AFFRECA   GILBERT,
Lord of Galloway   m. Olaf Godredsson,   Lord of Galloway
murdered 1174   King of Man   d. 1185

ROLAND,   DUNCAN,
Lord of Galloway   Earl of Carrick
d. 1199   d. 1250

(first wife) m. ALAN,   m. (2) Margaret, daughter of David,   NEIL,
Lord of Galloway   Earl of Huntingdon   Earl of Carrick
d. 1233   d. 1256

ELENA   THOMAS   CHRISTINA   DERVORGUILLA   MARJORIE,
m. Roger de Quency,   (illegitimate)   m. William de Fortez,   d. 1290   Countess of Carrick
Earl of Winchester   claimant to the   Earl of Albermarle   m. John Balliol   d. 1292
lordship of Galloway   d.s.p. 1246   m. Robert Bruce,
Lord of Annandale
d. 1304

JOHN Balliol   ROBERT I Bruce,
King of Scots   King of Scots
(1292–1296)   (1306–1329)

KINGS of MAN

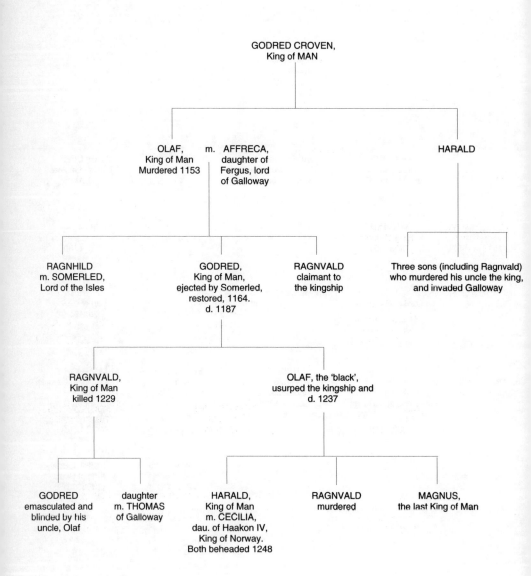

GODRED CROVEN,
King of MAN

OLAF, m. AFFRECA,
King of Man daughter of
Murdered 1153 Fergus, lord
of Galloway

HARALD

RAGNHILD
m. SOMERLED,
Lord of the Isles

GODRED,
King of Man,
ejected by Somerled,
restored, 1164.
d. 1187

RAGNVALD
claimant to
the kingship

Three sons (including Ragnvald)
who murdered his uncle the king,
and invaded Galloway

RAGNVALD,
King of Man
killed 1229

OLAF, the 'black',
usurped the kingship and
d. 1237

GODRED
emasculated and
blinded by his
uncle, Olaf

daughter
m. THOMAS
of Galloway

HARALD,
King of Man
m. CECILIA,
dau. of Haakon IV,
King of Norway.
Both beheaded 1248

RAGNVALD
murdered

MAGNUS,
the last King of Man

THE DISPUTED SUCCESSION

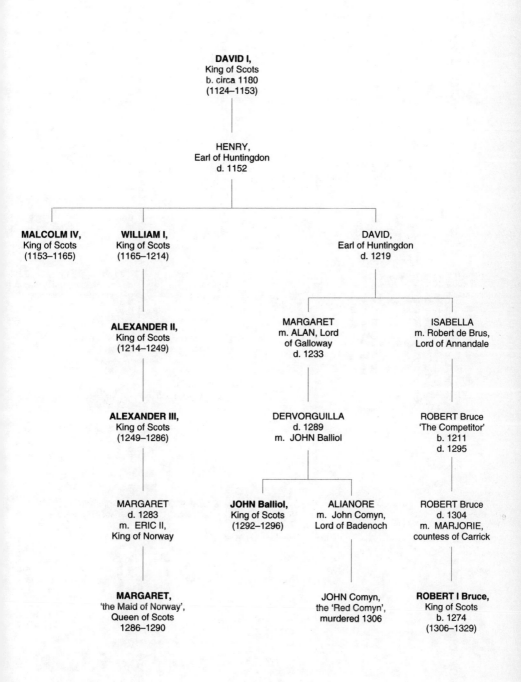

THE COMYNS

COMYNS, earls of BUCHAN

BADENOCH COMYNS

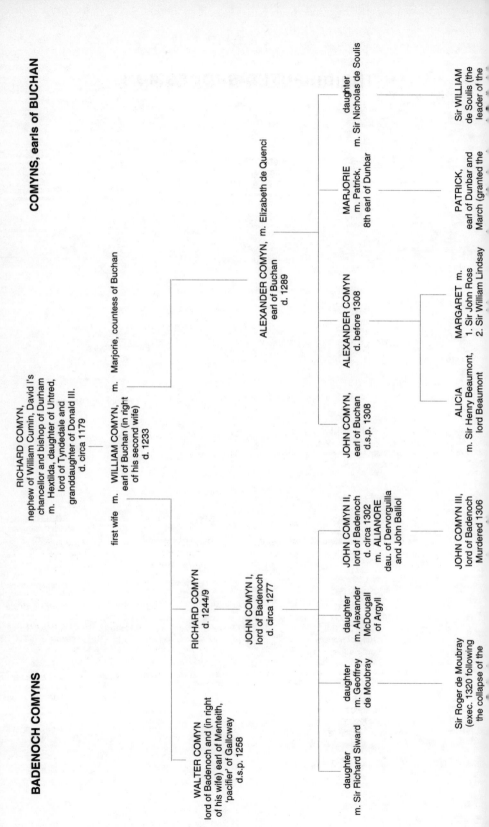

RICHARD COMYN,
nephew of William Cumin, David I's
chancellor and bishop of Durham
m. Hextilda, daughter of Uhtred,
lord of Tyndedale and
granddaughter of Donald III.
d. circa 1179

first wife m. WILLIAM COMYN, m. Marjorie, countess of Buchan
                earl of Buchan (in right
                of his second wife)
                d. 1233

RICHARD COMYN
d. 1244/9

ALEXANDER COMYN, m. Elizabeth de Quenci
earl of Buchan
d. 1289

JOHN COMYN I,
lord of Badenoch
d. circa 1277

WALTER COMYN
lord of Badenoch and (in right
of his wife) earl of Menteith,
'pacifier' of Galloway
d.s.p. 1258

daughter
m. Sir Richard Siward

daughter
m. Geoffrey
de Moubray

daughter
m. Alexander
McDougall
of Argyll

JOHN COMYN II,
lord of Badenoch
d. circa 1302
m. ALIANORE
dau. of Dervorguilla
and John Balliol

JOHN COMYN,
earl of Buchan
d.s.p. 1308

ALEXANDER COMYN
d. before 1308

MARJORIE
m. Patrick,
8th earl of Dunbar

daughter
m. Sir Nicholas de Soulis

Sir Roger de Moubray
(exec. 1320 following
the collapse of the

JOHN COMYN III,
lord of Badenoch
Murdered 1306

ALICIA
m. Sir Henry Beaumont,
lord Beaumont

MARGARET m.
1. Sir John Ross
2. Sir William Lindsay

PATRICK,
earl of Dunbar and
March (granted the

Sir WILLIAM
de Soulis (the
leader of the

HEIRS of ELENA de QUENCI

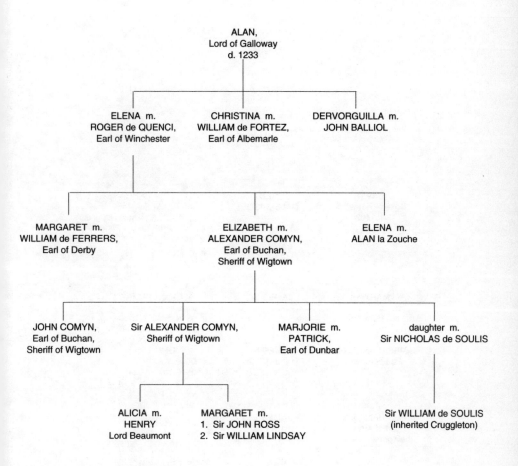

ALAN,
Lord of Galloway
d. 1233

ELENA m.
ROGER de QUENCI,
Earl of Winchester

CHRISTINA m.
WILLIAM de FORTEZ,
Earl of Albemarle

DERVORGUILLA m.
JOHN BALLIOL

MARGARET m.
WILLIAM de FERRERS,
Earl of Derby

ELIZABETH m.
ALEXANDER COMYN,
Earl of Buchan,
Sheriff of Wigtown

ELENA m.
ALAN la Zouche

JOHN COMYN,
Earl of Buchan,
Sheriff of Wigtown

Sir ALEXANDER COMYN,
Sheriff of Wigtown

MARJORIE m.
PATRICK,
Earl of Dunbar

daughter m.
Sir NICHOLAS de SOULIS

ALICIA m.
HENRY
Lord Beaumont

MARGARET m.
1. Sir JOHN ROSS
2. Sir WILLIAM LINDSAY

Sir WILLIAM de SOULIS
(inherited Cruggleton)

THE LATER KINGS of SCOTLAND

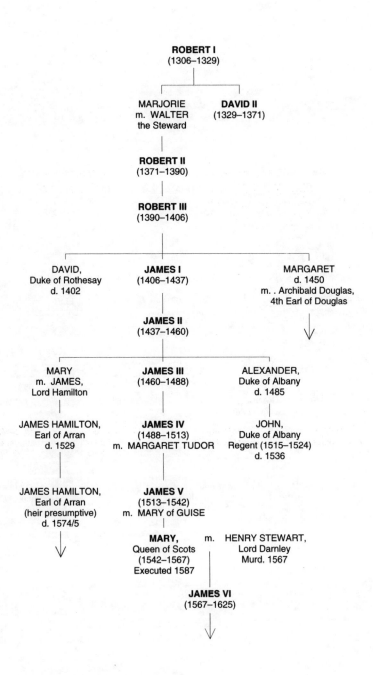

ROBERT I
(1306–1329)

MARJORIE
m. WALTER
the Steward

DAVID II
(1329–1371)

ROBERT II
(1371–1390)

ROBERT III
(1390–1406)

DAVID,
Duke of Rothesay
d. 1402

JAMES I
(1406–1437)

MARGARET
d. 1450
m. . Archibald Douglas,
4th Earl of Douglas

JAMES II
(1437–1460)

MARY
m. JAMES,
Lord Hamilton

JAMES III
(1460–1488)

ALEXANDER,
Duke of Albany
d. 1485

JAMES HAMILTON,
Earl of Arran
d. 1529

JAMES IV
(1488–1513)
m. MARGARET TUDOR

JOHN,
Duke of Albany
Regent (1515–1524)
d. 1536

JAMES HAMILTON,
Earl of Arran
(heir presumptive)
d. 1574/5

JAMES V
(1513–1542)
m. MARY of GUISE

MARY,
Queen of Scots
(1542–1567)
Executed 1587

m.   HENRY STEWART,
Lord Darnley
Murd. 1567

JAMES VI
(1567–1625)

THE HOUSE of DOUGLAS

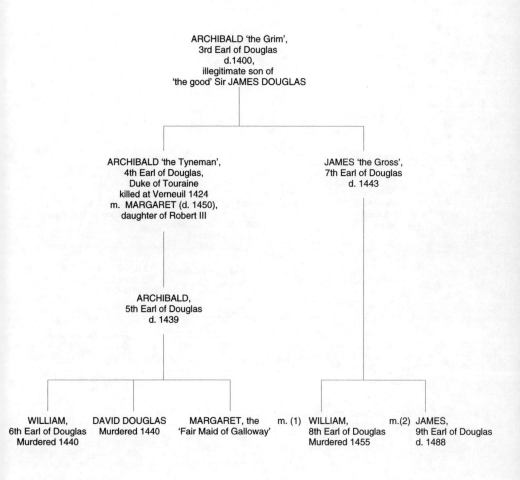

ARCHIBALD 'the Grim',
3rd Earl of Douglas
d.1400,
illegitimate son of
'the good' Sir JAMES DOUGLAS

ARCHIBALD 'the Tyneman',
4th Earl of Douglas,
Duke of Touraine
killed at Verneuil 1424
m. MARGARET (d. 1450),
daughter of Robert III

JAMES 'the Gross',
7th Earl of Douglas
d. 1443

ARCHIBALD,
5th Earl of Douglas
d. 1439

WILLIAM,
6th Earl of Douglas
Murdered 1440

DAVID DOUGLAS
Murdered 1440

MARGARET, the
'Fair Maid of Galloway'

m. (1)

WILLIAM,
8th Earl of Douglas
Murdered 1455

m.(2)

JAMES,
9th Earl of Douglas
d. 1488

KENNEDYS, EARLS of CASSILIS

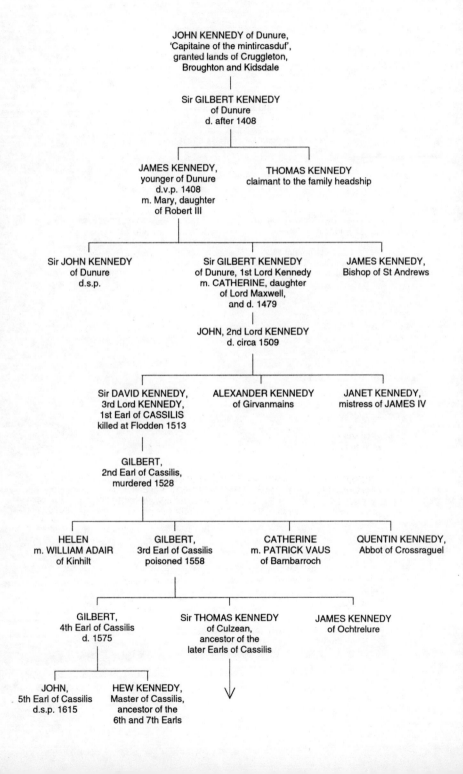

JOHN KENNEDY of Dunure,
'Capitaine of the mintircasduf',
granted lands of Cruggleton,
Broughton and Kidsdale

Sir GILBERT KENNEDY
of Dunure
d. after 1408

JAMES KENNEDY,
younger of Dunure
d.v.p. 1408
m. Mary, daughter
of Robert III

THOMAS KENNEDY
claimant to the family headship

Sir JOHN KENNEDY
of Dunure
d.s.p.

Sir GILBERT KENNEDY
of Dunure, 1st Lord Kennedy
m. CATHERINE, daughter
of Lord Maxwell,
and d. 1479

JAMES KENNEDY,
Bishop of St Andrews

JOHN, 2nd Lord KENNEDY
d. circa 1509

Sir DAVID KENNEDY,
3rd Lord KENNEDY,
1st Earl of CASSILIS
killed at Flodden 1513

ALEXANDER KENNEDY
of Girvanmains

JANET KENNEDY,
mistress of JAMES IV

GILBERT,
2nd Earl of Cassilis,
murdered 1528

HELEN
m. WILLIAM ADAIR
of Kinhilt

GILBERT,
3rd Earl of Cassilis
poisoned 1558

CATHERINE
m. PATRICK VAUS
of Barnbarroch

QUENTIN KENNEDY,
Abbot of Crossraguel

GILBERT,
4th Earl of Cassilis
d. 1575

Sir THOMAS KENNEDY
of Culzean,
ancestor of the
later Earls of Cassilis

JAMES KENNEDY
of Ochtrelure

JOHN,
5th Earl of Cassilis
d.s.p. 1615

HEW KENNEDY,
Master of Cassilis,
ancestor of the
6th and 7th Earls

LORDS MAXWELL and HERRIES

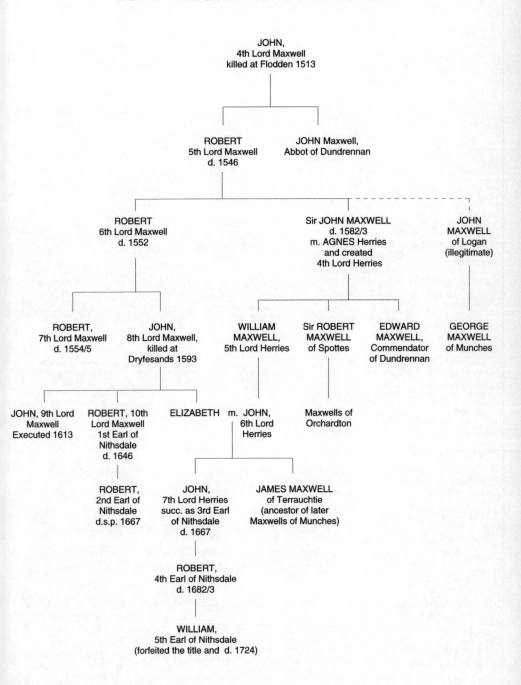

JOHN,
4th Lord Maxwell
killed at Flodden 1513

ROBERT
5th Lord Maxwell
d. 1546

JOHN Maxwell,
Abbot of Dundrennan

ROBERT
6th Lord Maxwell
d. 1552

Sir JOHN MAXWELL
d. 1582/3
m. AGNES Herries
and created
4th Lord Herries

JOHN
MAXWELL
of Logan
(illegitimate)

ROBERT,
7th Lord Maxwell
d. 1554/5

JOHN,
8th Lord Maxwell,
killed at
Dryfesands 1593

WILLIAM
MAXWELL,
5th Lord Herries

Sir ROBERT
MAXWELL
of Spottes

EDWARD
MAXWELL,
Commendator
of Dundrennan

GEORGE
MAXWELL
of Munches

JOHN, 9th Lord
Maxwell
Executed 1613

ROBERT, 10th
Lord Maxwell
1st Earl of
Nithsdale
d. 1646

ELIZABETH m. JOHN,
6th Lord
Herries

Maxwells of
Orchardton

ROBERT,
2nd Earl of
Nithsdale
d.s.p. 1667

JOHN,
7th Lord Herries
succ. as 3rd Earl
of Nithsdale
d. 1667

JAMES MAXWELL
of Terrauchtie
(ancestor of later
Maxwells of Munches)

ROBERT,
4th Earl of Nithsdale
d. 1682/3

WILLIAM,
5th Earl of Nithsdale
(forfeited the title and d. 1724)

GORDONS of KENMURE

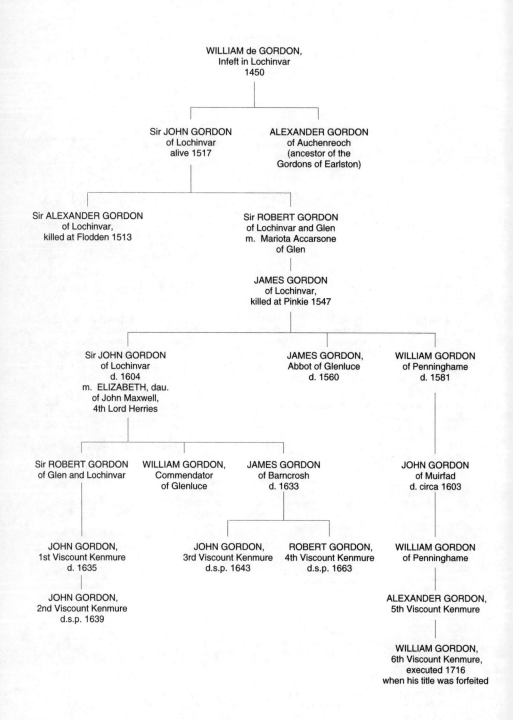

EARLS of GALLOWAY

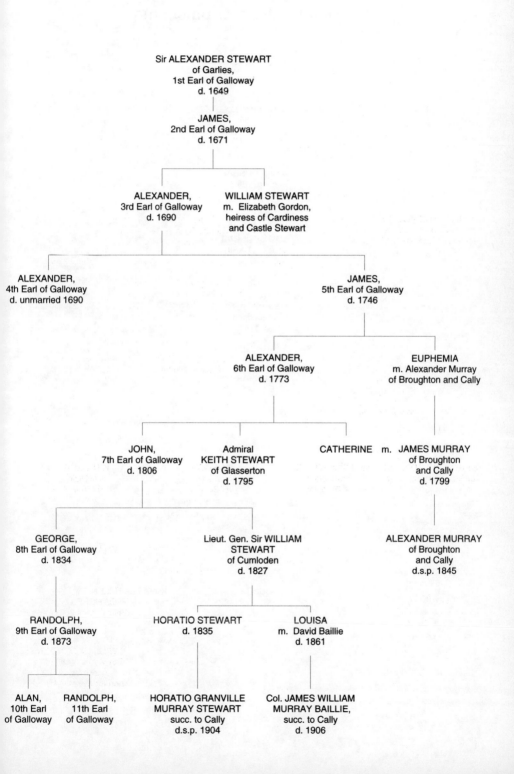

Sir ALEXANDER STEWART
of Garlies,
1st Earl of Galloway
d. 1649

JAMES,
2nd Earl of Galloway
d. 1671

ALEXANDER,
3rd Earl of Galloway
d. 1690

WILLIAM STEWART
m. Elizabeth Gordon,
heiress of Cardiness
and Castle Stewart

ALEXANDER,
4th Earl of Galloway
d. unmarried 1690

JAMES,
5th Earl of Galloway
d. 1746

ALEXANDER,
6th Earl of Galloway
d. 1773

EUPHEMIA
m. Alexander Murray
of Broughton and Cally

JOHN,
7th Earl of Galloway
d. 1806

Admiral
KEITH STEWART
of Glasserton
d. 1795

CATHERINE   m.   JAMES MURRAY
of Broughton
and Cally
d. 1799

GEORGE,
8th Earl of Galloway
d. 1834

Lieut. Gen. Sir WILLIAM
STEWART
of Cumloden
d. 1827

ALEXANDER MURRAY
of Broughton
and Cally
d.s.p. 1845

RANDOLPH,
9th Earl of Galloway
d. 1873

HORATIO STEWART
d. 1835

LOUISA
m. David Baillie
d. 1861

ALAN,
10th Earl
of Galloway

RANDOLPH,
11th Earl
of Galloway

HORATIO GRANVILLE
MURRAY STEWART
succ. to Cally
d.s.p. 1904

Col. JAMES WILLIAM
MURRAY BAILLIE,
succ. to Cally
d. 1906

EARLS of SELKIRK
(and Dunbars of Baldoon)

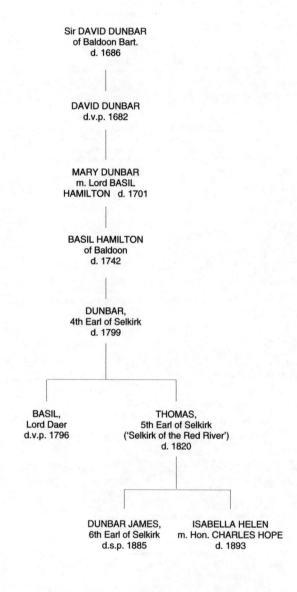

Sir DAVID DUNBAR
of Baldoon Bart.
d. 1686

DAVID DUNBAR
d.v.p. 1682

MARY DUNBAR
m. Lord BASIL
HAMILTON   d. 1701

BASIL HAMILTON
of Baldoon
d. 1742

DUNBAR,
4th Earl of Selkirk
d. 1799

BASIL,
Lord Daer
d.v.p. 1796

THOMAS,
5th Earl of Selkirk
('Selkirk of the Red River')
d. 1820

DUNBAR JAMES,
6th Earl of Selkirk
d.s.p. 1885

ISABELLA HELEN
m. Hon. CHARLES HOPE
d. 1893

EARLS of STAIR

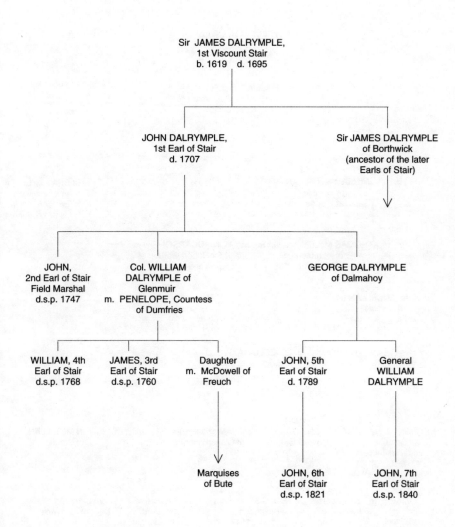

Sir JAMES DALRYMPLE,
1st Viscount Stair
b. 1619   d. 1695

JOHN DALRYMPLE,
1st Earl of Stair
d. 1707

Sir JAMES DALRYMPLE
of Borthwick
(ancestor of the later
Earls of Stair)

JOHN,
2nd Earl of Stair
Field Marshal
d.s.p. 1747

Col. WILLIAM
DALRYMPLE of
Glenmuir
m. PENELOPE, Countess
of Dumfries

GEORGE DALRYMPLE
of Dalmahoy

WILLIAM, 4th
Earl of Stair
d.s.p. 1768

JAMES, 3rd
Earl of Stair
d.s.p. 1760

Daughter
m. McDowell of
Freuch

JOHN, 5th
Earl of Stair
d. 1789

General
WILLIAM
DALRYMPLE

Marquises
of Bute

JOHN, 6th
Earl of Stair
d.s.p. 1821

JOHN, 7th
Earl of Stair
d.s.p. 1840

McLELLANS of BOMBIE,
Lords KIRKCUDBRIGHT

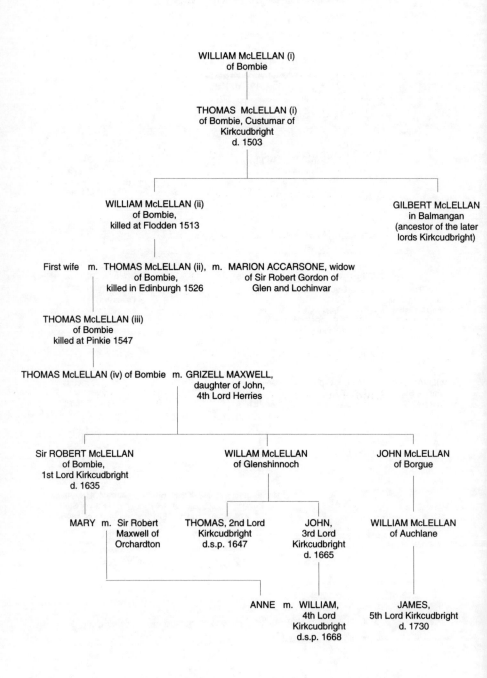

WILLIAM McLELLAN (i)
of Bombie

THOMAS McLELLAN (i)
of Bombie, Custumar of
Kirkcudbright
d. 1503

WILLIAM McLELLAN (ii)
of Bombie,
killed at Flodden 1513

GILBERT McLELLAN
in Balmangan
(ancestor of the later
lords Kirkcudbright)

First wife   m.   THOMAS McLELLAN (ii),   m.   MARION ACCARSONE, widow
of Bombie,   of Sir Robert Gordon of
killed in Edinburgh 1526   Glen and Lochinvar

THOMAS McLELLAN (iii)
of Bombie
killed at Pinkie 1547

THOMAS McLELLAN (iv) of Bombie   m.   GRIZELL MAXWELL,
daughter of John,
4th Lord Herries

Sir ROBERT McLELLAN
of Bombie,
1st Lord Kirkcudbright
d. 1635

WILLAM McLELLAN
of Glenshinnoch

JOHN McLELLAN
of Borgue

MARY   m.   Sir Robert
Maxwell of
Orchardton

THOMAS, 2nd Lord
Kirkcudbright
d.s.p. 1647

JOHN,
3rd Lord
Kirkcudbright
d. 1665

WILLIAM McLELLAN
of Auchlane

ANNE   m.   WILLIAM,
4th Lord
Kirkcudbright
d.s.p. 1668

JAMES,
5th Lord Kirkcudbright
d. 1730

LIST OF MAPS

Galloway – Physical Geography

Galloway Parishes

The Coastline of Galloway in Post-Ice Age Times

Anglian Settlements in Galloway

Cumbric Parish and Estate Names in Galloway

Parish and Settlement Names of Scandinavian Origin

Medieval Religious Houses in Galloway

Railway System in Galloway

Lands Forfeited by the 9th Earl of Douglas in 1456

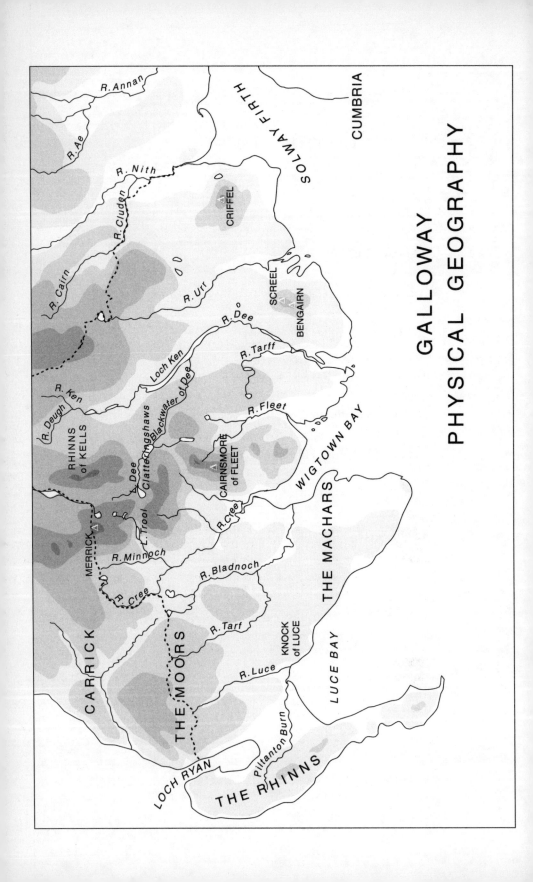

R. Annan

R. Ae

R. Nith

R. Cluden

R. Cairn

CRIFFEL

SOLWAY FIRTH

CUMBRIA

R. Urr

R. Dee

SCREEL

BENGAIRN

Loch Ken

R. Tarff

R. Ken

R. Deugh

RHINNS
of KELLS

R. Dee

Clatteringshaws

Blackwater of Dee

R. Fleet

CAIRNSMORE
of FLEET

WIGTOWN BAY

CARRICK

MERRICK

L. Trool

R. Minnoch

R. Cree

R. Cree

R. Bladnoch

THE MACHARS

THE MOORS

R. Tarf

KNOCK
of LUCE

R. Luce

LUCE BAY

Piltanton Burn

LOCH RYAN

THE RHINNS

GALLOWAY

PHYSICAL GEOGRAPHY

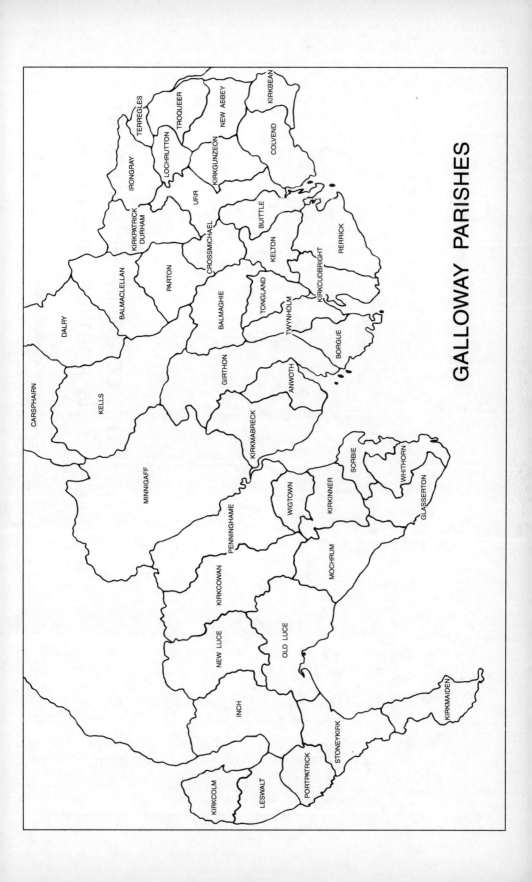

GALLOWAY PARISHES

THE COASTLINE of GALLOWAY
in POST-ICE AGE TIMES

———— post-ice age coastline ·············· modern coastline

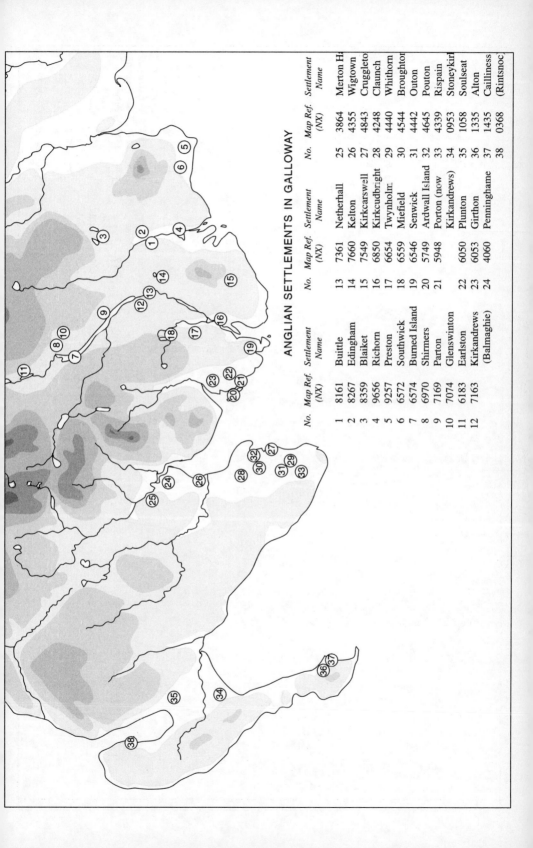

ANGLIAN SETTLEMENTS IN GALLOWAY

No.	Map Ref. (NX)	Settlement Name	No.	Map Ref. (NX)	Settlement Name	No.	Map Ref. (NX)	Settlement Name
1	8161	Buittle	13	7361	Netherhall	25	3864	Merton Ha
2	8267	Edingham	14	7660	Kelton	26	4355	Wigtown
3	8359	Blaiket	15	7549	Kirkcarswell	27	4843	Cruggleto
4	9656	Richorn	16	6850	Kirkcudbright	28	4248	Claunch
5	9257	Preston	17	6654	Twynholm	29	4440	Whithorn
6	6572	Southwick	18	6559	Miefield	30	4544	Broughton
7	6574	Burned Island	19	6546	Senwick	31	4442	Outon
8	6970	Shirmers	20	5749	Ardwall Island	32	4645	Pouton
9	7169	Parton	21	5948	Porton (now	33	4339	Rispain
10	7074	Glenswinton			Kirkandrews)	34	0953	Stoneykir
11	6183	Earlston	22	6050	Plunton	35	1058	Soulseat
12	7163	Kirkandrews	23	6053	Girthon	36	1335	Alton
		(Balmaghie)	24	4060	Penninghame	37	1435	Cailliness
						38	0368	(Rintsnoc

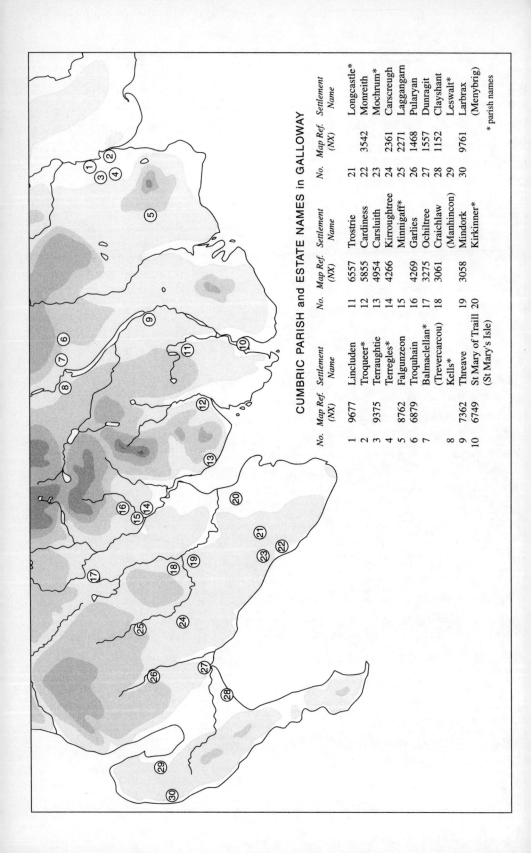

CUMBRIC PARISH and ESTATE NAMES in GALLOWAY

No.	Map Ref. (NX)	Settlement Name	No.	Map Ref. (NX)	Settlement Name	No.	Map Ref. (NX)	Settlement Name
1	9677	Lincluden	11	6557	Trostrie	21		Longcastle*
2		Troqueer*	12	5855	Cardiness	22	3542	Monreith
3	9375	Terraughtie	13	4954	Carsluith	23		Mochrum*
4		Terregles*	14	4266	Kirroughtree	24	2361	Carscreugh
5	8762	Falgunzeon	15		Minnigaff*	25	2271	Laggangarn
6	6879	Troquhain	16	4269	Garlies	26	1468	Pularyan
7		Balmaclellan* (Trevercarcou)	17	3275	Ochiltree	27	1557	Dunragit
8		Kells*	18	3061	Craichlaw (Manhincon)	28	1152	Clayshant
9	7362	Threave	19	3058	Mindork	29		Leswalt*
10	6749	St Mary of Traill (St Mary's Isle)	20		Kirkinner*	30	9761	Larbrax (Menybrig)

* parish names

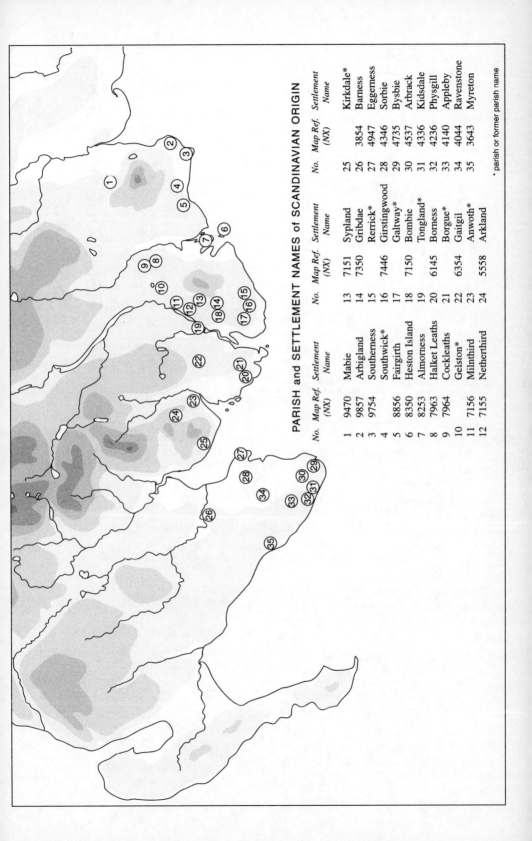

PARISH and SETTLEMENT NAMES of SCANDINAVIAN ORIGIN

No.	Map Ref. (NX)	Settlement Name	No.	Map Ref. (NX)	Settlement Name	No.	Map Ref. (NX)	Settlement Name
1	9470	Mabie	13	7151	Sypland	25		Kirkdale*
2	9857	Arbigland	14	7350	Gribdae	26	3854	Barness
3	9754	Southerness	15	7446	Rerrick*	27	4947	Eggerness
4		Southwick*	16		Girstingwood	28	4346	Sorbie
5	8856	Fairgirth	17	7150	Galtway*	29	4735	Bysbie
6	8350	Heston Island	18		Bombie	30	4537	Arbrack
7	8253	Almorness	19		Tongland*	31	4336	Kidsdale
8	7963	Halket Leaths	20	6145	Borness	32	4236	Physgill
9	7964	Cockleaths	21		Borgue*	33	4140	Appleby
10		Gelston*	22	6354	Gaitgil	34	4044	Ravenstone
11	7156	Milnthird	23	5558	Anwoth*	35	3643	Myreton
12	7155	Netherthird	24		Arkland			

* parish or former parish name

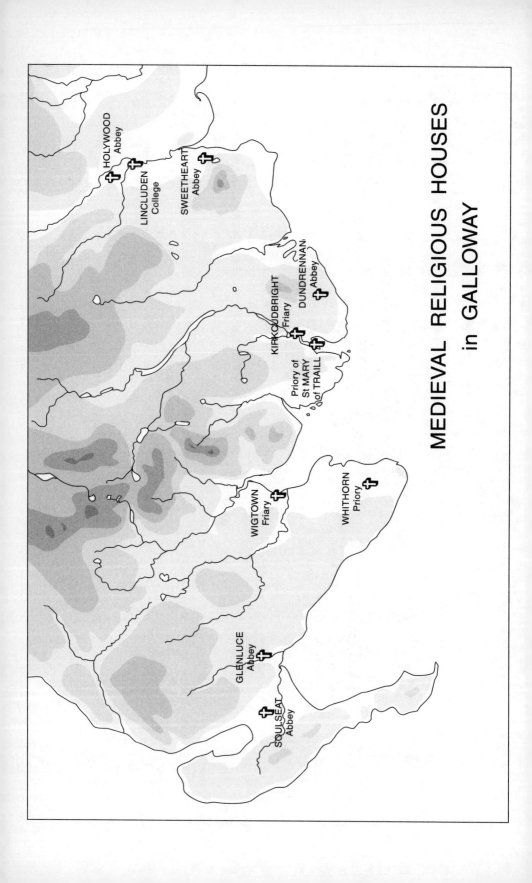

MEDIEVAL RELIGIOUS HOUSES
in GALLOWAY

HOLYWOOD Abbey

LINCLUDEN College

SWEETHEART Abbey

DUNDRENNAN Abbey

KIRKCUDBRIGHT Friary

Priory of St MARY of TRAILL

WIGTOWN Friary

WHITHORN Priory

GLENLUCE Abbey

SOULSEAT Abbey

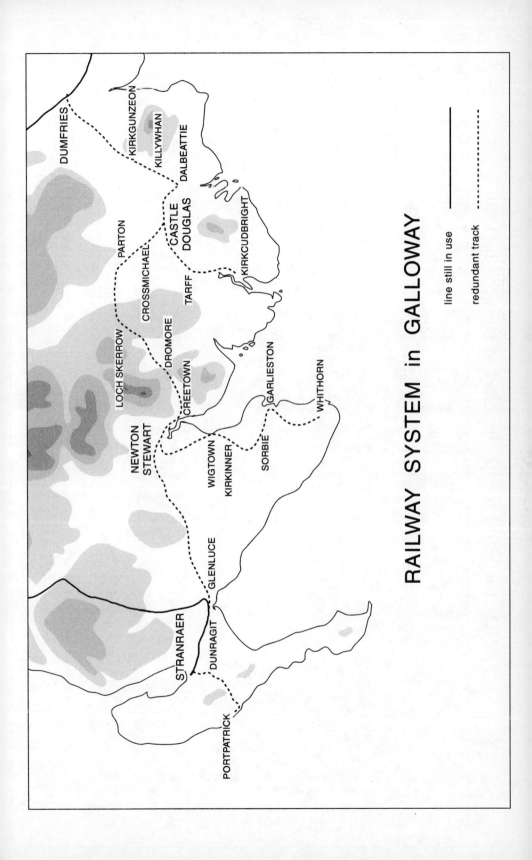

RAILWAY SYSTEM in GALLOWAY

——— line still in use

········· redundant track

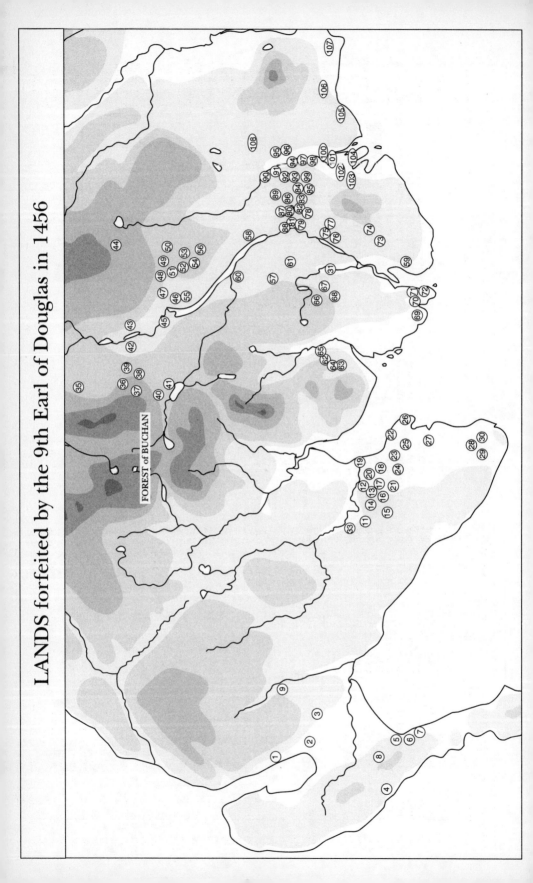

LANDS forfeited by the 9th Earl of Douglas in 1456

FOREST of BUCHAN

Lands in western Galloway:

No.	Map ref. (NX)	Original Name	Present Name
1	0765	LEFFYNNOLLOK	Leffnoll
2	0961	CLOUTURPLAK	Clachanpluck
3	1259	CUYLTIS	Cults
4	0152	MARRAUCH	Morroch
5	0951	CULYNGROUT	Culgroat
6	0850	BALLYNGRAGANE	Balgreggan
7	0948	LACHT	Lake
8	1753	CALLONES	Caldons
9	1664	LARGIS	Larg
10		CORWAR	(unidentifiable)

Lands in the Machars:

No.	Map ref. (NX)	Original Name	Present Name
11	4054	KEROWBRUCHYN	Kirbreen
12	4054	KERWALCOK	Kirwaugh
13	4053	CLACHARE	Clauchrie
14	3752	CLONTHAG	Clutag
15	3850	KYLDARACH	Kildarroch
16	3951	BERNBERACH	Barnbarroch
17	4051	BERNGLASS	Barglass
18	4151	KNOCAN	Knockann
19	4352	BALLYNDONNE*	Baldoon
20	4052	TALLOLAGATH	Tahall
21	3950	SLEUNDUNNULL	Slochabbert (?)
22		LYBRIG*	Lybrack
23	4249	KNOKYNCUR	Knockencurr
24	4249	KNOCKEFFRIC	Knockeffrick
25	4347	BLAREMAUKYN	Low Blair
26	4947	EGYRNES	Eggerness
27	4442	ALTOUNE	Outon
28	4437	IRSYKE	Ersock
29	4436	LYTILAROW*	Little Arrow
30	4537	ARBORG*	Arbrack
31	4336	KIDDISDALE*	Kidsdale
32		KWONQUHORNE	(unidentifiable)
33	3556	KYLADAM	Kiladam
34		Forest of BUCHAN	

Lands in the Glenkens:

No.	Map ref. (NX)	Original Name	Present Name
35	5589	CASTELMADDY	Castlemaddy
36	5684	LARGVEY	Largvey
37	5582	CLUNNAREE	Clenrie
38	5682	LARGMOR	Largmore
39	5682	DRUMBOY	Drumbuie
40	5379	GARWERE	Garrary
41	5578	CRAGYNBAY	Craigenbay
42	5882	BARNSCHEACH	Barskeoch
43	6183	ERLISTONE	Earlston
44	7386	CRAGMOY	Craigmuie
45	6379	FYNTELLACH	Fintloch
46	6477	CUBBOYS	Cubbox
47	6579	BALMAKKLELLAN	Balmaclellan
48	6779	ARNGLOSK	Ironlosh
49	7079	LOWYS	Lowes
50	7278	CALDOW	Caldow
51	6878	BARTAGARE	Bartaggart
52	6877	BAYRLEY	Barlay
53	6877	CARSYNVEY	Cassenvey
54	6776	CORSE	Corse
55	6475	Le PARK	Low Park
56	6875	CRAG	Craig
57	6665	CULLYNDACH	Cullenoch
58	7267	ARDIS	Airds
59	7147	GALTWAY	Galtway

Other lands:

No.	Map ref. (NX)	Original Name	Present Name
60	6769	DUCHRAY	Duchrae (Hensol)
61	6863	BARGALTOUN	Bargatton
62	5858	KILHERN	Killern
63	5655	KIRKBRYDE	Kirkbride
64	5756	LAGANE	King's Laggan
65	5858	POLLINCRE	Pulcree
66	6559	MEYTHFELDE	Miefield
67	6558	CULGAGRE	Culcaigrie
68	6557	TROSTAREE	Trostrie

Other lands (continued):

No.	Map ref. (NX)	Original Name	Present Name
69	6244	DUNRODSANNAK*	Dunrod
70	6446	SANNAKGRANG*	Senwick
71	6546	NEDDYRSANNAK	}
72	6446	OVYRSANNAK	
73	7251	BALGREDANE	Balgreddan
74	7251	MARKIS	Marks
75	7356	MYDDYLLOCHDOUGANE	}
76	7357	NEDDYRLOCHDOUGANE	Lochdougan
77	7457	OVIRLOCHDOUGANE	
78	7458	SLEUNGNAW	Slagnaw
79	7359	DANDAWAN	Dildawn
80	7461	NEDDYRKELTOUN	Kelton Mains
81	7660	KELTOUNGRANG*	Midkelton
82	7560	OVYRKELTOUNE	Kelton Hill
83	7760	CULE	Cuil
84	7861	COYWAYR	Corra
85	7860	BREKHALCH	Breoch
86	7661	QUHITPARK	Whitepark
87	7661	CARLYNWERK	Carlingwark
88	7362	TREVE*	Threave
89	7965	CORBARTOUNE	Corbieton
90	8067	OVYRSPOTTISGRANG*	Spottes
91	8164	MOTE de UR	Mote of Urr
92	7963	HANCOKLATHIS	Halketleaths
93	7962	MIKILKNOX	Meikle Knox
94	8062	GUFFOKLAND	Guffogland
95	8263	FYRTHE	} Meikle and Little
96		FYRTHEND	Firth-head
97	8161	BUTIL	Buittle
98	8060	LYTILKNOX	Little Knox
99	8059	CAULGNAW	Cullinaw
100	8359	LYTYL RICHHYRN	Little Richorn
101	8258	MOUNCHES	Munches
102	8158	CLUNE	Clone
103	8058	MARYNACH	Marnoch
104	8253	AUMORNES	Almorness
105	8654	CULWEN	Colvend
106	9257	SUTHEK	Southwick
107	9657	PRESTOUN	Preston
108	8369	CULMEN	Culmain

* indicates grange lands

INDEX

Note: only individuals, place-names, battles, sources, acts of parliament, or other matters which have a direct bearing on Galloway or its inhabitants are included.